Innovations in Social Finance

Thomas Walker · Jane McGaughey ·
Sherif Goubran · Nadra Wagdy
Editors

Innovations in Social Finance

Transitioning Beyond Economic Value

palgrave
macmillan

Editors
Thomas Walker
Department of Finance
Concordia University
Montreal, QC, Canada

Jane McGaughey
School of Irish Studies
Concordia University
Montreal, QC, Canada

Sherif Goubran
Department of Architecture
School of Sciences and Engineering
The American University in Cairo
Cairo, Egypt

Nadra Wagdy
CID Consulting
Cairo, Egypt

ISBN 978-3-030-72534-1 ISBN 978-3-030-72535-8 (eBook)
https://doi.org/10.1007/978-3-030-72535-8

This Palgrave Macmillan imprint is published by the registered company Springer Nature Switzerland AG
The registered company address is: Gewerbestrasse 11, 6330 Cham, Switzerland

Acknowledgments

We acknowledge the financial support provided through the Autorité des marchés financiers, the David O'Brien Centre for Sustainable Enterprise at Concordia University, and the Higher Education Institutional Excellence Program 2020 of the Ministry of Innovation and Technology (TKP2020-IKA-02) at Corvinus University of Budapest. In addition, we appreciate the research and administrative assistance provided by Tyler Schwartz as well as the excellent copy-editing and editorial assistance we received from Adele Dumont-Bergeron, Brenda Ordria, Gabrielle Machnik-Kekesi, Julie Brown, and Maya Michaeli. Finally, we feel greatly indebted to Arlene Segal, Joseph Capano, Stephane Brutus, Anne-Marie Croteau, and Norma Paradis (all at Concordia University) who in various ways supported this project.

Contents

Notes on Contributors

Ajibola Anthony Akanji holds degrees in Law and Public Administration. He is an advocate and solicitor of the Supreme Court of Nigeria. He is a Lecturer at the Faculty of Law, Lead City University, and an adjunct at the Department of Politics and International Relations of the same institution. He served as a trainer on cooperative law at the International Co-operative Alliance (ICA) organized Global Youth Forum at Kuching, Malaysia. He is a consultant to the Cooperative Federation of Nigeria and a member of the ICA Africa region's law committee. He is an organizer with the Cooperative Working Group of the Young Scholars Initiative(YSI) and a development team member of the finance and economics Knowledge-Action Network of Future earth.

Asier Ansorena has a B.A. in Economics and Political Science from the University of Michigan. His early professional career has focused on youth empowerment and entrepreneurship through AIESEC in the USA, Jordan, and several countries in Latin America. From 2009 to 2018, he was part of Instituto Palmas where his different roles included leading the microcredit team, developing a youth innovation and research lab, establishing new partnerships, and implementing new technologies and areas of work. He was Mel-King Community Fellow on Transnational Economic Democracy at MIT-Colab from 2016 to 2018 and has served as the Diaspora Networks director at Ashoka since 2019.

Sureyya Burcu Avci holds a Ph.D. in Business from Ozyegin University (2016). After conducting research at the University of Michigan and the University of Notre Dame as a post-doctoral researcher, she began teaching finance at Sabanci University. Dr. Avci's research focuses on corporate finance, corporate ethics, insider trading, and sustainability. Her research agenda includes current topics such as new technologies used in finance and sustainability, traditional topics such as IPO underpricing, optimal debt level, optimal incentive levels for executives, and the performance of an asset class.

Erica Barbosa Vargas is Director of Solutions Finance at The J.W. McConnell Family Foundation, where she leads strategies for financial innovation and integration of the Foundation's financial assets to support social and economic system transformation. She oversees the management of a multi-asset impact investing portfolio, which includes blended finance approaches, and ESG integration within the Foundation's endowment. She also leads a portfolio of national market-building initiatives. She completed her undergraduate studies in behavioral psychology and neuroscience, and holds an MPA in Public and Economic Policy from the London School of Economics & Political Science. She specializes in innovation and systems dynamics for inclusive economic development.

Belinda Bell is the Programme Director of Cambridge Social Ventures at the Cambridge Judge Business School Centre for Social Innovation. Belinda is a social entrepreneur and has established a range of social ventures including those focusing on finance, aging, and young people. She has acted as a mentor and advisor to many social entrepreneurs and has developed a broad knowledge of business models for social innovation. Belinda's academic research explores social finance. She holds a professional doctorate in Public Works, a master's degree in Community Enterprise, and a bachelor's degree in Social Anthropology.

Lars Boggild, CFA is a creative thinker working at the intersection of finance and social change. He supports new business relationships for Vancity Community Investment Bank, Canada's first bank dedicated to social and environmental impact. Previously, he worked at Purpose Capital, leading impact investing advisory projects that built practical strategies for asset owners to deploy more of their investments toward social and environmental good. Lars sits on the Canadian Community Economic Development Network's Policy Council, the Investment

Committee of the Evangelical Lutheran Foundation of Eastern Canada, and is the Chair of Not Far from the Tree, Toronto's urban fruit picking project.

Julie Brown is a writer, editor, and technical content developer for Genetec Inc. She previously worked as a research associate at the Emerging Risks Information Centre (ERIC) at Concordia University, Montreal.

Ignazio Castellucci, Ph.D., FCIArb is a lawyer, admitted before the Italian Supreme Court and Associate Professor of Comparative Law at the University of Teramo (Italy). Ignazio has been an invited or visiting professor at several universities worldwide. His legal research, publications, and teaching are in the areas of general comparative law and methodology, Chinese law, Asian laws and other legal area studies, global legal issues, arbitration, and geo-legal issues. He is Vice President of the Juris Diversitas International Society of Legal Research and editor of the Juris Diversitas Book Series (Routledge).

Israel Cedillo Lazcano is a Lecturer/Researcher in Banking and IP/IT Law at Universidad de las Américas Puebla (UDLAP) (Mexico). He has worked as an intellectual property advisor and in personal data protection for different institutions, and as editor on intellectual property for SCRIPTed. His academic research focuses on intellectual property, artificial intelligence, financial innovation, and the legal nature of money. He has won different national and international research prizes, such as the First Prize of the Fifth Edition of the Competition of Legal Monographs for Lawyers under 35 years old in 2013, sponsored by the Latin American Banks Federation (FELABAN).

Wendy Cukier, M.A., M.B.A., Ph.D., DU (HC), LLD (HC), M.Sc. is one of Canada's leading experts in disruptive technologies, innovation processes, and diversity. She is the Founder of Ryerson University's Diversity Institute, leading numerous projects aimed at promoting the participation and advancement of underrepresented groups, including women, racialized people, and Indigenous peoples. Dr. Cukier has assisted organizations in becoming more inclusive through innovative programs such as DiversityLeads (funded by the Social Sciences and Humanities Research Council), which tracks the progress, impediments, and evidenced-based strategies for promoting diversity in organizations.

Eduardo H. Diniz earned his Ph.D. in Business Administration from Fundação Getúlio Vargas-SP in 2000. Since 1999, he has worked as a Professor at the Business School of São Paulo at Fundação Getulio Vargas (EAESP-FGV). He was editor-in-chief of Revista de Administração de Empresas (RAE), GVexecutivo, and GVcasos, from January 2009 to December 2015. He is currently Chief Department of Technology and Data Science (TDS). He was a visiting scholar at the University of California, Berkeley (1996–1998), at HEC Montréal (2007), and at Erasmus University (2016–2017). He is a Bellagio Fellow, appointed by the Rockefeller Foundation in 2014, and has been a researcher at the Center for Microfinance and Financial Inclusion at FGV, GVcemif since 2007.

Barbara Dömötör is an Associate Professor in the Department of Finance at Corvinus University of Budapest. She received her Ph.D. in 2014. Her doctoral thesis modeled corporate hedging behavior. Her research interests include financial markets, financial risk management, and financial regulation. She is the co-director of the Hungarian Chapter of Professional Risk Managers' International Association.

Adele Dumont-Bergeron is an M.A. student in English Literature and Creative Writing at Concordia University, Montreal. She currently serves as a Research Assistant for the finance department. Adèle has copyedited over a hundred chapters and articles by professionals in finance for publication. She recently completed a research project about plastic taxes and has co-authored an article on the topic. Her research now focuses on water risks and their impacts on the financial system and society.

Adam Fleming works on the investment team of an Irish technology firm, with a particular focus on corporate venture capital. Prior to this, Adam spent several years in Dubai where he worked for an asset management company, helping them to establish a commodity-based fund. He holds a master's degree in International Finance from Trinity College Dublin.

Dave Gorman is Director for Social Responsibility and Sustainability at the University of Edinburgh. Prior to this, he served as the Head of Strategy at the Scottish Environment Protection Agency. After qualifying as an engineer, Dave dedicated two years to a wide variety of community work, before returning to do a master's degree in Energy and Environmental Systems at Glasgow Caledonian University. His current role involves senior leadership of the University's social responsibility and sustainability activities, as well as strategic advice on climate change issues, energy, and a wide range of social responsibility and investment issues. Dave is a chartered environmentalist, a chartered manager, and a fellow of the RSA, EAUC, CMI, and IEMA.

Sherif Goubran is an Assistant Professor in the Department of Architecture (School of Sciences and Engineering) at the American University in Cairo. His research focus includes building sustainability and sustainability assessment, sustainability in architectural design, and human approaches in design.

Constantin Gurdgiev teaches investments, impact finance, corporate finance, and risk analysis at Northeastern University (Boston, USA), Trinity College Dublin (Ireland), and the Presidio Graduate School (San Francisco, USA). His expertise and academic research concentrate on the fields of investment markets, geopolitical and macroeconomic risk, uncertainty and complexity analysis, and ESG impact finance. Professor Gurdgiev is a co-founder and board member of two charities working on issues related to financial inclusion and empowerment in Europe. He chairs the board of directors in a regulated financial services nonprofit organization and serves on the risk and audit committee of another organization.

Zohreh Hassannezhad Chavoushi, Ph.D. is currently a Postdoctoral Research Fellow at the Diversity Institute, Ryerson University, where she uses insights from gender and diversity theories to reveal the barriers and opportunities that are associated with women and immigrants' entrepreneurship development. She is currently working on reports and research papers describing the pathway toward a more inclusive innovation ecosystem in Canada, the exploration of women and underrepresented groups' barriers in entrepreneurial activities, and the application of a critical ecological lens to address existing issues in entrepreneurial ecosystem.

Dániel Havran is Associate Professor at the Department of Finance at Corvinus University of Budapest, where he obtained his Ph.D. in Economics. He teaches corporate finance, credit risk management, and econometrics for finance. His research interests are related to corporate finance, market liquidity, and household debt.

Julia Qermezi Huang is a Lecturer in Anthropology of Development at the University of Edinburgh and Fellow at the Edinburgh Futures Institute. She is the author of *To Be an Entrepreneur: Social Enterprise and Disruptive Development in Bangladesh* (Cornell University Press, 2020) and *Tribeswomen of Iran: Weaving Memories among Qashqa'i Nomads* (I.B. Tauris, 2014). Her research focuses on social enterprise and the use of new technologies, data, and markets for poverty alleviation.

Stephan A. Jansen is coordinator of the Digital Urban Center for Aging & Health (DUCAH) at the Alexander von Humboldt Institute for Internet & Society (HIIG) and Professor of Management, Innovation & Finance as well as Director of the Center for Philanthropy & Civil Society (PhiCS) at Karlshochschule, Karlsruhe. He is Managing Partner of BICICLI Holding GmbH (Corporate Bike Mobility as a Service) and partner of the Societas for Digital & Social Transformation, "The 18th Camel & Accomplices" in Berlin, Hamburg, and Vienna. He has been listed on the "Thinkers 50" global ranking.

Péter Kerényi is a PhD student at the Department of Finance at Corvinus University of Budapest. He earned his master's degree in Financial Mathematics at Eötvös Loránd University. His research interests include dynamic contract theory.

Maxime Lakat is a fourth-year student at McGill University, studying Managing for Sustainability and Social Entrepreneurship. Maxime has been the Co-President of the Desautels Sustainability Network (DSN) for the past three years. He helped to co-create McGill's first course on sustainable finance and organize the Montreal Youth Summit on Sustainable Business. Maxime is the Chair of the Canadian Business Youth Council for Sustainable Development, Canada's largest youth-led movement to change the way we do and teach business. He also co-founded the Montreal Social Value Fund (MSVF), Québec's first student-led impact investing group.

Bruno Lam is the Research Manager at the University of British Columbia's (UBC) Sauder Centre for Social Innovation & Impact Investing (SauderS3i) and Senior Advisor to the National Social Value Fund. He leads projects with impact investors that focus on cleantech venture capital and climate finance. Previously, he contributed to piloting income share agreements to finance higher education in Ghana with Brighter Investment, and helped to create Vancouver's first mug-sharing program through mugshare. Bruno is a graduate of UBC's Sauder School of Business with a B.Com. (Hons.) in Finance and Sustainability.

Lorenzo Liotta formerly managed the Impact & Financial Services business unit at ItaliaCamp, and aimed to foster the social impact assessment approach in strategic planning as a way to integrate both financial and non-financial results. He coordinated the company research team and the teaching activities carried out in partnership with LUISS Guido Carli University as well as other prestigious Italian universities. Previously, he held the role of assistant manager at KPMG Advisory S.p.A in strategic advisory. Lorenzo continues to work in consulting.

Brenda Odria Loayza is an undergraduate student in English Literature and Professional Writing at Concordia University in Montreal, QC. She works as a Research Assistant for Emerging Risks Information Center (ERIC).

Gabrielle Kathleen Machnik-Kekesi holds an Individualized Program master's degree from Concordia University and a master's in Information Studies from McGill University. Her research interests include the Irish Revolution, food history, cultural heritage, and ethnobotany.

Mariana Martinez Rubio is a soon-to-be Entrepreneurship undergraduate from the University of British Columbia. She is grateful to work and learn in the ancestral and unceded territories of the xʷməθkʷəy̓əm (Musqueam), Sḵwx̱wú7mesh (Squamish), and Sel̓íl̓witulh (Tsleil-Waututh) Nations. Since the beginning of her career, she has taken on a variety of roles advocating for youth leadership and gender issues. She has worked at the SauderS3i and Canvas Impact Advisors on various advisory projects with social ventures, investors, and nonprofits. Mariana's roots in Mexico, upbringing in South Africa, and undergraduate career in Canada fuel her desire to work toward female economic empowerment through a social justice and equity lens.

Clemens Mast is Strategy and Business Development Manager at Siemens AG and a guest lecturer for business model innovation and entrepreneurship at the Zeppelin University (ZU), Germany. He studied Business Administration, as well as Corporate Management and Economics, and has prior work experience as group controller at Bertrandt AG. Until 2016, he was an associate researcher at the Chair of Strategic Organization & Financing and the Civil Society Center at the

ZU. His doctoral studies focused on entrepreneurship and business model innovation; in 2017, he published his thesis on how new business models influence and change established industries.

Jane McGaughey is an Associate Professor of diaspora studies at Concordia University's School of Irish Studies, holding a Ph.D. in Irish history from the University of London. Her research focuses on the intersections of historical and contemporary migration, gender, and ethnic discrimination.

Marguerite Mendell is Distinguished Professor Emerita, School of Community and Public Affairs and Director, Karl Polanyi Institute of Political Economy, Concordia University. For over thirty years, she has contributed to research on community economic development, the social economy in Québec and internationally, social finance, and economic democracy. She has collaborated with international organizations including the OECD, ILO, European Commission, the United Nations Research Institute on Social Development (UNRISD) as well local and national governments in Canada and abroad. She continues to work in close collaboration with actors in the social economy and social finance in Québec. She is co-founder of CAP Finance, a network of social finance institutions in Québec. Marguerite is an Officer of the Order of Québec, a Member of the Order of Canada, and a recipient of a Prix du Québec.

Maya Michaeli currently works as a Research Assistant in the Department of Finance, at Concordia University, Montreal. She has a natural passion and enthusiasm for financial markets, which has led her to further pursue her studies in this field. As a current undergraduate, she has expanded her interests and began undertaking her personal endeavors in portfolio management. Her focus ranges from risk management, speculative investing, real estate investment trusts, and sustainable investment opportunities.

Guang Ying Mo is a senior research associate at the Diversity Institute, Ryerson University. Dr. Mo obtained her Ph.D. in Sociology from the University of Toronto. Her research fields are organizational communication, collaboration and innovation, social support for underrepresented groups, and social media. Prior to joining the Diversity Institute, she conducted research projects on organizational communication and technology use by underrepresented groups such as older adults, adolescents, and caregivers of people with dementia. Her current work focuses on entrepreneurship and employment equity for underrepresented groups.

Nancy Neamtan is a founding member and the first CEO (1996–2015) of the Chantier de l'économie sociale, a province-wide organization representing Québec's social economy. She was the founder and president of the Board of Directors of RISQ (1997–2007), the first investment fund dedicated to collective enterprises and the Chantier de l'économie sociale Trust (2007–2015). With over thirty years of experience in the field of community economic development, social economy, and social finance, her expertise is recognized internationally. Neamtan is an Officer of the Order of Québec and a Member of the Order of Canada. She is the recipient of honorary doctorates from Concordia University, Montréal and the University of Québec in Outaouias.

Tímea Ölvedi started her Ph.D. studies in 2018 at the Department of Finance of Corvinus University of Budapest. Her research interests include social lending and different forms of financial intermediation. She works as a senior consultant at Ernst & Young Hungary in the Financial Services and Risk Management team, focusing on credit risk related projects.

Stefania Paladini, Ph.D. is Reader in Economics and Global Security and a former Trade Commissioner in East Asia, where she spent several years. In the last decade, she has taken part in EU projects on smart cities, sustainability, innovation technologies (including blockchain), and the benefits of space exploration. She recently published *The New Frontiers of Space* (Palgrave Macmillan, 2019) and co-edited *Emerging Markets & Sustainable Economies* (Routledge, 2019).

Steve Petterson is a co-founder of the National Social Value Fund and a manager at the HSBC Social Innovation Academy. At National Social Value Fund, Steve is working to develop a network of community-based funding mechanisms for high-impact social purpose organizations. He is an advocate for the empowerment and involvement of young leaders in this mission. To date, he has helped launch five social value funds across Canada. To begin his career, Steve worked at Helder Ventures, an impact investment firm in Vancouver, where he advised on investment deals and helped to manage portfolio ventures. It was during this time, with the support of the Helder Ventures team, that the genesis of the National Social Value Fund was realized.

Marlei Pozzebon is a Professor at HEC Montréal and at FGV/EAESP (joint appointment). She earned her Ph.D. at McGill University. Marlei's research interests are social change, social technologies, community-based projects, and post-development. These interests are linked to the relationship between communities and social technologies, as well as to the possibilities of better understanding and promoting social change. She was a visiting scholar at LUISS (Italy), University of Cape Town (South Africa), Université Paris-Dauphine (France), Universidad Nacional de Colombia, London School of Economics (UK), University of Siegen (Germany), and Erasmus University (The Netherlands).

Jason Prince is an urban planner with nearly three decades experience in community economic development, coaches collective enterprises in the social economy at PME MTL Centre Ville. Prince has worked with entrepreneurs on a wide variety of projects from community housing, to retail cooperatives, placemaking, food security projects, makerspaces, community energy projects, daycares, and seniors' services. Prince teaches the social economy part-time at Concordia University and has co-edited a few books on problems facing the city. Prince has two children aged 13 and 14 years.

Alessandro Rizzello holds a Ph.D. from the University Magna Graecia of Catanzaro, where he currently teaches social and sustainable finance. His dissertation focuses on social impact investing and social impact bonds in the healthcare sector. His research interests are impact investing, social impact bonds, sustainable finance and banking, and the crowdfunding of social ventures. His working experience includes a position of head of the Budgetary and Financial Office in the Italian public administration. He received his degree in Economics from LUISS Guido Carli University, Rome.

Tyler Schwartz is a M.Sc. candidate at HEC Montreal studying Data Science and Business Analytics. He currently serves as a Research Assistant in the Department of Finance at Concordia University. Tyler completed his undergraduate degree at the John Molson School of Business in which he received an Honours in Finance. He was also presented with the CUSRA scholarship in 2016, which is awarded to undergraduate students who have an interest in pursuing research activities. His research interests include predictive modeling, machine learning, sports analytics, and sustainable finance.

Elisabetta Scognamiglio received her Ph.D. from the University of Naples Federico II, with a dissertation that focused on the nature of risks in social impact bonds. Currently, she is Head of Communities Domain in Italiacamp, where she has worked since 2017 and was previously a project manager. Her main activities are the management of and advisory on impact evaluation, strategy, and impact assessment processes. She also coordinates the activities of the Governance Innovations and Impact Management (GIIM) Observatory, a LUISS research observatory founded and supported by Italiacamp. Prior to this, she was project manager for a leading microfinance institution.

Julie Segal is a graduate of McGill University's Desautels Faculty of Management. She works in impact investing at The J.W. McConnell Family Foundation, one of Canada's largest private philanthropic foundations, which is distinguished by its application of social innovation and social finance. She is a board member of a Montreal community organization and is engaged in environmental activism.

Molly Sinderbrand is a higher education professional in the Nonprofit Leadership Program at the University of Pennsylvania. She held a Post-doctoral Research Fellowship at the Center for High Impact Philanthropy at Penn, where she focused on philanthropic impact on domestic K-12 education. Molly's research and teaching revolve around ethics, social norms theory, and behavior change. She earned her Ph.D. in Philosophy from the University of Pennsylvania, her M.A. in Applied Ethics through a joint program between Utrecht University and Linkoping University, and her BA in Philosophy from Washington University in St Louis.

Érica S. Siqueira is a researcher at CEMIF/FGV. She recently obtained a Ph.D. from Fundação Getulio Vargas (FGV). Her research is related to digital platforms as well as financial and digital inclusion. She is particularly interested in critical studies in information systems and ICT4D.

Anne Snick works as an independent researcher. She obtained a Ph.D. in Philosophy in Education at KU Leuven (Belgium) in 1994. After a period of academic research, she engaged in fieldwork in the domains of gender, poverty, and the social economy for about twenty years. Her focus is on systemic drivers of exploitation and regenerative alternatives, especially in finance. She has written several contributions to peer-reviewed publications, serves the wider community through public speaking and workshops, and engages in various organizations that promote social justice and sustainability. Her current projects focus on sustainable higher education and transformative learning.

Vanessa Sorin holds a master's degree in sociology and local development. She has over 15 years of experience in community economic development, and for the past five years, she has been working as a transfer advisor for Territoires innovants en économie sociale et solidaire (TIESS) in Montreal, where she coordinates work on community bonds.

Wolfgang Spiess-Knafl is Co-Director of the European Center for Social Finance and Director of Next Generation Impact. After completing his studies in Management Engineering, he worked as an analyst in the investment banking division of Morgan Stanley. Between 2009 and 2016, he wrote his doctoral thesis with a focus on social finance at the TU Munich and worked as a Postdoctoral Research Fellow at the Zeppelin University. Since 2016, he has worked on the development of the social finance market for the European Commission, conducted studies for the European Parliament (among others), and published a book on impact investing with Palgrave Macmillan.

James Tansey is an Associate Professor at the University of British Columbia's Sauder School of Business and Executive Director of UBC's Sauder Centre for Social Innovation & Impact Investing. For the last 20 years, he has served as a faculty member in the business schools of University of Oxford and UBC. He is the founder of Offsetters, NatureBank Asset Management, and Canvas Impact Advisors. He has served as an advisor to the federal and provincial governments on social innovation and impact investing, and was awarded the Queen's Diamond Jubilee Award for service to the environment in 2014.

Ludovica Testa graduated with a degree in Economics and Management from LUISS Guido Carli University in Rome. Since 2018, she has been a project manager at ItaliaCamp, where her work is dedicated to impact assessment and measurement as well as impact strategy. She provided research contributions on impact measurement to several research and development activities of ItaliaCamp. She also contributed to academic activities focused on impact measurement and management held by the company in research groups and conferences.

Percy Venegas is Chief Scientist at Economy Monitor. He conducts research on post-quantum and decentralized artificial intelligence and advises family offices on risk, resilience, and responsible investment. He is a former Intel engineer, and a member of the New England Complex Systems Institute, the International Institute of Forecasters, and the International Association for Applied Econometrics. Percy pioneered the study of asymmetric trust and fields finance; he has published and presented on the topic at the University of Cambridge and MIT, among others. Venegas holds degrees in engineering, business, sustainability, and recently completed the Artificial Intelligence program at the University of Oxford.

Kalima Amber Vico is a research associate at the Emerging Risks Information Centre (ERIC) at Concordia University, Montreal, Canada. She previously worked for Concordia's David O'Brien Centre for Sustainable Enterprise.

Attila A. Víg is a Ph.D. student in the Department of Finance at Corvinus University of Budapest. He earned his master's degree in Financial Mathematics at Eötvös Loránd University. His main research interests are asset price dynamics and the population dynamics of financial markets.

Nadra Wagdy is an associate consultant at CID Consulting in Egypt. She is contributing to the development and scaling of an Extended Producer Responsibility program, working with the informal waste sector. She has extensive experience supporting cooperatives and not-for-profit organizations across their development phases: starting from validating their business plan and governance model to scaling-up their operations.

Thomas Walker is a full Professor of finance at Concordia University in Montreal, Canada. He previously served as an associate dean, department chair, and director of Concordia's David O'Brien Centre for Sustainable Enterprise. Prior to his academic career, he worked for firms such as Mercedes Benz, KPMG, and Utility Consultants International. He has published over 70 journal articles and books.

Erez Yerushalmi is a senior Lecturer at Birmingham City Business School and director of the Centre for Applied Finance and Economics (CAFÉ). Previously, he was a Research Fellow at the Institute for Employment Research (IER) at the University of Warwick (and remains an honorary research associate). His research focuses on applied policy analysis using computable general equilibrium (CGE) modeling and other quantitative methods. He has studied topics in labor modeling, environmental economics, health economics, tax policy, infrastructure and transportation assessment, and energy modeling. He teaches advanced economic theory, macroeconomics, and industrial organization. Erez has a Ph.D. in Economics from the University of Warwick, UK.

List of Figures

Social Finance Investments with a Focus on Digital Social Business Models

From Community Bank to Solidarity Fintech: The Case of Palmas e-Dinheiro in Brazil

Social Finance and Agricultural Funding

Public Governance of the Blockchain Revolution and Its Implications for Social Finance: A Comparative Analysis

Blockchain Consortia for the Social Good: An Introduction for Non-Technical Audiences

The Financial Intermediary Role of Peer-To-Peer Lenders

Evaluating Impact Investments: Frameworks and Applications for Social Ventures

The New Venture Philanthropy

List of Tables

Social Finance Investments with a Focus on Digital Social Business Models

Social Finance and Agricultural Funding

Informational Efficiency and Cybersecurity: Systemic Threats to Blockchain Applications

The Financial Intermediary Role of Peer-To-Peer Lenders

Evaluating Impact Investments: Frameworks and Applications for Social Ventures

The New Venture Philanthropy

Introduction

Expanding Our Understanding of Value Through Innovations in Social Finance

Thomas Walker, Jane McGaughey, Sherif Goubran, and Nadra Wagdy

1 Introduction

Our world is experiencing increasingly intricate social and environmental challenges, and we are struggling to meet them. Prevailing business models and the capitalist world order are commonly blamed for this failure, due to their neglect of social and environmental value in favour

T. Walker
Department of Finance, John Molson School of Business, Concordia University, Montreal, QC, Canada
e-mail: twalker@jmsb.concordia.ca

J. McGaughey
School of Irish Studies, Faculty of Arts and Science, Concordia University, Montreal, QC, Canada
e-mail: jane.mcgaughey@concordia.ca

S. Goubran (✉)
Department of Architecture, The School of Sciences and Engineering, The American University in Cairo (AUC), Cairo, Egypt
e-mail: sherifg@aucegypt.edu

N. Wagdy
CID Consulting, Cairo, Egypt

T. Walker et al. (eds.), *Innovations in Social Finance*,
https://doi.org/10.1007/978-3-030-72535-8_1

of financial return. Within this context, social finance has attracted the attention of governments, organizations, entrepreneurs, and researchers as a way to mobilize resources and harness innovation in establishing effective long-term solutions. While some economists suggest that social finance can be understood as the new paradigm of our age, other practitioners and researchers propose that social investments are closely related to practices that have long been understood in mainstream finance. At its core, social finance has the potential to redefine the philosophy of how money is raised and used, moving beyond economic value and incorporating the social and environmental externalities that have long been neglected. The disruptive (and generative) capacity of social finance lies in its intent to reconcile two distinct capital allocation traditions that were previously perceived as incompatible.

2 Outlining Innovation Within Social Finance

All organizations generate economic, social, and environmental outcomes. Even though the traditional approach of the financial sector is focused on creating positive financial and economic value, it also affects our society and the environment (Hebb, 2013; Nicholls & Emerson, 2015). Yet, these effects are considered externalities, which are neither managed nor optimized in the traditional approach. Over the past decade, there has been a growing interest in understanding, managing, and creating non-economic outcomes. This approach underlines the simplest definition of social finance, "refer[ing] to the allocation of capital primarily for social and environmental returns, as well as in some cases, a financial return" (Nicholls & Emerson, 2015, p. 4). However, this definition is contested, highlighting that social finance is variously understood as a policy tool for innovatively tackling social challenges, an outcome of social innovation or as a tool to facilitate it, and as a space for growing social business activities (Kiron et al., 2012; Moore et al., 2012; Standing Committee on Human Resources Skills and Social Development and the Status of Persons with Disabilities, 2015).

Thus, we can understand social finance as an umbrella term representing an attitude towards the utilization and flow of capital towards creating positive economic externalities, including its supply, intermediation, and demand (Hebb, 2013). Additionally, the term may represent a critique of the present financial system and its consequential negative impact, which includes social inequality and environmental degradation. While the creation of non-financial returns and the allocation of capital for social purposes are not new developments, these approaches are historically linked to government spending and different philanthropic organizations. What is currently changing is the gradual institutionalization of social finance approaches and their increased adoption by mainstream private organizations, thus creating new opportunities, challenges, and risks.

Some of the most popular tools within the social finance sector are investment-focused. This includes social investing, where capital is allocated to create measurable positive social and environmental impacts, or socially responsible investment (SRI), where social, environmental, and ethical dimensions are integrated into investment decisions (Hangl, 2014). These approaches vary significantly in their focus and priorities, ranging from an "impact first" approach, in which lower financial returns are accepted for the sake of better social or environmental effects, to "finance first" investments, which attempt to generate both non-financial outcomes and reasonable risk-adjusted rates of return (Hebb, 2013). Other established tools within the social finance sector include approaches that aim to alleviate poverty (such as microfinance), as well as tools that create contracts between governments and private investors (such as social impact bonds, SIBs). Social entrepreneurship is another important term within the social finance field, often perceived as being at the intersection of creating social value through market-based strategies and simultaneous income generation (Hangl, 2014). Additionally, new types of financial institutions, such as social banks, aim to serve social missions (Weber & Remer, 2011).

Innovation is a critical part of the development and progress of social finance. This has led some to view social innovation and social finance as a nexus that can potentially enhance and scale existing ideas for delivering broader impact (Standing Committee on Human Resources Skills and Social Development and the Status of Persons with Disabilities, 2015). While social financial innovation does present some risks, such as those associated with microfinance explored by Langevin (2019), innovation is nevertheless needed to channel different forms of capital towards tackling today's multifaceted social and ecological challenges. While social finance development makes available the capital needed for societal innovation to happen, the relationship between these two concepts is not linear. The broader impact of social finance innovations may extend far beyond directing capital flows and include supporting new collaborations, new sectorial developments, establishing and institutionalizing disruptive technologies, and even revealing new understandings of human socio-economic systems (Goldenberg et al., 2009). Thus, innovation, in the context of social finance, can be understood as cross-cutting across all levels of the sector: rethinking internal and external organizations and processes, creating new products and services, generating and measuring value in new ways, and developing new hybrids that combine the established and untried (Geobey et al., 2012; Moore et al., 2012). This collection argues that emerging innovation in social finance can help us chart the global transition to a new epoch, in which the social and financial dimensions of a given investment are reconciled.

3 Overview of the Collection

Innovations in Social Finance—Transitioning Beyond Economic Value summarizes, discusses, and analyses new innovative social finance trends. The collection includes contributions from scholars, practitioners, and industry experts that underscore the opportunities, challenges, and risks associated with new products, tools, and processes in the social finance field. These are supported by a range of case studies that vary in their geographic scope and coverage. The collection offers more than a snapshot of the current social finance field by highlighting the major challenges and difficulties that require policymakers' and social entrepreneurs' urgent attention. Additionally, the contributions shed light on how disruptive social finance innovations are redefining mainstream finance. The collection places a significant focus on the digital innovations that are reshaping cash flows, money creation, and financial governance. The collection approaches social finance and its innovations as a catalyst for the transition of the broader financial sector towards a new epistemology of value creation that extends beyond the fiscal dimension. This approach distinguishes *Innovations in Social Finance—Transitioning Beyond Economic Value* from the currently available publications on the topic.

The book is divided into five main sections. In the first section, a collection of four chapters presents the diverse developmental potential of social finance on societal, institutional, and individual levels. In the chapter "Social Finance in the Anthropocene", *Snick* proposes that resilient social finance initiatives are living labs where humans can reconnect with nature and each other. The chapter views social finance as a new paradigm for making capital function as a means for human and natural wellbeing.

Similarly, in their chapter "Social Finance in Quebec: An Ecosystemic Approach to Financial Innovation", *Mendell and Neamtan* offer an overview of the evolution of social finance in Québec and present its social economy and social finance ecosystem as a model that can be replicated globally, as explored in the case of South Korea. In the next chapter "Social Finance for Women's Entrepreneurship in Canada", *Chavoushi, Ying Mo, and Cukier* present and analyse successful Canadian examples of social finance that are helping women in business and entrepreneurship. They propose that social finance can help women in overcoming the systemic gender barriers they face in their access to financing. Finally, in the chapter "The Role of Youth in Scaling Social Value Investing: The Case of Canada's National Social Value Fund", *Lam, Petterson, Tansey, Rubio,* and *Lakat* explore the stewardship role and the responsibility that youth hold in advancing finance towards a more equitable and social value-driven field. They present a case of a youth-led social fund as an example of innovation that embodies the new generation's ethics and values.

In the second section, the collection explores emerging innovation in capital flows. In the chapter "The Community Bond Experience in Montreal, Quebec", *Prince* and *Sorin* present community bonds as a social financial tool for achieving social missions. They focus on Québec's experience and present the emerging trend of coupling crowd-lending with community bond issues. In the next chapter, "Let's Get Explicit: The Emergence of Impact-Linked Returns in the Commercial Debt Market", *Boggild* studies and compares a range of impact-linked debt instruments that can enable practitioners to manage and balance between return, impact, and risk. The subsequent chapter, "A University Model of Social Finance: Reflections on the University of Edinburgh's Social Investment Fund", *Gorman* and *Huang* provide an overview of the University of Edinburgh's Social Investment Fund. They suggest that the university's model—which is based on engagement from the entire institution as well as new kinds of capital flows and local collaborations—can provide insights into existing institutions and inform mainstream practices. Finally, *Segal* and *Vargas* introduce the concept and applications of patient investment capital in their chapter "Opportunities in Patient Capital Financing". They review the applicability of patient capital across investment types, using it to advance social and sustainability outcomes in private market transactions.

In the third section, four chapters present an array of digital innovations that are advancing social finance and creating new local and community-focused developments. *Lazcano* opens the section with his chapter "Inside Money Creation in the Digital Era" by revisiting the development and institutionalization of money and cryptoassets. The chapter explores the possibility of creating "social cryptoassets" that move beyond the definitions of speculative commodities and securities. His work is followed by the chapter "Social Finance Investments with a Focus on Digital Social Business Models", in which *Jansen, Mast,* and *Spiess-Knafl* observe and analyse a split between non-tech and tech investments in portfolios of social venture capital funds. They offer insights into the potential of the digital tools presented, as well as the limits of digital business models. Next, in their chapter "From Community Bank to Solidarity Fintech: The Case of Palmas e-Dinheiro in Brazil", *Ansorena, Diniz, Siqueira,* and *Pozzebon* present the case of the Palmas e-Dinheiro, a local digital currency. They delve into the digital currency's history, connection to community banks, in addition to its role in financial inclusion and local development. Finally, in their chapter "Social Finance and Agricultural Funding", *Havran, Kerényi,* and *Víg* explore how social finance, in the form of digital crowdfunding, can play integrative and entrepreneurial roles, in the case of consumer-supported agricultural farmers.

Section four continues this emphasis on digital innovation, focusing specifically on blockchain technology. The section starts with the chapter "Public Governance of the Blockchain Revolution and Its Implications for Social Finance: A Comparative Analysis", in which *Paladini, Yerushalmi,* and *Castellucci* investigate the potential for blockchain applications beyond the monetary system. They study the limits to the technology's social applications by comparing laws and regulations in multiple countries, and propose the potential characteristics of a blockchain-friendly regulatory framework. In the next chapter "Blockchain Consortia for the Social Good: An Introduction for Non-Technical Audiences", *Venegas* presents the idea of blockchain consortia, which provide a balance between privacy and transparency. They argue that a blockchain consortium offers a viable alternative to addressing the gaps that emerge from the social application of traditional financial architectures. In the last chapter, *Gurdgiev* and *Fleming* study the cybersecurity threats of blockchains and cryptocurrencies, highlighting that there may be major risks to their imminent wide application in social finance.

Finally, section five concludes the collection by concentrating on the role of different institutions, exploring governance issues, and critiquing the social finance field. In the chapter "Who Should Fund Social Innovation?", *Sinderbrand* focuses on the issue of social innovation and the actors that are most suited to its undertaking. The chapter argues that social enterprises are more fit to innovate than governments, but that governments are better suited at scaling these innovations. *Dömötör* and *Ölvedi* offer an overview of P2P lending in their chapter "The Financial Intermediary Role of Peer-to-Peer Lenders". They identify the main differences and competitive advantages of different P2P lending platforms and compare them to traditional banks, finding the model relevant and highlighting its contribution to social welfare. Their work is followed by the chapter "The Role of Social Financing in Sustainable Development: The Case of Nigerian Co-operatives", in which *Ajibola* examines social financing challenges in the Nigerian context that are a result of top-down development mechanics. The chapter proposes that the cooperative model, in which resources are mobilized into close-knit units, and the upscaling of the financial sector are viable solutions to Nigeria's sustainable development challenges. Next, in their chapter "Evaluating Impact Investments: Frameworks and Applications for Social Ventures", *Rizzello, Scognamiglio, Testa,* and *Liotta* study both the impacts and their assessment in the social finance field. In the subsequent chapter "Social Investment in the UK: The Emergence of a Hollow Field", *Bell* proposes that social finance in the UK is a hollow field, with much institutional work, but surprisingly few investment deals. Finally, in her chapter "The New Venture Philanthropy", *Avci* presents the concept of venture philanthropy, which is reshaping our understanding of donations. The chapter argues that funding ideas and initiatives that have growth potential increases donations' efficiency and leads to innovation.

This edited collection underscores the wide range of topics that comprise social finance. By combining contributions from both practitioners and scholars, the book presents new insights into the transition of innovations from theory to practice. It highlights that digital tools and emerging technologies offer new avenues for social finance. However, questions related to the impact, definition, and assessment of innovations in social finance require further investigation.

References

Geobey, S., Westley, F. R., & Weber, O. (2012). Enabling social innovation through developmental social finance. *Journal of Social Entrepreneurship, 3*(2), 151–165. https://doi.org/10.1080/19420676.2012.726006.

Goldenberg, M., Kamoji, W., Orton, L., & Williamson, M. (2009). *Social innovation in Canada: An update.* Canadian Policy Research Networks Inc.

Hangl, C. (2014). A literature review about the landscape of social finance. *ACRN Journal of Finance and Risk Perspectives, 3*(4), 64–98.

Hebb, T. (2013). Impact investing and responsible investing: What does it mean? *Journal of Sustainable Finance and Investment, 3*(2), 71–74. https://doi.org/10.1080/20430795.2013.776255.

Kiron, B. D., Palmer, D., Phillips, A. N., & Kruschwitz, N. (2012). Social business: What are companies really doing? *MIT Sloan Management Review, 31.*

Langevin, M. (2019). Big data for (not so) small loans: Technological infrastructures and the massification of fringe finance. *Review of International Political Economy, 26*(5), 790–814. https://doi.org/10.1080/09692290.2019.1616597.

Moore, M.-L. L., Westley, F. R., & Nicholls, A. (2012). The social finance and social innovation nexus. *Journal of Social Entrepreneurship, 3*(2), 115–132. https://doi.org/10.1080/19420676.2012.725824.

Nicholls, A., & Emerson, J. (2015). Social finance. In *Social finance* (pp. 1–42). Oxford University Press. https://doi.org/10.1093/acprof:oso/9780198703761.003.0001.

Standing Committee on Human Resources Skills and Social Development and the Status of Persons with Disabilities. (2015). *Exploring the potential of social finance in Canada.* Parliament of Canada. https://www.ourcommons.ca/DocumentViewer/en/41-2/HUMA/report-12.

Weber, O., & Remer, S. (Eds.). (2011). *Social banks and the future of sustainable finance.* Routledge. https://doi.org/10.4324/9780203827871.

Exploring the Potential of Social Finance

Social Finance in the Anthropocene

Anne Snick

1 Introduction: Why a New Paradigm?

Today, social finance initiatives remain small niches, unable to alter the capitalist system's destructive course. We call that system destructive because since the 1950s, when the economy globalized, most natural resources have been depleted or destroyed at an increasing (or even exponential) rate, disrupting the balance of living ecosystems (Crist, 2019; McNeill & Engelke, 2014). Niche innovations like "organic food" or "circular economy" are aimed toward sustainability, yet until now remain side-branches of an extractive production system. The same is true for social finance. Most of the research and governance for sustainability focus on marketable technologies or environmental regulations, remaining blind toward using social finance as leverage to change our economic model and "restore the balance." This chapter proposes a framework for understanding under what conditions social finance can foster sustainability.

Scientists call the current era "Anthropocene" since human activity impacts the Earth's geophysical processes (Crist, 2019; Rockström et al.,

A. Snick (✉)
Club of Rome, Winterthur, Switzerland
e-mail: anne.snick@scarlet.be

T. Walker et al. (eds.), *Innovations in Social Finance*,
https://doi.org/10.1007/978-3-030-72535-8_2

2009). Since the 1950s, *socio-economic* trends reveal growth at exponential rates; the *Earth system* trends reveal the price we pay in rising CO2 levels, ocean acidification, biosphere degradation, etc. (McNeill & Engelke, 2014). This "great acceleration" causes disruptions of the ecosystems that human life depends on. Since most of our societal institutions originated in the previous epoch, viz. the Holocene period of relative stability, they are not designed to cope with these novel conditions. They merely aim to control each subsystem separately while assuming the others remain stable, and neglect how feedback among the various subsystems affects the planet as a whole. However, "unpredicted" or "unintended" outcomes such as antibiotics resistance or global warming prove this paradigm wrong.

The financial system, as well, is mostly studied as a separate sector with its proper rationale and pursuing its own growth while concealing its interdependency with social and ecological subsystems. Investigating how money, e.g., could drive a *decrease* in antibiotics consumption or CO_2 emissions, is crucial today. Therefore, the first paragraph explains what the complexity of the new epoch means and how it affects science. Secondly, we explain why, in this context, the current money system is inadequate for human survival. In a third step, we propose an alternative framework for the role and design of finance. The last paragraph explores how and under what conditions social finance can foster sustainable development.

2 Entering the Anthropocene Epoch

2.1 Ontology: Understanding Reality as Increasing Complexity

Life on Earth as we know it began as simple cells that could reproduce themselves (Capra & Luisi, 2014; Chapman, 2015; Ulanowicz, 2009). As their numbers increased, these cells frequently collided, and from these interactions, multicellular life forms emerged. These then started to combine, leading to even more complex life forms and so on. Evolution is a self-propelling process of interactions that auto-catalyze into increasingly complex systems. At each next level of complexity, the natural system reveals new, "emergent" behaviors and characteristics, different from those of the previous (sub)systems (Chapman, 2015). Kitchen salt, e.g., consists of sodium and chloride, and since none of these components taste like salt, the salty taste is called an "emergent" characteristic. Similarly, to understand the intelligence of beehives, studying single bees is useless; what matters is how they *interact* with each other and their environment.

Since some decennia, our planet shows characteristics such as weather patterns and oceanic currents unseen in history (Watch the Ocean, 2020). The physics and chemical cycles of the Earth are changing, indicating that *life is evolving into a next level of complexity*. Scientists agree that humans play an essential role in this evolution (Capra & Luisi, 2014; Crist, 2019; Daly & Farley, 2011). Intense interactions between human-made and natural systems bring our planet's evolution into a new stage, called the Anthropocene (from Anthropos, meaning man).

2.2 Epistemology: From Linear to Complex Systems Thinking

The Anthropocene system is more complex than the previous one and this forces scientific models to adapt. The past era, the Holocene, started about 12,000 years ago when the climate stabilized. Humans no longer had to migrate to find food and shelter, as in the times of ice ages and interglacial periods. This exceptional stability allowed humankind to build settlements and cities, invent agriculture, and develop writing, culture, and science. It let scientists believe that reality functions like clockwork.

Research takes place in laboratories focusing on specific subdomains and parameters while disregarding (interdependencies with) others. By manipulating parameters and measuring the outcomes, researchers look for regularities to be expressed in mathematical equations (Hossenfelder, 2018). They assume subsystems also remain stable outside the lab (as the formula "ceteris paribus" used by economists expresses). A scientific experiment may reveal that "if (in the lab) we do A, the outcome is B." Scientists take that as proof that "if (in society) we do more of A, more of B will be the result"; ultimately, they use a *linear* (mechanistic) paradigm. If a subdomain impacts others in ways the equations did not predict (e.g., the economy causing ecological degradation), scientists treat this as "externalities" they leave out of their models.

Faced with these complex and unintended outcomes of the mechanistic worldview, a more holistic scientific approach emerged in the twentieth century: systems thinking. To understand the behavior of complex technical, social, or ecological systems, systems thinkers study patterns of interactions and feedbacks among its various parts or subsystems (Capra & Luisi, 2014; Meadows, 2008). If, for example, traffic jams occur, a "linear" solution is to construct more roads. However, in turn, these attract more cars (since drivers believe traffic will now be smoother), and traffic jams increase again, calling for more roads, etc. Mutually reinforcing feedbacks thus create a vicious cycle that results in the traffic system developing in an unintended direction. If a teacher praises a pupil for her or his qualities, the learner will be motivated to work hard, eliciting more praise, etc. In that case, the feedback creates a virtuous cycle, serving a desirable goal.

A prevailing solution to increasingly severe heatwaves is to sell air-conditioners to stabilize the climate inside houses, assuming (linearly) that "the more cooling devices consumers buy, the more the problem is solved." However, producing and using these devices require energy and cause increasing gashouse emissions that spur global warming: a vicious cycle. A balanced system at *a small* scale (house) can in the long run become part of an escalating system at *a large* scale (climate). This insight helps avoid unwanted effects; planting trees around houses may be recognized as a more *sustainable* (long-term) solution. Similarly, animal-borne diseases emerge from human intrusion into wild nature and a standard reaction is to develop vaccines to kill specific viruses. That, however, fosters the belief that humanity can safely continue conquering wilderness areas, which paradoxically increases the risk of animal-borne pandemics.

The whole is more than the sum of the parts. The difference between a mechanical system and a living ecosystem is that in the latter, both the parts and the relationships evolve (Gorissen, 2020). Consequently, if *specialist* (mechanistic) science reveals truth about life on Earth, it is not the *whole* (holistic) truth. Linear thinking has to make room for complex system analyses in which (large-scale, long-term) interactions between subsystems—*including finance*—are center-stage (Meadows, 2008). In Anthropocene conditions, transcending the disciplinary lens and co-creating knowledge from as many sources and perspectives as possible (a trans-disciplinary paradigm) are crucial. In systemic terms, the current economic model is caught in vicious circles and we need a financial system that drives virtuous ones, contributing to social and ecological goals.

2.3 A Shifting Paradigm for Sustainable Co-Evolution

It is crucial to understand what keeps prevailing systems from adapting to emergent planetary conditions. Since the 1970s, scientific reports warned that a growing (fossil-fuel based) industrial economy would run into planetary boundaries (Meadows et al., 1972). A recent graph by the

Global Footprint Network shows the Human Development Index, i.e., a combined metric of health, education, income, and housing (on the horizontal axis) in relation to the ecological footprint—the hectares needed per person per year to achieve this "development" (on the vertical axis). It reveals that "highly developed" countries all overshoot the world's bio-capacity (Fig. 1).

The way scientists and politicians define and organize "development" is manifestly not adapted to the planetary reality (Latour, 2017). The pursuit of human "progress" thus paradoxically increases the risk that (human life will disappear, as the result of an interplay among the following three spheres:

1. The *biophysical* domain creates the conditions for life to evolve and circumscribes Nature's capacity to remain balanced and replenish its offerings. It depends on (the right amount of) solar energy and is governed by thermodynamics (entropy) and autocatalysis. Some of these offerings are renewable (on a human time scale), and others

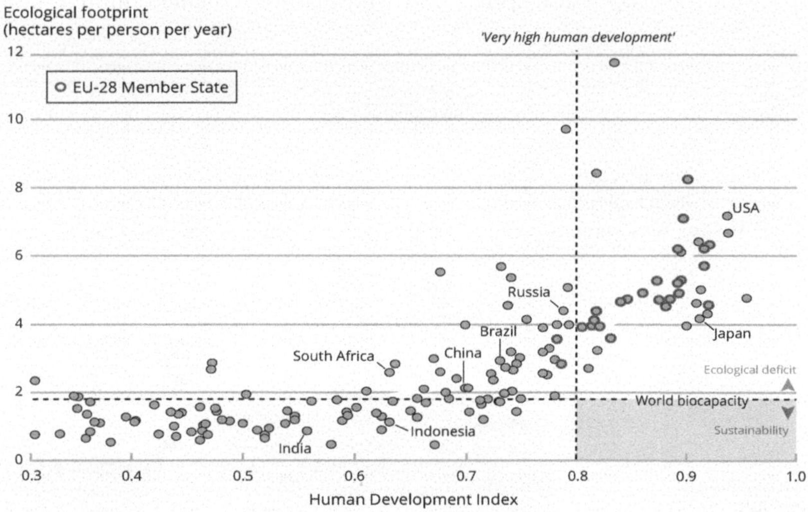

Fig. 1 Correlation of the ecological footprint and Human Development Index (*Source* Global Footprint Network)

(like soils, minerals, or metals) are not (Sverdrup & Ragnarsdottir, 2014).

2. *Values and narratives* concern how people define a "good life." Indigenous people recognize Nature as their life base and treat it with restraint, respect, and reciprocity (Crist, 2019; Kimmerer, 2013). Indo-European cultures claim that God created humans in his image and gave them Nature to own and use; "progress" for them is proportional to the unrestrained exploitation of Nature (Lent, 2017).
3. The *economic-technological sphere* is how people organize and institutionalize relations among themselves and with the biophysical domain for achieving (what they define as) a "good life"; this includes financial tools.

Figure 2 depicts how these spheres, themselves complex entanglements of subsystems, interact over time; it shows non-linear processes, mutual interactions, and feedbacks among the three spheres engendering the *co-evolution* of life on Earth. As long as the human population was small, its impact on the biophysical sphere and wild Nature remained limited; in a

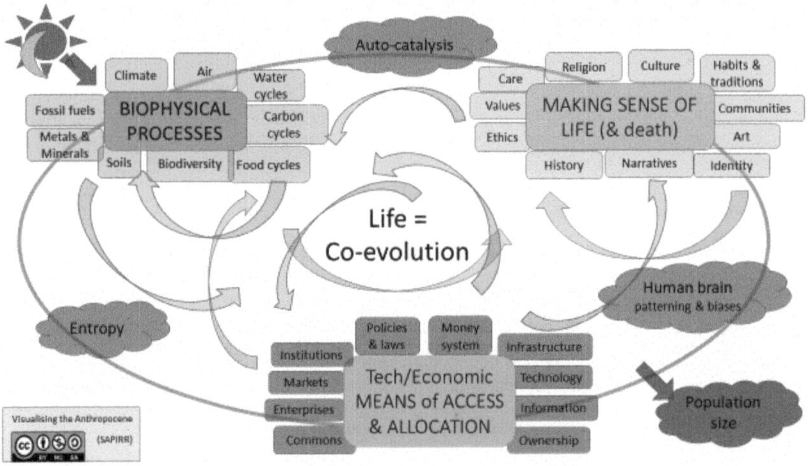

Fig. 2 Visualizing the complexity of the anthropocene co-evolution (*Source* Snick, 2020)

globalized extractive economy, however, it may lead to the extinction of all life as we know it.

The feedback mechanisms (bent arrows) mean that, e.g., cultural narratives that equate human progress with the domination of Nature foster extractive economic, financial, and technological regimes. These, in turn, strengthen the belief (narrative) that wellbeing is impossible without the ongoing exploitation of Nature. As natural buffers decline, more aggressive technologies are deployed and this requires investments that increase the pressure to extract and ensure a financial return on investment: a race to the bottom.

Western culture defines human development without considering how this impacts the biosphere. It imposes this capitalist narrative (via institutions like the World Trade Organization and World Bank) on nations globally. However, communities worldwide start questioning this narrative and its economic-technological regime because of the social and ecological destruction it causes (Mignolo & Walsh, 2018). The COVID-19 pandemic highlights the interconnectedness of life and the need for a regenerative economy. Only through a *systemic* response can we ensure a fair transition (Forslund, 2020).

3 Deconstructing Money

3.1 Money Is an Agreement Based on Trust

To be able to adapt finance to the Anthropocene, one needs to understand what it is. Money is an *agreement within a community* to use something as a medium of exchange, a unit of account, and a store of value. Throughout history, people have used many things as money, yet metal coins are the best known. During World War I, soldiers in the trenches used cigarettes as money; non-smokers accepted them as payment, for they *trusted* they could exchange them for things they needed (e.g., food). Money lets society run smoothly (as long) as it gives users access to things of *real* value (like food, clothing, or housing). It facilitates the economy because it can be used to give entrepreneurs credits, allowing them to launch a business; it expresses trust that the debtors will pay back later. *Credit* comes from the Latin *credere*, which means *believing*.

Today, governments have bestowed the sole power (or the “fiat”) to create money upon (mostly private) banks. Hence, this money is also called "fiat-money." Banks bring money into circulation by providing loans (debts) to economic actors *they* deem trustworthy, i.e., capable of bringing back more money. Money is created by putting numbers on debtors' accounts, and since numbers are unlimited, bank money can grow endlessly. Only a fraction of the money brought into circulation has to be deposited in the National Bank or Federal Reserve ("Fractional Reserve Banking"). Therefore, if the community loses trust in the financial system and "runs to the banks" to take their money out, the system may collapse.

3.2 *Monetary Means-Ends Reversal*

Bank debts must be paid back with interest. Debtors cannot create this interest themselves (i.e., a bank monopoly), so they must "extract" it from their dealings with each other and Nature. In sum, there is always less money around than we collectively owe the banks, and "to make money" becomes the aim of all economic activity, a means-ends reversal (Pogany, 2015). Companies that do not make a profit go bankrupt, and this permanent menace fuels short-term thinking (Lietaer et al., 2012). It feeds the ideology that competition is necessary for economic progress and that eternal growth is possible. That, in turn, encourages economists and bankers to develop increasingly speculative financial instruments, losing connection with society's real needs and the planet's real carrying capacity.

In order to keep up with an ever-increasing amount of (money as) debt, the economy needs to keep growing. Since growth always involves (energy captured by) natural processes, planetary overshoot is *inevitable* (Chang, 2011). Compound interests grow exponentially; however, on our planet, exponential growth is impossible. If a gold coin at the start of the Christian era would have grown at a rate of 3% annually, it would now represent a golden globe larger than Earth. In this system, disasters like traffic accidents or cleared rainforests are *good* for the economy, as they stimulate sales of medical care, insurance products, or air-conditioners (Raworth, 2017). Knowledge, rather than being freely shared among all people, is privatized as "intellectual property." Research results—even of publicly funded studies—are commodified, and society has to pay again to access them. Most of today's financial instruments, institutions, and markets have been purposed to maximize direct wealth creation, rather than achieving universal, long-term goals (Patel & Hansmeyer, 2020).

3.3 Social Finance Framed as "Redistribution"

How do nations organize wellbeing with a money system designed for exploitation? Wellbeing is usually defined in terms of education, health care, elderly care, and access to culture and Nature. Those are services that companies are hardly interested in, since they do not yield high financial returns. In most cases, governments finance them by *redistributing* (via taxes) a percentage of income. So, in a redistributive system that uses bank money, raising *wellbeing* inevitably requires economic growth, which paradoxically increases *exploitation*.

During the COVID-19 pandemic, the global economy came to a halt for several weeks, and as a result, the global carbon footprint was reduced by 14.5% from 2019 (Overshootday, 2020). People rediscovered the importance of Nature for their health and immune system. If economists claim that "after" the pandemic, the economy has to grow again to finance health care, this shows how unfit their linear thinking is for human survival. In a world where pandemics and heatwaves risk to become the new normal, care and wellbeing cannot be organized solely by redistributing bank money. Using money to repair the damage money causes is like putting out a fire with a torch.

For a long time, extractive money appeared successful since it spurred productivity and wealth (at least in some parts of the world). Pursuing the growth of capital (capital-ism) seemed the best pathway, and many leaders still believe more capitalism will bring more wellbeing. However, experts have warned for "externalities" from the early stages of capitalism, pointing towards gender inequality, workers' exploitation, pollution, or the depletion of Nature. Through redistribution mechanisms (via taxes), governments built social welfare provisions to absorb those frictions, and after World War II, this seemed to work well. Rather than correct the extractive system, redistribution made it bearable, and so reinforced it.

COVID-19 reveals the limitations of this approach. During the lockdown money-making was halted to save lives, yet, to pay for their housing, e.g., people still depended on making money; most governments addressed this "housing instability" by redistributing money. A more systemic approach, however, starts by re-thinking "how to guarantee secure housing for all, even in pandemic times" and then redesigns financial and legal tools accordingly (City of Cambridge, 2020). Given the planet's dire condition and the suffering of people, we must adapt our financial system to foster wellbeing because without innovating finance, sustainability is impossible (Lietaer et al., 2012; Snick, 2019). Our societies, trapped in a race to the bottom, face a dilemma between stopping the economic engine (and suffer) or keep growing (and suffocate). If the COVID-19 pandemic manages to slow the economy down long enough, this may well signal a bifurcation where societally responsible money systems can emerge as "the new normal," allowing mankind to survive the Anthropocene.

4 A Framework for Social Finance in the Anthropocene

Initiatives in social finance have emerged in response to the toxic effects of bank money. At the core of social finance is the capacity to think of money again as a *social construct*, an agreement in a community on how to achieve *shared goals*. How can finance be redesigned to serve social goals and foster Nature's regeneration?

The Anthropocene reminds us that humans either co-evolve with Nature or collapse (see Fig. 2). Therefore, our best strategy is *to learn from Nature how to fit in*. For millions of years, Nature has been a laboratory brimming with innovative solutions nurturing the abundance of life. By imitating Nature (bio-mimicry), humanity can learn to thrive again (Gorissen, 2020). For ages (often until colonialism disrupted their lives), many indigenous cultures thrived in balance with their natural surroundings, treating other life forms not as private property but as a common good to be respected and nurtured. Western civilization can learn from them how to adapt (Mignolo & Walsh, 2018).

4.1 Learning from and Adapting to Nature's Dynamic Systems

The framework for social finance proposed here builds on insights into sustainable ecosystems revealed by process ecology, a scientific model used to study the organization of complex flows of energy and nutrients within (natural and technical) ecosystems (Ulanowicz, 2009). Systems turn out to be sustainable when they achieve a balance between two opposite characteristics: ascendency and resilience (see Fig. 3).

Ascendency is the capacity to channel activity along the most efficient pathway by streamlining processes and eliminating superfluous pathways. Monocultures, for example, are extremely ordered, efficient ways to grow plants. However, pursuing maximum ascendency means decreasing the

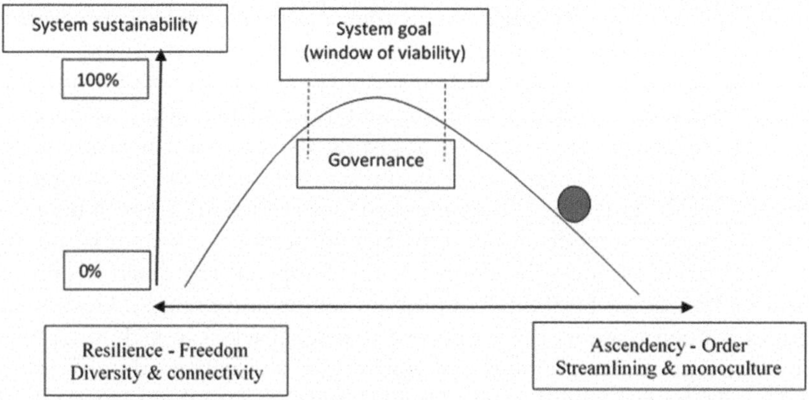

Fig. 3 Sustainability curve understood from the perspective of process ecology (*Source* Adapted from Lietaer et al. [2009])

number of alternative pathways that can take over the system's vital activities if the usual processes falter; therefore, monocultures score low on sustainability. A single disease or storm can destroy the entire crop, and the system may collapse (the red dot in Fig. 3).

Therefore, systems also need a degree of resilience, i.e., the capacity to create redundant (inefficient) pathways that can keep the system functioning in case of a crisis. A farm may survive a storm or drought by growing diverse plants with varying harvesting dates and complementary ecosystem functions. Nevertheless, in an ecosystem only consisting of tiny niches competing for resources (high resilience and low efficiency), the energy gets dissipated and the system stagnates (low sustainability). This curve explains why agro-ecological and indigenous farming is sustainable: they select combinations of diverse crops (resilience), allowing maximum productivity on a given surface (ascendency). It combines plants that optimally share light, water, and nutrients while feeding nutrients back into the soil (Kimmerer, 2013).

Sustainable systems keep both parameters in balance, and in multiple habitats and environments, they show a surprising consistency in their degrees of efficiency at *around 40%* (Ulanowicz, 2016). Resilience is often misunderstood as the system's capacity to return to its *former* state (and "sustain" established patterns, which, in fact, increases ascendency).

In dynamic systems, resilience means the capacity to establish *innovative* pathways toward a new balance, pursuing long-term co-evolution.

"Governance" refers to mechanisms maintaining (or restoring) the balance between (resilient) freedom and (ascendant) order at optimal levels. It regulates the system by adjusting its processes in response to context changes. For example, a thermostat adjusts flows (by closing or opening valves) in response to context changes (fluctuating room temperature). Correcting feedbacks have to kick in before the system is too far removed from its goal (the desired room temperature), thus keeping it within a "window of viability" (a pleasant temperature range). Governing should happen close to the system, so that feedbacks can kick in rapidly. Cities or regions, for example, can put in place alternative solutions more swiftly and more adapted to local conditions than central governments or international bodies.

This framework allows us to understand why the capitalist financial system is unfit for sustainable goals. Since governments bestowed the "governance" of finance upon banks, it serves banks' private (financial) goals, not (social and ecological) needs in the real world. Most banks are private companies whose aim is to produce a financial return for shareholders. They trade (speculative) assets without reflecting on how this impacts people or Nature (as ongoing investments in fossil fuels demonstrate). Financial headquarters are alienated from the real needs and dreams of people and the suffering of Nature, and they feel justified in dumping the costs for "externalities" of economic exploitation on society.

The current financial system is extremely streamlined (ascendant). Currencies like the dollar, euro, and yen are interchangeable worldwide; money moves in nanoseconds across continents. Global finance processes all societal transactions and boosts the economy (high efficiency), yet makes the system brittle, like a row of domino stones. If one bank fails, the whole global system may collapse (as in 2008). The system lacks diversity and connectivity. Banks can hardly adapt after financial crises: they became so powerful that they are "too big to fail." Governments, the business world, and even scientists treat bank money as the only possible pathway (with no room for resilience). This belief that "there is no alternative" in turn makes bank money even more ascendant. Legislation, taxation, and social welfare are organized almost entirely around it. As a result, people are convinced that without purchasing power, they cannot live or take care of each other, and that social or ecological policies are bad for them as soon as they "cost money."

The process-ecology framework also reveals how social finance can let humanity and Nature thrive again. At the most basic level, money facilitates both the investments that *create* surpluses and the trade that *distributes* them. Social finance should allow communities to create surpluses that are not extractive but regenerative, and distribute them in a way that "leaves no living being behind." Communities must assume the (decentralized) governance of the money system, for they have the knowledge allowing them to verify what kind of scheme effectively mobilizes capabilities to address local needs (Renn, 2020).

The planet is itself a rich tapestry of human-Nature ecosystems, each with its specific assets and capacities. Therefore, it is an illusion to believe all societal goals are achievable with only one kind of money. Rather than a monoculture, a reliable money system should become a living ecosystem of various financial leverages and a high diversity that uses the globally mainstream money system for around 40% of transactions only. The abundance of social finance initiatives shows that resilience is growing, but this has to speed up and become more ascendant (efficient) for humanity to survive. During the COVID-19 lockdown, alternative economic pathways emerged spontaneously. Citizens produced and donated the face masks and respiratory devices that private and public sectors were unable to provide, neighbors took care of each other, and local farms were rediscovered as reliable food suppliers. Nevertheless, these niches were too fragmented (low in ascendency) to take over the entire economy when the lockdown brought it to a standstill.

4.2 The Goals for Finance to Serve

Decentralized, democratically controlled monetary platforms may allow communities to assume the governance of finance. Nevertheless, decentralizing money does not automatically foster the common good. Blockchain technologies, e.g., break the bank monopoly on money creation and escape centralized control. However, a currency like Bitcoin still serves speculative goals and, moreover, it comes with an enormous energy footprint. Social money schemes, on the contrary, aim to restore communities' health and natural ecosystems (Cordon, 2019). Distributed ledgers allow people to create systems that *mutualize* the main provisioning systems (rather than commodifying them for private profit), and introduce collaborative forms of accounting that recognize both the positive and negative social and ecological externalities (Bauwens & Pazaitis, 2019). The downside of these systems is that they currently operate as disconnected niches in an overwhelmingly extractive environment. That means that either they remain marginal, separate from the dominant money system (like time banks or time dollars, and Local Exchange and Trade Systems—LETS) or, if they are interchangeable with the dominant financial system, they are vulnerable to being subsumed within its extractive logic again (Bruchhaus, 2016).

In a sustainable economy, economic growth can only mean *increasing* a community's capacity to foster the wellbeing of all, including future generations, while restoring ecosystem health. For example, in the United Nations Global Agenda 2030, "economic growth" is one of the sustainable development goals to be achieved *along with* human and planetary wellbeing. Many people recognize how economic growth damages our ecosystems; yet, their standard reaction is: "but we *need* money to live." The yellow vests movement in France in 2018, for example, called for lower fuel taxes and a minimum-wage increase. That is a way of saying: "given the current financial system, we have no other choice than to keep extracting Nature." Social finance initiatives transform that into: "given the current challenges, we have no other choice than to change finance." Social finance initiatives allow humans to "de-grow" levels of exploitation and extraction as well as increase collaboration and solidarity; they both stem from *and* contribute to changing narratives, thus creating virtuous circles (Snick, 2017). Only by experiencing how social finance increases happiness and restores environmental health can citizens "unlearn" the old narrative and feel empowered and hopeful (Grancitelli et al., 2020).

The economy can be defined as "the way societies organize themselves and allocate resources to fulfill their needs" (a description generally accepted in economics) (Daly & Farley, 2011). In that sense, fire brigades fulfill an *economic* function. They are organized to allocate resources (engines, technologies, water) for meeting a societal need (fire security). The *less* firefighters have to work, the *more* the societal goal is achieved. However, if society would value their contribution using standard monetary indicators ("how much did they make?"), fire brigades would have an interest in soaring conflagrations. When private penitentiary facilities appeared in the USA, the result was an increase in incarcerations. Since the jailing business had to remain profitable, criminal behavior in citizens became a source of wealth. When finance provides prisons with incentives to remain full, this causes arrests, indictments, and convictions that need to remain high, regardless of public safety needs (Kirkham, 2013). A social financial system helps us live better, safer, healthier, and freer lives while working, producing, extracting, or jailing *less*. If the economic function is to organize work and resources for increased wellbeing, this requires weaving a web of alternative monetary tools that can serve various societal purposes. Although their coherence (ascendency) is still frail, many social finance initiatives are already available.

5 Social Finance as an Emerging Sustainable Ecosystem

The following metaphor may help visualize the transition from a financial *monoculture* to a sustainable *ecosystem*. If the current system is like a tanker heading toward an iceberg, social finance is a *fleet* of maneuverable vessels of multiple types and sizes (increasing resilience), navigating turbulent waters in a cooperative, coordinated way. With ICT tools, this coordination (governance) may be decentralized in the long run, but leverage by powerful institutions is currently needed to guarantee a timely transition.

Knowing what the fleet will or should look like is impossible since currents (planetary and societal changes) are unpredictable. Moreover, the vessels influence not only each other but also their environment (human-Nature co-evolution). Framing science as the discovery of unchangeable truths that society then has to implement is obsolete because the future depends on the choices humans make. A complexity-based paradigm is an ongoing design process of action research transcending the disciplinary (linear) approach and trying out innovations in "living labs." That allows communities to swiftly register local feedback and apply correcting measures, staying on a safe course in turbulent conditions.

In that light, social finance initiatives are not research *objects* but transdisciplinary *laboratories* where societal actors test ideas about finance and sustainable co-evolution. However, current (academic, business, and political) leaders are slow to understand and accept this, as they have been educated in the Holocene paradigm. For finance to provide the basis of the next civilization, society needs to re-engineer the entire system, including how politics, economies, societies, and individuals work and measure success (Patel & Hansmeyer, 2020).

5.1 *Social Finance Increases Societal Resilience*

Whereas pursuing wellbeing through bank money re-distribution fuels accelerated exploitation, regenerative money schemes facilitate transactions that "pre-distribute" the offerings of Nature and human labor to the wellbeing of all life. Today, a myriad of regenerative initiatives implement innovative financing schemes. Some of them correct the extractive pull of bank money by improving the governance, e.g., by including "pollution" in taxing or pricing mechanisms or promoting ethical banking. Others increase resilience by installing complementary or "redundant" pathways for economic transactions. From the established system's perspective, these are "inefficient" and therefore are labeled "social" rather than "economic", even though for finance to become sustainable, they should actually take care of about 60% of transactions.

Time banks and LETS reward people for contributing to community goals using time as a unit of value; an hour of service by a computer specialist is given the same value as garden work, which reduces social inequality. Time banks' demonstrated outcomes include improved intergenerational relations, increased employability, confidence and self-esteem for individuals, access to public services for marginalized groups, reduced discrimination, and greater community cohesion (Slay, 2011).

Other initiatives use bank money to create local exchange schemes; they need a stringent set of rules and governance mechanisms to avoid "contamination" by the extractive mindset this money engenders. Crowdfunding initiatives provide interest-free credits to social or ecological pursuits, and civil society organizations facilitate their uptake by providing rules and (insurance) mechanisms fostering participants' trust. Bandcamp, a payment platform for online music, designed a business model aligning its interests with those of the artist community it serves and collects donations for musicians whose income fell during COVID-19 (Bandcamp, 2020). In precariousness contexts, lending circles (or "tontines") increase the economic security of their members (especially women) by pooling and sharing money fairly. They collect a fixed amount at regular intervals that participants can use in turn; some also put aside small sums to donate to members faced with exceptional expenses (such as funerals). The formal financial sector is interested in integrating tontines into its business, which boosts tontines' capacities and facilitates significant investments, increasing their ascendency. However, private profit-oriented micro-finance schemes require strict governance, for they often lead to over-indebtedness of poor people; moreover, tontine savings may be used for speculation, thwarting their core purpose (Bruchhaus, 2016).

Local governments or mission-driven businesses address local needs (like recidivism, waste, marginalized groups' participation, etc.) with complementary currencies; they valorize all citizens' contributions to the chosen goals with a token which participants can then spend on services or products that foster their wellbeing (e.g., public transportation, food, or education) (Lietaer & Belgin, 2012). In coastal communities, the "Plastic Bank" exchanges plastic waste collected by inhabitants for coins they can use for housing, education, or health; it also promotes a circular economy using recycled plastic (*Empowering the World to Stop Ocean Plastic—Plastic Bank*, n.d.). The Curitiba currency (Brazil) addressed garbage-related health issues in slums by rewarding inhabitants who collected trash with coins that could be used to pay for fresh food and public transportation (Lietaer & Belgin, 2012). In South Africa, the Sustainable Food Fund supports farming communities that nurture their soil and environment (Jones, 2020). In Switzerland, the local economy protects itself from international money's cyclical instability utilizing WIR, a business-to-business currency. In Italy, the Sardex currency rewards participants for spending money locally; with over half a billion registered sales, it creates an additional market for thousands of local small and medium enterprises.

Social finance engenders new ownership models returning profits to the community and preventing speculation (Forslund, 2020; Kelly, 2012). Even if many people perceive these initiatives as social rather than economic, they bridge the immense gap bank money created between societal and economic pursuits; they do so by fostering exchanges (of goods and services) that serve the common good.

5.2 *Increasing the Ascendency of Social Finance*

Emerging social finance initiatives display a highly resilient landscape. However, interfaces between them and the prevailing financial regime are lacking. Regime actors may perceive them as unfair *competition* (although they foster cooperation) or accuse them of tax *evasion* (even if they prevent negative externalities and increase wellbeing). Therefore, governance mechanisms to make social finance mainstream are needed. If we want to achieve a societal transition before reaching points of no return in ecological degradation, these governance leverages are urgent. Since finance is deeply embedded in most societal practices, institutions, and worldviews, this demands a coherent set of policies across many domains.

The future depends on the choices humans make, so a scientific account of what the future of finance *will* look like is impossible. Nor is science entitled to determine what the future of humanity *should* be like (Jasanoff, 2018). This paragraph outlines institutional leverages that *can* contribute to a social finance system (*Towards a Sustainable Financial Ecosystem*, n.d.) summarized by the acronym ALERT, short for Agenda 2030, Legislation, Education, Research, and Taxation.

5.3 *Agenda 2030*

Countries worldwide signed the United Nations Agenda 2030 that has 17 sustainable development goals (SDGs), calling for policies in all domains. Economic actors increasingly support this Agenda. However, studies reveal that (with the *current* financial system) people-oriented goals—e.g., no poverty, education, equality—cannot be achieved without undermining ecological ones; consequently, the SDGs are mostly treated as a choice menu, not a coherent vision of *interdependent* goals. Since social finance facilitates regenerative transactions, it is a cornerstone of Agenda 2030 to be integrated transversally in all SDG policies, and only mission-driven companies operating with social finance can claim to contribute to SDGs.

5.4 *Legislation*

In an extractive system, legal *constraints* on the creation and circulation of money are needed to protect society; in a regenerative financial system, however, legislation should *facilitate* financial innovation for the common good. Governments at all levels can put in place legislation to stimulate social finance. States can adopt laws supporting the development of currencies by non-profits (Orsi, 2012). Cities and regions can explore legal systems that protect rather than commodify the common good (Capra & Mattei, 2015). The Swiss WIR network has bank status, which fosters trust and guarantees secure money transfers.

5.5 *Education*

Education for the twenty-first century requires unlearning human-centrism and embracing ecocentrism (Grancitelli et al., 2020). Higher education can create the conditions for young people to share a process of ecocentric learning with their peers, give them credits for it, or even make it mandatory. Funding mechanisms and ranking systems for universities can take that into account.

All students (and teachers) must understand that money is a social construct that *can and should be* redesigned for sustaining life. Economic faculties can teach students how to set up regenerative businesses using social finance tools and cooperative ownership models, presenting social finance as the vanguard of sustainable economic innovation.

5.6 *Research*

All publicly funded research and innovation results can be protected against privatization and commodification, and be governed as a publicly shared common good. Knowledge vouchers can represent the value people generate whenever they exchange ideas and co-create knowledge, allowing community members to freely access new knowledge.

Social finance initiatives can be recognized as innovation labs and subsidized accordingly, giving them access to research funding. Funding agencies and governments can stimulate research into legal and political leverages to increase the societal impact of social finance and to better understand the governance it requires in a volatile and uncertain context.

5.7 *Taxation*

If (local) governments ask citizens to pay a certain percentage of their taxes in social currencies designed to serve community goals, this incentivizes people to earn those currencies and contribute to the achievement of those goals. Since social finance prevents or heals the negative externalities of the extractive money system (reducing the need for redistribution), governments can tax transactions in extractive money more heavily than those invested (via ethical banks or social finance initiatives) in projects fostering the regenerative economy and Agenda 2030.

6 Conclusion

When the COVID-19 pandemic halted the extractive economy, many analysts treated this as a crisis *for* the system and hope we will make up for losses once a vaccine is available. A more in-depth systemic analysis reveals that pandemics like this are caused (in non-linear ways) by the anthropocentric system's pursuit of financial gains. They signal a crisis *of* the system. A financial system can be sustainable if it is designed and governed like natural ecosystems, and growth (including that of the human population) is no longer seen as a desirable goal but as a risk (Crist, 2019). Indigenous and postcolonial practices and discourses treat Nature as a living being with intelligence, feelings, and spirituality of which humans are part; however, they are vulnerable in the face of global finance and "cheap oil" (Mignolo & Walsh, 2018). Social finance may offer crucial leverage to realize their vision in a globalized world.

For achieving wellbeing for all within planetary boundaries, social finance should no longer be conceived as a corrective mechanism to a primarily extractive money system but as a model for a new financial system that fosters regenerative practices. This chapter explored a framework for such an innovative model based on scientific insights into sustainable systems. Communities worldwide show resilience by creating a wide variety of monetary tools serving social and ecological goals. However, the shift toward a sustainable financial system requires governance leverages that increase their ascendency. In this chapter, we explored five possible leverages, but many more are conceivable.

References

Bandcamp. (2020). *Bandcamp fair trade music policy*. https://bandcamp.com/fair_trade_music_policy.

Bauwens, M., & Pazaitis, A. (2019). *P2P accounting for planetary survival*. https://p2pfoundation.net/wp-content/uploads/2019/06/AccountingForPlanetarySurvival_def.pdf.

Bruchhaus, E. M. (2016). Flexible and disciplined. *D+C E-Paper*, *11*, 38–39.

Capra, F., & Luisi, P. L. (2014). *The systems view of life*. Cambridge University Press.

Capra, F., & Mattei, U. (2015). *The ecology of law*. Berrett-Koehler Publishers.

Chang, H.-J. (2011). *23 Things they don't tell you about capitalism*. Penguin.

Chapman, K. (2015). *Complexity and creative capacity*. Routledge.

City of Cambridge. (2020). *City of Cambridge launches $1.5 million COVID-19 housing stabilization program.* https://www.cambridgema.gov/covid19/News/2020/07/housingfund.
Cordon, R. (2019). *How blockchain can transform our financial, climate & political crises all at once.* Seeds Library. https://seedslibrary.com/how-blockchain-can-transform-our-political-environmental-and-financial-crises-all-at-once/.
Crist, E. (2019). *Abundant earth.* University of Chicago Press.
Daly, H. E., & Farley, J. (2011). *Ecological economics.* Island Press.
Empowering the World to Stop Ocean Plastic—Plastic Bank. (n.d.). Retrieved December 20, 2020, from https://plasticbank.com/.
Forslund, T. (2020). Ten seeds for a circular ecosystem. *Sitra.* https://www.sitra.fi/en/publications/ten-seeds-for-a-circular-ecosystem/.
Gorissen, L. (2020). *Natural intelligence.* Studio Transitio.
Grancitelli, L., Himpens, J., Smeers, I., & Snick, A. (2020). Unlearning human-centrism: A bumpy road. *Ecological Citizen, 4*(1), 11–13.
Hossenfelder, S. (2018). *Lost in math.* Basic Books.
Jasanoff, S. (2018). *Can science make sense of life?* Polity Press.
Jones, B. (2020). *Sustainable food fund: A new economic model for the future of food.* https://challenges.openideo.com/challenge/food-system-vision-prize/evaluation-2/food-credits-new-economic-model-to-develop-african-farming-networks-communities.
Kelly, M. (2012). *Owning our future: The emerging ownership revolution.* Berrett-Koehler Publishers.
Kimmerer, R. W. (2013). *Braiding sweetgrass: Indigenous wisdom, scientific knowledge and the teachings of plants.* Milkweed Editions.
Kirkham. (2013). Prison quotas push lawmakers to fill beds, derail reform. *Huffington Post.* https://www.huffpost.com/entry/private-prison-quotas_n_3953483?1379606057.
Latour, B. (2017). *Où atterrir?* La Découverte.
Lent, J. (2017). *The patterning instinct: A cultural history of humanity's search for meaning.* Prometheus Books.
Lietaer, B., Arnsperger, C., Goerner, S., & Brunnhuber, S. (2012). *Money and sustainability: The missing link.* Triarchy Press.
Lietaer, B., & Belgin, S. (2012). *New money for a new world.* Qitera Press.
Lietaer, B., Ulanowicz, R., & Goerner, S. (2009). Options for managing a systemic bank crisis. *S.A.P.I E.N.S, 1*(2), 1–15.
McNeill, J. R., & Engelke, P. (2014). *The great acceleration.* Harvard University Press.
Meadows, D. (2008). *Thinking in systems.* Chelsea Green.
Meadows, D. H., Meadows, D. L., Randers, J., & Behrens, W. (1972). *Limits to growth.* Universe Books.

Mignolo, W. D., & Walsh, C. E. (2018). *On decoloniality*. Duke University Press.
Orsi, J. (2012). *Practicing law in the sharing economy*. American Bar Association Publishing.
Overshootday. (2020). https://www.overshootday.org/.
Patel, K., & Hansmeyer, C. (2020). The role of finance in solving global issues and in the transition to a new civilisation. *Cadmus, 4*(2), 46–55.
Pogany, P. (2015). *Havoc, thy name is twenty-first century*. IUniverse.
Raworth, K. (2017). *Doughnut economics*. Random House.
Renn, J. (2020). *The evolution of knowledge: Rethinking science for the Anthropocene*. Princeton University Press.
Rockström, J., Steffen, W., Noone, K., Persson, Å., Chapin, F. S., Lambin, E. F., Lenton, T. M., Scheffer, M., Folke, C., Schellnhuber, H. J., Nykvist, B., de Wit, C. A., Hughes, T., van der Leeuw, S., Rodhe, H., Sörlin, S., Snyder, P. K., Costanza, R., Svedin, U., ... Foley, J. A. (2009). A safe operating space for humanity. *Nature, 461*(7263), 472–475. https://doi.org/10.1038/461472a.
Slay, J. (2011). *More than money*. NESTA. https://media.nesta.org.uk/documents/more_than_money_literature_review.pdf.
Snick, A. (2017). EU Politics for sustainability: Systemic lock-ins and opportunities. In A. Diemer, F. Dierickx, G. Gladkykh, M. E. Morales, & J. Torres (Eds.), *Europe and sustainable development: Challenges and prospects* (pp. 3–22). Editions Oeconomia.
Snick, A. (2019). Aging policy ideas. In D. Gu & M. E. Dupre (Eds.), *Encyclopedia of gerontology and population aging* (pp. 1–7). Springer International Publishing. https://doi.org/10.1007/978-3-319-69892-2_214-1.
Snick, A. (2020). Wiser than Vikings? Redefining sustainability in the Anthropocene. In A. Diemer, M. E. Morales, M. Nedelciu, & M. Oostdijk (Eds.), *Paradigms, models, scenarios and practices for strong sustainability* (pp. 69–83). Editions Oeconomia.
Sverdrup, H., & Ragnarsdottir, K.V. (2014). Natural resources in a planetary perspective. *Geochemical perspectives, 3*(2).
Towards a Sustainable Financial Ecosystem. (n.d.). The Club of Rome-EU Chapter. Retrieved December 20, 2020, from https://www.clubofrome.eu/towards-a-sustainable-financial.
Ulanowicz, R. (2009). *A third window: Natural life beyond Newton and Darwin*. Templeton Foundation Press.
Ulanowicz, R. (2016). Process ecology: Philosophy passes into praxis. *Process Studies, 45*(2), 199–222.
Watch the Ocean [Editorial]. (2020). *Nature, 556*(149). https://www.nature.com/articles/d41586-018-04322-x. https://doi.org/10.1038/d41586-018-04322-x.

Social Finance in Quebec: An Ecosystemic Approach to Financial Innovation

Marguerite Mendell and Nancy Neamtan

1 Introduction

Throughout history, civil society has played a pivotal role in economic development. The creation of the cooperative movement and the labor movement illustrates but two social movements with lasting impact on the economic organization of enterprises and working life. For the past several decades, social movements across the globe have spearheaded citizen-based economic initiatives. Although the terminology to describe these movements varies in different contexts, what these movements have in common is a commitment to prioritize people over capital, to

This chapter has been adapted from "Strategy for knowlsedge transfer of social finance—Best practices of Quebec and strategy for adaptation to Seoul." CITIES, 2018.
We wish to thank Ralph Rouzier for his invaluable assistance.

M. Mendell (✉)
Concordia University, Montreal, QC, Canada
e-mail: marguerite.mendell@concordia.ca

N. Neamtan
Chantier de L'Économie Sociale, Montreal, QC, Canada
e-mail: nancy@nancyneamtan.quebec

T. Walker et al. (eds.), *Innovations in Social Finance*,
https://doi.org/10.1007/978-3-030-72535-8_3

orient economic development in response to collective needs and aspirations, and to introduce democratic and participatory processes into entrepreneurial and territorial development. In all cases, access to capital is a crucial issue, often representing the greatest challenge for initiatives to succeed and to scale up. In a financialized global economy, challenging the logic that drives private investment undermines the dominant economic paradigm. Social finance presents such a challenge as it integrates social, economic, and environmental goals into financial decisions. No longer on the fringes, it draws the attention of financial analysts, policy-makers, savers, and investors into a new and burgeoning financial market in which finance becomes a means to achieve societal goals, all the while generating returns for investors. The 2008–2009 crisis was a tipping point as investors were drawn to social and ethical financial tools and institutions. Today, social finance is growing apace and providing opportunities for innovative solutions to address the climate crisis and deepening income disparities within and between countries.

In this context, interest in the social economy and social finance in Quebec continues to grow internationally. Since it is embedded in the socioeconomic landscape and is recognized as a significant economic actor, the Quebec social economy (and its social finance ecosystem) is considered a model or a "template" in many regions and countries. The long history of the cooperative movement and its presence in numerous sectors of activity, as well as the strong and expanding presence of non-profit organizations that are meeting social needs with economic means (including the provision of social services not previously provided by the state nor by the private sector), attract the attention of civil society actors, governments, and researchers around the world.

The example of the social economy in Quebec, especially over the last 20 years, allows for bold statements about its capacity to contest the dominant paradigm through practice. Its resilience in the face of the post-2008 economic crisis and the COVID-19 pandemic is testimony to the viability of collective enterprises when supported by a community-based social infrastructure and a network of social finance institutions. The response was immediate. In the early weeks of the pandemic, social finance institutions revised their reimbursement and interest payment requirements. The network of social finance institutions continues to meet regularly to share information and collaborate in order to assure the viability of the enterprises in which they invest. Measures include moratoriums on capital repayments, the suspension of both interest payments and service fees, reduced credit rating requirements, and increased services to accompany enterprises through the crisis. The three levels of government—federal, provincial, and municipal—coordinated their efforts to assist small and medium-sized enterprises (SMEs), including collective enterprises, with new programs and considerable financial support. The economic impact of the pandemic is yet to be fully realized. This collaboration and cooperation between all social economy actors, including social finance institutions, during this unprecedented moment are rooted in the history of the social economy in Quebec and its capacity to work collectively during difficult times.

International interest in the Quebec experience also raises the question of how these innovations can be transferred from one country to another, given the diversity of contexts and opportunities. Knowledge transfer requires a capacity to synthesize lessons that reach beyond local realities and to capture the fundamental components of successful social innovations. Such efforts have been at the heart of recent work by social economy and social finance actors in Quebec and beyond.

The following chapter offers a portrait of social finance in Quebec and proposes a synthesis of the major lessons learned from the past three decades. It presents one example of efforts to transfer this knowledge to South Korea, where interest in the Quebec model has led to numerous bilateral exchanges.

2 A Brief Overview of the Social Economy in Quebec

In Quebec, the social economy includes more than 11,200 collective enterprises, 75% of which are non-profits, 22% are non-financial cooperatives, and 3% are financial cooperatives or mutuals. Collectively, these enterprises have 13.4 million members of which 2.4 million are members of non-financial cooperatives, 4.5 million are members of non-profits, and 5.6 million are members of financial cooperatives (Institut de la statistique du Québec, 2019). Framework legislation for the social economy, adopted unanimously by Quebec's National Assembly in 2013, recognizes the social economy as an integral and essential component of Quebec's socioeconomic infrastructure (Social Economy Act, CQLR, c. E-1.1.1, 2019).

Quebec has several distinctive characteristics that provided fertile ground for the development of its social economy and social finance.

The long history of the cooperative movement and credit unions is foundational in its development. The aspirations of a majority francophone population within Canada, the commitment to greater autonomy for the provincial government across political parties, the strong presence of the state in economic development, and a tradition of dialogue between government, unions, and employers have all shaped the history of the social economy in Quebec.

However, the recent history of the social economy is indebted to the citizen-based community economic development organizations that grew out of the early 1980s in urban neighborhoods struggling against economic restructuring and the recession. The strategies for economic revitalization proposed by these organizations planted the seeds for what we refer to today as "place-based strategies" and for comprehensive public policy to meet the needs of communities devastated by mass layoffs, plant closures, and accompanying urban decay. They successfully pressed for the integration of policy—in the labor market, enterprise services and business development, social integration through economic initiatives, and local revitalization—insisting upon the limits of homogeneous and undifferentiated programs designed in ministerial silos. They successfully pressed for multi-stakeholder dialogue with all social and economic actor/community organizations, the labor movement, the private sector, and the government, prefiguring a process of co-construction of public policy that would be applied more broadly, transforming the top-down relation between the state and civil society to one of collaboration and co-determination. This period marks a watershed in the recent history of the social economy as well as its commitment and capacity to work across boundaries, across sectors, and with different levels of government. The comprehensive and coordinated approach that characterizes the social economy in Quebec today is rooted in the collective actions of community movements from the 1980s.

The term "social economy" gained recognition in Quebec at a specific moment in Quebec's history. In October 1996, Lucien Bouchard, then Prime Minister of Quebec, convened a summit on the economy and employment; the Premier called upon government, employers, trade unions, community organizations, and social movements to discuss how to address the dilemma of an urgent need to create jobs without increasing the deficit.[1] This was the first time community organizations and social movements convened at such a summit, which in the past had been limited to participation by the labor movement and the private sector. A vast mobilization by the women's movement thrust the concept of the social economy into the limelight, and a working group on the social economy was among those created to prepare the summit.

The report presented by the working group on the social economy at the 1996 summit was well received. It called for institutional recognition of this third component of a plural economy and presented several innovative solutions to create new jobs in response to needs that neither the market nor the public sector could meet. It identified 20 social economy projects that would create 20,000 jobs within two years, including urgently needed services such as childcare, perinatal services, home care, social housing, and programs for workforce integration and local development. In fact, the working group's proposed initiatives exceeded their objectives. It also called for the creation of an investment fund unlike any existing entity, dedicated entirely to cooperative and non-profit enterprises. Though modest in size, with a capitalization of $10 million, the creation of Réseau d'investissement social du Québec (RISQ) represented a major step in the evolution of social finance in Quebec.

In 1999, the working group created for the summit became an independent non-profit organization to continue to promote and develop the social economy. The Chantier de l'économie sociale, a network of networks, is now a non-profit organization that represents all social economy actors throughout Quebec. Its members include sectoral networks of collective enterprises, social movements, and local development intermediaries. The Assembly of First Nations Quebec Labrador joined the Board of Directors in 2013.

Over the past decades, social finance has diversified and expanded as more and more collective enterprises have emerged and as existing enterprises undertake increasingly ambitious projects. New approaches to financing traditional sectors, such as housing or community real estate, have also enriched the development of the Quebec social finance ecosystem.

[1] *October Summit Conference on the Economy and Employment.* An initial conference, the *Conference on the Social and Economic Future of Quebec* was held in March, during which the Task Force on the Social Economy was created.

Although the social economy in Quebec was long associated with activity on the margins of the economy, or exclusively with non-market social services in the past, this is no longer the case. The lengthy process leading to the adoption of framework legislation in 2013, coupled with increased visibility, resulted in wide recognition of the role of the social economy and its important contribution to inclusive growth, certainly in Quebec and increasingly across Canada. The Quebec experience has been characterized by its institutional innovations, deliberative processes, and collaboration between a wide range of actors engaged in designing democratic strategies of socioeconomic transformation. Alliances between social movements, labor, the cooperative movement, and community organizations have been at the heart of this initiative. The construction of an institutional context for multi-stakeholder partnerships, as well as distributed and democratic governance, was critical to its development.

Social economy actors engage in institutional innovation at several levels. In addition to the creation of the Chantier de l'économie sociale, and through its initiatives, a series of partners have contributed to the creation of enabling instruments, such as finance, training, enterprise services, knowledge transfer, public policy, and research. Practitioners are re-embedding the economy in society, designing sustainable approaches to development that respond to the needs and desires of communities and provide appropriate tools to achieve these. The strength of the social economy is rooted in the capacity of its practitioners to work across sectors collaboratively and to negotiate with different levels of government. The social economy movement in Quebec has historically insisted on the complementarity between social economy actors and the state, resisting a trend common in other parts of the world to question or to reduce the primary regulatory and redistributive role of the state. It has been active in calling for a new sociopolitical architecture, for more horizontal policy settings to address the hybrid needs of the social economy within government, and for a process of collaborative policy formation situated in new institutional dialogic spaces.

3 Social Finance Initiatives and Enabling Policy Measures: A Brief Overview[2]

Unlike many other parts of the world, the social finance tools and institutions created in Quebec over the past decades were designed by social movements; they embody citizen mobilization at local, regional, and national levels (Table 1). Many have benefited from government support through a variety of measures including direct injection of capital, credit enhancement, legislation, and fiscal measures. The following section offers an overview of the existing social finance instruments and the policy measures that have supported their growth.

3.1 Community-Based Funds

Community-based funds refer to small loan circles and local funds created by civil society organizations. Le Réseau québécois du crédit communautaire (the Quebec Network of Community Credit Funds) represents community-based funds including loan circles, small micro-credit organizations, and loan funds across Quebec that provide loans between $500 and $2000. Larger loan funds, such as the Montreal Community Loan Association (MCLA), lend up to a maximum of $20,000. The mission of community-based funds is to serve the marginalized populations that are denied access to conventional loans. Community-based funds either provide individual loans and/or work in close partnership with other social finance actors and institutions to structure larger investments. As such, these community-based funds act as important leverage for additional investment. In Quebec, unlike elsewhere, many community-based funds were established in close collaboration with local development organizations to provide financial opportunities for initiatives embedded in local development strategies.

The Quebec government has supported community-based funds through direct financial support or indirect support through employment promotion programs. Still, this support is often not enough to cover the funds' operating costs. This is true for community-based funds in many parts of the world and is an ongoing challenge.

[2] On the evolution of solidarity finance and development capital in Quebec, see Table 1, Annex 1.

Table 1 Key historical moments in the evolution of solidarity finance and development capital in Quebec

1800	*1900*	*1970s*	*1980s*	*1990s*	*2000+*
Sociétés de secours mutuels (1840)	***Mouvement des caisses d'épargne et d'économie Desjardins*** (1900)	***Caisse d'économie solidaire (Caisse d'économie des travailleuses et travailleurs—Québec)*** (1971)	***Fonds de solidarité (FTQ)*** (1983)	***SOLIDE*** (1991)	***Filaction*** (2000)
			Community Economic Development Corporations (CDEC) (1984)	***Fondaction de la CSN*** (1995)	***Réseau québécois du crédit communautaire*** (2000)
			Régime d'investissement coopératif (1985)	***Société de développement des entreprises culturelles*** (1995)	***Capital régional et coopératif Desjardins*** (2001)
			Réseau des sociétés d'aide au développement des collectivités (SADC) et des centres d'aide aux entreprises (CAE)/Community Futures (1986)	***Fonds régionaux de solidarité*** (1996)	***Fiducie du Chantier de l'économie sociale*** (2007)
				Fonds locaux de solidarité (1996)	***Plan d'action gouvernemental pour l'entrepreneuriat collectif*** (2008)
				Réseau d'investissement social du Québec (1997)	***Fonds d'initiative et de rayonnement de la métropole*** (2009)
				Fonds d'investissement de Montréal (FIM) (1997)	Cycle Capital Management (previously, the ***Fonds d'investissement en développement durable***) (2009)
				Fonds d'investissement pour la culture et communication (1997)	Local solidarity fund—social economy (2009)

1800	*1900*	*1970s*	*1980s*	*1990s*	*2000+*
				Investissement Québec (1998) — cooperative, social economy, ***Fonds du développement économique***	***Fonds d'investissement pour la relève agricole*** (2011)
				Local Development Centers (1998)—Local investment fund, Social economy enterprise development fund	***Financement IMPLIQ*** (2012)
					Capitalization of Social Economy Enterprises Program (2013)
					Social Economy Act (2013)
					Plan d'action gouvernemental en économie sociale 2015–2020
					Fonds Essor et Coopération (2013)
					PME MTL, SDE, etc. (2015)
					PUSH Fund (2016)
					Fonds INNOGEC (2017)
					Community Bonds (2017)
					Fonds d'investissement pour le logement étudiant (2018)
					Fonds Écoleader (2019)

3.2 *Co-Operative Funds*

The Mouvement Desjardins (Desjardins Group) was the first savings and credit cooperative established in North America. From a small local credit union created by Alphonse Desjardins and local stakeholders in December 1900, it achieved legal status in 1906 with the adoption of legislation for cooperatives by the Quebec Legislative Assembly (Desjardins, n.d.). Today, it is a large federation of many independent institutions and has become a major international financial player. It played a fundamental role in the development of the social economy in Quebec, and in particular in the creation of social finance tools. We highlight two examples of credit unions and cooperative funds in Quebec.

The Caisse d'économie solidaire (CES)—formerly the Caisse d'économie Desjardins des travailleurs et travailleuses—was created in 1971 by the labor movement (Maheux, 2016).[3] Its mission is to contribute to social justice and solidarity by supporting collective and social enterprises and the cooperative movement. The Caisse d'économie solidaire Desjardins provides guaranteed loans to social economy enterprises and organizations. With other social finance actors, it also contributes to the financial structuring of social economy enterprises across Quebec. Since it was established by unionized workers affiliated with the Confédération des syndicats nationaux (CSN; Confederation of National Unions) and because it is dedicated to the social economy, this Caisse is distinct from other members of the federation. In 2019, its total assets were $1.1 billion; in 2019, it invested a total of $666.6 million in collective enterprises and social housing, of which $7.2 million was invested in private enterprises (Caisse d'économie solidaire [CES], 2020).

The second example, Capital régional et coopératif Desjardins (CRCD; Desjardins Capital for Regional and Co-Operative Development), was established in 2001 by the Mouvement Desjardins to promote employment in Quebec. Its creation was formalized in 2006 through legislation. It offers a 40 percent provincial tax credit to investors with a seven-year commitment (Capital régional et coopératif Desjardins [CRCD], 2015). The CRCD and its partner funds have contributed to the growth of 530 enterprises, cooperatives, and funds across Quebec, investing over $1.3 billion. As of 2019, it has contributed to the creation or maintenance of more than 80,000 jobs (CRCD, 2019).

[3] More particularly by the CSN, which was founded in 1921 and has more than 300,000 members.

3.3 Labor Solidarity Funds

Labor solidarity funds also distinguish the social finance landscape in Quebec from other parts of the world. Economic restructuring and the recession of the early 1980s transformed Quebec's economy and the lives of numerous structurally and cyclically unemployed workers. The labor movement acted on behalf of workers to create new jobs and to maintain those that could be preserved by designing an innovative investment tool with worker retirement funds. This commitment by the labor movement to job creation (job maintenance, in many cases) and to the economic development of Quebec is unique and has marked the development of Quebec's economy for almost three decades. The Fédération des travailleurs et travailleuses du Quebec (FTQ; Quebec Federation of Labour)[4] established the first union-controlled investment fund, Fonds de solidarité FTQ, in 1983 (Fonds de solidarité FTQ, 2020). Inspired by its success, the CSN established a second labor solidarity fund, Fondaction CSN pour la cooperation et l'emploi (CSN Action Fund for cooperation and employment), in 1995 (Fondaction, 2021).

The creation of the Fonds de solidarité FTQ was made possible by the establishment of a tax credit by the Quebec government, followed by the federal government. The tax credit was offered to encourage workers to put aside money for their retirement while contributing to job creation within the local economy.[5] Since the creation of these funds, their performance and competitive returns have attracted investors throughout the province of Quebec, in addition to its members. The two labor funds play an important role in the Quebec economy and are widely supported by all economic actors.

Given that they do not invest exclusively in social economy enterprises but also pursue socioeconomic and environmental objectives, Fondaction CSN and Fonds de solidarité FTQ are classified as development capital. However, as investment in the social economy proves to be low risk and offers stable returns, an increasing proportion of these funds is currently invested in the social economy, often blurring the distinction between development capital and solidarity finance. Moreover, in 2007,

[4] The FTQ which was officially founded in 1957 and has more than 600,000 members.

[5] A non-refundable tax credit exists both in Quebec and at the federal level for labor-sponsored funds (Fondaction: 20% in Quebec and 15% at the federal level; Fonds de solidarité: 15% for each level of government).

Fondaction CSN and Fonds de solidarité FTQ invested $8 million and $12 million, respectively, to create the Fiducie du Chantier de l'économie sociale (Chantier Social Economy Trust–Fiducie), the first patient capital fund for the social economy (Government of Canada, 2006).

In 2019, the total net assets of the Fonds de solidarité FTQ were $15.6 billion. The Fonds has invested almost $10 billion in 3126 enterprises, creating or maintaining over 215,000 jobs (Fonds de solidarité FTQ, 2019a, 2019b). The total net assets of Fondaction CSN are almost $2.2 billion. Fondaction has invested a total of approximately $1.5 billion, in more than 1200 enterprises, creating or maintaining over 39,500 jobs (Fondaction, 2019).

Over the years, both labor solidarity funds have established local, regional, and sectoral funds, contributing extensively to the financial architecture of Quebec, to regional and local development, and job creation. Many of these funds now invest in the social economy, most often with other partners, including the government.

3.4 Hybrid Funds

Hybrid funds in Quebec refer to funds that are capitalized by several partners, including the government and the private sector, but managed by civil society organizations. Their sources of capitalization vary from government and labor/civil society sector or government and private enterprises, private enterprises and the labor/civil society sector, or government, private enterprises, and the labor/civil society sector. The Fonds d'innovation pour la gouvernance et la gestion des entreprises collectives (Fonds INNOGEC; the Innovative Fund for the Governance and Management of Collective Enterprises) is an example of hybrid funds. The INNOGEC Fund provides access to professional management consulting and governance services by contributing to the payment of professional fees for these purposes. The Fund was initially capitalized by the ministère de l'Économie et de l'Innovation, Fondaction, Filaction and the Caisse d'économie solidaire (Filaction, 2020).

Following the summit on the economy, the Chantier, with contributions by the Quebec government and private investors employment, created RISQ in 1997 (Neamtan, 2019). The Quebec government invested 50 percent of the initial capital of $10.5 million. RISQ was the first fund entirely dedicated to financing social economy enterprises.

From 1997 to 2019, RISQ provided pre-start-up loans and capitalization, with a total value of $30.2 million, for 926 projects and created or maintained 11,215 jobs (Réseau d'investissement social du Quebec [RISQ], 2020). In 2016, the Government of Quebec invested an additional $5 million in RISQ and provided a non-repayable subsidy of $5 million (Gouvernement du Québec, 2016).

The Fiducie was created in 2007 to meet the need for long-term capital for social economy enterprises. An initial subsidy of $23.8 million by the Government of Canada leveraged additional investment by the two labor solidarity funds and the Government of Quebec (Mendell, 2014). The Fonds de solidarité FTQ and Fondaction CSN invested $12 million and $8 million, respectively; the Government of Quebec invested $10 million. The Fiducie provides patient capital or quasi-equity ranging from $50,000 to $1.5 million, repayable in 15 years. Only interest payments are made throughout the 15-year term of the investment; the principal is repaid at the end. The Fiducie invests in start-up, expansion, and consolidation as well as in the improvement and/or adaptation of goods and services produced by social economy enterprises. It also invests in real estate. From 2007 to 2018, it invested $59.9 million in 190 enterprises and created 3497 jobs, including work insertion positions (Fiducie, 2019).[6]

In 2020, a new hybrid fund was established in Montreal to enable community organizations to stabilize their infrastructure costs in a speculative real estate market by becoming owners of their own buildings (J. Charest, personal communication, January 13, 2020). With an initial capitalization of $16.6 million from foundations ($10.6 million) and the Quebec Solidarity Fund ($6 million), the initiative combines three financial products: short-term loans for the development phase ($1.65 million), a fund to rapidly acquire property ($4.95 million), and patient capital for the final project ($10 million) (Charest, January 13, 2021). Centraide (United Way) launched the initiative with support from several foundations, the Chantier de l'économie sociale, and other social finance

[6] Work insertion enterprises offer training opportunities to men and women otherwise unable to access the labor market. In Quebec, the network of "entreprises d'insertion" includes 50 such enterprise members in 14 regions across the province. The mission of the network is to support the social and professional integration of people in vulnerable situations and contribute to the further development of integration enterprises and their unique model.

actors (Charest, January 13, 2021). The fund will be managed by the Fiducie (Charest, January 13, 2021).

3.5 Private Funds

Private sector businesses, foundations, and some high net-worth individuals also contribute to social finance. Following the 1996 summit and with the broad participation of the private sector, architect and philanthropist Phyllis Lambert founded the Fonds d'investissement de Montréal (FIM; Montréal Investment Fund) for the purchase and renovation of real estate for cooperative and non-profit housing. The initial fund mobilized additional investors, including the Fonds de solidarité FTQ ($2.5 million), the Desjardins Credit Union Federation of Montreal and Western Quebec ($1.25 million), the National Bank of Canada ($400,000), the Royal Bank of Canada ($400,000), Hydro-Québec ($400,000), and Claridge Investments Ltd. ($100,000). As the fund for social housing proved to be low risk and profitable, two private sector foundations, the Fondation J. Armand Bombardier and the McConnell Family Foundation, have also invested in the FIM. There have been four investment phases (1997, 2007, 2011, and 2016) which have made it possible to acquire, preserve, or improve community housing. From 1997 to 2019, 12 investment partners invested $22.6 million ($85.2 million in investments), which generated the building of 1053 community housing units and the acquisition and preservation of 39 affordable rental buildings (Bâtir son quartier, 2019).

3.6 State Funds

Investissement Québec (IQ) is a state-owned public corporation that aims to finance various enterprises in Quebec. In 2001, it created La Financière du Québec (Quebec Financier), a subsidiary that provides loans and loan guarantees to collective enterprises. The guarantee provided by IQ is an important credit enhancement tool, reducing risk for other investors. Currently, IQ has two major programs for the capitalization of the social economy: Capitalisation des entreprises de l'économie sociale (CAES) and a support program for the collective buyouts of enterprises. CAES IQ invests a minimum of $50,000 in long-term financing for a period up to 25 years (Investissement Québec, 2016). Only non-profit organizations, cooperatives, federations, and confederations of cooperatives are admissible to this program. IQ plays a unique role as a public institution that partners with social finance and development capital to invest in collective enterprises. The returns to the government can be invested in new initiatives, generating significant multiplier effects.

Initiated by the Government of Quebec in 2019, the Fonds Écoleader is a major project coordinated by the Fonds d'action québécois pour le développement durable (Quebec Action Fund for Sustainable Development), in collaboration with the Centre québécois de développement durable (Quebec Center for Sustainable Development and Écotech Québec) (Fonds Écoleader, 2021).[7] Its objective is to reach 50,000 Quebec enterprises in order to guide and support them in the implementation of a wide range of eco-responsible business practices and clean technologies.

3.7 *Local Development Funds*

Both the governments of Canada and Quebec have equipped local development organizations with the financial tools to invest in SMEs. Some of these funds have been made available for social economy enterprises, though the majority have been invested in traditional private initiatives.

Supported by the federal government, 57 Community Futures Development Corporations invest an average of $60 million in SMEs located in low-income rural communities (Réseau des SADC et CDE, 2016). Local development centers created by the government of Quebec invest in private and collective enterprises with public funds. In Montreal, PME Montreal offers a full range of professional support services for private-sector and social economy entrepreneurs, including financial assistance. From 2015 to 2019, it allocated $7.6 million to social economy enterprises through its Social Economy Development Fund, with individual grants of up to $50,000 (PME MTL, 2015–2019).

[7] From a sustainable development perspective, Écotech Quebec mobilizes key players in the green economy to create the most favorable conditions for the development and growth of companies, and encourages end-users to increase the deployment of clean technologies.

3.8 Community Bonds

Community bonds and crowdfunding are recent innovations in social finance in Quebec, though they have a long history in other contexts (municipal bonds and love money, for example). Community bonds are debt securities and have characteristics similar to any bond, i.e., face value, maturity, remuneration (interest rate), etc. They are accessible to everyone but can only be issued by non-profit organizations. They are offered to the community without an intermediary and constitute a peer-to-peer crowdfunding model. Community bonds not only mobilize finance, but also offer investment opportunities to citizens wishing to allocate savings toward collective initiatives that generate social, environmental, and economic returns. Large-scale community bonds launched with success in Toronto inspired Quebec actors to test the model locally.

A first community bond was issued in 2002, by the Centre récréatif au fil des ans–Centre des ainés Sorel-Tracy,[8] which made it possible to test the potential of this financial tool. In 2017, three community bonds launched with immediate success in Montreal with the guidance of Territoires innovants en économie sociale et solidaire (TIESS), a knowledge transfer organization contributing to innovations in social finance and to accelerating the development of the social economy across sectors and regions throughout Quebec. TIESS published a guide to assist those social economy enterprises wishing to issue a community bond to complement other sources of finance (Territoires innovants en économie sociale et solidaire [TIESS], 2017). The involvement of the community through proximity investment raises the visibility and awareness of the social economy and is being utilized by more and more social economy enterprises. Today, there are 15 community bonds, some that are in an experimentation phase. Others are being considered and designed. Interest in these bonds has accelerated considerably since 2017.

4 A Formal Platform Collaboration: CAP Finance

The strength of Quebec's culture of collaboration is manifest in the trajectory of social finance. Social finance institutions and organizations, including solidarity finance, development capital, and state funds, have

[8] This community bond still exists.

frequently worked together in structuring finance for social economy enterprises. They have several collective projects, including the publication of the *Portrait of Socially Responsible Finance across Quebec* every four years and, most recently, the publication of the second edition of the *Guide for the Analysis of Social Economy Enterprises*, an invaluable tool for financial analysts assessing social economy initiatives seeking investments (CAP Finance, 2019). This guide provides a range of tools for analysis, evaluation, and development of social economy business plans. Accounting is customized for NPOs and cooperatives. In addition, face-to-face training is offered for advisors, analysts, and managers of collective enterprises to use the *Guide* effectively. The training's aim is to prepare the participants to evaluate the set of elements that compose a social economy enterprise.

In 2009, this collaboration led to the creation of CAP Finance, a network for "socially responsible finance" (development capital and solidarity finance) (CAP Finance, n.d.). Formalizing this collaboration was important in order to demonstrate the collective capacity of these financial actors to contribute to Quebec's socioeconomic well-being. CAP Finance provides an institutional space for dialogue, knowledge mobilization, and collective representation, fully respecting the autonomy of each of its members who share a commitment to economic democracy, promoting the public awareness of social finance, and influencing the financial sector to become socially responsible.

Building a network of social finance organizations was considered essential for: (a) the development of professional expertise in social finance; (b) collective action to influence government policy and the practices of conventional finance; and (c) creating a community of practice (CAP Finance, 2017). Since its creation, CAP Finance has continued to collaborate on various issues, including a Canadian government policy initiative on social finance and a response to the COVID-19 pandemic (CAP Finance, 2021).

5 Key Lessons from the Quebec Social Finance Experience

The construction of a social finance ecosystem in Quebec involved a long process that included building new partnerships, developing and strengthening capacity within the civil society and government, and allowing space for creative thinking in favor of innovative financial products. The success of this experience is rooted in several key principles.

5.1 A Bottom-Up Approach: Responding to Demand

The development of social finance tools in Quebec was, from the outset, a bottom-up approach. The creation of RISQ emerged from a need expressed by the community-based organizations involved in local development initiatives. As more and more entrepreneurial initiatives with social goals emerged, the lack of access to both investment products and guarantees was identified as an obstacle to development. RISQ was created to respond to that need. Its financial products have been continuously adapted to emerging demand. From the beginning, RISQ offered small high-risk loans to social economy enterprises for technical assistance. Rather than simply rejecting an initiative that clearly responded to local needs due to an incomplete business plan, for example, a small loan instrument was created to provide the necessary professional support for the project to become "investment ready." Since then, other new financial products have been developed, constantly adapting to identified needs. These include pre-start-up financing, development capital for the enterprises in the digital economy, and security for enterprises responding to public tenders.

As the number of collective enterprises increased and the internal capacities of social economy enterprises in all sectors expanded, access to equity for sustainable growth became a priority. The Fiducie responded to that need with patient capital or quasi-equity long-term finance for social economy enterprises.

The creation of both RISQ and the Fiducie marked significant milestones for the social economy in the decade following the 1996 summit, as they were designed to meet the specific investment needs of collective enterprises. As described above, they became part of a growing constellation of social finance institutions that already existed in Quebec. The Fiducie was an innovation in venture capital, widening the objectives of investment capital to consider both social and economic returns, bringing it closer to socially responsible investment, but with a marked difference. Social finance in Quebec involved direct investment by financial institutions into initiatives, in contrast to the more indirect practice of socially responsible investment (SRI) mediated by fund managers and most often pooled.

In the early 1990s, the network of community credit institutions, starting with the MCLA Fund, also emerged in response to a need for access to credit or non-guaranteed loans for small entrepreneurial initiatives among new immigrants and people living in conditions of poverty and social exclusion (Mendell, 2000). Added to this was the creation of regional and local investment funds by labor solidarity funds, bringing financial tools closer to communities, thereby aligning the supply of capital with local and regional demand, and thus reducing the risk to investors.

Proximity finance has proven its effectiveness in risk management. A recent example is the long process of collaboration between a university student association, a collective of young social economy entrepreneurs, and the Fiducie to finance the construction of a cooperative student housing initiative. In Montreal, the Concordia University Student Association established the Popular University Student Housing (PUSH) Fund, a revolving loan fund with an initial investment of $1.8 million to finance the first housing collective initially for Concordia University students (Government of Canada, 2020). The project benefitted from the collaboration of the Off-Campus Housing, the Job Resource Centre at the university, and the Unité de travail pour l'implantation de logement étudiant (UTILE), the latter well known for its expertise in student housing across Quebec. The initial investment leveraged a combination of loans and subsidies from the City of Montreal ($1.6 million), the Fonds d'investissement pour le logement étudiant (Fund for student housing, $3 million) newly created by the Fiducie as well as the Caisse d'économie solidaire ($7 million), the Canada Mortgage and Housing Corporation (federal government, $3 million), the Fonds immobilier de solidarité FTQ ($500,000), the RISQ ($100,000), and the Mouvement Desjardins ($200,000) (Fonds de solidarité FTQ, 2019a, 2019b). This is an excellent illustration of the collaboration between social finance institutions across Quebec and their support for innovative collective projects. The first cohort of students moved into the new student housing cooperative, a 90-unit building in Montreal named "Woodnote," in September 2020 (Woodnote, 2018).

Social finance institutions continuously innovate not only to provide access to capital (their core business, so to speak), but also to contribute to investment readiness, viability, and build capacity to enable enterprises to scale. For example, RISQ, originally created to invest directly in collective enterprises, is on a continuous innovation path. Two recent examples are illustrative. Launched on November 7, 2019, the Réseau des relayeurs du RISQ (network of "torchbearers")—a network of 27 social economy organizations across Quebec—was established to provide necessary support services to assure that collective enterprises could meet their objectives (RISQ). More recently, RISQ has launched a pilot project to respond to the diversity of financial needs throughout the lifecycle of social economy enterprises. Inspired by the venture capital model of repayment based on revenue, the proposed Fund to promote innovation and growth of collective enterprises, the Fonds d'innovation et croissance en économie sociale, now in a pilot phase, will introduce more flexibility into repayment schedules based on earnings of the enterprise, in contrast to fixed repayment schedules that often hamper the ability of enterprises to grow.

In summary, one of the key success factors of the Quebec experience was the choice to build new financial instruments based on the analysis of concrete needs expressed by social economy enterprises and entrepreneurs. These financial innovations are customized to meet these needs. Most importantly, they align the supply of social finance with the demand for investment tools and products. These contrast sharply with current trends to create new forms of social finance and impact investing; these are largely supply driven and risk misalignment with needs and/or non-dispersal, as investment pipelines are structured.

5.2 A Process of Co-Construction and Co-Ownership Among Diverse Partners

The bottom-up approach to building new financial products to respond to needs expressed on the ground went hand in hand with a process of co-construction and co-ownership of these newly created funds. Throughout this process, future users collaborated in the conception and structuring of the funds to assure that they remained closely aligned with their expressed needs. When compromises were necessary because of investors' requirements (financial stability or rate of return), these issues were transparent and resolved consensually. More importantly, the principle of shared governance, involving all stakeholders in governance structures, was applied to all new investment tools.

Shared governance was designed to assure a professional and objective selection process for investments based on strict due diligence. For example, the Board of the Chantier de l'économie sociale has veto power over any changes in the investment policy of the Fiducie, but the individual investment decisions are based on rigorous analysis and recommendations by an investment committee for approval by the Fiducie's Board of Trustees.

5.3 An Ecosystemic Approach with a Diversity of Tools Working in Collaboration

Private for-profit enterprises benefit from a wide variety of financial products and can choose the best vehicle depending on their sector, size, and stage of development. Over the years, social economy actors, in partnership with the government and other investors, have strived to ensure similar access to a diversity of financial products to correspond to a range of needs. Each financial product has its specificity; the goal is to achieve complementarity between the various products. This allows enterprises to choose the best product for their needs.

Simultaneously, funds are often partners in supporting the development of the same enterprise. It is indeed rare that investment in an enterprise is made by only one entity. This ongoing collaboration benefits all. It allows for a pooling of risk among investors and a sharing of the work involved in pre-investment analysis and tracking investments. These ongoing collaborations have been formalized with the creation of CAP Finance in 2010, raising the public profile of social finance and the visibility of the diverse actors in this market (CAP Finance, n.d.). There is no substitute for this collaboration. Its collective professional expertise, and influence on policy and practice, is invaluable. Speaking with one voice strengthens the entire sector without compromising the autonomy of each of its members.

This ecosystemic approach constantly evolves to meet changing needs, but the principle of collaboration versus competition remains unchanged and has been fundamental to the success of Quebec's social economy and social finance.

5.4 Continuing Training, Research, and Knowledge Transfer to Strengthen Supply and Demand Sides

The building of a social finance ecosystem in Quebec was a process of innovation nourished and accelerated by ongoing mobilization of knowledge, as well as learning from both international and national experiences. At every step of the journey, from inception until today, it has been necessary to accompany financial analyses and new investors with training, research, and knowledge transfer. These ongoing learning processes take place within civil society organizations, government, and the financial sector.

As a first step, social economy actors in Quebec worked in close partnership with academic researchers to learn of examples in other countries and to better understand the functioning of the financial sector so as to attract investors to social finance initiatives in Quebec. This "community-university research alliance" was also extremely important in the evolution of public policy, as it provided legitimacy and a clear articulation of issues to policy-makers that were called upon to support the social finance sector.

Training has been an ongoing activity since the emergence of the social finance sector. Its first objective was to reinforce the capacity of social economy entrepreneurs, employees, and their board of directors to use new financial instruments other than the traditional grants or contributions to which they were accustomed. This training contributed to an increased number of investment-ready projects and helped to accelerate investments. Capacity building on the demand side has been an essential component of Quebec's social finance successes.

However, training and knowledge transfer were also essential elements on the supply side within the financial world. The *Guide for the Analysis of Social Economy Enterprises*, the first edition published by RISQ in 2002, is an excellent example of the importance of ongoing training for those working in social finance (CAP Finance, 2019). As social economy actors created new financial instruments, it quickly became evident that it was also necessary to train those offering support to these enterprises. Traditional training for financial analysts focuses exclusively on for-profit private companies and does not consider distinctions in mission, business approaches, and legal structures specific to social economy enterprises. The guide produced by RISQ in partnership with other social finance actors synthesized the lessons learned from analyzing feasibility and the level of risk associated with investment in the social economy. It has become a key training tool for all those involved, directly or indirectly, in investing in collective enterprises.

After almost two decades of systematic research and training, the transition to systematic knowledge transfer was enabled by the creation of TIESS, a center of liaison and knowledge transfer in social innovation created by the Chantier de l'économie sociale and its partners: TIESS' 26 members bring together civil society actors, research networks, and institutions to accelerate the process of mutual learning based on best practice and best research. As social finance accelerates its development and diversifies its forms of intervention, the capacity to rapidly transfer knowledge to reinforce development work has been critical to the success in scaling up Quebec's social finance.

5.5 *A Coherent Policy Framework Built Through Ongoing Dialogue Between Government and Civil Society*

Public policy has played a vital role in the construction of Quebec's social economy and social finance ecosystem. The successful development of policy measures has been largely attributed to deliberative dialogue and processes of co-construction. A coherent and integrated policy framework, which incorporates support for strengthening enterprise development and the creation of new investment instruments, has resulted from this dialogue between representatives of the social economy and government. The social economy file is a challenge for government because it embraces a wide range of intersecting issues, sectors, and strategies. In Quebec, the mandate for the social economy and social finance in government given to several ministries over the years reflects this diversity. A silo approach that characterizes most public institutions is counterproductive in the development of social economy/social finance policy and required institutional innovation. For example, government action plans on the social economy have involved a wide range of ministries, but actions taken by government have not necessarily been well coordinated. The contribution of social economy actors best able to articulate the needs and how to integrate a variety of interventions to achieve results has imposed coherence on these inter-ministerial processes. Despite advances, the challenge for better coherence across ministries remains.

This is particularly true in the field of social finance. The involvement of civil society actors in a deliberative dialogue with government has been instrumental in identifying the most strategic ways that public funds can leverage private investment. This dialogue has also facilitated the evolution of the legislative framework to adapt to new needs and aspirations in developing new social finance instruments.

5.6 *Mobilization of Support from the Labor Movement*

In Quebec, the labor movement has been important in developing the social economy, especially in recent years, during which it has become increasingly evident that investing in collective enterprises generates stable returns. This follows from the earlier reticence by the labor movement's risk assessment of collective enterprises and the myth that these enterprises were marginal and potentially not viable. In addition, there was the concern that new sectors in the social economy, particularly those providing services, would displace secure, well-paid, public-sector jobs. These views are no longer held. The labor movement is a key partner in social finance and the development of the social economy.

5.7 *Maintaining the Focus on Local Realities and a Long-Term Vision of Sustainable and Inclusive Development*

During recent decades, social finance in Quebec has evolved in response to local needs; it has also sought inspiration and lessons from experiences around the world. There is evidence of a clear choice to create a "made in Quebec" response rather than riding fashionable trends or proposals with a tendency to dominate the landscape for a certain period and be sold as "the answer" to current challenges. Two examples stand out. Inspired by the experience of the Grameen Bank, microcredit and microfinance institutions that provide small loans to those who could not apply for bank loans or access any form of capital investment underwent an intense period of development. Quebec was no different. The creation of community loan funds was partially inspired by this approach. However, history has revealed the mitigated results of microcredit experiences in different parts of the world. Additionally, the skepticism many felt about its capacity to considerably reduce poverty has been confirmed. Microcredit is only one among many tools necessary to lift millions of people out of poverty throughout the world, and it is grossly inadequate to address endemic poverty and social exclusion. Its ambitions were unrealistic, even if these small loans have certainly made a difference in the lives of many people. However, critical evaluations of microcredit experiences have revealed the limitations of a homogeneous approach to poverty alleviation without enabling policy measures and without raising the capacity of microcredit to leverage larger sums with the availability of diverse financial tools, thereby increasing its transformative potential; this is why microcredit or community loan funds have always been considered one component on a broader continuum of social finance tools.

Another more current example is the Quebec response to the more recent trend in what is called "impact investment." This new term is promoted by a growing number of financial actors, including large international financial institutions and investment banks, eager to enter this growing market. Today, impact investment is considered a new asset class. It is distinct in its capacity (or at least promised potential) to mobilize large pools of capital from institutional investors such as pension funds, insurance companies, foundations, high net-worth individuals, and increasingly from retail and investment banks. It is the new face of socially responsible investment that began as a means to filter negative investment opportunities. Impact investing is capitalizing on the large international SRI market to transform negative screening into proactive or intentional investment in social enterprises and organizations with the capacity to achieve social outcomes while generating economic returns. It is not surprising that interest in impact investing has increased exponentially since the 2008 financial crisis as investors seek more "ethical" investment opportunities.

However, the major proponents of impact investing do not include a vision of the democratization of capital as a long-term objective. In Quebec, however, solidarity finance has always been seen as a means to democratize capital in the context of a new development model. Hence, impact investing finds an uncomfortable cultural fit in Quebec; solidarity among social actors determines how and where this capital is deployed as a concrete manifestation of a process of economic democratization. The landscape is shifting, but the unity and cohesiveness of the social economy will determine how this new source of capital can best serve its organizations and enterprises in Quebec.

The growing interest in social enterprise internationally has also raised interest in certain circles in Quebec. Behind the concept of social enterprise, in many cases, is the desire to encourage the commercialization of non-profit organizations and the development of social purpose or public benefit businesses by the private sector. This "enterprise" focus is gaining ground in Canada and often conforms to prevailing global trends to privatize public services more generally and/or to replace government programs with "pay for success" approaches by government, such as social impact bonds. It focuses on individual initiatives, not comprehensive approaches. Once again, the Quebec social economy movement has been cautious about this approach. It has maintained its insistence on the importance of collective ownership, the embedding of the social economy and social finance in a broader movement for economic democracy, and inclusive growth.

6 The Challenge of Knowledge Sharing: An Example from Quebec and South Korea[9]

The Quebec experience of the social economy and social finance is enriched by learning from the experiences of other countries, both their successes and failures. In return, Quebec has been called upon by many international partners to share its experiences (Mendell & Neamtan, 2018). Over the past decade, social economy actors have chosen to invest considerable resources in international networking with numerous countries including France, Brazil, Argentina, Mexico, Mali, Morocco, Cuba, and Cameroon. More specifically, since 2014, strong links have been built with South Korea. At the initiative of the former Mayor of Seoul,[10] who was inspired by the Quebec model, social economy actors, researchers, and representatives of government have participated in numerous bilateral exchanges and have joined forces to create the Global Social Economy Forum (GSEF).

Despite strong alignment on values, the challenge of knowledge sharing between Quebec and South Korea is considerable. While both Korea and Quebec have a shared history of civic activism, the turn to economic democracy in Quebec by community activists, especially in the 1980s, saw a departure from common experience (Mendell, 2006; Neamtan, 2019). A developmental state model is also characteristic of both regions; however, in Quebec, this shifted toward a partnership state in the 1980s. While there are still publicly funded programs and initiatives, the history of the social economy and social finance in Quebec is embedded in such a partnership model (Laville et al., 2007). In Korea, the recent evolution of the social economy has been spearheaded by government, beginning with the former Mayor of Seoul. That said, the role

[9] We wish to thank Jinhwan Kim for his assistance in updating information on the current state of social finance in South Korea.

[10] Mayor Won-soon Park passed away in the spring of 2020. He was a passionate advocate for the social economy in Seoul and worked closely with social economy actors in Quebec, including the authors of this chapter. He pioneered many initiatives in his own country, South Korea, and internationally.

of the Seoul metropolitan government in promoting and supporting the social economy in the city is emblematic and is now certainly a model for Quebec and elsewhere; it was, to a large extent, itself inspired by the social economy in Quebec.

Social finance is underdeveloped in Seoul and throughout South Korea, despite the availability of primarily publicly funded tools, micro-finance, and a history of credit unions. What was especially interesting for social economy actors in Seoul was the existence of customized financial tools within the social economy itself in Quebec. Although these tools have the support of government, they were designed by practitioners who could best identify the needs for capital by social economy enterprises and develop financial products to correspond with these needs.

Knowledge sharing and transfer are not unidirectional nor formulaic; experiences cannot be mechanically transposed from one place to another. In the case of Seoul, a municipal government dedicated to the social economy established an infrastructure that now exceeds government involvement in Quebec. Yet, even in Seoul, it is now apparent that more devolution to social economy actors at the municipal level would ease their capacity to design enabling financial tools in collaboration with government at all levels. The election of the current national government in South Korea in 2016 has opened up new opportunities.

Seoul's social finance ecosystem has rapidly evolved in recent years, mainly due to social finance activation programs initiated by the country's current President Moon Jae-In's administration. These programs combine community-based and impact investment approaches. Major new developments since 2018 include the creation of the Social Value and Solidarity Foundation (SVSF), a wholesale social finance fund proposed in the national government activation plan by a pan-ministry task force on social finance (Social Value and Solidarity Foundation, n.d.). The SVSF is an independent organization governed by consumer cooperatives, social finance organizations, and commercial banks, each of which contributes to its capitalization. Networks have also emerged as spaces for dialogue and collaboration, such as a social finance forum made up of 21 organizations, among others. Work to foster the establishment of retail social finance intermediaries is receiving support from ministries at the national level, as well as local governments, and is enhancing the role of conventional credit unions to support the social economy. In addition to this work in progress, the Korea Credit Guarantee Fund launched a digital evaluation platform to assess the social value of social economy enterprises in April 2020, providing an assessment tool for government, conventional banks, and social finance institutions.[11] Of course, how this social value is determined is key.

While there is clearly progress in developing a social finance sector, the government's social finance activation program is, for the most part, a supply-driven impact investment approach. It promoted the establishment of three large funds for social economy enterprises, as well as social ventures operated by for-profit financial enterprises, including asset management companies and venture capital firms. The social finance activation program also includes venture capital firms and new technology companies as important types of retail social finance intermediaries to be fostered by the government.

The social finance ecosystem in Seoul will be significantly influenced by the ongoing reform programs initiated by the national government of South Korea, whereas the autonomy of local governments is still largely limited, given the national government's dominant power in regulation and fiscal allocation. Nonetheless, the establishing of the Seoul Social Innovation Fund by the Seoul metropolitan government is encouraging as it challenges established government-led initiatives. It is too soon to say if it will succeed, as most of its financing comes from government, large companies, corporate social responsibility portfolios, and philanthropic investors. Self-financing remains weak, despite efforts to create mutual aid funds for cooperatives or social enterprises in recent years. The mismatch between supply and demand for social financing is an ongoing concern raised by analysts in South Korea. Access to capital enabling the growth of social economy enterprises remains limited while seed capital or start-up funds are relatively abundant. The most significant barrier to the development of a social finance ecosystem that responds to the needs of the social economy is the absence of collaboration between the public sector, civil society, and the private sector in South Korea, where current legislation curbs such cooperation.

Under these circumstances, Korean actors identified four major lessons from Quebec's successful experience to build a coherent ecosystem for social finance in Seoul. The needs-based or demand-based approach (as opposed to a supply-driven approach) has been identified as a key

[11] Korea Credit Guarantee Fund Social Economy Enterprises Evaluation Platform can be accessed here: https://www.kodit.co.kr/social/main/main.do (Korean only).

challenge, as has the importance of community-based social finance intermediaries. The democratization of capital, reflected in mechanisms that allow those who use social finance tools to have a say in how these tools are developed and operated, has also been identified as a key success factor. The last lesson has to do with the absence of collaboration between government, the social economy sector, and the private sector in building a social finance ecosystem as noted above. This remains at the forefront of the Quebec experience. While these lessons are universal, their applications are very different in the Quebec and Korean contexts.

The process of knowledge transfer in the field of social finance was facilitated by the publication of *Strategy for Knowledge Transfer of Social Finance: Best practices of Quebec* and strategy for adaptation to Seoul by CITIES, an international center for knowledge transfer linked to the Global Social Economy Forum, from which this chapter is adapted. Numerous other exchanges between practitioners, researchers, and government representatives generate an ongoing conversation within Korea.

7 Conclusion

The Quebec experience of the social economy and social finance is one example of the growing international trend to redefine the relationship between economic and social development, between globalization and localization, as well as between profit-driven and mission-driven organizations and enterprises. The COVID-19 pandemic reinforces the limits of the dominant development model that is already strongly challenged by the climate crisis. The Korean experience, while seeking inspiration from Quebec, has shown the need to adapt initiatives to different institutional contexts. However, it has also demonstrated the limitations of conventional financial institutions and models to respond to the specificities of social economy enterprises in countries across the globe.

Many questions remain. Will social finance progress rapidly enough to make a significant contribution to the urgently needed ecological and social transition? Many indicators allow for optimism, but vigilance is required. The role that capital plays in perpetuating the dominant economic paradigm is fundamental and it can be expected that attempts will continue to deviate social finance from its transformative trajectory. However, through citizen mobilization and strong links with social movements, as is the case in Quebec, there is great potential for social finance to contribute significantly to the building of a sustainable and inclusive economy, and society, across the planet.

The COVID-19 pandemic has unleashed an unprecedented global social and economic crisis. Not since the Second World War have governments intervened so rapidly to prevent economic collapse while prioritizing the health of citizens.[12] In many contexts, supporting local economic initiatives has been integrated into larger macro-strategies. A scan of the social economy internationally reveals its rootedness in territory, as well as its generative and regenerative capacity that is now key to the livelihoods of communities around the world. Much as all sectors in the economy are required to transform many of their established practices, social finance institutions must also adapt to a new reality beyond assuring the survival of existing collective and social enterprises. The determination of risk and return will require rethinking; social finance institutions need to become more flexible, more agile. And they will. The model that underlies social finance integrates social, environmental, and economic objectives. As instability and disruption define a new reality requiring integrated approaches, social finance needs no lessons. It needs to stay connected to new realities and evolve as it has over these last decades in Quebec. It needs to be reflexive and adapt its own practices. And it will.

References

Bâtir son quartier. (2019, June 7). *Le Fonds d'Investissement de Montréal célèbre son 1 000ᵉ logement communautaire à Montréal*. Bâtir son quartier. https://www.batirsonquartier.com/le-fonds-dinvestissement-de-montreal-celebre-son-1-000e-logement-communautaire-a-montreal/.

Caisse d'économie solidaire (CES). (2020). *Rapport annuel 2019*. https://caissesolidaire.coop/wp-content/uploads/2020/05/2019_Revue-annuelle_Caisse-solidaire.pdf.

CAP Finance. (2017). *Charte de CAP finance*. http://capfinance.ca/wp-content/uploads/2017/08/Charte-de-CAP-Finance.pdf.

CAP Finance. (2019). *Guide for the analysis of social economy enterprises* (2nd ed[A2].).

CAP Finance. (2021). *CAP finance—Le réseau de la finance solidaire et responsable*. https://capfinance.ca/.

[12] Indeed, there are exceptions to how this is being played out. While mostly ad hoc, quickly baked measures to mitigate economic chaos, a new policy framework will surely emerge from this crisis.

Capital régional et coopératif Desjardins (CRCD). (2015). *Who we are*. https://www.capitalregional.com/about-us/who-we-are.

Capital régional et coopératif Desjardins (CRCD). (2019). *Rapport financier annuel 2019*. https://www.capitalregional.com/media/1821/31-decembre-2019-rapport-financier.pdf.

Desjardins. (n.d). *Timeline: Desjardins*. https://www.desjardins.com/ca/about-us/desjardins/who-we-are/our-history-museum/timeline/index.jsp#tiroir-first-steps.

Fiducie. (2019). *Rapport annuel 2018*. http://fiducieduchantier.qc.ca/wp-content/uploads/2019/03/FCES_rapportAnnuel018_FR_LR.pdf.

Filaction: Fonds de développement. (2020). *Innogec fund*. https://filaction.qc.ca/innogec-fund.

Fondaction. (2019). *Rapport annuel 2018–2019*. https://www.fondaction.com/pdf/rap_financiers/FONDACTION_rapportannuel2020.pdf.

Fondaction. (2021). *À propos*. https://www.fondaction.com/a-propos.php.

Fonds de solidarité FTQ. (2019a). *Rapport d'activité et de développement durable 2019*. https://www.fondsftq.com/-/media/Site-Corporatif/Fichiers/2019/FondsFTQ_RADD2019_FR.pdf?la=fr-CA.

Fonds de solidarité FTQ. (2019b, April 17). *Montréal's first-ever affordable student housing building breaks ground* [Press release]. https://www.fondsftq.com/en/salle-de-presse/liste-communiques-de-presse/communique.aspx?nom=20190417-logement-etudiants-montreal.

Fonds de solidarité FTQ. (2020). *Qui sommes-nous?* https://www.fondsftq.com/fr-ca/a-propos/qui-sommes-nous.aspx.

Fonds Écoleader. (2021). *Qui sommes-nous?* https://www.fondsecoleader.ca/le-fonds-ecoleader/qui-sommes-nous/.

Gouvernement du Québec. (2016, May 17). *Attribution de 10 millions de dollars pour soutenir les entreprises d'économie sociale au Québec*. Québec Social Investment Network. [Press release]. https://www.economie.gouv.qc.ca/ministere/salle-de-presse/communiques-de-presse/communique-de-presse/?no_cache=1&tx_ttnews%5Btt_news%5D=19034&cHash=208cf3a86893491df168fe4f0fa7c8d9.

Government of Canada. (2006, January 6). *Canada's new government grants $22,8 million for the growth of Quebec social economy enterprises*. https://www.canada.ca/en/news/archive/2007/01/canada-new-government-grants-22-8-million-growth-quebec-social-economy-enterprises.html.

Government of Canada. (2020, August 14). *New affordable housing options for students in Montreal*. National housing strategy. https://www.placetocallhome.ca/stories/071-new-affordable-housing-options-students-montreal.

Institut de la statistique du Québec. (2019). *L'économie sociale au Québec – Portrait statistique 2016*. https://www.stat.gouv.qc.ca/statistiques/economie-sociale/portrait-economie-sociale-2016.pdf.

Investissement Québec. (2016). *Collective entrepreneurship*. All our solutions. https://www.investquebec.com/quebec/en/financial-products/all-our-solutions/collective-entrepreneurship.html.

Korean Social Value and Solidarity Foundation (SVS). (n.d.). https://www.svsfund.org/en.

Laville, J. L., Lévesque, B., & Mendell, M. (2007). The social economy: Diverse approaches and practices in Europe and Canada. In A. Noya & E. Clarence (Eds.), In *The social economy: building inclusive economies* (pp. 155–187). OECD Local Economic and Employment Development (LEED) Programme. https://www.oecd.org/cfe/leed/thesocialeconomybuildinginclusiveeconomies.htm#getbook.

Maheux, P. (2016). L'émergence d'un "Deuxième Front": Vers la création d'un nouveau type de caisse (1945–1970). In P.-O. Maheux (Ed.), *Histoire de la Caisse d'économie solidaire Desjardins: La Passion des Êtres* (pp. 33–62). Septentrion. https://caissesolidaire.coop/wp-content/uploads/2018/10/histoire-de-la-caisse-deconomie-solidaire-desjardins.pdf.

Mendell, M. (2000). Chapter 5: Local finance in a global economy: Palliative or Panacea? In P. Hamel, H. Lustiger-Thaler, & M. Mayuer (Eds.),*Urban movements in a globalising world* (pp. 101–123). Routledge. https://books.google.ca/books?hl=en&lr=&id=etGAAgAAQBAJ&oi=fnd&pg=PA101&dq=:+Local+Finance+in+a+Global+Economy:+Palliative+or+Panacea%3F&ots=VJUzaWB9a-&sig=AN7kUdKT3tQBNrWMfwK39a4SuGs&redir_esc=y#v=onepage&q=%3A%20Local%20Finance%20in%20a%20Global%20Economy%3A%20Palliative%20or%20Panacea%3F&f=false.

Mendell, M. (2006). L'empowerment au Canada et au Québec: Enjeux et opportunités. *Géographie, Économie, Société, 8*(1), 63–85. https://doi.org/10.3166/ges.8.63-86.

Mendell, M. (2014). *Improving social inclusion at the local level through the social economy: Designing an enabling policy framework* (p. 15). OECD LEED. https://www.oecd.org/employment/leed/Improving-Social-Inclusion-Capacity.pdf.

Mendell, M., & Neamtan, N. (2018). Chapter 2: Developing an ecosystem of social finance: Quebec's experience. In C.I.T.I.E.S., *Strategy for knowledge transfer of social finance: Best practices of Québec and strategy for adaptation to Seoul* (pp. 5–32). CITIES. http://cities-ess.org/wp-content/uploads/2018/08/Strategy-for-the-Knowledge-Transfer-of-Social-Finance.pdf.

Neamtan, N. (2019). *Trente ans d'économie sociale au Québec: Un mouvement en chantier*. Fides.

PME MTL. (2015–2019). *Résultats annuels du réseau PME MTL*. https://pmemtl.com/a-propos/publications.

Réseau des SADC et CDE. (2016). *Résultats*. https://www.sadc-cae.ca/en/.

Réseau d'investissement social du Québec (RISQ). (2020). *Rapport annuel 2019*. https://fonds-risq.qc.ca/rapport-annuel/2019/.
Réseau d'investissement social du Québec (RISQ). (2020). *Réseau de relayeurs du RISQ*. https://fonds-risq.qc.ca/reseau-de-relayeurs-du-risq/?lang=en.
Social Economy Act, CQLR, c. E-1.1.1. (2019). http://legisquebec.gouv.qc.ca/en/ShowDoc/cs/E-1.1.1.
Territoires innovants en économie sociale et solidaire (TIESS). (2017). *Guide d'émission pour les entreprises d'économie sociale*. Obligations communautaires. https://tiess.ca/guide-demission-pour-les-entreprises-deconomie-sociale-obligations-communautaires-2017/.
Woodnote. (2018). *History*. https://woodnote.coop/about/history/.

Social Finance for Women's Entrepreneurship in Canada

Zohreh Hassannezhad Chavoushi, Guang Ying Mo, and Wendy Cukier

1 Introduction

Supporting women entrepreneurs is a global priority. Countries worldwide have developed policies and programs for women that bring new ideas, services, products, and approaches to the economic community. Canada is considered a global leader with its Women Entrepreneurship Strategy (WES), which aims to double the number of women entrepreneurs by 2025 (Government of Canada, 2019a).

Despite these interventions, women and other under-represented entrepreneurs often face barriers to starting and growing their businesses. Per Cukier et al. (2020), "while organizations supporting women entrepreneurs in Canada have made important strides over the last two decades, the resources available to women are not as significant as those

Z. Hassannezhad Chavoushi · G. Y. Mo · W. Cukier (✉)
Diversity Institute, Ryerson University, Toronto, ON, Canada
e-mail: wcukier@ryerson.ca

Z. Hassannezhad Chavoushi
e-mail: zhassannezhad@ryerson.ca

G. Y. Mo
e-mail: g.mo@ryerson.ca

T. Walker et al. (eds.), *Innovations in Social Finance*,
https://doi.org/10.1007/978-3-030-72535-8_4

available for individuals considered to be mainstream or stereotypical entrepreneurs" (Cukier et al., 2020, p. iv). Women working on social enterprises and women in low-income brackets face additional barriers. While there has been progress in this area, gender inequality persists in entrepreneurial activities due to discrimination, the underrepresentation of women in many economic and political spheres, as well as social norms and attitudes that disadvantage women (United Nations, 2019). For example, women are less likely to have incorporated businesses, and the majority of them are self-employed and active in the service sector (55.2%), health care and social assistance (69.7%), and educational services (66%) (Government of Canada, 2019b) which are easily approachable sector for entrepreneurship and require low investment and easy made infrastructure.

All around the world, social finance initiatives have emerged in order to facilitate women's pathways in entrepreneurial activities. These initiatives range from crowdfunding to impact investing and appear to be an effective mechanism for this goal. Social finance is "a sustainable approach to managing money that delivers social [and] environmental dividends [as well as] economic return through social enterprises operating in the non-profit or public sector" (Draimin, 2008, p. 12). This type of financing is one of the new methods for funding civil society initiatives and social entrepreneurship. The Federal Government of Canada created a new committee to explore ways to accelerate social finance, including the use of dormant funds and tax incentives. While there is extensive academic literature on social finance, the research that focuses on Canada specifically remains limited (Phillips et al., 2008).

In order to shed light on social finance initiatives that support women entrepreneurs in Canada, this chapter starts with a brief review of the social finance literature and the taxonomy of social finance based on models and types, functions, and implications. A comparative case study follows; it analyzes seven Canadian cases that are active in financing women-owned businesses. By way of conclusion, we offer recommendations to inform the development and use of social finance in supporting women entrepreneurs and helping them overcome the barriers that they face.

While social finance is increasingly used to mobilize private capital for the public good in Canada, research dedicated to social finance in support of women entrepreneurs in the Canadian context remains limited (Phillips et al., 2008). This study, therefore, raises two research questions:

1. What are the different types of social finance that can be used to support women entrepreneurs?
2. What are the actual social finance initiatives that have been successful in supporting women entrepreneurs in Canada?

2 Social Finance

Social finance is an investment in which investors deploy financial resources primarily for social and environmental return and in some cases, a financial return (Moore et al., 2012; Weber & Duan, 2012). Such finance initiatives mobilize private capital to achieve social and environmental goals (Government of Canada, 2015); gender equality is often one of these goals. In general, social finance exists in various forms, such as impact investing, microfinance, and social banking (Geobey & Weber, 2013). Other models, such as crowdfunding and pay-for-performance, have also emerged in support of women entrepreneurs (Tapestry Community Capital, 2019). The funding provided to women entrepreneurs does not need to be repaid; grants, gifts, or money given unconditionally are as important to social enterprises as equity and grants are to private and public companies (Varga & Hayday, 2019). Social finance can meet the financial needs of entrepreneurs by providing simple and easily understood structures, and by being more flexible regarding the terms on which financing is provided. This flexibility depends on the source of the funds (Varga & Hayday, 2019). Table 1 shows a variety of financial resources that are available to entrepreneurs. Resources are organized on a continuum that range from higher expectation for social returns to greater obligation for financial returns, as the type of investor indicates. This chapter focuses on the five models used for achieving social returns.

2.1 Social Impact Bonds and Pay for Success

The social impact bond (SIB), also known as a "social benefit good" or "social bond," is a relatively new mechanism for governments to fund social services (Tan et al., 2019). SIBs combine a pay-for-performance element with an investment-based approach: private investors provide up-front capital to fund interventions and can expect to get back their principal investments and a financial return if the results are achieved (Government of Canada, 2013). In other words, this funding model asks private investors to fund social service projects. If the project meets

Table 1 Financial resources available for entrepreneurs

Finance model	*Explanation*	*Examples*
Crowdfunding	A collective effort by people who network and pool their money together in order to invest in and support efforts initiated by other people or organizations	The Pebble E-Paper Watch, Star Citizen (on kickstarter.com)
Microfinance	Financial services striving to mitigate poverty through microloans and other microfinance products, such as micro insurance	"Saving Up" campaign (India), "Saving Through" campaign (Kenya)
Social banking	Banking services with the main objectives to promote economic sustainability, provide opportunity for the disadvantaged, and support social, environmental, and ethical agenda	Members of the Global Alliance for Banking on Values (the Netherlands)
Impact investing	Investment for both social and financial returns, where positive societal impact has a higher priority than financial returns	United Nations Capital Development Fund (the UN), Bridges Fund Management (the UK)
Social impact bonds and Pay for Success	A model in which private investors fund social service projects, success of which (meeting certain targets) allows investors to get their money back from the government with a return	El Futuro en Mis Manos (Mexico), Aspire Social Impact Bond (Australia)
Socially responsible investing	An investment strategy that takes into account societal and/or environmental benefits when making financial investment decisions	Dwight Hall Socially Responsible Investment Fund (the U.S.), Calvert Mid Cap Value Fund (the U.S.)
Responsible investing	A strategy or practice that incorporates environmental, social, and governance factors into the selection and management of investments	Mackenzie Investments (Canada), Canadian Focused Equity Fund, Government Employee Pension Fund (South Africa)

(continued)

Table 1 (continued)

Finance model	*Explanation*	*Examples*
Traditional debt	The act of committing money or capital to an endeavor with the expectation of obtaining an additional income or profit	CI Investments Inc. (Canada), BlackRock Asset Management Canada Ltd. (Canada)

certain targets, investors get their money back from the government, with a return. If the project fails, the investors do not receive anything, which signals high risk. Therefore, since its introduction, SIB has been controversial, due to higher costs and payments to private investors (Hajer, 2019).

2.2 *Impact Investing*

Impact investing refers to investing for both social and financial returns, where positive societal impact has a higher priority than financial returns (Hangl, 2014; Weber & Feltmate, 2016). Impact investing differs from socially responsible investing. While socially responsible investing encompasses avoidance of harm, impact investing actively seeks to make a positive impact via investment (Chen, 2019). Impact investing is poised to address investment inequalities and can mobilize more private capital to close the equity gap for entrepreneurship funding. This framework views gender inequality as a relational issue and a matter of structural inequality that needs addressing by women, institutions, governments, and wider society.

2.3 *Social Banking*

Legal banks (as well as cooperative banks, on occasion, and credit unions who provide social finance products and services under the legal form of a bank) primarily engage social banking in conducting banking activities (Geobey & Weber, 2013). The structures of these products and services are often similar to conventional ones, such as loans, mortgages, or funds. In the 1950s, Canada's credit union system considered most women eligible for loans and mortgages, which contributed to gender equality in the country (Geobey & Weber, 2013). In 2017, the Government of Canada created the Social Innovation & Social Finance Strategy Co-Creation Steering Group. The group provided twelve recommendations to advance social innovation and mobilize social finance in Canada. In November 2018, the Fall Economic Statement from the federal government outlined a proposed $755 M Social Finance Fund to invest in socially innovative projects (Rainey et al., 2017).

2.4 *Microfinance*

Another type of social finance that has successfully contributed to gender equality and the empowerment of women is microfinance (Geobey & Weber, 2013). Microfinance includes financial products and services, such as loans, saving products, insurance, and other financial services which help impoverished demographics that usually do not have access to capital in improving their financial circumstances. This term subsumes micro-credit, micro-savings, and microinsurance (Weber & Feltmate, 2016). For example, microcredit allows loans ranging from $500 to $50,000. These loans must be paid back on a short-term basis. About 58% of Canada's small business owners start out with less than $5000 (Intuit Canada, n.d.). Some organizations even provide micro-loans starting from $60 (Opportunity International Canada, n.d.). Microfinance has a great impact on small enterprises. Small enterprises often have high returns to capital, but it is difficult for them to access credit from official banks. Small enterprises that operate at low levels of capital may find it hard to return capital if production functions display decreasing returns (Bruhn et al., 2012). Commercial banks often refuse the loan applications of small enterprises since the revenue generated by small loan amounts is low compared to fixed costs and the operational costs of lending to micro-firms (World Bank, 2009).

To illustrate, microfinance, especially microcredit, proves to be effective for fighting poverty in Bangladesh. Microfinance pioneer Muhammad Yunus was awarded the Nobel Prize for Peace in 2016 (Geobey & Weber, 2013). Microfinance programs have been quite effective in contributing to women's ability to earn an income and have resulted in economic empowerment, increased well-being for women and their families, and wider social and political empowerment. Essentially, there are three paradigms on microfinance and gender: financial self-sustainability paradigm, poverty alleviation paradigm, and feminist empowerment paradigm (Mayoux, 2000). However, the existing evidence of the impact of microfinance programs on gender relations is limited. In Canada, 58% of small businesses are started with less than $5000.

There are multiple microfinance programs in Canada that support women entrepreneurs, e.g., Paro Micro loans, Alterna Micro Finance, Microcredit Montréal, and Oasis Centre des femmes, the latter targeting francophone women entrepreneurs specifically. Additionally, the programs and/or services that aim to empower women can significantly help toward achieving gender equality (Mayoux, 2006). For example, CAUSE Canada's Microfinance program supported 128 girls in Sierra Leone through Junior and Senior secondary schools and University. In addition, they provide small loans and business training to women entrepreneurs in the rural regions of central America and West Africa.

While there is extensive research available on the impact of micro-loans and grants in international contexts (e.g., Hussain et al., 2015; Sharma et al., 2012), there is little research on programs in Canada, although anecdotal evidence suggests these loans are one of the major gaps in the current finance system. For example, many microfinance programs in Canada are location based—you have to be living in a particular region to qualify (Intuit Canada, n.d.).

2.5 *Crowdfunding*

A recent model for impact investing is crowdfunding. The term describes a collaborative finance system that pools small amounts of money from numerous people, usually via web platforms, to fund a specific project (Braund & Schwittay, 2016). There is an increasing number of investment funds tied to social causes and specifically to gender equality (Orser et al., 2020). Crowdfunding has proven to be a successful mechanism in helping women entrepreneurs raise capital when resources are scarce (Greenberg & Gerber, 2012; Schwienbacher & Larralde, 2010). Capital is often raised through online social networks in which the large audience (the "crowd") contribute a small amount of money (Kuppuswamy & Bayus, 2018; Mollick, 2014). When raising financial resources to start a business, crowdfunding may offer an attractive alternative for women entrepreneurs who face more barriers to access traditional financing.

3 Canada's Social Finance Ecosystem

Social finance is still at an early stage of development in Canada. To include investors, social enterprises, and intermediaries in the same framework for a thorough discussion, we use an innovation ecosystem approach to examine the landscape of social finance for women-led innovation in Canada. The ecosystem lens uses the critical ecological approach as a holistic model that allows the analysis of complex systems which constrain and advance entrepreneurship of diverse groups ranging from macro-level factors (policies, cultures, and values), meso-level factors (organizational policies and practices), and micro-level factors (opportunities, preferences, choices) (Cukier et al., 2014). In other words, the model depicts the interactions of macro (societal), meso (organizational), and micro (individual) level influences associated with the economic and social challenges that individuals and businesses face (Cukier & Chavoushi, 2020).

In Canada, governments at all levels implement policies, procedures, and/or practices to encourage and support the growth of social finance in tackling intractable societal problems. For instance, in 2011, the British Columbia Social Innovation Council recommended that the private and non-for-profit (NFP) sectors partner with the provincial government to create SIBs that fund services, improve social outcomes, and attract new sources of social investment capital. It further recommended that social enterprises gain access to the government programs and support that are typically provided to small and medium social enterprises (Government of Canada, 2013). In Ontario, the 2012 Commission on the Reform of Ontario's Public Services, also known as the "Drummond Report," recommended pilot projects to test SIBs across a range of applications (Government of Canada, 2013). Social finance initiatives are also developing at the municipal level. The City of Toronto started the Toronto Atmospheric Fund (TAF) in 1993 to address emissions from buildings and transportation (Government of Canada, 2013). Boasting ten programs, TAF uses a new carbon emission inventory to develop climate solutions (The Atmospheric Fund, 2019).

With such a pro-social-finance climate, many national or local initiatives are successfully operating in the private and NFP sectors. Among all types of social finance, impact investing is seeing an outstanding growth in market size. Impact assets under management (AUM) in Canada grew from $8.15 billion in 2015 to $14.75 billion in 2017, representing

81% growth over a two-year period (Responsible Investment Association, 2019). One successful example is the Youth Social Innovation Capital Fund (YSI-CF), created in 2011 in Toronto. It supports young social innovators by providing finance through loans, resource support, networking and mentoring, as well as impact measurement support. In particular, YSI-CF applies a gender lens to support women entrepreneurs by offering flexibility in funding diverse ventures, as they are aware of the fact that most women entrepreneurs are more likely to fail the meeting of funding criteria because their ventures are not as product-focused as those of their male counterparts (Youth Social Innovation, 2011).

The YWCA Toronto was the first organization that issued a "community bond." In December 2011, the community bond launched to raise $1 million in flexible development capital to fund 300 low-income women and women-led single-parent households. Inspired by this model, Toronto Community Housing Corporation (TCHC) also issued a $450 million bond to solve housing issues for low-income households. These two community bonds are consistently cited as leading examples of impact investing (Housing Services Corporation, 2013).

Despite the fast growth, social enterprises that seek funding through impact investing are often challenged with the high, and sometimes prohibitive, costs associated with investing in social enterprises, in addition to the lack of champions and anchor investors (Lam & Tansey, 2019). Women entrepreneurs of early-stage social enterprises are particularly frustrated with fundraising as they face a different, more critical investor perspective throughout the process, exemplified through the asking of questions that suggest failure instead of future aspiration or past successes (Lam & Tansey, 2019). For example, Kanze et al. (2018) observe Q&A interactions between 140 prominent venture capitalists and find out that 67% of the questions posed to men entrepreneurs were promotion-oriented, while 67% of the questions posed to women entrepreneurs were prevention-oriented, i.e., questions about customer acquisition vs. customer retention, respectively (Kanze et al., 2018). In response, researchers and social entrepreneurs are calling for the adoption of a gender-lens in investing, or the incorporating of a gender analysis into financial analysis, to understand how value is assigned, how relationships are structured, and how processes work (Quinlan & VanderBrug, 2016; Roberts, 2016).

In the mid-1980s, Metrofund focused on serving women who were disadvantaged in comparison with men, in terms of access to business credit due to the lack of social capital and the absence of a gender strategy, which is often overlooked by most microfinance organizations (Cheston & Kuhn, 2002; Frankiewicz, 2001; Gomez & Santor, 2001; Mayoux, 2002). In November 2011, in British Columbia, the Vancouver Foundation and credit union Vancity created the Vancity Resilient Capital Fund with a grant from the Government of British Columbia. The pool of $15 million dollars was earmarked for investment in social enterprises. In two years, the program collaborated with more than twenty institutional and individual depositors who, together, contributed about $13.5 million in Resilient Capital Term Deposits and provided $4 million in financing to eleven enterprises that address social and environmental challenges and build resilient communities. Since its launch, the Resilient Capital Program model has been seen as a pioneering approach with the potential for replication in other jurisdictions (Vancity, 2013). Another successful case in Canada is the investment fund developed by the Quebec credit union Mouvement des Caisses Desjardins. The "Placement à rendement social" focuses on housing, environmental, and cultural projects that allow the public to invest via their retirement vehicles (RRSPs) or tax-free savings accounts (Government of Canada, 2013).

Social banking in Canada often uses the credit union model, which has been in usage for the past 120 years. The first credit union movement, the "Caisse Populaire," started in Quebec (Colman, 2004). The credit union movement in Canada is the largest per capita in the world—about one-third of the population are members. In the early 1960s, Vancity began lending to women without a male co-signer (Vancity, 2019). However, gender stereotypes and gender relationships for women continue to act as barriers, and women are unable to fully benefit from the service of credit unions (Cheston & Kuhn, 2002). For example, on average women's loan sizes are smaller than those offered to men, even when they are in the same credit program, the same community, and/or the same lending group with men (Cheston & Kuhn, 2002).

SIBs, unlike standard bonds, are not a form of debt security in which interest is paid by the issuer of the bond to the holder at maturity. This model allows the government to use funds otherwise spent on services like counseling, health care, or detention to reward investors who fund programs that reduce the need for these services in the first place (Government of Canada, 2013). In 2016, MaRS launched Canada's first SIB in health. It used a social impact bond model to provide a stable source of funding from government and private investors to support a project aimed to help seniors get their blood pressure levels under control, started by Heart & Stroke Foundation (MaRS Centre of Impact Investing, 2016).

As macro-level policy-making grows, meso-level initiatives and activities thrive, micro-level individual investors and entrepreneurs engage with the ecosystem, and interactions across the three levels increase. From November 2012 to January 2013, the Government of Canada asked Canadians to participate in the National Call for Concepts for Social Finance that aimed to research the potential of social finance to augment existing programs with new capital and new ideas. Citizens, businesses, charities, and other groups from eight provinces provided more than 150 responses on the topic of innovative and collaborative solutions (Government of Canada, 2013). The responses addressed issues in a wide array of demographics and issues, such as youth, health, Indigenous peoples, persons with disabilities, public safety, housing and homelessness, the unemployed, seniors, and new Canadians. The responses also suggested the use of SIBs, social investment funds, pay-for-performance contract, and social enterprise among others (Government of Canada, 2013).

As a result of the responses, the Government of Canada developed new social finance initiatives. For instance, Career Focus pilot projects provided funding to targeted organizations to support the creation of career-related work experiences for post-secondary graduates and to help them develop advanced employability skills. This pilot developed into Career Focus, which is a part of the Youth Employment Strategy, a horizontal initiative involving eleven federal departments and agencies. A community partnership pilot, Calgary's Community Kitchen Program, aimed to leverage public and private funding to engage and mobilize community volunteers who work with vulnerable individuals and families. This pilot is now a self-empowering model that addresses the needs of marginalized Calgarians and operates five programs, including food rescue and a feeding program designed for children in low-income communities (Government of Canada, 2020).

4 Methods

We use the comparative case study approach to conduct a systematic comparison of multiple cases to analyze cases representing the various models of social finance in Canada (Fox-Wolfgramm, 1997; Goodrick, 2014; Kaarbo & Beasley, 1999). We collect data from publicly accessible sources, such as the cases' Web sites, industry and reports, and/or news about them.

Our comparative case study approach allows us to examine in rich detail the context and features of several typical forms of social finance, as well as how each form supports women. This allows us to present a rich description of each case and to discover contrasts in addition to similarities across the cases. This approach may in turn contribute to the creation of a holistic picture of social finance initiatives in Canada and the development of theory (Mills et al., 2009).

In this study, we conduct a comparative case study using the following steps (Kaarbo & Beasley, 1999):

1. *Identify variables:* We investigate and interpret the cases using six critical components: objective, strategic focus, fund receivers, funding process, resources and services, and socioeconomic effects.
2. *Case selection:* The theoretical basis of this study is the typology of "social finance" activities that support women entrepreneurs. Thus, we look for organizations that have strategies to support women entrepreneurs. Evidently, there are many of cases that could benefit from study, but to allow for variations in significant contextual factors, we used inclusion and exclusion criteria to select cases. To ensure the comparability of cases, we identify four major aspects when selecting cases: time of founding, geographic area, type of social finance, and the existence of a plan to support women entrepreneurs. Firstly, we look at social finance organizations that were founded at a range of different times. The inclusion of cases at different stages of growth enables us to tease out common factors and identify distinctive features of social finance that occur at different stages. The second criterion is geographic area. We select organizations that provide social finance on various scales, from specific regions in Canada to global markets. For those practicing at the local level, we select cases from geographical areas that are dispersed across the country so that we include the factors of language (i.e., francophone vs. anglophone areas) and urbanization (i.e., big cities vs. outskirts) in the comparison. Next, the type of social finance is a crucial aspect. We include cases representing various types, such as impact investing and microfinance, to compare their strategies. Finally, as social finance activities are diverse and have different targets, and our focus is only on cases that have plans

for supporting women entrepreneurs, we intentionally include a case that targets women who are not entrepreneurs in order to cover a diverse range of cases and programs. We also have exclusion criteria: local social finance initiatives outside of Canada are excluded. We exclude institutions that only focus on environmental or community support. Finally, we select cases as a representative of each type of social finance. In total, we select seven cases across Canada for analysis.

3. *Coding:* We use a "codebook" as a guide to check the type of data that are needed from the cases. We create the codebook on the basis of the research questions and a database for the cases, with the focus on the key variables (Table 2).
4. *Comparison and implications for theory and practice:* We compare and contrast the cases to identify similarities and differences across the cases and to note implications for theory development and practice. Through the case studies, we aim to identify gaps in social finance theory and to provide recommendations for researchers, practitioners, and policy-makers.

5 Findings

To analyze the cases in this study, we compare and contrast their objectives, mission, strategic focus, commitment of resources, and their impact.

5.1 Objective

Our objective is to focus on output efficacy (measures of quantity of desired outputs created), output efficiency (measures of the inputs required to create the desired output), and/or as simple inputs (activity/effort measures of utilization or consumption of inputs, regardless of their effect on the creation of outputs). In organizations, strategy development is the process of formulating policies with the focus on organizational objectives. The objectives vary in time scope from short-range objectives, to middle-range, and long-term objectives.

Table 2 Social finance activities to support women entrepreneurs

Case	*Year of founding*	*Objective*	*Strategic focus*	*Fund receivers*	*Funding process*	*Resources and services*	*Socioeconomic effects*	*SF type*	*Scale*
SheEO	2013	Support women-owned and women-led ventures	Assistance to fund and grow women-owned enterprises	Women entrepreneurs & Activators	Open call for Activators and the voting process by 500 Activators	Resources, funding, mentorship, and network	Job creation, supporting ventures	Crowdfunding	Global
Vancity	1946	Help improve the financial well-being of its members, especially women members	Value-based financial co-operation	Local businesses, community members, investors	Investment in local businesses and organizations with grants, microcredit, start-up financing, traditional loans, mortgages and lines of credit with cash-flow and growth financing	Expertise, advice, network, financing solutions	Building healthy communities that are socially, economically, and environmentally sustainable	Social banking	Local (British Columbia)
Equality Fund	2019	To support women's rights organizations and feminist movements in Canada and around the world	Providing sustainable funding for women around the globe (e.g. in Congo Afghanistan, Iraq, and Mexico)	Women's rights organizations, feminist movements, individual women and girls	Crowdfunding to provide sustainable funding and invest in women's movements globally	Financial resources and strengthen organizations active at the grassroots level and on the global stage	Working with over 650 women's organizations in 71 countries, Equality Fund invested nearly $12 million in women and girls	Crowdfunding and Impact investing	Global

Case	*Year of founding*	*Objective*	*Strategic focus*	*Fund receivers*	*Funding process*	*Resources and services*	*Socioeconomic effects*	*SF type*	*Scale*
Alterna Savings	1908	Help new and marginalized people and women in Ontario to start a business	Supporting small and developing businesses through community-based micro-lending	Members	Loan funds administered in partnership with local community organizations	Financial services, wealth management, sharing skills and knowledge, sharing time and money	Sponsorships to support community groups, community funds for environment, homelessness, and children's issues	Microfinance	Local (Ontario)
Marigold Capital	2016	Allocating capital for a more just and equitable world while earning a generative return on investment	Applying a gender lens to the investment process to revalue and empower women	Women and any group of individuals that are marginalized or disadvantaged, social companies that are overlooked in traditional investing	Help clients to reach a strategic plan, and invest in their business with further help in risk management, support services, and more. They also partner with other organizations for collective impact investing	Customized strategic consulting for developing a strategy, executing the strategy, and managing the funds	Social change in diversity and inclusivity. Empower individuals with the capacity, skills and confidence to participate and benefit society	Impact investing	National (Canada and US)

(continued)

Table 2 (continued)

Case	*Year of founding*	*Objective*	*Strategic focus*	*Fund receivers*	*Funding process*	*Resources and services*	*Socioeconomic effects*	*SF type*	*Scale*
Restoring the Sacred Bond	2019	Support at-risk women with pregnancy and following childbirth	Providing emotional and physical support to women in Indigenous communities to reduce the number of days their children spend in care	A child and family services authority named Southern First Nations Network of Care	Private investors fund social services projects. If the project meets certain targets, investors get their money back from the provincial government, plus a return	Social services	Social service works with an Indigenous doula group to match moms-to-be with doulas who will provide emotional support, Indigenous ceremonial knowledge and more	Social impact bond	Local (Manitoba)
Mastercard Foundation	2006	Help economically disadvantaged people and support women-led businesses	Working in a diverse group of countries with high levels of young people and women living in poverty	Women and young people	Scholarship	Education, financial services, and skills training	Partnership with more than 150 organizations to increase financial inclusion and access to youth learning in Africa	Impact investing	Global

5.2 *Strategic Focus*

The social finance providers' strategies reflect their objectives and the chosen dominant logic. Using a single set of objectives and logic, different strategic choices are possible for different social finance activities, including a sectoral focus (women, youth, marginalized groups), lifecycle stage (newcomers, early start-ups), as well as desired impact over time (short-term vs long-term) and across space (specific locale or community). These strategic choices operationalize through the design of a business model, including the choice of a source of funding and the choice of an investment structure. Even in a single strategy, multiple business models are possible for different social finance activities.

5.3 *Fund Receivers*

Each social finance activity aims to support special sectors, ranging from women to marginalized groups. They can also have an environmental focus and target other social groups.

5.4 *Funding Process*

The funding process aims to exhibit a particular structure of intake, value-adding interventions, and final investment activity. Through this process, social finance providers may provide various value-adding interventions (see Resources and Services below).

5.5 *Resources and Services*

A key decision for a social financier to make is how to translate the chosen strategic focus into the suite of resources and services provided. To make this choice, they may decide to provide what is "typical" of similar investment institutions or what is specifically wanted or needed to make a real social impact.

5.6 *Social Finance Type*

Based on the types of social finance that the literature review section above explains, Table 2 groups the cases into the categories. The different types of social finance activities include social impact bonds or pay-for-performance, impact investing, social banking, crowdfunding, and microfinance. Table 2 is a summary of the strategic features from the cases. There is a wide range in the year of organizations' respective founding's, from rather new initiatives, such as the Equality Fund and Restoring the Sacred Bond, to full-fledged organizations in maturity like Alterna and Vancity. Meanwhile, SheEO, Mastercard Foundation, and Marigold Capital are in the middle stage of their business cycle. The objectives for social finance are similar for all of the organizations: their plans focus on supporting women in various ways. SheEO, Marigold, Alterna, and Mastercard Foundation mainly focus on equality in distributing available funds to women entrepreneurs, whereas Restoring the Sacred Bond supports women who are at risk. Equality Fund provides direct and indirect support for women by funding women's rights organizations in Canada and around the world.

Out of the seven cases in the study that aim to support women entrepreneurs, three are in impact investing (Equality Fund, Marigold Capital, and Mastercard Foundation), two are involved in crowdfunding (Equality Fund, SheEO), one engages in social impact bonds (Alterna), and one is a social bank (Vancity). Equality Fund, Marigold Capital, and Mastercard Foundation seek to strengthen women's rights organizations, encourage social change by alleviating inequality, and promote financial inclusion, respectively. The Equality Fund is also involved in crowdfunding, along with SheEO. However, SheEO is more innovative than its counterpart in a way that women get together to activate a forever fund that creates benefits beyond currency flow. Vancity and Alterna are the two oldest organizations and use traditional methods of supporting women and marginalized people. Vancity, as a social banker, is committed to value-based banking and joined the Global Alliance for Banking on Values in 2010. As a value-based financial cooperative, Vancity is dedicated to helping members and local communities thrive financially, socially, and environmentally. Alterna Savings is the oldest local credit union and is a member of the Deposit Insurance Corporation of Ontario. For over a decade, Alterna has been known for supporting small and developing businesses through community-based micro-lending. Social impact bonds and pay-for-performance activities have not yet been developed extensively in Canada. These types of activities are even rarer in initiatives that are specifically designed to support women, although some initiatives do exist: a relatively new pilot project in Manitoba, Restoring the Sacred Bond, aims to help Indigenous women who maybe at risk of having their infant apprehended into the child welfare system. The program aims to support 200 at-risk expected mothers.

Generally, the objectives and performance measures of social finance activities are poorly defined and under-reported. Although the seven cases share the common goal to support women, their performances and/or effectiveness are not easily assessed by the same measurements due to the differences in their specific objectives. These cases differ in their resources, procedures, and the ultimate recipients of funding. For example, SheEO receives some government funding for operations and programs, but the global perpetual funding of women-led enterprises is generated by individual women, called Activators, who contribute \$1100 a year (\$1000 goes into the fund and \$100 as a program fee). Activators are customers and promoters, and can serve as local advisors around the world. This is a key part of accelerating the impact of social innovations and getting them out to the world market. Activators vote for the Ventures, that receive the funding as a zero percent interest loan, which gets paid back over five years and is then reinvested into new Ventures (SheEO, 2019). As of 2019, SheEO brought together a network of 4000 Activators globally, resulting in \$4 million in Activator loans, contributed to the funding of 53 Ventures, and supported the development of three jobs created on average, per year (SheEO, 2019).

Vancity is a value-based financial cooperative that serves the needs of its more than 543,000 member-owners and their communities in the Coast Salish and Kwakwaka'wakw territories. It boasts 60 branches in Metro Vancouver, the Fraser Valley, Victoria, Squamish, and Alert Bay in British Columbia. With \$28.2 billion in assets plus assets under administration, Vancity is Canada's largest community credit union. Vancity uses its assets to help improve its members' financial well-being while helping to develop healthy communities that are socially, economically, and environmentally sustainable.

Similarly, Alterna Savings is a local credit union and a member of the Deposit Insurance Corporation of Ontario. For over a decade, Alterna has supported small and developing businesses through community-based micro-lending. As securing credit and accessing banking services are major roadblocks for new and marginalized Ontarians looking to start a business, Alterna has set its goal to help them in these specific areas. Alterna Savings provides programs that are exclusive to women entrepreneurs. Their "Working Women Loan Program" supports women looking to gain financial independence or who are looking for self-employment to gain the job flexibility that they need to balance multiple demands with loans of up to $25,000.

Marigold Capital offers customized "[s]trategic consulting and fund management in the private-market impact investing space, with a focus on social justice in domestic, emerging, and frontier markets" (Beyond the Billion, n.d.). The firm applies a gender lens to the investment process with the aim of revaluing and empowering women, whether through funding female entrepreneurs or creating gender equity in senior positions. It also means investing in products created by women, for women. Overall, the idea is to increase women's purchasing power and involvement in formal and informal economic processes. Marigold aims to use the gender equity-driven model as the foundation for supporting groups of people that are marginalized or disadvantaged. Areas in which it hopes to create diversity and inclusivity range from financial inclusion and reproductive health to education, food security, and responsible procurement. Finance is not an intuitive tool to create systematic change, and its power in this regard is thus underestimated. Strategic investments are able to shift norms, perspectives, and methods. Moreover, these remove structural barriers and serve to empower individuals through participation and its subsequent benefits. Marigold utilizes a gender and inclusivity lens to invest in an equitable and prosperous social change.

The Equality Fund is a new innovation that provides sustainable funding for women around the globe. They have partnered with organizations that advocate for women from Congo to Afghanistan, and Iraq to Mexico. The Equality Fund has received awards from The Government of Canada with an historic $300 million contribution in building a new global funding mechanism and leveraging more resources for gender equality around the world (Equality Fund, 2020).

The Mastercard Foundation seeks a world where everyone has the opportunity to learn and prosper. The organization believes that all people, regardless of their starting point in life, should have an equal chance to succeed. They believe that with access to education, financial services, and skills training, people have that chance. Their focus is on helping economically disadvantaged young people in Africa to find opportunities to move themselves, their families, and their communities out of poverty and into a better life.

Restoring the Sacred Bond is a two-year pilot project that supports women at-risk during pregnancy and during childcare through funded social services. They have up to 200 at-risk expectant mothers, and they hope to support them throughout pregnancy and beyond childbirth. The Initiative is led by The Southern Network in partnership with Wiiji-i'idiwag Ikwewag, the service provider, in order to identify expectant mothers in Winnipeg who may not have resources to effectively parent their baby. These mothers are then connected the women who are trained to help with childbirth and early care (Birth Helpers). Each Birth Helper will serve up to ten to twelve mothers at a time for nine to twelve months per mother (Restoring the Sacred Bond, 2019). It is the first foray into social impact bonds in the province of Manitoba. If the project meets certain targets, investors get their money back from the province, plus a return. In this case, the province has budgeted up to $3 million to repay investors if the project reduces the average number of days in care for children in the program by 25, as compared to similar children outside the program. Although it does not target women entrepreneurs, this initiative is similar to other cases in terms of its socioeconomic outcomes.

6 Discussion and Conclusion

By comparing the features of cases systematically along a common set of dimensions, our analysis captures variation across different forms of social finance programs and initiatives that target social innovation for women. We reveal the focus on support for women entrepreneurship in the seven cases as reflected in their key objectives, strategic focus, funding processes, resources and services, socioeconomic effects, and social finance types. Several compelling insights emerge from this analysis.

Firstly, women's social innovation and social finance place more emphasis on social returns rather than financial returns. Although traditional social innovation models tend to use financial returns as a criterion for their funding decisions, the programs that support social innovation for women use funding criteria that are more flexible to achieve greater social impacts.

Secondly, unlike other social innovation programs, those that focus on women do not concentrate on technology or tangible products. Since women entrepreneurs are more likely to start businesses in the service sector, these programs support innovative businesses that service community members, particularly marginalized people (Ward, 2019). As a result, these programs are also more focused on innovative solutions to issues in certain areas, such as employment (e.g., Mastercard Foundation) and health (e.g., Restoring the Sacred Bond).

Thirdly, as women's social networks are composed of more family members and friends than those of their male counterparts, many women-led businesses are grounded in certain communities and bound to specific geographical areas (Renzulli et al., 2000). Social innovation and social finance programs for women often provide networking and mentorship opportunities that help them overcome this barrier. For example, SheEO aims to offer a platform to facilitate connection among members.

Finally, in response to the long-lasting issues of barriers to access to credit that women entrepreneurs face, social finance programs targeting women often adopt microfinance and crowdfunding as low-risk models to provide funding for them. Multiple microfinance programs operate in Canada and are aimed at supporting women entrepreneurs. Crowdfunding, as a collaborative system of financing, pools small amounts of money from numerous people, to fund a specific project and has proved to be a successful mechanism for women entrepreneurs to raise capital when other resources are scarce.

6.1 Recommendations

We use the comparative case study approach to examine heterogeneous examples of successful social innovation and social finance programs for women, which are, in general, growing fast in Canada. However, it is important to note that social finance programs are embedded in the innovation ecological system in Canada, which includes factors at the macro-, meso-, and micro-levels. Through our examination of these case studies, we offer recommendations to better support women entrepreneurs through various social finance models.

We should continue to apply a gender and diversity lens and collect disaggregated data on the effectiveness of these programs to support women entrepreneurs. Women who also identify with other marginalized groups, such as Indigenous women, immigrant women, and women with disabilities, need more support as they are challenged by additional structural inequalities. Therefore, social finance programs should extend flexible or individualized services to women with intersectional identities. Also, using a gendered and intersectional lens to examine the financial status of women entrepreneurs in the entrepreneurial ecosystem helps industry players and policy-makers to implement effective policies and practices and better support women entrepreneurs through financing.

Government and social innovation programs should also ensure that definitions of entrepreneurship are inclusive for self-employed women and owners of small and medium enterprises across various sectors, including services, arts, and social enterprises.

Stakeholders at both macro- and meso-levels should use innovative approaches to meet the needs of women entrepreneurs and innovators through, for instance, crowdfunding, microgrants, SIBs, as well as services like customized counseling, mentoring, and sponsorship,

Both government and community stakeholders should strengthen the capacity for financial and digital literacy programs to assist women by considering digitization for financing, commercialization, marketing, and exporting. Policies should be further developed to provide human capital to support research development and implementation. One example is to harness student subsidies to provide support to women entrepreneurs.

Adequate attention should also be paid to help women overcome barriers at the micro-level, such as affordable and accessible childcare, as well as language programs for immigrant women. Experts argue childcare should be considered an essential service (Vermes, 2020). Women's associations and supporting organizations should advocate for the inclusion of women business owners as active participants in economic decision-making.

References

Beyond the Billion (n.d.). *Our fund partners: Marigold capital.* Beyond the Billion. https://beyondthebillion.com/our-partners/marigold-capital/.

Braund, P., & Schwittay, A. (2016). Scaling inclusive digital innovation successfully: The case of crowdfunding social enterprises. *Innovation and Development, 6*(1), 15–29. https://doi.org/10.1080/2157930X.2015.1067392

Bruhn, M., Carpena, F., & Zia, B. (2012). Microfinance for entrepreneurs. In D. Cumming (Ed.), *The Oxford handbook of entrepreneurial finance* (pp. 825–858). Oxford University Press.

Chen, J. (2019). *Impact investing.* Investopedia. https://www.investopedia.com/terms/i/impact-investing.asp#:~:text=Impacting%20investing%20aims%20to%20generate,in%20addition%20to%20financial%20gains.&text=Impact%20investing%20refers%20to%20an,but%20also%20creates%20constructive%20outcomes.

Cheston, S., & Kuhn, L. (2002). Empowering women through microfinance. *Draft, Opportunity International, 64*. http://chs.ubc.ca/srilanka/PDFs/Empoweringwomenthroughmicrofinance.pdf.

Colman, R. (2004). Broad vision, local support. *CMA Management, 78*(2), 36–36.

Cukier, W., Gagnon, S., Hodson, J., Saba, T., Grandy, G., Morton, S., Elmi, M., & Chavoushi, Z.H. (2020). *The state of women's entrepreneurship in Canada*. Women Entrepreneurship Knowledge Hub. https://wekh.ca/wp-content/uploads/2020/09/WEKH_State_of_Womens_Entrepreneurship_in_Canada_2020_EN.pdf.

Cukier, W., Gagnon, S., Mae Lindo, L., Hannan, C., & Amato, S. (2014). A [Critical] ecological model to enabling change: Promoting diversity and inclusion. In V. Malin, J. Murphy, & M. Siltaoja (Eds.), *Getting things done* (pp. 245–275). Emerald Publishing.

Cukier, W., & Chavoushi, Z. H. (2020). Facilitating women entrepreneurship in Canada: The case of WEKH. *Gender in Management, 35*(3), 303–318. https://doi.org/10.1108/GM-11-2019-0204

Draimin, T. (2008). *Innovation and social enterprise: Building financial capacity*. AFP fundraising day. Tides Canada. www.tidescanada.org/wp-content/uploads/files/innovation_social_enterprise.pdf.

Equality Fund. (2020). *Equality fund: Funding feminist futures*. Equality Fund. https://equalityfund.ca/.

Fox-Wolfgramm, S. J. (1997). Towards developing a methodology for doing qualitative research: The dynamic-comparative case study method. *Scandinavian Journal of Management, 13*(4), 439–455.

Frankiewicz, C. (April, 2001). *Calmeadow metrofund: A Canadian experiment in sustainable microfinance*. https://www.gdrc.org/icm/calmeadow-metrofund.html.

Geobey, S., & Weber, O. (2013). Lessons in operationalizing social finance: The case of Vancouver City Savings Credit Union. *Journal of Sustainable Finance & Investment, 3*(2), 124–137.

Gomez, R., & Santor, E. (2001). Membership has its privileges: The effect of social capital and neighbourhood characteristics on the earnings of microfinance borrowers. *Canadian Journal of Economics, 34*(4), 943–966. https://doi.org/10.1111/0008-4085.00107

Goodrick, D. (2014). *Methodological briefs: Impact evaluation, No. 9: Comparative case studies*. UNICEF. http://www.dmeforpeace.org/wp-content/uploads/2017/06/Comparative_Case_Studies_ENG.pdf.

Government of Canada. (2013). *Harnessing the power of social finance: Canadians respond to the national call for concepts for social finance*. Human

Resources and Skills Development Canada, Government of Canada. https://www.canada.ca/en/employment-social-development/programs/social-finance/consultations-report.html.
Government of Canada. (2015). *Social finance*. Employment and Social Development Canada. https://www.canada.ca/en/employment-social-development/programs/social-finance.html.
Government of Canada. (2019a). *Women entrepreneurship strategy.* Innovation, Science and Economic Development (ISED) Canada, Government of Canada. https://www.ic.gc.ca/eic/site/107.nsf/eng/home.
Government of Canada. (2019b). *Key small business statistics—January 2019*. Innovation, Science and Economic Development (ISED) Canada, Government of Canada. https://www.ic.gc.ca/eic/site/061.nsf/eng/h_03090.html.
Government of Canada. (2020). *Funding: Career focus local and regional projects—Overview.* Employment and Social Development Canada, Government of Canada. https://www.canada.ca/en/employment-social-development/services/funding/career-focus.html.
Greenberg, M., & Gerber, E. (2012). *Crowdfunding: A survey and taxonomy—Technical Report 12–03.* Northwestern University Segal Design Institute.
Hajer, J. (2019, January 16). *Fast facts: Social impact bonds: A costly innovation.* Canadian Centre for Policy Alternatives (CCPA). https://www.policyalternatives.ca/publications/commentary/fast-facts-social-impact-bonds.
Hangl, C. (2014). A literature review about the landscape of social finance. *Journal of Finance and Risk Perspectives, 3*(4), 64–98.
Housing Services Corporation. (2013). *Blended financing for impact: Toolkit for social finance & supportive housing.* Convergence Blending Global Finance. https://assets.ctfassets.net/4cgqlwde6qy0/5wJhaQdNleOIaKk0sCOi8s/87f535d061f207553de73b971a2ff41d/MaRS__Blended_Financing_for_Impact_Toolkit_for_Social_Finance___Supportive_Housing.pdf.
Hussain, J. G., Mahmood, S., & Scott, J. M. (2015). *Entrepreneurial finance, poverty reduction and gender: The case of women entrepreneurs' microloans in Pakistan.* Edward Elgar Publishing.
Innovation, Science and Economic Development Canada. (2018). *Survey on financing and growth of small and medium enterprises (SFGSME), 2017.* Innovation, Science and Economic Development (ISED) Canada, Government of Canada. https://www.ic.gc.ca/eic/site/061.nsf/eng/03087.html.
Intuit Canada. (n.d.). *The $5,000 question: The keys to small-business success.* http://intuitglobal.intuit.com/delivery/cms/prod/sites/default/intuit.ca/downloads/quickbooks/intuit_5000_report.pdf.
Kaarbo, J., & Beasley, R. K. (1999). A practical guide to the comparative case study method in political psychology. *Political Psychology, 20*(2), 369–391.

Kanze, D., Huang, L., Conley, M. A., & Higgins, E. T. (2018). We ask men to win and women not to lose: Closing the gender gap in startup funding. *Academy of Management Journal, 61*(2), 586–614.

Kuppuswamy, V., & Bayus, B. L. (2018). Crowdfunding creative ideas: The dynamics of project backers. In D. Cumming & L. Hornuf (Eds.), *The economics of crowdfunding: Startups, portals, and investor behavior* (pp. 151–182). Palgrave Macmillan.

Lam, B., & Tansey, J. (2019, February). *Social venture impact investing: The Canadian landscape.* Centre for Social Innovation & Impact Investing. https://www.sauder.ubc.ca/sites/default/files/2019-03/SVII_Canada_S3i_FINAL_Report.pdf.

MaRS Centre for Impact Investing. (2016). *Community hypertension prevention initiative.* MaRS Centre for Impact Investing. https://impactinvesting.marsdd.com/chpi/.

Mayoux, L. (2000). *Micro-finance and the empowerment of women: A review of the key issues* (No. 993441343402676). International Labour Organization.

Mayoux, L. (2002). Women's empowerment through sustainable microfinance: Rethinking "Best practice." *Development Bulletin, 57*, 76–81.

Mayoux, L. (2006, January). Women's *empowerment through sustainable microfinance: Rethinking "Best Practice."* Eldis. https://www.eldis.org/document/A20744.

Mills, A. J., Durepos, G., & Wiebe, E. (Eds.). (2009). *Encyclopedia of case study research* (Vols. 1–0). Sage. https://doi.org/10.4135/9781412957397.

Mollick, E. R. (2014). The dynamics of crowdfunding: An exploratory study. *Journal of Business Venturing, 29*(1), 1–16.

Moore, M. L., Westley, F. R., & Nicholls, A. (2012). The social finance and social innovation nexus. *Journal of Social Entrepreneurship, 3*(2), 112–135.

Opportunity International Canada. (n.d.). *Products and services: Loans*. Opportunity International Canada. https://www.opportunityinternational.ca/what-we-do/products-and-services/global-loans.

Orser, B., Coleman, S., & Li, Y. (2020). Progress or pinkwashing: Who benefits from digital women-focused capital funds? *Small Business Economics, 55*(2), 363–378.

Phillips, J., Deiglmeier, K., & Miller, D. (2008). Rediscovering social innovation. *Stanford Social Innovation Review, 6*(4), 34–43.

Quinlan, J., & VanderBrug, J. (2016). *Gender lens investing: Uncovering opportunities for growth, returns, and impact.* John Wiley & Sons.

Rainey, M., & Sagalongos, S., Tansey, J. & Srivatsan, V. (2017, November). *Equity crowdfunding: A new model for financing start-ups and small businesses.* Centre for Social Innovation and Impact Investing. https://static1.squarespace.com/static/598b47ff6a49631e85d75e53/t/5a20764cc8302566a3a23863/1512076878794/SauderS3i_Equity_Crowdfunding_FINAL.pdf.

Renzulli, L., Aldrich, H., & Moody, J. (2000). Family matters: Gender, networks, and entrepreneurial outcomes. *Social Forces, 79*(2), 523–546.

Responsible Investment Association. (2019, February). *2018 Canadian impact investment trends report*. Responsible Investment Association (RIA). https://www.riacanada.ca/research/2018-impact-trends-report/.

Restoring the Sacred Bond. (2019). *News release: Restoring the sacred bond community launch*. Restoring the Sacred Bod Initiative led by Southern First Nations Network of Care. https://www.restoringthesacredbond.ca/site/blog-posts/2019/06/14/news-release-restoring-the-sacred-bond-community-launch.

Roberts, A. (2016). The limitations of transnational business feminism: The case of gender lens investing. *Soundings, 62*(62), 68–83.

Schwienbacher, A., & Larralde, B. (2010). Crowdfunding of small entrepreneurial ventures. In *Handbook of entrepreneurial finance*. Oxford University Press. Forthcoming. https://www.em-a.eu/fileadmin/content/REALISE_IT_2/REALISE_IT_3/CROWD_OUP_Final_Version.pdf.

Sharma, A., Dua, S., & Hatwal, V. (2012). Micro enterprise development and rural women entrepreneurship: Way for economic empowerment. *Arth Prabhand: A Journal of Economics and Management, 1*(6), 114–127.

SheEO. (2019). *About us. SheEO is a radically generous community supporting women + non-binary people working on the World's To-Do List*. SheEO. https://sheeo.world/about-us/.

Tan, S., Fraser, A., McHugh, N., & Warner, M. (2019). Widening perspectives on social impact bonds. *Journal of Economic Policy Reform*. https://doi.org/10.1080/17487870.2019.1568249.

Tapestry Community Capital. (2019). *Differentiating community bonds and social impact bonds*. Tapestry Community Capital. http://tapestrycapital.ca/socialimpactbonds/.

The Atmospheric Fund. (2019). *The atmospheric fund: About us*. TAF. https://taf.ca/about-us/.

United Nations. (2019). *Sustainable development goal #5: Achieve gender equality and empower all women and girls*. Department of Economic and Social Affairs, United Nations. https://www.un.org/sustainabledevelopment/gender-equality/.

Vancity. (2013). *$13.5M Resilient Capital Program recognized as a model for addressing social and economic challenges*. Vancity. https://www.vancity.com/AboutVancity/News/MediaReleases/Archives/MediaReleases2013/July18_2013_Resilient_Capital/.

Vancity. (2019). *Vancity's commitment to the full participation of women*. Vancity. https://www.vancity.com/AboutVancity/News/Backgrounders/ParticipationOfWomen/.

Varga, E., & Hayday, M. (2019). *A recipe book for social finance*. Publications Office of the European Commission.

Ward, S. (2019, February). *Statistics on Canadian women in business*. The balance small business. https://www.thebalancesmb.com/statistics-on-canadian-women-in-business-2948029.

Weber, O., & Duan, Y. (2012). Social finance and banking. In K. Baker & J. R. Nofsinger (Eds.), *Socially responsible finance and investing: Financial institutions, corporations, investors, and activists* (pp. 160, 180). John Wiley & Sons.

Weber, O., & Feltmate, B. (2016). *Sustainable banking: Managing the social and environmental impact of financial institutions*. University of Toronto Press.

World Bank. (2009). *Doing business 2009: Comparing regulations in 181 economies*. World Bank and the International Finance Corporation. https://openknowledge.worldbank.org/handle/10986/6313?show=full.

Youth Social Innovation. (2011). *Youth social innovation capital fund, revenue reach*. YSI. https://static1.squarespace.com/static/5b92b50e297114aace73e2f7/t/5fb82b7d0b4259424ea3f7a0/1605905278633/Revenue+Reach.pdf.

The Role of Youth in Scaling Social Value Investing: The Case of Canada's National Social Value Fund

Bruno Lam, Steve Petterson, James Tansey, Mariana Martinez Rubio, and Maxime Lakat

B. Lam (✉) · J. Tansey · M. Martinez Rubio
Centre for Social Innovation & Impact Investing (S3i), Sauder School of Business, University of British Columbia, Vancouver, BC V6T 1Z2, Canada
e-mail: bruno.lam@ubc.ca

J. Tansey
e-mail: james.tansey@sauder.ubc.ca

M. Martinez Rubio
e-mail: mmrubio@mail.ubc.ca

S. Petterson
National Social Value Fund, 3505 W 20th Ave, Vancouver, BC V6S1E6, Canada
e-mail: steve@nsvf.ca

M. Lakat
Montreal Social Value Fund, 1333 rue Sainte rose, Montreal, QC H2L2J7, Canada
e-mail: maxime.montreal@nsvf.ca

T. Walker et al. (eds.), *Innovations in Social Finance*,
https://doi.org/10.1007/978-3-030-72535-8_5

1 Introduction

In 2017, the Canadian federal government convened its Social Innovation and Social Finance Strategy Co-Creation Steering Committee which resulted in twelve recommendations to grow the sector. This includes actions sranging from coordinating a national social innovation and social finance campaign, to addressing regulatory barriers preventing charities and nonprofits from integrating social innovation tools into their organizations (Employment & Social Development Canada, 2018). A common thread across these recommendations is the inclusive definition of social innovation, manifested in the term "social purpose organizations" (SPOs). SPOs are defined as "the diverse range of organizations engaged in these ecosystems, including charities, nonprofit organizations, cooperatives, and private businesses advancing a social or environmental mission" (Employment & Social Development Canada, 2018, p. 2).

With this definition, a wide-ranging approach to the definition of SPO organizational structure has emerged to guide the future of the sector. This approach recognizes that solutions to social issues will not be solved exclusively by one subset of organizational form such as charitable entities. Instead, non-traditional actors such as for-profit start-ups, cooperatives, and investment firms will need to play an intentional role as well. This organization-agnostic approach has long been adopted by academics and practitioners. The Canadian Task Force on Social Finance (2010) similarly defines social enterprise as any organization, regardless of form, that takes a market approach to pursue a social or environmental mission. The transdisciplinary nature of the sector has also given rise to hybrid organizational structures (Mair & Noboa, 2003; Perrini & Vurro, 2006), which lie outside of traditional structures used to advance social and environmental mandates. Across Canada, structures such as Community Contribution Companies (British Columbia) and Community Interest Companies (Nova Scotia) have emerged. With the emergence of hybrid organizations as well as the range of existing organizational structures set up to address social and environmental challenges, all with core mandates centered around a social and environmental mission, the term "social purpose organization" reduces the need to debate structure-based boundaries when we discuss the private sector's role in addressing social and environmental issues. Our view is that we should approach society's greatest challenges with an organizational agnostic mindset. What matters most is making logical decisions around supporting those organizations that would best advance solutions to the problem at hand.

Austin et al. (2006) argue that the central driver for SPOs is the social or environmental issue, and that "the particular organizational form a social enterprise takes should be a decision based on which format would most effectively mobilize the resources needed to address that problem" (p. 2). One such resource is financial capital. Social finance, which refers to the deployment of financial resources for social and environmental returns, and sometimes financial returns (Moore & Westely, 2012), has emerged as a type of financial capital available for social purpose organizations. Within social finance lies various mechanisms, such as impact investing and grant capital. Impact investment is a form of social finance that seeks a return, whereas grant capital is an example of a social finance mechanism that does not seek returns (Moore & Westely, 2012). Höchstädter and Scheck (2015) reviews various interpretations and definitions of impact investing, and concludes that there are two approaches to defining the term: "one that limits impact investing to certain organization types—for example, unlisted organizations and/or organizations that place the mission above the business side... and one that ignores organizational characteristics completely and considers only the ultimate impact to be achieved with the investment." The latter is consistent with the organization-agnostic definition of social purpose organizations. However, it requires that the impact investment capital deployed is purpose-built to best serve the organizational structures used to address the social or environmental problem.

While traditional investment approaches such as venture capital and private equity may work for specific types of social purpose organizations (such as high-growth start-ups), the investment mechanisms deployed such as common and preferred equity, convertible notes, and market-rate debt may not allow an SPO to effectively and efficiently mobilize resources to achieve their mission. When an investor stipulates that their funding is limited to structures such as those mentioned earlier, it implicitly limits the types of organizations that they are willing to fund. For investors who wish to support social purpose organizations meaningfully, using only venture capital as a means of investment into SPOs may limit their ability to achieve the desired social and environmental outcomes. The limitations of the venture capital approach toward supporting social and environmental-focused ventures have been documented extensively, discussed in the next section.

The widespread integration of social innovation in various organizational structures requires an equally diverse set of financing mechanisms. These mechanisms have risen in popularity in the past decade: demand dividends, revenue-share loans, impact-adjusted debt, and variations to grants (Armeni & De Bone, 2017; Bannick et al., 2015; Benink & Winters, 2016; Kohler et al., 2011). Those who have effectively deployed these mechanisms have used several terms to define their methodology, such as patient capital and impact-first investment (Svedova et al., 2014). We refer to this as the Social Value Investing (SVI) approach. SVI refers to a capital deployment approach that places the social or environmental value creation of a social purpose organization at its core. SVI is not limited to a set of financial mechanisms. Instead, it focuses on the organization's ultimate impact and subsequently utilizes the appropriate financing mechanism to best fit the SPO's characteristics. This contrasts with traditional approaches in which the SPO's organizational characteristics influence whether or not they can receive the financing mechanisms deployed by the investor.

In order to effectively deploy SVI capital, the social or environmental issue addressed must be well-understood, which requires meaningful stakeholder engagement (International Finance Corporation, 2010). The SPO's organizational structure must be analyzed in order to properly design a financing mechanism conducive to the SPO's success in reaching its impact goals. Finally, properly engaging stakeholders, crafting proper financing mechanisms that fit the SPO's impact goals, and providing post-investment support requires a prohibitive level of resources. How then can SVI scale in a meaningful manner? We postulate that empowering local community stakeholders is vital to the success of scaling SVI. More specifically, youth in these local communities can occupy a unique role in scaling Social Value Investing.

This chapter will examine the concept of Social Value Investing and how youth can play a role in scaling the approach. In Sect. 2, we will situate Social Value Investing in the history and context of other investment approaches, namely venture capital and philanthropy. We will also discuss the principles of Social Value Investing. In Sect. 3, we discuss youth's unique role in scaling SVI through an in-depth case study on the National Social Value Fund, an organization aimed at scaling SVI by empowering youth involvement in Canada. Finally, Sect. 4 provides a discussion and conclusion of Social Value Investing and youth community development.

2 Investment Approaches and Social Value Investing

As discussed in the previous section, investment in the social innovation sector requires capital to flow toward a diverse set of organizational structures. This section situates Social Value Investing in the context of two other investment methods: venture capital (VC) and philanthropy. The two approaches have evolved to fund specific organization types: venture capital invests primarily in for-profit start-ups, while philanthropy funds charities and nonprofits. We can draw lessons from the VC and philanthropy mindsets to inform how Social Value Investing can best serve social purpose organizations.

2.1 *Overview of Venture Capital and Philanthropy Approaches*

Venture capital played a major role in the high-tech boom that began in the 1990s, making considerable impact on sectors such as communications, social media, and entertainment (Marcus et al., 2013). In the period between 1999 and 2009, over 60% of IPOs have been backed by venture capital, which is particularly impressive, considering only 0.17% of all companies receive VC funding (Kaplan & Lerner, 2010). Zider (1998) suggests that venture capital's ability to provide relatively affordable funding for high-risk companies has carved out a unique niche for itself within the investment market, in which traditional lending sources are unable to charge adequately high interest rates for loans to entrepreneurs with new disruptive ideas or products.

How are venture capital investments (VC) structured? One way to analyze VC investments is through the lens of agency theory. Agency theory holds that a manager will maximize their own value—not that of shareholders—unless proper governance mechanisms are in place to prevent opportunistic shirking (Hölmstrom, 1979). Several factors lead to such opportunistic behavior. For example, bargaining power will not be completely equal between the investor and the entrepreneur. If the entrepreneur leaves, she takes with her an irreplaceable set of skills. The hold-up problem occurs when two parties cannot work efficiently because there are concerns that one party will have more bargaining power than the other (Hart & Moore, 1994). Asymmetric information issues occur when the entrepreneur knows more about their venture and their own ability than the venture capitalist (Akerlof, 1970). Due to uncertainty about the venture's success, the venture capitalist will want control in some states (mainly bad ones) to maximize their own investment value and protect themselves from loss (Aghion & Bolton, 1992; Dewatripont & Tirole, 1994).

As a result, venture capital investments feature characteristics that aim to limit principal-agent problems. To deal with moral hazard, VCs tie the entrepreneur's compensation to their performance (Kaplan & Strömberg, 2003, 2004; Prendergast, 2002). To limit hold-up problems, the entrepreneur's shares are either time-vested or performance-vested (Kaplan & Strömberg, 2001, 2003, 2004). Due to asymmetric information, the VC will implement monitoring mechanisms such as board control and increased voting rights (Aghion & Bolton, 1992; Barney et al., 1989; Kaplan & Strömberg, 2003).

These VC investment characteristics prioritize the protection of the investor from any downside and allow the investor to participate in the firm's profits. As a result, VC has developed several limitations as an investment method of social innovation. Lam and Seidel (2020) argue that venture capital has developed a "hypergrowth exit mindset" within our innovation ecosystems in which entrepreneurs prioritize exits before understanding the long-term societal benefits of their product. The clean technology sector offers an illustrative example: clean technology companies developing new chemicals and processes require a long-term investment horizon in which the investment is illiquid beyond the shorter time frame of 3–5 years with which venture capitalists are familiar (Gaddy et al., 2016; Marcus et al., 2013). Incumbent energy firms and utilities were unwilling to acquire start-ups with pre-commercial products, further extending the potential exit time horizon leading to investor unwillingness to invest in early-stage ventures (Ghosh & Nanda, 2010). As a result, clean technology venture capital investment plummeted from over $5 billion in investments in 2008 to $2 billion in 2013 (Gaddy et al., 2016).

On the other end of the investment, spectrum lies philanthropy. Rooted in stewardship theory, which holds that the manager is not an opportunistic shirker but is motivated by non-financial factors that can benefit both the principal and themselves (Donaldson & Davis, 1991; Muth & Donaldson, 1998), philanthropy is less focused on meeting financial returns or mitigating agency risks. The recipients of the philanthropic funding are not subject to stringent contractual mechanisms that are designed to mitigate any financial risks to the investor if certain milestones are not achieved.

To illustrate how philanthropic capital differs from venture capital, Steinberg (1987) argues that when information asymmetry exists between a principal and agent, the goal of maximizing profits may incentivize the agent to reduce their effort, while the non-distribution constraint in which nonprofits cannot re-distribute earnings to their managers, will not. Furthermore, Caers et al. (2006) argue that since job applicants for nonprofit organizations have to compare offers between the for-profit sector and the nonprofit sector, those who choose to work with nonprofit organizations tend to reflect the sector's values and are likely to be committed to the mission (Callen & Falk, 1993; Handy & Katz, 1998), have a personal desire to serve the public (Wittmer, 1991), and prefer to work with an organization whose fiduciary policies correspond to their own (Hansmann, 1986).

Suppose a social purpose organization's decision on its organizational structure is based on that which most effectively mobilizes financial resources for its mission (Austin et al., 2006), and venture capital provides the majority of funding. In that case, SPOs may naturally gravitate toward taking on a for-profit venture form. Similarly, if philanthropic capital is perceived as the primary funding source, SPOs may gravitate toward incorporating as a nonprofit or charity. Alternative structures, however, may be better designed to mobilize non-financial capital such as human, community, or natural capital. Other organizational structures blend the characteristics of for-profits, nonprofits, and charities, such as cooperatives that can issue shares like for-profits but can be constrained from distributing earnings like a nonprofit (BC Co-op Association, 2018; Zeuli et al., 2004). British Columbia's Community Contribution Company (C3) cap dividends at 40% of assets that can be paid to shareholders, while the rest must be used for community purposes or transferred to a charitable entity (Bouw, 2013). With the emergence of these diverse hybrid models, venture capital or philanthropy are limited as the main approaches to financing social innovation in Canada. *Within these alternative models, should investments be structured to reduce principal-agent problems, or should they be rooted in stewardship? Or should investments be structured around both approaches?* What is required is an adaptive, flexible investment approach whose structure is based on what can maximize the SPO's impact. In the next section, we discuss Social Value Investing as an alternative approach to financing social innovation.

2.2 Social Value Investing

Social Value Investing (SVI) is rooted in the concepts of collective impact and patient capital. Kania and Kramer (2011) define collective impact as "the commitment of a group of important actors from different sectors to a common agenda for solving a specific social problem" (p. 36). They argue that cross-sector collaboration is actually more effective than the isolated and siloed approaches by individual organizations for desired societal or environmental outcomes to be achieved. From this concept we define the first characteristic of SVI: a systemic approach to investing that recognizes how a variety of organizations achieves outcomes. Novogratz (2010) defines patient capital as "money invested over a longer period of time with the acknowledgment that returns might be below market, but with a wide range of management support services to nurture the company to liftoff and beyond" (p. 229). Patient capital is deployed in a flexible manner to meet the SPO's organizational requirements and ensure the SPO prioritizes its stakeholders' well-being over its shareholders (Acumen, n.d.). Ultimately, it takes the role of a steward to the SPO because it is providing flexible capital that first and foremost aims to meet the needs of the SPO.

While venture capital and philanthropic investments have been structured to meet the characteristics of high-growth start-ups and impact-first charities or nonprofits, respectively, SVI recognizes that social and environmental outcomes can be generated by not only these two types of organizations but also through other diverse structures. We do not situate SVI in opposition to VC nor philanthropy's return profiles because it is possible to make both market-rate and concessionary returns with SVI. Rather, SVI is an approach that prioritizes the organizational needs of the investee and stakeholders first. SVI can use vehicles from the two approaches, and at times also alternative/innovative investment vehicles that do not fit into the VC and philanthropic buckets, so long as the vehicle used is deemed most appropriate for the investees' ability to achieve its desired social and environmental outcomes. Next, we explore some defining characteristics of Social Value Investing.

2.2.1 Systemic Approach and Organization-Agnosticism

Social value investors recognize that one size does not fit all when it comes to advancing social and environmental solutions and thus, they must be organizational structure-agnostic. Similar to Kania and

Kramer (2011)'s framework for collective impact, SVI recognizes that the desired societal or environmental outcomes can only be achieved through a system-based approach in which charities, nonprofits, cooperatives, small businesses, advocacy campaigns and more initiatives collaborate toward collective action. Existing investment approaches like venture capital funding and philanthropic funding are primarily designed for start-ups and nonprofit or charitable organizations, respectively. Social value investors are outcome-seeking investors that intend to address one or many social and environmental issues. They recognize that in order to address systemic issues, a wide array of stakeholders must be supported. There are start-up companies that can innovate the field, traditional companies that can build more sustainable and inclusive practices, nonprofits and charities who can adopt enterprising programs, and cooperatives that can enable community-led change. By employing an impact-first lens, combined with the stewardship mindset of capital, social value investors view all of these structures as viable investment initiatives in pursuit of the funder's social or environmental mission(s).

2.2.2 Stewardship and Impact-Adjusted Returns

Social value investors prioritize an SPO's ability to generate positive social and environmental impacts for its stakeholders over its shareholders' financial potential (Acumen, n.d.; Novogratz, 2010). Social value investors take a philanthropic mindset and apply it to non-philanthropic funding mechanisms and tools such as venture capital-like equity investments, debt instruments, and quasi-debt and equity tools. The stewardship component of social value investors is both a mindset change and an organizational strategy approach. Stewardship requires that one view their capital disbursements as a responsibility for the greater good of the world.

There have been various attempts to understand the social or environmental return on investment that impact investors are making with their capital. Social return on investment (SROI) has been one such attempt that has seen various positive and negative reviews (Fujiwara, 2015). SROI is traditionally used for public organizations, such as city governments, to demonstrate the potential return on capital from an initiative if undertaken. It also helps to bolster the understood return by valuing stakeholder effects from the initiative in dollar terms. While this is a positive step forward, it does not help the challenge of impact investors that are still primarily viewing their investment decisions through a financial-return-only lens. Social Value Investing has adopted an impact-adjusted return model to investments.

In contrast to SROI, which is used to amplify the return on investment feasible by including other quantifiable societal returns in the cost–benefit analysis calculation, impact-adjusted return investment decision-making builds a venture's core social or environmental mission into the actual financing terms. By incentivizing venture seeking funding to continue to pursue its original social or environmental mission in rewarding the venture through impact-adjusted financing terms, it can ensure that the values between funder and venture are clearly aligned and that the funder is put in a position to continue the stewardship role it has chosen rather than an extraction of returns (Hehenberger & Harling, 2018). Impact-adjusted investment instruments allow social value investors to accept lower financial returns in place of measurable social returns without translating that social return into dollar values as within SROI.

Social value investors bring these principles together in their investment thesis and policies. By approaching investments with a systems and structure-agnostic lens as well as using stewardship-based impact-adjusted financial instruments, social value investors can use a funding methodology that allows for the financial return of an investment portfolio to be identified *ex post*, or after the social and environmental outcomes have been considered and evaluated, and the financing period has concluded. In turn, this allows social value investors to put the social or environmental outcomes intended as the *ex ante* determining factor in investment evaluation.

In practice, SVI has been implemented through a variety of forms by organizations in the USA like Acumen Fund, Omidyar Network, and Calvert Impact Capital. In Canada, there are fewer applied cases of SVI. In Sect. 3, we explore how one emerging fund, the National Social Value Fund, is implementing SVI in a Canadian context through communities of youth. We explore the dynamics of youth in local community development in the next section.

3 The Role of Youth

Social Value Investing requires meaningful interaction with the community in which the investees, i.e., the social purpose organizations, operate. It requires a deep level of understanding regarding the issue at hand and systemic and structural dynamics. Additionally, relationship building with community stakeholders is essential to developing a better understanding of the organizational and community needs. Therefore, SVI is typically implemented within a regional community, rather than at the national or international scale. In other words, SVI is place-based.

Youth can play a critical role in the development of Social Value Investing in local communities. This section will review the role of youth in community development and how youth community development initiatives are evolving toward approaches that go beyond education and training, leveraging their ability to enact meaningful change.

3.1 *Youth and Community Development*

We define community using Brennan et al. (2009a)'s framework: "the community is a process of interrelated actions through which diverse segments of local society express their common interests and needs" (p. 332). This framework suggests that each community is made up of many distinct and diverse types of individuals and organizations acting to achieve the common and collective goals of the residents. When members of the community come together to identify common issues and goals, "community agency," or people's ability to manage and utilize resources to address local issues, arises (Brennan, 2006; Brennan & Luloff, 2007; Wilkinson, 1991). One such resource is financial capital. We postulate that youth represent a vast and untapped community segment for directing financial capital to social purpose organizations. We recognize that youth can represent many different identities based on school grades, age, and developmental stages. In our case study of the National Social Value Fund, youth is defined as university students that span across multiple faculties and disciplines.

Studies show that both youth and communities prosper when youth are meaningfully engaged in the community development process (Brennan et al., 2009b). Youth hold a unique position in the community that allows them to cut through different fields, sectors, and niches within the community (Brennan et al., 2009a). The role of youth in a community is a unique position that can cut across many diverse stakeholders (Brennan et al., 2009a). Ranging from the neighborhoods in which they reside, the schools where they study, and the organizations with which they volunteer and work, youth represent a community stakeholder group permeating through the local economy. Furthermore, youth's approaches to community development are often diverse: they are intergenerational, multicultural, and interfaith. Studies have shown that youth organizing effectively engages diverse youth (Christens & Dolan, 2011; Yee, 2008). When youth are in decision-making and leadership positions, they "alternately and collaboratively assume roles as learners, researchers, and educators of other youth and adults" (Dolan, 2010). The cross-sector collaboration is consistent with Social Value Investing's systems-approach that necessitates participation from various types of organizations in the community. Ultimately, engaged youth represent the community's future leaders who will influence the locale's well-being and continue evolving throughout the years.

3.2 *Youth Community Development Approaches*

There are many different approaches that youth have taken toward community development, which we can characterize on a spectrum between pro-sustainability behavior and actions (de Vreede et al., 2013; Schusler et al., 2009; Schusler & Krasny, 2010) and social justice youth development and youth organizing (Christens & Dolan, 2011; Ginwright & Cammarota, 2002; Ginwright & James, 2002). A common thread among these approaches is the contrast between individual, micro-level activities, and collective, systemic action.

In the first approach of pro-sustainability education, micro-level activities include: recycling, reducing waste, and energy usage (de Vreede et al., 2013). Kudryavtsev et al. (2012) found that educational programs that promote environmental skills development and monitoring were successful in increasing ecological place meaning (the symbolic meaning people ascribe to places), but was not successful in strengthening youth's sense of place attachment (the strength of the bond between people and places). While successful in increasing youth's sense of ownership within their community, this approach is in conflict with the latter approach of viewing youth as a fundamental part of community development.

Approaches such as social justice youth development (SJYD) and youth organizing take a systemic approach, including strategizing and acting to change policies and protocols (Ginwright & James, 2002). Ginwright and James (2002) suggest this approach differs from traditional youth development in two ways. First, by being explicit about societal problems that people face: SJYD fosters critical consciousness for youth and brings to the forefront how traditional institutions and systemic forces have failed people and communities. Second, SJYD differs from traditional youth development by viewing youth "not only as assets but also as agents capable of transforming their toxic environments, not simply developing resiliency and resistance to them." In organizations that utilize this approach, youth are often in a decision-making role, whereas adults take on a supporting role (Christens & Dolan, 2011).

Two examples of youth-led organizations that subscribe to the latter approach of creating SJYD are the University of British Columbia's Climate Hub (UBC Climate Hub) and CityHive. The UBC Climate Hub is a university-wide initiative that aims to connect and empower university and community stakeholders to take bold climate action for a just future. In late 2019, the UBC Board of Governors endorsed a Declaration on the Climate Emergency, responding to the advocacy from groups like the UBC Climate Hub and UBC C350, a global political climate action group. As a response to the Climate Hub's student engagement and activism, UBC created the Climate Emergency Task Force comprised of UBC students, staff, and faculty to conduct a university-wide community engagement. The work of the Climate Emergency Task Force will result in a set of recommendations to embed principles of climate justice and ambitious climate targets in UBC's university-wide policies, affecting many of the practices of the university ranging from campus operations to teaching, hiring, and recruitment policies. While staff and faculty have played an essential role in supporting this initiative, the Climate Hub youth-leaders' energy and ambition have been instrumental in creating inclusive and bold recommendations for UBC. Similar to the Climate Hub, CityHive is a nonprofit that seeks to involve youth in civic planning, shaping and decision-making at municipal levels. They have run multiple initiatives that amplify Vancouver's youth leaders to be involved in policy-making processes that affect their communities in their respective cities. The innovative approach that CityHive takes is having a unique hub or program in each city to reflect every city's differing issues and structures across British Columbia, allowing youth to understand the different needs and ways to propose solutions.

While the UBC Climate Hub and CityHive are examples from the local community in Vancouver and British Columbia, we can see youth taking on vital leadership roles in the global organization Fridays for Future (Greta Thunberg), the Sunrise Movement in the USA, and Future Majority in Canada. All these organizations have a "by youth, for youth" focus, which are then supported by their boards of directors—older adults who offer mentorship, guidance, and subject matter expertise when necessary.

The National Social Value Fund subscribes to this approach by implementing social value investing, where the engaged youth are the decision-makers and primary drivers of community development. When examining youth's role in scaling Social Value Investing, we base the analysis on the following two principles: (1) systemic approach and organizational structure-agnosticism, (2) stewardship and impact-adjusted returns. These principles are grounded in a case study on the National Social Value Fund (NSVF).

3.3 Case Study: The National Social Value Fund

The National Social Value Fund is a nonprofit that supports and connects place-based social value funds across Canada. Social value funds invest in social purpose organizations that are addressing local gaps in communities across Canada. The National Social Value Fund runs an experiential education program for undergraduate students that sees youth from diverse faculties take control of running a local community fund with support from advisors, mentors, co-investors, and NSVF personnel. NSVF provides opportunities for students, investors, and advisors to connect across Canada and share learnings to ensure our approach is local in scope, but national in scale. In the model, youth are put in an uncommon position of executive responsibility. The youth team running the Vancouver Social Value Fund through NSVFs experiential education program takes a leading role in all aspects of the fund's mechanisms from identifying SPOs, to completing research and due diligence, and most importantly, to the final decision-making process of investments into community SPOs.

The Social Value Investing methodology is being trialed across Canada's country by a network of youth-led social value investment teams. The National Social Value Fund model began three years ago in Vancouver, British Columbia and is now expanding to support four additional place-based social value funds in major cities across Canada in Calgary, Montreal, London, and Kingston. There are plans for an additional place-based, youth-led social value funds in Canada pending the successful expansion and proof points of the current social value fund community models. Figure 1 illustrates the organizational structure of NSVF.

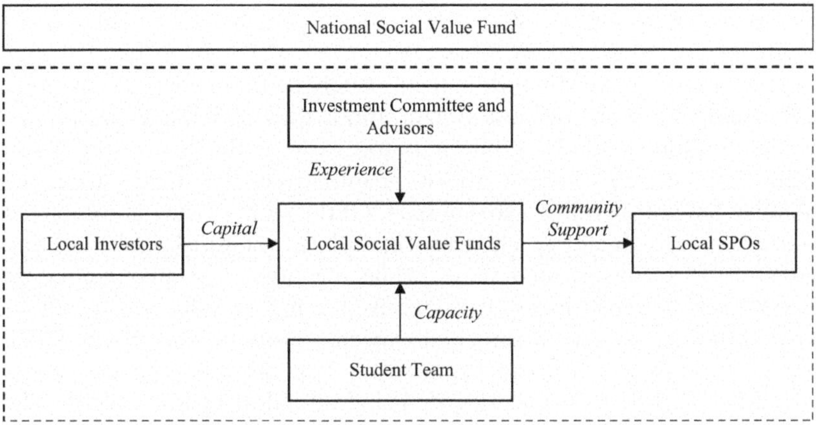

Fig. 1 National Social Value Fund Structure

The social value fund model initiated by the National Social Value Fund is governed by the principles laid out previously as the defining qualities of Social Value Investing: a systemic approach, organization structure indifference, stewardship, and impact-adjusted returns.

Here, by reviewing the first years of the National Social Value Fund's inaugural fund in Vancouver, we examine how the authentic empowerment of youth is not only an additional benefit to social value investors but may be, in fact, at times a necessity to the approach.

3.3.1 Systemic Approach and Organizational Agnosticism

The Vancouver Social Value Fund's stated goal is to direct social value investment capital to community-based social purpose organizations to solve social and environmental problems prevalent in Vancouver, British Columbia, and Canada. During the first two years of operation, we have seen success in implementing the social value investment methodology. VSVF's model has resulted in just under $400,000 of community capital invested in local SPOs. A team of engaged youth has directed these investment decisions. As described above, when youth are given a seat at the decision-making table, their ability to cut through different sectors, fields, and niches within communities results in a more systemic view of issues and analysis (Brennan et al., 2009a). This is an important factor in making judgments on investments into social purpose organizations, as private investment decisions are often the result of personal judgment (Cueto & Zhang, 2013). The VSVF has operated on the theory that a democratic group of engaged youth may ultimately be more adept at investing and supporting social purpose organizations than individual investors or smaller traditional funds. While it is too early in the Vancouver Social Value Fund model's lifespan to say quantitatively that this is true, the initiative has gotten off to a strong start. Of the six investments completed to date, one has already reached a successful exit via initial public offering (IPO) at 15× the invested value, while the other five investments are all on track to repay loans, have received a higher valuation in subsequent funding, or have maintained expected growth. This places VSVF in a position in which it can begin to say that the fund is experiencing strong financial performance despite being intentionally impact-first. The argument for leading with impact seems apparent although it is worth stating that the current results have significant limitations.

It is also worth touching on organizational agnosticism. Of the six investments completed to date, five have been in what would traditionally be seen as start-up SPOs. The sixth, which will be touched on briefly, was categorized as a project-based financing initiative for a social enterprise SME. While VSVF aims to provide investment into nonprofits, charitable organizations, community contribution companies and more, this has not been the case so far. This is a limitation to the outstanding financial results achieved. The assumption can be made that the model's financial return will decrease as more attention is paid to investing in a wider array or organizational structures, although it is good to see the model begin to prove the original theory that a youth-led team can generate significant results. While the financial returns are interesting, the purpose of the VSVF model is to attempt to derive superior social and environmental returns with their capital. To this end, we examine their results so far in the next section.

3.3.2 *Stewardship and Impact-Adjusted Returns*

Measuring an organization's aggregate social and environmental return that supports an array of issues is challenging (Reeder & Colantonio, 2013). We will look at an investment example from the Vancouver Social Value Fund to understand how a financial mechanism was designed to incentivize the venture to drive stronger social and environmental returns.

Our example will be an investee of VSVF called CleanStart. CleanStart is a community contribution company that hires individuals with barriers to employment and completes pest control, junk removal, and hoarding cleanup. They provide training, external support, and more to their employees who often come from disadvantaged backgrounds. CleanStart approached VSVF to receive financial support in order to expand operations. To properly support CleanStart, an SPO operating with thin margins due to their attention to supporting their workforce, concessionary financing was needed. VSVF demonstrated the stewardship mindset, previously defined by Donaldson and Davis (1991) and Muth and Donaldson (1998), as one motivated by non-financial factors that can benefit both the principal and themselves by developing their first impact-adjusted debt instrument. CleanStart would receive a patient and flexible loan with a variety of important terms: (1) grace period, meaning no interest would accrue for the first year of the loan; (2) variable interest rate, meaning interest rate and interest payable would be re-measured each quarter based on social metrics achieved by CleanStart. If their social impact metrics reached certain thresholds during the quarter, the interest rate applicable to that quarter would be reduced from 5% to 2.5%. The core impact metrics measured with this instrument were: (1) percentage of employment hours by individuals with barriers to employment and (2) percentage of employment hours by females with barriers to employment. At the time of the loan, the respective percentages were at around 40% and 0%. Today, they have increased to 75% and 40%, respectively. Here, we see the power of youth play a major role in implementing Social Value Investing. By connecting deeply with the issues that CleanStart is trying to tackle via a social enterprise model, the VSVF team could identify and build a financial instrument that would not extract returns. Instead, lifting the investee up toward creating further impact within the organization and the community.

The National Social Value Fund is an example of a youth-led community development initiative that integrates Social Value Investing principles. The importance of empowering youth to take on a leadership role in deploying capital toward community development is underscored by the $30 trillion wealth transfer to youth that will take place over the next few decades (Emerson & Norcott, 2014). This transfer represents an opportunity for social finance and impact investing to become widely adopted, as the investors of the next generation are being taught to evaluate, analyze, and construct impact investment portfolios critically.

4 Discussion and Conclusion

Social innovation in Canada has gained considerable momentum during the past decade. The sector has been catalyzed by the supply of social finance capital through the federal government's Investment Readiness Program and the Social Finance Fund. Additionally, private sector actors such as corporate venture capital arms, family offices, and financial institutions have also deployed capital toward Canadian social innovation. On the demand side, various types of organizations now make up a vibrant ecosystem of social purpose organizations, ranging from charities and nonprofits to cooperatives, start-ups, and hybrid organizations like Community Contribution Companies.

As more organizations from various sectors of the economy begin to actively participate in the social innovation ecosystem, the approach in which resources are distributed must be examined carefully and deployed meaningfully. Approaches such as venture capital and philanthropy have shaped the development of the technology entrepreneurship and charitable sectors, respectively, throughout the past decades. As the social innovation and social finance sector begins to grow to maturity in Canada, traditional financing approaches may not be able to fully satisfy the diverse needs of impact-focused organizations.

This leads us to a key question: *What, then, is required to serve social purpose organizations best?* We argue for an approach—Social Value Investing—that considers investment beyond solely recognizing returns as financial in nature. This systemic approach takes an organization-agnostic lens that first considers the social or environmental outcomes desired and recognizes that outcomes are achieved only through meaningful engagement from a diverse set of organizations and community stakeholders. As a result, investment vehicles are subsequently designed to primarily facilitate the generation of impact rather than to solely extract returns. Investment terms are structured so returns are dependent on an organization's ability to reach impact milestones such as reducing barriers to employment.

From a practical perspective, Social Value Investing necessitates several elements. First, a thorough understanding of the issue and desired outcomes is required. To achieve this, engagement beyond solely shareholders must be considered. Stakeholders such as community members and the potential beneficiaries of the SPO's product or service must be properly engaged. Youth occupy a unique position in the community that cuts across various fields and sectors that allows them to engage with stakeholders effectively. Youth engagement models can be characterized using two approaches: pro-sustainability education and social justice youth development (SJYD). The former approach promotes and trains youth to engage in micro-level activities, while the latter empowers youth to take on an ownership role in which they are the very agents capable of creating change. SJYD initiatives have shown an ability to increase youth's sense of place attachment, further strengthening youth's ability to meaningfully engage community stakeholders.

The National Social Value Fund (NSVF) represents an initiative at the intersection of Social Value Investing and social justice youth development. Its six local social value funds engage youth—university students across Canada—to identify local issues, engage community stakeholders, and structure investments into social purpose organizations. At the same time, they are given ownership of the fund decisions and operations. This intentional shift in power toward the NSVF associates and fund managers is aligned with social justice youth development principles. Since its inception in 2017, NSVF has facilitated over $400,000 in investments and has realized returns on one exit.

Through new organizational structures that put trust in youth to direct local capital, such as the National Social Value Fund model, communities will be able to authentically empower their next generation of leaders to support a new mindset of financing private-based organization that actively benefit the public good.

References

Acumen. (n.d.). *Acumen's patient capital model is a new approach to solving poverty*. https://acumen.org/about/patient-capital/.

Aghion, P., & Bolton, P. (1992). An incomplete contracts approach to financial contracting. *The Review of Economic Studies, 59*(3), 473–494.

Akerlof, G. (1970). The market for 'lemons': Quality uncertainty and the market mechanism. *Quarterly Journal of Economics*, *84*(3), 488–500.

Armeni, A., & De Bone, M. F. (2017). *Innovations in financing structures for impact enterprises: Spotlight on Latin America*. Inter-American Development Bank.

Austin, J., Stevenson, H., & Wei-Skillern, J. (2006). Social and commercial entrepreneurship: Same, different, or both? *Entrepreneurship Theory and Practice, 30*(1), 1–22.

Bannick, M., Goldman, P., & Kubzansky, M. (2015). *Frontier capital: Early stage investing for financial returns and social impact in emerging markets*. Omidyar Network. https://omidyar.com/news/new-report-helps-investors-who-want-to-achieve-financial-returns-and-social-impact-find-the-right-opportunities/.

Barney, J. B., Busenitz, L., Fiet, J. O., & Moesel, D. (1989, August). The structure of venture capital governance: An organizational economic analysis of relations between venture capital firms and new ventures. In G. Atinc (Ed.), *Academy of management proceedings* (Vol. 1989, No. 1, pp. 64–68). Academy of Management.

BC Co-op Association. (2018). *Cultivating co-ops: A cooperative development workbook for emerging and existing cooperative enterprises in British Columbia*. https://bcca.coop/knowledge-centre/starting-a-co-op/cultivating-coops-guide/.

Benink, E., & Winters, R. (2016). *New perspectives on financing small cap SMEs in emerging markets: The case for mezzanine finance*. Dutch Good Growth Fund, Ministry of Foreign Affairs. https://english.dggf.nl/publications/publications/2018/5/18/news---new-perspectives-on-financing-small-cap-smes.

Bouw, B. (2013). BC's new business model makes it easier to make money and give back. *The Globe and Mail*. https://www.theglobeandmail.com/report-on-business/small-business/going-global/new-business-model-lets-bc-companies-blend-social-values-into-bottom-line/article13631725/.

Brennan, M. A. (2006). The development of community in the west of Ireland: A return to Killala twenty years on. *Community Development Journal, 42*(3), 330–374.

Brennan, M. A., Barnett, R. V., & Lesmeister, M. K. (2009a). Enhancing local capacity and youth involvement in the community development process. *Community Development, 38*(4), 13–27.

Brennan, M. A., Barnett, R. V., & McGrath, B. (2009b). The intersection of youth and community development in Ireland and Florida: Building stronger communities through youth civic engagement. *Community Development, 40*(4), 331–345.

Brennan, M. A., & Luloff, A. E. (2007). Exploring rural community agency differences in Ireland and Pennsylvania. *Journal of Rural Studies, 23*(1), 52–61.

Caers, R., Bois, C. D., Jegers, M., Gieter, S. D., Schepers, C., & Pepermans, R. (2006). Principal–agent relationships on the stewardship-agency axis. *Nonprofit Management and Leadership, 17*(1), 25–47.

Callen, J. L., & Falk, H. (1993). Agency and efficiency in nonprofit organizations: The case of 'specific health focus' charities. *The Accounting Review, 68*(1), 48–65.

Canadian Task Force on Social Finance. (2010). *Mobilizing private capital for public good*. Canadian Task Force for Social Finance. https://learn.marsdd.com/article/mobilizing-private-capital-for-public-good-canadian-task-force-on-social-finance/.

Christens, B. D., & Dolan, T. (2011). Interweaving youth development, community development, and social change through youth organizing. *Youth & Society, 43*(2), 528–548.

Cueto, J. I., & Zhang, S. H. (2013). New venture decisions: A literature review of the entrepreneurial heuristics and biases. http://gebrc.nccu.edu.tw/proceedings/APDSI/2013/proc/P130122002.pdf.

Dewatripont, M., & Tirole, J. (1994). A theory of debt and equity: Diversity of securities and manager-shareholder congruence. *The Quarterly Journal of Economics, 109*(4), 1027–1054.

Dolan, T. (2010). *Youth organizing for education reform: A case study*. The Claremont Graduate University.

Donaldson, L., & Davis, J. H. (1991). Stewardship theory or agency theory: CEO governance and shareholder returns. *Australian Journal of Management, 16*(1), 49–64.

de Vreede, C., Warner, A., & Pitter, R. (2013). Facilitating youth to take sustainability actions: The potential of peer education. *The Journal of Environmental Education, 45*(1), 37–56.

Emerson, J., & Norcott, L. (2014). Millennials will bring impact investing mainstream. *Stanford Social Innovation Review*. https://ssir.org/articles/entry/millennials_will_bring_impact_investing_mainstream.

Employment and Social Development Canada. (2018). *Inclusive innovation: New ideas and new partnerships for stronger communities*. Employment and Social Development Canada. https://sisfs.ca.

Fujiwara, D. (2015). *The seven principle problems of SROI*. Simetrica Ltd.

Gaddy, B., Sivaram, V., & O'Sullivan, F. (2016). Venture capital and Cleantech: The wrong model for clean energy innovation. *MIT Energy Initiative*.

Ghosh, S., & Nanda, R. (2010). Venture capital investment in the clean energy sector. *Harvard Business School Entrepreneurial Management Working Paper* (pp. 11–020).

Ginwright, S., & Cammarota, J. (2002). New terrain in youth development: The promise of a social justice approach. *Crime and Social Justice, 29*(4).

Ginwright, S., & James, T. (2002). From assets to agents of change: Social justice, organizing, and youth development. *New Directions for Youth Development, 96*, 27–46.

Handy, F., & Katz, E. (1998). The wage differential between nonprofit institutions and corporations: Getting more by paying less? *Journal of Comparative Economics, 26*(2), 246–261.

Hansmann, H. (1986). The role of nonprofit enterprise. In S. Rose-Ackerman (Ed.), *The economics of nonprofit institutions*. Oxford University Press.

Hart, O., & Moore, J. (1994). A theory of debt based on the inalienability of human capital. *The Quarterly Journal of Economics, 109*(4), 841–879.

Hehenberger, L., & Harling, A. M. (2018). Moving toward "impact-adjusted" financial returns: Closing remarks. *American Journal of Evaluation, 39*(3), 408–412.

Höchstädter, A. K., & Scheck, B. (2015). What's in a name: An analysis of impact investing understandings by academics and practitioners. *Journal of Business Ethics, 132*, 449–475.

Hölmstrom, B. (1979). Moral hazard and observability. *The Bell Journal of Economics*, 74–91.

International Finance Corporation. (2010). *Strategic community investment: A good practice handbook for companies doing business in emerging markets*. International Finance Corporation. https://www.ifc.org/wps/wcm/connect/topics_ext_content/ifc_external_corporate_site/sustainability-at-ifc/publications/publications_handbook_communityinvestment__wci__1s319576907570.

Kania, J., & Kramer, M. (2011). Collective impact. *Stanford Social Innovation Review*, 2011, 36–41.

Kaplan, S. N., & Lerner, J. (2010). It ain't broke: The past, present, and future of venture capital. *Journal of Applied Corporate Finance, 22*(2), 36–47.

Kaplan, S. N., & Strömberg, P. (2001). Venture capitals as principals: Contracting, screening, and monitoring. *American Economic Review, 91*(2), 426–430.

Kaplan, S. N., & Strömberg, P. (2003). Financial contracting theory meets the real world: An empirical analysis of venture capital contracts. *The Review of Economic Studies, 70*(2), 281–315.

Kaplan, S. N., & Strömberg, P. E. (2004). Characteristics, contracts, and actions: Evidence from venture capitalist analyses. *The Journal of Finance, 59*(5), 2177–2210.

Kohler, J., Kreiner, T., & Sawhney, J. (2011, July). Coordinating impact capital: A new approach to investing in small and growing businesses. *Santa Clara University and The Aspen Network of Development Entrepreneurs (ANDE)*, Santa Clara, California.

Kudryavtsev, A., Krasny, M. E., & Stedman, R. C. (2012). The impact of environmental education on sense of place among urban youth. *Ecosphere, 3*(4), 1–15.

Lam, L., & Seidel, M. L. (2020). Hypergrowth exit mindset: Destroying societal wellbeing through venture capital biased social construction of value. *Journal of Management Inquiry, 29*(4), 471–474. https://doi.org/10.1177/1056492620929085.

Mair, J., & Noboa, E. (2003). *Emergence of social enterprises and their place in the new organizational landscape*. University of Navarra.

Marcus, A., Malen, J., & Ellis, S. (2013). The promise and pitfalls of venture capital as an asset class for clean energy investment: Research questions for organization and natural environment scholars. *Organization & Environment, 26*(1), 31–60.

Moore, M., & Westely, F. (2012). The social finance and social innovation nexus. *Journal of Social Entrepreneurship, 3*(2), 115–132.

Muth, M., & Donaldson, L. (1998). Stewardship theory and board structure: A contingency approach. *Corporate Governance: An International Review, 6*(1), 5–28.

Novogratz, J. (2010). *The blue sweater: Bridging the gap between rich and poor in an interconnected world*. Rodale.

Perrini, F., & Vurro, C. (2006). Social entrepreneurship: Innovation and social change across theory and practice. In J. Mair, J. Robinson, & K. Hockerts (Eds.), *Social Entrepreneurship* (pp. 57–86). Palgrave Macmillan.

Prendergast, C. (2002). The tenuous trade-off between risk and incentives. *Journal of Political Economy, 110*(5), 1071–1102.

Reeder, N., & Colantonio, A. (2013). *Measuring impact and non-financial returns in impact investing: A critical overview of concepts and practice*. The London School of Economics and the European Investment Bank Institute.

Schusler, T. M., Peters, S. J., & Decker, D. J. (2009). Developing citizens and communities through youth environmental action. *Environmental Education Research, 15*(1), 111–127.

Schusler, T. M., & Krasny, M. E. (2010). Environmental action as context for youth development. *Journal of Environmental Education, 41*, 208–223.

Steinberg, R. (1987). Nonprofit organizations and the market. In W. W. Powell (Ed.), *The nonprofit sector: A research handbook* (p. 1987). Yale University Press.

Svedova, J., Cuyegkeng, A., & Tansey, J. (2014). Demystifying impact investing. *UBC Sauder Centre for Social Innovation & Impact Investing*. https://www.sauder.ubc.ca/sites/default/files/2019-02/DemystifyingImpactInvestingFinalVersionApril2014.pdf.

Wilkinson, K. (1991). *The community in rural America*. Greenwood Press.

Wittmer, D. (1991). Serving the people or serving for pay: Reward preferences among government, hybrid sector and business managers. *Public Productivity and Management Review, 14*(4), 369–383.

Yee, S. M. (2008). Developing the field of youth organizing and advocacy: What foundations can do. *New Directions for Youth Development, 117*, 109–124.

Zeuli, K. A., Cropp, R. A., & Schaars, M. A. (2004). *Cooperatives: Principles and practices in the 21st century*. University of Wisconsin Extension-Madison.

Zider, B. (1998). How venture capital works. *Harvard Business Review, 76*(6), 131–139.

Innovations in Social Investing

The Community Bond Experience in Montreal, Quebec

Jason Prince and Vanessa Sorin

1 Introduction

Quebec is Canada's French province and, accordingly, it has its own distinct history, legal system, language, and cauldron of experimentation in collective finance and property ownership. Quebec has a long and rich cooperative movement dating back to the early 1900s with large and established parts of the formal economy owned and managed collectively; notably in the milk, forestry and finance sectors, and more recently, in housing. As is often the case, collective solutions arise out of stark need: Quebec's credit union movement was a response by French-speaking communities to the lack of credit from English capital in a nascent Canada (Rudin, 1982). Starting at the end of the twentieth century, and under the leadership of the *Chantier de l'economie sociale* (a dynamic network of networks), Quebec has seen an increase in new models of collectively owned economic activity in culture, social services, professional services, and even manufacturing. Quebec continues to innovate in the kinds of

J. Prince (✉)
PME MTL Centre-Ville, Montreal, QC, Canada
e-mail: jprince@pmemtl.com

V. Sorin
TIESS, Montreal, QC, Canada

T. Walker et al. (eds.), *Innovations in Social Finance*,
https://doi.org/10.1007/978-3-030-72535-8_6

financing that can be used at start-up, consolidation, and expansion of these collective ventures.

In this chapter, we will first explore the support context in which these social economy enterprises have grown and thrived, followed by a general overview of the range of financing that is available to this emerging business network, the so-called financial ecosystem. Next, we will explore the community bond, linking the Canadian experience to such innovations going back to the 1980s in Nova Scotia but also explored in Quebec and Ontario as early as the 1990s, in order to anchor it to a definition of "community bond." In the third section, we will describe an ongoing pilot project by a social economy do-tank to research and legitimize the use of community bonds as a finance tool for ongoing concerns in the social economy, which started in 2016. We will conclude with some observations on how this experience could be scaled up and transferred to other jurisdictions in Canada as well as elsewhere in the world—and under what conditions—and offer some general comments on what financial tools we think are necessary to support a vibrant, innovative, and entrepreneurial third sector, in any jurisdiction.

2 Context

Where did this vibrant movement to transform Quebec's economy come from? How did it arise, and what carries it forward? To answer this, we must grasp the profound economic transformation that has been shaping post-industrial Montreal and understand the social economy as a (radical) response to that transformation.

With the opening of the Saint Lawrence Seaway at the end of the 1950s, rendering the industrial heartland of Canada's economy obsolete, Montreal's South-West district began its long slow decline. Along with containerization, this new waterway brought ships deeper into the heart of Canada and Montreal's function as an exchange point suffered a major blow. By the 1980s, community leaders in the South-West were grappling with chronic, entrenched unemployment from hundreds of closed factories, and the cocktail of social ills that accompany it: alcoholism, spousal abuse, school dropouts, and lack of hope for a future (Garneau, 1990). The signing of the Canada-US Free Trade Agreement in 1987, which was followed shortly after by the North American Free Trade Agreement in 1994, killed any hope for bringing life back to the manufacturing sector around the Lachine Canal, yet community efforts to kick start the economy had started to produce (albeit very modest) results.

The multi-stakeholder approach to finding economic solutions, piloted by Nancy Neamtan and others in the South-West (Garneau, 1990) with Federal support from conservative governments at the federal level, was adopted as official City of Montreal policy under a progressive local government in 1992 with the installation of community economic development corporations (CDECs) in all of Montreal's struggling neighborhoods. Unions, residents, community organizations, and local businesses as well as in some cases ethnic minorities and elected representatives from various levels of government, participated in this approach (Richard, 2004). Its success has been amply demonstrated, most recently in two detailed evaluations of their economic impact, contributions in tax revenue, numbers of jobs created and survival rates (Kabanguka & Bazinet, 2017a, b).

At the core of the economic project of the newly founded CDECs was an effort to take some measure of control back from the other levels of government and from big capital over the economic destinies of the now decimated inner city. The CDECs were a locus of community control and a rallying point for those seeking to construct a new kind of economy that would not be subject to the whims of free trade deals, large-scale private investment (that can disappear as quickly as it arrives), or massive government investments to politically connected captains of industry to stimulate economic development (for a time). The CDECs were born out of a frustration over failed efforts in the past (Fontan, 1993; Perry, 1982) and a hope that it was possible to construct a new economy truly rooted in the local—community owned and community controlled—that would create permanent long-term employment for Montreal residents (Cabaj, 2004; Neamtan, 2019).

The rebranding of counter-capitalism modes of business development under the term "social economy" happened after the 1996 economic summit meeting in Quebec City. Leaders of groups representing the unemployed and underemployed, the women's movement, and anti-poverty groups, after fighting for it, were given a seat at the table and worked out their proposals in one of several working groups or "chantiers" during the summit meeting. The "chantier" on the social economy continued to meet after the conference as the *Chantier de l'économie sociale*, now an important lobby and clearing house for ideas and innovations in the field. One major initiative following this summit was a new decentralized economic development model aimed at stimulating small- and medium-sized businesses with revolving loan funds, which also included subsidies to stimulate local "social economy" projects. The new structures were modeled on Montreal's experiences in community economic development (Fontan & Shragge, 1997) and were rolled out and funded in 1998, across the entire territory of Quebec: *les Centres locaux de développement* (CLDs).

Embedded in the mandate of the CDEC/CLD was the stimulation, with grants and coaching, of the "new social economy." One observer at the time summarizes the opportunity as a "vast space" between the public and the private spheres:

> New alternatives are also being explored. The "new social economy" is one of them. It came to light during the Summit on the Economy and Employment, and is an approach integrating both the economic and social, explains sociologist Louis Favreau. Strongly territorialized, its interventions are based on a partnership between the public, associative and private sectors, linked organically by agreements, contracts or by projects. Financed in part by public funds and by the sale of goods or services, its preferred field of action is in the areas of health and social services, but it also tends to extend to the vast space between what the public sector cannot do and what the private sector does not want to do (author's translation). (Desrosiers, 1998)

3 Social Economy Movement in Quebec

The *Chantier de l'économie sociale* continued to meet after the 1996 Quebec City economic summit. Its function, as one observer noted by evoking a decidedly Canadian metaphor, is to act as a snowplow, clearing the way for other actors in civil society to build an alternative economy and society.[1] Within a year, it had developed a set of principles that would define a social economy enterprise, which continue to this day. By 1997, the Chantier founded the *Reseau d'investissement social du Quebec* (RISQ). The RISQ is a first-order lender to social economy enterprises

[1] As described by Robert Cohen, one of the key legal and social architects of the Milton Park community land trust, and founding director of the *Société d'habitation et de développement de Montréal* (SHDM), in conversation with one of the authors, circa October 2001. For information on the SHDM and its crucial partnership role in social economy housing ventures, see Vaillancourt et al. (2001).

across Quebec. After finalizing its policy and procedures and hiring its first cohort of financial analysts, the RISQ made its first loans in 1998.

In the intervening years, the *Chantier de l'économie sociale* and other actors in the emerging ecosystem have put into place a variety of tools, procedures, policies, and laws in support of collective enterprise (CITIES, 2018). The Patient Capital Fund founded in 2006 by the *Chantier* has enabled the purchase and construction of dozens of collectively owned buildings; a procurement policy adopted in 2009 by the City of Montreal favors social economy enterprises in the allocation of municipal contracts; and the framework Social Economy Act, adopted unanimously by Quebec's National Assembly in 2013, recognizes and favors the social economy in all government business.

The work of the *Chantier de l'économie sociale* and other interveners in the social economy is, in our view, best understood as a social movement to transform the nature of the economy away from private models of ownership toward collective ownership (Mendell, 2009).

4 Financial Ecosystem

Any description of the social economy's financial ecosystem in Quebec would have to start with the "front line" support organizations and decisions taken by the Social Economy Fund selection committee.

The Social Economy Fund of the CDECs (CLDs), financed by all three levels of government from 1998 to 2015, played a critical support role and "accreditation" function for the social economy.[2] Even after a government restructuring in 2015 under "austerity measures," leaving the Quebec CLD network in tatters and funding for local economic development considerably reduced, the decentralized model is still pursued, at least in Montreal, via a new structure called PME MTL.

Not all social economy enterprises in Quebec have been supported by these organizations. For example, only around 350 enterprises had been funded by the CDECs in downtown Montreal (Kabanguka & Bazinet,

[2] The local level continues to play an important "accreditation" function, acting as "judge" on whether a project or business truly fits the definition of "social economy": by providing a grant to a venture, the local CLD selection committee effectively "validates" or accredits a venture as a bone fide "social economy" venture. Practically speaking, the decision was taken by the local social economy selection committee composed of representatives appointed by the CLD (in Montreal, the CLD mandates were held by Community Economic Development Corporations, now the PME-MTL structure).

2017a) while Bouchard's careful measure of Montreal's social economy completed in 2008 put the number of existing social economy enterprises at over 1500 (Bouchard, 2008). However, the CDEC/CLD/PME MTL would be the first port of call for any organization seeking financial or other support. As one financial analyst at *Filaction* once put it: "(the 'front line' CLD) is the eyes and ears" of all the other funders in the social economy ecosystem.[3] Sometimes, especially for larger-scale projects, politically important ones, or new projects initiated by existing social economy enterprises, initiatives are referred back to the CDEC/CLD from other funders. But in most cases, though modest, the Social Economy Fund investment is a crucial first step.

Social economy enterprises come in all sizes. In 2018, the PME MTL Centre Ville selection committee financed a micro-enterprise with an annual revenue of $50,000 that had a strong social impact but produced only one part-time job, and a non-profit real-estate developer in pre-start-up phase for a $126 million real-estate project on a government-owned parking lot, both within a few short months of each other. Depending on the scale of the enterprise, there may be multiple sources of financing: loans, patient capital, a mortgage, one or more loan guarantees, lines of credit, bridge financing, or other. Most projects have at least one other source of quasi-equity and some larger or more complex projects include as many as 5 or 6 financial instruments. In addition to the subsidy provided by the CLD, additional equity is often provided by the owner's contribution: the "owner" is a non-profit or cooperative and their "ownership" must be understood as such. This "down payment" can come from foundations, crowdfunding, privileged shares (for coops), and more recently community bonds.

[3] The "front line" buttresses collective enterprises by playing a hand-holding role that translates badly in English as "accompaniment." "Accompaniment" plays out in practice as different things to different enterprises at different times: coach, critic, counsellor, match-maker, cheerleader, confidante, advisor and editor, capture some of the facets of the job. So-called front-line services also validate the business model, assure an adequate governance structure is in place for the collective enterprise and validate the network within which the enterprise is evolving: all crucial aspects and indicators of success in the social economy. See report on this matter: TIESS, 2019.

Table 1 Typical montage financier for a small start-up

Costs		*Financing*		*Confirmed*
3 months salaries	$10,500	Crowdfunding	$8,000	$8,000
Marketing	$4,000	Salary subsidy	$5,800	$5,000
Leasehold improvements	$5,000	Social Economy Fund	$12,500	
Administrative costs	$4,800	Loan RISQ	$20,000	
Equipment	$22,000			
Total	$46,300	Total	$46,300	$13,000

The equity that accumulates in the social economy is not public and not private, but "collective": what is fundamentally social in the social economy is the capital.[4]

Other government grants can also be solicited on a project-by-project basis but recurring subsidies are rare, with notable exceptions in some priority sectors such as Quebec's non-profit daycare network, cultural industries, seniors' homecare, and social reinsertion enterprises (CITIES, 2018). There is also some funding for cooperative and non-profit housing from both the federal and provincial level for both capital costs and on an ongoing basis, to help reduce the financial barriers for low-income residents, but it should be noted that the Canadian government—to their shame—spends much more every year to promote private homeownership than they do on de-commodified (i.e., collectively owned social economy) models of housing (Hulchanski, 2007) (Table 1).

[4] A key litmus test and perhaps paradoxical at first glance: what is fundamentally social in the social economy is the capital. Social economy ventures must be collectively owned: once collectively owned, the property never returns to the private market. To achieve this, they must be incorporated as either a not-for-profit (under Part Three of the Quebec Companies act or sometimes—rarely—federally incorporated as a non-profit) or a cooperative; their statutes must state that any remaining assets after dissolution must be transferred to another non-profit with a similar mission; and they should be embedded in broader networks with complex governance. Ideally, the property rights themselves should also be complex. According to the Chantier's 1997 definition, it should also meet a variety of other social and economic tests, notably around governance and links in appropriate networks; these tests are also reflected in the 2013 law on the social economy.

4.1 *The Funding Ladder*

The financial ecosystem is often described as funding "ladder," the first rung being a subsidy from the Social Economy Fund (FDES) that unlocks access to the others. The higher up the ladder, the larger the role played by the funding source. A rare social economy enterprise, at least in its initial years of existence, will access the highest rungs of the ladder where millions may be invested or loaned.

The second rung, and most commonly accessed, is occupied by the RISQ. Half of the social economy enterprises presented to the Social Economy Fund investment committee of PME MTL Centre-Ville also had a loan from the RISQ in the montage financier (author's analysis, unpublished). The RISQ invests in three ways: a small high-risk loan of 5k to help the enterprise better define its business model or to complete a technical study; a pre-start-up loan up to a maximum of 100k, but only when there is a strong team in place, a solid network of support and a viable business plan; and third, to help purchase buildings or equipment, often with the participation of other funders. The RISQ sometimes protects its investment with a ranking in Quebec's register of property rights or a lien on equipment. Interest rates are around 8% for RISQ products; importantly, responsibility for repayment of the loan attaches to the legal person, not the members of the board or staff; in contrast, Canada's acclaimed Futurpreneur loan must be personally guaranteed by the founders, which puts the financial risk directly on their shoulders. For this reason, Futurpreneur loans are practically invisible in Quebec's social economy.

Microcredit Montreal (formerly the Montreal Community Loan Association) (described elsewhere in this paper), the oldest microcredit institution in Quebec, can also play a role at this rung in the investment ladder with a small investment at 8% interest, based on the quality of the business case. They also offer a unique bridge loan product for non-profit organizations that have received a promise of funding but must wait months to receive it: the bridge allows the project to start spending right away. A bridge loan can be signed rapidly with a funding confirmation.

The other principal rungs in the ladder, described in detail elsewhere in the literature (CITIES, 2018) include:

- Where the enterprise is purchasing a building (or, as owner, is making important leasehold improvements that will improve the value of the real estate), recourse can be made to the *Chantier de l'économie sociale*'s Patient Capital Fund.

- *Investissement Québec* (IQ), a quasi-government institution whose mandate is to support business development in Quebec and which invests directly in for-profit and social economy enterprises, can enter into the financing of viable businesses whose financial needs surpass those that can be met by the lower rungs of the ladder.
- The *Caisse d'économie solidaire* has built a solid reputation within the Desjardins Credit Union movement as a major player in the social and solidarity economy in Quebec and participates financially in many social economy enterprises across Quebec.
- The *Fonds de solidarité* and *Fondaction* are two investment funds founded, funded, and operated by Quebec unions. While there are exceptions, these funds will enter into the portrait only when the scale of the project warrants it. In 2001, *Fondaction* founded *Filaction* with a specific mandate to participate financially in social economy ventures.

In the past few years, and playing a foundational role in a growing number of social economy enterprises, we see crowdfunding campaigns that produce sometimes significant sums at the start-up and in expansion of ventures (author's internal source, unpublished). While they often include pre-sales, in some notable cases, a significant percentage is unfettered cold hard cash. While a successful campaign can be an indicator of the strength of the community's support, it cannot be the only evidence; these funds are considered equity.

With this panoply of funding sources, why the need for a community bond? Paradoxically, it was a little over a year and a half after the adoption of the social economy framework law in 2013, with the unanimous support of Quebec's National Assembly, that Quebec government funding in support of the social economy was drastically slashed, as reported widely in the media at this time.

Social economy enterprises were facing growing capital needs as government supplies of capital dried up just when it was most needed. New ventures were rapidly arising from an increasingly effervescent start-up culture bubbling away in Montreal's universities, Montreal was rapidly expanding co-working spaces and specialized incubators thanks to an accelerating transfer of new ideas and techniques via idea-sharing Web sites on the Internet and the collaborative economy. Enterprising organizations, some seeking a quick financial fix, with a solid community of support start seeking out new ideas for financing.

Enter the community bond.

5 The Community Bond: A Short History

Perhaps the earliest precedents for what we are calling now the community bond are found in paper money issues bearing a 3% interest rate and sealed by reputable members of the community at the time of Khublai Khan, as reported by Marco Polo (1993). By the late 1800s, promissory notes had become commonplace in capitalism's Wild West: a lightweight loan instrument quickly settled between issuer and lender, payable within a defined period of time, often with interest—and recourse in case of default. But there were abuses. By 1934, the promissory note had been boxed in somewhat thanks to the initiative of several countries in the League of Nations (United Nations Treaty Collection; Hammett, 1975).

For our purposes, the immediate precursor to the community bond found an early application in the creative efforts of Dr. Greg MacLeod in Cape Breton, Canada with the launch of a community investment vehicle called BCA Holdings (for Banking Community Assets). The not-for-profit BCA Holdings raised over 500,000$ from its first issue of promissory notes to its community of support, before launching in 1989 with matching funds in a no-interest loan from the Canadian government (Johnstone, 1995). The mission of BCA Holdings was as clear as it was simple: to create jobs. Industrial Cape Breton's dependence on coal and steel, both in steady decline since the 1940s and 1950s, coupled with the closing of the fisheries, made the economic situation in Cape Breton dire. In its first few years, starting with a capital fund of $1 million, BCA bought and reinvented eight defunct companies, most often via joint ventures with private sector companies who had a demonstrated expertise; in every case, BCA Holdings guarded a majority shareholder position—and controlling interest—for the not-for-profit. The original investment board was composed of retired successful businessmen who had agreed to contribute their skills to better the community (MacAulay, 2001). According to an independent economic impact assessment, by 2011 the BCA Group, including its sister organization New Dawn Enterprises, had created 522 direct jobs (full-time equivalents) with over $15 million in direct wages and salaries and over $53 million in direct sales in the Cape

Breton economy (Foster et al., 2011). That same assessment estimated its contribution to the local Gross Domestic Product at $26.5 million, concluding: "relative to its size, (the BCA group) has been a significant contributor to the Cape Breton economy." MacLeod called his model of community economic development "community enterprise" to distinguish it from the stricter adherence to collective ownership, seeking the best hybrid possible to create lasting jobs in the Cape Breton economy (MacLeod, 2010). As a matter of principle, BCA Holdings accepted no government subsidy (Johnstone, 1995).

The Montreal Community Loan Association launched around the same time as BCA Holdings, in 1990, in Montreal, Quebec. One of the key architects of this new loan instrument was Lance Evoy, an activist and professor at Concordia University. The mission of the Montreal Community Loan Association (now Microcredit Montréal) is to fight against poverty and exclusion by lending to those neglected by traditional lenders (CITIES, 2018, p. 22). It accomplishes its mission by offering microcredit to vulnerable populations, an opportunity to develop their potential and start their own business. The model was inspired from the work of the Institute for Community Economics in New England (Evoy, 1997). The fund is capitalized solely from socially responsible investments from the community: their community bond issue capitalized the fund. Lenders invest for a defined period, at 2% interest; the loan is transferable under certain circumstances. In 2020, ACEM reported $4.4 million in authorized loans, 65% of businesses as still active after 5 years, a 93% reimbursement rate and 70% ethnocultural diversity. The organization reported leveraging $19 million in the local economy and 9500 people supported, over the past 30 years (Investor's Report, June 2020). ACEM's experience subsequently spread across Quebec and now includes 15 entrepreneurial microcredit organizations, spread across 12 regions and grouped within MicroEntreprendre.

Jacques Patenaude, social economy agent at the Sorel-Tracy Local Development Center (the CLD in Sorel, Quebec), was the first in Quebec to identify the possibility for direct investment in non-profit organizations via bond issues for specific projects. In 2002, he experimented first with a non-profit recreation center "Au fil des ans," which the authors believe was the first non-profit to be directly financed by a community bond in Quebec. The non-profit sold the bonds directly to the community it targeted, without intermediaries. After this initial success, a handful of community bond issues were carried out in Sorel, but the practice did not spread, due in part to lack of any organized effort to transfer knowledge on the subject.

In 2010, under the leadership of Tonya Surman in Ontario, the Center for Social Innovation (CSI) issued its first community bonds to finance the purchase and founding of a co-working space in downtown Toronto. CSI pioneered this practice by issuing $1.4 million in bonds for the acquisition of their building and, shortly afterward, produced a "how to" guide based on its experience (CSI, 2012). Others followed: Solar Shares, Zoo Share, London Innovation Work, 10 Carden Community, and the West End Food Coop among others.

Finally, 15 years after its first successful implementation in Quebec, and at a moment social economy enterprises were facing major government cutbacks while the support ecosystem found itself in an (imposed) period of restructuring, a university-backed research-action do-tank and its partners in the social economy "rediscovered" the community bond.

In 2017, key participants in Montreal's financial ecosystem participated in the launch of three community bonds, under the guidance of TIESS: the *Grand Costumier* (a non-profit that purchased a priceless collection of costumes and props from the Canadian Broadcasting Corporation in 2015, and now rents out the collection to film productions and others in the culture industry), the *Cinema du Parc* (a non-profit repertory cinema), and *7 a Nous* (a horizontally managed non-profit that transformed an empty industrial building in Pointe-Saint-Charles into an alternative gathering place called Batiment 7). It also worked with the Empress Theater (a non-profit proposing a neighborhood cinema in an empty building) but this organization decided finally not to emit a bond (TIESS, 2017a).

6 TIESS Pilot Project: Goals, Process, Results

Territoires innovants en Économie sociale et solidaire (TIESS) is a "liaison and transfer organisation" for social innovation (OLTIS), founded by university researchers and practitioners in the social economy, and funded by Quebec's Ministry of Economy and Innovation (MEI) (TIESS, 2017a). In close collaboration with key stakeholders and researchers, TIESS identifies, documents, and co-constructs practical innovations in the social economy. It also produces easy-to-use handbooks, guides and toolkits, and assures their dissemination across Quebec, fostering the uptake of this knowledge by other actors and enterprises in Quebec's social economy network.

Securing adequate financing for social economy enterprises has always been a challenge. Even if Quebec has benefitted from a solid solidarity finance ecosystem, it takes time and it remains a challenge for NPOs to capitalize, to find the first partners who will take the risk to support the development of a new project or a new service. Over the past 20 years of practice, many collective enterprises have struggled with problems arising from inadequate capitalization at start-up and subsequent difficulty in procuring appropriate financing for development and growth. In recent years, the traditional funding ecosystem for the social economy has seen the introduction of new players and new ways of doing things: crowd-funding, credit unions, foundations, and even private banks have entered the field.

Community bonds for non-profits are perhaps an analog to privileged shares for cooperatives. Privileged shares have been used by cooperatives to permit members to invest directly in their enterprise; they are well understood and relatively common, in the Quebec experience. Community bonds and privileged shares are both forms of what is called "participatory financing." TIESS has been actively documenting participatory financing in the social economy, since 2016: along with crowdfunding they are considered by TIESS to be major opportunities for mobilization and financing for social economy enterprises.[5]

However, because they are new and/or complex and misunderstood, they have been ignored and remain underused by social economy enterprises as well as the ecosystem supporting the social economy itself. The TIESS network has mobilized its efforts with a view to documenting, deploying, and perpetuating these tools and practices across Quebec.

6.1 *What Are Community Bonds?*

Community bonds are an easy-to-issue debt instrument that can be emitted by non-profit organizations (incorporated under Part Three of the Quebec Companies Act) and sold to support members in their community (users, clients, members, partners) to enable the purchase of

[5] TIESS also produced a practical guide to crowdfunding in 2017: crowdfunding can transform social capital into financial capital (TIESS, 2017b, 2).

a building, to carry out a project, to contribute to a mission, and/or to serve its community.

Like all bonds and promissory notes, they carry an issue price, a duration, and a rate of remuneration, and the principal is repayable at maturity.

Community bonds are part of the "exempt market" and are therefore not regulated by the *Autorité des marchés financiers* (AMF). Under Quebec law, these Part Three not-for-profit organizations may issue bonds and are explicitly exempted by the Securities Act from filing a prospectus and registering as brokers, provided that no intermediary is paid on the sale or purchase of these bonds. It is this power—which has existed in the law for some time but (rarely) exercised—that enables the issuing of what actors in the social economy are now calling "the community bond." But this power is not limitless: in case of abuse, the granting of this exemption may be withdrawn by the Administrative Court of Financial Markets and there is already at least one precedent. To be able to enjoy this power, the non-profit organization is responsible for providing all information necessary to allow for informed decision-making by members of its community of support: it is expected that the non-profit will act with diligence and transparency when issuing community bonds.

The treatment of the community bond by analysts and other lenders is slippery: is it a loan? an equity investment? quasi-equity? or perhaps a quasi-donation? Perhaps, after all, this will depend on the nature of the relationship the bond issuer has with its community of support, the assessment of risk, and the characteristics of the community bond issue.

Community bonds are not to be confused with Social Impact Bonds, sometimes called "pay for success" bonds. From a financial point of view, it is important to note that these tools are not obligations in the traditional financial sense (fixed interest and predetermined duration) but rather contracts or investment programs, hence the diversity of terminologies used. Social Impact Bonds (SIBs), also called social impact contracts, propose a restructuring of the relationships between public authorities, social organizations, and private donors. First appearing in 2010 in the UK, SIBs have since spread to several other countries, generating much debate: sometimes enthusiasm and sometimes mistrust of the actors concerned (Rijpens et al., 2020). Through this mechanism, social services provided by actors independent of the state are financed by private investors on the basis of a reimbursement contract with a government (municipality, region, state, etc.). This contract links the financial return on these investments to the social benefits of the program thus financed. At the end of the program, its social effects (impacts) are evaluated (measured) in order to translate them into financial returns (Gruet, 2017).

6.2 *What Is the Promise of a Community Bond?*

In a world where investment is increasingly disconnected from the real economy (especially in the financial sector), community bonds bring citizens an opportunity to make a transformational investment in their local economy and to directly experience the power of their investment in neighborhood assets and local employment. An "ethical investment" portfolio might have stocks purchased on a secondary market in a company with ethical filters: collective agreements, zero emissions, or other value, but the cash does not go directly to the company. On the contrary, a community bond is a direct investment in local assets. It reinforces the social bond between the investor and the enterprise, strengthening its community roots. A successful launch of a community bond issue can send a strong signal to other sources of finance that the project has the support of the community and not just moral or symbolic support, but is backed by "skin in the game." A successful bond issue also provides an opportunity to convey citizens' aspirations, the expectations of the financial ecosystem, and the needs of social economy enterprises. Community bonds are a direct way to contribute to the democratization of the economy and must be considered an important vector that permits responsible investment, impact investing and an extension of the now common practice of crowdfunding (Gruet, 2016).

However, issuing bonds requires social economy enterprises' foresight, rigor, and transparency: it will require ongoing institutional support to assure the appropriate application and influence of this tool.

6.3 *Documenting the Community Bond*

Between 2016 and 2017, TIESS researched and modeled the process of issuing community bonds in an innovative process of co-construction and collaboration with experts, researchers, and entrepreneurs in community bond issues for three enterprises: Le Grand Costumier ($20,000), Cinéma du Parc ($150,000), and Bâtiment 7 ($50,000).

The pilot project resulted in the publication of a comprehensive guide on how to issue a community bond for social economy enterprises (TIESS, 2017a). Made up of five booklets, the guide attempts to equip collective businesses at all stages of the issuance process. The guide starts with a description of the nature of community bonds, outlines how to conduct a serious reflection by the board surrounding the decision to issue a bond (are we genuinely "community bond ready"?), and then details the process of issuing and managing the bond. The guide aims to facilitate the issuing of bonds by social economy enterprises, but not at any cost. The underlying ambition is that a greater number of social economy enterprises will use this financial tool. It is crucial to its survival to assure its prudent application, beyond mere legalities, rooted in the ideal practice: a successful bond issue can only be measured after a successful bond *repayment*.

These avenues of funding are currently attracting great interest from the support ecosystem, social economy businesses, and even the general public. After the publishing of the guidebooks, at least forty Quebec non-profits have expressed interest in issuing short-term as well as medium-term community bonds and about 20 have or are in the process of issuing a community bond. TIESS and its partners have carried out some 30 dissemination and transfer activities throughout Quebec since April 2016. These dissemination activities have raised awareness of this new funding method, but it is not sufficient for them to fully master it. So, in the spring of 2018, TIESS launched the next step of knowledge transfer in an effort to enable the social economy ecosystem to take full advantage of the opportunities offered by participatory investment.

7 Toward the Institutionalization of Participatory Investment

TIESS's second phase of knowledge mobilization aims at institutionalizing the use of the community bond. The goal is to ensure that, throughout Quebec, social economy support structures understand these tools and are equipped to inform and support social economy enterprises who seek to issue a bond for their collective enterprise. The hope is that any social economy enterprise, anywhere in Quebec, will be able to benefit from a local expert who can guide them through the process of successfully issuing a community bond to its community of support.

So, at this stage of knowledge/practice deployment, TIESS will proceed along two axes:

1. Equip and strengthen the capacity of the social economy support ecosystem to inform enterprises that wish to issue community bonds, with reference to relevant resources.
2. Continue to document the actual application of the community bond: as noted above, enterprises are already innovating in the use of community bonds that were not intended or foreseen by TIESS when the model was initially launched.

The transfer strategy focuses on 3 main elements: (1) ongoing efforts by the *Chantier de l'économie sociale* to remove barriers to the use and deployment of this alternative financing by social economy enterprises—the *Chantier* will develop and maintain expertise in this mode of financing and hopes to become *the* reference for best practice across Quebec; (2) the appropriation of practical knowledge by territorial support agencies and social economy enterprises through the establishment of a community of practice that allows professionals to learn and share their experiences on an ongoing basis, while also allowing enterprises to pool their experiences and learn from each other; (3) the production of new practical tools, which allows information to be easily updated, adapted to the different audiences targeted by diverse sources of funding (social enterprises and their communities of support, support organizations and investors). A web space dedicated to participatory finance in the social economy (crowdfunding and community bond and others) will be launched in the winter of 2021.

7.1 A Common Vision for the Development of This Innovative Social Finance Practice

To ensure the successful deployment of community bonds across Quebec, it is essential that the players in the social economy and solidarity finance adopt a common vision.

An important lesson of the TIESS pilot project is that project governance is essential to ensure successful community bond issues.

Throughout the process, an oversight committee composed of participating enterprises and experienced actors from the collective enterprise support community ensured the monitoring, implementation, development, and collective evaluation of the project. Also, at a higher level, a broader committee of partners, made up of major players in the social economy, representatives from the solidarity finance sector in Quebec and practitioners and researchers brought their expertise and contributions to the table, in the ongoing fostering of the appropriation of knowledge by all partners in the financial ecosystem.

The co-construction of knowledge via experiential learning—which is at the core of the TIESS pilòt project—will continue to be refined in a long-lasting dynamic of co-construction and knowledge transfer. But as is often the case, practice spreads faster than expected when the preliminary results are promising: community bonds have seeded quickly and are already taking root in Quebec's financial landscape. While we counted a handful of community bond issues in 2016, in 2020, according to the field survey carried out by TIESS and its partners there are now 16 community bond issues, accounting for more than $1.5 m issued. Excitement about the "community bond" is spreading rapidly. First, a section on community bonds has been included in the second edition of the influential *Guide to the Analysis of Social Economy Enterprises* published in 2017 by the RISQ (Charette et al., 2017). While the PME MTL network has had the legal power to purchase community bonds from social economy enterprises via the Social Economy Fund since 2015, it was only in early 2018 that this power was first exercised by a PME MTL selection committee. These moves, while not anticipated by the TIESS in 2016, will certainly contribute to a more rapid deployment of the community bond.

7.2 Responsible Practices and "Self-Regulation"

The multiplication of uses of the community bond appears to be inevitable: the pilot project has stirred considerable excitement and attention in the media, the financial ecosystem and among collective enterprises. But while this rapid recognition of community bonds is important and favorable, it is also crucial to establish common standards for the responsible use of this tool.

Community bonds benefit from a relatively flexible legal framework; this flexibility reduced the barriers considerably when launching this financial innovation. However, the institutionalization of this innovation requires collective work and considerable "self-regulation" to ensure careful and prudent use of this tool, promote its credibility, and assure its continued and successful use in the social economy.

As mentioned above: a successful issue is only assured when the bond is finally *repaid*. The success of community bonds is based on the trust between the social economy enterprise and its community of support. It is important that this bond of trust is never broken; that bond issues are carried out with rigor and transparency; and that investors' confidence and interests are a top priority. Investor protection is paramount. While the motivation is above all social and not financial, the fact remains that each "solidarity" investor must be made aware of the risks associated with the bonds, the conditions of transfer, pre-term redemption, and redemption.

Therefore, adequate as well as complete (and honest) documentation produced by the non-profit issuing the bond is fundamental.

7.3 A Common Front to Promote the Scaling Up of Community Obligations in Quebec

While the legal hurdles facing non-profits, who seek to issue community bonds were relatively light, there remain many other legal and administrative barriers that will slow down efforts to popularize this new investment instrument. Tax incentives, loan guarantees, and putting in place an adequate administrative support for non-profits that want to issue bonds are but three areas under active scrutiny by TIESS and its communities of practice. Changes in these areas would make it possible to consider larger-scale issues in Quebec; a change in tax law, for example, would immediately expand the pool of potential investors by securing an even broader community of support. A loan guarantee, even only partial, would sweeten the deal for prospective investors who might be willing to take a greater risk if the possible loss is (even partly) covered. Finally, facilitating the management issues arising from issuing financial securities for non-profits that often have limited administrative teams would go a long way to reducing barriers, for reasons that may be obvious: what volunteer board wants to complicate their lives by getting into the business of issuing and managing loans, especially a lot of small loans to a large community of support? Also, the innovative use of digital and crowdfunding platforms will also be explored in the coming months: can we expand access to investors via the power of web-based crowdfunding platforms? As we write these lines, the private sector is already piloting these platforms in Quebec and there is at least one that is exploring community bond issues. Finally, many other uses of community bonds are beginning to be explored by non-profit enterprises such as: the issuing of community bond "credits" to founders in recognition of the time they have invested (and not been paid for); and a bond issue, payable in 5–10 years, "pays" for assets in the context of a purchase of a private company by a collective enterprise. Evidently, such bond issues should only be repaid if in repaying, it does not put the enterprise in financial trouble and the bond issue should make this clear.

TIESS continues to document, facilitate, and cultivate these innovations, in a rapidly evolving and always fascinating financial ecosystem.

7.4 *Applicability in Other Jurisdictions, Transferability*

But can the model find traction in other jurisdictions? United States and British law and custom have provided the legal fragments that allow the creation of non-profit organizations, community benefit organizations, associations and the like—such models are not uncommon in many jurisdictions around the world. Equally, some analog to the "securities and exchange commission" exist in virtually all jurisdictions, at this stage in the neoliberal project, aimed toward enabling safe passage of capital to all four corners of the planet.

A quick survey of legislations that provide for the creation of not-for-profit companies suggests the power to issue bonds or even "shares" is not uncommon. In New York state, according to article 506, non-profit corporations can issue bonds, but the interest rate must be "reasonable" (NY State Senate, 2021). In the UK, at least since 2005, Community Interest Corporations (CICs) can issue bonds and preferred shares that bear interest; the board is not obliged to pay the interest if the CIC does not post a surplus. CICs' assets are "locked" to assure that they are used only for community benefit, but there are loopholes; in that issues are government regulated (Office of the Regulator, 2016). According to the Community Shares Unit (CSU), a joint initiative of the non-government organization Locality and Co-operatives UK financed by the Department for Communities and Local Government, the term "community shares" refers to withdrawable share capital, non-transferable, in an incorporated society with a voluntary or statutory asset lock. According to CSU, the term is applied to societies with at least £10,000 in share capital and at least 20 members, in an effort to distinguish genuine community-owned ventures. Community shares can be invested to save local shops and pubs, finance renewable energy schemes, transform community facilities, support local food growing, fund new football clubs, restore heritage buildings, and "build stronger, more vibrant, and independent communities." Between 2009 and 2016, almost 120,000 people had invested over £100 m to support 350 such community businesses throughout the UK (Community Shares, 2016).

While India and Hong Kong have long had legislation allowing for the creation of non-profit societies, the authors have found no explicit provisions for issuing bonds.[6] Loans by NGOs in India must be approved by the government.[7] Brazil has a vibrant solidarity economy, but we have found no trace of anything like the community bond in a keyword scan of the literature. In 2020, partly in reaction to the international pandemic, India's Securities and Exchange Board is actively exploring a "social stock exchange" where non-profits can list bond issuances (SEBI, 2020).

While the examples from Canada to buttress the social mission and effective economic reach of non-profit organizations pursuing a strong social mission using the collective ownership model with community bond issues may be exceptional, it is important to stress that these stretches of "business as usual" have been made possible by exceptional innovators. Leaders like Nancy Neamtan and Tonya Surman, Lance Evoy and Jacques Patenaude—and Dr. Gregory McLeod—were willing to take a risk and did not take "that can't be done" as an answer. Things only change when there is force pushing for that change: we think this is one of important lessons learned from a review of the community bond experience in Canada and Quebec.

6 [4] See, for example, article 11 of the Societies Registration Act, 1860 which refers to bond issues for societies, without further comment (Societies Registration Act, 1860) and these helpful articles on NGOs in India: https://ngosindia.com/ngo-registration/difference-between-trust-society-and-company/ https://ngosindia.com/process-and-techniques-of-fund-raising/.

7 See, for example, Council of Foundations guide to India, Section III.A.1: Trusts https://www.cof.org/content/india.

8 Conclusion

Solidarity finance offers a mechanism for individuals and institutions to invest directly in viable, innovative collectively owned enterprises that are making a real difference in local communities and increasingly, as they scale up, in other provinces as well as internationally. Community bonds will never replace other sources of financing, but it can allow them to diversify, consolidate, and anchor projects in their community.

Investors in our world are increasingly hungry to make investments that make a real difference: a Financial Post article published in October 2020 notes an eightfold increase in social bond issues in the last year. Socially responsible investments, buying abstract "shares" in companies on a secondary market, are an indirect way to support ethical businesses. Your investment goes to a seller shedding their shares in an anonymous transaction on the stock market via the web: it typically doesn't directly find its way into the company, doing the hard work you want it to do of building windfarms or supporting a unionized, diverse workforce. But with a community bond, you can invest directly and tangibly into a local business that you can see and touch. Because the social economy enterprise is collectively owned, you can also be sure that the growth that your investment permits can never be pocketed by a private owner: at dissolution, under Quebec law, a social economy enterprise incorporated under part three of the Companies Act is obliged to transfer any remaining capital to a non-profit with the same mission. In principle, your investment and the fruit of your investment will continue—in perpetuity—to serve the original mission you supported.

With the introduction of the community bond and this very direct opportunity to invest in the social mission of the non-profit enterprise, we are now standing at the doorway to new space within ethical investment: permitting investors to connect directly to non-profit ventures seeking capital. There are numerous institutional lenders that could be persuaded to participate now that the door is open: capital funds managed by student unions; the investment side of foundations, both large and small; capital reserve funds managed by the non-profit housing sector; ethical investment clubs; church groups, etc. University communities have been mobilizing for years now in a move to encourage their boards of governors to invest ethically (e.g., McGill University's Committee to Advise on Matters of Social Responsibility, active since the South Africa divestment movement in the 1980s, recently recommended carbon reduction targets in its portfolio (CAMSR, 2021)). If even a fraction of the investment portfolio of a major university endowment fund or foundation invested locally in community bond issues, it would transform the financial landscape for social economy enterprises (Plant, 2002). The list goes on.

As evoked above, we need a polico-institutional entrepreneur to advocate for legislative changes that would enable changes that permit tax-sheltered eligibility for community bonds: that said, there must be reasonable limits to protect the investor. Perhaps only real-estate backed community bonds could be eligible for a tax-shelter: the ranking of the bond should be clearly signaled so the investors understand the risk.

One thing is quite clear: socially responsible investment is on the rise—with RBC reporting a substantial increase since 2016 across the globe, as reported by Global Sustainable Investment Alliance in 2018. There is also an interest in this more direct form of ethical investment made possible by the community bond, as evidenced by the work of TIESS. Clearly also, there are growing capital needs for ever expanding collective enterprises.

Crucial to the long-term successful roll-out of this new investment instrument will be maintaining trust among investors. Indeed, underpinning the legal exemption for the regulatory authority is the notion that non-profits operate in a network of support and draw from that network of support when they issue a community bond—the bond is cemented by trust. A high-profile failure would poison the well: such an unfortunate event might also provoke a response from the AMF (our securities commission) and a more authoritarian regulation of this instrument. Perhaps we can safely conclude our chapter with the word "prudence"—while it is true that the three emissions in Montreal succeeded in soliciting investments, we will not know if the bond issue is a success until after they have been reimbursed, in a few years from now. In the meantime, let us act with great prudence, as we explore this new, and hopefully fruitful, investment terrain. And all the more reason to equip the front-line social economy coaches and collective enterprises with clear guidelines to broadcast good practices, as is the case with Tapestry Community Capital in Ontario or Community Share Unit in the UK. In short, to collectively build the institutionalization of the model and perpetuate the innovation via a softer ecosystem-supported, instead of the strict government regulation that could complicate and stifle the application of this tool, which offers to democratize our economy.

References

Bouchard, M. J. (Dir.). (2008). *Portrait statistique de l'économie sociale de la région de Montréal*. Chaire de recherche du Canada en économie sociale de Université du Québec à Montréal (UQAM) et Conférence régionale des élus de Montréal (CRÉ de Montréal). https://www.economie.gouv.qc.ca/fileadmin/contenu/publications/administratives/economie_sociale/portrait_economie_sociale_montreal.pdf.

"Bonds and Security Interests." *NY State Senate*, The New York State Senate, 9 January 2021. www.nysenate.gov/legislation/laws/NPC/506.

Cabaj, M. (2004). CED and social economy in Canada: A people's history. *Making Waves, 15*(1), 13–20. http://communityrenewal.ca/sites/all/files/resource/MW150113.pdf.

Centre for Social Innovation (CSI). (2012). *The community bond: An innovation in social finance*. The Centre for Social Innovation.

Charette, P., Dorion, C., & Mendell, M. (2017). *Le guide d'analyse des entreprises d'économie sociale* (2nd ed.). Cap Finance et Réseau d'investissement social du Québec.

Committee to Advise on Matters of Social Responsibility (CAMSR). (2021). *Approval of CAMSR report implementation plan*. www.mcgill.ca/boardofgovernors/files/boardofgovernors/06._gd19-50_camsr_report.pdf.

Convention for the Settlement of Certain Conflicts of Laws in connection with Bills of Exchange and Promissory Notes, 7 June 1930, League of Nations, *Treaty Series*, *143*, p. 317. https://treaties.un.org/Pages/LONViewDetails.aspx?src=LON&id=551&chapter=30&clang=_en.

Desrosiers, É. (1998). Le débat idéologique. In R. Boily (Ed.), *L'année politique au Québec 1996–1997*. Les presses de l'Université de Montréal.

Evoy, L. (1997). *The Montreal Community Loan Association and social partnerships*. Caledon Institute of Social Policy. https://maytree.com/wp-content/uploads/mcla.pdf.

Fontan, J.-M. (1993). Pointe St. Charles-Building a community voice. In E. Shragge (Ed.), *Community economic development* (pp. 76–92). Black Rose Books.

Fontan, J.-M., & Shragge, E. (1997). CED in Montreal: Community versus state control. In E. Shragge (Ed.), *Community economic development* (2nd ed., pp. 87–109). Black Rose Books.

Foster, M., Duff, R., Peters, K., & Currie, C. (2011). *Tompkins Institute—An economic impact statement*. Canmac Economics Limited. http://bcagroup.ca/images/stories/files/CANMAC-Impact-2011-Sept.pdf.

Garneau, J.-M. (1990). *Le programme économique de Pointe Saint-Charles 1983–1989: La percée du développement économique communautaire dans le Sud-Ouest de Montréal*. Institut de formation en developpement economique communautaire (IFDEC). https://ccednet-rcdec.ca/en/node/15961.

Gruet, É. (2016). Les nouvelles pratiques de financement des entreprises d'économie sociale. *Revue Vie économique, 8*(1), 1–8. http://base.socioeco.org/docs/rve_vol8_no1_gruet.pdf.

Gruet, É. (2017). *Obligations à impact social, un glissement des responsabilités vers le secteur privé*. Territoires innovants en économie sociale et solidaire (TIESS). https://tiess.ca/obligations-a-impact-social-un-glissement-des-responsabilites-vers-le-secteur-prive/.

Hammett, H. D. (1975). Any promissory note: The obscene security: A search for the non-commercial investment. *Texas Tech Law Review, 7*(25), 25–77.

Hulchanski, J. D. (2007). Canada's dual housing policy: Assisting owners, neglecting renters. *Centre for Urban and Community Studies Research Bulletin, 38*, 1–8. http://www.urbancentre.utoronto.ca/pdfs/researchbulletins/CUCSRB38Hulchanski.pdf.

Johnstone, H. (1995). Financing ventures in a depleted community. In G. A. Macintyre (Ed.), *Active partners: Education and local development*. University College of Cape Breton Press.

Kabanguka, A., & Bazinet, G. (2017a). Impacts économiques des financements réalisés dans le cadre des Fonds de Développement de l'Économie Sociale (FDÉS) 1998–2016. Document interne, PME MTL Centre-Ville. https://pmemtl.com/files/Reseau/Documents/PMEMTL_CentreVille_EtudeImpacts_FDES.pdf.

Kabanguka, A., & Bazinet, G. (2017b). Impacts économiques des financements réalisés dans le cadre des Fonds PME MTL et Fonds local d'investissement (FLI) 1998–2016. Document interne, PME MTL Centre-Ville. https://pmemtl.com/files/Reseau/Documents/PMEMTL_CentreVille_EtudeImpacts_FondsPMEMTL.pdf.

MacAulay, S. (2001). The community economic development tradition in Eastern Nova Scotia, Canada: Ideological continuities and discontinuities between the Antigonish Movement and the Family of community development corporation. *Community Development Journal, 36*(2), 111–121. https://doi.org/10.1093/cdj/36.2.111.

MacLeod, G. (2010). *How to start a community enterprise: A personal approach*. Cape Breton University.

Mendell, M. (2009). The three pillars of the social economy: The Quebec experience. In A. Amin (Ed.), *The social economy: International perspectives on economic solidarity* (pp. 176–207). Zed Books.

Mendell, M., Neamtan, N., Jang., J., Gruet, E., Sorin, V., Kim, J., & Lee, G. (2018). *Strategy for knowledge transfer of social finance: Best practices of Québec and strategy for adaptation to Seoul*. Centre international de transfert d'innovations et de connaissances en économie sociale et solidaire (CITIES).

Neamtan, N. (2019). *Trente ans d'économie sociale au Québec: Un mouvement en chantier*. Fides.

Office of the Regulator of Community Interest Companies. (2016). Chapter 7: Financing community interest companies. *Office of the Regulator of Community Interest Companies: Information and guidance notes*. United Kingdom, Department for Business, Energy & Industrial Strategy. https://assets.publishing.service.gov.uk/government/uploads/system/uploads/attachment_data/file/641476/14-1090-community-interest-companies-chapter-7-financing-cics.pdf.

Perry, S. (1982). Evolving a new economic perspective. In E. Ticoll & C. J. Dorsey (Eds.), *The nuts and bolts of community economic development* (pp. 5–13). Edmonton Social Planning Council. https://ccednet-rcdec.ca/sites/ccednet-rcdec.ca/files/1982_nutsandbolts.pdf.

Plant, B. A. (2002). *Mission-based investing: Practices & perceptions among foundations and endowments in Quebec* (Master's Thesis, École des Hautes Études Commerciales de Montréal). Institut de Recherche en Économie Contemporaine. https://irec.quebec/ressources/repertoire/memoires-theses/BrendaAnn_Plant.pdf.

Polo, M. (1993). *The travels of Marco Polo: The complete Yule-Cordier edition* (3rd ed.). Dover Publications

Richard, P. (2004). Transformed by community economic development: Southwest Montréal now has a future as well as a past. *Making Waves, 15*(1), 21–25. https://auspace.athabascau.ca/bitstream/handle/2149/1000/MW150121.pdf;jsessionid=DA95E8DA6AC83DCEF5FB9AB8E2C71775?sequence=1.

Rijpens, J., Bouchard, M., Gruet, É., & Salathé-Beaulieu, G. (2020). *Social impact bonds: Promises versus facts. What does the recent scientific literature tell us?* CIRIEC International Working Group on Impact Measurement of the Social Economy. https://ssrn.com/abstract=3672377.

Rudin, R. (1982). Montreal Banks and the Urban Development of Quebec, 1840–1914. In G. A. Stelter & A. F. J. Artibise (Eds.), *Shaping the urban landscape: Aspects of the Canadian city-building process* (pp. 65–83). Carleton University Press.

Securities and Exchange Board of India (SEBI). (2020). *Working group report on social stock exchange*. https://www.sebi.gov.in/reports-and-statistics/reports/jun-2020/report-of-the-working-group-on-social-stock-exchange_46751.html.

Societies Registration Act, 1860, Legislative Department in the Ministry of Law and Justice, India. www.indiacode.nic.in/handle/123456789/2262?view_type=browse&sam_handle=123456789/1362.

Territoires innovants en économie sociale et solidaire (TIESS). (2017a). *Guide d'émission d'obligations communautaires pour les entreprises d'économie sociale*. http://www.tiess.ca/wp-content/uploads/2017/12/TIESS_guide_obligations_commun_Guide-complet_8dec017.pdf.

Territoires innovants en économie sociale et solidaire (TIESS). (2017b). *Guide sur le financement participatif pour les entreprises d'économie sociale*. http://tiess.ca/wp-content/uploads/2017/04/TIESS_Guide_Financement_Participatif.pdf.

TIESS. (2019). *Accompagnement en économie sociale et développement territorial: État exploratoire des lieux*. https://tiess.ca/etat-exploratoire-des-lieux-delaccompagnement-en-economie-sociale-et-developpement-territorial/#:~:text=Accompagnement-,%C3%89tat%20exploratoire%20des%20lieux%20de%20l'accompagnement,%C3%A9conomie%20sociale%20et%20d%C3%A9veloppement%20territorial%amp%text=L'accompagnement%20est%20un%20facteur,au%20d%C3%A9veloppement%20territorial%20(DT).

Vaillancourt, Y., Ducharme, M.-N., Cohen, R., Roy, C., & Jetté, C. (2001). *Social housing—A key component of social policies in transformation: The Quebec experience*. Caledon Institute of Social Policy. http://www.urbancenter.utoronto.ca/pdfs/elibrary/CaledonSocialHousing.pdf.

"What Are Community Shares?" *Community Shares*, Community Shares Unit, 15 November 2016, http://communityshares.org.uk/find-out-more/what-are-community-shares.

Let's Get Explicit: The Emergence of Impact-Linked Returns in the Commercial Debt Market

Lars Boggild

1 Introduction

The most common definition of impact investing is "investments made with the intention to generate positive, measurable social and environmental impact alongside a financial return" (*Core Characteristics of Impact Investing*, 2019). The critical idea in this definition is that positive impacts are intended ***alongside*** financial returns, not solely as a means to drive additional financial returns. The degree to which these positive impacts are prioritized, and given financial bearing in decision-making, will naturally vary between investors. To help understand these investor preferences, a common approach has been to categorize investors as either "finance first" investors willing to concede intended impacts in exchange for additional financial returns, or "impact first" investors likewise willing to concede financial returns in exchange for further intended impacts (Freireich & Fulton, 2009).

This approach raises the question of how investors that fall along this continuum manage trade-offs between impact and financial return.

L. Boggild (✉)
Vancity Community Investment Bank, Toronto, Ontario, Canada
e-mail: lboggild@vcib.ca

T. Walker et al. (eds.), *Innovations in Social Finance*,
https://doi.org/10.1007/978-3-030-72535-8_7

Managing such trade-offs fundamentally requires wrestling with how much financial value is being placed on intended impact, and how that translates into the pricing of impact investments. Directly pricing impact into investments by tying returns to an investee business's observed impact has been limited in practice. This gap in widely available financial tools and precedents is important because it limits professional impact investors' ability to efficiently manage trade-offs between impact and financial goals.

This chapter will focus on emerging practices that address this gap. Recently, a growing number of innovative transactions in both private impact investments and mainstream capital markets are actively encouraging positive impact by explicitly tying investor returns to the observed impacts of an investee business. These are exciting developments with the potential to reshape the impact investing market and create common footing between parts of the capital markets that wouldn't have previously been considered part of the impact investing marketplace.

Firstly, the chapter will begin by clarifying the scope of the research. This will be followed by illustrating where in the investment value chain there is the greatest activity in linking investor financial returns to impact, while simultaneously recognizing those areas of activity that fall outside of scope. The chapter will address Sustainability-Linked Loans, as one type of investment product and an active area within the capital markets providing impact-linked returns. This sets the stage for a discussion on a sample of private market impact investments that have similarly demonstrated impact-linked returns. A case study demonstrates such a deal in practice, examining the mechanics and application of these approaches in a loan product. The chapter will explore the theoretical foundations that these different tools share. It will then conclude with a discussion of the challenges and opportunities to support further adoption in the market by practitioners.

2 Narrowing in on the Most Relevant Parts of the Value Chain

Linking investor returns to intended outcomes can occur at multiple stages within an investment value chain. This is the sequence of activities and relationships between different actors involved in both investment activity and a business's operation. This can be conceptualized as beginning with the original asset owner and ending with the business's customers. Illustrated in Fig. 1 is a simplified value chain, describing core relationships in the upper boxes, and hypothetical approaches for compensating for intended outcomes within these relationships in the lower boxes.

The link between investor returns and intended impacts can be assessed by any additional value creation, as well as the distribution of that value, for different actors along the value chain. For example, additional payments by end customers for a more impactful product could drive additional revenues for a business. If representing a stronger margin, it will ultimately lead to additional returns for the equity owners of the operating business. It could be as simple as a one-time premium price for a good or service believed to be more socially and environmentally sustainable (e.g. fair trade or organic produce). This could also come from recurring payments aligned with shared goals (e.g. solar as a service, or shared efficiency savings).

Earlier research and market development efforts have assessed the relationship between asset owners and asset managers as an area to explicitly price impact (see Bouri et al., 2011). A primary concern of these efforts has been to align the incentives of an asset manager with an asset owner's goals. To eliminate any conflicts of interest, efforts have

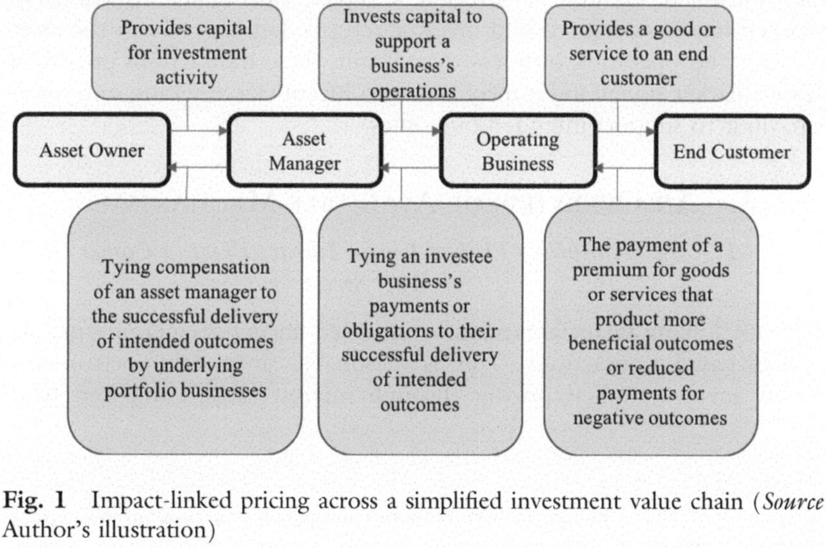

Fig. 1 Impact-linked pricing across a simplified investment value chain (*Source* Author's illustration)

focused on managing the risk of drifting away from intended goals, when opportunities present themselves that are financially lucrative but not mission-aligned (Armeni, 2016). Linking asset manager compensation to impact, usually by adjusting any "carried interest" with non-financial indicators, is an example of linking asset owner returns to impact to manage this risk. However, this approach presents clear limitations. By focusing on the relationship between asset owners and asset managers, it only indirectly addresses operating businesses' actual behaviours where intended impacts are produced. The relationship between asset managers and operating businesses is a key relationship in the value chain. This is the area in the value chain that directly resources what goods and services are produced, how they are produced, and to whom they are provided.

Although there is a growing level of relevant market activity between asset managers and operating businesses explored here, these are not examples of straightforward concessionary financing.[1] Such concessions are usually made at the start of an investment transaction and do not necessarily involve the pricing of observed impacts. This could be defined as implicitly pricing impact, where financial return is varied based on assumed impact, and that relationship may be unquantified or unknown to an operating business. The mechanisms examined below all involve an explicit link between financial returns and intended impacts. This link is explicit because it involves a direct, quantifiable relationship between impacts achieved and investor returns, known to both the asset manager and operating business. As a result, these transactions provide a clearer market signal and a mechanism to incentivize ongoing enterprise behaviour to support intended outcomes.

3 An Overview of Available Mechanisms

3.1 Sustainability-Linked Loans: Impact Pricing Comes to Wall Street

Explicitly linking financial returns to intended impact is emerging mainly in debt-based transactions. This is reasonable since debt instruments already involve explicit pricing through interest rates, compared to a

[1] Where favourable terms might be provided to an operating business on the basis of its expected impacts.

reliance on future valuations and appreciation in equity-based investments. Debt instruments already involve contractual monitoring and behavioural covenants to restrict borrowers' activity. They provide fruitful ground for introducing a link between interest rates and social and environmental impacts while being relatively consistent with existing market norms. A Sustainability-Linked Loan (SLL) is defined as "any type of loan instruments and/or contingent facilities... which incentivize the borrower's achievement of ambitious, predetermined sustainability performance objectives" (LTSA, 2019). Under this definition, all of the core characteristics of impact investing are in place, including an intention of the investor and operating business to generate a positive impact, an expectation of financial return, and impact measurement (*Core Characteristics of Impact Investing*, 2019). Nonetheless, this activity takes place in distinctly mainstream, commercial settings. The first reported instance of a SLL was in 2017, with a EUR 1 billion syndicated revolving credit facility for Royal Philips, a Dutch health technology firm. The facility, arranged by ING with sixteen participating lenders, has an interest rate margin that reduces with year-on-year improvements in Environmental, Social, and Governance (ESG) scores, currently assessed by Sustainalytics (Royal Philips, 2017). From this initial deal, there has been substantial growth, with total reported issuance of US 62.4 billion in 2019, reported by Bloomberg (Poh, 2019b).

Sustainability-Linked Loans are distinct from other forms of sustainable finance, such as green bonds. Green bonds are typically defined by having a dedicated use of proceeds related to environmental impact, such as new clean energy generation or transit development. SLLs are more flexible as the use of proceeds isn't tied to a specific use, but are used for general purposes with incentives tied to agreed performance targets. This makes the tool more open to sectors and industries that are less likely to qualify for green bond issuance. That flexibility can be a positive characteristic by providing more room for adaptation in how goals are achieved. For example, over the lifetime of a loan, new or existing technologies might improve to the point of making previously unavailable options viable and effective. This openness to sectors is already being demonstrated, with examples active in manufacturing, food processing, housing, education, airlines, and storage industries (Poh, 2019c; *The Economist*, 2020; Virmani, 2019).

As of mid-2020, Europe has been the most active market for SLLs, with ING and BNP Paribas taking early leadership roles in supporting issuance, which supports their own commitments regarding sustainable financing. Nonetheless, it is far from a uniquely European phenomenon with US examples including Prologis receiving a US $3.5 billion Line of Credit with a margin reduction based on the achievement of annual sustainability benchmarks (Prologis, 2019). In Canada, the first SLL was struck between BMO and Maple Leaf Foods in 2019, using a variety of measures on water use, material waste, and electricity consumption as targets. This deal was quickly followed by other Canadian deals with WSP Global and Brookfield Renewable Energy Partners (BMO Financial, 2019; BNP Paribas, 2020; WSP, 2020).

The growth in SLLs should attract scrutiny on whether they provide strong enough incentives or ambitious targets to support corporate behaviour change. While full disclosure of terms is rare, existing coverage suggests that interest rate discounts for the successful achievement of targets in an SLL have hovered around 5–10 bps, with a low end of 1.25 bps (Poh, 2019a; *The Economist*, 2020). At the other extreme, Enel, which was the first company to issue a Sustainability-Linked Bond, has a penalty of 25 bps for failing to meet their sustainability targets, primarily tied to growing their proportion of renewable power generations (Société Générale, 2019). While these are small percentages, spread across billion-dollar-plus lending facilities, they do provide a clear incentive to focus executive attention.

In an effort to ensure that the integrity of this nascent market is upheld, many of the major loan industry associations have recently published frameworks to guide these deals. These frameworks could help pave the way for wider adoption in the market. The Loan Syndications and Trading Association, based out of New York, has identified four principles that SLLs should follow (LTSA, 2019; Virmani, 2019):

1. A clear relationship between the selected targets embedded in the loan and the borrower's overall sustainability, and social responsibility strategies;
2. Clear and objective target setting that extends beyond what is already being achieved;
3. Reporting on borrower performance against these targets, usually on an annual basis;
4. Require an external review, whether at the target setting or review stages.

In the context of these principles, the relationship between a lead lender and borrower is adjusted. A lender may also need to act as a "Sustainability Coordinator" (sometimes referred to as a Sustainability Structuring Agent) working with the borrower and any syndicate partners to determine targets (including their accompanying measurement and frequency) that are embedded in a loan (Gossin & Lewis, 2019). Focusing on more ambitious target setting, that stretches beyond current achievements, aligns well with the impact investing market's focus on additionality (i.e. ensuring what has occurred wouldn't have happened anyways absent an investment) and provides greater legitimacy to this early market.

Given the need for objective target setting, it is unsurprising that the majority of early SLLs have tied interest rates to environmental indicators, such as clean energy generation or physical waste. This is partly due to more opportunities to measure and access data, which may have been gathered routinely before the introduction of the loan. It is also more likely that industry peer data will be available to help establish baselines and determine what an ambitious goal is in context. Many SLLs have occurred in industries such as utilities or heavy industry that have significant energy and material intensity (and sometimes pair SLLs with green bond financing as a complementary source of capital). Nonetheless, the definition of "sustainability" in SLLs is applied inclusively to a variety of non-environmental targets, which reinforces the flexibility of the tool and framework. For example, WSP, a Canadian professional services firm, has a US $1.2 billion syndicated credit facility for which BNP Paribas acted as the Sustainability Coordinator. Targets included the proportion of its revenues derived from services having a positive environmental impact and the increase in the percentage of women in management positions by the end of 2021. Neither target would generally fit within a green bond framework. Likewise, L&Q, a UK-based housing provider, has a five-year, £100m credit facility with BNP Paribas that includes an interest-rate reduction based on L&Q's ability to support 600 unemployed residents to find and retain employment, in line with their existing "Independent Lives" support programming. The loan facility, which has the option to extend for an additional two years, places a rising floor on this target, such that the number of residents required to be successfully supported increases by 25 for each year (L&Q Group, 2018).

3.2 Impact-Linked Returns in Private Market Impact Investments

Private market investment has been a core area of activity in impact investing, with private debt attracting a large majority of both deal numbers and volume of capital deployed (Hand et al., 2020). Debt is also the area in the market where linking financial returns to impact is gaining the most traction in the private market, although in more varied forms. One such model is the "Social Impact Incentive" (SIINC) designed by the consultancy Roots of Impact. The SIINC provides additional revenues, usually from a third-party donor to an organization for successfully achieving certain impact milestones. A core aim of the SIINC model is to support enterprises where there is a clear trade-off between positive impacts and financial results. This is more often the case for businesses serving bottom-of-the-pyramid customers, where the business would be better off commercially by shifting upmarket. A SIINC can de-risk earlier stage impact investment by providing additional revenues to incent more commercially focused investors into these businesses. They also enable impact-focused investors to drive a long-term business focus on lower-income beneficiaries with the help of donors that provide the additional SIINC payment (Baic et al., 2019; Price, 2016).

In an early example, Clinicas del Azucar, a group of diabetes treatment facilities, received up to US $275,000 over 2.5 years for providing treatment and prevention services to low-income patients. The additional potential revenue, which is being provided by the Swiss development agency SDC and managed by the Inter-American Development Bank, is intended to prove the commercial viability of serving these customers, with the goal to crowd in US $6 to $10 million of additional private investment as part of a $1.6 million pilot across four companies (Pothering, 2017a; Price, 2016).

Another example involves Impact Water, a Ugandan provider of water purification systems for schools, which will receive a US $200,000 bonus payment in a "Social Success Note" from the Rockefeller Foundation. In order to obtain this bonus payment, Impact Water must hit an installation target reaching 1.4 million school children over 5 years. The SIINC is being used in parallel with a $500,000 loan provided by the UBS Foundation, and it is intended to crowd in further commercial financing, while allowing the Rockefeller Foundation to incentivize intended outcomes (Pothering, 2018b). The model could apply in many contexts where trade-offs in delivering goods and services to the neediest customers create perceived risks that scare off commercial investors. Scaling the approach, outcome funds have been considered and put in practice in sectors such as off-grid clean energy at both the enterprise and fund level to create similar incentives (Patton Power, 2020; Roots of Impact, 2018).

Additional models that directly link investor returns to impact, while providing incentives to drive corporate behaviour, are also being tested in the market. In an "impact tranche", investors can agree to accept a lower return if certain impact goals are met, thereby increasing the returns of other equity investors in a deal. This structure allows investors to segment by their individual preferences for risk, return, and impact, while providing an operating business the incentive of lower cost capital to deliver on goals that might fall outside of normal commercial expectations. New Forests, an Australian timberland investor with AUD 3.5 billion in assets under management, set aside $40m of a $300m fund in an impact tranche that was anchored by the David and Lucile Packard Foundation with a $10m equity investment. This tranche is intended to enable New Forests to deliver climate and conservation measures where there isn't yet direct revenue-generation potential such as peatland restoration, and targeted logging bans, going beyond existing sustainability practices (Bank, 2019).

Intended impacts can also be incentivized where there is less of a trade-off between these goals and commercial success. For example, Beneficial Returns, a US-based impact loan fund manager, has made working capital loans to two Mexican social enterprises incorporating impact incentives. Sistema Bibolsa, a provider of biodigesters for farmers, received a $75,000 working capital loan to purchase materials and carry inventory with a fully forgivable final payment if 50,000 new systems are sold in the next five years (Pothering, 2018a). A similar structure has been applied with Ilumexico, a provider of affordable home solar systems in Mexico. Their five-year loan, which will provide working capital for vendor financing to end customers, has a forgivable final payment if 20,000 solar panel installations take place over the next five years (Pothering, 2017b). These targets, which had been self-selected by the enterprises, demonstrate a clear alignment between the asset manager and operating business. The impacts are embedded in the underlying products' sale and use, creating a shared understanding that additional sales success also contributes to the investor's desired impact goals. Likewise, revenue-loans (explored in greater detail in the case study below) are an example of an investment model where a tight connection between intended impacts and commercial success can support shared goals and aligned incentives.

3.3 An Impact-Linked Deal in Practice: Being BOLD

To help further illustrate the mechanics of impact-linked pricing and how they could be replicated, consider the case of Xceptional and their Beneficial Outcomes Linked Debt (BOLD) loan. The Impact Investment Group (IIG), an Australian Impact Fund Manager, developed the BOLD contract as a mechanism to incentivize an ongoing focus on impact while providing founder-friendly financing.

The first BOLD contract was developed to support Xceptional, an Australian technology platform founded in 2017. Xceptional operates as a social enterprise supporting people on the autism spectrum to gain employment in specialized roles in IT and software development. They allow job seekers to demonstrate their strengths through activity-based assessments rather than formats such as interviews, which can be challenging for people on the autism spectrum. The founder, Mike Tozer, is a mission-driven entrepreneur who was seeking growth capital to address strong employer interest in employee placements and grow Xceptional's core staffing team. He also wanted to engage investors that shared a commitment to effective job placements as a key indicator of success (Palmer-Derrien, 2019).

The loan was signed in October 2019 and was invested in by IIG's Catalyst Fund alongside co-investors Tripple, the Community Impact Fund, the Disability Impact Fund, and the Snow Foundation (Williams, 2019).

The BOLD instrument combines the key features of a revenue-loan with impact-linked repayments. A revenue-loan has repayments that are made as a share of revenues, instead of a fixed interest rate. Typically, a specific return on capital (e.g. 1.5× the original loan) is determined, and the loan is considered repaid when that specific return amount is reached. Revenue-loans are a flexible tool that can be attractive for social enterprises. Since they are self-liquidating, revenue-loans don't rely on a future liquidity event such as an acquisition, which is less likely for such niche social enterprises. As well, because repayments vary with revenue they don't create a fixed cash-drag like a conventional amortizing loan, behaving more as quasi-equity on a balance sheet by relying on a business's operating performance. As a debt instrument, they don't rely on the sale of an equity stake, which also makes the instrument a practical investment tool for non-profits and co-ops who cannot sell equity shares.

The BOLD financing for Xceptional uses impact-linked repayments to create a financial incentive to achieve positive impact aligned with the business's mission, as the loan amount is reduced based on their impact. The faster that Xceptional grows, the sooner the loan is repaid, increasing their investors' Internal Rate of Return. The greater their success at delivering job placements, the more the amount owed is reduced. In the base case, Xceptional is expected to repay their BOLD loan in 4–4.5 years, delivering an IRR between 5 and 15% depending on their impact. A maximum term is set for 10 years. The calculation and adjustment of their loan based on impact goes as follows (Impact Investment Group, 2019):

After the Repayment Holiday, which is a grace period at the loan start where no cash payments are due, Xceptional begins repayment with a negotiated share of revenue. They will continue to repay until the Return Amount is reached. The Return Amount is defined as "A" as follows:

$$A = (B \times C) - D$$

Return Amount (A)	The amount investors can receive back from their investment in dollars.
Principal Amount (B)	The amount originally loaned in dollars.
Multiplier (C)	The figure, absent any adjust which would determine the Return Amount (e.g. 1.5× the Principal Amount, 2.0× the Principal Amount, etc.). This is determined by commercial negotiation.
Impact Adjustment Amount (D)	A variable, expressed in dollars, determined by the degree of Impact, which reduces the maximum return. This creates the incentive, where

$$D = (E - F) \times G$$

Impact Metric (E)	The quantitative value chosen to represent a positive impact. Care is needed to guard against perverse incentives and ensure that goals shared by both the investor and borrower are being rewarded. In the Xceptional BOLD example, this is "people placed in jobs, who are also happy with their role", as determined through a wellbeing survey. Including satisfaction is meant to protect against placements for individuals with autism that aren't suitable.
Minimum Impact Level (F)	A baseline for success of the same impact metric. This is so the instrument incentivizes success beyond this level.
Impact Value (G)	This is the dollar value associated with each instance of impact.

By providing an investment instrument that is flexible and accessible to different types of organizations (including for-profits and non-profits), while incentivizing impact through explicit impact pricing, the BOLD contract combines two areas of innovative activity in impact investing.

4 Summary and Comparison of Presented Mechanisms

So far, a variety of impact-linked debt instruments including Sustainability-Linked Loans, Social Impact Incentives, Beneficial Outcomes Linked Debt, and other variants have been covered. Before turning to a discussion of the theoretical connections between these mechanisms, the Table 1 provides a summary of the basic characteristics of these tools.

Table 1 Comparison of presented investment tools

Feature	*Sustainability-Linked Loans (SLLs)*	*Beneficial Outcomes Linked Debt (BOLD)*	*Social Impact Incentive (SIINC)*	*Loan with payment forgiveness*
Codified link between impact and return	Link is explicitly codified in transaction terms			
Positive or negative incentive for operating business	Both, generally positive	Positive		
Maturity of tool	More mature with recurrent activity	Least mature with bespoke private transactions still emerging		
Data source for impact measures	ESG scores or internal measures	Reliant on agreed, usually company produced measures		
Third-Party Involvement	Yes, often a validator	No	Yes, donor	No
Continuous or lump sum benefit	Continuous		Lump-Sum	
Benefit during or at end	During		At end	

5 Discussion

5.1 Common Foundations

Despite varied applications, these examples of impact-linked returns (and their buffet of acronyms) share some common theoretical underpinning. These tools operate at different scales and in different parts of the capital market, but all are involved in bringing previously less-priced characteristics of an operating business's performance into their financing in explicit terms. This can be understood as a process of internalizing what were previously considered externalities to a business. They might be desirable positive externalities, such as the successful resident employment of L&G, or negative externalities being avoided, such as the waste and water reductions by Maple Leaf Foods. Whether approached from the lens of the conventional capital markets or from an impact investor's viewpoint, there is a legitimate basis for providing an operating business a lower cost of capital based on internalizing these factors.

From a more conventional perspective, non-financial factors such as Environmental, Social, and Governance (ESG) risks are increasingly understood as material risk factors that influence asset pricing and valuation. As the number of investors with explicit "Socially Responsible Investment" mandates grows, the cost of capital for so-called sin stocks (e.g. alcohol, tobacco, and pornography) and those producing negative externalities (e.g. fossil fuels) can increase. Through market segmentation and the expression of investor preferences, more norm-constrained investors will refuse to hold certain investments or participate in specific loan syndications, reducing the risk-sharing benefit of other investors and correspondingly reducing the supply of available capital at a cost to the company (Fama & French, 2007). This has been demonstrated to be most pronounced for sin stocks, as these industry sectors are most "negatively screened" by institutional investors that have introduced responsible investment practices (El Ghoul et al., 2011; Hong & Kacperczyk, 2009). Beyond individual sectors, the costs of both equity and debt capital have shown to vary with the environmental risk profile of their firm. This is the result of multiple factors, including the impacts of the diversification of ownership described above, as fewer bank lenders and investors participate in the most at-risk sectors, as well as from additional risk premiums applied by investors (Bauer & Hann, 2010; Cai et al., 2016; Chava, 2014).

Generalizing further beyond just the "Environment" in "ESG", research has demonstrated that CSR scores do have an independent effect, albeit relatively small, on equity costs in public markets (Friede et al., 2015). Results show that the introduction of voluntary non-financial disclosures of CSR activities contributes to reductions in subsequent equity financing costs, and that the best scoring companies can arrange lower cost capital (Dhaliwal et al., 2011; El Ghoul et al., 2011). Additional analysis relying on data provided by Sustainalytics, the same third-party ESG rating agency involved in the very first SLL to Royal Phillips, demonstrated that changes to ESG ratings are associated with a subsequent repricing in Canadian markets (Sodjahin et al., 2018). ESG ratings have also been analysed with regard to bank loans, with socially irresponsible firms encountering a 7–18 bps increase in borrowing costs, most in evidence with unsecure loans (Goss & Roberts, 2011). It is notable that this range is similar to that observed in SLLs and

Enel's Sustainability-Linked Bond described above. These results, which are directionally similar across different sectors and equity and debt markets, are all consistent with investors "re-pricing" their investments by reducing the risk premium associated with the investment as overall investor demand increases.

While the evidence above describes how non-financial factors are being incorporated into public market asset pricing in general, it is worth noting the similarities and differences to the Sustainability-Linked Loans and private market instruments covered here. The evidence demonstrates that non-financial factors affect pricing most deeply in sectors at the extremes of social acceptability (Hong & Kacperczyk, 2009). While research supports that anti-social and anti-environmental behaviour has a cost over time, this may not produce a consistent signal regarding corporate behaviour. Longitudinal reviews have shown that the influence of these non-financial factors on firm equity costs vary substantially over time (Girerd-Potin et al., 2014). Sustainability-Linked Loans, in directly adjusting a firm's cost of debt financing, are consistent with investors and lenders generally re-pricing risk based on company-specific or sector behaviour.[2] At the same time, SLLs make the mechanism and pricing of intended outcomes explicit between the asset manager and operating business, allowing applications outside of the most socially or environmentally damaging firms. Further, while the evidence discussed demonstrates a relationship between non-financial performance and asset pricing, it is important to note that in a conventional financial market these non-financial risks are presumably being analysed as a means to support superior financial performance.

Distinctly, within an impact investing framework, intended impacts are desired intrinsically. Impact investors are expected to value impacts at different amounts. An investor might value positive impact by considerably more than the actual effect that these behaviours will have on financial performance. Impact investors that receive impact-linked returns, regardless of the instrument used, compensate the operating business for delivering a desired outcome, while concurrently incentivizing the business to achieve those shared goals. In this way, investors are using a financial means to achieve non-financial end goals. Both a conventional

[2] It is perhaps unsurprising that proponents have therefore suggested that banks involved in such loans should carry a lower regulatory cost of capital for such lending (Thomä et al., 2018).

and impact investing framework can be understood as internalizing positive or negative externalities, with differences emerging as to why that internalization is itself desirable.

5.2 *Challenges and Opportunities for Deeper Adoption*

All instruments examined here, whether on a large or small scale, seek to attach value to objective measures of desired impact. Given this reliance on clear, refutable metrics, there will be a need to support organizations' capacity to produce quality information and reporting needed to justify substantial incentives. Many smaller-scale companies will not have the internal systems to provide data on a longitudinal basis. Even among larger public companies, outside of ESG leaders, there is likely to be a relative scarcity of robust non-financial reporting. Even third-party, independent ESG ratings, which have provided a clear basis for instruments such as Sustainability-Linked Loans, have demonstrated significant divergence in ratings based on their individual scopes and rating categories (Berg et al., 2020).

Rather than seeking to introduce new and additional measures, a potential area of opportunity is introducing impact-linked pricing against existing measures that are already gathered for core business purposes (e.g. revenue from certain activity types). Lower associated incentives could be initially applied as a margin of safety to compensate for the risk that the measures may not adequately or fully capture the intended impact. This approach could establish the framework and build needed relationships with operating businesses to transition to more robust measures over time. It also recognizes that the most relevant priorities for positive impact will vary substantially between industries, which will inhibit standardization. Impact-linked return instruments will also need periodic reporting. Early efforts suggest including contractual protections to allow for the retroactive recovery of any financial difference, perhaps with additional penalties, if there is incorrect reporting under any impact targets (Virmani, 2019).

The design of intended impact metrics in impact-linked transactions needs careful attention to maintain operating business flexibility, while avoiding perverse incentives. Measures in impact-linked deals that are too broadly defined, perhaps around a customer group or product type, can lead to perverse incentives by privileging easier to serve clients at the expense of intended beneficiaries. This risk, sometimes referred to as "creaming" (as in skimming the cream from the top), has been well discussed with regard to Pay-for-Success transactions as another (non-debt) type of impact-linked investment structure (Giantris & Pinakiewicz, 2013; McGahey & Willis, 2017). While Pay-for-Success typically attaches a greater proportion of investment value to outcomes than the debt-based structures discussed, impact-linked debts create similar questions about incentives. Poorly designed measures could focus corporate attention on delivery against that metric, while ultimately distracting from the transaction's truly intended goals. This is especially relevant where the intended impacts might not be directly embedded in the sale of a product or service (as an output), but require additional consumer behaviour change (the intended outcome). For example, an investor looking to support health improvement through the use of clean cookstoves is ultimately looking for consumer behaviour (the ongoing use of the cleaner cooking method), which might receive less ongoing support from a clean cookstove seller if they are purely incentivized to sell more units or expand sales geographically.

To balance rigour with rightsizing requirements for operating businesses, it will be critical to examine what intended outcomes are truly core to a business's mission and be comfortable with "robust-enough" solutions. These design efforts can also serve as an opportunity to explore the use of alternative data that may be valuable in a business's operation, regardless of the impact-linked investment. For example, 60 Decibel's Lean Data approach to impact measurement relies on customer data surveys collected accessibly through mobile devices. This method supports and builds a clear understanding of impact on end customers while providing valuable insights into businesses regarding their product or services used in the field (Baic et al., 2019).

Efforts to create impact-linked pricing in investments can ultimately strengthen the relationship and trust between the asset manager and investee operating business. This will require meaningful buy-in from the investee enterprise, as effort needs to be invested in the upfront design of measurement systems and regular internal effort to produce reporting. Even businesses that have not traditionally seen themselves as mission-driven companies would need to focus more on planning and impact management. This will be particularly important to deliver genuine alignment to set targets that go beyond existing achievements, creating greater additionality in goals. Alongside the work of individual practitioners, existing efforts to support better impact management by both large and small companies, such as the B Impact Assessment and the Impact Management Project, will also support the market conditions needed for impact-linked deals to be repeated and become more commonplace.

6 Conclusion

As examined here through various tools, the use of impact-linked returns has the potential to support many goals in impact investing. It provides avenues to incentivize positive outcomes through organizational behaviour at both large-scale corporations, which have often been seen as outside the sphere of impact investing, as well as the mission-driven businesses and social enterprises that have been near the heart of this market. These approaches provide a useful basis to see how impact investing can be approached with integrity even within mainstream markets. No less important, through these instruments' actual mechanics, they can explicitly focus on the delivery of net new benefits and additionality. Given this potential, opportunities to support this emergent area's continued growth merit attention. By using measures that already carry meaning to investee businesses for new impact-linked transactions, focusing efforts upfront around an investee business's use of value-adding data, and supporting broader industry efforts around impact management, there are opportunities to apply such investments with both large and small businesses.

As this chapter has explored, investments with impact-linked returns have emerged in both the mainstream capital markets at multi-billion dollar scales down to small scale social enterprise loans in private markets in the tens of thousands of dollars. These practices are still relatively early in the market but hold meaningful potential to reward the delivery of positive impacts and to build shared norms and practices between disparate parts of the market. Despite varied applications, different investment tools are supported by strong theoretical similarities. The emergence of explicit pricing of impact across a variety of instruments should be expected to continue to grow and mainstream in parallel as impact measurement and management practices also mature. Impact-linked tools will ultimately be of strong benefit to impact investing practitioners seeking more and better options to manage the trade-offs, between risk, return, and impact.

References

Armeni, A. (2016). *Tying fund manager compensation to impact outcomes*. Transform Finance Investor Network. https://static1.squarespace.com/static/54cfca5be4b06d2d0d7c0f1d/t/57e285d1bebafb329d4a71fa/1474463185846/TFIN+Issue+Brief+-+Tying+Carry+to+Impact+2016-09-12+v3.pdf.

Baic, A., Struewer, B., Doerner, W., Henderson, B., Maennig, M., Kammerer, L., Baffioni, P., & Montgomery, B. (2019). *Accelerating impact-linked finance*. Roots of Impact. https://www.roots-of-impact.org/wp-content/uploads/2019/01/Roots-of-Impact-BCG-Accelerating-Impact-Linked-Finance-2019.pdf.

Bank, D. (2019, April 30). Taking an 'impact tranche,' Packard Foundation pushes forest fund beyond business as usual. *ImpactAlpha*. https://impactalpha.com/taking-an-impact-tranche-packard-foundation-pushes-forest-fund-beyond-business-as-usual/.

Bauer, R., & Hann, D. (2010). *Corporate environmental management and credit risk* (SSRN Scholarly Paper ID 1660470). Social Science Research Network. https://doi.org/10.2139/ssrn.1660470.

Berg, F., Kölbel, J. F., & Rigobon, R. (2020). *Aggregate confusion: The divergence of ESG ratings* (SSRN Scholarly Paper ID 3438533). Social Science Research Network. https://doi.org/10.2139/ssrn.3438533.

BMO Financial. (2019, December 11). *Maple leaf foods and BMO capital markets enter into first sustainability-linked loan in Canada—Dec 11, 2019*. https://newsroom.bmo.com/2019-12-11-Maple-Leaf-Foods-and-BMO-Capital-Markets-enter-into-First-Sustainability-Linked-Loan-in-Canada.

BNP Paribas. (2020, June 1). *BNP Paribas closes sustainability-linked RCF with Brookfield renewable partners*. GlobeNewswire News Room. http://www.globenewswire.com/news-release/2020/01/06/1966554/0/en/BNP-Paribas-Closes-Sustainability-Linked-RCF-with-Brookfield-Renewable-Partners.html.

Bouri, A., Lankester, K., Leung, G., Meyer, M., Ragin, Jr., L., Schmidlapp, C., Schmidlapp, C., & Shah, S. (2011). *Impact-based incentive structures: Aligning fund manager compensation with social and environmental performance*. The Global Impact Investing Network. https://thegiin.org/research/publication/impact-based-incentive-structures-aligning-fund-manager-compensation-with-soci.

Cai, L., Cui, J., & Jo, H. (2016). Corporate environmental responsibility and firm risk. *Journal of Business Ethics, 139*(3), 563–594.

Chava, S. (2014). Environmental externalities and cost of capital. *Management Science, 60*(9), 2223–2247.

Core Characteristics of Impact Investing. (2019). Global Impact Investing Network. https://thegiin.org/characteristics.

Dhaliwal, D. S., Li, O. Z., Tsang, A., & Yang, Y. G. (2011). Voluntary nonfinancial disclosure and the cost of equity capital: The initiation of corporate social responsibility reporting. *The Accounting Review, 86*(1), 59–100. JSTOR.

El Ghoul, S., Guedhami, O., Kwok, C. C. Y., & Mishra, D. R. (2011). Does corporate social responsibility affect the cost of capital? *Journal of Banking & Finance, 35*(9), 2388–2406. https://doi.org/10.1016/j.jbankfin.2011.02.007

Fama, E. F., & French, K. R. (2007). Disagreement, tastes, and asset prices. *Journal of Financial Economics, 83*(3), 667–689. https://doi.org/10.1016/j.jfineco.2006.01.003

Freireich, J., & Fulton, K. (2009). *Investing for social and environmental impact*. Monitor Institute. https://www2.deloitte.com/content/dam/Deloitte/global/Documents/Financial-Services/gx-fsi-monitor-Investing-for-Social-and-Environmental-Impact-2009.pdf.

Friede, G., Busch, T., & Bassen, A. (2015). ESG and financial performance: Aggregated evidence from more than 2000 empirical studies. *Journal of Sustainable Finance & Investment, 5*(4), 210–233. https://doi.org/10.1080/20430795.2015.1118917

Giantris, K., & Pinakiewicz, B. (2013). Pay for success: Understanding the risk trade-offs. *Community Development Investment Review, 9*(1), 35–39.

Girerd-Potin, I., Jimenez-Garcès, S., & Louvet, P. (2014). Which dimensions of social responsibility concern financial investors? *Journal of Business Ethics, 121*(4), 559–576. JSTOR.

Goss, A., & Roberts, G. S. (2011). The impact of corporate social responsibility on the cost of bank loans. *Journal of Banking & Finance, 35*(7), 1794–1810. https://doi.org/10.1016/j.jbankfin.2010.12.002

Gossin, A., & Lewis, R. J. (2019). *Sustainability-linked loans: Financing the green transition*. https://www.lsta.org/content/sustainability-linked-loans-financing-the-green-transition/.

Hand, D., Dithrich, H., Sunderji, S., & Nova, N. (2020). *2020 Annual impact investor survey*. The Global Impact Investing Network. https://thegiin.org/research/publication/impinv-survey-2020.

Hong, H., & Kacperczyk, M. (2009). The price of sin: The effects of social norms on markets. *Journal of Financial Economics, 93*(1), 15–36. https://doi.org/10.1016/j.jfineco.2008.09.001

Impact Investment Group. (2019). *The BOLD contract*. http://www.impact-group.com.au/wp-content/uploads/2019/11/IIG-BOLD-Contract-Explainer.pdf.

L&Q Group. (2018, June 26). *L&Q completes landmark £100 million "positive incentive loan" with BNP Paribas*. https://www.lqgroup.org.uk/about/media-centre/news/details/111.

LTSA. (2019). *Sustainability Linked Loan Principles (SLLP)*. Loan Syndications and Trading Association. https://www.lsta.org/content/sustainability-linked-loan-principles-sllp/.

McGahey, R., & Willis, M. (2017). The promise and reality of social impact bonds. In *What matters: Investing in results to build strong, vibrant communities* (pp. 420–427). Federal Reserve Bank of San Francisco and Nonprofit Finance Fund.

Palmer-Derrien, S. (2019, November 25). Australia's new performance-based, debt funding facility invests $600,000 in Xceptional. *SmartCompany*. https://www.smartcompany.com.au/startupsmart/news/australias-new-performance-based-debt-funding-facility-invests-600000-in-xceptional/.

Patton Power, A. (2020, July 7). Incentives for driving impact in deal and fund structures. *ImpactAlpha*. https://impactalpha.com/incentives-for-driving-impact-in-deal-and-fund-structures/.

Poh, J. (2019a, March 6). Banks can't afford to ignore the $23 trillion market for doing good. *Bloomberg.Com*. https://www.bloomberg.com/news/articles/2019-03-06/banks-can-t-afford-to-ignore-the-23-trillion-market-for-doing-good.

Poh, J. (2019b, October 16). ESG debt: A user's guide to ever-growing menu of bonds and loans. *Bloomberg.Com*. https://www.bloomberg.com/news/articles/2019-10-16/esg-debt-a-user-s-guide-to-ever-growing-menu-of-bonds-and-loans.

Poh, J. (2019c, November 13). How companies get cheaper loans for doing social good. *Bloomberg Professional Services*. https://www.bloomberg.com/professional/blog/how-companies-get-cheaper-loans-for-doing-social-good/.

Pothering, J. (2017a, June 15). "Social impact incentives" introduced in Mexico and Honduras. *ImpactAlpha*. https://impactalpha.com/social-impact-incentives-introduced-in-mexico-and-honduras-bf0ca2621bf3/.

Pothering, J. (2017b, September 16). Beneficial returns includes impact incentives in loan to Iluméxico. *ImpactAlpha*. https://impactalpha.com/beneficial-returns-includes-impact-incentives-in-loan-to-ilumexico/.

Pothering, J. (2018a, March 2). Sistema Biobolsa gets working capital to bring biodigesters to smallholder farmers. *ImpactAlpha*. https://impactalpha.com/sistema-biobolsa-gets-working-capital-to-bring-biodigesters-to-smallholder-farmers-8fc34ec2b1c/.

Pothering, J. (2018b, April 23). Rockefeller and UBS Optimus test pay-for-success model for water purification. *ImpactAlpha*. https://impactalpha.com/rockefeller-and-ubs-optimus-test-pay-for-success-model-for-water-purification/.

Price, D. (2016, January 19). Social impact incentives aim to tilt businesses toward the needs of the poor. *ImpactAlpha*. https://impactalpha.com/social-impact-incentives-aim-to-tilt-businesses-toward-the-needs-of-the-poor-a64c70f99142/.

Prologis. (2019, January 16). *Prologis recasts and upsizes $3.5 billion global line of credit*. https://www.prnewswire.com/news-releases/prologis-recasts-and-upsizes-3-5-billion-global-line-of-credit-300779678.html.

Roots of Impact. (2018). *Blueprint for an outcomes fund in off-grid clean energy*. Roots of Impact. https://www.roots-of-impact.org/wp-content/uploads/2018/12/Roots-of-Impact_Blueprint-for-an-Outcomes-Fund_FINAL.pdf.

Royal Philips. (2017, April 19). *Philips couples sustainability performance to interest rate of its new EUR 1 billion revolving credit facility*. Philips. https://www.philips.com/a-w/about/news/archive/standard/news/press/2017/20170419-philips-couples-sustainability-performance-to-interest-rate-of-its-new-eur-1-billion-revolving-credit-facility.html.

Société Générale. (2019, September 19). *Enel electrifies sustainability market with inaugural green-linked bond and swap*. Société Générale. https://wholesale.banking.societegenerale.com/en/about/news-press-room/news-details/news/enel-electrifies-sustainability-market-with-inaugural-green-linked-bond-and-swap/.

Sodjahin, A., Champagne, C., & Coggins, F. (2018). Are changes in extra-financial ratings a (un)sustainable source of abnormal returns? *Academy of Accounting and Financial Studies Journal, 22*(1), 1B–. Gale Academic OneFile.

The Economist. (2020, February 15). Green paper; Sustainability-linked debt. *The Economist, 434*(9181), 65(US). Gale Academic OneFile.

Thomä, J., Caldecott, B., & Ralite, S. (2018). *Sustainability improvement loans*. 2 Degree Investing Initiative. https://2degrees-investing.org/wp-content/uploads/2019/09/SI-paper_v8.pdf.

Virmani, T. (2019, November 13). *The rise of sustainability linked loans*. LSTA. https://www.lsta.org/news-resources/the-rise-of-sustainability-linked-loans/.

Williams, W. (2019, December 4). Bold new way to invest for social change | PBA. *Pro Bono Australia*. https://probonoaustralia.com.au/news/2019/12/bold-new-way-to-invest-for-social-change/.

WSP. (2020, February 4). *WSP becomes the first professional services firm to sign sustainability-linked syndicated credit facility in the Americas*. https://www.wsp.com/en-GL/investors/press-releases/details/WSP-Becomes-the-First-Professional-Services-Firm-to-Sign-SustainabilityLinked-Syndicated-Credit-Facility-in-the-Americas/1979420/2020.

A University Model of Social Finance: Reflections on the University of Edinburgh's Social Investment Fund

Dave Gorman and Julia Qermezi Huang

1 Introduction

Universities are frequently seen as organizations with potential to generate positive impact through the manner in which they operate, given their knowledge base, organizational scale, and longevity (Barnett, 2018). As heterarchical organizations (Stark, 2000) with "enduring institutional complexity" (Kraatz & Block, 2008), universities pursue multiple purposes and embody multiple values, a multiplicity that can be (but is rarely) reflected in the investment program of their endowments (Dyer et al., 2020; Humphreys et al., 2012). Additionally, many universities are key anchor institutions for their local areas, by providing knowledge, skills, and employment and supporting local economic activity (Oxford Economics, 2017). While the literature contains a number of studies

D. Gorman (✉)
Department for Social Responsibility and Sustainability,
University of Edinburgh, Edinburgh, UK
e-mail: dave.gorman@ed.ac.uk

J. Q. Huang
School of Social and Political Science, University of Edinburgh, Edinburgh, UK
e-mail: juli.huang@ed.ac.uk

T. Walker et al. (eds.), *Innovations in Social Finance*,
https://doi.org/10.1007/978-3-030-72535-8_8

about ethical investment funds, or the performance and governance of university endowments, or notions of the social responsibility of universities in their locales, little is known about how these themes might interconnect. The potential for universities to leverage their endowments (or parts of them) to invest in positive social impact for the communities in which they are embedded is an under-recognized opportunity.

In this chapter, we suggest that a university model of social finance (as exemplified by the case presented here) is not only a distinct model, but it also provides insights relevant to mainstream social finance and university sustainability agendas. First, a review of the literature on social investments and universities in the context of the United Kingdom and the United States is examined. Then, a case study, which examines the University of Edinburgh's Social Investment Fund (SIF), is assessed in detail. The study furthermore summarizes the experience of developing the Edinburgh fund and compares it to existing good practice in a US/UK context, from which we suggest a series of innovations of relevance to universities considering making social investments. Finally, a discussion is raised on the prospects for such a model, as well as its limitations, including future opportunities and risks for the fund, such as scaling up, impact measurement, organizational change, and external shocks like the unforeseen COVID-19 outbreak.

2 University Social Investments, in Historical and Institutional Context

Socially oriented organizations, such as universities and churches, were among the first innovators in institutional ethical investing. The first known examples of ethical investment funds were led by churches and appeared in the mid-1960s in Sweden and in the early-1970s in the United States (Kreander et al., 2004). In the United Kingdom, "religious groups were to the fore in the development of the social investment movement" (Gray et al., 1996: p. 246). University and college endowments in the United States led innovations in social and environmental investment in the 1960s and 1970s in response to campaigns for more responsible endowment management, often driven by the advocacy of diverse stakeholder groups such as students, faculty, and community members (Humphreys et al., 2012). Yet despite their early pioneering role, endowments and church ethical funds are not represented today among industry best practice in the impact investment sector. There is little formal understanding of the values, decision-making processes, and management structures of these university (and church) funds, or of how these early innovations are related to present-day initiatives of universities to render their endowments more responsible. While universities and churches are different institutions with disparate objectives, what they possess in common is their institutional complexity and pursuit of multiple organizational logics and values, such as those of society and economy, or religion and finance. Such organizations have long navigated a multiplicity of logics and values. Unlike faith-based organizations, universities operate endowments with complex stakeholder relations, which include students, faculty, administrators, trustees, donors, alumni, community groups, and civil society organizations, all exerting competing stakes and claims on the investments' implications.

In subsequent decades, the circumstances that led to the possibility of universities being impact investors in contemporary markets are tied to wider political and ideological shifts. In the United States and the United Kingdom, higher education was integrated to varying degrees into the neoliberal capitalist economy from the 1990s (Vernon, 2018). The defunding of public universities, the introduction of student fees, the management of scholarship by metrics, and other policies and practices of marketization influence how universities deliver a public service for the common good (Maisuria & Cole, 2017). Initiatives like the Social Investment Fund (SIF) arise within this context of the marketization of higher education institutions, the increase of university assets under investment, and the expectations of students and staff for such investments to be responsible (Bergman, 2018). In the broadest sense, initiatives such as SIF invoke the general question of what universities are for and to what extent it is justified for them to undertake these activities. Yet university endowments possess more than $400 billion in combined assets under management in the United States (Ryan & Marsicano, 2020) and at least $21 billion in the United Kingdom (authors' estimate).

Within this context, universities position themselves as both highly connected and enmeshed in their local area, and concerned with the grand challenges of the day (Barnett, 2018) such as poverty or climate change. Following over a decade of UK government spending cuts after the financial crisis of 2008, local services are much smaller, less coordinated, and possess diminishing ability to offer the support available ten years ago. University involvement in social investments does raise the challenge of whether and to what extent a university can and should plan a role in meeting social needs, what frameworks should guide its activities in this area, and how to avoid the danger of attempting to replace services that should be provided by the government. The discussions included in this chapter are situated within these broader questions.

The 1980s–1990s restructuring of the relationship between the public, private, and civil society sectors also led to the proliferation of social enterprises—businesses that pursue social good while also engaging in trading activities—and thus also the introduction of social impact investment. Social enterprises emerged from a variety of directions: non-profits adding income-generating initiatives (Alexander, 2010; Gunn, 2004), corporations developing social responsibility (CSR) agendas and socially focused spin-offs (Rajak, 2011), and newly formed organizations entwining multiple sets of value(s) in their core business models (Cross & Street, 2004; Huang, 2020).

Social impact investment, as a set of vehicles for financing social enterprises, is "a relatively new umbrella term for monetary investment in both emerging and developed markets that aims to integrate the creation of positive social or environmental impact with financial return on capital" (Andreu, 2018: p. 708). It invokes the dual (or triple) creation of financial value with social value (and environmental value), invests finance with ethical discourses, and draws affective solidarities with disadvantaged others. The explicit emphasis on multiple regimes of worth (or, heterarchies) and multiple criteria for evaluating potential investments, and measuring their impacts, is a defining feature of a range of social enterprises and impact investors. As "heterarchical firms" (Stark, 2000), enterprises and investment firms self-organize around competing and coexisting value systems, which add complexity to the meaning of success. While this chapter focuses on what is specific about a *university* model of social investment, the burgeoning literature examines what the meaning of social value becomes when linked to the pursuit of profit in general (Andreu, 2018; Barman, 2016; Huang, 2020; Ortner, 2017).

A university is no stranger to heterarchical modes of operation. Universities are said to pursue the triple mission of research (knowledge creation), teaching (knowledge dissemination and education), and the third mission (knowledge exchange and impact); all delivered alongside revenue streams that span public funds, customer fees, investment returns, and other commercial profits. The vaguely formulated third mission is generally understood in terms of the commercialization of knowledge, such as technology transfer, patents, and spin-off companies (Arocena et al., 2018), but it is also increasingly becoming associated with social innovation activities (Bayuo et al., 2020). Despite a growing literature on university engagement with social innovation, little attention is placed on the range or impact of these activities. In particular, universities' involvement in social finance (and the institutional structures and processes required to pursue these activities) remains unaddressed.

While university social responsibility (USR) is defined as "a philosophy of a university to use an ethical approach to develop and engage with the local and global community in order to sustain the social, ecological, environmental, technical, and economic development" (Shu-Hsiang et al., 2015), the emerging literature on USR focuses primarily on the conduct of internal operational practices. Based on websites and annual-report information, top global universities communicate their social responsibility through organizational governance (accountability, transparency); labor practices; respect for environment (preservation, divestment); fair operating practices (fair contracts and supply chains); and community involvement and development (Nejati et al., 2011). The focus of these USR initiatives is often concerned with legitimacy and public image, rather than proactively addressing societal needs, challenges, demands, and expectations (Tetrevova & Sabolova, 2010).

Similarly, much activity, publicity, and research on university endowments have focused on acts of divestment and their impact on fund performance (Ryan & Marsicano, 2020). Between 2011 and 2018, thirty-five US universities have divested or partially divested from fossil fuels (ibid., 2). Indeed, the majority of activity related to incorporating environmental, social, or governance criteria into fund management is in single-issue "negative screening" (that responds to ethical concerns by choosing not to invest in a sector considered problematic, such as tobacco), or "voting with its feet" away from industries that are perceived to be harmful, as opposed to direct efforts to influence positive behavior (Smith & Smith, 2016: p. 877). Some small-scale experimentation exists in micro-finance and investments into student-run social funds and green loan funds, though these are primarily made from operational accounts, not from endowment funds (Humphreys et al., 2012). The largest such initiative, the Omidyar-Tufts Microfinance Fund (established in 2005 with $100 million in eBay stock), is part of the Tufts University Endowment but is structured as a separate trust with its own governance structure. In recent years, universities such as Arizona State University (2019), Becker College (2017), California State University (2019), and North Carolina

State University (2012) have established foundations with explicit social responsibility mandates (Dyer et al., 2020). To our knowledge, none of them invest through local partnerships for community development investments in the same way as the University of Edinburgh Social Investment Fund does.

3 Case Study—The Edinburgh Social Investment Fund Model

3.1 Background

The University of Edinburgh is the largest university in Scotland with a turnover of over £1.1 billion[1] and with investments and treasury funds approaching £1 billion. The University of Edinburgh holdings are the third largest UK endowment after Oxford and Cambridge, albeit modest by US standards. The University is committed to making a positive contribution to the world through the combined impact of its teaching, research, knowledge management, operations, and investments. Between 2014 and 2015, universities added £21.5 billion to UK GDP and supported over 1 million jobs (Oxford Economics, 2017).

Since 2013, the University of Edinburgh has developed a responsible-investment policy and strategy.[2] Addressing first the question of divestment (from coal and tar sands in 2015, and from fossil fuels by 2020), the University moved toward proactive investment in renewable energy and sustainable technology and began monitoring the carbon footprint and risks associated with its investments. Building on these commitments, in 2017, the University's governing body agreed to create a Social Investment Fund (SIF) to promote positive impact for society alongside financial return.

This institutional journey—from emissions reductions and divestment from harmful industries to investments that prioritize social value, and set within a broader organizational commitment to social impact—has yielded key lessons for *a university model of social investment*. Such a model involves a specific set of innovations that we believe are new to both the university sector and the impact investment industry. The paragraphs summarize the process of development of the SIF and future plans,

[1] https://www.ed.ac.uk/finance/accounts.

[2] https://www.ed.ac.uk/sustainability.

and the subsequent discussion identifies the innovations that we believe go beyond existing best practice to have relevance to universities wishing to link their social impact to their investments.

3.2 *Development of the Social Investment Fund*

In 2017, the University of Edinburgh's governing body agreed to the creation of a Social Investment Fund of £8 million to promote impact for society and financial return. This decision evolved from two linked discussions: first about the operationalization of "social responsibility" across the whole institution and second recognizing that progress on divestment had been a polarized issue concerning what the University stood against, rather than what it stood for.

Discussions initially focused on what return should be sought from this new activity. Market intelligence and discussions with key providers suggested that 2–4% returns were most readily available for UK impact investment funds, unlike the 6–8% commonly achieved by the main endowment fund. A mandate of UK inflation plus 1.5% (approximating to a fund range of c3–4%) was therefore agreed with an explicit desire to help fill a gap in provision. This agreement then raised the question of governance and the source of the funds. It became clear that a combination of mixing mandates at Investment Committee (the committee overseeing the endowment fund), the relatively small size of the fund, and the lack of expertise in this area (at the time) from Investment Committee members made it not suitable to place the SIF under Investment Committee governance.[3] These observations also suggested that using the main endowment fund to provide capital for the SIF was premature.

Therefore, it was decided to draw SIF from treasury funds, capped at 2% of total treasury funds held. The University made a decision to link its social investments to core activities in its other two missions, in research and teaching (including student experience), culminating in the agreement of a five-year social enterprise and social investment strategy in 2019. This strategy pursued broader aims than merely financial performance and attempted to highlight the need to support and nourish an

[3] https://www.ed.ac.uk/finance/about/sections/financial-information-reporting-strategy-team/investments-and-endowments/investment-committee/reports.

ecosystem of student and staff social enterprise within the University's teaching, research, and commercial activities.

The strategy agreed success criteria and priorities for the fund including financial return (capital preservation); value for the University (such as positive impact on reputation, opportunity to engage with new partners); and social/environmental impact (including for young people, low income households and communities, environmental sustainability and climate change, homelessness and social housing, and international development).

A sample of fund rules is included in Table 1. Finally, the University took the decision to move from relying on individual impact frameworks supplied by investees, to a simple dashboard of impact metrics to be monitored by the University for the overall fund.

Table 1 Sample of Social Investment Fund rules

Diversification	We will normally limit our investments in individual investees to one investment at any one time, and we will spread our investments across a variety of themes from housing to sustainability and from poverty to the arts
Investment mix	We are neutral on whether to invest in equity or debt
Geographical spread	The balance of investments should ensure a substantial allocation of funds for the Edinburgh and City Region Deal for Scotland, with lesser sums allocated to the United Kingdom and to global investments
Capital preservation	We will prioritize capital protection; investments that are underwritten or where co-investors take first-loss capital positions are particularly attractive
Opportunities for impact in the relevant area or scaling	We are particularly interested in investments that support wider University objectives, generate innovation to tackle complex social and environmental issues, and present opportunities to scale up over time

Source University of Edinburgh Social Investment Fund portfolio document (2019), unpublished

At the time of writing (September 2020), the University has allocated £3.75 m to six investments, with two more under active consideration, and a further six rejected at various stages of due diligence. The investment examples we consider below—a student social enterprise, a collaborative early-stage social enterprise debt fund, and a large-scale growth-stage investment fund—are investments of varying size and purpose to illustrate the range of innovation with which this type of model can engage.

4 Discussion of Key Innovations

The development of the University governance and rules was seen to provide significant comfort that the activities being undertaken did fit within an acceptable and well-managed framework for prioritization, due diligence, risk management, and reporting, similar to the main investments. The University needed to undertake significant innovations to create and manage a fund that could deliver social impact and meet financial and governance criteria.

4.1 Innovation 1: Whole-Institution Approach to Social Change

As heterarchical organizations (Stark, 2000), universities are fundamentally geared toward pursuing and balancing multiple values, beyond economic value. Universities are considered to act as agents of change through their three recognized missions of teaching, research, and engagement with society. Additionally, universities pursue wider social responsibility agendas that are embedded in core governance and operations.

The SIF is a key element of the University's responsible investment strategy, which itself is nested within a conscious, long-term, and institution-wide attempt to deliver a more socially responsible and sustainable approach. The University's new strategic plan, Strategy 2030,[4] makes this commitment explicit.

Therefore, the first innovation highlighted flows from the idea that the theory of change of a university social finance model is (or should be) hitched to the wider university theory of change, and that the sphere

[4] https://www.ed.ac.uk/about/strategy-2030.

of impact of any University social finance program has the potential to be amplified. There is a gap in the literature in identifying the significant potential for existing university objectives to be delivered through a program of social investments. We believe this lesson has general relevance to any university considering making a social investment. This view is illustrated below with examples from Edinburgh.

Current avenues for change arise from a number of already existing activities. Firstly, through its research, a university has the opportunity to tackle some of the most profound and pressing challenges of the twenty-first century, to create the new knowledge required to underpin delivery of the sustainable development goals (SDGs) (United Nations, 2015). Secondly, each decade sees tens to hundreds of thousands of students progress their education through a university, forming their capacity for independent thought and critical thinking forevermore. To raise student consciousness about social and environmental concerns, the extent to which sustainability and the SDGs are embedded in the curriculum is vital. Thirdly, the scale, organizational research, and reputation of universities give these institutions significant potential to drive forward socially responsible and sustainable aims. Finally, the nature of a university potentially grants it the ability to take a long-term view and to consider matters of public good and positive impact.

In sum, this combination of factors—curation of young minds, creation of new knowledge, ability to take a long view and focus on public good—underpins a theory of change that provides the opportunity to experiment, learn lessons, tell a story, influence others, then review, and improve.

A social investment fund therefore joins other university mechanisms that demonstrate its commitment to the city or locality, to regional or national social objectives, and to long-term positive impact for society. For example, the University of Edinburgh has the benefit of flexibility in the deployment of its investable resources and to accept lower returns should the social and environmental impact justify doing so.

Further scope exists for universities in creating formal learning opportunities and programs of impact-led research (and research-validated impact) associated with the investments made. The decision to bring together University of Edinburgh's activity on social investment with broader action on social enterprise, student engagement, and teaching, learning, and research, offers the chance to amplify the value created by sparking conversations that otherwise might not happen.

The University's institution-wide strategy provides a platform continuously to try and build toward the ultimate vision of being the leading university in the United Kingdom for this topic,[5] and to harness the expected continued growth in young people's interest in mission-led, values-first enterprise. Anecdotally but powerfully, many students have communicated to the authors that becoming involved in the social enterprise and social investment elements of the program was a highlight of their University experience. The University seeks to teach about social enterprise, social investment, and lessons learned from the SIF, through the program.

On the research front, impact-driven investments yield the opportunity to stimulate and draw research from the activities of the SIF. The UK Research Excellence Framework for judging the quality of research and providing the basis for much UK university research funding increasingly requires real-world impact to be demonstrated by research activities.[6] Clear opportunities exist to investigate a wide range of questions: from the development of the University social investment strategy itself, to the evaluation of its social and environmental impacts, to how it fits in the broader context of social investment and philanthropy, and its repeatability and scalability across the university sector. An abundance of research work exists across the University on the subjects of impact investment (Chen & Harrison, 2020), social enterprise and the community sector (Cross & Street, 2004; Henderson & McWilliams, 2017; Huang, 2020), and social innovation (Kwon, 2019). Further mobilizing the interdisciplinary expertise of these often-disaggregated research activities, discussions, and outputs around the themes of the University's social finance projects would benefit both scholarly impacts and learning processes for the SIF. Recurrently, an opportunity exists to link the increasing need to demonstrate the real-world impact of research with the activities of a university social investment approach.

As an illustration of the type of engagements activated at the intersection of the student experience and social responsibility agenda, the

[5] University of Edinburgh Investing for Good—A Strategy for Social Enterprise and Social Investment, December 2019. https://www.ed.ac.uk/sustainability/what-we-do/responsible-investment/policy/positive-investment-and-social-finance.

[6] https://www.ref.ac.uk/about/.

University committed a total of £50,000 over five years to a student-led Community Interest Company (CIC)[7] called Prosper.[8] As noted on its website: "Prosper Social Finance is the first student-run socially responsible-investment fund in the United Kingdom, founded and run entirely by students at the University of Edinburgh." The company aims to not only deliver socially responsible benchmark-beating returns, but also empower and train a cadre of students on financial investment skills and to use surplus profits to secure local social impact. To date, hundreds of students have now applied for and passed through the company's training program, and the investment returns are above the benchmark. We believe the point of innovation here is the explicit linking of the missions of student experience and teaching with social investment and social impact.

4.2 *Innovation 2: New Finance Flows*

As noted above, the University decided to use treasury funds to finance SIF investments. This is an unusual decision—to use funds normally designed to be as liquid as possible—to fund long-term commitments with third parties. The model is predicated on the SIF outperforming standard treasury funds in a continued low-interest environment, with expenditure capped at 2% of average treasury funds to avoid solvency events. If the success of the model could be demonstrated, then it is expected to be of wider relevance to universities across the United Kingdom. The relevance of the model would include those institutions that may not have endowment funds to invest but that, in common with all universities, would have treasury funds (as the average size of University endowment in the United Kingdom is only £21 m; Sutton Trust, 2014).

The University's reliance on treasury funds as the source of funding thus appears innovative. Instead of social investments being perceived negatively due to generating lower returns when compared to main endowment funds, the perception can be reversed. Now, the argument can be made that a university could deliver significant social impact in line

[7] A CIC is a special type of UK limited company which exists to benefit the community rather than private shareholders. See https://www.gov.uk/set-up-a-social-enterprise

[8] https://prospersocialfinance.co.uk.

with its mission *and* at a higher financial return than comparator treasury funds, while the 2% cap on overall use of treasury funds is introduced to limit risks.

Some of the University investments made are 10–15 year commitments, raising the issue that the model effectively relies on a relatively low-interest environment. A question for the long-term is whether and to what extent this model is viable to what extent this model is viable should interest rates return to more historic interest rates to return more toward historic levels.

4.3 Innovation 3: Collaborative Model

The decision to locate the SIF within the existing Social Responsibility and Sustainability (SRS) model at the University has been fruitful, by bringing together disparate sets of skills and experience and to address topics rarely discussed together (e.g., sustainability, social investment, homelessness, community engagement).

Externally, the SIF has allowed the University to have discussions with the Scottish Government, with major investment managers and advisers, and with a range of social enterprises, community groups, and third-sector bodies. SIF and related activities provide significant opportunities to engage with individuals, organizations, and investors that might not otherwise arise. Opportunities to leverage our activities continue to expand for attracting potential future partners, such as donors and major corporations seeking to enhance their social and environmental activities.

The need for the social investment funds, like any innovative sustainability or social initiative, to align to broader organizational objectives has been assisted by taking a proactive, collaborative investment approach. This lesson has broader relevance for universities in developing the business case for such investment.

To illustrate how the collaborative model plays out, two further examples are highlighted from among the SIF's active investments. The first, Power Up Scotland, shows how an inter-networked model allows for the hedging of university risk. The second, the Scottish Growth Fund 2, shows how the SIF is able to achieve its overall target returns through alliances with established social investment leaders.

The first investment of the SIF was a £500 k investment with the Big Issue Invest (BII) in 2017. BII's newly established corporate social venturing fund "Power Up Scotland" (PUS) was launched in 2018 and aims to enable more than twenty Scottish early-stage social ventures to access loan funding of up to £50 k in 2018–2021. The program, funded by partners Aberdeen Standard Investments (ASI), the University, and the Scottish Government, was developed for organizations likely to be accessing finance for the first time. The program has supported a series of start-ups with innovative approaches.[9]

Although returns are set to 0% (unusual for investment in risky new ventures), the University was able to commit due to the innovative nature of the partnership, with ASI providing the funding to support management costs. The Scottish Government provides the "first-loss" capital to allow the University the comfort to invest a larger sum as senior debt, and Brodies (a leading law firm) provides in-kind legal and practical advice. The design of the program allows for more than just loan finance, with detailed and extended mentoring from partner organizations' employees, providing a win for start-ups but also personal development for the mentors. We believe several elements of this approach are innovative and present broader lessons for any university. A larger size investment from the University was enabled first by the combination of underwriting of risk from the Scottish Government, and second from the nature of the contributions from partners. The payment of management costs from ASI from their CSR funds and the in-kind legal advice from Brodies allowed the University to accept 0% returns in the knowledge that every penny of its investment went straight to investees. The wide distribution of knowledge and skills among the partners added strength to the due diligence and monitoring process.

To generalize the lesson learned, the University's investment at 50% was a key enabler of an innovative model that delivered a new approach, while it also allowed each partner to contribute in ways best suited to their financial and impact drivers.

A second investment made by the University in 2018 was in Scottish Growth Fund 2, a £17 m partnership with the Scottish Government and Big Society Capital (BSC) and managed by Social Investment Scotland (SIS), Scotland's leading provider of affordable, flexible investment for social enterprises.[10] BSC was formed in 2012 and is a UK-wide independent social investment institution with £1.2 bn of capital providing

[9] See, for example, https://bigissueinvest.com/case-studies/invisible-cities/.

[10] https://www.socialinvestmentscotland.com.

finance to organizations that support front-line social sector entities. The Scottish Growth Fund 2 aims to make £17 m of investment available to charities and social enterprises in Scotland over 2018–2022. Investing in this fund provides a number of advantages for the University: the opportunity to support the Scottish Government's social enterprise strategy,[11] work with new skillful partners, and join a well-structured follow-on fund with an experienced fund manager. The key learning point here was not the investment in a limited-partnership debt-led fund (which is relatively common in the United Kingdom), but rather the ability to give confidence to other investors by signaling support for such ventures. This fits with the University's desire to both catalyze new partnerships and facilitate deals that would otherwise not happen, drawing on our size and reputation as much as the funding offered.

5 Conclusion

This chapter suggests three innovative elements to the University of Edinburgh experience—the whole-institution approach; the identification of new financial flows; and the collaborative model adopted to leverage diverse institutional strengths. We believe these innovations address gaps in existing best practice: 1) the opportunity to link social investments to a broader organizational commitment and purpose; 2) the continual shortage of funds in this area and lack of flexibility in terms of returns accepted; 3) the under-recognized unconventional ability to use treasury funds for long-term results; and 4) the impact of working innovatively with partners to create structures that deliver new investment.

As mentioned above, at the highest level, the SIF receives its mandate from and achieves legitimacy within the University of Edinburgh's Strategic Plan 2030. Operationally, the SIF is embedded in multiple existing structures and processes. An early decision linked action required for delivering the SIF to existing job roles and functions. Overhead costs have been borne in-house and justified on the basis that the SIF delivers on multiple objectives. This has helped ensure that the relatively small fund size is not adversely affected by running costs eating into returns.

The University's experience of setting up the fund is worth reflecting on to understand how universities (as organizations) learn, how they

[11] https://www.gov.scot/publications/building-sustainable-social-enterprise-sector-scotland-2017-20.

introduce and adopt new ideas, and how innovative projects are sold up the ladder and through key decision-making bodies.

The process of generating support relied heavily on a number of key factors: the organizational context and SRS commitments; the support of key individuals including an Investment Committee chair committed to responsible investment and a supportive Director of Finance, and a successfully expanding University with a growing income and endowment. Even with these elements in place, securing agreement on fundamental questions of financial objectives, sources of funding, social and environmental priorities, and governance and investment strategy was slow and complex. The ambition to make change often ran up against a tendency for risk aversion. In the authors' experience, the finance and investment community tends to be cautious and reluctant to experiment in areas where returns may be modest or sums relatively small. Real concerns existed over the degree of risk that was acceptable for using University funds for non-traditional activities. It would not be unreasonable to ask—with the degree of effort required for a major, relatively wealthy UK university with a strong organizational commitment to SRS issues—whether the model could survive contact with a more hostile organizational context. This struggle frames our attempt to suggest a model with which other universities can begin.

Considerable time was spent in 2017–2019 generating the structures, governance, and rules that are now in place. Although the University underestimated the effort and time required to pursue a social investment model successfully, it gained distinct advantages from wrestling with the process and creating a sound organizational fit. We hope that the innovations explored here can be scaled up and operationalized in other university contexts, and that engagement with this model may facilitate other institutions to venture more easily into new forms of social finance.

We now reflect on the potential process of transitioning the SIF from "pilot" project to a scaled-up fund within the University of Edinburgh that is also possibly absorbed into the endowment. A challenge arises from the very nature of the model itself. Since it was developed in 2017 with an ambition to carve £8 m from a larger slice of c£500 m and return 3–4%, new questions are posed. Is the relatively small sum committed simply too small to be of consequence? If a larger sum is needed to make a larger impact, would and could the University commit to doing so with returns of 3–4%, well below the standard of 6–8%+ achieved for the main investment portfolio?

If the case were made that larger funds were required, a further conversation would be needed about whether the University would require the same returns as from the standard portfolio. This issue would further trigger the question of whether such returns would rule out impactful, responsible investments. Discussions with partners in the UK social investment space suggest that the University's model meets a clear need. But questions keep arising about whether both (university and social investment sector) are being too modest in terms of ambition, and whether the revised aim should be a much larger deployment, at higher return, and considered as a key component of future mainstream investment portfolios.

To date, early judgment of the University and peers appears to be that SIF and the general commitment to act in this space have been a success. Clear linkages in conceptual terms exist between the investments and broader University objectives for social responsibility, the principle of being a responsible investor, and using all levers at our disposal to make positive, real-world change.

The achievements in linking to learning, teaching, and research are real but currently work on a modest scale. A number of student studies have been completed, one of the authors is actively researching questions associated with SIF, and a vibrant but small community of researchers, commercial professional staff, and committed students exists. Social enterprise and social investment remains a recognized but modest component of University research (£300 m per annum) and teaching (£300 m + per annum) activities and would not yet register as a key driver of either research or teaching and learning strategy.

Utilization of treasury funds advances an argument that social investments can generate higher returns than standard treasury funds. Hence, it has the potential to be attractive to universities that do not wish to see diminishing returns or which lack large endowment funds. Taking a portfolio approach to returns allows for some investments with no or low returns, buttressed by investments with more generic impacts but higher returns. This is an obvious way in which the model could be scaled; universities could trial the model with its concepts and rules already developed, as all organizations will have treasury funds. However, the strength of the model also contains the seeds of potential risks—namely, whether a low-interest environment will endure over the long timeframe required for social investment, and whether the entire concept of carving out a small percentage of funds at intermediate rates of returns locks in a mindset that this will always be an ancillary, optional, and modest-impact activity. In addition, the global financial outlook at the time of writing (2020) is badly affected by the global outbreak of COVID-19 and is very different from 2017 when the model was agreed. Questions emerge about whether such a fund is overly dependent on the coincidence of positive situational factors to secure agreement and is overly susceptible to external shocks.

Deciding an appropriate size for social investment funds would depend on better evidence to questions such as the impact of the SIF to date and an analysis of the Scottish/UK social investment landscape; the degree to which broader objectives such as research and teaching opportunities are important compared to investment-driven social impact alone; and the degree to which University funds could be the key catalyzing element to seal more and larger deals for funds.

A further topic of research would be whether a fund could be designed from more mainstream endowment funds, aimed at a similar return (i.e., higher returns instead of intermediate ones) but still allowing for substantial social impacts (i.e., the higher returns not preventing investment from achieving a socially beneficial footprint), or similar returns but over a more flexible timeline.

Overall, we believe the Edinburgh model developed is useful to consider within a university context but could also be applied more widely. The lessons learned from the Edinburgh experience should allow others to build a model based on that approach and reduce their development time. At the same time, key questions remain unanswered about scalability, measurement of social impact, and the ability to grow the wider benefits to research, teaching, and the student experience.

References

Alexander, C. (2010). The third sector. In K. Hart, J.-L. Laville, & A.D. Cattani (Eds.), *The human economy: A citizen's guide* (pp. 213–224). Polity.

Andreu, M. (2018). A responsibility to profit? Social impact bonds as a form of 'humanitarian finance.' *New Political Science, 40*(4), 708–726.

Arocena, R., Göransson, B., & Sutz, J. (2018). *Developmental universities in inclusive innovation systems*. Palgrave Macmillan.

Barman, E. (2016). *Caring capitalism: The meaning and measure of social value*. Cambridge University Press.

Barnett, R. (2018). *The ecological university—A feasible Utopia*. Routledge.

Bayuo, B. B., Chaminade, C., & Göransson, B. (2020). Unpacking the role of universities in the emergence, development and impact of social innovations—A systemic review of the literature. *Technological Forecasting & Social Change, 115*, 1–11.

Bergman, N. (2018). Impacts of the fossil fuel investment movement: Effects on finance, policy, and public discourse. *Sustainability, 10*(17), 2529.

Chen, S., & Harrison, R. (2020). Beyond profit vs. purpose: Transaction-relational practices in impact investment. *Journal of Business Venturing Insight, 14*, n.p.

Cross, J., & Street, A. (2004). Anthropology at the bottom of the pyramid. *Anthropology Today, 25*(4), 4–9.

Dyer, G., DonnaSelva, A., & Bowen, H. (2020). *Financial performance of sustainable investing: The state of the field and case studies for endowments.* Intentional Endowments Network Report. https://www.intentionalendowments.org/financial_performance_of_sustainable_investing.

Gray, R., Owen, D., & Adams, C. (1996). *Accounting and accountability.* Prentice-Hall Europe.

Gunn, C. (2004). *Third-sector development: Making up for the market.* Cornell University Press.

Henderson, J., & McWilliams, C. (2017). The UK community anchor model and its challenges for community sector theory and practice. *Urban Studies, 54*(16), 3826–3842.

Huang, J. (2020). *To be an entrepreneur: Social enterprise and disruptive development in Bangladesh.* Cornell University Press.

Humphreys, J., Solomon, A., Electris, C., & Ferrara, C. (2012). *Environmental, social and governance investing by college and university endowments in the United States: Social responsibility, sustainability, and stakeholder relations.* Study commissioned by the Investor Responsibility Research Center.

Kraatz, M. S., & Block, E. S. (2008). Organizational implications of institutional pluralism. In R. Greenwood, C. Oliver, R. Suddaby, & K. Sahlin-Andersson (Eds.), *The Sage hand-book of organizational institutionalism* (pp. 243–275). Sage.

Kreander, N., McPhail, K., & Molyneaux, D. (2004). God's fund managers: A critical study of stock market investment practices of the Church of England and UK methodists. *Accounting, Auditing & Accountability Journal, 17*(3), 408–441.

Kwon, W. (2019, July 4–6). Institutions, innovation and impact: A study of social innovators. *Conference proceedings from the 35th EGOS colloquium: enlightening the future: The challenge for organizations*, University of Edinburgh Business School.

Maisuria, A., & Cole, M. (2017). The neoliberalization of higher education in England: An alternative is possible. *Policy Futures in Education, 15*(5), 602–619.

Nejati, M., Shafaei, A., Salamzadeh, Y., & Daraei, M. (2011). Corporate social responsibility and universities: A study of top 10 world universities' websites. *African Journal of Business Management, 5*(2), 440–447.

Ortner, S. B. (2017). Social impact without social justice: Film and politics in the neoliberal landscape. *American Ethnologist, 44*(3), 528–539.

Oxford Economics. (2017). *The economic impact of universities in 2014–15: Report for universities UK*. https://www.universitiesuk.ac.uk/policy-and-analysis/reports/Documents/2017/the-economic-impact-of-universities.pdf.

Rajak, D. (2011). *In good company: An anatomy of corporate social responsibility*. Stanford University Press.

Ryan, C., & Marsicano, C. (2020). Examining the impact of divestment from fossil fuels on university endowments. *New York University Journal of Law and Business, 17*, 1–48.

Scottish Government. (2016). *Scotland's social enterprise strategy 2016–26*. https://www.gov.scot/publications/scotlands-social-enterprise-strategy-2016-2026/.

Shu-Hsiang, C., Nasongkhla, J., & Donaldson, J. A. (2015). University social responsibility (USR): Identifying an ethical foundation within higher education institutions. *TOJET, 14*(4), 165–172.

Smith, J. K., & Smith, R. L. (2016). Socially responsible investing by universities and colleges. *Financial Management Winter, 45*(4), 877–922.

Stark, D. (2000). *For a sociology of worth*. Working Paper Series, Center on Organizational Innovation, Columbia University, New York. http://www.columbia-coi.com/media/papers/stark_fsw2.pdf.

Sutton Trust. (2014). *Academic assets: University fundraising—An update*. https://www.suttontrust.com/wp-content/uploads/2019/12/academic-assets-final.pdf.

Tetrevova, L., & Sabolova, V. (2010). University stakeholder management and university social responsibility. *WSEAS Transactions on Advances in Engineering Education, 7*(7), 224–233.

United Nations. (2015). *Transforming our world: The 2030 agenda for sustainable development*. Resolution adopted by the General Assembly on 25 September. https://en.wikipedia.org/wiki/File:N1529189.pdf.

Vernon, J. (2018). The making of the neoliberal university in Britain. *Critical Historical Studies, 5*(2), 267–280.

Opportunities in Patient Capital Financing

Julie Segal and Erica Barbosa Vargas

1 Introduction

Long-term thinking can be a decisive factor for investment outcomes. "Patient capital" is long-term financial capital that can take many different forms, yet it almost always includes a degree of investor flexibility. Common examples of patient investment capital include debt, equity, and hybrid instruments. Each structure confers distinct outcomes to the receivers and distributors of capital. While there are reviews elsewhere of patient capital's value at the national level in macroeconomic policy or foreign-direct investing, this chapter evaluates the use of patient capital by institutional investors. There is disagreement on how long an investment must be held before it can be categorized as "patient," as well as who constitutes a patient investor; likewise, most other characteristics of patient versus impatient capital are not consistently defined. There is,

J. Segal (✉)
The J.W. McConnell Family Foundation, Montréal, QC, Canada
e-mail: jsegal@mcconnellfoundation.ca

E. Barbosa Vargas
SecondMuse Capital, Montréal, QC, Canada
e-mail: erica.barbosa@secondmuse.com

T. Walker et al. (eds.), *Innovations in Social Finance*,
https://doi.org/10.1007/978-3-030-72535-8_9

however, majority consensus on what patient capital can achieve and what its providers aim to do.

Patient capital is commonly understood as "the expectation of holding an asset for an indefinite period of time by an investor with the capability to do so" (World Economic Forum, 2011, p. 9), practiced through low portfolio turnover and non-cyclical investment strategies (OECD). Importantly, the patience of capital is a relative concept, corresponding to the type of financing being provided and the underlying asset being financed—in short, the minimum duration for a patient capital investment greatly depends on the asset class. While patient capital in infrastructure investing is typically seen as an investment exceeding 10 years, patience in venture capital is generally considered to be around seven (Lin & Wang, 2017). Practitioners such as Blackstone (2014) define patience across all private markets as exceeding a minimum of 10 years, while academic definitions can range from holds as brief as 5 years (Ivashina & Lerner, 2019) to those that equate patient capital with multi-generational transfers of wealth (Van Loon, 2016).

1.1 Asset Classification

The boundaries defining how patient capital can be applied have altered and progressed, initially by practitioners positing new ways of investing and then subsequently through academic confirmation. There is an evolving definition for two key aspects of patient capital: who constitutes a patient investor, and which asset classes patient capital can apply to. Although traditional definitions emphasize the length of an investor's hold, Deeg and Hardie (2016) support a revisionist definition of patient capital, eschewing a minimum duration and focusing instead on an investor's intentions. This emerging line of thought differentiates between "the *holding period* of a shareholder [and] her *orientation*," indicating that a more important metric of patience is whether an investor makes decisions based on long-term information (Edmans, 2017). A long-term orientation style would avoid basing investment decisions on short-term falls in financial markets or organization profitability and would instead prioritize long-term outcomes, often assimilating social impact considerations with the financial data. This analysis prioritizes an investor's *ex ante* holding plan and investment style rather than her resulting holding timeline, evading the debate of minimum investment term.

Another central question related to patient capital is the type of asset(s) it can apply to. Ivashina and Lerner (2019), in their titular book on patient capital, often equate the concept to exclusively risky, private market investments, proposing a contrast between long-term investments and easily tradeable liquid assets. Various practitioners and organizations have likewise applied this reductionist definition by limiting patient capital transactions to the private markets of venture capital, equity, debt, infrastructure, or real estate (Blackstone, 2014; Pensions and Lifetime Savings Association, 2019; World Economic Forum, 2011). Although patient capital is a valuable and frequently applied tool in these asset classes, this decisive conflation, which is made even by proponents of long-term investing, incorrectly implies that patient capital necessitates complexity and illiquidity. By instead concentrating on investor orientation, patient capital can apply to any type of asset for which the "providers maintain their investment even in the face of adverse short-term conditions" (Deeg et al., 2016, p. 18). This permits even liquid publicly traded investments to enter the category. An investor would be a supplier of patient capital when responding flexibly to short-term vicissitudes and, instead, prioritizing long-term results.

Other analyses that document an association between patient capital and a particular investment structure still recognize that a patient investor would prioritize long-term growth (Mendell & Nogales, 2012). This moves toward the common recognition that long repayment terms must be matched with a focus on long-term metrics for an investment to properly qualify as patient capital. Removing the rigid boundaries of investment term and product structure and focusing instead on the investor's approach open a nuanced discussion that encourages more progressive applications of patient capital.

A natural alignment between patient capital and social impact investments emerges when considering an investor's intentions and goals. Many investors with long-term orientations, driven by obligations to multiple generations of beneficiaries, imbue their investment strategies with social impact considerations. For example, the Church of England states that assessing social and environmental factors "is an intrinsic part of being a good long-term investor" (The Church of England). The Japanese Government Pension Investment Fund similarly advocates for "the sustainable and stable growth of the overall capital market," recognizing that their position as a "universal [...] super long-term investor" brings in a wider universe of factors affecting investment performance (Government Pension Investment Fund, 2018). By prioritizing cross-generational, sustainable growth, these investors are inclined to permit short-term financial fluctuations in pursuit of longer-term goals. This flexibility enables capital recipients to develop sustainably, generating long-term value for both the capital recipient and the investor.

2 History of Patient Capital in Institutional Finance

2.1 Emergence

Patient capital has a prominent history within mainstream institutional finance and a demonstrable link to these organizations' sustainability objectives. For many organizations and types of institutions, patient investing originated from diversifying into alternative and direct investing. Select historical cases illustrate a patient approach across structures and asset types, and emerging uses continue to explore broader applicability. Patient capital serves a unique role in many institutional investors' portfolios. It can benefit these portfolios through diversification and counter-cyclical behavior; it is also a distinct form of capital for financing the social impact economy and generating social value.

Like many innovations in social finance, the application of long-term, patient investment capital emerged first in family wealth management and subsequently in university endowments, finally diffusing to pension portfolios, life insurance groups, and sovereign wealth funds (Ivashina & Lerner, 2019 p. 31). Multi-generational transfer of family firm ownership was one of the initial forms of patient capital; non-financial considerations, "such as social capital and reputation," encouraged family firms to take a sensible long-term investment strategy (Van Loon, 2016, p. 710). This initially niche financial tool evolved substantially in its diffusion throughout the 1980s onward (Ivashina & Lerner, 2019) but "the interest of other stakeholders" remains paramount for many long-term investors (Deeg & Hardie, 2016, p. 633). The association with social and environmental outcomes remains notable in the strategies of multi-generational investors such as pension funds, religious groups, and endowments.

J.M. Keynes' management of Cambridge University's Kings College endowment from 1921 to 1946 is one of the earliest examples of institutionalized patient capital use (presented in Ivashina & Lerner, 2019, pp. 25–27). It is also an instructive example for patient investing in public markets. Keynes implemented a patient buy-and-hold strategy of select public equities, arguing that the College's "investment strategy should capitalize on [its] long investment horizon" (presented in Ivashina & Lerner, 2019, p. 26). He achieved an impressive risk-adjusted return. This philosophy of long-term, active management of a university endowment was rather uncommon at the time but has since spread substantially. The celebration of the eponymous "Yale Model" of long-term active investing highlights the shift of opinion toward appreciating long-term asset alignment. While Keynes favored public equity investments, Yale's model (since the 1980s) targets private markets and alternative investments. These contrasting implementations demonstrate that there are diverse opportunities for an investor who privileges a patient time horizon.

2.2 Patient Capital in Pension Funds

Patient capital became more prominent as pension funds began to explore the potential of flexible long-term investing. Its applicability to social and environmental outcomes likewise became more notable. Given the relative weight of pension fund assets (as of year-end 2019, the OECD estimates that pensions across its member states hold 32 trillion USD in cumulative assets under management—over one-fifth of the year's global GDP), the proclivities of pension funds play a critical role in shaping capital markets. Pension funds are logical proponents of patient investing given the long-term nature of their liabilities to pension members. They have an unusual level of certainty about their future financial position, created by their actuarial ability to forecast contributions and withdrawals. Pensions which choose to leverage this "long-time horizon, scale and certainty of assets" are in a unique position to generate illiquidity premiums and withstand market volatilities (Common Wealth, 2017, p. 9). Shifts in pension fund dispositions toward patient capital have had a notable impact on popularizing and normalizing the approach.

Despite the key characteristics aligning pension funds with the long term, they, like all investor types, are not inevitable providers of patient capital. This heterogeneity holds true regardless of patient capital's fluctuating primacy. This is clear when analyzing the differing levels of pensions' patience both within and across countries. The adoption of a patient approach remains largely dependent on policy, business, and labor actors (see Dixon, 2011; Estevez-Abe, 2001; Naczyk, 2013, 2016, as cited in McCarthy et al., 2016). In certain cases, the differing choices and orientations of these actors yield a connection between patient investing and the intentional integration of social and environmental factors. We examine this relationship in the dispositions of pension funds in the United States, France, and Canada.

The history of patient capital in the US pension system, for example, clearly illustrates the linkage between patient capital and a long-term orientation toward sustainability. A change in US Department of Labour regulation in 1979 permitted pensions to diversify into alternative asset classes and created an opportunity for more innovative investment strategies (Ivashina & Lerner, 2019). However, pensions did not interpret this ruling as an opportunity for patient capital, and patient investing is not contemporarily the dominant strategy among US pensions. Rather, the more prominent driver of patient investing was union activism in the 1980s; pensioners advocated for a larger role in pension governance and more strategic, intentional long-term investment strategies (McCarthy et al., 2016). Notably, socially oriented worker-controlled pensions in the country continue to demonstrate more patient investment strategies than their firm-controlled counterparts (McCarthy et al., 2016).

Long-term investment strategies in French pension funds are also connected to environmental, social, and governmental (ESG) considerations (Naczyk, 2016). In France, the 2001 *Fabius Act* established new variants of worker saving streams along with the requirement to specify ESG considerations in investment purchases and sales. The ESG requirement in France's *Fabius Act* is widely seen as a harbinger of pension funds in the country increasing their patient investment activity.

Pension funds in Canada have been quite progressive in applying patient investing (Common Wealth, 2017). Most pensions in the country are acclaimed for their long-term, alternative investments: the country's largest state-sponsored funds, Canadian Pension Plan and Ontario Teachers' Pension Plan, target long-term investments in social and physical infrastructure (CPP Investment Board, 2013; Ontario Teachers' Pension Plan). However, this long-term investment orientation has only recently converged with a growing emphasis on sustainable investing and ESG outcomes. Although pension funds across the country are beginning to explore ESG, intentional sustainability integration is seen almost exclusively in the Canadian province of Quebec's public pension fund. The *Caisse de dépôt et placement du Québec* has demonstrated leadership in combining a long-term, macroeconomic perspective with ESG criteria and measurable carbon-reduction targets (Common Wealth, 2017; O'Neill, 2009).

These country-level comparisons reiterate the connection between patient capital and investor orientation, highlighting the differing approaches to patient capital. They introduce the interrelation between patient capital and ESG-guided stewardship and convey pension capital's prominent role in advancing both.

Increasingly, institutional investors of all types are applying the principles of patient capital to ESG objectives. As new classes of investors implement a patient approach, it proliferates to novel strategies and asset classes. For example, a connection between patient capital and ESG is only recently applied in the public markets—asset managers are engaging across their public equity holdings to oppose corporate short-termism. Leading investor membership and research groups including the UN Principles of Responsible Investment (2016), Cambridge University's Investment Leaders Group (2016), CERES (2019), and studies such as the British Government's Kay Commission (2012) call on investors to move past short-term and toward long-term, more sustainable orientations in their public equity mandates. This growing body of industry research and coordinated activities highlights that patient and persistent engagement in public equity can have positive results. While there is academic evidence that patient and active engagement in public equity markets generate financial return (Cremers & Pareek, 2017) and that shareholder advocacy for long-term corporate orientation can improve financial performance (Bansal & Flammer, 2016), the connection between social impact outcomes and persistent, longer-term engagement remains an area for further academic research.

3 Benefits of Use

The strategy of patient capital confers notable benefits to both its providers and receivers. These benefits are distinct from the outcomes that are achievable in traditional and short-term investments. Industry advocates have called on investors to apply their capital to "long-term, productive activities that support sustainable growth" (Della Corce et al., 2011, p. 1), noting that these strategies are also effective at meeting traditional financial goals. Long-term capital benefits its providers by creating counter-cyclical financial stability, escaping short-term market inefficiencies, and delivering risk-adjusted return premiums to investors taking on reduced liquidity (Blackstone, 2014; Edmans, 2017; OECD). Investors also use long-term investment strategies to create social relations complementary to transactional ones, creating alignment, interdependencies, and increased transparency between provider and receiver of capital (Deeg et al., 2016). This relational strategy is increasingly applied to encourage ESG considerations.

Patience by shareholders and creditors can achieve better alignment for the capital receivers, as well. Patient capital signals support for the long-term interests of the organization. Long-term, patient investment timelines provide organizations with reprieve from focusing on short-term quarterly or annual indicators. This encourages future-oriented gains and enables maturation through longer-term capital planning. This longer-term thinking permits organizations to integrate extra-financial objectives into their priorities and apply a wider stakeholder approach, too (Mendell & Nogales, 2012; Naczyk, 2016; Van Loon, 2016). This flexibility is especially critical for nascent ventures in the social impact economy, most frequently financed by the private markets, who are reluctant to deviate from their stakeholder-oriented missions.

At a macro-scale, patient investment capital has been studied as a critical factor in economic growth and social development. Long-term financing and a patient capital approach, particularly when invested into physical and social infrastructure, can create a notable advantage for an economy's development and can be important for its stabilization (Deeg et al., 2016; Lin & Wang, 2017; World Economic Forum, 2011). Other authors such as Van Loon (2016) and Mazzucato (2016) have explored patient capital in both the private and public sectors as an important hindrance of the over-financialization process.

It is important to note that long-term investments are not unconditionally positive for each associated stakeholder: passive index fund investors are often loyal to their holdings but are primarily conscious of short-term market signals, and long-term active investors may have myopic priorities. However, when applied properly and thoughtfully, truly patient capital is an important instrument. It is a fundamental mechanism to foster innovation and sustainability across organizations, particularly in the private market and social economy.

4 Patient Capital in the Private Markets: Toward Sustainable Outcomes

Understanding patient capital as a long-term, flexible form of investment capital contingent on investor intention reveals multiple and diverse applications. The following case studies present a selection of common forms of patient capital within the social impact economy: patient debt, venture debt quasi-equity, revenue-sharing quasi-equity, repayable grant arrangements, and long-term debt guarantees.[1] The different cases depict a spectrum of risk, return, and investor involvement across the investment sub-classifications; within each type, there is likewise the opportunity to accommodate various investor types and risk-return preferences. The investment structures deliberately respond to the needs of the capital receivers, reconciling the gaps of traditional, impatient capital.

The cases differ in their sector, risk source, and income type. It is therefore possible for an investor to achieve portfolio diversification while prioritizing patient capital goals. For example, three of the case studies outlined (*Fiducie du Chantier de l'économie sociale*, ABSCAN First Nation's Precursor Housing Fund, and the *Garantie Solidaire* Program) are held within the J.W. McConnell Family Foundation's impact investment portfolio.

4.1 *Patient Debt:* Fiducie du Chantier de l'économie sociale

The prominence of sustainability-oriented capital in Quebec, Canada, extends to financial institutions in banking and asset management. Patient capital has been a common tool in the province, beginning with the government-sponsored capitalization of the *Fiducie du Chantier de l'économie sociale* in 2007. The network of patient capital providers in Quebec coalesces to form a "social economy," i.e., one focused on community reinvestment and social solidarity. This "social economy" is credited to intentional political collaboration with labor during the mid-1990s and early 2000s, exemplified by the establishment of the *Fiducie*. Patient debt remains most prominent in the province's social economy space, despite a growth of other patient capital instruments (Mendell & Neamtan, 2008; Mendell & Nogales, 2012).

[1] The details included in these cases studies are sourced from the authors' conversations with investment fund managers, if not otherwise cited.

The *Fiducie*'s landmark application of patient debt creates an equalizing opportunity for the non-profit sector to access financing. Under many jurisdictions, including Quebec, non-profits cannot issue equity shares—patient debt facilitates long-term investments without creating an ownership vehicle. The *Fiducie* provides long-term loans to actors in the social economy for real estate activities or working capital financing. The *Fiducie* additionally manages two funds in affordable real estate, both of which apply patient capital to improve affordable housing in Quebec. These funds achieve risk-adjusted market rates of return for the pension funds, foundations, and insurance groups participating as investors.

The *Fonds d'aide à la renovation de l'habitation Communautaire (FondsARHC)* was launched in 2015. In this Fund, the *Fiducie's* unique patient debt structuring enables building operators to improve living conditions in existing affordable real estate buildings through repairs or renovations. Critically, the loan financing is structured to ensure tenants' rents remain stagnant despite the building taking on additional debt. *FondsARHC* aligns the debt repayment schedule with each buildings' existing mortgage terms, offering a moratorium on principal repayment of up to 15 years (*Fonds d'aide à la renovation de l'habitation Communautaire,* 2020*)*. When borrowers enter the market to renegotiate and recapitalize their mortgage at end of term, they include the value of their loan from *FondsARHC*. This allows building operators to renovate their real estate before it dilapidates, while deferring the principal costs of these renovations to the end of their outstanding mortgages. Without *FondsARHC* postponing the principal repayment, the building operators would either have to transfer the cost to tenants through raised rents or defer necessary renovations. Similar financial terms are applied in *Fiducie*'s *Fonds d'investissement pour logement étudiant (FILE),* founded in 2018, which provides financing for construction of new student housing buildings. The loan principal payments are likewise postponed until the end of the mortgage's term (*Fonds d'investissement pour logement étudiant,* 2020). In the interim period, investors in *FILE* and *FondsARHC* receive fixed annual interest payments.

In both products, the *Fiducie* ensures that a building's annual debt servicing costs are capped at a limited percentage of revenues to safeguard its long-term sustainability. The extensive use of impact-oriented patient capital by the *Fiducie* in these two funds demonstrates how patient capital can be deployed to confront specific structural challenges for social organizations.

4.2 *Venture Debt in Quasi-Equity: The European Investment Bank (EIB)*

Venture debt is a form of mezzanine quasi-equity, another common structure for patient capital investing. The European Investment Bank (EIB) introduced quasi-equity into its portfolio in 2014 through its *Investment Plan for Europe*, including innovative structures such as venture debt. The EIB defines quasi-equity (through its fi-compass platform) as:

> a type of financing that ranks between equity and debt, having a higher risk than senior debt and a lower risk than common equity. Quasi-equity investments can be structured as debt, typically unsecured and subordinated and in some cases convertible into equity. (fi-compass, n.d.)

Venture debt, a subcategory of quasi-equity, is a hybrid instrument that blends aspects of debt and venture capital to enhance flexibility for capital receivers. It accommodates early stage organizations by accomplishing the flexible, participatory relationship of shareholder arrangements without diluting ownership. It avoids the typical burdens associated with heightened debt exposure through a flexible and patient approach.

The EIB introduced venture debt to incentivize sustainable growth for smaller, higher-risk, or more experimental organizations. The model is intentionally well suited to companies undergoing research and innovation activities as it prioritizes growth metrics over prompt capital repayment. The EIB's venture debt investments aim to encourage additional financing to new companies that may otherwise be perceived by the market as high-risk investments. An example is the EIB's 20 million EUR loan to Heliatek, a renewable energy technology company originating from Germany's Technical University. Heliatek raised an 80 million EUR financing round in late 2016 to build a new manufacturing facility. The EIB's quasi-equity stake in Heliatek was instrumental in this raise; the EIB's flexible capital was complementary to the 42 million EUR of traditional equity capital from groups including ENGIE and BNP-Paribas (European Investment Bank, 2016). Without sacrificing the EIB's required rate of return, their application of a flexible investment structure allowed the company to expand operations without unmanageable dilution or debt burdens.

4.3 *Revenue Sharing in Quasi-Equity: Mirova Natural Capital Land Degradation Neutrality Fund*

Revenue-sharing agreements are a variant of quasi-equity in which the receiver's future revenue streams are explicitly linked to repayment of the financing principal. Like other forms of quasi-equity, revenue-sharing agreements are beneficial to projects with high upfront capital investment. Revenue-sharing agreements emulate the reality of initial costs being offset by future earned revenues, enabling projects to prioritize development without being hampered by high debt servicing costs.

Mirova Natural Capital applies this structure in its Land Degradation Neutrality Fund. The Fund, launched in 2018 in association with the United Nations' Convention to Combat Diversification (UNCCD), targets a 300 million USD raise from private and public sector investors. It invests in sustainable agriculture and forestry projects across Latin America and the Asian Pacific, aligning its financial terms with the long-term goal of land degradation neutrality. To match the project timelines, the initial Fund structure has a 15-year term, which the manager hopes to continually extend through raising subsequent vehicles (Mirova, 2017). Investors in the fund include government organizations and pensions.

While each investment matches a project's unique needs and timelines, the Fund overlays key criteria to accommodate high upfront costs. The quasi-equity financing is achieved through junior debt positions with profit-sharing mechanisms; the payment of the profit-related incentive, conditional on a future date or business performance, supplements the return to Mirova's flexible junior position. The debt repayment schedule includes a 1–3 year moratorium on loan servicing costs followed by cash-flow-oriented repayments. This structure confers substantial flexibility to the project operators during their initial, highly capital-intensive years of land transformation before profitability. These initial years are critical to the projects' sustainability, and the cash-flow-oriented repayments enable project operators the flexibility to remain patient during the start-up period of low profitability. Furthermore, this structure remains adaptable in case of short-term variations, recognizing the potential volatility of land-based projects to weather and climate changes.

Additional to the environmental outcomes and the benefits to project operators, this patient approach yields market-rate returns to investors over the Fund's lifetime. The low returns in early years are offset by long-term sustainable cash flows, which accrue both to Mirova's investors and to the local project operators.

4.4 *Repayable Grant: ABSCAN First Nation's Precursor Housing Fund*

A repayable grant is a flexible instrument that mirrors the risk-reward trade-offs of venture capital investing. It is typically applied by foundation investors willing to share the initial risk with an organization that is incapable of issuing shares. This applies to pioneering organizations in the social impact economy, which are often registered as non-profits and therefore not eligible for shareholder structures. In venture capital, angel investors take on the risk that the receiving organization may be unsuccessful in returning their initial investment capital; similarly, in a repayable grant structure, the investor provides capital with the understanding that their capital may not be repaid. However, if the receiving organization is successful in its endeavor, the grant would be converted to a repayable debt instrument. Like venture capital, repayable grant structures require a flexible investor with a patient approach.

In 2015, the J.W. McConnell Family Foundation issued a repayable grant to the Aboriginal Savings Corporation of Canada (ABSCAN), an Aboriginal Financial Institution in Quebec, Canada. ABSCAN provides credit services to Indigenous communities and individuals in Canada. The repayable grant structure permitted ABSCAN to expand its home ownership mortgage services and initiate a new product without risking its existing lines of business.

For on-reserve Indigenous communities in Canada, home ownership remains a highly complex and underfinanced issue, in part due to prohibitive regulations around land ownership. After successfully supporting the development of a housing market in the Huron-Wendat community of Wendake, Quebec, ABSCAN received increased demand for its mortgage services from on-reserve communities that did not have access to traditional credit services. The repayable grant supported the organization to respond to this demand by initiating the First Nations Precursor Housing Fund. ABSCAN expanded its services with the knowledge that it would only be required to repay its financing if the project were successful. Once converted to debt, the loan repayment amortized for up to 25 years to match ABSCAN's cash-flow expectations from borrowers.

The flexibility of the Foundation's repayable grant enabled a blended finance structure, which pooled a non-reimbursable contribution from the Canadian Federal government and a senior-positioned line of credit from a mainstream financial banking institution. The flexibility of the financing from the government and foundation reduced the risk for the mainstream financial institution. The banking institution deployed capital in a market in which it would not otherwise engage and ABSCAN developed a track record for its mortgage lending program. The pilot fund successfully financed over 27 housing projects across four First Nations communities. All investors are being repaid according to their expectations; the Foundation's grant was converted to a loan instrument and is being paid back with inflation-matching interest over 15 years. Most notably, the success of this Precursor Fund is facilitating ABSCAN to scale its services to additional communities. This example profiles how creative applications of patient capital can target broader changes in a market.

4.5 *Debt Guarantees:* Garantie Solidaire *Program*

Debt guarantees are a common source of collateral in traditional finance and have interesting applications in social impact investing. In loan guarantee structures, a guarantor assumes the risk of a debt instrument between a creditor and borrower. The guarantor undertakes the responsibility of a debt obligation in the case of the borrower's default. The structure mitigates the risk for lenders, often reducing the borrower's cost of capital as a result. Debt guarantees are an opportunity to increase the affordability of investment capital for social impact organizations. Furthermore, many of the reasons that social impact organizations have difficulty accessing finance—such as perceived risk from traditional financial institutions, lack of balance sheet collateral, and lack of relational experience for both lender and non-profit borrower—could be reduced by normalizing transactions between lenders and social impact organizations.

The *Garantie Solidaire* program was established to address this market gap. It is a 15 million CAD loan guarantee program structured as a partnership between three Canadian private family foundations (Lucie et Andre Chagnon, Lino and Mirella Saputo and J.W. McConnell) and the financial institution *Caisse d'economie solidaire Desjardins*. By providing unfunded guarantees on loans made by the *Caisse*, the foundations leverage their asset-heavy balance sheets to facilitate financing to social impact organizations. Within one year of its launch, the *Garantie Solidaire* Program has enabled over 24 million CAD of financing to 12 social impact organizations through a guaranteed amount of 1.2 million CAD.

While this initial program is contracted for a maximum of 5–7 years, the participating foundations have the option to roll over and extend their commitments to the program. This long-term orientation has benefits for all participating institutions. Rather than the foundations partnering with the *Caisse* on a deal-by-deal basis, the multi-year partnership achieves transactional efficiencies, reducing costs, and due diligence requirements. These efficiencies enable the partners to support more social impact organizations. The structure offers loans up to a maximum of 7 years, allowing borrowing organizations a long-term repayment schedule; this flexibility is achieved in part because of the risk-reducing role of the foundations' guarantee. This risk reduction likewise facilitates loans of larger amounts.

This patient, relationship-based structure creates numerous opportunities for the banking institutions, the foundations, and the social impact organizations. The borrowers access loans at an affordable cost of capital and develop credibility with mainstream financial institutions; the financial institution shares risk with credible partner organizations; the foundations support social impact organizations while generating their traditional investment returns (since the guarantee is unfunded). The foundation partners as well as the financial institution generate market rates of return.

5 Conclusion

In each of the outlined cases, the nuances of patient capital are instrumental in facilitating the capital receivers' pursuit of long-term social outcomes. This is illustrated by examples in real estate, agriculture real assets, and credit services. The investors' patient approaches reduce the primacy of short-term financial outcomes typical to traditional financing. The case studies begin to illustrate the value of patient capital approaches—particularly for early stage, socially oriented organizations.

This chapter introduces the multiple forms of patient capital and outlines a selection of the distinct uses and outcomes. It advances the opinion that the patience of capital is contingent on investor intention rather than being unequivocally linked to specific investment structures.

By highlighting the history of patient capital across institutional investors' portfolio, the chapter begins to explore the breadth of its applicability. Through an analysis of patient capital in pension funds, the chapter identifies an emerging connection between patient investment orientation and sustainability outcomes. The case studies and the overview of patient capital's benefits solidify this relationship. Further research could explore the effectiveness of socially oriented patient capital in public investment case studies, examining the association between a long-term, patient orientation, and successful advocacy for social value creation.

References

Bansal, P., & Flammer, F. (2016). Does a long-term orientation create value? Evidence from a regression discontinuity. *Strategic Management Journal, 38*(9), 1827–1847. https://doi.org/10.1002/smj.2629

Besoin de rénover vos logements sans impact sur les loyers? (n.d.). *Fonds d'aide à la nrénovation de l'habitation communautaire*. Retrieved July 7, 2020, from http://fondsarhc.quebec/.

Cremers, M., & Pareek, A. (2017). Patient capital outperformance: The investment skill of high active share managers who trade infrequently. *Journal of Financial Economics, 122*(2), 288–306. https://doi.org/10.1016/j.jfineco.2016.08.003

Deeg, R., & Hardie, I. (2016). What is patient capital and who supplies it? *Socio-Economic Review, 14*(4), 627–645. https://doi.org/10.1093/ser/mww025.

Deeg, R., Hardie, I., & Maxfield, S. (2016). What is patient capital, and where does it exist? *Socio-Economic Review, 14*(4), 615–625. https://doi.org/10.1093/ser/mww030.

Della Corce, R., Stewart, F., & Yermo, J. (2011). Promoting longer-term investment by institutional investors: Selected issues and policies. *OECD Journal: Financial Market Trends, 2011*(1), 145–164. https://doi.org/10.1787/fmt-2011-5kg55b0z1ktb

Edmans, A. (2017). The answer to short-termism isn't asking investors to be patient. *Harvard Business Review*. https://hbr.org/2017/07/the-answer-to-short-termism-isnt-asking-investors-to-be-patient?registration=success.

Fi-compass. (n.d). Glossary: https://www.fi-compass.eu/info/glossary/q.

Financement spécifique destiné au développement de logements étudiants abordables. (n.d.). *Fonds d'investissement pour logement étudiant*. Retrieved July 7, 2020, from http://fondsetudiants.org/.

Financer les entreprises d'économie sociale. *Fiducie du Chantier de l'économie sociale*. Retrieved July 7, 2020, from http://fiducieduchantier.qc.ca/.

Financial Instrument Products. (2015). *Loans, guarantees, equity and quasi-equity*. https://www.fi-compass.eu/sites/default/files/publications/ESIF-factsheet-FI-products.pdf.

First Investment for the LDN Fund. (2019). *Mirova*. https://www.mirova.com/en/news/first-investment-ldn-fund.

Germany: Heliatek raises EUR 80 million to finance large manufacturing expansion and support worldwide market development. (2016). European Investment Bank. https://www.eib.org/en/press/all/2016-213-heliatek-raises-eur80-million-to-finance-large-manufacturing-expansion-and-support-worldwide-market-development.

How asset owners can drive responsible investment. (2016). UN Principles for Responsible Investment. https://www.unpri.org/download?ac=1398.

How we invest. (n.d.). The Church of England. https://www.churchofengland.org/about/leadership-and-governance/church-commissioners-england/how-we-invest.

Investing for long term value. (2013). CPP Investment Board. https://www.cppinvestments.com/wp-content/uploads/2019/10/CPPIB_Responsible_Investing_Report_2013_KnYCvdK.pdf.

Ivashina, V., & Lerner, J. (2019). *Patient capital: The challenges and promises of long-term investing*. Princeton University Press.

Land Degradation Neutrality Fund. An innovative fund project dedicated to sustainable land use. (2017). Mirova. https://www.cbd.int/financial/un/unccd-ldnfund2017.pdf.

Lin, J., & Wang, Y. (2017). The new structural economics: Patient capital as a comparative advantage. *Journal of Infrastructure, Policy and Development, 1*(1), 4–23. https://doi.org/10.24294/jipd.v1i1.28.

Mazzucato, M. (2016). Innovation, the state and patient capital. *Rethinking Capitalism, 86*(S1), 98–118. https://doi.org/10.1111/1467-923X.12235

McCarthy, M., Sorsa, V., & van der Zwan, N. (2016). Investment preferences and patient capital: Financing, governance, and regulation in pension fund capitalism. *Socio-Economic Review, 14*(4), 751–769. https://doi.org/10.1093/ser/mww020.

Mendell, M., & Neamtan, N. (2008). *The social economy in Quebec: Towards a new political economy*. https://sec.oise.utoronto.ca/english/project_outputs/proVanLoon,2ject33_February09Report.pdf.

Mendell, M, R. (2012). Solidarity finance: An evolving landscale. *Universitas Forum, 3*(2). https://doig.org/10.3138/9781442695092-009.

Naczyk, M. (2016). Creating French-style pensions funds: Business, labour and the battle over patient capital. *Journal of European Social Policy, 26*(3), 205–218. https://doi.org/10.1177/0958928716642944

O'Neill, L. (2009). Pension fund investment and disclosure: Acknowledging environmental, social and governance considerations. *Shareholder Association for Research & Education*. http://www.share.ca/files/16_03_2009_Canada_Fed_Department_of_Finance_Pension_Consultation.pdf.

Our beliefs. (n.d.). Ontario Teachers' Pension Plan. https://www.otpp.com/investments/performance/investment-strategy/our-beliefs.

Patient capital made simple. (2019). Pensions and Lifetime Savings Association. https://www.plsa.co.uk/Policy-and-Research/Document-library/Patient-Capital-Made-Simple.

Patient capital, private opportunity. The benefits and challenges of illiquid alternatives. (2014). Blackstone. http://www.heritagegroup.ca/sites/default/files/users/db/PDFs/Patient%20Capital%20-%20Private%20Opportunity.pdf.

Pension markets in focus. (2019). OECD. http://www.oecd.org/daf/fin/private-pensions/Pension-Markets-in-Focus-2019.pdf.

Stewardship activities report. (2018). Government Pension Investment Fund. https://www.gpif.go.jp/en/investment/gpif_stewardship_activities_report_2018.pdf.

Taking the long view. (2016). The University of Cambridge Investment Leaders Group. https://www.cisl.cam.ac.uk/resources/publication-pdfs/taking-the-long-view-ilg-mandates-report.pdf.

The evolution of the Canadian pension model: practical lessons for building world-class pension organizations. (2017). Common Wealth and the World Bank Group. https://www.cwretirement.com/wp-content/uploads/2017/11/WBG-The-Evolution-of-the-Canadian-Pension-Model.pdf.

The Future of long-term investing. (2011). World Economic Forum. http://www3.weforum.org/docs/WEF_Future_of_Long_term_Investing.pdf.

The Kay review of UK equity markets and long-term decision making. (2012). https://assets.publishing.service.gov.uk/government/uploads/system/uploads/attachment_data/file/253454/bis-12-917-kay-review-of-equity-markets-final-report.pdf.

The OECD long-term investment project. (n.d.). OECD. https://www.oecd.org/pensions/private-pensions/institutionalinvestorsandlong-terminvestment.htm#:~:text=Patient%20capital%20allows%20investors%20to,leading%20to%20better%20corporate%20governance.

The role of investors in supporting better corporate ESG performance. (2019). CERES. https://www.ceres.org/sites/default/files/reports/2019-04/Investor_Influence_report.pdf.

Van Loon, J. (2016). Patient versus impatient capital: The (non-)financialization of real estate developers in the Low Countries. *Socio-Economic Review, 14*(4), 709–728. https://doi.org/10.1093/ser/mww021

Digitalizing Social Finance

Inside Money Creation in the Digital Era

Israel Cedillo Lazcano

1 Introduction

After the global markets' disruption that followed the Global Financial Crisis (GFC), we have witnessed how the historical hostility against traditional intermediaries has been made evident (Ferguson, 2008, p. 2). Unsurprisingly, this aversion has fostered the development of new socio-technological answers, commonly labeled under the term Financial Technology (FinTech) (Arner et al., 2016). These solutions aim to deliver alternative financial solutions to face the excessive infrastructural and political influence held by those institutions, which are considered Too-Big-To-Fail (TBTF) and/or Too-Complex-To-Fail (TCTF) and promote competition and financial inclusion. Within the FinTech universe, "cryptoassets" tend to be described in social media and among enthusiasts as the purest materialization of these objectives, which would eliminate the need for the government and the existing financial infrastructures to form bonds of trust on our behalf (Cohney et al., 2019, p. 593).

The creation and evolution of "cryptoassets" offer us a rather interesting scenario to work with. Just as it will be developed further in the

I. Cedillo Lazcano (✉)
Universidad de las Américas Puebla (UDLAP), Cholula, Mexico
e-mail: israel.cedillo@udlap.mx

T. Walker et al. (eds.), *Innovations in Social Finance*,
https://doi.org/10.1007/978-3-030-72535-8_10

next lines, the introduction of new technologies and social arrangements has fostered the development of financial innovations, which have posed challenges for social scientists in their respective contexts. For instance, Bill Maurer (2006) discusses the relevance of the materiality of money in different contexts from commodity monies to current electronic monies, while Andreas Rahmatian (2018) focuses his attention on the relationships incorporated within them, independent of whether they are made of paper or electrons. At the core of these challenges, we find two common but key questions: "What is money?" and "Are these innovations money?" Generally, money tends to be defined in terms of its economic functions: money as store of value, money as unit of account, and money as means of payment. For our purposes, this is a good starting point. However, these elements by themselves are not enough to define and understand money and/or "cryptoassets." Money does not emerge nor evolve in isolation through these functions; it needs the repetition and diffusion of uses and conventions that reflect the content of social agreements and network effects that force us to ask the complementary question: "who can create money?"

Building on this question, I will argue that Distributed Ledger Technologies (DLT) represents a means to incorporate social relationships, which have been the source of liquidity for every monetary instrument found throughout the financial history of the world (Kiyotaki & Wright, 1989, p. 950). In monetary matters, most of the time, we tend to identify the relationships developed between individuals and sovereign stakeholders, which are incorporated within sovereign currencies through constitutional conventions. However, if we want to understand innovations, such as "cryptoassets," we have to consider that relationships developed within individual markets. Within these latter, we can find organizational "families" (Liptrap, 2020) that are structured around different social agreements represented not through constitutions, but through licenses that contain the terms and conditions of the interactions developed within these "families," which are endogenous sources of liquidity. Accordingly, just as in the case of sovereign currencies, a "cryptoasset," for it to be credible beyond speculative purposes, has to reflect social conventions that are under development to mitigate the speculative uncertainty and coordinate social expectations (Shenai, 2018, p. 47). To see how these emerging digital conventions can configure sources of liquidity for different social finance paradigms, this chapter will open with an effort to answer the following questions: "what is money?" and "who can create money?" Building upon the answers to these questions, we will then highlight the differences between "inside money" and "outside money" as well as the role of the former in the configuration of new digital conventions that act as endogenous sources of liquidity in certain DLT networks.

2 What Is Money?

When looking to answer this question, we find a myriad of interpretations that are focused exclusively either on the socio-legal element or on the economic ones. Furthermore, most of the analyses relevant to the proper understanding of the origins of money argue that this social innovation must have started somewhere, but their authors simply cannot agree on exactly where and what money was originally (Dodd, 2014, p. 15). Consequently, one can find academic biases among anthropologists, economists, and legal scholars that tend to ignore the emergence of different states with money, merchants, and commercial institutions in different contexts (Smith, 2004, p. 78) that go beyond the commodity standards found in the famous Karl Menger (1892)'s *On the Origin of Money*, and Moses I. Finley (1973)'s *The Ancient Economy.*

If one wishes to understand past, current, and future monetary developments, we first have to tackle these academic biases. For this purpose, it is worth going beyond the analysis of the traditional functions associated with money and Metallist arguments,[1] starting the analysis with the relationships incorporated in promissory texts found in different banknotes and smart contracts issued around the orb by which the issuer promises to pay the bearer on demand the sum of certain amount of money. Beyond the evolutionary analyses and the comparisons between these instruments, it is possible to argue that these pieces of text, independently of their representation, are the remnants of proto-monetary forms used to constitute and incorporate conventional claims and debts within different objects, which probably worked like the *Vaygu'a* of the *Kula*[2]

[1] The Metallist theory argues that money emerged through the use of different commodities like metals as means of exchange before their respective adoption and regulation, and it can be identified in the work of authors, such as Karl Menger.

[2] The Kula ring is a system of exchange that is strictly ceremonially regulated by which several tokens of value known as Vaygu'a are exchanged periodic overseas expeditions, which link together the various Kula communities on the Trobriand Islands.

ring described by Bronislaw Malinowski (1961) and Rolf Ziegler (2008). These acts of incorporation rely on the level of commercialization of each society, the recognition of different political arrangements (Smith, 2004, p. 79), and the nature of the trust incorporated in each transfer (Ziegler, 2008, pp. 107–108). For a proper analysis of "cryptoassets," the elements that define each context are rather important given that these transfers show how fundamental socio-legal relations are developed as "opposites" and "correlatives" designed around those conventions recognized by a specific community in a specific context (Hohfeld, 1914, p. 30), which are then incorporated within different payment instruments.

We can say that the referred "opposites" and "correlatives" can be identified, on the active side, with the creditor whose right will be called "claim" and, on the passive side, we will find the debtor whose obligation will be called "debt" (Rahmatian, 2018, p. 215). Consequently, it is possible to argue that the idea of debt must pre-date the idea of money if we are talking about cacao seeds or cryptographic instruments like Bitcoin (Gleeson, 2018, p. 32), since these debts are the type of property or *res* that will be incorporated into different monetary *reifiers* depending on the context (Rahmatian, 2018, p. 208).

Now, to constitute this *res* and incorporate it within certain tangible and intangible assets, we first need to separate commodities from nature and/or create new goods through a process of manufacture. After all, a cacao seed or a piece of code by itself cannot be considered money per se (Rahmatian, 2018, p. 209). In the absence of perfect information and conventions, these goods are employed based on different exchange rates (Banerjee & Maskin, 1996). In scenarios featuring two commodities (A and B) that are exchanged in the absence of externalities, innovation, and convention, as described by Arrow and Debreu (1954), it is easy to claim that we do not need money and that we can rely only on trust. Yet, one can argue accurately that barter was not a great system. Following the discussions introduced by Léon Walras (1926, pp. 145, 157) and the evolution of the "cryptoassets" market, we can highlight that: first, one or both goods can become useless or unlimited in quantity (something that would decrease their value in exchange), and second, this gets complicated when we introduce additional goods (C, D, E…). Consequently, in both scenarios, the absence of standardized and explicable acts of incorporation will result in only imperfect equilibriums. To ease exchange processes, money is introduced to keep a stable reference just as one can read in the whitepapers of different "cryptoassets"—particularly "stablecoins"—and in the central banks' constitutional mandates. However, just as Satoshi Nakamoto (2008) noted in his famous whitepaper, the root problem with money "is all the trust that's required to make it work." In other words, trust and network effects that derive from it is what will make our money useful (Marwala & Hurwitz, 2017, p. 3).

These commodities, among which we found our "cryptoassets," are adopted as means of payment by virtue of the conventional relationships of trust developed among persons with regard to these things and the social obligations incorporated within them in a particular socioeconomic context. After all, money was designed to circulate and transfer messages within individual communities, not to hoard (Benedikter, 2011, p. 56). That is why, we incorporate cultural elements, such as animals, flowers, gods, among others within our currencies (Doty, 1978, p. 24). However, Malinowski (1961, p. 143) warned us about the risks relating to the use of the word "money" to describe and/or classify different objects and commodities that are used under certain conventional exchange/gift schemes such as the *Kula*, and the Bitcoin network. For him, these units are not used as means of exchange nor as denominators of value following the traditional economic theories. To face this argument, Marcel Mauss (2002, pp. 127–128) tried to defend the applicability of the use of the referred term to institutions like the *Kula's Vaygu'a* arguing that:

> These precious objects have the same function as money in our societies and consequently deserve at least to be placed in the same category. They have purchasing power, and this power has a figure set on it… The idea of number is present, even if that number is fixed in a different way from the authority of the state, and varies during the succession of kula and potlatches. Moreover, this purchasing power does indeed discharge debts.

From an initial point of view, these words could be applicable to "cryptoassets." Now building on Mauss' argument, if we want to refine our understanding of the nature of these innovations, the original question (What is money?) has to be refined, and instead, ask "what does money do?"

We can argue that during the first stages of monetary innovation, culturally valuable substances and/or goods, such as silver, whales' teeth, or *Vaygu'a*, could have served as: firstly, commodities valuable for ornamental/ritual purposes; secondly, incorporated wealth that enhanced the prestige and influence of the holder; thirdly, a medium of exchange; and finally, a standard measure of value (Jevons, 1875, pp. 15–16; Kiyotaki & Wright, 1989, p. 950). A similar process can be verified in the "cryptoassets" market. For instance, the first "cryptoassets" emerged as commodities described in court decisions, such as *Commodity Futures Trading Commission v Patrick K. McDonnell and Cabbagetech, Corp. d/b/a Coin Drop Markets* ([2018] 18-CV-361 [US], pp. 17–20); the second, as witnessed through the emergence of Proof-of-Stake (PoS) protocols, these innovations gradually started to be used as instruments to enhance the influence of the holder within a particular network; and, finally, "cryptoassets" are evolving to become a uniformed and stable means of payment as seen through the emergence of "stablecoins."

One can differ and argue that these functions emerged following a different order, particularly between the third and fourth transition. However, we lack the proper legal-archaeological evidence to make a definitive statement on a specific order. Independent of this, it can be argued that the custom relating to the use of esteemed/sacred articles as store of value probably precedes their employment as a trusted medium of exchange, independently if we are talking about pre-capitalist societies or digital networks in the Fourth Industrial Revolution (FIR). As one can see through the case of the "cryptoassets" market, value is not a property that belongs to an object like color, taste, or smell. It is a third category incorporated in an asset to create a cultural link between the members of a community and the objects they use to transact and communicate with each other (Simmel, 2004, p. 68).

3 *Lex monetae* and Network Effects

During the first existential stages of practically every monetary innovation, the private sector tends to be in charge of what one could label as a proto-*lex monetae*.[3] This fact can be verified in the behavior developed within DLT networks, which are designed around a *crypto lex monetae* exercised through Intellectual Property Rights (IPRs). As it can be seen through the cases of Mesopotamia and Mesoamerica, at the beginning

[3] The *ius cudendae monetae/lex monetae* is understood as the power over the monetary system by which a stakeholder defines the unit of account, regulates the creation and circulation of currency within its territory, the right to determine and change the value of the currency, and its interaction with foreign currencies (Avgouleas & Blair, 2020, p. 25).

sovereign entities do not concern themselves with the public supply of monetary commodities like silver, cacao, or code which, at this point, are pure forms of "inside money" based on relationships *reified* within the private sector whose acceptability increases through network effects by which new conventions started their diffusion and gradual consolidation. However, the diversity of goods used as means of payment and the qualitative asymmetries found among them eventually are seen as a problem (Goodhart, 1998, p. 412). To face this practical obstacle, the sovereign recognition and/or the adoption of certain goods and social customs, as reflected in documents like the Mendoza Codex and the discussions related to the creation of Central Bank Digital Currencies (CBDCs), is set as the imposed standard of value and regulated to some extent by sovereign stakeholders (Baron, 2018, p. 213; Eagleton & Williams, 2013, p. 19; Goodhart, 1998, p. 412). It can be argued that standardization eases the creation of an external source of liquidity by grouping together all the heterogeneous items used as money and grading them in regimented ways (Baron, 2018, p. 214). Consequently, one can infer that private parties, gradually, transferred the control of the referred proto-*lex monetae* to a sovereign stakeholder that will recognize the monetary convention within the social contract (Ashworth, 2004, p. 1314; O'Keefe, 1966, pp. 1–2).

Building upon this fact, economists, anthropologists, and lawyers have been looking for a definition of "money" that could transcend specific institutional arrangements (Geva, 2011, p. 18) and have reached partial consensus that is reflected in judicial definitions like the one provided by Darling J in *Moss v Hancock* ([1899], 2 QBD 111 [UK], p. 116), which defines this socio-legal institution as:

> that which passes freely from hand to hand throughout the community in final discharge of debts and full payment for commodities, being accepted equally without reference to the character or credit of the person who offers it and without the intention of the person who receives it to consume it.

This definition is very useful given that it goes beyond the three main characteristics (money as unit of account, medium of exchange, and store of value) that tend to be used to define money and instead highlights the role of trust and network effects that emerge from the general acceptability of money that gradually evolves into new monetary conventions. For our purposes, we can develop our efforts upon it.

4 "Inside" and "Outside" Money

John C. Gurley and Edward S. Shaw (1960, p. 364), in their book *Money in a Theory of Finance*, ease our efforts to understand the referred transition in the exercise of *lex monetae*, using the terms "outside money" and "inside money." The former can be identified with our traditional coins and notes denominated in terms of "dollars," "pesos," "renmimbis," "pounds," among others, and it is defined as "money that is backed by foreign or government securities or gold; or fiat money issued by the government" (Gurley & Shaw, 1960, p. 364). This means that the money supply is an exogenous economic variable that is set independently of the market forces by a sovereign entity like a central bank (Wu et al., 2009). On the other hand, its complement, "inside money" can be defined as privately issued liabilities that respond to the behavior of regulated and non-regulated intermediaries, individuals, and companies as result of the internal factors of our economic systems (Lagos, 2006; Sissoko, 2007, p. 2097; Wu et al., 2009). It is important to highlight that both terms are not opposites but actually complement each other in different contexts through different governance paradigms structured around different stakeholders. Based on that interaction between endogenous and exogenous sources of liquidity, authors like Hayek (1978, p. 41), Sargent and Wallace (1982) argue that it does not make sense to assign the State the full control of the *lex monetae*.

Why is this distinction relevant to the proper understanding of "cryptoassets"? If we want to understand the nature of these cryptographic innovations, we cannot analyze them as antagonists to current paradigms or as substitutes to current expressions of "outside money." After all, they are not offering a new constitutional arrangement. They are not even a consolidated monetary convention that could act as a source for a social contract. Consequently, we have to focus our attention on who creates them and who accepts them under the light of "inside money" based on the gradual constitution of different social agreements that act as the underlying source of liquidity of these instruments. Most of the time, "inside money" is analyzed based on the monetary creation developed by commercial banking. When we open a banking law or economics textbook, we tend to find that the conceptual and modeling framework employed to analyze and define banking is the intermediation of the loanable funds (ILF) model. This model takes our minds to the original functions of banking as storehouses and mere intermediaries that distribute a fixed amount of "outside" money (Jakab & Kumhof, 2019; McLeay et al., 2014). Under the ILF model, authors, such as Phillip E. Strahan (2010, p. 112), argue that commercial banks produce credit and provide liquidity through a process that "involves channeling resources from entities with excess of funds (savers) to entities with a scarcity of funds (investors [or businesses])." Furthermore, many orthodox policy prescriptions and even banking regulations in practice are designed around this vision; in particular, the view that money's value is linked to its scarcity (Wray, 2016, p. 631).

In opposition to this academic anachronism, Zoltan Jakab and Michael Kumhof (2019) present the financing through money creation (FMC) model, which is structured around the fact that the amount of money in our economies is determined less by the need to buy things—or pay taxes—and more by the supply of credit created by the private sector banks responding to the demand from borrowers (King, 2016, pp. 61–63). Thus, one cannot say that saving sovereign chattels by itself creates funds available for banks to lend (McLeay et al., 2014). Of course, again, this is not a new business model. As explained by Sir Charles Morgan-Webb (1935, pp. 19–20), when a bank receives a loan application, it does not peer into its vault to determine how many depositors' funds are on hand to lend to third parties, and it does not typically do so by giving them thousands of pounds, dollars, or pesos worth of banknotes. In practice, following a well-established convention known as fractional reserve banking, banks hold only cash enough to process their legal obligations and, under a FMC model, they fund new loans by creating new ledger-entry deposits for their borrowers with no saver involved (Jakab & Kumhof, 2019). For this reason, James Tobin (1963) put the "money created by bankers' fountain pens" and the "money created by public printing presses" at the same level, given that both rely on well-defined conventions that have evolved from the commercial practices developed in the Middle Ages.

5 The GFC and the Emergence of New Suppliers of "Inside Money"

Following the GFC, Nigel Dodd (2014, p. 234) argued that "the era in which money was defined by the State is coming to an end." However, is this possible and/or is this a new idea? Studies of non-sovereign means of payment show that throughout history, people constantly disrupt "monetary uniformity" through the design and periodical introduction of different schemes by which they offer private and semi-private means of payment sometimes adopted and integrated into the legal monetary infrastructure. The intended purpose of these "inside money" schemes has had very different targets, ranging from meeting local credit demand and stimulating local economies, to achieving social and political reforms (Naqvi & Southgate, 2013).

These complementary means of payment reified within the private sector can be broadly categorized into three groups following the underlying source of trusted liquidity: backed tokens, un-backed tokens, and mutual credit system tokens (Pfajfar et al., 2012, p. 48). Backed tokens are backed by commodities for which they can be exchanged at a fixed fee. Among these asset-backed tokens, we find some of the earliest examples of incorporation of assets/rights since we can verify through the tokens of Mureybet (Schmandt-Besserat, 2019, p. 11). Today, we are witnessing the emergence of digital versions such as those "stablecoins" propounded by companies like IBM and Facebook who rely on their IPRs and/or the nature of the assets incorporated within their "cryptoassets" to create trust. Unbacked tokens are typically tied to the provision of some services or simply one hour of labor, as it can be seen through the famous case of the Ithaca Hours[4] used in Ithaca, New York. Finally, mutual credit systems work through networks like the Edinburgh Local Exchange Trading System (LETS)[5] that can be considered a form of payment club by which, after paying a fee, its users transform working time, products, and/or services into an underlying obligation that will give form to an alternative unit (Pfajfar et al., 2012, p. 48)—in the case of the LETS of Edinburgh it is the Reekie.

[4] See http://ithacahours.com/.

[5] See https://www.letsedinburgh.org.uk/.

Just as we are witnessing through the "utility tokens" issued as integral parts of some Initial Coin Offerings (ICOs[6]), the regular issue of tokens by general stores, bakers, barbers, hoteliers, transportation, among other different companies and businesses, has been a common practice. These chattels are useful for merchants given that they are designed as: forms of inexpensive advertising, schemes to receive money in advance to face unpredicted scenarios like the one posed by COVID-19, alternative or complementary means of payment for small purchases, and a customer loyalty practice considering that these tokens can be redeemed only at the establishment of the issuing merchant. For examples of these tokens, we can find the dairy tokens issued by Clark Dairy Ltd and National Milk Co. in Canada during the nineteenth century (Berry & Bevan, 2008), and some DLT utility tokens that are designed to act as means of payment on the issuer's platform, which cannot exist and/or be used outside their respective platforms (Li & Mann, 2018).

On monetary matters, the State—in exercise of its *lex monetae*—has shown a double approach toward these "inside" monies. In most cases, the State decides to stamp them out, but occasionally, the same State decides to enable the use of these units (Dowd, 2015, Loc 3457) depending on their conventional nature and potential to disrupt its ability to meet monetary and financial stability objectives (Naqvi & Southgate, 2013). Now, can we say that these tokens are money? Our answer will depend on the design of each *reifier*. They can be labeled as money if they constitute complementary forms of payment that incorporate an obligation accepted *erga omnes* within a community; independently, they cannot be seen as proper currencies as described in *Vick v Howard* ([1923] 116 S.E. 465 [US], p. 214). So far, they have been conceived for limited use—for example, for emergency money in times of crisis, for the revitalization of depressed neighborhoods, or for the joy of social experimentation (Huber, 2017, p. 11) (Fig. 1).

Following this view, one can argue that these units also act as cornerstones for the development of governance paradigms by means of which

[6] They are known as Initial Coin Offerings given that they present similarities to traditional initial public offerings (IPOs), which involve "a fundraising event in which an entity offers participants a unique digital asset – often described as a 'coin' or 'token' – in exchange for consideration (most commonly Bitcoin, Ether, U.S. dollars, or other fiat currency)." See *U.S. Securities and Exchange Commission v Kik Interactive Inc.* ([2019], 19cv-5244 [US], p. 8).

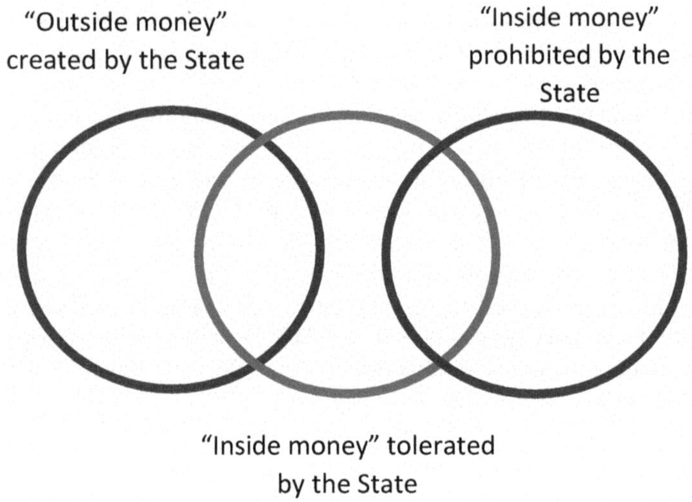

Fig. 1 Monies interacting under the exercise of *Lex monetae*

sovereign entities and private sector parties agree to introduce a monetary unit, structured around a sovereign unit of reference, to fulfill social and/or political goals in different administrative levels. An example of this can be found in municipal complementary monies, such as the program developed by the government of Ichikawa in Japan, which is designed around a local monetary unit to promote generalized trust among citizens by rewarding civic engagement and encouraging social interaction (Richey, 2007, p. 70). In this case, again, we see a social contract is incorporated within a payment instrument. After the GFC, in countries like France, the spirit of these efforts can be found in new legislations like the French Law No. 2014-856 of July 31, 2014, whose Section V, Article 16 established that Social and Solidarity Economy Organizations referred in Article 1 of the referred law can issue local forms of money to promote the development of social and solidary economies.

6 Are "Cryptoassets" Money?

During an interview on June 25th, 2018, Agustín Carstens, the former governor of Banxico and current General Manager of the Bank for International Settlements, stated that "[cryptoassets] are not money" (Egli & Hirter, 2018); an answer that has been repeated by several central bankers around the world, such as the Governor of the Sveriges Riksbank, Stefan Ingves (2018, p. 12). This viewpoint was also inserted in new regulations like the Directive (EU) 2018/843 of the European Parliament and the Council on the prevention of the use of the financial system for the purposes of money laundering or terrorist financing, popularly known as 5MLD.[7]

In the same spirit and resulting in the words of Betts J found in *O'Dea v Merchants Trade Expansion Group Ltd* ([1938] 37 AR NSW [AU], at 417), it may be possible to argue that these "cryptoasset" innovations cannot be labeled as money. One could even argue that a contract by which the parties involved agree on an exchange of goods for anything other than money can be treated as a barter instead of a sale. On this point, Sarah Green (2019b, p. 20) argues that contracts of barter differ significantly from those transactions materialized using non-sovereign means of exchange. Set in cases, such as *Quality Publications Australia Pty Ltd v Commissioner of Taxation* ([2012] FCA 256 [AU], at 48), where a monetary value assigned to the goods introduced the element of fungibility by which the parties retained their ultimate right to be paid on a trusted sovereign currency.

Throughout this paper, it has been highlighted that if you can uniform and incorporate an underlying obligation accepted within a community, building upon relationships of trust and network effects, these cryptographic instruments could be considered money. So if we look for potential answers to the question "are 'cryptoassets' money?" the first thing that one will find in academic sources relating to economics and banking law is the statement that money is a good that has to act as a medium of exchange, a unit of account, and a store of value. Despite the quasi-universal adoption of this definition, this is only a partial answer. If

[7] Article 2(d) defines "virtual currencies" as "digital representation of value that is not issued or guaranteed by a central bank or a public authority, is not necessarily attached to a legally established currency and does not possess a legal status of currency or money, but is accepted by natural or legal persons as a means of exchange and which can be transferred, stored and traded electronically."

we look at the definition of money provided in *Moss v Hancock* ([1899], 2 Q.B. 111 [UK], p. 116), we will find that the referred answer depends on three central elements that characterize both "inside" and "outside" monies: (1) the definition of the underlying source of trusted liquidity set by a stakeholder, (2) the community in which the monetary convention emerged, and (3) the necessities and oddities of this latter.

On this point, in different forums where this argument has been presented, some people have argued that one cannot use any available good to act as money and, in a certain way, they are right. If one desires to fulfill certain obligations using an artwork, one could do it, but only under exceptional circumstances, and these goods would not be considered as money per se. These goods and transactions are unique, and they do not represent the uniformed practices recognized *erga omnes* by a particular community. They represent an expression of the *lex contractus*, which is isolated from the remaining uniformed interactions, taking some authors like Randall Wray (2013, p. 139) to highlight accurately that, under this argumentative line, goods cannot buy goods.

Therefore, just as in the case of the complementary monies analyzed above, "cryptoassets" depend on different sets of underlying obligations, stakeholders, governance arrangements based on computational codes, and private entities that are currently not backed by any sovereign entity to create trust. However, how can we create trust and diffuse a new monetary convention in a decentralized environment like Internet? And, consequently, how can we create new expressions of "inside money" in such environments? The answers to these questions are important, if we consider that the development of these environments have generated alarmist reactions, such as the "cypherpunk" movement, which claimed that Internet fosters the configuration of Foucauldian panopticons[8] by which the State violates the terms of the social contract that acts as the underlying source of liquidity of our national currencies.

To avoid the creation of digital panopticons, innovators have looked for answers to a well-known computer science problem commonly known as the "Byzantine Generals Problem" (Lamport et al., 1982), which highlights the need for well-defined stakeholders and intermediaries to create

[8] Uta Kohl (2012, pp. 187–188) argues, constructing on the work of Bentham and Foucault, that technology can be employed as a regulatory "panopticon" where sovereign control is pervasive and hidden in technological structures and designs.

trust. The initial answer to this problem was introduced through a "cryptoasset" known as Bitcoin. The first generation of these instruments relied on a public ledger commonly denominated as the blockchain, which relies on a "cryptographic proof instead of trust" known as Proof-of-Work (PoW) (Nakamoto, 2008). Through this protocol, nodes can transfer information over the network through a "work" aimed to solve a mathematical problem denominated hash puzzle (Doguet, 2013, p. 1125; Green, 2019a, p. 3). In this point, as explained in the lines above, we are talking about a valuable commodity found in certain DLT networks, whose monetary acceptability relies on network effects that try to diffuse a digital use. Unfortunately, the lack of a well-defined stakeholder has fostered the emergence of parties that hold these assets to increase their influence within the network and for the introduction of intermediaries like exchanges, but not to transfer the messages found in Nakamoto's (2008) whitepaper. Consequently, following the example set by other monetary innovations, we are witnessing the development of protocols of second and third generation that rely on IPRs and well-defined institutions. These take the well-defined commercial conventions in order to exercise a digital proto-*lex monetae*, which will eventually be transferred to a sovereign stakeholder (Cedillo-Lazcano, 2020).

So, at this stage, "cryptoassets" have the potential to evolve into fully-recognized monetary assets relying solely on the expectation, on the part of private agents, that they will be accepted following extrinsic beliefs, social customs, and technology preferences (Kiyotaki & Wright, 1989, p. 928; Lo & Wang, 2014). After all, as seen in cases like *White v Elmdene Estates Ltd* ([1959] 2 All ER 605 [US], at 610-611) and the decision SCR 100 of the Supreme Court of Canada in the Matter of Three Bills Passed by the Legislative Assembly of the Province of Alberta at the 1937 (Third Session) ([1938] *RE Alberta Statutes* SCR 100 [CA], p. 116), it is possible to say that not being a liability of a central bank does not prevent "cryptoassets" from being used as money (Ali et al., 2014), based on the following set of arguments.

First, the analyses that claim that these instruments are not money take the characteristics of sovereign currencies in one context and try to extrapolate the main social contract in different scenarios, ignoring the existence of governance arrangements and different underlying social obligations that have been generated outside this paradigm. Second, it has been argued that money has to act as store of value, means of payment, and/or unit of account. If it does not fulfill one or all of these functions in an optimal way, that is matter for a different discussion. Following the experience set by the monetary union between Scotland and England in the eighteenth century, it is possible to argue that different assets may, in different contexts, play some or all of these roles (Ali et al., 2014) and they may offer them for some people, but not for others, as Milton Friedman (1991) illustrated accurately through the case of the stone money of Yap.

Third, again, the argument against classifying "cryptoassets" as money is based on the unsupported assumption that all the instruments that constitute this market work using Proof-of-Work (PoW) protocols and follow Bitcoin's design. This ultimately ignores the existence and potential of protocols, such as PoS, Proof-of-Location (PoL), and Proof-of-Authority (PoA), to create permissioned networks with regulated and well-defined categories of nodes that could act as issuers/payers, payees, or beneficiaries, among other figures. Fourth, it is possible to say that these arguments tend to ignore the potential evolution of currently accepted commercial conventions that act as the source of liquidity for these instruments. This last point is very important given that the pre-existence of these conventions could ease their gradual definition under existing regulations applicable to payment systems and electronic money.

7 Conclusion

Money is a socio-legal institution by which societies transfer information and stabilize their economic conventions; after all, these conventions cannot extend their network effects without a social agreement extending its influence at the same time and in direct relation (Durkheim, 1960, p. 65). Of course, we agree that social agreements can be expressed in algorithmic code following the needs of specific communities. However, the creation and diffusion of a convention is not an easy task, particularly in decentralized and global environments, considering that we cannot develop global conventions to incorporate within universal agreements. However, that does not mean that "cryptoassets" are not useful for the development of social finance paradigms.

Currently, "cryptoassets" go beyond the protocol of Bitcoin and its network where Nakamoto's (2008) whitepaper circulates more than the asset that is hoarded; cryptographic codes are reproducing different schemes of interaction developed by different communities. As we can see in PoW, PoS, and PoA, these rules are constituted not by a repetition of the Nakamotian asset, but by a system of different rules of interaction and intermediaries reflecting different societal structures that could diffuse digital conventions within new free banking paradigms.

Throughout our financial history, we have witnessed the emergence of these paradigms by which the private sector provides complementary payment schemes based on regional social contracts. Despite that most of these schemes tend to be associated with marginal communities and networks, we are witnessing how some communities are taking advantage of new technologies like DLT to incorporate the referred agreements. During the Monetary Innovation and Complementary Currencies Researcher Symposium held on October 25, 2018, in the Palace of Nations in Geneva, we listened to different and interesting presentations relating to certain "community currencies" developed in countries like Portugal, Spain, and Switzerland that are making the transition from paper-based instruments to digital representations using DLT and protocols like PoL. As an illustration of these projects, we found the *léman*[9] and its crypto-wallet *Biletujo*. According to the General Secretary of the project, Antonin Calderon, this unit was introduced in Geneva in 2015 and is currently used to acquire products and services in different local shops and businesses within the referred city—thus, reflecting a social contract within it that acts as its source of liquidity.

Working on the same argument, despite the fact that most DLT units are not restricted to geographical areas, it is evident that they are integral parts of digital communities structured around their own social agreements and networks in which digital personas, as those described by Roger Clarke,[10] interact with each other using the technologies developed in the FIR. One can go further on this argument. Most of the analyses are focused on the role of "cryptoassets" as money, thus putting them at the same level of our sovereign currencies. However, we think that these innovations are money for Darwinian reasons.

Accordingly, at their current state, "cryptoassets" can follow two paths. First, they can evolve and become a form of electronic money as defined in Section 2(1) of the Electronic Money Regulations 2011 of the UK and Article 2(2) of the 2EMD, which would be the cornerstone for: (a) the development of CBDCs structured around governance paradigms,

[9] See http://monnaie-leman.org/ou-depenser-mes-lemans/.

[10] Clarke, above n 52.

following the models set by Visa, Mastercard, SWIFT, among others; and/or (b) set in place different free banking models designed around complementary monies like the *léman*, whose stakeholders will be the Social and Solidarity Economy Organizations like those described in the French Law No. 2014-856 of July 31, 2014.

Second, following the spirit set in cases such as *Oxigen Evironmental Ltd v Mullan* ([2012] NIQB 17 [IRL]), these instruments could be considered equivalents to cash just as we do with other instruments like checks and bills of exchange. After all, following the spirit of the *crypto lex mercatoria*, and the content of cases, such as *Miliangos v George Frank (Textiles) Ltd* ([1972] M. No. 2957 [UK], p. 506), one can argue that money adapts itself to the necessities of trade. In this view, we can think on the JPM Coin, Diem, and the other instruments that will follow them, which, in simpler terms, could be designed to act as encrypted digital checks to keep building upon current commercial conventions that emerged from the social practices developed in the Middle Ages.

References

Ali, R., Barrdear, J., Clews, R., & Southgate, J. (2014). *The economics of digital currencies.* Bank of England. Accessed on 10 October 2018. https://www.bankofengland.co.uk/-/media/boe/files/digital-currencies/the-economics-of-digital-currencies.

Arner, D. W., Barberis, J., & Buckley, R. P. (2016). 150 years of Fintech. An evolutionary analysis. *The Finsia Journal of Applied Finance, 3,* 22–29.

Arrow, K. J., & Debreu, G. (1954). Existence of an equilibrium for a competitive economy. *Econometrica, 22*(3), 265–290.

Ashworth, W. J. (2004). Metrology and the state: Science, revenue, and commerce. *Science, 306*(5700), 1314–1317.

Avgouleas, E., & Blair, W. (2020). The concept of money in the 4th industrial revolution—A legal and economic analysis. *Singapore Journal of Legal Studies,* 4–34.

Banerjee, A. V., & Maskin, E. S. (1996). A Walrasian theory of money and barter. *Quarterly Journal of Economics, 111*(4), 955–1005.

Benedikter, R. (2011). *Social banking and social finance. Answers to the economic crisis.* Springer.

Berry, P. S., & Bevan, K. (2008). *Ottawa dairy tokens. An overview of the dairy tokens of Ottawa and their issuers.* Bank of Canada. Accessed on 20 July 2018. https://www.bankofcanadamuseum.ca/wp-content/uploads/2014/07/ottawa-dairy-tokens.pdf.

Baron, J. P. (2018). Making money in Mesoamerica: Currency production and procurement in the Classic Maya financial system. *Economic Anthropology, 5*(2), 210–223.

Cedillo-Lazcano, I. (2020). A new approach for "cryptoassets" regulation. *Banking & Finance Law Review, 35*(1), 37–61.

Cohney, S., Hoffman, D., Sklaroff, J., & Wishnick, D. (2019). Coin-operated capitalism. *Columbia Law Review, 119*(3), 591–676.

Doguet, J. J. (2013). The nature of the form: Legal and regulatory issues surrounding the bitcoin digital currency system. *Lousiana Law Review, 73*(4), 1119–1154.

Dodd, N. (2014). *The social life of money.* Princeton University Press.

Doty, R. (1978). *Money of the world.* Ridge Press.

Dowd, K. (2015). Contemporary private monetary systems. In L. H. White, V. J. Vanberg & E. A. Köhler (Eds), Loc 3442-4029. *Renewing the search for a monetary constitution. Reforming government's role in the monetary system.* Cato Institute. Kindle EBook.

Durkheim, E. (1960). *Division of labor in society.* The Free Press of Glencoe.

Eagleton, C., & Williams, J. (2013). *Money. A history.* The British Museum Press.

Egli, C., & Hirter, C. (2018). *My message to young people: Stop trying to create money.* Bank for International Settlements. Accessed on 5 October 2018. https://www.bis.org/speeches/sp180704a.htm.

Ferguson, N. (2008). *The ascent of money. A financial history of the world.* The Penguin Press.

Finley, M. I. (1973). *The ancient economy.* University of California Press.

Friedman, M. (1991). The Island of stone money. *Hoover Institution Working Papers, 91*(3), 1–5.

Geva, B. (2011). *The payment order of antiquity and the middle ages. A legal history.* Hart Publishing.

Gleeson, S. (2018). *The legal concept of money.* Oxford University Press.

Goodhart, C. A. E. (1998). The two concepts of money. Implications for the analysis of optimal currency areas. *European Journal of Political Economy, 14*(3), 407–432.

Green, S. (2019). Cryptocurrencies: The underlying technology. In D. Fox & S. Green (Eds.), *Cryptocurrencies in public and private law* (pp. 1–12). Oxford University Press.

Green, S. (2019). It's virtually money. In D. Fox & S. Green (Eds.), *Cryptocurrencies in public and private law* (pp. 13–31). Oxford University Press.

Gurley, J. G., & Shaw, E. S. (1960). *Money in a theory of finance.* The Brookings Institution.

Hayek, F. A. (1978). *Denationalisation of money. The argument refined.* Institute of Economic Affairs.

Hohfeld, W. (1914). Some fundamental legal conceptions as applied in judicial reasoning. *Yale Law Journal, 26*(8), 16–59.

Huber, J. (2017). *Sovereign money. Beyond reserve banking*. Palgrave Macmillan.

Ingves, S. (2018). Going cashless. *Finance & Development, 55*(2), 11–12.

Jakab, Z., & Kumhof, M. (2019). *Banks are not intermediaries of loanable funds. Facts, theory and evidence.* Bank of England. Accessed on 7 September 2019. https://www.bankofengland.co.uk/-/media/boe/files/working-paper/2018/banks-are-not-intermediaries-of-loanable-funds-facts-theory-and-evidence.pdf?la=en&hash=5FCDED87A783AA0483319CD4351170DB94C8A771.

Jevons, W. S. (1875). *Money and the mechanism of exchange.* D. Appleton and Company.

King, M. (2016). *The end of alchemy. Money, banking and the future of the global economy.* Little, Brown.

Kiyotaki, N., & Wright, R. (1989). On money as a medium of exchange. *Journal of Political Economy, 97*(4), 927–954.

Kohl, U. (2012). The rise of online intermediaries in the governance of the internet and beyond. *International Review of Law, Computers & Technology, 26,* 185–210.

Lagos, R. (2006). Inside and outside money. *Federal Reserve Bank of Minneapolis Research Department Staff Report, 374,* 1–8.

Lamport, L. R., Shostak, R., & Pease, M. (1982). The Byzantine generals problem. *ACM Transactions on Programming Languages and Systems, 4*(3), 382–401.

Li, J., & Mann, W. (2018). *Initial coin offering and platform building.* University of Cambridge. Accessed on 24 July 2018. https://www.jbs.cam.ac.uk/fileadmin/user_upload/research/centres/alternative-finance/downloads/2018-af-conference/paper-li.pdf.

Liptrap, J. S. (2020). *A social enterprise company in EU organisational law?* University of Cambridge. Accessed on 1 October 2020. https://papers.ssrn.com/sol3/papers.cfm?abstract_id=3703147.

Lo, S., & Wang, J. C. (2014). *Bitcoin as money?* Boston FED. Accessed on 6 November 2017. https://www.bostonfed.org/publications/current-policy-perspectives/2014/bitcoin-as-money.aspx.

Malinowski, B. (1961). *Argonauts of the Western Pacific. An account of native enterprise and adventure in the archipelagos of Melanesian New Guinea.* Dutton.

Marwala, T., & Hurwitz, E. (2017). *Artificial intelligence and economic theory: Skynet in the market.* Springer Nature.

Maurer, B. (2006). The anthropology of money. *Annual Review of Anthropology, 35,* 15–36.

Mauss, M. (2002). *The gift*. Routledge Classics (Published originally in 1967).

McLeay, M., Radia, A., & Thomas, R. (2014). *Money creation in the modern economy*. Bank of England. Accessed on 21 August 2017. http://www.bankofengland.co.uk/publications/Documents/quarterly bulletin/2014/qb14q1prereleasemoneycreation.pdf.
Menger, K. (1892). On the origin of money. *The Economic Journal, 2*(6), 239–255.
Morgan-Webb, C. (1935). *The money revolution*. Economic Forum Inc.
Nakamoto, S. (2008). *Bitcoin: A peer-to-peer electronic cash system*. Bitcoin.org. Accessed on 10 January 2016. https://bitcoin.org/bitcoin.pdf.
Naqvi, M., & Southgate, J. (2013). *Banknotes, local currencies and central bank objectives*. Bank of England. Accessed on 30 September 2017. http://www.bankofengland.co.uk/publications/Documents/quarterly bulletin/2013/qb130403.pdf.
O'Keefe, J. A. (1966). *The law of weights and measures*. Butterworths.
Pfajfar, D., Sgro, G., & Wagner, W. (2012). Are alternative currencies a substitute or complement to fiat money? Evidence form cross-country data. *International Journal of Community Currency Research, 16*(2012), 46–56.
Rahmatian, A. (2018). Money as a legally enforceable debt. *European Business Law Review, 29*(2), 205–236.
Richey, S. (2007). Manufacturing trust: Community currencies and the creation of social capital. *Political Behavior, 29*(2007), 69–88.
Sargent, T., & Wallace, N. (1982). The real bills doctrine versus the quantity theory. A reconsideration. *The Journal of Political Economy, 90*(6), 1212–1236.
Schmandt-Besserat, D. (2019). The invention of tokens. In A. Crisà, M. Grikaki & C. Rowan (Eds.), *Tokens. Culture, connections, communities* (pp. 11–18). Royal Numismatic Society.
Shenai, N. (2018). *Social finance. Shadow banking during the global financial crisis*. Palgrave Macmillan.
Simmel, G. (2004). *The philosophy of money*. Routledge Classics (Published originally in 1900).
Sissoko, C. (2007). Why inside money matters? *Journal of Money, Credit and Banking, 39*(8), 2097–2105.
Smith, M. E. (2004). The archaeology of ancient state economies. *Annual Review of Anthropology, 33*(2004), 73–102.
Strahan, P. E. (2010). Liquidity production in twenty-first-century banking. In A. N. Berger, P. Molyneux & J. O. Wilson (Eds.), *The Oxford handbook of banking* (pp. 112–145). Oxford University Press.
Tobin, J. (1963). *Commercial banks as creators of money*. Yale University. Accessed on 19 July 2018. https://cowles.yale.edu/sites/default/files/files/pub/d01/d0159.pdf.
Walras, L. (1926). *Elements of pure economics*. Richard D. Irwin.

Wray, L. R. (2013). Money. In G. C. Harcourt & P. Kriesler (Eds.), *Oxford handbook of post-Keynesian economics, Volume 1: Theory and origins* (pp. 139–151). Oxford University Press.

Wray, L. R. (2016). From the state theory of money to modern money. In D. Fox & W. Ernst (Eds.), *Money in the Western legal tradition. Middle ages to Bretton woods* (pp. 631–652). Oxford University Press.

Wu, L., Zhang, N., Chen, C., & Liu, J. (2009). *Electronic payment instruments and endogenous money supply.* IEE Xplore. Accessed on 8 October 2017. http://ieeexplore.ieee.org.ezproxy.is.ed.ac.uk/stamp/stamp.jsp?arnumber=5279897.

Ziegler, R. (2008). What makes the Kula go round? A simulation model of the spontaneous emergence of a ceremonial exchange system. *Social Networks, 30*(2), 107–126.

Social Finance Investments with a Focus on Digital Social Business Models

Stephan A. Jansen, Clemens Mast, and Wolfgang Spiess-Knafl

1 Introduction

Social venture capital funds follow the approach of traditional venture capital funds. They pool capital in their fund, apply relatively strict selection criteria, and only invest in a limited number of social enterprises with growth potential. These enterprises follow a social mission by either delivering products and services with a social value or by integrating the target group in the production process (e.g., Okpara & Halkias, 2011; Zahra et al., 2009).

S. A. Jansen
Karlshochschule International University, Karlsruhe, Germany

Alexander von Humboldt Institute for Internet & Society, Berlin, Germany

S. A. Jansen
e-mail: sjansen@karlshochschule.de

C. Mast
Siemens AG, Munich, Germany

W. Spiess-Knafl (✉)
European Center for Social Finance, Munich Business School, Munich, Germany

T. Walker et al. (eds.), *Innovations in Social Finance*,
https://doi.org/10.1007/978-3-030-72535-8_11

Some funds are now operating in their second decade while others have been launched more recently. The industry itself is in a growth phase in which strategies and approaches are still evolving rapidly. While some funds prioritize the social impact, others put a focus on the financial side of the investments.

The early years were a period of relatively low return expectations. Capital owners such as wealthy families and individuals were willing to accept low returns, and investment managers had to pioneer concepts which were successful when they have managed to return the invested capital. Fundraising volumes as well as return expectations have been on an uphill slope ever since, and some funds target financial returns as high as or even above 20% (Spiess-Knafl & Scheck, 2019).

Growing fund volumes and higher return expectations have an impact on investment strategies, which have led some fund managers to focus more on tech-related investments because these products and services are scalable and promise higher margins, since funds have to offer their investors a certain return. These returns seem easier with scalable digital business models that have low marginal costs in either production or delivery.

Given all the potentials, it is also important to keep the criticisms and risks in mind. One of the main criticisms of digital business models is that they are putting pressure on workforces. Platform workers have rarely access to full social benefits although their work is comparable to those of employees (e.g., Forde et al., 2017). There is also a widespread fear of a loss of good-paying jobs for large segments of the population (e.g., Frey & Osborne, 2017). Consequently, it becomes necessary to understand the implications at a time when digital business models are becoming increasingly relevant and transferred to emerging social business models.

It is also important to keep in mind that there are still open questions around biases in algorithms or the exclusion of certain target groups. There have been many cases where minorities have been discriminated against. It can include cases such as loan applications but also the fact that darker-skinned females are more likely to be misclassified in commercial gender classification systems (Buolamwini & Gebru, 2018).

This is the background for the analysis of 203 social enterprises focused on tech out of a sample of 397 investments by social venture funds. It aims to provide insights and categorize the types of digital social business models.

The models we discuss in this chapter show that digital technologies can help tackle social challenges in health care and education, among other social services. It is interesting to note that there is no strong evidence that social business models are at the forefront of advancing digital technologies. It is rarely the case that they are pioneering new digital technologies, but they are adapting already existing models to create social value. It is interesting to note that it is usually the other way round. Social innovations such as urban farming, couch surfing, coworking, or shared economy are developed in non-commercial domains and then commercialized in the more traditional parts of the economy (e.g., Rüede & Lurtz, 2012).

2 Theoretical Background

2.1 Business Model Innovation

Business models and business model innovation are frequently discussed topics in both research and practice when using an ecosystemic stakeholder and governmental perspective. Even though the discussion about business model innovation in social enterprises has received limited attention so far, the question of what a suitable business model is is not only important for profit-oriented organizations, but also highly relevant for social enterprises, when very different revenue models like fees, memberships, donations, grants, and service or product prices are concerned (Spiess-Knafl et al., 2015).

While business models have been crucial for trade and business activities since pre-classical times (Teece, 2010), the concept of the business model has been rising with the so-called dot.com era of the 1990s and has received a lot of attention since then (Zott et al., 2011). A business model describes the rationale behind how an organization creates, delivers, and captures value in economic, social, cultural, or other contexts. A significant change, e.g., the integration of a new technology, leads to a reconfiguration of this logic and thus to a new business model—a business model innovation. Accordingly, a business model is a logic or system of specific and interrelated activities that are carried out to satisfy the perceived market needs and generate profit.

The design elements that characterize the activity system of a business model are content, structure, and governance. Content is defined as the selection of activities to be performed, structure describes the link between the activities and their sequence, and governance refers to the entities performing the activities. Changing one or more of these elements means changing the whole model (Zott & Amit, 2017).

2.2 *Digitalization*

Digital technologies enable—and perhaps even force—an enterprise to reconsider and redesign its business model. This is true in the case of both for-profit and social enterprises. Digitalization is a broad term and therefore reveals little about what it is. For example, the emergence of digital technologies and applications, such as the Internet of Things (IoT), Industry 4.0, artificial intelligence, automation, remote monitoring, predictive maintenance, big data analytics, and other connected products, offer many business opportunities that are associated with digitalization. Further, digitalization touches almost all areas from the use of technologies to the narratives.

We define digitalization as the "use of digital technologies to innovate a business model and provide new revenue streams and value-producing opportunities in industrial ecosystems" (Parida et al., 2019). At its core, this definition takes the view that digitalization is much more than just the application of various digital technologies. Rather, digitalization facilitates new products, services, and business models.

Among other consequences, digitalization and big data analytics reshape existing business models in different ways (Loebbecke & Picot, 2015). Research studies show different ways in which digital technologies influence and change enterprises and their business models. They include optimization of the existing business model (e.g., process and cost optimization), transformation and scaling of the existing business models (e.g., redesign of existing models and an expansion of established business), and development of a new business model (e.g., displacement of established market participants and new products/services) (Bressanelli et al., 2018; Cenamor et al., 2017; Lenka et al., 2017; Loebbecke & Picot, 2015). Consequently, digital technologies like Industry 4.0, big data, blockchain, and artificial intelligence can be used to develop a business model on the content level through the digitalization of products and services, on the structure level through the digitalization of processes and decision-making, and on the governance level through the digital transformation of the value proposition and the operating model (Matzler et al., 2016).

Social enterprises seem to have another important and advantageous level: The narrative level of digitalization serves social enterprises as an advantage in the acceptance of digitalization as well as the scaling of digital products and services. The narrative foundation of a social venture is an important point because it often differs from the for-profit enterprises.

Social enterprises not only create services and values, but also produce social capital in the form of bonds and networks. However, these are always structured narratively and are created and developed through narratives. This narrative foundation influences the business model of a social enterprise, because the narrative delivers positive emotions that a for-profit company does not have.

The narratives can also build on trust. Although social enterprises are different from non-profits, there are still certain aspects that can be transferred. Non-profits enjoy a high degree of trust for various reasons driven by regulatory requirements such as the non-distribution constraints but also through the reputation of the sector and voluntary accountability efforts (Achleitner et al., 2013; Handy, 1995; Hansmann, 1980; Steinberg, 2006).

In line with the structure of the business model, the following figure illustrates the various aspects to consider (Fig. 1).

Every dimension can be combined and specified for the digitalization of existing or newly created business models. Some social business models might focus on the narrative side, while others might focus on digital processes or digital services.

2.3 *Social Finance*

Social finance is related to the financing of social enterprises. While impact investing is related to those investments which have positive financial return expectations, investors in social finance expect both positive social change and financial returns. It includes grant-giving institutions, among others, and thus encompasses a complete set of instruments to fund social innovation and social change in general.

While there are many aspects to consider, we focus on three main aspects. These elements are the reduction of transaction costs, an increase of trust, and a rise in productivity.

Economic activities are associated with costs. It is expensive to gather information, contract services, and monitor and control the quality. Firms

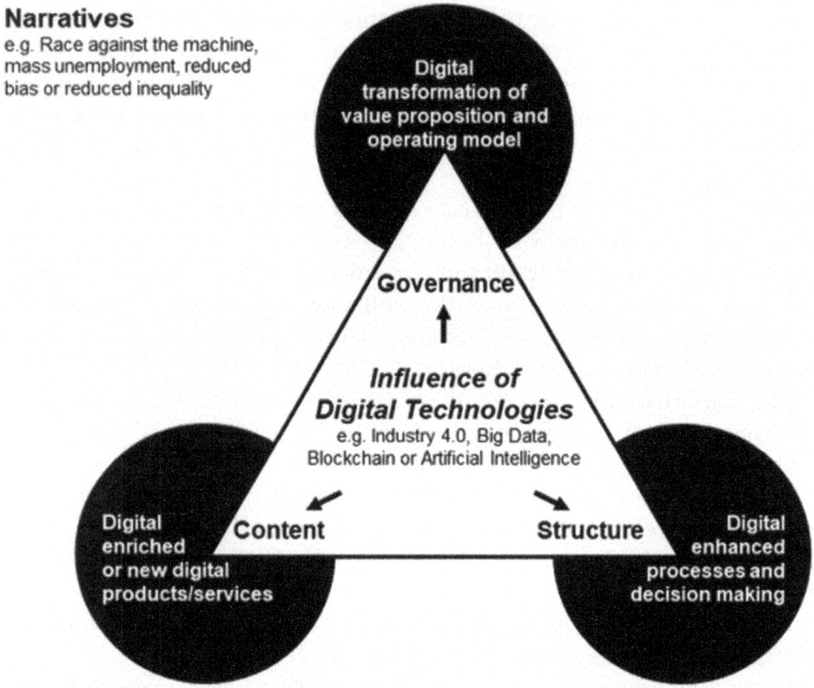

Fig. 1 Different levels of a social business model

exist to internalize those processes and avoid transaction costs with third parties (Coase, 1937). The ongoing digitalization has reduced the transaction costs for almost any industry and facilitated the use of markets. The most visible examples can be found in the gig and platform economy (e.g., Drahokoupil & Fabo, 2016; Kenney & Zysman, 2016). Lower transaction costs also open possibilities for disintermediation as intermediaries are no longer needed. Therefore, we expect to see an increase in investments taking advantage of the lower transaction costs.

Social enterprises and non-profits in general enjoy high levels of trust which is often an enabler to deliver their services (e.g., Handy, 1995; Steinberg, 2006). It seems likely that social enterprises will use digital tools to increase transparency and find other ways to reduce information asymmetries. The reduction of information asymmetries might ultimately enhance the trust in a certain product or service. There are various ways to enhance trust. One prominent example is the blockchain technology, which uses cryptographic methods to store information publicly and securely.

Digitalization can also contribute to higher productivity. It is sometimes compared to the steam engine and electrification when it comes to radical changes (e.g., McGowan et al., 2015). It can be related to data analysis or the decision-making process regarding the allocation and distribution of goods and services. This is in line with the general view that the allocation of capital should go to enterprises that promise the highest productivity.

In addition, there are aspects that might be less intuitive. For example, digital tools could be used in situations where human rights are violated, as well as to track supply chains or enable the delivery of services outside of the reach of oppressive regimes (Scheck & Spiess-Knafl, 2020).

3 Empirical Analysis

This chapter is an exploratory study on the emerging topic of social finance. As there are no existing databases, it was necessary to create a database for the analysis. In line with other explanatory studies (e.g., Spiess-Knafl et al., 2015), the data collection follows a two-phase approach.

The first step was the identification of relevant social venture capital funds in this area which have an investment portfolio with publicly available data. The funds listed below provide the basis for this analysis.

The selection of the funds was decided to ensure a globally balanced dataset. It includes funds active in North America, Europe, and across other continents. The investors use different financing instruments in the funds and invest in different stages of the entrepreneurial life cycle. This analysis is based on 13 funds with an overall portfolio of 397 investments (Table 1)

In the second step, all portfolio companies were identified, and a description of the business model was added to the database to classify the business model. The classification was conducted independently by at least two of the authors. In case of divergences, the classification was discussed to reach a conclusion.

4 Findings

The analysis reveals a few interesting findings. The main one is that there is a relatively high amount of non-tech-related investments. Overall, the

Table 1 Overview of funds and number of investments

Nr.	*Fund*	*Headquarter*	*Regional focus*	*Number of investments*
1	Aavishkaar	India	India, South and South East Asia	35
2	Acumen Fund	USA	Global	39
3	Ananda Impact Ventures	Germany	Europe	23
4	Bamboo Capital	Luxembourg	Global	22
5	BonVenture	Germany	German-speaking countries	18
6	INCO	France	Global	43
7	LGT Venture Philanthropy	Switzerland	Global	14
8	MAZE	Portugal	Europe	19
9	PG Impact Investments	Switzerland	Global	6
10	The Rise Fund	USA	Global	25
11	Working Capital Fund	USA	Global	8
12	Obvious Ventures	USA	Mostly North America	55
13	Village Capital	USA	Global	90
Total				397

Source Own illustration

technology implemented is rather well established and mature. There are also a few dominant clusters of technology deployed.

4.1 Proportion of Tech-Related Investments

Out of the 397 investments, 203 focused on a technology, leaving slightly less than half of the investments (194 to be precise) as non-tech-related investments. This is a relatively high proportion for non-tech-related investments.

Most of the cases are less focused on innovation or new services and more on providing basic services, such as in the department of energy or infrastructure. Some examples include social housing, waste management, micro-warehouses, sustainable home construction, biogas facilities, or solar energy. Agriculture is also a popular investment target, which includes investments in dairy brands, alternative meat producers, cocoa

Table 2 Sector classification of tech-related investments

Healthcare	39	19.2%
Education	36	17.7%
Fintech	36	17.7%
Sustainable Consumption and Fairtrade	19	9.4%
Mobility and Logistics	11	5.4%
Energy	16	7.9%
Labor Market and Inclusion	7	3.4%
Agriculture	9	4.4%
Other	30	14.8%
Total	203	100.0%

farming, and irrigation systems. These investments are focused more on developing countries and less on industrialized countries.

Education and health care are other topics with significant investment needs. Examples include learning kits, the operations of schools, and the provision of affordable or emergency healthcare services. Finance is another big investment area that is often connected to other topics. Student loans, for instance, are linked to education while energy finance is linked to energy-generating assets such as solar panels.

In addition, employment schemes for target groups, the design for artisanal product, or traditional food delivery do not rely on technology. Many business models related to the circular economy or sustainability, such as sustainable fashion or sustainable tourism, do not need technology to be successful.

4.2 *Fields of Investment Activity*

The investments in this database often combine different fields. For example, education and financial services, energy and financial services, and healthcare and mobility services are fields which we have seen in the database. Table 2 shows the number of investments in each investment and the proportion of the total number.

4.3 *Specific Fields in the Database*

Health care offers many opportunities to digitalize existing processes. There are many examples of app-based communication channels between doctor and patient. Other examples include artificial intelligence for medical data analysis, information systems for medications or medical bills, and datasets for nutrition. One of the biggest investments in this field is for a company delivering medical products via drones.

Agriculture primarily requires assets such as machinery, land, or warehouses. However, there are opportunities to transform some of the processes. Some examples include artificial intelligence solutions to find the best timing for feeding, cultivating, and harvesting. Solutions might use weather forecasts and historical yields to determine the optimal timing. Farmers might also be willing to pay for price data to sell their products at higher prices or at different markets.

Education offers many opportunities to introduce digital solutions. The examples in the database are built around tutoring and mentoring via online tools, registration tools for childcare, recruiting platforms, recognition of handwriting, automatic grading of assignments, or AI-based language learning. The need to generate revenues excludes some more inclusive business models, which might be the focus of more philanthropic initiatives.

Concepts in energy are built around software-based management of energy consumption. In industrial countries, the investments concentrate on reducing the carbon footprint.

Many concepts are based on the integration of financial services that might be considered as "unbanked." Reducing the transaction costs involved by implementing digital solutions might provide an answer to this problem. Examples in the database include financial services for small business owners, last mile payments, and microfinance institutions introducing not only digital processes, but also wealth-building strategies.

There are relatively few examples of concepts focusing on the labor market and the integration of a certain target group in it. It seems that social enterprises operating in work integration can hardly rely on digital tools as they need to communicate and interact directly with their employees. Some examples in the database include the opportunity to generate income on platforms to sell products or on gig economy platforms.

There are a few examples of logistics companies that optimize logistics and delivery services in emerging countries. Other examples include apps, which have become an integral part of the sharing economy and can, for instance, help to share car rides or even cars.

It seems that sustainable consumption and digitalization have a big overlap in terms of new business models. There are various online marketplaces in which sellers can put sustainable products for sale or where valuable products can be resold. Other examples are either part of the sharing economy or producing alternatives to unsustainable products. A few examples are based on better data to assess the supply chain of products.

Examples that could not be classified in the other categories include a range of different concepts. These include cross-family organization apps, satellite data to answer specific questions, match-making platforms between campers and landowners, and supply chain data analytics concepts.

4.4 *Technological Capabilities*

It emerged from the data analysis that the business concepts financed by social venture funds in the technological area have a lower level of technological capabilities than those currently financed by venture capital funds when it comes to for-profit enterprises. Accordingly, social venture funds are increasingly investing in social business models that have a less sophisticated digital technology at their core. These so-called low technologies (low tech) are, in contrast to high technologies, already established (e.g., in another industry) and largely mature. The term "low tech" is not clearly defined, and its definition is strongly dependent on the current state of development in the respective market. What is considered high tech at the moment can be classified as low tech in due course. Correspondingly, the amount of investments by social venture funds in digital low-tech-based social business is significantly smaller.

Within the sample, the regular case is that the technologies have been well established until they were rolled out for social purposes. This pattern suggests that digitalization in the social business sector is catching up to the for-profit enterprises.

In a subsequent study, it would be worthwhile to analyze if social enterprises are better at working around the governance aspects of business model innovation. Indeed, they might be better suited to work on the narratives of new business models.

4.5 *Digital Social Business Model*

Digitalization is revolutionizing the way organizations can generate added value within their sector. Through the use and dissemination of the Internet of Things (IoT) technologies, intensive data exchange, and predictive analysis, new opportunities exist for generating additional value or entirely new added value (Zott & Amit, 2017).

However, technological application alone is not enough to generate benefit from digitalization. It requires an adaptation of existing business models or a complete redesign of an innovative business model based on digital technology. This shift applies to both for-profit companies and social enterprises.

The analysis has shown that many social enterprises are using established digital business models, which confirms the assumption that digital business models are becoming increasingly relevant and important in the context of social enterprises. This widespread adoption might also be related to an increased willingness to pay.

The analysis of the digital social business models indicates that increasing digitalization has influenced the activities of social enterprises within their digital business model on the system levels of content, structure, and governance.

On a content level, digitalization has enabled social enterprises to create new products and service offerings that were not possible before. For example, one company offers real-time insights in aquaculture based on their AI-driven data management platform and empowers farms and research centers to track and manage their aquatic populations to contribute to food sustainability.

On a structure level, digital technologies enable social enterprises to create new forms of relationships with their target group and offer completely new ways to communicate their added value. Another example worth mentioning is an AI-powered companion for cancer patients and their caretakers. The company provides health monitoring, psychological coaching, and medication management for more effective treatment processes.

On a governance level, digital business models provide social enterprises with the opportunity to scale faster and more cost-effectively in order to expand their influence. For example, a German social enterprises offers a tool for people with hearing impairment which helps them to particapte in education and society via speech transcriptions. Transcriptions are transmitted live on canvas, live streaming, or smartphone.

5 Conclusion

Our analysis shows that investments in the social finance sector continue to target non-tech investments to a significant extent. Simultaneously, investments in tech-related social enterprises are responsible for a large share of investments in the analyzed sample.

The main results are the observed time lag, the potential to create impact, and the limitations of digital business models.

Investments in technologies seem to lag for for-profit businesses. New technological developments, which could be observed in traditional segments, are being implemented much later in social enterprises. There are various potential arguments to explain this lag. It might have to do with competition for tech-talent and less appealing compensation structures for employees. Other reasons might be that the initial costs are too high for social enterprises and they need to wait until decreased prices allow them to enter the market, or that social venture funds themselves may not have the due diligence to analyze a range of technology-based ventures.

The examples mentioned have shown that digital technologies can help ease social challenges, such as facilitating access to education, improving health care, or contributing to environmental and climate protection. It can be expected that these elements will continue to play a role.

However, not every social challenge can be solved with digital technologies. Digital solutions seem to reach their limits when interpersonal relationships predominate in a social business model. This aspect of personal commitment may have less affinity for digitalization.

The chapter uses an exploratory set of data, which has some limitations in terms of size and potential selection bias. The level of technology is hard to assess based on online research, and the limited number of funds might impact the representation of the sample.

However, the analysis reveals some insights as well as further questions, which point toward a need for further research. Although there is evidence that social enterprises are late adapters of technologies, it is less clear how this process works. Future research might look at the temporal and material relationship between technology financing and technology receptivity in the social space and the more traditional space.

This question also has policy implications as social finance could be a force for general productivity growth. There is potential for governments to adapt their funding strategies.

A final question relates to the ethical dimensions. In line with Bostrom (2016), one could ask if social enterprises should be more critical of their use of technologies due to ethical questions of data governance as well as the "indirect normativity" of algorithms.

References

Achleitner, A.-K., Lutz, E., Mayer, J., & Spiess-Knafl, W. (2013). Disentangling gut feeling: Assessing the integrity of social entrepreneurs. *Voluntas: International Journal of Voluntary and Nonprofit Organizations, 24*(1), 93–124.

Bostrom, N. (2016). *Superintelligence: Paths, dangers, strategies* (Reprint). Oxford University Press.

Bressanelli, G., Adrodegari, F., Perona, M., & Saccani, N. (2018). Exploring how usage-focused business models enable circular economy through digital technologies. *Sustainability, 10*(3), 639.

Buolamwini, J., & Gebru, T. (2018, January). Gender shades: Intersectional accuracy disparities in commercial gender classification. In *Conference on fairness, accountability and transparency* (pp. 77–91). PMLR.

Cenamor, J., Sjödin, D. R., & Parida, V. (2017). Adopting a platform approach in servitization: Leveraging the value of digitalization. *International Journal of Production Economics, 192*, 54–65.

Coase, R. H. (1937). The nature of the firm. *Economica, 4*(16), 386–405.

Drahokoupil, J., & Fabo, B. (2016). The platform economy and the disruption of the employment relationship. *ETUI Research Paper-Policy Brief*, *5*.

Forde, C., Stuart, M., Joyce, S., Oliver, L., Valizade, D., Alberti, G., Hardy, K., Trappmann, V., Umney, C., & Carson C. (2017). *The social protection of workers in the platform economy*. Policy Department A of the European Parliament.

Frey, C. B., & Osborne, M. A. (2017). The future of employment: How susceptible are jobs to computerisation? *Technological Forecasting and Social Change, 114*, 254–280.

Handy, F. (1995). Reputation as collateral: An economic analysis of the role of trustees of nonprofits. *Nonprofit and Voluntary Sector Quarterly, 24*(4), 293–305.

Hansmann, H. B. (1980). The role of nonprofit enterprise. *The Yale Law Journal, 89*(5), 835–901. JSTOR. https://doi.org/10.2307/796089.

Kenney, M., & Zysman, J. (2016). The rise of the platform economy. *Issues in Science and Technology, 32*(3), 61.
Lenka, S., Parida, V., & Wincent, J. (2017). Digitalization capabilities as enablers of value co-creation in servitizing firms. *Psychology & Marketing, 34*(1), 92–100.
Loebbecke, C., & Picot, A. (2015). Reflections on societal and business model transformation arising from digitization and big data analytics: A research agenda. *The Journal of Strategic Information Systems, 24*(3), 149–157.
Matzler, K., Bailom, F., & von den Eichen, S. F. (2016). *Digital disruption: Wie Sie Ihr Unternehmen auf das digitale Zeitalter vorbereiten*. Vahlen.
McGowan, M. A., Andrews, D., Criscuolo, C., & Nicoletti, Giuseppe. (2015). *The future of productivity*. OECD. http://www.oecd.org/eco/OECD-2015-The-future-of-productivity-book.pdf.
Okpara, J. O., & Halkias, D. (2011). Social entrepreneurship: An overview of its theoretical evolution and proposed research model. *International Journal of Social Entrepreneurship and Innovation, 1*(1), 4–20.
Parida, V., Sjödin, D., & Reim, W. (2019). *Reviewing literature on digitalization, business model innovation, and sustainable industry: Past achievements and future promises*. Multidisciplinary Digital Publishing Institute.
Rüede, D., & Lurtz, K. (2012). Mapping the various meanings of social innovation: Towards a differentiated understanding of an emerging concept. *SSRN Electronic Journal*. https://doi.org/10.2139/ssrn.2091039.
Spiess-Knafl, W., & Scheck, B. (2019). *Social enterprise finance market analysis and recommendations for delivery options*. Publications Office of the European Union.
Scheck, B., & Spiess-Knafl, W. (2020). *Impact investing in the framework of business and human rights*. European Parliament. https://www.europarl.europa.eu/thinktank/de/document.html?reference=EXPO_IDA(2020)603490.
Spiess-Knafl, W., Mast, C., & Jansen, S. A. (2015). On the nature of social business model innovation. *Social Business, 5*(2), 113–130.
Steinberg, R. (2006). Economic theories of nonprofit organizations. In *The nonprofit sector: A research handbook* (pp. 117–139). Yale University Press.
Teece, D. J. (2010). Business models, business strategy and innovation. *Long Range Planning, 43*(2–3), 172–194.
Zahra, S. A., Gedajlovic, E., Neubaum, D. O., & Shulman, J. M. (2009). A typology of social entrepreneurs: Motives, search processes and ethical challenges. *Journal of Business Venturing, 24*(5), 519–532.
Zott, C., & Amit, R. (2017). Business model innovation: How to create value in a digital world. *GfK Marketing Intelligence Review, 9*(1), 18–23.
Zott, C., Amit, R., & Massa, L. (2011). The business model: Recent developments and future research. *Journal of Management, 37*(4), 1019–1042.

From Community Bank to Solidarity Fintech: The Case of Palmas e-Dinheiro in Brazil

Asier Ansorena, Eduardo H. Diniz, Erica S. Siqueira, and Marlei Pozzebon

1 Introduction

Fifty million Brazilian people live below the poverty line. This means that at least 25% of Brazilian families live with a monthly income that is less than or equal to 5.5 dollars a day. In the Northeast region, the poorest part of the country, the percentage of families below the poverty line has increased to 43.5% (Oliveira, 2017). In addition, the Brazilian financial system is characterized by a continuous concentration process that limits its expansion and curbs the inclusion of the impoverished part of

A. Ansorena (✉)
Banco Palmas, Fortaleza, Brazil

E. H. Diniz · E. S. Siqueira
FGV EAESP, São Paulo, Brazil
e-mail: eduardo.diniz@fgv.br

E. S. Siqueira
e-mail: erica.siqueira@fgv.br

M. Pozzebon
HEC Montréal e FGV EAESP, São Paulo, Brazil
e-mail: marlei.pozzebon@hec.ca

T. Walker et al. (eds.), *Innovations in Social Finance*,
https://doi.org/10.1007/978-3-030-72535-8_12

the population. In Brazil, as of 2017, four banks held 72.7% of the country's commercial financial assets and high-interest rate consumer loans (Furche et al., 2017). Banking concentration has its historical origin in the explosion of foreign debt in 1982 in which Brazil's development pattern became even more dependent on foreign capital, resulting in persistent volatility in interest rates, inflation, and the reorientation of banks toward the market segments that are considered safer and more profitable (Souza, 2015). This scenario contributes to persistent access inequality to the traditional financial system, excluding mostly young adults, the less educated, and those who work outside of the formal labor force (Demirguc-Kunt et al., 2018).

To overcome this inequality, social organizations that seek a more sustainable development model have attempted to build effective solidarity finance instruments, with the hope that those efforts can help eradicate poverty by guaranteeing access to financial services and thus fostering local development and community empowerment (Freire, 2013). An example of a solidarity finance instrument includes community banks offering microcredit and a form of social currency. Such instruments also articulate themselves alongside traditional banks through the correspondent banking system, in addition to mapping local production and consumption activities (Diniz et al., 2014).

Parallel to the efforts of community banks, technology has greatly contributed to the emergence of more efficient alternatives that provide access to financial services. Mobile technologies, in particular, offer a way to overcome the rigidity and resistance to change that characterizes the conventional financial system. These technological advancements foster new business models, such as financial startup companies operating on digital platforms, widely known as fintech, an acronym for "financial technology" (Siqueira et al., 2018).

In this chapter, we describe Palmas e-Dinheiro, a Solidarity Fintech owned by Banco Palmas, which we define as a *digital endeavor focused on financial inclusion and local development* that has a strong identification with the community banks' movement. We start by presenting the context that characterizes the 20 years since the creation of Banco Palmas in 1998, including a description of the solidarity tools developed during this period and up to launching the e-Dinheiro mobile payment platform to support operations of the community banks. We close this chapter by describing Banco Mumbuca, a community bank with the largest e-Dinheiro operation, with more than fifty thousand users receiving social benefits from a city government. The Mumbuca case will be analyzed using the multilevel framework model proposed by Pozzebon and Diniz (2012) to explain the process in which "social innovations and community arrangements shape a solidarity fintech."

The facts presented in this chapter come from many sources reported on the Palmas case over its 20 years of existence: Meyer (2012), França Filho et al. (2012), Blanc and Fare (2013), Fare et al. (2013) and Rigo and França Filho (2017). Moreover, three of the authors have made regular local visits and published research about the Palmas experience for more than ten years, and the first author has been closely involved in the Palmas evolution for the last ten years.

2 Background—From a Local Bank to a Replicable Model

In 1997 the residents of Conjunto Palmeiras, a poor neighborhood in the outskirts of Fortaleza in Ceará state, developed a research project to better understand the way their local economy worked and answer the question: "why are we poor?" The consumption map generated from this research initiative showcased that most of the income residents generated was spent outside of their neighborhood and that they needed to implement solutions to foster local consumption in their own neighborhood. Such a modest initiative ended up with the launching of Banco Palmas in January 1998, with only R$2,000 in capital donated by a local NGO (Faria, 2018). The bank, an initiative born with the self-determination and solidarity spirit of the Conjunto Palmeiras neighborhood, would become a concrete financial alternative to the people living in that community.

Soon after its creation in March 1999 Banco Palmas' operation was legally authorized under Brazilian Law 9790, thus approved to promote nonprofit experimentation in commerce and credit through alternative production systems, and allowed to partner with public and private entities to promote financial inclusion (Diniz et al., 2016). After that, community banks achieved legal recognition as civil society organizations aiming to provide financial services to foster local development.

PalmaCard was Banco Palmas' first social innovation, created to facilitate access to credit and promote the local economy. It was a small paper card where all client transactions were registered by hand. As this tool became successfully adopted by a growing number of users, a more efficient liquidity process was necessary to deal with a larger scale of operation. To respond to this increased demand for a local payment instrument, Palmas issued a community currency in 2001 (Ansorena, 2020).

The first community currency in Brazil faced some aversion by Brazilian financial regulators. The Central Bank refused to accept it as a valid currency, determining it was a "fake currency" instead. Banco Palmas defended itself in court and won the right to issue a local currency paired one-to-one with the national currency. In 2011, the Central Bank apologized to Banco Palmas, additionally recognizing the role of community currencies to empower local economies around Brazil and attesting to the legal character of community banks operations. At that time, community currencies were already a reality in other parts of the world, usually with circulation restricted geographically. Mostly created and operated by self-managed associations, community currencies defy the domination of national payment means by promoting local payment systems as instruments to fight the money concentration in the capitalist system (Ansorena, 2020).

Therefore, community currency use is related to the tools used to improve financial inclusion and strengthen solidarity relations (Diniz et al., 2018). Although frequently focused on promoting local development, community currencies vary enormously in their goals and strategies. They can be found in refugee camps that suffer from a shortage of local currency and resources, as well as in affluent neighborhoods aiming to promote consumption from local farmers. They can be as old as "Wir," operating without interruption for more than 80 years to support small entrepreneurs in Switzerland, and reach a few million users, such as the case of the "Club de Trueque" in Argentina during the financial crisis of the 2000s.

What is particular in the case of Banco Palmas and its "Palma" currency is that it became more than a solution for the problems of a single neighborhood, eventually growing to represent a model that spread its social technologies to other communities around the country. In 2005, Banco Palmas established the Instituto Palmas to disseminate its model by teaching its methodology in other communities. Two important partnerships were established to serve these goals: with the National Secretary of the Solidarity Economy (SENAES), which was responsible for promoting solidarity economy in the country and with Banco do Brasil, the largest commercial bank in the country. While the SENAES provided logistic and financial support for the expansion of the community bank model,

Banco do Brasil became a correspondent bank, allowing Palmas to have more access to credit resources and providing more credit to the local population (Melo Neto Segundo & Magalhães, 2009).

As far as 2018, Instituto Palmas helped deliver over 14 million reais in microcredit to thousands of entrepreneurs, mostly women, who had not yet had access to formal financial services. Moreover, it taught other communities to build their own community banks, develop their own microcredit methodology, create their own local currencies, and operate within the banking correspondent network. With the knowledge imparted, the community banks grew in numbers; ultimately, benefiting local communities through the ease of accessing credit and financial services (Ansorena, 2020).

Banco Palmas was able to scale up its operations from a few hundred people in Fortaleza to hundreds of thousands of people located in diverse and widely spread poverty-stricken areas all over the country. More than one hundred community banks were created following the Banco Palmas model, supported by partnerships with the public sector and the use of the correspondent banking model. This meant that despite applying their own credit scoring methodology, community banks had to operate within the rules and technological infrastructure of the partner public banks.

From the beginning, when Banco Palmas was first created, the community residents knew that they needed to create their own bank. Beyond answering a question regarding access to financial services, the bank's establishment represented the need for constituting local power. Following the rules and technology of traditional banks limited the autonomy that community banks envisioned. However, the digitalization process opened new opportunities for realignment.

3 Digital Social Currency—Questioning the Limits of the Paper Format

The expansion of the community banks also brought up the issue of the high costs of printing and managing a physical currency. In 2013, during the 3rd meeting of the community bank network, community bank coordinators cast doubts on the limits of the social currency in paper format (Diniz et al., 2016). At the time, even the circulation of the Palmas currency was decreasing, although local residents kept in mind the idea of consumption within the neighborhood (Rigo & França Filho, 2017).

Therefore, new questions arose: Had the Palmas currency already fulfilled its role as a catalyzer for local consumption and development? Was it about to disappear, or could it take on a different role? According to Joaquim de Melo Neto, co-founder and coordinator of Banco Palmas, social currencies should be seen as a mechanism, even if temporary, to stimulate the local consumption and appreciation of local products: "the social currencies cannot, therefore, be viewed romantically or as a panacea, but as an instrument with roles to play" (Rigo & França Filho, 2017).

While mobile payments have been considered a solution for leveraging the spread of currency use in poor communities around the world, particularly in Africa and Asia (de Albuquerque et al., 2016), Instituto Palmas started to support the idea of creating a digital platform for managing community currency payments. In addition to supporting a higher scale, a mobile payment approach could lower the costs of creating and managing a paper currency. Therefore, digital payments have the potential to encourage greater local economic development (Cernev et al., 2009; Duncombe & Boateng, 2009; Ramada-Sarasola, 2012). Next, we will explore Palmas' initial experiences of digitalization.

4 First Digital Experience—Partnerships and the Lack of Control Over the Platform

In 2012, Banco Palmas wanted to develop a digital community currency within Conjunto Palmeiras with the expectation that digitalization of the social currency would increase: the speed of money circulation, the currency management efficiency, and the local monetary multiplier (Hernandes et al., 2018). At that time, the only legal way for a community bank to issue a digital currency was to partner with traditional organizations from the telecommunication and financial sectors. Financial inclusion through mobile platforms can be inaccessible to some users due to their lack of electricity and/or internet connection. Additionally, the population could be lacking in technological literacy and confidence in mobile payments (Suresh & Namdeo, 2018).

Despite its potential, the first mobile experience of Banco Palmas was unsuccessful. Operational issues, conflict of interests, and divergent expectations among partners were reported as the main factors responsible for the project's failure (Diniz et al., 2013). The Banco Palmas managers felt excluded from the decision-making process by the other partners, as most of their suggestions were either not approved or took a long time to be approved. The low adoption of this mobile payment solution by users and merchants in Conjunto Palmeiras reflected this lack of coordination among partners. The lack of success in this initiative from Banco Palmas, the first and best organized community bank in the country, meant that other community banks would not attempt the project in Brazil.

By the end of 2013 the country's political and economic mood began to shift (Arcanjo & Oliveira, 2017), in that the Brazilian federal government changed its perception of what its role should be in supporting the solidarity economy. Because of this process the SENAES, despite its 10 years of investment in community banks and positive impact on hundreds of thousands of people, slowly lost the relevance and the ability to establish public policies (Ansorena, 2020).

This change triggered the internal debate that community banks have had over the years about the need to diversify their financing strategy in order to gain autonomy from public sources. Such autonomy was necessary to expand the ability to deliver solidarity-based financial services beyond the limited approach adopted during the years of public sector support. Although this political and economic downturn was challenging, there was still room for community banks to develop new opportunities.

Some old aspirations of the community banks, such as the opening of bank accounts and the issuing of currency by community banks as part of the legal framework, came to consideration when a new regulation for payment platforms was issued by Central Bank in November 2013. This new regulation included ideas of the solidarity economy movement expressed in a never approved bill project dated from 2006, designed to institutionalize the solidarity finance system (Ansorena, 2020).

Based on the new regulation, community banks would be able to establish their own digital payment systems. Banks could offer digital checking accounts on their own digital payment platform and nonfinancial institutions could issue digital currency. This new Brazilian regulation for digital payments claims that by proposing the replacement of community paper currencies with a digital version, Instituto Palmas was about to become a solidarity fintech.

For the first time in 20 years, community banks would have a regulatory framework more in tune with their mandate of achieving greater financial inclusion; allowing them to provide a wider range of financial services and adopt their own digital payment platform without the need to partner with traditional actors from the financial or telecommunication markets. Although it did not include the values of the solidarity economy, the new regulation gave the community banks room to grow in an autonomous manner and to keep up with the opportunities arising around digital payments.

5 Palmas e-Dinheiro—A Solidarity Fintech Experience in Brazil

In mid-2015 Instituto Palmas launched e-Dinheiro in partnership with MoneyClip, a Brazilian startup, interested in building a digital platform for financial inclusion. As had happened in previous cases, the platform was first implemented as a pilot project at Conjunto Palmeiras. With this new platform, community banks could deliver solidarity financial services through SMS, mobile apps, and web channels. As e-Dinheiro became more widely used, the paper community currency after almost 15 years of operations, would be phased out to become an educational tool, used mostly in financial literacy classes and in solidarity economy workshops.

Built around a partnership between a tech startup and Instituto Palmas, e-Dinheiro had to take into account the different values and approaches of each partner. Nevertheless, Instituto Palmas and MoneyClip were able to work toward common goals and avoid the problems experienced in the first digital payment project that had been tried a couple of years earlier. This time the community bank kept the lead role over the platform, so the design and implementation of the solution was more bottom-up than it had been in the previous failed project (Ansorena, 2020).

Palmas e-Dinheiro faced challenges inherent to other fintech initiatives, such as the need for scale, since expanding the operation required investments and the search for capital led to targeting financial performance indicators (Carraher et al., 2016; Battilana & Dorado, 2010; Zahra et al., 2009). In addition to facing the complexity and costs of the technology infrastructure, Palmas managers had to overcome the challenges that come with being a solidarity fintech—in particular regarding the governance model—which is critical for maintaining control over the decision-making process on the platform (Diniz et al., 2018).

A year and a half after the implementation of Palmas e-Dinheiro, the network of community banks took control over it. While MoneyClip, the for-profit partner, was expecting the platform to become financially sustainable within two years, guided by solidarity economy principles, the view of Instituto Palmas was more long term, knowing that other mobile payment experiences around the world had taken a few years to reach the breakeven point.

In 2018 81 community banks were registered in the Palmas e-Dinheiro platform, among them 48 used it for local operations and 21 actively implemented it in their communities. However, the impact and usage vary greatly. In Banco Mumbuca, founded in 2013 in the city of Maricá, state of Rio de Janeiro, there are thousands of users and a conditional cash transfer program from the city government is delivered in the social currency of the community bank and also through e-Dinheiro (Bolsa Mumbuca). In other cases, community banks struggled to get the platform off the ground because they were not able to convince other partners and stakeholders to participate, as well as, convince anchor institutions to adopt it. Although there is still much room for e-Dinheiro to grow, its platform and the opportunities it presents are already making a difference for banks around Brazil. This potential is seen in the Banco Mumbuca case, which is explained in the next section.

6 The Case of Banco Mumbuca—The Largest e-Dinheiro Operation

To better explain the Banco Mumbuca case, we apply the multilevel framework model proposed by Pozzebon and Diniz (2012), which deals with technology's implications at the community level. It does so by describing the relevant actors, the negotiation mechanisms among them, and the resulting technology-in-practice. Figure 1 illustrates the dimensions of the multilevel framework.

The context refers to the social, cultural, and political sphere where a given technology has been implemented and used. Analyzing a context implies identifying relevant social groups and recognizing similar and conflicting interpretive frames among them. The process consists of understanding the way the various social groups negotiate to achieve a resultant solution. Finally, the content refers to the technology-in-practice as a result of the negotiation process, i.e., the expected and unexpected consequences of the implementation and use of a given technology.

The main social groups involved in the creation of Banco Mumbuca are as follows: the 12,000 families that benefit from the complementary cash transfer program in the city of Maricá; the local community bank staff responsible for all the operations of Banco Mumbuca; Instituto Palmas, which is in charge of the training of Banco Mumbuca's staff and

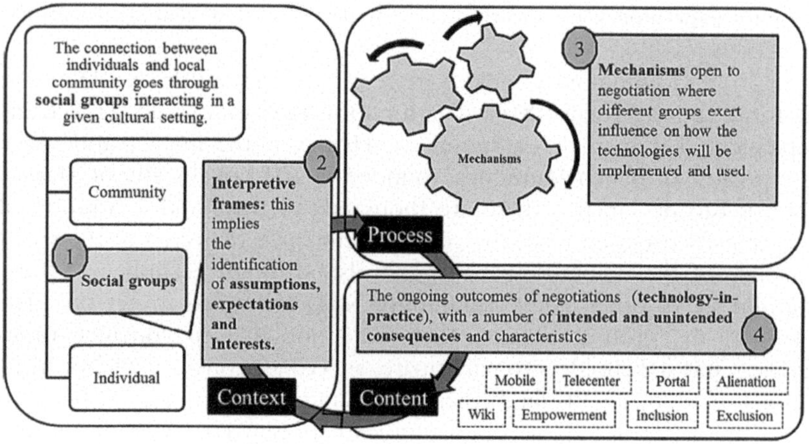

Fig. 1 Multilevel framework (*Source* Pozzebon and Diniz [2012])

the dissemination of the solidarity economy principles; the city government of Maricá, which provides financial resources for the beneficiaries and supports the regulatory conditions needed by Banco Mumbuca's operations; local businesses of Maricá that have registered at Banco Mumbuca to accept "mumbucas"; residents of the city of Maricá other than the beneficiaries, who can also open accounts at Banco Mumbuca; and technology providers, first related to the POS card platform and then the MoneyClip team that initially ran the e-Dinheiro platform before Instituto Palmas took over the operations of the platform.

Next, we describe the negotiation mechanisms that the socially relevant groups had to engage into make Banco Mumbuca a reality. The facts described below are based on the authors' knowledge of the case and is documented in detail from the following three sources: Faria (2018), Nascimento (2015), and Freitas and Egydio (2014).

The first movement to create Banco Mumbuca took place in 2011 when the mayor of Maricá at the time decided to distribute a small part of the oil royalties, that the city had begun to receive, as a social benefit. The amount to be distributed would be added to the benefit that the poorest families already received through the Bolsa Família program. Bolsa Família is a federal income transfer program for the poorest families created in 2003. It is an income transfer program with wide national coverage, whose benefits are conditional on keeping children vaccinated and attending school. The circulation of this benefit was restricted to the city of Maricá to promote local commerce.

Although the mayor had been inspired by the Palmas model, no municipality in Brazil had the right to issue local currencies. The solution was to hire a local community bank that was to deliver the benefit on behalf of the city administration. That solution had two main problems: First, there was no community bank in Maricá, and second, the city could not give money to a third party (the community bank) and allow it to convert city resources into a type of "local currency."

In June 2013, part of the problem was solved when the city council approved the Municipal Program of the Solidarity Economy. This new regulation guaranteed that the city government could enter into "agreements with civil society organizations certified by the Brazilian Network of Community Banks, granting them financial and structural contributions to its operation" (Freitas & Egydio, 2014). In addition to approving this new regulation, it was necessary to create a community bank in Maricá, and Instituto Palmas seemed to be the right choice to advise in this process.

There were at least three challenges to creating the local community bank in Maricá. First, this local bank was a top-down initiative created by a city law, while Instituto Palmas was used to incentivize local initiatives in a bottom-up manner, such that "community banks should be created and managed by local social organizations" (Ansorena, 2020). In this case, the "local social organization" should be fostered by an "external" social organization, with the role being played by Instituto Palmas. Second, despite the strong belief in the digital future of community currencies, in 2013, the only digital experience of Instituto Palmas was its first failed project. Because of the previous experience of beneficiaries with the Bolsa Família Program and the concern of the city government staff to avoid the spending of city money on alcohol and drugs, the decision was that the benefit should be paid electronically with a plastic card. Third, the estimated scale of the project was several times larger than the scale of any other project Instituto Palmas had been involved in. While most of the previous community currency projects were limited to a single neighborhood, the Mumbuca project was designed to serve the whole city as well as thousands of poverty-stricken families.

Two main reasons can explain why Instituto Palmas decided to join the Maricá project, despite the relevant challenges it would face. First, the approval of the new regulation for payment systems allowed Instituto Palmas to charge a fee for managing the payment infrastructure, which was not possible when it was managing a printed paper currency. Since the SENAES was not considered a funding partner, a new source of income was very welcome. Second, the solid belief was that the future of community banks would be digital. After winning a public bidding, Instituto Palmas signed a contract with the municipality of Maricá in late 2013 to begin the activities of a local community bank, which would manage the delivery of the benefit (Cernev & Proença, 2016).

In 2013, the technology behind e-Dinheiro was not yet available; therefore, despite some discomfort with the fact that the community bank would not control the technology to read mumbuca cards, a POS card provider was hired to deliver the magnetic cards and manage the IT system behind the payment system.

The first year of operation experienced certain problems. First, differing from the creation of other community banks where community leaders took a leading role in the implementation of the community bank, in the case of Banco Mumbuca, Palmas relied more heavily on city employees. This was because the city government of Maricá considered Banco Mumbuca a strategic priority and had requested Palmas to provide support to implement the community bank. In the examples of the other community banks, it had been civil society and community-based organizations that had made the request to Palmas, and their city governments usually played a supporting role. Second, the whole scale of the operation attracted a multitude of beneficiaries, and it was not easy for Banco Mumbuca's staff to manage the demand to deliver mumbuca cards. Third, many local merchants did not want to accept mumbucas since it seemed to them that this was just "another political initiative" that they did not want to be associated with (Ansorena, 2020). Fourth, the system offered by the company hired to address the technological infrastructure of POS cards was unavailable. Finally, all major decisions about the project, such as control on beneficiaries' registration and change in the values of the benefit, were made by the city government without discussion with either the Palmas or Mumbuca staff.

In 2015 the number of registered beneficiaries steadily grew, operations became more stable and local merchants started to notice the project as an important source of income. The whole scale of the operation attracted a multitude of beneficiaries and, accordingly, it was not easy for Banco Mumbuca's staff to manage the demand to deliver mumbuca cards.

Certain frustration still remained among the Mumbuca staff since their role in the project was not clearly defined—it was the city government, the Palmas staff, or the POS card company that made most decisions. Moreover, many local merchants did not want to accept mumbucas since it seemed to them that this was just “another political initiative” that they did not want to be associated, and the mumbucas were restricted only to beneficiaries’ payments to the merchants; in turn, the merchants could not spend the mumbucas on their suppliers but could only exchange them for Brazilian cash. This meant that mumbucas did not circulate as a currency around the city the way the Palmas staff had envisioned and as had happened in other areas where Palmas had helped to create community banks.

Another problem was that Banco Mumbuca did not offer any service other than distributing and controlling plastic cards. The vision of a community bank with a community currency and microcredit was not in place, since there were no resources available for activities other than distributing the benefit. According to Joaquim Melo, the Banco Palmas founder, they were no longer in an environment of “few resources and more freedom”; but on the contrary they were dealing with an experience that, on the one hand, injected a significant amount of money into the local economy, but on the other, was tied to the dependencies of a partnership governed by a specific agreement with the municipality. In 2017, the situation changed significantly. By that time the e-Dinheiro platform was already in stable operation within Banco Palmas in Fortaleza, and in a new public bidding, e-Dinheiro replaced the POS card system as a channel to deliver mumbucas in Maricá.

E-Dinheiro was not only cheaper than the magnetic card system but also allowed the beneficiaries to have access to a mobile platform for other regular banking services, such as checking accounts, savings, P2P transfers, and buying credit for phones, features that were not available with the card technology. Following the solidarity economy principles, e-Dinheiro charge lower fees, and all profits made by Banco Mumbuca would be reinvested back into the territory. The entrance of e-Dinheiro as the Mumbuca platform would open the opportunity to make mumbucas circulate as a real currency within Maricá and to start microcredit operations. To fulfill the financial inclusion goals, e-Dinheiro beneficiaries also received a regular electronic “checking” account, allowing them to pay bills and make P2P transfers, as they could with any other bank account.

The proximity of users/clients/beneficiaries/business with the community bank and the e-Dinheiro maintenance team allowed an iteration process directed toward attending to local needs. The e-Dinheiro case proposes a different model than most traditional fintechs do. While in a regular fintech, the upgrade, development, and roll out phases are highly centralized, in the case of the e-Dinheiro, there is more space to develop features and services based on the specific demands of a territory.

E-Dinheiro is a nonprofit platform that fosters local governance through community banks. It efficiently allocates investment from the revenue generated in each community. Furthermore, since it is not-for-profit and is based on the principles of the solidarity economy, it has built-in incentives to reinvest its profits in improving the platform as well as investing in the human and physical capital of its community banks. These are key elements that enable it to achieve the highest impact possible in the communities where it is used and has set it apart as a social fintech.

During the COVID-19 crisis, the city of Maricá included new benefits paid in mumbucas to microentrepreneurs who lost income all in the form of salaries to companies that did not lay off their workers, all through the e-Dinheiro app in the form of emergency basic income initiatives (Gonzalez et al., 2020). With the inclusion of this group of users, e-Dinheiro reached almost half of the population of the whole city of Maricá, with approximately 80 thousand users (Yeung, 2020).

E-Dinheiro was created for the unbanked, just as community banks are, but it is a digital solution available to anyone interested. The Banco Mumbuca case is an extraordinary example of the struggle of a community committed to solidarity economy principles that managed to evolve to a larger operation platform and offer a promising experience of a solidarity fintech, to be better observed in the near future.

7 Conclusion and Lessons Learned

In this chapter, we have shown how the evolution of social innovations, such as a community credit card, a social currency, mobile money, and a digital platform, occurred in the field of the solidarity economy, particularly in the field of solidarity finance in Brazil and how it intertwined with the periods of social struggle of the community banks. We present how these innovations first arose without government support and gained a larger scale when supported by a government committed to the solidarity economy.

One of the objectives of the e-Dinheiro platform is to provide a reliable platform to support a digital community bank that is capable of generating enough income to sustain its own activities and finance initiatives within the community. Furthermore, it illustrates how a solidarity economy approach related to public investment, especially at the municipal level, can foster a solidarity fintech that intends to be a strategic way to leverage community banks in Brazil.

In summary, this chapter discussed how solidarity fintech evolved as an alternative to the traditional financial system, starting from a small, low-tech social organization, and becoming a larger-scale digital platform. The chapter described how the fintech was challenged in its autonomy and by the scarcity of resources, how it dealt with different sources of public funding without losing the focus on disseminating the principles of financial inclusion and local development, and how it preserved its sustainability and a democratic decision-making process connected with the goals of the community.

References

Ansorena, A. (2020). Field notes. *Palmas Institute.*

Arcanjo, M. A. S., & Oliveira, A. L. M. (2017). A criação da Secretaria Nacional de Economia Solidária: avanços e retrocessos. *Perseu: História, Memória e Política* (13).

Battilana, J., & Dorado, S. (2010). Building sustainable hybrid organizations: The case of commercial microfinance organizations. *Academy of Management Journal, 53,* 1419–1440.

Blanc, J., & Fare, M. (2013). Understanding the role of governments and administrations in the implementation of community and complementary currencies. *Annals of Public and Cooperative Economics, 84*(1), 63–81.

Carraher, S. M., Welsh, D. H. B., & Svilokos, A. (2016). Validation of a measure of social entrepreneurship. *European Journal of International Management, 16*(4), 386–402.

Cernev, A. K., & Proença, B. A. (2016). Mumbuca: A primeira moeda social digital do Brasil/Mumbuca: The first digital social currency in Brazil. *GVcasos, 6*(2).

Cernev, A., Diniz, E., & Jayo, M. (2009). Emergência da quinta onda de inovação bancária. *AMCIS 2009 Proceedings*, 4.

de Albuquerque, J. P., Diniz, E. H., & Cernev, A. K. (2016). Mobile payments: A scoping study of the literature and issues for future research. *Information Development, 32*(3), 527–553.

Demirguc-Kunt, A., Klapper, L., Singer, D., Ansar, S., & Hess, J. (2018). *The Global Findex Database 2017: Measuring financial inclusion and the fintech revolution*. The World Bank.

Diniz, E. H., Cernev, A. K., Gonzalez, L., & Albuquerque, J. P. (2013). Mobile payments in Brazil: How to make them happen. *The European Financial Review*, 55–58.

Diniz, E. H., Jayo, M., Pozzebon, M., Lavoie, F., & Foguel, F. H. S. (2014). ICT helping to scale up microfinance: The case of a successful bank-MFI partnership in Brazil. *Journal of Global Information Management (JGIM), 22*(1), 34–50.

Diniz, E. H., Siqueira, E. S., & van Heck, E. (2018). Taxonomy of digital community currency platforms. *Information Technology for Development*, 1–23.

Diniz, E. H., Cernev, A. K., & Nascimento, E. (2016). Mobile social money: An exploratory study of the views of managers of community banks. *Revista de Administração (São Paulo), 51*(3), 299–309.

Duncombe, R., & Boateng, R. (2009). Mobile phones and financial services in developing countries: A review of concepts, methods, issues, evidence and future research directions. *Third World Quarterly, 30*(7), 1237–1258.

Fare, M., Freitas, C., & Meyer, C. (2013) Community currencies in Brazilian community development banks: What role in territorial development? The case of Banco Palmas. In *International conference on social and complementary currencies*, 2, Haia, Holanda, Anais. Haia.

Faria, L. A. S. (2018) *Digitalizações de moedas sociais no Brasil e suas pré(histórias): tensões e mediações com Estados, mercados e tecnologias*. Tese (Doutorado em História das Ciências e das Técnicas e Epistemologia) – Programa em História das Ciências e das Técnicas e Epistemologia, Universidade Federal do Rio de Janeiro.

França Filho, G. C. D., Júnior, S., Torres, J., & Rigo, A. S. (2012). Solidarity finance through community development banks as a strategy for reshaping local economies: Lessons from Banco Palmas. *Revista de Administração (São Paulo), 47*(3), 500–515.

Freire, M. (2013). A importância dos bancos comunitários para a inclusão financeira. Instituto Palmas & NESOL-USP (Eds.), *Banco Palmas, 15*, 41–60.

Freitas, H., & Egydio, O. (2014). Programa Moeda Social Mumbuca: Inovação Social, Digital e Econômica. Relatório de Pesquisa. *Projeto Conexão Local*. GVpesquisa. São Paulo. Retrieved from https://pesquisa-eaesp.fgv.br/sites/gvpesquisa.fgv.br/files/conexao-local/relatorio_conexao_local_final_-_mumbuca_henrique_e_olavo.pdf.

Furche, P., Madeira, C., Marcel, M., & Medel, C. (2017). *FinTech and the future of central banking at a crossroads*. Central Bank of Chile.

Gonzalez, L., Cernev, A. K., & Diniz, E. H. (2016). O Desafio da Inclusão Financeira e a Promessa das Fintechs. In A. Dodl, R. L. Troster, (Org.), *Sistema Financeiro Nacional: o que fazer?* (Vol. 1, pp. 157–168) Elsevier Editora Ltda.

Gonzalez, L., Cernev, A. K., Araujo, M. H. D., & Diniz, E. H. (2020). Digital complementary currencies and public policies during the COVID-19 pandemic. *Revista de Administração Pública, 54*(4), 1146–1160.

Hernandes, E. G. S., Siqueira, E. S., Diniz, E. H., & Pozzebon, M. (2018). A digital community bank: Mapping negotiation mechanisms in its consolidation as an alternative to commercial banks. *International Journal of Community Currency Research, 22*(2), 56–70.

Melo Neto Segundo, J. J. D., & Magalhães, S. (2009). Bancos comunitários. In Mercado de trabalho - Conjuntura e análise. *Instituto de Pesquisa Econômica Aplicada* (Ipea) (pp 59–64).

Meyer, C. (2012). *Les finances solidaires comme biens communs durables: étude de cas de la banque communautaire de dévelopment Palmas (Brésil)*. Memoire du Master, Faculte de sciences sociales et politiques, Université Libre de Bruxelle.

Nascimento, E. P. C. C. D. (2015). Moedas sociais digitais: estudo de caso de duas experiências em bancos comunitários. Dissertação de Mestrado. *Escola de Administração de Empresas de São Paulo* (pp. 129). Fundação Getulio Vargas.

Pozzebon, M., & Diniz, E. H. (2012). Theorizing ICT and society in the Brazilian context: A multilevel, pluralistic and remixable framework. *BAR-Brazilian Administration Review, 9*(3), 287–307.

Oliveira, N. (2017). IBGE: 50 milhões de brasileiros vivem na linha de pobreza. *Agência Brasil (EBC)*. Retrieved on March 2018 from http://agenciabrasil.ebc.com.br/economia/noticia/2017-12/ibge-brasil-tem-14-de-sua-popula cao-vivendo-na-linha-de-pobreza.

Ramada-Sarasola, M. (2012). Can mobile money systems have a measurable impact on local development? *Research Report for the International Development Research Centre (IDRC)*. Innovation & Research Multiplier and Social Trade Organization (STRO).

Rigo, A. S., & França Filho, G. C. D. (2017). The Palmas' paradox: Analysis of social currency in the "neighborhood of the solidarity economy". *Cadernos EBAPE. BR, 15*(1), 169–193.

Siqueira, E., Diniz, E., & Albino, R. (2018). Fintech Social: Definição, Categorização e Ilustrações Empíricas-Social Fintech: Definition, Categorization and Empirical Illustration.

Souza, H. P. B. (2015). Desregulamentação financeira, concentração bancária e exclusão financeira no Brasil na década de 1990. XI Congresso Brasileiro de História Econômica. Vitória – ES.

Suresh, A. S., & Namdeo, V. (2018). A critical review: Mobile banking services and its significant impact on rural customer behaviour patterns.

Yeung, P. (2020). *Short on money, cities around the world try making their own*. Bloomberg CityLab. https://www.bloomberg.com/news/articles/2020-08-07/a-depression-era-idea-gets-a-new-look-local-money.

Zahra, S. A., Gedajlovic, E., Neubaum, D. O., & Shulman, J. M. (2009). A typology of social entrepreneurs: Motives, search processes and ethical challenges. *Journal of Business Venturing, 24*(5), 519–553.

Social Finance and Agricultural Funding

Dániel Havran, Péter Kerényi, and Attila A. Víg

1 Introduction

In response to the challenges that traditional agricultural production faces globally, an increasing number of farmers have established community-supported agriculture (CSA) farms in the last two decades. Agricultural business models traditionally run on the logic of the wholesale and retail markets with economies of scale, standardization, price competition, and impersonal distribution, while short food supply chains (SFSCs)

This research was supported by the Higher Education Institutional Excellence Program of the Ministry of Human Capacities in the framework of the "Financial and Public Services" research project (20764-3/2018/FEKUTSTRAT) at Corvinus University of Budapest.

D. Havran (✉) · P. Kerényi · A. A. Víg
Corvinus University of Budapest, Budapest, Hungary
e-mail: daniel.havran@uni-corvinus.hu

P. Kerényi
e-mail: peter.kerenyi@uni-corvinus.hu

A. A. Víg
e-mail: attila.vig@uni-corvinus.hu

T. Walker et al. (eds.), *Innovations in Social Finance*,
https://doi.org/10.1007/978-3-030-72535-8_13

are usually based on ecological farming and consumers' awareness of goods' provenance. CSA farmers sustainably produce a diverse mix of species and provide high-quality vegetables, fruits, dairy, livestock, and poultry as part of their operations. Beyond biodiversity and controlled product quality, CSA farms can become workplaces as well. Together, community-supported "foodsheds" confer biological and organic, social, and economic advantages on local communities (Chiffoleau et al., 2016; Chorn et al., 2010; Kloppenburg et al., 1996; Woods et al., 2017). The direct information flow between consumers and farmers is key. SFSCs share the "common characteristic of reduced numbers of intermediaries between the farmer or food producer, and the consumer," and while neither the number of times a product is handled nor the distance over which it is ultimately transported is determinative, "the product reaches the consumer embedded with information" (EIP-AGRI Focus Groups, 2015, p. 3; Marsden et al., 2000, p. 425). From the perspective of consumer inclusion, involving consumers in the process creates value by familiarizing them with farmers, applying joint distribution systems, and utilizing the authenticity of local sourcing with joint branding. In this way, CSAs establish a more democratic framework for farmer-consumer cooperation (Balázs et al., 2016). Based on existing practices, Kneafsey et al. (2013) highlight four major methods of involvement: CSAs, on-farm sales (e.g., farm shops), off-farm sales (e.g., hospitality, catering, and restaurants), and farm direct deliveries (e.g., online sales). In this study, we focus our analysis on CSAs and their financing, which often lie beyond the scope of traditional banking.

Commonly, micro- and small-sized farms, such as CSA farms, have limited access to finance. The small size and high risk of this type of agricultural production makes it challenging to evaluate the debt capacities of farmers as borrowers. The costs of lending, credit scoring, and monitoring often exceed potential benefits for traditional banks. Further, the costs of establishing close contact and exchanging reliable information between banks and farmers create major barriers for finance. However, more online solutions have appeared recently that connect people and businesses through social media and other platforms of exchange or finance. In this regard, the broader concept of crowdfunding relies on the strength of online communities and social interactions.

Our study explores how offline and online personal relationships reduce information asymmetry and create value during funding activities. The first section deals with theory-building. To better understand the business model, we introduce and identify two roles related to the work of farmers: the entrepreneurial and integrative roles. We model the way in which these supportive roles contribute to production efficiency and the reduction of information asymmetry. Overall, we derive a debt contract model of farm financing in which the actors share the revenue.

In the study's second section, we present practical examples of these two roles. We illustrate start-up financing by a CSA crowdfunding campaign (MyFarm Harta from Hungary) and evaluate the components of the services offered by a crowdfunding platform (Indiegogo, USA). We share the experiences of working capital finance with the contribution of cooperative consumer communities (TVE and Szatyorbolt from Hungary) and with a "crowdfarming" platform (CrowdFarming, Spain). We also review how peer-to-peer lending platforms distribute micro-farm investment loans (Steward, USA, and Crowde, Indonesia) and consider the example of an urban CSA farm (ACRE, USA). Finally, in the Lessons Learned section, we summarize and evaluate the roles that the listed actors fulfill to exemplify the theory introduced in our study's first section.

Using the debt contract approach, this study suggests an analytical framework to explain how social finance utilizes the advantages of direct (online) relations to enhance cultivation projects.

2 Theory

2.1 *Institutional Roles at the CSAs*

A sustainable farm aims to meet many requirements, including business success through care for efficient allocation of resources, humanitarianism through care for society, and environmental consciousness through care for the environment (Silvestre, 2016). Thus, despite overseeing a typically small cultivation size, the management of such farms requires versatile knowledge that is rarely possessed by just one person. As a rule, multiple actors collaborate in a CSA farm, including a farmer and assistants that handle cultivation. Consumers in turn can be organized in many other ways. There can be a professional network, which knows the best practices in business; Chorn et al. (2010) provide some examples of these. Indeed, the small number of intermediary actors at CSAs does not necessarily signal a lack of participants in transactions.

To develop an analytical framework, we introduce two distinct intermediary roles from the institutional perspective: the entrepreneurial and the integrative roles. We note that many other roles exist from the technological or societal perspectives, such as in Gorton et al.'s (2013) conceptual framework, but this study's focus on the institutional perspective directs our attention to the above-mentioned roles.

The main tasks of those performing the entrepreneurial role are distributing products to consumers, managing operations, undertaking food processing, and managing emerging risks related to product quality or quantity, operational liquidity, or human resources. Distribution includes marketing, product engineering, and delivery solutions, while production and risk management involve responding to issues related to product quality or quantity. The entrepreneur can be seen either as a retailer who develops and maintains a marketplace, platform, or service to connect consumers and farmers, or as an individual who transforms raw materials into high-value processed goods or catering services. The integrative role entails creating and maintaining contact with farmers, personally advising and observing them, as well as coordinating and developing consumers' and farmers' communities. The integrator can be either a non-profit hub (association), a profit-oriented distributor firm, or the farm itself.

These roles not only serve as substitutes for retailers/wholesalers in traditional supply chains, but also enhance information dispersion. Figure 1 depicts the combination of the two distinct roles in a schematic SFSC compared to traditional food supply chains. In traditional food supply chains, personal information is lost during the exchange between retail and wholesale traders. In this case, information about price, quantity and quality frames the transactions. In the SFSCs, consumers know farmers well and are mutually committed to transacting with each other.

2.2 A Debt Contract Model of CSAs

In this subsection, we develop an economic model in which a CSA can ease finance by using the introduced entrepreneurial and integrative roles. Our approach borrows from the debt contract and incentive theories, for example, in Holmström and Tirole (1997), Tirole (1999), and Hart (2017), and studies on funding contracts design in agriculture by Baumann (2000) and McMichael (2013). Our model derives the conditions of the integrative and entrepreneurial roles to add more value. Without compromising the general applicability of our model, we posit the farmer, consumer (who lends to the project as well), entrepreneur,

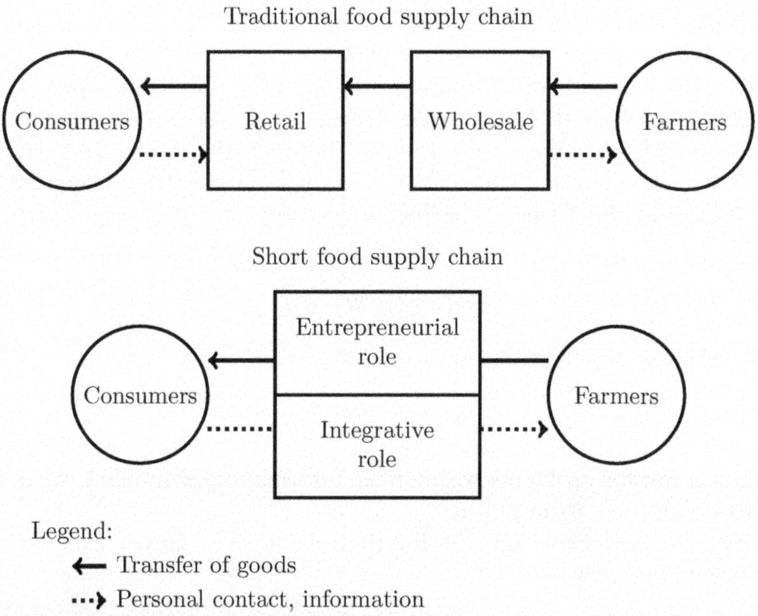

Fig. 1 Traditional and short food supply chains

and integrator as independent actors even though these roles may appear jointly in practice.

Consider a farmer who produces and then sells food to the consumer. The farmer has $A_f > 0$ private wealth but needs to invest $I > A_f$ in the seed phase (I can be considered a fixed asset or working capital). The project lasts for a finite period of time, and it is risky; production yields $R > I$ with probability p, and 0 otherwise. Moral hazard arises when production is financed externally, because in this case the farmer will be less motivated to expend more effort on the project. If the farmer borrows amount $I - A_f$ from the lender-consumer (consumer buys the product in advance), they may decide to exert more effort (behave), causing the probability of success to be p_H, or may shirk effort, resulting in a lower ($p_L < p_H$) probability of success and some private benefit. Thus, a behaving farmer can reach $p_H R$ expected net profit.

We model two types of farmers regarding their creditability. A farmer of the *reliable* type can obtain b_f private benefit, while the *unreliable* type may obtain a higher $B_f > b_f$ benefit with shirking. The lender-consumer knows that the population ratio of reliable type farmers is $\alpha \in (0, 1)$, and the rest $1 - \alpha$ of the population is classified as the unreliable type.

Let R_f and R_c with $R = R_f + R_c$ denote the shares of the profit (or the produced food that they can consume) between the farmer and lender-consumer, respectively. The lender-consumer must offer an agreement that motivates the farmer. The incentive constraint of a reliable farmer is:

$$p_H R_f \geq p_L R_f + b_f \tag{1}$$

and that of an unreliable farmer is:

$$p_H R_f \geq p_L R_f + B_f \tag{2}$$

To account for problems arising from information asymmetry, we make the following two assumptions:

First, the pledgeable income for the reliable type farmer exceeds the borrowed amount:

$$p_H\left(R - \frac{b_f}{\Delta p}\right) > I - A_f, \tag{3}$$

where $\Delta p = p_H - p_L$, while it is less than the borrowed amount for the unreliable type farmer:

$$p_H\left(R - \frac{B_f}{\Delta p}\right) < I - A_f \tag{4}$$

Any lender would prefer to finance the reliable farmer. However, the consumer, without any direct contact to or personal knowledge of the farmer, is not able to be so selective in their choice to endorse reliable versus unreliable type farmers. Thus, the non-informed consumer expects the weighted average net pledgeable income for their lending.

Second, we assume that the weighted average net pledgeable income is lower than the borrowed amount:

$$m_0\left(R - \frac{b_f}{\Delta p}\right) < I - A_f, \tag{5}$$

where $m_0 \equiv \alpha p_H + (1 - \alpha) p_L$ is the probability of success. In other words, the farmer does not have the required capital to start the project:

$$A_f < \bar{A}_f^0 \equiv I - m_0 \left(R - \frac{b_f}{\Delta p} \right) \tag{6}$$

With this inequality, the market collapses, and the entrepreneur will not finance the project. This situation often occurs in traditional agribusinesses, in which state subsidies contribute the required capital.

Next, we consider the entrepreneurial role. The entrepreneur knows how to sell products to conscious consumers, which means higher profitability for the project. When the entrepreneur advises the farmer, the project's probability of success increases from p to $p + q$. However, the entrepreneur also endures r_e cost while advising, for which they expect a share R_e of the profits with $R_c + R_f + R_e \leq R$. Calculations similar to those shown above demonstrate that the minimum capital requirement in this case becomes:

$$\bar{A}_f^e \equiv I - m_e \left(R - R_e - \frac{b_f}{\Delta p} \right), \tag{7}$$

where the probability of success is $m_e \equiv \alpha(p_H + q) + (1 - \alpha)(p_L + q)$. The entrepreneur makes financing possible if $\bar{A}_f > \bar{A}_f^e$ and their added value to the project is greater than their cost:

$$q \left(R - \frac{b_f}{\Delta p} \right) > m_e R_e \geq r_e \tag{8}$$

Considering the integrative role, the integrator can accurately reveal the type of farmer through their sustained personal contact with the farmer in question. However, this activity costs $r_i > 0$, which is covered by a share R_i of the profit, with $R_f + R_e + R_i \leq R$. With the support of the integrator, a reliable type farmer is contracted with probability $\beta \in [0, 1]$ instead of α, with $\beta > \alpha$. The minimum capital requirement in this case becomes:

$$\bar{A}_f^i \equiv I - m_i \left(R - R_i - \frac{b_f}{\Delta p} \right), \tag{9}$$

where the probability of success is $m_i \equiv \beta p_H + (1-\beta)p_L$. The integrator makes funding possible, if $\bar{A}_f > \bar{A}^i_f$ and the benefits exceed the costs:

$$(\beta - \alpha) \cdot \Delta p \cdot \left(R - \frac{b_f}{\Delta p}\right) > m_i R_i \geq r_i \tag{10}$$

Financing further eases if both the entrepreneur and integrator contribute, and if profit is divided among all four: $R_f + R_c + R_e + R_i \leq R$. The capital requirement is even lower:

$$\bar{A}_f = I - m\left(R - R_e - R_i - \frac{b_f}{\Delta p}\right), \tag{11}$$

where $m = \beta(p_H + q) + (1-\beta)(p_L + q)$.

We can define the contract set that offers acceptable conditions for the four actors. For the fixed set of $(I, R, A_f, b_f, \Delta p, m, r_e, r_i)$, the contract between farmer, lender-consumer, entrepreneur, and integrator is acceptable if the (R_f, R_c, R_e, R_i) profit shares satisfy the inequalities of:

$$R_f \geq \frac{A_f}{m} \tag{12}$$

$$R_f \geq \frac{b_f}{\Delta p} \tag{13}$$

$$R_e \geq \frac{r_e}{m} \tag{14}$$

$$R_i \geq \frac{r_i}{m} \tag{16}$$

$$R_c \geq \frac{I - A_f}{m} \tag{16}$$

$$R_f + R_e + R_i + R_c \leq R \tag{17}$$

The entrepreneur and the integrator together increase the probability of success by $m - m_0 = q + (\beta - \alpha)\Delta p$. When moral hazard exists, the capital requirement of the farmer can be expressed as:

$$A_f \geq \bar{A}_f \equiv I - (m_0 + q + (\beta - \alpha)\Delta p)\left(R - \frac{b_f}{\Delta p}\right) + r_e + r_i \tag{18}$$

Per our equations, the minimum level of capital $\bar{A}_f$ decreases *ceteris paribus* if the selective efficiency β of the integrator or the advising efficiency q of the entrepreneur increases.

At this abstraction level, the model does not specify the techniques applied by the integrator and entrepreneur. With online social finance technologies such as crowdfunding, the described roles can be implemented at a low cost. Several authors, including Jenik et al. (2017), believe that crowdfunding can be an efficient tool of financial inclusion. Yet, other authors critique this tool. Strausz (2017) shows that crowdfunding improves the choice of promising projects and reduces the aggregate investment demand uncertainty. Mollick (2014) finds that the assessment of a project's quality by funders is key to a successful campaign. More so than trust in the borrowers, the characteristics of the crowdfunding platforms and the quality of information are often more relevant (Moysidou & Hausberg, 2020).

Overall, the model suggests that entrepreneurial and integrative roles can extend business feasibility. The entrepreneur enhances the probability of success (with their engagement to support the project) and the integrator helps to solve information asymmetry issues (by publishing personal information, stories, updates, and reliable data about the farmer). In the presence of integrative and entrepreneurial activities, consumers are willing to finance farmers even if they would not do so otherwise. In the following section, we survey some practical cases of typical funding situations.

3 Farmers and Social Finance: Practical Examples

Herein, we present an overview of the methods related to startup finance, working capital finance, and investment loan funding for CSAs. In each subsection, we review the leading social financing solutions and/or platforms. Subsequently, using our analytical model framework, we present examples of how farms access finance through integrative and entrepreneurial roles.

3.1 Startup with a Crowdfunding Campaign

The start-up phase hinges on devising innovative ideas and networking. Galli and Brunori (2013) emphasize the importance of consumer involvement, the skills and knowledge required by the main participants, the work overload for farmers in the case of excessive diversification of production, distribution costs, and other investment expenses during this stage. The key lesson that practitioners imbibe is that knowledge support is necessary for a successful start (Cannella et al., 2012). Such support comes in the form of advice from experts and activists in the fields of marketing, entrepreneurship, law, agricultural production, technology, transportation, trade, civic organizations, local government, and funding. Notable advisory examples are Short supply chains Knowledge & Innovation Network (SKIN), with a food focus, as well as the European Network for Rural Development (ENRD) and their LEADER Toolkit, which has a broader scope than SKIN's. From a financial perspective, this stage involves procuring fixed assets and building a consumer community. Based on practical experience, farmers and/or their families acquire sufficient land and elementary tools. However, initial activities require seed working capital for raw material purchases and operating expenses.

3.1.1 Finding Consumers and Investors in One Step

A crowdfunding campaign may extend the initial equity and decrease the capital requirement of external funding. In general, the campaign helps commit new consumers willing to buy for a whole season, which induces a higher q probability of success in the model due to the higher certainty of revenues. Furthermore, publicity provides the farmers' operations with more visibility and transparency. The result is that the lender-consumers can discover the reliability of the farmer with a higher (β) chance compared to the "no crowdfunding case" (α). In sum, the campaign takes on the integrative role.

Global crowdfunding platforms, such as Indiegogo or Kickstarter, serve as efficient facilities for capitalizing start-ups. However, these platforms do not offer any specialized services for SFSC businesses. Many CSA farmers use these reward-based crowdfunding tools to acquire their first-year capital. As of September 2020, a search for the term "organic farms" on Kickstarter's page results in 390 projects, while a search for "CSA" locates 72 projects. Indiegogo provides a platform for funding tech and "businesses for social good" projects. It also runs many campaigns for farmers and CSA borrowers. In addition, the website offers a fixed or flexible funding campaign through this website. In this theoretical model, r_i (cost of the integrator) plays a decisive role from the point of view of rentability. Currently, the platform itself charges 5% of the final amount fundraised and an extra 2.9% +0.30 USD per pledge for credit card fees. Kickstarter, its main competitor, provides a platform to run fix-funding campaigns for a wide range of businesses that create a product for funders. It charges 5% for the platform service and an extra 3% +0.2 USD per pledge for credit card payments.

Recent examples of successful mixed funding schemes exist as well. A collection of case studies provided by EIP-AGRI Focus Groups (2015) offers structured insight into the existing practice. The report mentions a successful "part loan, part grant and part community crowdfunding" (EIP-AGRI Focus Group, 2015, p. 10) structure in the UK. In terms of the theoretical model, the grantor extends the initial capital A_f. Beyond the lender-consumers, a professional lender offers capital and shares from revenue (R). From these examples, we glean that crowdfunding can be more efficient if associated with subsidies such as tax relief for donors. Funding Enlightened Agriculture (a UK network comprising funders, social entrepreneurs, social investors, investment and business development advisers, as well as food and farming experts) conducted a program titled "Just Growth" to encourage the growth of community-based farming microbusinesses between 2015 and 2017. Cooperative & Community Finance sourced one-third of the funding, a commercial bank sourced another third, and the local community raised the remaining third. The latter contribution served to strengthen the commitment of consumers to the project.

3.1.2 *Case: MyFarm Harta*

The case of MyFarm Harta (Hungary) illustrates how a crowdfunding platform can play an integrative role at the start-up stage. The micro-sized entrepreneurial venture launched in 2018. The staff decided to reduce business risk, and hence obtain first-year revenues in advance, through a crowdfunding campaign. At the time, MyFarm Harta did not have an established community, nor specific goods to sell. The company already owned agricultural land in the Harta village, close to the river Danube, and the founder's father had extensive experience in farming. Attuned to the risks associated with cultivation, the founder's father imposed a condition from the very beginning: the first-year subscriptions, thus the revenues, had to be accessible at the start of the season. The company organized a fundraising campaign on Indiegogo in 2019, defining the business prerequisite at 100 subscriptions for vegetable baskets (EUR 3,000) for the first year. According to the farmers' estimation, the maximum capacity of production was around 300–400 baskets. Finally, they collected EUR 3,665, around 20% of the EUR 18,000 goal. Since the amount was above the targeted threshold, the campaign was regarded as a success, even more so as new investors doubled as consumers for one year (Table 1).

Today, MyFarm Harta directly collects next-year subscriptions. It supplies three types of sustainably sourced products: vegetables, smoke-dried meat, and egg baskets. It also offers seasonal foods and mixed baskets for an annual period; it accepts new orders until the next season. The team comprises three farmers and five part-time assistants. Since the fundraising campaign, the farm performs tasks related to the integrative role: it manages a Facebook site (with two to four posts a week), runs a homepage (www.myfarmharta.com), and organizes live meetings. Two of the part-time staff create online content and develop the community network. Further, the farm offers an online streaming service for the consumers ("follow how your garden evolves") and strengthens its brand's philosophy through advertising, exemplified by the "rent a part of a land, follow the evolution, eat healthy foods, and give some for charity purposes" slogan. The farm collaborates with a local charity to fulfill the

Table 1 Analyzing MyFarm Harta using the debt contract approach

Participant	*Role*	*Effect*	*Associated parameters*
Indiegogo	Integrator and entrepreneur	Provides an online platform for crowdfunding projects. The platform helps consumers by revealing the type of the farmer, who can be of the reliable or unreliable type The site also increases profitability by reaching conscious consumers who are able and willing to pay more for quality products	$\beta > \alpha$ q
MyFarm Harta	Farmer	Can behave or shirk, which affects profitability Can be of the reliable or unreliable type, which affects their private benefit when shirking	$p_H > p_L$ $b_f < B_f$

latter part of its mission. Furthermore, it collaborates with a food magazine to generate broader publicity. The founder, Gábor Kövesdi, and two of his colleagues occupy the entrepreneurial roles. The marketing staff handles the design of the basket system (pricing, conditions, and subscriptions), and their delivery coordination. Although MyFarm Harta successfully attained a financially sustainable way of production, its' relatively small company size and limited number of consumers suggest that there is still much room to grow.

3.2 Working Capital Finance

After starting a business, further capital may be needed. To meet the additional operational expenses and working capital requirements, CSA farms often offer subscription-based services. Online solutions are thus essential in farmer-consumer communication. Usually, consumers follow the farm online, leading to a commitment to ordering throughout the season. The commitment lowers the risk of revenue loss, which is an essential contribution to preserving operational stability.

3.2.1 Subscription Systems: Lessons from Hungarian CSAs

The Association of Conscious Consumers (TVE, "Tudatos Vásárlók Egyesülete," Hungary) supports and develops an eco-conscious community network that both incorporates and offers advice to CSA farmers. With the help of TVE, one author of this study led a one-day workshop on the financial problems that its member CSA farmers face. During the event, held in the summer of 2019, around a dozen Hungarian CSA farmers shared their financial challenges as well as their techniques.

During the workshop, the farmers shared their basic financial plans based on their then-current business operations and their best practices. The participants were from various regions in Hungary, owning around two to six hectares, and employing two to six workers. The farms produce a wide range of vegetable species with the aim of fostering biodiversity. They generally sell freshly harvested vegetables and eventually process extra crops for future winter deliveries. The farmers also often extend their activities to producing fruits, rearing poultry for eggs and meat, or rearing rabbits. Farms with larger plots sometimes raise other animals, such as goats, alpacas, or cattle, and use part of their land as pasture. Smaller farms have a team of two to three people and 20–30 consumers, while larger farms have four to six team members and 30–60 consumers.

The price of a half basket is HUF 4–6,000 (13–18 USD), and the full baskets are priced at HUF 5–7,000 (20–25 USD). The farms usually offer large and small size baskets year-round and the consumers make payments a month before to receive weekly baskets from March to December. The baskets are slightly more expensive than alternatives purchased from long supply chains. However, they are still affordable for middle-class consumers: these are usually young, educated families, often with small children, working in the capital or larger cities. However, the subscription system results in low profitability. The farmers of the workshop usually do not incorporate the costs of asset deprivation and vacant winter months in the pricing of the boxes because many would see this as overpricing, and thus unethical. To cover their expenses, they undertake other activities and contract with restaurants to target more revenue. They also mention bank loans as a financial possibility but ignored the option of crowd-funding (CSA farmers at the TVE Workshop, personal communication, July 19, 2019).

Considering the integrative role, the farmers explicated that they build their consumer communities themselves as opposed to practices in the USA where communities search for farmers. The farmers relay that they start by appealing to their friends, former colleagues, and members of local communities. All of them use Facebook and many of them organize weekly delivery events on their homepages. In addition, all farms have open days during which consumers are invited to visit. In this regard, the farmers spoke of difficulties with pricing and the consumer community understanding the issues and challenges they face. These farmers often fulfill entrepreneurial functions themselves. They place great emphasis on delivery, production, risk management, and employee care. However, they face time and knowledge constraints in managing their sales activity and marketing strategy satisfactorily (CSA farmers at the TVE Workshop, personal communication, July 19, 2019).

3.2.2 Prepaid Baskets on Cooperative Webshops

Sometimes, independent companies establish online marketplaces and offer cooperative platforms for food distribution. Typically, two kinds of platforms exist: cooperative webshops and crowdfarming sites. In both cases, online platforms play certain integrative roles. In the case of online marketplaces, technology is primarily used for distribution and secondarily for finance. Szatyorbolt ("bag shop") is an online webshop in Hungary. It is supported by a civic association of consumers ("Bag Association") that is interested in knowing the origin of products. This association organizes workshops and farmer-consumer meetings. Hence, the association fulfills some entrepreneurial roles, and the online shop fulfills some of the integrative roles. The online shop directly distributes food from the producers and offers prepaid "season tickets" for ten bags. The support team puts together these bags using products sourced from dedicated farmers. Except for the prepaid "season tickets," no other method of funding is used. Other examples of online webshops include Rechtstreex, a Dutch case that Marjon Krol EIP-AGRI Focus Groups (2015) documents.

3.2.3 Online Adoption Projects

Adoption projects are the latest alternatives to working capital funding. The idea stems from farm contracting, which is "a system where a central processing or exporting unit purchases the harvests of independent farmers and the terms of the purchase are arranged in advance through contracts" (Baumann, 2000, p. 7).

The pioneer of adoption projects is Crowdfarming, a profit-oriented company that works as a global internet platform in supporting sustainable agriculture. The platform facilitates adoption projects and operates a marketplace for prepaid baskets similar to the webshops mentioned above. The founders of Crowdfarming are two brothers from Spain, Gabriel and Gonzalo Úrculo, who are also farmers themselves. They took over their grandparents' abandoned farm in 2010 and started their homepage in order to sell their fruit directly to consumers. More farmers later joined and there are currently over 60 projects that can be backed by consumers, with a majority of projects based in Europe, and in Spain more particularly.

Adoption helps farmers to sell their products in advance and without substantial risk. The consumer opens an account and initiates adoption by a cash transfer to the farmer. Here, the farmers decide and fix the price. In general, an adoption lasts for a season, but consumers can renew in the subsequent season. The adopter can also name the selected plants or animals, and a personal plaque is attached to the farm. During the time of production, farmers periodically photograph the adopted productive units. To diversify the risk of returns, the adopter consumers share the harvest of all adoptions. Beyond the adoption cost to start the delivery, consumers contribute to processing costs, delivery fees, and taxes.

3.2.4 *Case: Bio Dió*

To illustrate the use of crowdfarming, we showcase the example of Bio Dió. The farm is located in Osli, a small village in Northwest Hungary. It grows 8,000 walnut trees on 42 hectares. The trees were planted in the year 2000. The farm received a bio certificate (conforming to EU standards) in 2019, is well-equipped, and has the capital required for production. To find an alternative selling channel, Bio Dió joined the Crowdfarming platform in 2019. By offering adoptions on the Crowdfarming platform, the farm has been able to increase and diversify its revenue and finance the harvest in advance. Once consumers adopt a walnut tree, they receive the harvest (around 10 kg of walnuts) in November through delivery. The price of the adoption is EUR 100 (HUF 35,000), which covers a period of one year. This price is about 50% higher than that of the other non-organic walnuts in the region. The company runs a Facebook page, which provides weekly updates from the farm. Parallel to the adoption project, the farm also runs a webshop and recently started processing and selling walnut oil. Thus, adoption is a supplementary revenue that both funds and increases business activity (Table 2).

3.3 *Investment Loans Through Peer-to-Peer Lending*

At the maturing stage, companies require capital for growth, as well as for the repair and/or replacement of equipment. However, operational revenues alone cannot sustain growth. In this phase, a lack of capital creates significant challenges for growth, even though the size of investments is small. Farms usually require debt or other loan-type financing forms. They often possess a credit history, a stable consumer network, and a positive operative cash flow. Their operation also follows traditional business logic. However, these organizations often find conventional borrowing too difficult and seek funding by peer-to-peer lending.

3.3.1 *Peer-to-Peer Lending Platforms*

Peer-to-peer agricultural variants to financing often relate to CSA, but not always. This form of financing usually follows traditional loan construction, in which lenders receive interest and capital redemption in return for the loan amount.

We focus on platforms that have some sustainable agriculture profiles. We overviewed the homepages of the platforms, e.g. GoSteward, Crowde,

Table 2 Analyzing Bio Dió's crowdfarming using the debt contract approach

Participant	*Role*	*Effect*	*Associated parameters*
Crowdfarming	Entrepreneur	Increases profitability by providing an online platform for adoption	q
	Integrator	Stays connected with the farmer through the adoption scheme, thus increasing the probability that the farmer is of the reliable type	$\beta > \alpha$
Consumer	Lender-consumer	Provides funding by pre-purchasing the harvest (adopting)	$I - A_f$
Bio Dió	Farmer	Is incentivized to behave instead of shirk, which increases the probability of success Can be of reliable or unreliable type, which affects their private benefit when shirking	$p_H > p_L$ $b_f < B_f$

iGrow, Agryo, Dirt Capital, and FarmTogether. Through these peer-to-peer platforms, investors show high commitment to the project and respect its values. These lenders may know the farmers in person or online through the platform, and lenders can follow the farmers' activity and updates. We note that this engagement may be typically lower than in the reward-based crowdfunding construction introduced in the previous parts. We investigate the practices of Crowde and Steward.

Crowde is a notable Indonesian platform, connecting micro- and small-sized farms, as well as both individual and institutional investors. The platform was founded in 2015 and has since financed more than 5,071 farmers in 276 villages in Indonesia. In 2018, a venture company funded Crowde, and in 2019, it secured 1M USD in funding. Avisha et al. (2019) analyze Crowde's business concept by interviewing farmers, investors, and Crowde employees. The authors expressed that the interviewed farmers had proven success in their businesses, and Crowde's financial aid helped them increase their revenues. The platform offers financial possibilities for cultivation projects, inventory financing, and invoice financing, but only for those with bank accounts. After a farmer applies to the platform, Crowde undertakes credit scoring: it assesses the farmers' financial requirements and evaluates the project. If required, the team helps farmers develop their business plans. The fundraising period is 14 days on the website and in the case of a successful campaign, Crowde sets a provision fee of 3% of collected investments. During the redemption period, farmers regularly provide updates on the ongoing project. At the end of the year, farmers pay an agreed share of the revenues instead of interest. For the institutional lenders, who buy loan portfolio shares, the rate of return varies between 6 and 18% for the repayment period, which is from one to twelve months. The platform also regularly publishes the 90-day non-performance-loan ratio, which is below 5%; this ratio seems to be permanently low. However, there is no public information available about the rejection ratio.

Steward is a relatively new US-based crowdfunding platform for direct investment in sustainable farming projects. The Steward Holding Company runs the platform and offers flexible loans for small- and medium-sized farms in the USA. A separate entity, Steward Farm Trust, owns the loan portfolio. The fund is open to individual and institutional investors with US citizenship or US investor accreditation, and the minimum investment amount is 100 USD. The fund annually pays dividends, which are estimated at around 6% by the platform. Amelinckx (2020) reports that Steward has already invested more than 2.6M USD in 16 different farms, and more than 1,200 farmers have applied for funding through the platform. Steward's platform offers flexible loans up to 50,000 USD for farmers, usually for one to five years in duration. The cash flow of redemption is annuity-type in general. Moreover, farms may borrow a secured mortgage (in this case, a larger loan size is possible, ranging from 25,000 USD to 1M USD) or an unsecured loan to purchase land or equipment. The borrower's equity here should be at least 15%. The interest rates of flexible loans range from 6 to 10% per annum. Further, the platform charges 2.0% of the principal loan amount for origination and a 149–499 USD per month service fee from the farmers (including for a bookkeeping software that Steward supplies). The investors must pay 1.0% of invested capital annually for the services and bear the risk of default. They can finance a single project or a portfolio of the projects represented by Steward Farm Trust, which mostly comprise secured mortgage loans.

3.3.2 *Case: ACRE*

To illustrate the use of peer-to-peer lending, we present the example of ACRE. ACRE is a sustainable urban farm in Detroit, USA and was formed as a for-profit company. Pfleger (2018) notes that the owners, Ryan Anderson and Hannah Clark, joined the local food movement in 2016. In that year, the farm obtained 10,140 USD through the campaign Public Equity Detroit to cover the installation of water supply. The farmers offered stylish t-shirts for 30 USD and a badge with the names of the donors on the Wall of Heroes for 100 USD. The micro-sized farm took one step further and contacted Steward to finance the purchase of 0.69 acres of vacant land in Core City (a neighborhood in Detroit) and equipment. In 2017, the company targeted further financing of 75,000 USD and obtained 83,221 USD in loan amounts with five years of maturity and a 10% interest rate. The farm delivers vegetables to restaurants and sells on the local market as well, with the sales to restaurants being their primary source of income. They have also launched a limited-edition CSA subscription model with ten shares. The baskets include 30 selected vegetable species, which ACRE delivers during a 12-week season for 250 USD. The farmers also maintain contact with their community on Facebook (Table 3).

Table 3 Analyzing ACRE using the debt contract approach

Participant	*Role*	*Effect*	*Associated parameters*
Steward	Integrator	Helps by revealing the type of the farmer by providing an online platform for direct investment in sustainable farming projects	$\beta > \alpha$
Consumer	Lender-Consumer	Provides funding by investing in the selected farming project on www.gosteward.com	$I - A_f$
ACRE	Farmer	Can behave or shirk, which affects profitability Can be of the reliable or unreliable type, which affects their private benefit when shirking	$p_H > p_L$ $b_f < B_f$

4 Lessons Learned

There are many alternatives to traditional bank financing for micro- and small-sized farms committed to ecological, sustainable, or locally distributed cultivation. These alternatives take shape in the emergence of new platforms, communities, and financing facilities. Although online technologies amplify access as we have seen in the local examples, there is still no standardized solution for funding, and they cannot be labeled as global financing alternatives. However, platforms and communities appear to be taking steps in this direction, as many of these use the benefits of online payment systems, social media, and even the broad range of data provided by their digital environment in working toward their own solutions.

To compare the examples of the theoretical frameworks introduced, we provide an overview of the three kinds of financing. Small-firm size restricts traditional funding possibilities. However, social finance can resolve arising information asymmetry and provide more opportunities. Further, social finance platforms can capitalize on their advantages through their integrative role. Stories about the farm's origin, essential business data, photos, contact addresses, and regular posts make financing transparent. In the case of loan-based projects, platforms undertake credit scoring, and the lenders undertake the risk of funding. However, entrepreneurial activities are less supported by these platforms. To the best of our knowledge, there is no platform that provides advisory services. Despite good experiences, the success rate varies according to the form of financing. Extending the consumer community is a persistent challenge for CSA farmers. While new ways of financing enable socially and environmentally responsible farming across the world, there is still both a need, and an opportunity, for further evolution and innovation.

References

Amelinckx, A. (2020, January 11). *New crowdfarming platform looks to help sustainable farmers*. Modern Farmer. https://modernfarmer.com/2020/01/new-crowdfarming-platform-looks-to-help-sustainable-farmers/.

Avisha, A., Charina, A., Noor, T. I., & Mukti, G. W. (2019). Crowdfunding as alternative access to digital technology-based capital on agricultural activities, (Case study at PT Crowde Membangun Bangsa). *Mimbar Agribisnis: Jurnal Pemikiran Masyarakat Ilmiah Berwawasan Agribisnis*, 5(1), 1–22. http://dx.doi.org/10.25157/ma.v5i1.1571.

Balázs, B., Pataki, G., & Lazányi, O. (2016). Prospects for the future: Community supported agriculture in Hungary. *Futures, 83*, 100–111. https://doi.org/10.1016/j.futures.2016.03.005.

Baumann, P. (2000). *Equity and efficiency in contract farming schemes: The experience of agricultural tree crops*. Overseas Development Institute. Working Paper 139. https://www.odi.org/publications/2022-equity-and-efficiency-contract-farming-schemes-experience-agricultural-tree-crops.

Cannella, M., Holtzman, B., Peabody, M., Roche, E., Waterman, B., & Yandow, C. (2012). *Guide to financing the community supported farm. Ways for farms to acquire capital within communities*. University of Vermont Extension, Center of Sustainable Agriculture. http://www.uvm.edu/newfarmer/?Page=business/community-supported-farm-guide.html&SM=business/sub-menu.html.

Chiffoleau, Y., Millet-Amrani, S., & Canard, A. (2016). From short food supply chains to sustainable agriculture in urban food systems: Food democracy as a vector of transition. *Agriculture, 6*(4), 57. https://doi.org/10.3390/agriculture6040057.

Chorn, B., Sisco, C., & Pruzan-Jorgensen, P. M. (2010, December). *The business case for supply chain sustainability. A brief for business leaders*. Business for Social Responsibility. https://www.bsr.org/en/our-insights/report-view/the-business-case-for-supply-chain-sustainability-a-brief-for-business-lead.

EIP-AGRI Focus Groups. (2015, November 30). *Innovative short food supply chain management*. European Commission. https://ec.europa.eu/eip/agriculture/en/publications/eip-agri-focus-group-innovative-short-food-supply.

Galli, F., & Brunori, G. (2013). *Short food supply chains as drivers of sustainable development*. Evidence Document. https://orgprints.org/28858/1/evidence-document-sfsc-cop.pdf.

Gorton, M., Hubbard, C., & Fertő, I. (2013, December). *Theoretical background and conceptual framework*. COMPETE. http://www.compete-project.eu/fileadmin/compete/files/working_paper/COMPETE_Working_Paper_2_Conceptual_framework.pdf.

Hart, O. (2017). Incomplete contracts and control. *American Economic Review, 107*(7), 1731–1752. https://doi.org/10.1257/aer.107.7.1731.

Holmström, B., & Tirole, J. (1997). Financial intermediation, loanable funds, and the real sector. *The Quarterly Journal of Economics, 112*(3), 663–691. https://doi.org/10.1162/003355397555316.

Jenik, I., Lyman, T., & Nava, A. (2017, March). *Crowdfunding and financial inclusion*. CGAP (Consultative Group to Assist the Poor). https://www.cgap.org/research/publication/crowdfunding-and-financial-inclusion.

Kloppenburg, J., Hendrickson, J., & Stevenson, G. W. (1996). Coming into the foodshed. *Agriculture and Human Values, 13*(3), 33–42. https://doi.org/10.1007/BF01538225.

Kneafsey, M., Venn, L., Schmutz, U., Balázs, B., Trenchard, L., Eyden-Wood, T., & Blackett, M. (2013). Short food supply chains and local food systems in the EU. A state of play of their socio-economic characteristics. https://doi.org/10.2791/88784.

Marsden, T., Banks, J., & Bristow, G. (2000). Food supply chain approaches: Exploring their role in rural development. *Sociologia Ruralis, 40*(4), 424–438. https://doi.org/10.1111/1467-9523.00158.

McMichael, P. (2013). Value-chain agriculture and debt relations: Contradictory outcomes. *Third World Quarterly, 34*(4), 671–690. https://doi.org/10.1080/01436597.2013.786290.

Mollick, E. (2014). The dynamics of crowdfunding: An exploratory study. *Journal of Business Venturing, 29*(1), 1–16. https://doi.org/10.1016/j.jbusvent.2013.06.005.

Moysidou, K., & Hausberg, J. P. (2020). In crowdfunding we trust: A trust-building model in lending crowdfunding. *Journal of Small Business Management, 58*(3), 511–543. https://doi.org/10.1080/00472778.2019.1661682.

Pfleger, P. (Producer). (2018, January 16). *Detroit's urban farms: Engines of growth, omens of change* [Radio broadcast]. Michigan Radio. https://www.michiganradio.org/post/detroit-s-urban-farms-engines-growth-omens-change.

Silvestre, B. (2016). Sustainable supply chain management: Current debate and future directions. *Gestão and Produção, 23*(2), 235–249. https://www.scielo.br/scielo.php?pid=S0104-530X2016005007102&script=sci_arttext.

Strausz, R. (2017). A theory of crowdfunding: A mechanism design approach with demand uncertainty and moral hazard. *American Economic Review, 107*(6), 1430–1476. https://doi.org/10.1257/aer.20151700.

Tirole, J. (1999). Incomplete contracts: Where do we stand? *Econometrica, 67*(4), 741–781. https://doi.org/10.1111/1468-0262.00052.

Woods, T., Ernst, M., & Tropp, D. (2017, April 4). *Community supported agriculture. New models for changing markets*. US Department of Agriculture, Agricultural Marketing Service. https://www.ams.usda.gov/publications/content/community-supported-agriculture-new-models-changing-markets.

Blockchains in Social Finance

Public Governance of the Blockchain Revolution and Its Implications for Social Finance: A Comparative Analysis

Stefania Paladini, Erez Yerushalmi, and Ignazio Castellucci

1 Introduction

There is hardly anyone who has not heard of blockchain, even though an exact idea of what Blockchain is, and how it exactly works, is far from common. The knowledge most people seem to have of Nakamoto's (2008) original concept is related to cryptocurrencies (Doguet, 2013); to the point that blockchain itself is often referred to as the "Bitcoin protocol". The other clear association to blockchain is the Dark Web, since Bitcoins (and other cryptocurrencies) are commonly used for illegal transactions—as is illustrated by the 2015 FBI-led prosecution of the Silk Road (Bearman, 2015). However, Bitcoins are not illegal currencies. In fact, they are now widely used as a monetary exchange in the banking system

S. Paladini (✉) · I. Castellucci
Birmingham City Business School, Birmingham, UK
e-mail: stefania.paladini@bcu.ac.uk

I. Castellucci
e-mail: icastellucci@unite.it

E. Yerushalmi
University of Teramo, Birmingham, UK
e-mail: Erez.Yerushalmi@bcu.ac.uk

T. Walker et al. (eds.), *Innovations in Social Finance*,
https://doi.org/10.1007/978-3-030-72535-8_14

(Boulton, 2015; Caffyn, 2015), the stock exchange (Nasdaq, 2014), and other financial transactions (Gallippi, 2014).

Blockchain is not a cryptocurrency. Rather, it is a type of promising technology that extends beyond the financial sector and is now being developed for use in sectors such as energy (EnerChain, 2017*),* health (Deloitte, 2016), and aerospace (AIA, 2019). The key to understanding its potential is in the way that it functions. Blockchain is essentially "an open, distributed ledger that can record transactions between two parties efficiently and in a verifiable and permanent way" (Iansiti & Lakhani, 2017, online). It is highly configurable and secure by design. Blockchain will change how sectors of the production and individuals in society interact. Because of its fundamental characteristics and disruptive potential (both positively and negatively, as we explain in this chapter), it is crucial for governments to proactively update regulatory frameworks while considering blockchain. This is crucial and will make this technology either a success or a lost opportunity.

To consider these issues, the aim of this chapter is to highlight the potential that blockchain application has beyond the cryptocurrency and monetary system. We compare some of the existing laws that directly impact blockchain and highlight its potential for social finance and social innovation (as explored in Sect. 2). This is exemplified by the European Union's (The EU) European Innovation Council award. In June 2020, €5 million were committed to blockchain solutions for social innovation (The EU Commission, 2020), the largest to date, but was by no means the only institutional contribution. Opportunities for a more inclusive application of blockchain for social innovation are available to every country. While there is little doubt that emerging economies could greatly benefit from blockchain (Brito & Castillo, 2013), through its ability to foster their internal agendas of social inclusions and innovation, not all of them have at present the necessary technical ability or motivation; but nothing prevents this in the future. A few examples have been offered in this context. Section 3 is the core of this chapter because it considers blockchain's regulatory dimension in a comparative perspective. Its aim is to distil what a "blockchain-friendly" legal framework should look like, to utilize its benefits and highlight the challenges for wide-scale implementation.

The geographic areas selected for analysis are the EU, Israel, and East Asia, with reference to the Philippines. The rationale for these choices is as follows: (i) the EU is the largest single market in the world, but also the one where the regulatory framework can prove the most challenging for implementing blockchain technology (mainly due to the GDPR, a 2016 regulation entered into force in 2018). (ii) Israel is an example of a country with a high digital literacy, a leader in technology start-ups (BBC, 2020, online) and is located in a completely different economic and financial environment. Finally, (iii) East Asia represents the area of the world where blockchain had the most impressive growth in the past decade. One example is Japan, a country with a sophisticated financial system and an inclination for implementing blockchain on a large scale. It is rapidly emerging as one of the "leading blockchain hubs in Asia, and arguably, the world" (Hackernoon.com, 2019). Another example is the Philippines, which is surprisingly a prominent location for applying blockchain as a social finance tool. Section 4 will offer a few examples of what can be defined as "blockchain in action"—i.e., the current status of the application of blockchain technology, some challenges in implementation, and future possibilities. Section 5 concludes with a few words of caution regarding this new technology.

2 Social Finance, Innovation & Blockchain

A lot has been written both on the technical specifications of blockchain (Casino et al., 2019; Crosby et al., 2016;) and about the characteristics of privacy, reliability, security, and distributed access (Christidis & Devetsikiotis, 2016; Housley, 2004; Meng et al., 2018), which contribute in making the technology so valuable and flexible when it comes to widespread uses.

Most of the literature focuses on the economic benefits of cryptocurrency that lowers transaction costs and enables access to capital (Brito & Castillo, 2013). Cryptocurrency facilitates the elimination of third-party intermediaries, making it cheaper for small businesses to transact and lowers the cost of global remittances. It has, therefore, the potential to alleviate global poverty and improve access to capital. Furthermore, it protects individuals against various forms of capital control, and monetary censorship as well as protecting marginalized groups' privacy. However, an aspect less explored is how blockchain can become an enabler for social innovation. Some go further and define blockchain as a "fundamental for forwarding progress in society as Magna Charta or the Rosetta Stone" (Swan, 2015, p. 7). What is true is that "the blockchain technology potentially allows individuals and communities to redesign their interactions in politics, business and society at large, with an unprecedented process of disintermediation on large scale, based on automated and trustless transactions" (Atzori, 2016, p. 4), with immediate and fundamental consequences for social innovation dynamics.

In this chapter, we define social innovation as "a complex process of introducing new products, processes or programs that profoundly change the basic routines, resource and authority flows, or beliefs of the social system in which the innovation occurs. Such successful social innovations have durability and broad impact" (Westley & Antadze, 2010, p. 2; also Moore et al., 2012; Repetto, 2006;). If this is the case, then blockchain, with its characteristics of being open-source and immediately available for use by various forms of economic operators, private, public, and from the third sector, is an ideal candidate for social innovation. Section 4 provides some examples of potential and promising uses of blockchain.

Moreover, all social innovation projects need, as much as any other project, resources (Bloom & Chatterji, 2009; Harding, 2007). Here, the competitive advantage of blockchain lies in the fact that often traditional finance is not immediately available to social aims (Dees & Battle Anderson, 2006; Nicholls, 2010; Nicholls & Young, 2008), while examples in emerging economies show that blockchain applications in the financial sectors can and are currently being used to this extent. In this sense, blockchain for the financial sector can be usefully inserted within the more general category of instruments liable to promote social finance, subjected to the same constraints, and working with the same rules. This is an important point to note, considering that "social finance is more than just the flow of money into social or environmental projects. It is conceived as an ethos about the way money is used … social finance can be seen as the discourse around such flows that is developing in concrete terms in the new institutions of supply, intermediation, and demand. This is a discourse in flux with competing perspectives driving the debate" (Nicholls & Pharoah, 2007, p. 6).

While it is unclear how blockchain will affect the context of social finance, some applications provide a glimpse of the potential direction. One is crowdfunding, whereby blockchain tokens are used either as preorders of goods or as ownership shares. This enables businesses to mimic venture capital funding while reaching a much wider audience in comparison with traditional methods (Belleflamme et al., 2014). Another example is the specific blockchain fundraising initiative, ICO (initial coin offerings), that bypass traditional intermediaries in fundraising initiatives (Mollick, 2014) and are more appealing to global investors (Massey et al., 2017). Both cryptocurrencies and blockchain tokens can effectively work as crowdfunding enablers, albeit with different modalities that would require setting up smart contracts (Chen & Bellavitis, 2020). In addition, these are hailed as being potential Shariah-compliant methods for Islamic crowdfunding, which will spur the development of new opportunities (Muneeza et al., 2018).

Whatever the modality, it has been convincingly demonstrated that blockchain has the potential to enable social innovators in "democratis[ing] entrepreneurship by democratizing the access to capital [...] and disrupting traditional venture investments just as social media is disrupting traditional media" (Chen & Bellavitis, 2020, p. 7), tax inefficiency, regulatory hiccups, and uncertainty (O'Leary, 2017) notwithstanding. These forward-looking aspects of blockchain technology have been recently taken on board by most international organizations working towards one or more SDGs.[1] Given its complex nature and the limited space available to us, we chose to focus on a selected number of initiatives in a few specific geographic areas (as previously mentioned).

3 Adapting the Regulatory Framework for Blockchain

Given that blockchain technology is being implemented without a clear legal framework, the regulation vacuum is creating friction in both the real and virtual worlds. For example, because blockchain is meant to remove the *Third-Party Verification*,[2] creating a virtual alternative market (in which people can directly interact with one another) means that new rules need to develop and be upheld within the virtual world. Furthermore, at least some of the likely conflicts and irregularities in the virtual world could be resolved by real-world interventions (e.g. policing, legal

[1] Examples abound here. A good starting point is HSBC 2019 Report Blockchain. Gateway for Sustainability Linked Bonds. (2020). Retrieved 14 October 2020, from https://www.sustainablefinance.hsbc.com/mobilising-finance/blockchain-gateway-for-sustainability-linked-bonds.

[2] A process whereby an independent, trustworthy, actor confirms the accuracy and intent of the transacting parties.

disputes, etc.), in addition to the smart enforcement tools and protocols associated with the relevant transactions algorithms—with the legal dimension possibly being at conflict with algorithmic remedies, and/or with platforms' possibilities of intervention on selected transactions (e.g. to reverse them). A striking example of this tension is the Singapore case *Quoine Pte Ltd v. B2C2 Ltd*, recently decided by the Singapore Court of Appeal, following a first instance judgement delivered in 2019 by the Singapore International Commercial Court.

In this case, the courts had to deal with balancing contract law, unjust enrichment, automated protocols, and human mistakes and the consequent unilateral interventions on a performed "smart" transaction which wasn't actually that smart, in the particular case at hand.[3] Policy, law, and technology will, thus, need to adapt to one another accordingly, in all attempts to develop a regulated digital, or digital/real, environment. Which elements will have to adapt to which ones remains to be seen—the answers could vary depending on the different contexts. In the following sections, we examine three different regulatory frameworks and offer some perspectives on the likely key areas of future friction as well as their solutions.

3.1 The EU

The European Union (EU) is the second largest market for blockchain applications (after the USA) and yet also the area with the largest barrier for its adoption. The main sticking-point is the in-principle scarce compatibility of blockchain with GDPR rules (i.e. the EU regulation for privacy), which covers two fundamental technical aspects: (i) the encryption that ensures anonymity and decentralization and (ii) the systemic tracking of all transactions. Interestingly, these precise features are those that make blockchain so attractive and valuable.

The first issue is that GDPR requires at least one "data controller", a legal or personal entity to whom subjects can ask for the enforcement of their rights. However, the very nature of blockchain is that this central authority does not exist, and herein lies the value of the technology. Article (Art) 22 of GDPR states: "The data subject shall have

[3] See *Quoine Pte Ltd v. B2C2 Ltd* [2020] SGCA (I) 02, delivered by the Singapore Court of Appeal following [2019] SGHC (I) 03 by the Singapore International Commercial Court.

the right not to be subject to a decision based solely on automated processing, including profiling, which produces legal effects concerning him or her or similarly significantly affects him or her". This is, however, the precise mechanism that underpins blockchain technology. The second issue, touching another fundamental characteristic of blockchain, is its immutability of past transactions to ensure data integrity and the overall trust of the chain itself. This also clashes with GDPR, specifically Art 16 and 17 that require that all data must be subject to modification, or even erasure, when necessary for legal reasons. Art 16 (Rectification) states: "The data subject shall have the right to obtain from the controller without undue delay the rectification of inaccurate personal data concerning him or her. Taking into account the purposes of the processing, the data subject shall have the right to have incomplete personal data completed, including by means of providing a supplementary statement".

Even more stringent is the right to erasure (Art 17), also known as the right to be forgotten, which clearly contradicts one of the basic principles of blockchain technology. This point has attracted a lot of discussion in terms of mitigation strategies (as we discussed below).

Additional hurdles are created by the components of personal data and if anonymization techniques like hashing (used by blockchain technology to confirm its state) can successfully transform them and thus realign and comply with GDPR.[4] Finally, a further complication is the territorial scope of GDPR, as Art 3 clearly states. Even though it is an EU law, it has implications beyond EU borders. For example, whenever EU nationals and their personal data are involved (both as data subjects and data controller), GDPR provisions take precedence. Companies that adopt blockchain internationally must be mindful of this.

There are a few ongoing studies that explore ways to conciliate GDPR and blockchain, tackling one or all the above legal rifts. In most cases, the solution lies within sophisticated techniques that enable data controllers to have a separate treatment of their personal data from the others, as in the case of off-chain storages. This "would enable the rectification and erasure of personal data stored off-chain in appropriate databases in line

[4] About this specific point and in general on the anonymization procedures, the debate is still ongoing (Acar 2018; Felten, 2012).

with Articles 16 and 17 GDPR" (The EU Parliament, 2019, online).[5] Working on the configuration of the distributed ledger would partially address those concerns (Bacon et al., 2018; Berberich & Steiner, 2016; Finck, 2018).[6] A further approach is the outright destruction of data (e.g. The EU Parliament, 2019, online), including the destruction of private keys, as some cases at EUCJ prove (Case C-131/12 Google Spain [2014]).

No matter the specific solutions devised, there is a clear problem that requires correction. The GDPR obstacles are unique to the EU and tougher when compared to other countries with similar regulatory frameworks. For example, regulation in the USA is more blockchain-friendly. The only other exception is California, which recently introduced a new regulation (the California Consumer Privacy Act of 2018—CCPA) that has GDPR-like provisions for the digital sector, and is expected to have a direct impact on blockchain. Legal hurdles and technical obstacles aside, there is certain future for blockchain in Europe. Though GDPR is a major point of friction for blockchain, a friendlier regulatory environment is actively being encouraged in some European jurisdictions, designed to attract investments in this field. For example, Malta and San Marino are in the process of developing an attractive legal framework for blockchain applications. Its aim is to regulate blockchain through official channels, promote supervision and the development of certified best practices, attract global market actors in the field, and incentivize compliance within the growing blockchain market. How well this is going to be achieved in a GDPR-compliant framework remains to be seen.

The following issues represent significant legal challenges: the time required for the technology to mature and an indication of where it is heading; and, especially, a significant change in the legal framework as well

[5] Even though issues would still remain. "An open question in this regard is, however, that of the status of the remaining hash. Indeed, the data in off-chain storage will be linked to the database through a hash, and where the off-chain data is erased, that hash will remain on the ledger. To determine whether this hash remains personal data, the means reasonably likely to provoke identification need to be examined. However, this is an era where confusion reigns as many have expressed confusion as to how this ought to be determined" (The EU Parliament, 2019, online).

[6] Increasingly inventive solutions are currently under consideration, such as state channels for two-party smart contracts, which will share information in the event of a dispute (Butering, 2016), ring signatures hiding key information (European Blockchain Observatory and Forum, 2018), and the addition of noise to the data (MIT, 2019).

as a major cultural change in the very mind of legal systems' operators will be required. Domestic laws and the EU normative environment—both European States and the EU certainly having a long-term vested interest in developing both the blockchain economy and tools for its governance, whether hard or soft—certainly add complexity to this picture.

The EU appears fully committed to reaping the benefits of blockchain, across various potential applications, even though this poses a challenge and a contradiction towards its own regulatory framework. It recognizes the importance of the blockchain technology in the EU, in fields as different as health care, energy, financial market, global-supply chains, and agricultures, which are impossible to discuss in the limited space of this chapter. Some examples of recent blockchain development in the EU, both in general and with specific references to social innovation, are provided in Section 4.

In terms of institutional support, a lot of recent initiatives show the commitment of the EU to the development of the technology. To this extent, the EU Commission and the European Parliament launched in February 2018 the Blockchain Observatory and Forum aimed at the promotion and support of the blockchain initiatives that enable "cross border cooperation on practical use cases, bringing Europe's best experts together and promoting an open forum for blockchain technologists, innovators, citizens, industry stakeholders, public authorities, regulators and supervisors, to discuss and develop new ideas in order to learn, engage and contribute in an open way" (The EU Commission, 2018, online). Since its beginning, the EU Blockchain Observatory and Forum have organized workshops, issued expert reports on different topics, and mapped 700 + global blockchain projects on an interactive map available on the institutional website. The Observatory has also grown in scope together with the European blockchain landscape, both private and public, and it will continue to do so even after 2020 (The EU Commission, 2020).[7] Finally, in terms of financial support, the EU Commission has been funding blockchain projects since 2013 through their framework programmes FP7 and Horizon2020. The funds committed to projects

[7] For example, in October 2019, the EU Commission selected a consortium to operate together with the Forum, composed by a group of operators (INTRASOFT, the University of Nicosia, the Centre for Research and Technology Hellas (CERTH), and a series of subcontractors (including Bitfury Group, OpenForum Europe AISBL, White Research, PLANET S.A.).

that draw on blockchain technologies is up to €340 million by 2020 and, while details of the next framework programme for R&D are not available yet, they would probably keep rising in the future.

3.2 *Israel*

Israel is a country known for its high concentration of high-tech technological development. According to a report by StartupBlink (2020), which provides a ranking of the start-up ecosystems among a list of the top 1000 cities and 100 countries, Israel maintains its lead among the top four countries (including USA, UK, and Canada). Similarly, Deloitte (2016)reported Israel as the world's second-best entrepreneurial ecosystem.[8] The Israeli hi-tech sector is estimated at around USD 33.1 billion (bln) in 2016 (CBS, 2019)—roughly 10.3% of GDP.[9] Within Deloitte (it, 2016) estimates that 61 fintech Israeli firms raised USD 0.37 billion (bln) in 2014 and include firms working with blockchain. Recently, SPHINX (2020) focused on the narrower sub-sector, *blockchain and Bitcoin*, and estimate the amount of external raised capital at around USD 2.1 bln in 2020. Combining these two points in time is clear evidence that the sub-sector is growing very rapidly.[10]

As in other countries, blockchain in Israel is most closely linked to the financial intermediation sector and fintech. New developments are mainly focusing on electronic wallets, bitcoin, and other crypto

[8] Much of Israel's success originates from the military as a technology incubator. Young adults are recruited to various elite cyber units that are responsible for collecting signal intelligence and code decryption. Once these young 18–21-year-olds complete their compulsory army service, they enter the labour market, having already gained valuable and practical skills in IT and R&D. A most well-known example is Unit 8200.

[9] Using annual average Shekel/USD = 3.8406 from Bank of Israel, Foreign Currency Department.

[10] The SPHINX (2020) report collects a comprehensive list of 134 blockchain related companies. It finds that all firms are small medium enterprises (SME), i.e. most firms employ 1–10 workers, and only five employ above 50 that employ just under 1,800 workers as a sub-sector. Just above 50% of these firms are funded by outside sources and the rest by private funding. Furthermore, 37% of the firms have released a product to the market, while the rest are at various development stages (either R&D, alpha or beta versions). SPHINX (2020) is the most up-to-date market analysis on the blockchain and bitcoin sub-sector in Israel, commissioned by the Israeli Bitcoin Association https://www.bitcoin.org.il/. The report came out in February 2020 and provides information immediately prior to the COVID-19 pandemic in Israel that begin in March 2020.

digital currencies, and on utilizing initial coin offerings (ICO). But there are also examples of technologies being developed for other sectors, e.g. health care record, legal, intellectual property (IP), contract digitalization, fundraising, community regeneration projects, international shipping, food and product control, and many more applications. These new blockchain applications are either utilizing the open network or developing their own closed network.[11] (SPHINX [2020] collected a comprehensive excel list of blockchain firms in Israel that describes the products being developed, number of employees, and more.)

Even though Israel is a top innovator of blockchain technology, this technology's practical application is very limited. The Israeli consumer does not currently benefit from the social and economic potential. The main reason for this is due to the Israeli market being too small, and high-tech firms prefer to focus their energies on the much larger external markets. So far, the greatest scope for Israeli customers to benefit from blockchain technology has come from private banks and credit card companies who are incorporating fintech technologies to update themselves and move towards a digital business model (BoI, 2019). Yet one Israeli firm, *Colu*, is experimenting with blockchain technology called *colored coins* to associate digital assets with real assets (e.g. stocks, car, land, intellectual property, etc.). Their aim is to use the enhanced security features of Bitcoins to trade with non-financial products. Colu provides various applied impact case studies to promote their product.[12] One example is the creation of a local currency at the neighbourhood level of Jaffa (part of the Tel-Aviv Jaffa municipality). Its aim is to promote local shopping and regeneration in Jaffa's neighbourhood.[13] The project is being used to demonstrate transferability to other communities across the word, bypasses traditional intermediaries of exchange, and creates growth from the ground up. BoI (2019) provides other examples of blockchain related applications in Israel. They focus on payment apps, virtual banking services that use Artificial Intelligence (AI) and blockchain. These are developed by private banks together with Israeli Fintech Startup firms and academia. One specific application of blockchain is a partnership between

[11] One interesting example is the shipping giant, Maersk, and IBM developed a blockchain network for shipping called TradeLens.

[12] https://colu.com/case-studies/.

[13] https://colu.com/case-studies/urban-regeneration-in-tel-aviv-colu-civic-engagement/.

Bank Hapoalim and *Microsoft Israel* that uses the *Azure cloud-platform*. The platform enables the customer of the bank to become guarantors without the need to physically appear in the bank for validation (Walla, 2017).

Another example is *Bits of Gold.net*,[14] an Israeli firm that provides a platform for buying and selling Bitcoins and Ethereum. In 2013, it was the first cryptocurrency broker in Israel to receive a licence from the Israeli Money Laundering and Terror Financing Authority. Today three firms provide such a service. Bit of Gold is a well-known example that shows the new frictions emerging between incumbent "traditional" private banks, which want to incorporate blockchain technology into their services and yet hinder its adoption by potential non-bank (competitor) entrants. The legal dispute between *Bitsofgold.net* and *Bank Leomi* reveals the need to develop and update government regulation (CCLP & ISOC-IL, 2019; Katsiri, 2019a; Levush, 2018). In 2017, the courts agreed that Bank Leomi is not obliged to accept earnings that originate from profits produced by cryptocurrencies because of the possible illegal activities associated with cryptocurrencies. The outcome barred Bits of Gold from using "real world" current account services that were made in the "virtual world". This would have a serious impact on the abilities of new virtual coin application in entering the financial intermediation sector as alternative products.[15]

Like the contradictions between GDPR and blockchain in the EU, Israel's regulators are also grappling with this new emerging technology and its potential positive or negative consequences. In 2016, the *Supervision on Finance Services Law 5776-2016* was introduced in order to provide a licensing requirement for trading in virtual currency.[16] The new law deemed virtual currencies a "financial asset" and required persons

[14] https://www.bitsofgold.net/

[15] In 2018, Bits of Gold appealed to the Supreme Court, whereby a temporary injunction was issued prohibiting a bank from blocking activities of a company using virtual currency on the basis that the allegations are speculative rather than evidence based (Levush, 2018). In the same year, in a move to legitimize and regulate crypto currency activities, Bits of Gold agreed to declare its heavy cryptocurrency users of above NIS 50 K to the Israeli Tax Authority (Milman, 2018). Finally, in 2019, the Supreme Court agreed on the compromise made by both sides that allowed Bits of Gold to continue using Bank Leomi's financial services.

[16] For further details see Library of Congress, https://www.loc.gov/law/help/cryptocurrency/israel.php#_ftn3.

providing services in "virtual currencies" (i.e. cryptocurrencies) to obtain a licence. To manage control over fiat money, the Israeli tax authority (ITA) declared in January 2018 that virtual currencies cannot be used as official money or as foreign currency, as stipulated by the *Bank of Israel (BoI) Law 2010* and *Order of Income Tax* (ITA, 2018a, 2018b; Levush, 2018).[17] However, because virtual currencies are none-depreciable assets, their profits are taxable according to income tax rules or as value-added tax (VAT) if used as an intermediate payment. In other words, activities that generate profits using virtual currencies are obliged for tax reporting, including mining, payments for services, exchange, and others. In March 2018, ITA also published its new tax rules on Initial Coin Offerings (ICO) that uses blockchain technology, to clarify and close any regulatory leaks (ITA, 2018b).

In a detailed white paper on the emergence of blockchain technology in Israel, CCLP and ISOC-IL (2019) argue that the current regulatory framework in Israel is wide enough to encompass and regulate blockchain development and its use, including other technologies that compete with blockchain. For example, the main law in Israel is the *Economic Competition Law 5748-1988* (GOV.IL, 1988), which aims to protect market competition and the public interests. The law covers three themes: (i) the appropriate conduct of market players so that none impair the other or harm market competitiveness, (ii) the assessment of mergers and acquisitions that could impair competition and the public interest, and (iii) protect against anti-monopolistic behaviour (CCLP & ISOC-IL, 2019). Moreover, the law states the structure and role of the Israeli Competition Authority (ICA), the Director General of ICA, and the Competition Tribunal that deals with cases brought before it. CCLP and ISOC-IL (2019) explain that regulation relating to blockchain is currently reactive and piecemeal. They provide some examples as models that communicate how the Ministry of Finance and Bank of Israel (BoI) provide reactive policy and that a serious effort towards a proactive approach is lacking. The key characteristics that make blockchain incompatible with current real-world laws and regulations are highlighted by CCLP and ISOC-IL (2019). These are like those faced by the EU (e.g. the incompatibility of GDPR and Blockchain, as previously discussed). In Israel, so far, the focus has been on two issues: (i) the anonymity of blockchain users that hinders

[17] Also known as the Income tax law.

enforcement and (ii) the permanency of blockchain's limits rectifying anti-competitive actions, even when these were identified (i.e. also known as *unstoppable code*). CCLP and ISOC-IL (2019) and Katsiri (2019b) further explain that the lack of clear blockchain regulation in Israel creates a mismatch between short and long-run objectives. In the short run, the vacuum enables firms to save on costs because no regulatory considerations are required. But in the long run, this exposes them to risks because their platforms might not fit (or even oppose) future regulation. This lack of clarity and risk of mismatch hinders new developments from forming as well as limit the adoption of good technology.

Though regulation is undeniably required, it is not a simple task. Institutions such as the BoI, which are crucial for implementing policy, argue that blockchain and the virtual world are simply too new and that it is impossible to proactively develop appropriate regulation without knowing the direction that blockchain is heading towards (BoI, 2018a). However, as much as this makes sense, blockchain is unavoidable, and regulation must find ways to quickly accommodate and evolve. We expect further disruptions to occur, as the legal dispute between *Bits of Gold* and *Bank Leomi* showed—a highly cited example in Israel within the context of blockchain.

3.3 East Asia and the Philippines

After the USA and the EU, East Asia is the area of the world that has witnessed the most impressive growth both in cryptocurrency trading and blockchain technology in general, even though the approach and the regulatory framework of the individual countries are different and quite nuanced. Still, compared to other world regions outside the USA and the EU, the entirety of East Asia is one that has enthusiastically welcomed this new technology—not only by the technology-advanced countries (e.g. Japan, South Korea or Singapore), but also by the emerging economies.

For instance, the Philippines is among the Asian countries that are becoming increasingly blockchain-friendly. There are various indicators showing this. One example is the value of cryptocurrency transactions which rose from 189.18 million USD, in 2017, to 390.37 million USD in 2018—just the following year. There are a few reasons why the Philippines departed from the usual suspicious approach shared by other countries in the region and decided to support the technology. One is, maybe surprisingly, the relative backwardness of the Philippines' financial system. For example, many individuals still do not even have access to traditional banking (i.e. seven in ten, according to some recent estimates; International Finance, 2020). E-currencies provide, therefore, an inexpensive substitute (solution) to fill the void. But the largest driver for embracing blockchain comes from the local start-ups and SMEs, and the economic benefits it generates. These capital-starved firms are keen to integrate blockchain because of its cost saving decentralized nature, as discussed in Sect. 2. Compared to its neighbouring countries, access to the stock market is limited in the Philippines, which is ideal for fintech-powered capital market technology to flourish.

In the last few years, the adoption of blockchain solutions has grown parallel to the establishment of crypto exchanges for cryptocurrencies based in different areas of the country to make adoption easier. In addition to the 11 crypto exchanges approved by the central bank with a licence to the entire national territories (Bitcoin News, 2018), the government-owned CEZA (Cagayan Economic Zone Authority) authorized 37 crypto exchange operators with a smaller and/or more restricted trading scope. CEZA is an important case in this context: this special economic zone and freeport has been set up in the northeast of the Philippines, specifically to compete with Hong Kong and Singapore as an international financial hub. The authorization of crypto exchanges to operate in the zone signals the government's support of blockchain and its view that this is a "winning" future technology, which will make the country more internationally competitive.

There are also additional measures put in place to support the whole fintech sector and blockchain. For a start, the Philippines Securities and Exchange Commission also recently finalized crypto guidelines to make their application more transparent.

The government has also established what the press dubbed "the Crypto Valley of Asia" (SCMP, 2019) which is a cyber-park that shares the area with the already-mentioned cryptocurrency and fintech hub in CEZA economic zone. This was created with the participation of the property developer Northern Star Gaming & Resorts Inc., investing 100 million USD over a ten-year period (Bitcoin News, 2019b). As mentioned, the aim is to give the country a competitive advantage compared to the rest of ASEAN countries (e.g. Indonesia or Vietnam) and the rest of East Asia, which might be less inclined to offer such strong support towards the new technology. While Japan has embraced blockchain technology early on and it can be considered the leader of bitcoin transactions in Asia, other important players, like China and South Korea, have demonstrated enthusiasm but also a certain degree of caution.

Finally, there are concerns about blockchain, not only relevant to the Philippines but across East Asia. At the core of blockchain technology is its ability to maintain secure and decentralized virtual transactions, both legitimate and illegitimate. However, without appropriate safeguards, it is prone to be exploited by unlawful operations. For this reason, despite supporting the development of cryptocurrency hubs, the Philippines Central Bank also imposed some legal limits to their activities. First, all single transactions amounting to more than P 500,000 (about 10,000 USD) cannot be made by cryptocurrencies. Instead, the operation needs to be carried out by cheque or through direct credit to the bank accounts. Second, the Central Bank requires all exchanges in cryptocurrencies to adhere to the official guidelines, maintaining all the required records and filing reports on the activities, which, considered the inherent technology, looks quite difficult to achieve.

If the past is any guide, if not supervised and correctly configured with the right mix of checks and balances, the wide-scale adoption of the technology could also be used for money laundering and terrorist financing, enhancing security issues that currently exist everywhere in the world.

4 Blockchain in Action

Blockchain does not consist of just cryptocurrencies, but cryptocurrencies still represent the bulk of blockchain applications so far. The entire cryptocurrency sector has boomed since Bitcoin's appearance in 2009 and, as of April 22, 2020, approximately 5,392 cryptocurrencies are being traded with a total market capitalization of 201 billion USD around the world. Revenue from blockchain technology overall, beyond cryptocurrencies, are projected to continue growing to over 39 billion USD by 2025. Regional spending on blockchain solutions has been rising steadily since 2010, and the world's outlook is impressive both in sheer value and in growing trends. In 2022, the forecast for US spending on blockchain technology is about 4.2 billion USD, still the single largest country in terms of value.

As Fig. 1 shows, other regions have been gaining momentum, especially the EU and Asia-Pacific. As much as the cryptocurrencies are the

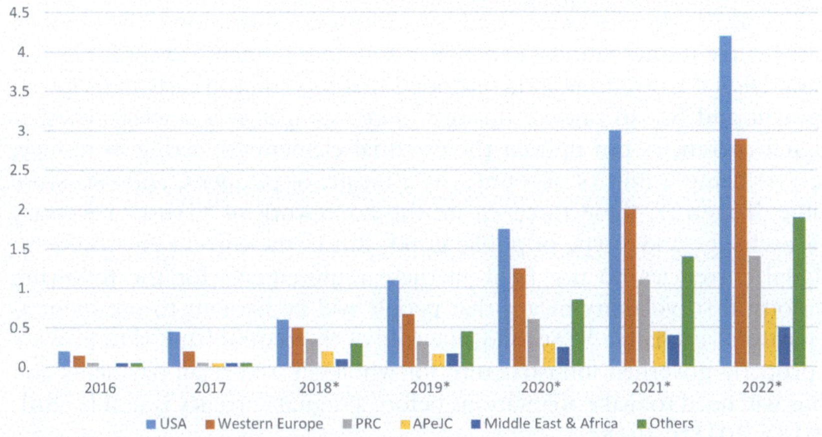

Fig. 1 Worldwide spending on blockchain solutions from 2016 to 2022 by region (in billions $) (*Source* Authors' elaboration on IDC and Statista data, 2020; PRC refers to Mainland China here, while ApeJC is the Asia-Pacific. Conclusive data still not available for 2018 and following years. Latin America is not present as a separate region in this article for a reason: it is one of the areas where the introduction of blockchain technology proved the slowest, with countries such as Bolivia and Ecuador banning the use of cryptocurrencies as means of payment)

lynchpin of blockchain applications, the financial sector represents its core, even though the technology, as mentioned before, is rapidly expanding.

The focus, so far, has been on private firms pushing to develop and integrate blockchain. But key state institutional players are also involved. For example, countries' central banks are considering the adoption of Distributed Ledger Technology (DLT) using Blockchain. Countries such as South Africa, Canada, Japan, Thailand, and Singapore are already testing a wholesaler digital coin for the financial and payment system (WEF, 2019). The aim is to improve the efficiency of interbank transfers and loans, and as a proof-of-concept before the introduction of a public e-currency for retail use. The Bank of Israel (BoI) had also deliberated on this in the working group that discussed the introduction of a digital e-Shekel. Ultimately, they decided against it for the time being due to the risks outweighing the gains. A similar conclusion was reached by the Central Bank of Denmark (BoI, 2018a).

The BoI's decision was based on various considerations: they looked at the current international experience and developments towards Central Bank Digital Currencies and concluded that it is still too early in its development and has an unclear future.[18] For example, it is unclear whether digital currencies can uphold the essential elements of acting as money, i.e., (i) being a unit of account, (ii) a means of payment, and (iii) store value. Together, these three create the framework of "Trust" necessary for exchange and a type of public good. But in the current environment, digital currencies do not fulfil all these requirements for the following reasons: first, volatility means that people will be hesitant to use them as a means of exchange.[19] Second, the role of the central bank is to provide a properly governed infrastructure for wholesale and retail payments and thus will need to make adaptations before a digital currency is usable (BoI, 2018a, 2018b, 2018c).

Finally, the aim of central banks is to create a price-stable environment, supervising private banks so that they maintain resilience with enough capital and generate good governance with Anti-Money Laundering and Finance Crime Protection. However, blockchain is currently incompatible with these. The risks and uncertainties inherent within digital currencies are still too large. Regulation and legal barriers must first be clarified before adoption (e.g. the anonymity of cryptocurrency users opens it up to money laundering, tax avoidance, and unclear legal disputes).

However, countries and institutions recognize that the potential of blockchain for social innovation is beyond financial intermediate—as discussed in Sect. 2. They, therefore, are willing to go to the extent of offering substantial institutional support. A telling case is the EU. Despite GDPR-related hurdles, the EU Commission has shown a clear intention to support blockchain when geared towards social innovation initiatives. For example, in June 2020, the EIC (European Innovation Council) awarded a €5 million prize to six institutions that use blockchains for "Social Good". The aim is to identify a series of high-impact and workable blockchain solutions to address societal challenges (The EU, 2020, online). In line with the original philosophy that inspired Bitcoin, an open-source protocol was one of the proposal requirements, to make

[18] BoI reviewed the experiences of the other central banks that have been testing a wholesaler digital coin for the financial and payment system.

[19] For example, people will hold-on-to them if prices are expected to rise, while others will not accept them when prices are expected to fall.

sure that access to the developed solutions was extended and available to a wide platform of users. The focus of the six winning proposals includes: solutions for fair trade, contribution to financial inclusion, circular economy, transparency in procurement and public work, management of public records, and renewable energy, each of which will receive €1 million (EnterpriseUk.com, 2020).

The six winners were the Dutch WordProof (quality content), the UK-based PPP (traceability and fair trade), GMeRitS (financial inclusion) by the Finnish University in Aalto, UnBlocked Cash Project OXBBU (aid and philanthropy) developed by the British Oxfam and the French start-up Sempo, CKH2020 (decentralized circular economy) by the French company Klero, and the Italian PROSUME (energy).

Beyond the EU Commission itself, there are further examples of several European start-ups that have focused on utilizing blockchain technology for social innovation. For example, the London-based Coinfirm, which since 2015, has developed an anti-money laundering (AML) system for virtual currencies to allow financial institutions and regulators to safely engage with the crypto world (Co-Infirm, 2020); the Swiss Odem, which applies blockchain to education and training accessible to everybody (Odem, 2020); and the Estonian Solve.Care. Since 2017, Care has raised €26.7 million to bring transparency and a more agile bureaucracy in the world healthcare systems (Solve.Care, 2020).

5 Conclusions

Twelve years after Nakamoto's paper, blockchain technology is booming, and the most widespread and comprehensive applications, like IoT (internet of things), are still in their infancy. In one of the most likely scenarios, in ten years from now, we will live in a world where so much more will be powered by highly sophisticated, anonymous, encrypted, and distributed ledger.

As for any technology, it is important to understand how things can go wrong before they can be used for good. If anything, the early issues with Bitcoin and its utilization on the Dark Web and lending blockchain a dubious reputation, also alerted all perspective users about its inherent dangers. This is, however, a good thing at the end of the day. Because the real challenges with blockchain are not the technology, but "the issues involved relating to implementation, organization and trust" (Werbach, as cited by WEF, 2018*)* a lot still remains to be done. If anything, a snapshot of the 2020 global outlook presents a quite diverse landscape (Chohan, 2017) when it comes to the regulatory framework and blockchain adoptions, and for countries that still ban the use of cryptocurrencies as means of payments, there are others that have provided a friendly and supportive environment.

Still, one point that clearly emerges from this synthetic overview is that countries and realities as different as Israel, EU, and East Asia are all dealing with similar issues when the adoption of the blockchain technology is scaled up for everyday use. The hurdle to overcome is the reconciliation and integration with the existing regulatory framework that exists to protect citizen rights and public interests in a fast-changing digital world. The stronger the rule of law and the protection granted to those rights, the more challenging it is to integrate blockchain, as the EU case illustrates.

But solutions do exist. What matters the most is the political will to adopt the technology and use it in the most inclusive way possible. Blockchain can not only dramatically alter our economic and technological landscape; it can be a force for good and social innovation, as our chapter demonstrates. This will likely pass for a necessary, and in some cases, overdue reflection on how to address the problematic points raised by regulations such as the GDPR and together make sure the technology is as inclusive and forward looking as it can possibly be.

References

Acar, G. (April 2018). *Four cents to deanonymize: Companies reverse hashed email addresses*. Freedom to Tinker. https://freedom-to-tinker.com/2018/04/09/four-cents-to-deanonymize-companies-reverse-hashed-email-addresses/. Accessed on 10 March 2020.

AIA. (2019). *Blockchain in aerospace & defense*, https://www.aia-aerospace.org/report/blockchain-in-aerospace/. Accessed on 2 March 2020.

Atzori, M. (2016). *Blockchain technology and decentralized governance: Is the state still necessary?* University College of London—Center for Blockchain Technologies.

Bacon, J., Michels, J. D., Millard, C., & Singh, J. (2018). Blockchain demystified: A technical and legal introduction to distributed and centralised ledgers. *Ledgers' Richmond Journal of Law and Technology, 1*(63), https://jolt.richmond.edu/blockchain-demystified-a-technical-and-legal-introduction-to-distributed-and-centralised-ledgers/. Accessed on 2 March 2020.

BBC News. (2020). *How Israel became a high-tech hub*. BBC Website. https://www.bbc.com/news/business-15797257. Accessed on 1 March 2020.

Bearman, J. (2015). *The rise and fall of silk road: Part I*. WIRED. http://www.wired.com/2015/04/silk-road-1. Accessed on 1 March 2020.

Berberich, M., & Steiner, M. (2016). Blockchain technology and the GDPR—How to reconcile privacy and distributed ledgers? *European Data Protection Law Review, 2*, 422–425.

Bitcoin News. (2019a). *Philippines increasingly crypto friendly*. Regulation Bitcoin News. https://news.bitcoin.com/philippines-crypto-friendly/.

Bitcoin News. (2019b). *48 crypto exchanges approved in the Philippines*. Regulation Bitcoin News. https://news.bitcoin.com/48-cryptocurrency-exchanges-philippines/. Accessed on 2 March 2020.

Bitcoin News. (2018). *Philippines building crypto valley of Asia*. Bitcoin News. https://news.bitcoin.com/philippines-crypto-valley-asia/. Accessed on 2 March 2020.

Bloom, P., & Chatterji, A. (2009). Scaling social entrepreneurial impact. *California Management Review, 51*(3), 114–133.

Bank of Israel. (2018a). *Report of the team to examine the issue of Central Bank Digital Currencies*. Bank of Israel.

Bank of Israel. (2018b). *Deputy Governor's Governor's Remarks at the Eli Hurvitz Conference on Economy and Society*. Bank of Israel (BoI).

Bank of Israel. (2018c). *Remarks by Bank of Israel Deputy Governor Dr. Nadine Baudot-Trajtenberg at the Knesset Finance Committee meeting on activity and use of virtual currencies*. Bank of Israel (BoI).

Bank of Israel. (2019). *Banking System Annual Report*. Bank of Israel (BoI), [Hebrew].

Boulton, C. (2015). BNY Mellon explores Bitcoin's potential. *Wall Street Journal*. http://blogs.wsj.com/cio/2015/04/05/bny-mellon-explores-bitcoins-potential. Accessed on 2 March 2020.

Brito, J., & Castillo, A. (2013). *Bitcoin: A primer for policymakers, Mercatus Center* (pp. 14–15). George Mason University. https://www.researchgate.net/publication/269707314_Bitcoin_A_Primer_for_Policymakers. Accessed on 2 March 2020.

Buterin, V. (January 2016). *Privacy on the blockchain*. https://blog.ethereum.org/2016/01/15/privacy-on-the-blockchain/.

Caffyn, G. (2015). *Barclays trials Bitcoin tech with pilot program, COINDESK*. http://www.coindesk.com/barclays-trials-bitcoin-tech-withpilot-program. Accessed on 1 March 2020.

Casino, F., Dasaklis, T. K., & Patsakis, C. (2019). A systematic literature review of blockchain based applications: Current status, classification and open issues. *Telematics and Informatics, 36*, 55–81.

CBS. (2019). *Israel in Numbers: Main Data from the Yearly Statics of Israel.* Israel Central Bureau of Statistics.

CCLP, ISOC-IL. (2019). *Blockchain technology in Israel: Disruptions, uses, challenges, and obstacles.* Center for Cyper Law & Policy (CCLP), University of Haifa and Israeli Internet Association (ISOC-IL).

Chen, Y., & Bellavitis, C. (2020). Blockchain disruption and decentralized finance: The rise of decentralized business models. *Journal of Business Venturing Insights, 13.*

Chohan, U. W. (2017). *Assessing the differences in bitcoin & other cryptocurrency legality across national jurisdictions.* Available at SSRN 3042248.

Christidis, K., & Devetsikiotis, M. (2016). Blockchains and smart contracts for the Internet of things. *IEEE Access., 4,* 1–1. https://doi.org/10.1109/ACCESS.2016.2566339.

CoinDesk. (2019). *Philippines Central Bank warns on risks of growing Cryptocurrency use.* https://www.coindesk.com/philippines-central-bank-warns-on-risks-of-growing-cryptocurrency-use. Accessed on 16 June 2020.

Co-Infirm. (2020). *Company website.* https://www.coinfirm.com/. Accessed on 2 March 2020.

CoinMarketCap. (2020) *Market capitalisation.* https://coinmarketcap.com/rankings/exchanges/. Accessed on 20 April 2020.

Crosby, M., Pattanayak, P., & Verma, S., (2016). *Blockchain technology: Beyond bitcoin.* http://scet.berkeley.edu/wp-content/uploads/AIR-2016-Blockchain.pdf. Accessed on 2 March 2020.

Dees, J. G., & Battle Anderson, B. (2006). Rhetoric, reality, and research: building a solid foundation for the practice of social entrepreneurship. In A. Nicholls (Ed.), *Social entrepreneurship: new models of sustainable social change* (pp. 144–168). Oxford: Oxford University Press.

Deloitte. (2016). *Blockchain: Opportunities for health care.* https://www2.deloitte.com/us/en/pages/public-sector/articles/blockchain-opportunities-for-health-care.html. Accessed on 1 March 2020.

Deloitte. (2016). *Israel: A hotspot for blockchain innovation.* Deloitte.

Doguet, J. (2013). The nature of the form: Legal and regulatory issues surrounding the Bitcoin digital currency system. *LA. L. REV., 73,* 1119, 1130. Accessed on 1 March 2020.

EnerChain. (2017). *Gridchain: Blockchain-based process integration for the smart grids of the future.* https://enerchain.ponton.de/index.php/16-gridchain-blockchain-based-process-integration-for-the-smart-grids-of-the-future. Accessed on 2 March 2020.

Entrerprises.UK. (2020). *Eic awards Euro 5 million for social innovations based on blockchain.* https://www.enterprisetimes.co.uk/2020/07/07/eic-awards-e5m-for-social-innovations-based-on-blockchain/. Accessed on 2 March 2020.

EPRS. (2019). *Can distributed ledgers be squared with European data protection law?* Available at European Parliamentary Research Service, EPRS_STU2019634445_EN.pdf. Accessed on 13 March 2020.

EUCJ. (2014). *Case C-131/12 Google Spain [2014] EU:C:2014:317*. http://curia.europa.eu/juris/liste.jsf?num=C-131/12. Accessed on 2 March 2020.

European Blockchain Observatory and Forum. (2018). *Blockchain and the GDPR*. https://www.eublockchainforum.eu/reports. Accessed on 6 October 2019.

Felten, E. (2012). *Does hashing make data "anonymous"?* Federal Trade Commission. https://www.ftc.gov/news-events/blogs/techftc/2012/04/does-hashing-make-data-anonymous. Accessed on 2 March 2020.

Finck, M. (2018). Blockchains and data protection in the European Union. *European Data Protection Law Review, 17*.

Gallippi, T. (2014). *ESPN and BitPay Enter 3-Year Deal To Produce NCAA Bowl Game*. Bitpay Blog. http://blog.bitpay.com/2014/06/18/espn-and-bitpay-enter-3-yeardeal-to-produce-ncaa-bowl-game.html. Accessed on 2 March 2020.

GOV.IL. (1988). *Economic Competition Law, 5748-1988*. Israel Competition Authority.

Hackermoon. (2019). *Japan is fast becoming the gold standard for blockchain adoption*. https://hackernoon.com/japan-is-fast-becoming-the-gold-standard-for-blockchain-adoption-p3s32kni. Accessed on 1 March 2020.

Harding, R. (2007). *Social entrepreneurship monitor*. London: London Business School and Barclays Bank.

Housley, R. (2004). *Public key infrastructure (PKI)*. The Internet Encyclopedia. https://papers.ssrn.com/sol3/papers.cfm?abstract_id=2709713. Accessed on 2 March 2020.

Iansiti, M., & Lakhani, K. R. (January 2017). The truth about blockchain. *Harvard Business Review*. Harvard University, https://hbr.org/2017/01/the-truth-about-blockchain. Accessed on 1 March 2020.

ITA. (2018a). *Taxation of activity by means of virtual payment*.

ITA. (2018b). *Initial Coin Offering (ICO) for providing services and/or developing products* (Utility Tokens) (Israel Tax Authority Circular No. No. 7/2018). Israel Tax Authority (ITA).

Katsiri, R. (2019a). *Israeli bitcoin holders take on banks*. Globes.

Katsiri, R. (2019b). *Israel missing out on blockchainBlockchain, study finds*. Globes.

Levush, R. (2018). *Regulation of cryptocurrency: Israel (Web page)*. Library of Congress.

Massey, R., Dalal, D., & Dakshinamoorthy, A. (2017). *Initial coin offering: A new paradigm*. Deloitte. https://www2.deloitte.com/content/dam/Del

oitte/us/Documents/process-and-operations/us-cons-new-paradigm.pdf. Accessed on 2 March 2020.

Meng, W., Tischhauser, E. W., Wang, Q., Wang, Y., & Han, J. (2018). When intrusion detection meets blockchain technology: A review. *Ieee Access, 6*, 10179–10188.

Milman, O. (2018). The tax authority will receive information on heavy crypto users. *Kalkalist Newspaper*.

MIT Media Lab. (2020). *Project overview enigma*. https://www.media.mit.edu/projects/enigma/overview/. Accessed on 27 July 2020.

Mollick, E. (2014). The dynamics of crowdfunding: An exploratory study. *Journal of Business Venturing, 29*(1), 1–16.

Moore, M.-L., Westley, F. R., Tjornbo, O., & Holroyd, C. (2012). The loop, the lens, and the lesson: Using resilience theory to examine public policy and social innovation. In A. Nicholls & A. Murdoch, (Eds.) *Social innovation* (pp. 89–113). Palgrave MacMillan.

Muneeza, A., Arshad, N. A., & Arifin, A. T. (2018). The application of blockchain technology in crowdfunding: Towards financial inclusion via technology. *International Journal of Management and Applied Research, 5*, 82–98.

Nakamoto, S. (2008). Bitcoin P2P e-cash paper. https://archive.is/20121228025845/http://article.gmane.org/gmane.comp.encryption.general/12588/ [Accessed on 1 March 2020]

NASDAQ. (2014). *Nasdaq launches enterprise-wide blockchain technology initiative*. http://ir.nasdaq.com/releasedetail.cfm?releaseid=912196 [Accessed on 1 March 2020]

Nicholls, A., & Pharoah, C. (2007). *The landscape of social investment: a holistic topology of opportunities and challenges*. Oxford: Skoll Centre for Social Entrepreneurship.

Nicholls, A., & Young, R. (2008). Introduction: The changing landscape of social entrepreneurship. In A. Nicholls, (Ed.), *Social entrepreneurship: New paradigms of sustainable social change* (pp. 7–23). Oxford University Press.

Nicholls, A. (2010). The institutionalization of social investment: The interplay of investment logics and investor rationalities. *Journal of Social Entrepreneurship, 1*(1), 70–100.

Odem. (2020). *Company website*. https://odem.cloud/. Accessed on 20 July 2020.

O'Leary, R. (2017). *South Korean regulator issues ICO ban*. CoinDesk. Available at https://www.coindesk.com/south-korean-regulator-issues-ico-ban/. Accessed on 2 March 2020.

Belleflamme, P., Lambert, T., Schwienbacher, A. (2014). *Crowdfunding: Tapping the right crowd*.

Repetto, R. (2006). *By fits and starts: punctuated equilibrium in US environmental policy*. New Haven, CT: Yale University Press.

SCMP. (2019) *CEZA's Crypto Valley of Asia is haven for foreign investors*. https://www.scmp.com/country-reports/country-reports/topics/philippines-business-report-2019/article/3013776/cezas. Accessed on 17 January 2021.

Solve.Care. (2020). *Company website*. https://solve.care/. Accessed on 20 August 2020.

SPHINX. (2020). *Market analysis of Bitcoin and Blockchain in Israel. SPHINX Research & Consulting*.

StartupBlink. (2020). *Start-up Ecosystem Rankings. Start-up Blink*.

Swan, M. (2015). *BlockchainL Blueprint For a New Economy*. Sebastopol, CA: O'Reilly.

Tax Authority Circular No. 05/2018. Israel Tax Authority (ITA).

The Economist. (2015). Who is Satoshi Nakatomo? https://www.economist.com/the-economist-explains/2015/11/02/who-is-satoshi-nakamoto. Accessed on 1 March 2020.

The EU. (2020). *Press release*. https://ec.europa.eu/digital-single-market/en/news/commissions-european-innovation-council-awards-eu5-million-blockchain-solutions-social. Accessed on 1 March 2020.

The EU Commission. (2016). The General Data Protection Regulation. GDPR. 2016/679

The EU Commission. (2018). European Commission launches the EU Blockchain Observatory and Forum: Shaping Europe's digital future. Retrieved 27 July 2020, from https://ec.europa.eu/digital-single-market/en/news/european-commission-launches-eu-blockchain-observatory-and-forum [Accessed on 2 March 2020]

The EU Commission. (2020). The European Commission has selected the new partner to operate the EU Blockchain observatory and forum: Shaping Europe's Europe's digital future, https://ec.europa.eu/digital-single-market/en/news/european-commission-has-selected-new-partner-operate-eu-blockchain-observatory-and-forum [Accessed on 27 July 2020]

The EU Parliament. (2019). *Blockchain and the general data protection regulation*.

Walla. (2017). *Bank Hapoalim will use blockchain to accept digital bank guarantees*. Walla Finance. https://finance.walla.co.il/item/3094864. Accessed on 2 March 2020.

WEF. (2018). *How blockchain brings social benefits to emerging economies*. Retrieved 28 July 2020 from https://www.weforum.org/agenda/2018/12/how-blockchain-brings-social-benefits-to-emerging-economies. Accessed on 2 March 2020.

WEF. (2019). *Central Banks and distributed ledger technology: How are Central Banks exploring blockchain today?* World Economic Forum.

Westley, F. R. & Antadze, N. (2010). Making a difference: Strategies for scaling social innovation for greater impact. *The Public Sector Innovation Journal, 15*(2), http://www.innovation.cc/scholarly-style/westley2antadze2make_difference_final.pdf.. Accessed on 2 March 2020.

Case Law

Quoine Pte Ltd v. B2C2 Ltd, [2020] SGCA (I) 02 (the Singapore Court of Appeal);

Quoine Pte Ltd v. B2C2 Ltd, [2019] SGHC (I) 03 (the Singapore International Commercial Court.)

Blockchain Consortia for the Social Good: An Introduction for Non-Technical Audiences

Percy Venegas

1 Introduction

Decentralized ledger technologies, among which blockchain is the most widely known, have been growing at a fast pace since the 2008–2009 financial meltdown and the crisis of trust that followed. The reason for this traction in adoption is not only the growing risk aversion toward centralized financial infrastructures, but also the realization that disintermediation of trust is necessary to build resilient systems in a globalized economy, where financial flows among developing and developed countries have to remain functional even after the most striking shocks. A special case of a blockchain-based financial construct takes the form of a consortium. In this case, a group of entities can operate by privately exchanging sensitive financial information while the regulators and the public can leverage the openness of distributed ledgers.

P. Venegas (✉)
King's College London, London, UK
e-mail: v.percy@economymonitor.com

T. Walker et al. (eds.), *Innovations in Social Finance*,
https://doi.org/10.1007/978-3-030-72535-8_15

1.1 Chapter Description

The chapter will begin with an overview and history of the technologies and the trends around consortium blockchains. This will be followed by case studies related to the deployment and operation of blockchain consortia for social good, including instances where the economics of established activities and processes, such as insurance and peer review research, are being disrupted. This experimental approach will make use of natural language tools to make programming concepts accessible to non-technical audiences, including explaining the key architectural components of distributed ledger systems (DLT) like certification and validation. Finally, by using examples from real-world events, we will illustrate how those DLT systems can handle non-economic externalities and risk. The expected outcome will be a comprehensive overview of the methods and technologies that global blockchain consortia use to provide effective, efficient, and innovative solutions for otherwise complex problems in society.

The chapter's goal is to present the blockchain consortia as a key building block in the future of social finance and social applications. A blockchain consortium offers a viable alternative to the sort of problems that traditional financial architectures have had issues with, in the context of social use cases, such as matching usage and incentives when coopetition exists. The objective is geared toward the direction of current research, namely presenting the different types of platforms that are used in consortia, and speaks to the urgency that non-technical researchers and practitioners need to understand this innovative technology better. The research question is: is blockchain consortia, as a tool for social finance, capable of enabling current and future applications in the presence of some level of cooperation and competition between operators. Some of the cases that will be discussed in detail later in the chapter are mentioned below:

1.2 Ant Financial

Ant Financial, is a part of the Chinese e-commerce giant Alibaba. It operates a mutual aid platform that caters to more than 100 million users. This platform, Xiang Hu Bao, uses a consortium blockchain to link the notary office and the e-certification center. During the COVID-19 pandemic, Xiang Hu Bao has further extended insurance coverage to those users affected by the coronavirus, effectively bringing emergency health care to a population that otherwise could not have afforded the expensive premiums during such unexpected and extraordinary events.

1.3 Bloxberg

In February 2019, the Max Planck Society and a group of leading research organizations founded the bloxberg blockchain consortium. The aim of the consortium is to operate an infrastructure for scientists from around the world so that they can have access to decentralized services. Bloxberg is based on a version of Ethereum and thus allows public decentralized applications or "dApps" to be built using Ethereum-compatible programming languages. Like many consortium-driven public networks, bloxberg hopes that the focus on the global scientific community will help lead and popularize dAPPs that assist in their community. This "permissioned public blockchain" (Bloxberg, 2019) is a type of network where only previously vetted institutions can add data. Decentralized applications are programs that are hosted across the multiple servers that power the network, without presenting a single point of failure. Many permissioned blockchains are based on Ethereum's computer code, making it one of the largest decentralized platforms for blockchains (Ethereum, 2020).

2 Consortia as New Use Cases Beyond P2P and B2B

What these emerging use cases (from the private sector and academia) have in common, is that the benefits transcend organization boundaries as well as current models of Peer-to-Peer and Business-to-Business (P2P and B2B) blockchains that bring innovation and value to entire societies. Moreover, the underlying human-machine systems are both non-monolithic and scalable. They adapt to new opportunities and new risks. Some of the special-purpose technologies covered in this chapter include Corda, which is being deployed in mainstream finance and holds promise as a tool in social finance.

3 Methodology

Given the novelty of this technology, the scholarly material available on the topic is very limited. Therefore, we complemented the academic sources with inputs from practitioners who have hands-on experience in industrial research and on the deployment of blockchain and blockchain consortia projects. In this manner, we will answer the research question by taking into account the different perspectives, market developments, and lessons learned by the key players in the field.

4 Literature Review

The literature on blockchain consortia is not abundant, but the topic of blockchain has been explored by multiple authors more frequently from the computer science perspective than from the economic perspective. Still, there are a few references we can cite regarding how to blockchain and how blockchain consortia can affect and become part of the fabric of social finance. Some important ones to note include:

4.1 Blockchain

Bartoletti et al. (2018) analyzed 120 projects where blockchain technology was used to address social problems, although the list included many "token" projects in which the role of blockchain was mainly fundraising. Al-Saqaf and Seidler (2017) have discussed applications of blockchain toward social issues such as surveillance, censorship, and human rights.

Mukkamala et al. (2018) identified and discussed principles and applications of Blockchain that enhance trust, transparency, and auditability in social business activities.

Kewell et al. (2017) explored key areas of blockchain innovation that appear to represent viable catalysts for achieving sustainable global development targets.

Jain and Simha (2018) reviewed the role of blockchain as a tool of citizen philanthropy.

Mukkamala et al. (2018) in their paper "Converging Blockchain and Social Business for Socio-Economic Development," analyzed a borrowing use-case.

4.2 Blockchain Consortia

On what appears to be one of the first works dealing with definitions, Dib et al. (2018) discussed how consortium blockchains emerged as an interesting architecture concept that benefits from the transactions' efficiency and privacy of private blockchains, while leveraging the decentralized governance of public blockchains. They also stated that although many studies have been made on the blockchain technology in general, the concept of consortium blockchains has not been widely addressed in academic literature.

Zavolokina and collaborators (2020) studied governance and value creation in blockchain consortia as well as what tension and problems emerge in such collaborations. This is one of the first works in the academic literature that explores debates in the context to technology.

Khan et al. (2017) studied a use case of a blockchain consortium in collaborative innovation, specifically in banks.

Schwabe (2019) investigated public-private partnerships in the context of blockchain consortia.

Venegas (2018) presented the paper "Asymmetric trust and causal reasoning in blockchain-based AIs" at The Network Interventions for the Social Good event in Cambridge, MA in 2018. This is the first academic source that associates blockchain-based artificial intelligence in the context of social finance and social applications.

Some of these publications attempted to study blockchain consortia in relation to social matters, but the field is still nascent and there is a distinct need for an authoritative source of academic information concerning this topic. However, throughout this chapter, we cite multiple gray literature sources, which points to the disconnect (or at least, lag) between the academic and practical dimensions of these new technologies. Therefore, we hope that by bringing these sources together, the present chapter will become an important introductory material to the topic of blockchain consortia for social good.

5 Blockchain in Finance and Social Platforms

5.1 *Blockchain Basics*

A blockchain is essentially a distributed database with data shared across a network of computers, and a consensus mechanism—rather than a central point of control—used to ensure the accuracy and trustworthiness of the shared data. Some experts insist that a correct definition must include a description of the economic incentives involved (Morningstar Institutional Equity Research, 2018) but there are many ways to think about the centrality of a public network—from complete centralized control of the database (as described with the database example previously) to perhaps a theoretical ideal where every user of the network operates a single complete node of their own (containing a copy of the shared data). In practice, we readily acknowledge that the actual degree of centralization varies with different public (or permissioned) blockchain systems.

Blockchain is a bit easier to define when another name is used—distributed ledger technology (DLT). Another way of thinking about distributed is simply as sharing the ledger among different participants the ledger portion of DLT is just as it would be described in accounting, which is the principle for recording and examining monetary transactions, technology is just as it sounds, software. Blockchain or DLT is a software that allows multiple participants to share the principle sources of records on the transactions.

With a basic understanding of blockchains (or DLT), as a software that shares records of transactions, we can return to the name "blockchain." The "block" comes from how transactions are grouped in "blocks" and then they are "chained" together through cryptographic references to the previous blocks. The monetary unit of a blockchain is called cryptocurrency, and it was designed as a medium of exchange to be used in transactions. These transactions of cryptocurrency occur from one account to another account and are listed in the ledger.

It is important to briefly discuss three highly influential blockchains: Bitcoin, Ethereum, and Hyperledger Burrow.

Bitcoin is the first public blockchain, originally described in the Bitcoin whitepaper "Bitcoin: A Peer-to-Peer Electronic Cash System," written by Satoshi Nakamoto in 2008 (2009). Bitcoin (CNN Money, 2020) is a public network where theoretically anyone can participate and, because of the economic incentives, it is heavily centralized. However, many third-generation public networks such as Cardano (2020) have created incentive structures that discourage centralization. On the other end of the spectrum, private blockchains are open only to those with the explicit permission to participate. A blockchain consortium belongs in the semi-private category. The existence of the consortium limits what entities can participate in the activity of the network. That participation can be limited in several ways: governance of the network (how it will change over time), operation of the network (who can host fully functional nodes that participate in the consensus or choosing transactions that determine the blocks), and finally who can participate in transactions on the network.

After noticing Bitcoin is limited to public transactions of the bitcoin cryptocurrency, Vitalik Buterin (Coindesk, 2020) designed the Ethereum blockchain to go beyond cryptocurrency transactions and add public programs between the participants called "smart contracts." These two public blockchains, Bitcoin and Ethereum, feature public activity (Deloitte, 2019); yet many organizations (and consortiums) realized they would want to keep access to the entire network private, or "permissioned" in blockchain jargon.

Hyperledger Burrow, now incubated at The Hyperledger Foundation, was one of the first permissioned blockchains to allow support for both transactions and smart contracts (using the same system as Ethereum, although it is their own implementation of that system or "virtual machine").

5.2 *Investment in Blockchain*

According to PitchBook Data, Inc., Finance and Social Platforms are among the top 5 associated industries for blockchain investment, within which Financial software accounts for 51.72% (2380 companies), Financial Services for 23.27% (1071 companies), and Social Platforms 14.54% (669 companies). A Social Platform is defined as a software that facilitates the production, distribution, or following of social content. This category includes online markets (Figs. 1 and 2).

Notoriously, the investment in blockchain technology still lags in most of the developing world, except for certain parts of Asia (Fig. 3).

5.3 *History of Blockchain Consortia*

Blockchain consortia are defined as a type of network where multiple organizations maintain the system. A group of companies thereby collaborate on advancing the state of blockchain technology adoption in the industry by establishing industry standards, drafting use cases, developing key infrastructure, and also operating commercial blockchain platforms (Finextra, 2020). By 2016, when the World Economic Forum released its first report on the future of financial infrastructure and blockchain (World Economic Forum, 2016), there were already 90 corporations working as part of a blockchain consortium. Within the next year, more than 40 blockchain consortia had formed globally attracting significant investments mostly from industry players in financial services like: Bank

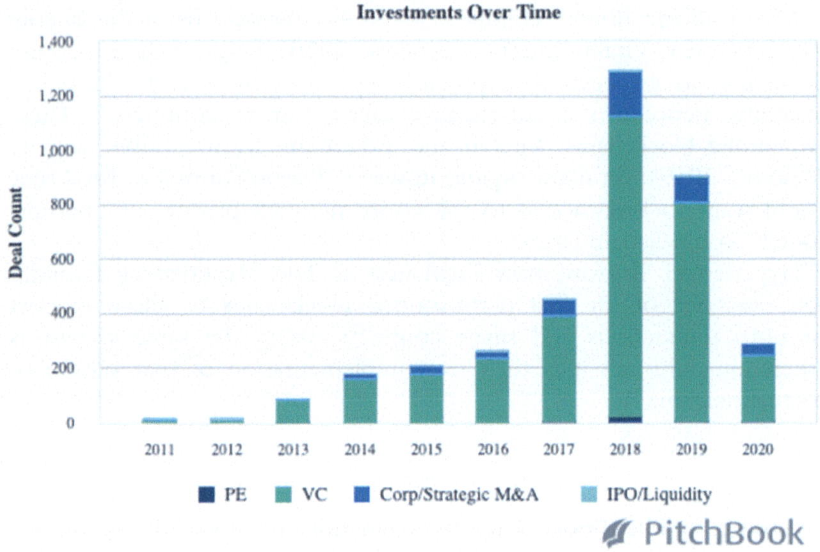

Fig. 1 Private market investments in blockchain technology (*Note* Data has not been reviewed by PitchBook analysts, June 28, 2020. *Source* PitchBook Data, Inc.)

of America Merrill Lynch, Citigroup, Credit Suisse, Goldman Sachs, and JP Morgan (Deloitte, 2020).

5.4 *Technology Penetration*

Blockchain, as a foundational technology, enables applications in a variety of problem domains like anything from digital currency to timestamping (Deloitte, 2020).

Consortia are a special case in the blockchain space because they are utilized usually across the same application domains but with different mechanics. An entity, sometimes a foundation, works as the main promoter of the technology and as the coordinator for the group of collaborating organizations. The most well-known consortium blockchain initiative is Hyperledger (www.hyperledger.org), an open-source collaborative effort created to advance cross-industry blockchain technologies. It is a global collaboration hosted by The Linux Foundation and includes

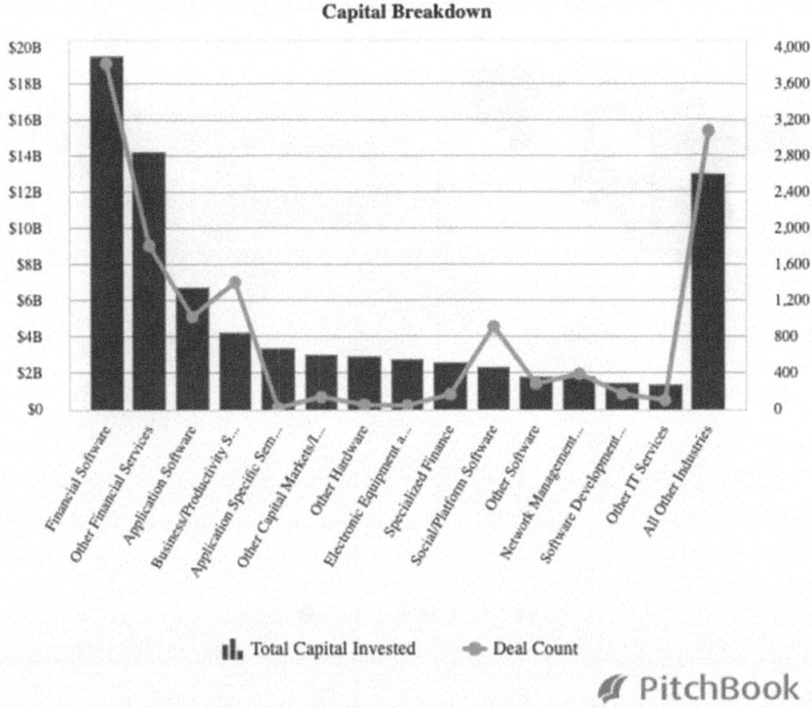

Fig. 2 Capital breakdown by blockchain application (*Note* Data has not been reviewed by PitchBook analysts, June 28, 2020. *Source* PitchBook Data, Inc.)

the leaders in finance, banking, Internet of Things, supply chain, manufacturing, and technology (PitchBook Data, Inc.; *Data has not been reviewed by PitchBook analysts, 2020). Some of the members include Microsoft, Walmart, Deutsche Boerse, among many other global corporations, governments, and organizations (Hyperledger, 2020).

6 Hyperledger

As mentioned earlier, Hyperledger Burrow, which is now incubated at The Hyperledger Foundation, was among the initial permissioned blockchains allowing support for smart contracts and transactions (using the same system as Ethereum, but their own implementation of it).

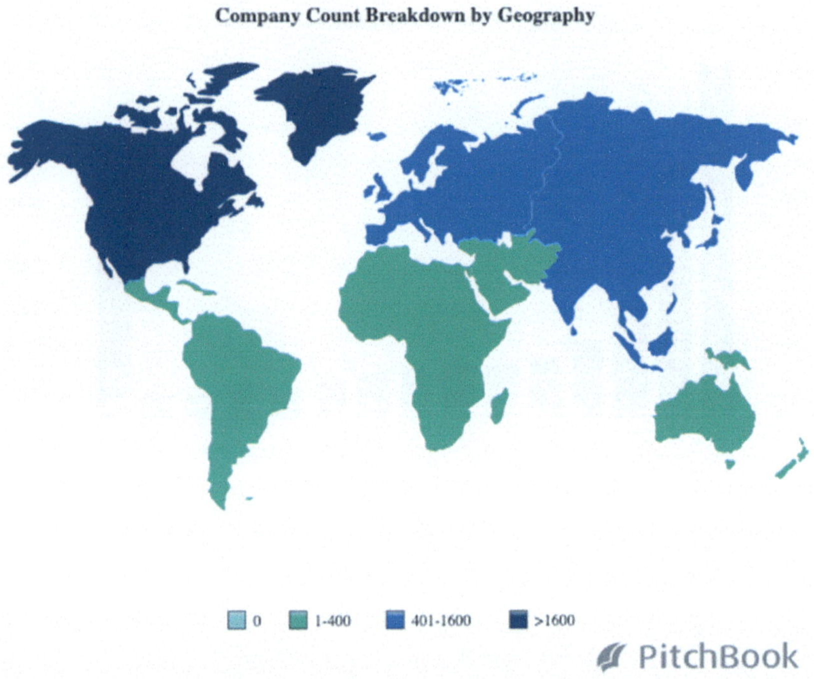

Fig. 3 Distribution of blockchain applications by continent (*Note* Data has not been reviewed by PitchBook analysts, June 28, 2020. *Source* PitchBook Data, Inc.)

Founded in 2015, The Hyperledger Foundation is an organization that serves as an environment to allow a variety of organizations, ranging from non-governmental organizations to for-profit institutions, to collaborate on permissioned blockchain systems and tools. While the most well-known Hyperledger Foundation software is Hyperledger Fabric, which was donated by IBM and Digital Asset (in practice people use two versions, IBM's version and The Hyperledger Foundation's version), there are six different DLT frameworks.

Thus, The Hyperledger Foundation itself could be thought of as the initial blockchain consortium for social good by lowering the threshold for organizations to use blockchain technologies. One can also say The

Hyperledger Foundation is the inaugural "blockchain consortium for social good."

Blockchains under The Hyperledger umbrella (on its different versions or "flavors," such Fabric and Sawtooth, or subprojects such as IBM Fabric and "open source" Fabric) are used in both commercial projects and social-oriented initiatives. The objective of the project is to advance cross-industry collaboration by developing blockchains and distributed ledgers, with a particular focus on improving the performance and reliability of these systems (in a privacy-preserving setting as compared to cryptocurrency designs) so that they are capable of supporting global business transactions by major technological, financial and supply chain companies (Hyperledger, 2016). An explanation of the attributes of blockchains, such as cryptocurrencies and related technologies such as smart contracts, is outside of the scope of this chapter. However, readers can refer to the author's previous publications on the subject for additional background (Venegas, 2017).

Other organizations have developed proprietary solutions to tackle societal challenges in topics such as health access and the integrity of research data. Both topics are of vital importance now given the new risk regime brought forth by the COVID-19 pandemic. Perhaps the most prevalent use case is the certification and verification of documents and identities.

There are multiple ways through which one can verify the existence of a document on the blockchain. The easiest is to re-upload the document to verify its existence. Upon re-uploading the document, the proof of its existence gets verified as the cryptographic digest and the marker for the transaction are also verified. The other ways are to check the transaction record of the blockchain to verify the existence of a time-stamped document. Returning to the verification page of the original time-stamped document also verifies its existence. Thus, the existence of a time-stamped document on a prior date gets proven. This helps banks, educational institutions, and healthcare industries verify documents in little time, cost, and effort (Blockchain Council, 2020) (Fig. 4).

7 Corda and Its Impact on Sustainable Finance

The public blockchain networks like Bitcoin and Ethereum represent phenomenal achievement and innovation. While Bitcoin brought the first "purely peer-to-peer version of electronic cash that would allow

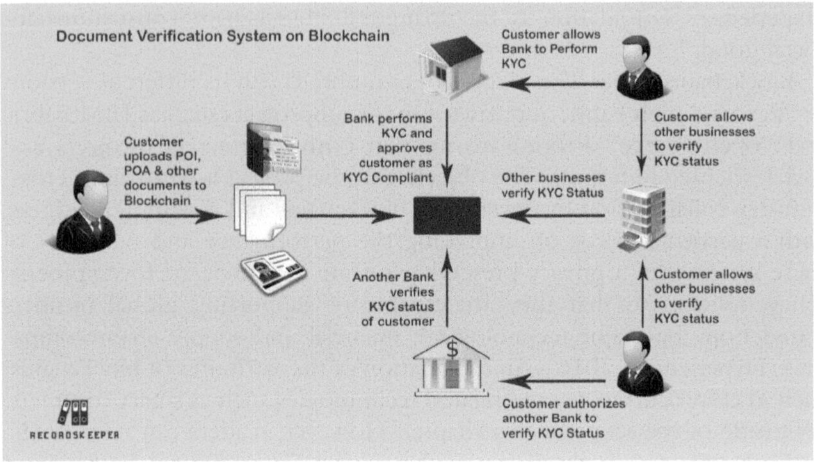

Fig. 4 The document verification system in blockchains (*Source* Blockchain Council)

online payments to be sent directly from one party to another without going through a financial institution" (Nakamoto, 2009), its network is unsuitable for building sustainable finance applications because it is not a general-purpose environment for blockchain application, but instead more or less a network narrowly focused on running programs related to the bitcoin cryptocurrency.

In comparison, the Ethereum network gives more flexibility due to the featured smart contracts. The current design of the Ethereum system requires each node (there were 9133 at the time this article was written)(EtherNodes, 2020) to process every single transaction on the entire network. This provides security and verifiability to the system but severely limits the scalability. While Ethereum's peak is an average of 15.6 transactions per second, VISA's global processing network, VisaNet, provides secure and reliable payments around the world and is capable of handling more than 65,000 transaction messages a second (VISA, 2020). **Secondly, d**ue to the volatile nature of the cryptocurrencies and the design of the system costs for Ethereum, the transaction fees are unpredictable and are reaching an all-time high (The Block Crypto, 2020). This unpredictability makes Ethereum less transparent and hard to use for environmental, social and governance purposes.

There is also a lack of privacy on Ethereum. As a public ledger where data is visible to everyone, there are plenty of reasons to keep sensitive information off the blockchain. Nevertheless, there are many applications where making private data accessible on the blockchain would be beneficial. For instance, consider applications that handle financial data or systems dealing with medical records. There needs to be a way people can conceal data while still allowing it to be used reliably in transactions on the blockchain.

At present, cryptocurrencies and public blockchains bring serious environmental and inefficiency concerns. Bitcoin's annualized total electrical energy is 58.93TWh (comparable to the power consumption of Switzerland), while Ethereum's annualized total electrical energy is 9.34 TWh (similar to the power consumption of Costa Rica). At the same time, the average bitcoin transaction now uses 330,000 times more energy than a credit card (Spending one bitcoin = 330,000 credit card transactions, 2020). Next, the nature of the public blockchain requires that every user should keep their private keys and that private keys are the only way to access their account. This means if a user loses their key, there is no fail-safe scenario and no one to help. This also limits the usage of the network to people unfamiliar with the complexities of the technology and increases the chances for loss and theft.

On the other hand, Corda is a distributed ledger technology created by R3, a technology company founded in 2014; R3 gained prominence in 2015 when a consortium of banks joined the initiative (Hamilton, 2019). At present, R3 is an enterprise software firm working with more than 350 partners internationally. In comparison with the public blockchains, Corda is private and permissioned with an emphasis on data privacy by sharing transactions only on a need-to-know basis. This is a huge boost to performance, as linear horizontal scalability can be achieved because all the data need not be shared with all the members of the network. Corda also has a set of procedures in case of a data breach and allows designs that are better suited to comply with the requirements of GDPR and data protection (Medium.com, 2019). Last but not least, Corda has "pluggable" consensus that allows notary clusters to choose a consensus algorithm based on their requirements in terms of privacy, scalability, legal-system compatibility, and algorithmic agility. Such solution represents serious environmental and efficiency improvement over the public blockchains.

7.1 *Corda's Applicability for Sustainable Finance in the Field of Improved Public Services*

There is a widening gap between public government services and the expectations of the public. Financial services organizations, governments, and regulators are increasingly turning to DLT to address the following challenges (Corda, 2018).

- Public service organizations want to retain their existing decentralized business models (budgets, decision making, process, partners, value proposition, and service design), yet they want to optimize and synchronize locally and nationally.
- Organizations would like to collaborate in the design and delivery of frictionless human-centric services.
- Organizations would also like to automate their adherence to regulations, policies, and procedures and improve the financial transparency across the public service value chain.

Many people hold banks responsible for creating the financial crisis of 2008 that triggered austerity (Skidelsky, 2018) and the continued downward trajectory in public service funding resulting in the major expectation gaps we see today. The only viable approach to close the expectation gap in a world of declining tax revenues, and therefore declining budgets, is to make a bigger impact with the existing resources. This can help remove friction, cost, and duplication so that services can be optimized and synchronized; thus enabling resources to be moved to the front-line services that deliver direct value for the citizen (Corda, 2018).

7.2 *Consortia Development on Corda*

A consortium is a collection of organizations that work together to implement DLT in a particular industry. Consortia enable the pooling of resources and the setting of common standards as well as reduce the risk of running proof of concept projects. Since the benefits of DLT can only be realized through coordination efforts and the utilization of multiple members, consortia serve as a facilitator to get corporates to work together (Welfare, 2019).

Consortia help to resolve the so-called coopetition paradox. Natural competitors are joining forces to create common standards for DLT usage, messaging, platforms, etc. to reduce market friction and improve interoperability. Consortia and other kinds of collaborative approaches are the mechanisms by which blockchain-interested companies, regulators, and governments can work together. From a sustainable finance perspective, blockchain consortia can act as a catalyst for coopetition toward the circular economy.

Trade finance consortia are aiming to bring significant efficiencies into existing ecosystems and build on Corda, such as projects like Contour (an open platform for documentary trade, targeting production) (R3, 2018), Marco Polo (a trade finance business network) (Partz, 2019), and B3i (an insurance network). What is interesting in these use cases is that unlike most other blockchains, business consortia play a key governance role when building applications and transactions together, on top of the Corda Network. Use of its infrastructure is shared by all the nodes. As a result, any node on the network can transact seamlessly with all the other nodes (otherwise known as "interoperability"). It is being used by many types of legal entities across different industries to transact together. The Corda Network is governed by an independent Dutch Foundation, which is a not-for-profit with no shareholders, but with a governing Board.

8 Results and Case Studies

The findings suggest there are at least two themes in which blockchain consortia can be mobilized for social good. One is financial applications and the other is non-financial but incentive-based. In each case, social good is measured using different key performance indicators. For the purely financial cases, problems such as access to insurance are solved through metrices like number of new users of digital "policies." For non-financial use cases, in the verification of research datasets, the metric is the number of users of validated data (here the incentive is intangible, since the units of digital currency used to run the system do not have any monetary value).

Use cases

The implementation of the certification and verification use cases is presented below, with examples of the private sector for social good and non-profit applications.

8.1 *Private Sector: Ant Financial*

Alibaba's Ant Financial unit has created a blockchain operated by a consortium to run Ant Financial's insurance services. It is called Open Chain, a consortium blockchain to link the notary office and the e-certification center in services such as insurance (Cointelegraph, 2020). The insurance service, Xiang Hu Bao, is built in the Alipay app. Given its modus operandi, Xiang Hu Bao might disrupt the process traditional insurance companies selling critical-illness cover were used to. Whoever joins the service is eligible for one-time cash payouts, with the entire membership, and now has 100 million participants as of November 2019 within one year of its launch, sharing the cost. Payouts are calculated based on the cases submitted, and that sum in turn determines the twice-monthly premiums that members must put in. Rather than the traditional business model of paying expensive premiums upfront for the promise (often qualified) of future protection, wherein a traditional insurer would use premiums to build an investment fund to generate returns for future obligations as well as to earn a return for the company, Xiang Hu Bao operates on a pay-as-you-go basis (DigFin, 2019). The majority of Xiang Hu Bao's participants are from middle or low-income communities who are at great risk of falling into poverty if they become critically ill (BusinessWire, 2020) (Fig. 5).

8.2 *Academia: Bloxberg*

The bloxberg infrastructure is a secure global blockchain established by a consortium of leading research organizations to provide scientists with decentralized services worldwide. Bloxberg broadens the scientific landscape of regionally and nationally governed blockchain networks to become the first truly globally maintained scientific decentralized network for scientists. By establishing the permissioned public blockchain, the network is safeguarded against the cryptographic power of third entities because the credibility of the research organizations maintaining the network constitutes trust in the system. The social problem that this type of blockchain consortia solves is in the tackling of data forgery and disinformation. Commercial companies, non-profits, and start-ups are both encouraged and supported by the bloxberg consortium to build new and innovative services on the bloxberg blockchain. Maintaining the network

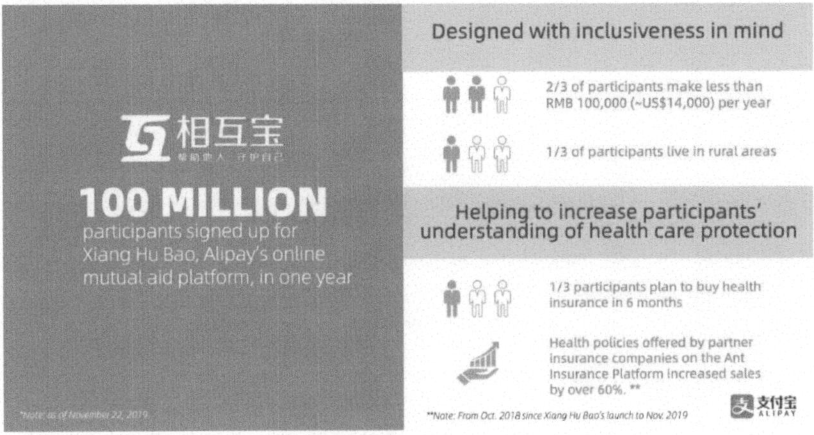

Fig. 5 Xiang Hu Bao's business approach leading to 100 million participants within one year (*Source* Business Wire)

and validating transactions is only administered by the bloxberg consortium of scientific organizations (which include the Max Planck Society, University College London, Carnegie Mellon University, among the twenty-odd global academic institutions) (Bloxberg Consortium, 2019) (Fig. 6).

With bloxberg, research claims need not be limited to one institution alone but can be confirmed by the whole trusted network. Additionally, researchers can leverage bloxberg to create a transparent footprint of their work, without revealing its content. You can then generate a certificate that proves you uploaded this data at a certain time, therefore protecting you from being scooped or the IP being stolen (Bloxberg, 2020).

8.3 *Fair Ai*

One initiative that uses academic blockchain consortia infrastructure and data for the public good is Fair Ai (www.fairai.uk), a group working to bring awareness about AI fairness, and simultaneously operationalizing a self-certification program aimed at creating an open dataset for the use of academics and the general public. The current focus is on work displacement due to macro events such as: the post-COVID world re-alignment;

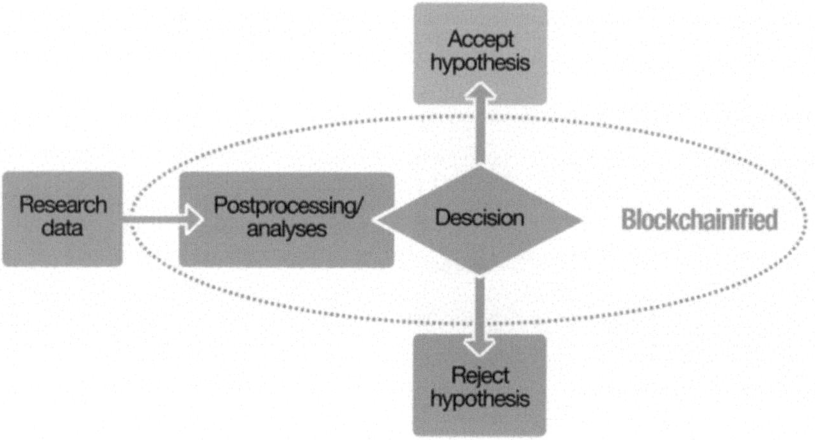

Fig. 6 Blockchain for science: Applying blockchains in scientific research

internal business matters, such as poorly deployed automation; and externalities, such as malicious agents (e.g., bot operators) that target the jobs of digital workers. Contributors to the project are encouraged to implement the verification step of the process using the Wolfram Language (Fig. 7).

The Wolfram Language has built-in capabilities for interacting with blockchains. It can retrieve detailed information from Bitcoin, Ethereum, ARK (Ark.io, 2020), and other blockchains as well as construct and submit transactions to blockchains (including bloxberg) (Wolfram Research, 2020). The main benefit for non-technical users is the facility to use a unified interface for all supported blockchains.

9 Corda

Two use cases with focus on sustainable finance that are currently being developed on Corda are presented.

9.1 Renewable Energy Certificate Trading

Renewable energy certificate trading is an application designed to improve the verification and exchange of renewable energy certificates (REC) for

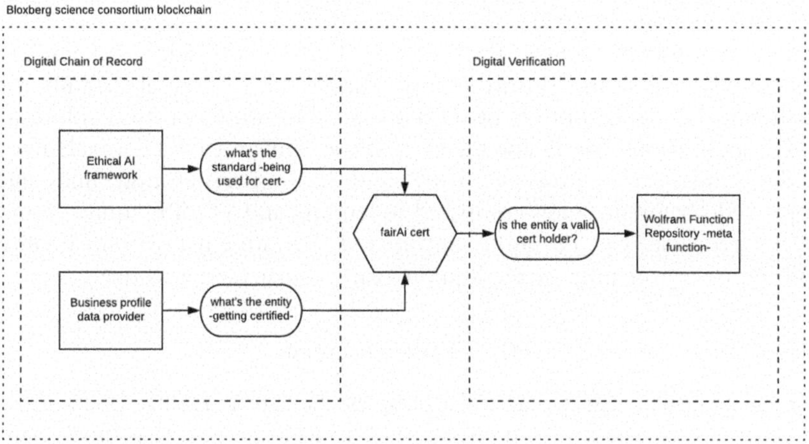

Fig. 7 Fair Ai certification architecture (*Source*: www.fairai.uk)

the US voluntary market and the implementation of R3's distributed ledger platform, Corda. The US renewable energy market is an estimated $2.6 billion industry, which is highly segmented among 29 state compliance markets and an active voluntary market. These markets are supported by a diverse set of stakeholders including generators, utilities, traders, brokers, marketers, regulators, ratepayers, Fortune 500 companies, tracking systems, and layers of third party-verifiers. These stakeholders are tied together by a complex web of financial agreements and burdened by redundant record-keeping and intermediaries designed to: protect the chain of custody, prevent double-counting, and mitigate risks between mutually distrusting counterparties. The application offers a significant opportunity to eliminate the need for these services and their associated costs through the DLT-based Corda.

9.2 SME Financing

Over 90% of all businesses worldwide are small and medium enterprises (SMEs) (IFAC, 2019). SMEs face an estimated unmet financing need of over $4.5 trillion every year (IFC, 2017). At the same time, trillions of Euros are raised and/or earmarked for the financing of SMEs by private and public sector institutions that never reach the intended beneficiaries.

The private equity industry alone is estimated to be sitting on over €2.3 trillion in unspent capital. For both SMEs (demand-side) and lenders or venture capital and private equity (supply-side), there are significant challenges to either option being a sustainable, wide-reaching solution. SME applications for financing in a shape similar to ETF (exchange-traded funds) can be processed with rapid decision turnaround times and improved acceptance rates compared to lending and VC/PE equity. Some of the processes can be highly automated. Investment portfolio quality will improve over time, while liquidity can be managed effectively.

10 Discussion

We have shown, using practical examples that are currently operational in applications ranging from energy trading to insurance, that blockchain consortia help resolve the so-called coopetition paradox. Natural competitors are joining forces to create common standards for DLT usage to reduce market friction and improve interoperability. Consortia collaborative approaches are the mechanisms by which blockchain-interested companies, regulators, and governments work. The experience from real use cases in SME finance and energy trading supports the academic literature, for instance, Dib et al (2018) discussed how consortium blockchains emerged as an interesting architecture concept that benefits from the transactions' efficiency and the privacy of private blockchains. The differentiating factor of the blockchain consortia from other blockchain applications is that the stakeholders do not need to engage in a contest to command resources, thus interoperability and value creation can co-exist.

Secondly, we discussed how public service organizations want to retain their existing decentralized business models (budgets, decision making, process, partners, value proposition, and service design) and yet they optimize and synchronize locally and nationally. Also, the consortia enable the pooling of resources and the setting of common standards as well as reduce the risk of running proof of concept projects. For the exchange of validated university research data where monetary incentives are not always apparent, the benefits of using blockchain consortia also seem clear and are supported by practical use cases. However, those experiences have been documented mainly in gray data sources such as "white papers," GitHub code repositories, etc. This opens new avenues for researchers who are already using those technologies to create taxonomies and document the knowledge in a systematic way.

The social benefit of applying blockchain consortia to insurance (and offer health access to the uninsured) is self-evident in light of the global COVID-19 pandemic. In this respect, the experience of Ant Financial in China offers valuable lessons. But here too, the academic literature is lagging, even if the press has covered the experience at length.

From our experience, the author and contributors to this chapter can state that there are multiple challenges, opportunities, and tangible benefits associated to the use of blockchain consortia vis-a-vis centralized systems and pure play blockchain approaches. The opportunities and benefits are similar to what the others have found, as per the use cases discussed. The challenges include the lack of education of the decision makers on this novel approach and the access to talent trained on the different consortium technologies. Readers from the international development and social science disciplines can think of their own perceived challenges or on the limitations for their teams to plan and execute strategies based on blockchain consortia. That includes literacy on a set of technologies that are not yet mainstream. The costs may be high if there are significant resources to acquire and if sponsors and managers do not understand the background and risks, the sign-off becomes difficult to obtain.

10.1 Risks and Negative Impacts

One of the issues commonly associated with blockchains is privacy. Public blockchains (also known as permission-less blockchains) are not suitable for applications that manage sensitive data, while private blockchains may lack the transparency and level of security required by regulators. Leaning too much on either side may create unwanted risk exposures and generate negative impacts that may include: limited functionality in the application for what the distributed ledger was first intended, reputational damage to the members of the blockchain network, or legal liabilities to the participants.

In order to navigate these risks, the consortia blockchain projects use technologies (such as advanced cryptography) to solve inherent problems relating to privacy, data confidentiality, and transaction unlinkability. One such project, the enterprise blockchain start-up HACERA, allows blockchain participants to transact freely without worrying about the others being able to profile them and see all their transaction history, prices, amounts, or even counterparties.

HACERA initiated a new blockchain platform, MiPasa, to help with the data aggregation and analytics for COVID-19. It partnered with IBM and Oracle, among others. The MiPasa project aims to synthesize data from separate sources and helps to reconcile them. It plans to ensure that the data in the system matches the original and that the public will report any data discrepancies. By aggregating data from numerous sources, the project hopes to be able to help public health officials and others study the information effectively and efficiently. The MiPasa platform is based on Hyperlerledger Fabric, a consortium blockchain technology (LedgerInsights, 2020).

Another risk involved is on the financial side. Blockchain consortia projects are by definition edge technology projects, where the total cost of ownership and return of investment are harder to realize. This can be mitigated in part by the pooling of resources that a consortium allows. However, policy makers, managers, and technical staff should maintain realistic expectations regarding the outcome of pilots and especially, large-scale implementations.

11 Conclusion

We set out to present the blockchain consortia as a key building block in the future of social finance and social applications. From our investigation of academic literature and practitioner documentation, we conclude that in fact, a blockchain consortium offers a viable alternative to the kind of cooperation and competition problems that traditional financial architectures are ill-equipped to handle when pertaining to social use cases. The practical examples include the validation of digital identities to allow access to insurance for millions who otherwise could not have afforded it and the validation of data where no market for data exists.

11.1 The Future of Blockchain Consortia

The *bloxberg* consortium and the 24 different consortia that form *unbounded*, the native network of HACERA (The Unbounded Network, 2020) are now operating across 15 categories: academia, asset tracking, business information services, communications, financial services, health care, identity management, internet of things, insurance, non-profits, privacy, security, social sector, supply chain management and transportation and warehousing. To have an idea of the expected growth, just one of these sectors (i.e., supply chain blockchain) is projected to reach a median market size of $9.85 billion by 2025, which implies a compounded annual growth rate of about 80% (Allied Market Research, 2020). It is also expected that the technology will continue to bring efficiencies to mainstream and social finance, especially since many of the codebases are public, and can be utilized by the smaller federations of organizations. The first applications to watch out for will be trade finance transparency, which is already seeing adoption growing from the banks and corporates (GTReview, 2020) and business-to-business payments (LedgerInsights, 2020). The interest around companies such as R3, the maker of CORDA, continues to grow (at the time of writing, it was in the top quartile of growth in terms of web visits and social network activity, according to PitchBook Data, Inc.; *Data has not been reviewed by PitchBook analysts, 2020).

The takeaway is clear: the interest in and the applications of blockchain consortia are growing, and the tangible benefits for social projects have been proven in real-world cases. Non-technical audiences engaged in social good projects will benefit from becoming versed on the topics discussed.

Acknowledgements Special thanks to Jon Woodard (CEO, Wolfram Blockchain Labs, jwoodard@wolfram.com) and Petko Karamotchev (Founder, Industria.tech, petko.karamotchev@industria.tech) for important contributions to this work.

Appendix

The Wolfram Language provides a sophisticated framework for accessing a wide variety of external services and APIs, including blockchain data. Download the notebook in the video class "Interacting with Blockchains" to follow interactively during a recorded live-coding session. This class showcases the latest features for reading and writing data to blockchains. A sample of Bloxberg specific functions is also included. Non-technical users can also interact with the code, which is available publicly on the following webpage: https://www.fairai.uk/consortium-blockchains-examples.

References

Allied Market Research. (July, 2020). *Blockchain supply chain market to reach 9.85 billion globally by 2025 at 80.2%.* CAGR. Retrieved September 8th, 2020, from https://www.prnewswire.com/news-releases/blockchain-supply-chain-market-to-reach-9-85-bn-globally-by-2025-at-80-2-cagr-allied-market-research-300867066.html.

Al-Saqaf, W., & Seidler, N. (2017). Blockchain technology for social impact: opportunities and challenges ahead. *Journal of Cyber Policy*, 1–17. https://doi.org/10.1080/23738871.2017.1400084.

Ark.io. (July, 2020). *Home Page*. https://ark.io/.

Bartling, S. (July, 2020). *Blockchain for science, 5 years later—What is going on?* [Powerpoint presentation]. Slideshare. https://www.slideshare.net/soenkeba/blockchain-for-science-5-years-later-what-is-going-on.

Bartoletti, M., Cimoli, T., Pompianu, L., & Serusi, S. (2018). *Blockchain for social good: A quantitative analysis*. https://doi.org/10.1145/3284869.3284881.

Bitcoin. (2020). *Bitcoin: A peer-to-peer electronic cash system*. Retrieved September 7th, 2020, from https://bitcoin.org/bitcoin.pdf.

Blockchain Council. (July, 2020). *Document verification system using blockchain*. Retrieved September 11th, 2020, fromhttps://www.blockchain-council.org/blockchain/document-verification-system-using-blockchain/.

Bloxberg Consortium. (February, 2019). *Bloxberg Whitepaper 1.0*. https://bloxberg.org/wp-content/uploads/2019/07/bloxberg_whitepaper.pdf.

Bloxberg. (2019). *Bloxberg: The trusted research infrastructure* (White paper). Bloxberg. https://bloxberg.org/wp-content/uploads/2019/07/bloxberg_whitepaper.pdf.

Bloxberg. (June, 2020). *Home Page*. https://bloxberg.org/.

Bocken, R., & Albareda, V. (2019). *Innovation for sustainability* (pp. 1–16). Springer. https://doi.org/10.1007/978-3-319-97385-2.

BusinessWire. (July, 2020). *Alipay Xiang Hu Bao online mutual aid*. Retrieved November 20th, 2020, from https://www.businesswire.com/news/home/20191126005952/en/Alipay%E2%80%99s-Xiang-Hu-Bao-Online-Mutual-Aid.

Cardano. (July, 2020). *Home Page*. https://www.cardano.org/.

Carolin, J. (October, 2019). B3i's blockchain re/insurance network begins to offer real-life industry solutions. *Insurance Journal*. Retrieved November 19th, 2020, from https://www.insurancejournal.com/news/international/2019/10/22/546184.htm.

CNN Money. (July, 2020). *What is Bitcoin*. Retrieved September 8th, 2020, from https://money.cnn.com/infographic/technology/what-is-bitcoin/index.html.

Coindesk. (2020). *Vitalik Buterin: Co-creator, Ethereum bockchain*. Coindesk. Retrieved November 20th, 2020, from https://www.coindesk.com/people/vitalik-buterin.

Coindesk. (May, 2019). *Bitcoin: A peer-to-peer electronic cash system*. Coindesk. Retrieved November 19th, 2020, from https://www.coindesk.com/bitcoin-peer-to-peer-electronic-cash-system/.

Cointelegraph. (July, 2020). *Alibaba subsidiary Ant Financial launches new consortium blockchain platform for SMEs*. Retrieved September 11th, 2020, from https://cointelegraph.com/news/alibaba-subsidiary-ant-financial-launches-new-consortium-blockchain-platform-for-smes.

Corda. (2018). *The Internet of public value*. Retrieved September 7th, 2020, from https://www.corda.net/blog/the-internet-of-public-value.

Deloitte. (December, 2019). *Deloitte's 2019 global blockchain survey: Blockchain gets down to business*. https://www2.deloitte.com/content/dam/Deloitte/se/Documents/risk/DI_2019-global-blockchain-survey.pdf.

Deloitte. (December, 2020). *Deloitte's 2020 global blockchain survey: From promise to reality*. https://www2.deloitte.com/content/dam/insights/us/articles/6608_2020-global-blockchain-survey/DI_CIR%202020%20global%20blockchain%20survey.pdf.

Deloitte. (July, 2020). *Emergence of blockchain consortia*. https://www2.deloitte.com/us/en/insights/focus/signals-for-strategists/emergence-of-blockchain-consortia.html.

Dib, O., Brousmiche, K., Durand, A., Thea, E., & Hamida, E. (2018). Consortium blockchains: Overview, applications and challenges. *International Journal on Advances in Telecommunications, 11*(1 & 2), 51–64. https://www.researchgate.net/profile/Omar_Dib/publication/328887130_Consortium_Blockchains_Overview_Applications_and_Challenges/links/5be99602299bf1124fce0ab9/Consortium-Blockchains-Overview-Applications-and-Challenges.pdf.

DigFin. (May, 2019). *How Ant Financial is disrupting insurance*. Retrieved September 9th, 2020, from https://www.digfingroup.com/insurtech-china-2/.

Ethereum. (July, 2020). *Home Page*. https://ethereum.org/en/.

EtherNodes. (July, 2020). *Home Page*. https://ethernodes.org/.

Finextra. (July, 2020). *Blockchain consortia need good governance but how*. Retrieved September 11th, 2020, from https://www.finextra.com/blogposting/18543/blockchain-consortia-need-good-governance-but-how.

GTReview. (July, 2020). *Trade finance blockchain consortia now*. Retrieved September 7th, 2020, from https://www.gtreview.com/magazine/volume-18-issue-2/trade-finance-blockchain-consortia-now/.

Hacera. (July, 2020). *Home Page*. https://hacera.com/.

Hamilton, C. (November, 2019). *Corda v Hyperledger v Quorum v Ethereum v Bitcoin* [online]. Retrieved November 30th, 2020, from https://medium.com/corda/corda-v-hyperledger-v-quorum-v-ethereum-v-bitcoin-58f2f0890dce.

Hyperledger. (February, 2016). *Linux foundation's hyperledger project announces 30 founding members and code proposals to advance blockchain technology*. Retrieved on February 17, 2016, from https://www.hyperledger.org/announcements/2016/02/09/linux-foundations-hyperledger-project-announces-30-founding-members-and-code-proposals-to-advance-blockchain-technology.

Hyperledger. (June, 2020). *Members*. https://www.hyperledger.org/about/members.

IFAC. (2019). *The foundation for economies worldwide is small business*. https://www.ifac.org/knowledge-gateway/contributing-global-economy/discussion/foundation-economies-worldwide-small-business-0.

IFC. (2017). *MSME Finance Gap Report*. World Bank Group. https://www.ifc.org/wps/wcm/connect/03522e90-a13d-4a02-87cd-9ee9a297b311/121264-WP-PUBLIC-MSMEReportFINAL.pdf?MOD=AJPERES&CVID=m5SwAQA.

INDUSTRIA. (2019). *The complicated relationship of blockchains, DLT and GDPR*. Retrieved September 7th, 2020, from https://medium.com/industria-tech/https-medium-com-industria-tech-the-complicated-relationship-of-blockchains-2888c04b3e9b.

Jain, S., & Simha, R. (2018). Blockchain for the common good: A digital currency for citizen philanthropy and social entrepreneurship. *Cybermatics*, 1387–1394. https://doi.org/10.1109/2018.2018.00238.

Kewell, B., Adams, R., & Parry, G. (2017). *Blockchain for good?. Strategic change* (forthcoming). https://doi.org/10.1002/jsc.2143.

Khan, C., Lewis, A., Rutland, E., Wan, C., Rutter, K., & Thompson, C. (2017). A distributed-ledger consortium model for collaborative innovation. *Computer, 50*, 29–37. https://doi.org/10.1109/MC.2017.3571057.

Kumar, V. (October, 2020). *16 biggest and most valuable fintech companies in the world, 2020 edition*. RankRed. Retrieved November 20th, 2020, from https://www.rankred.com/biggest-valuable-fintech-companies/.

LedgerInsights. (July, 2020a). *IBM, Oracle launch blockchain to integrate Covid-19 data from WHO, CDC*. Retrieved September 7th, 2020, from https://www.ledgerinsights.com/ibm-oracle-launch-blockchain-to-integrate-covid-19-data-from-world-health-organization-cdc/.

LedgerInsights. (July, 2020b). *Visa partners with IBM for B2B connect blockchain payments*. Retrieved September 9th, 2020, from https://www.ledgerinsights.com/visa-partners-with-ibm-for-b2b-connect-blockchain-payments/.

Leible, S., Schlager, S., & Schubotz, M. (2019). *A review on blockchain technology and blockchain projects fostering open science*. https://www.frontiersin.org/articles/10.3389/fbloc.2019.00016/full.

Medium.com. (2019). *The complicated relationship of blockchains, DLT and GDPR*. Retrieved July 20th, 2020, from https://medium.com/industria-tech/https-medium-com-industria-tech-the-complicated-relationship-of-blockchains-2888c04b3e9b.

Morningstar Institutional Equity Research. (April, 2018). *Blockchain observer: Disruption by decentralization?* Retrieved September 8th, 2020, from https://www.morningstar.com/articles/868019/blockchain-disruption-by-decentralization.

Mukkamala, R., Vatrapu, R., Ray, P., Sengupta, G., & Halder, S. (2018a). Blockchain for social business: Principles and applications. *IEEE Engineering Management Review*. (pp. 1–1). https://doi.org/10.1109/emr.2018.2881149.

Mukkamala, R., Vatrapu, R., Ray, P., Sengupta, G., & Halder, S. (2018b). *Converging blockchain and social business for socio-economic development* (pp. 3039–3048). https://doi.org/10.1109/bigdata.2018.8622238.

Nakamoto, S. (2009). *Bitcoin: A peer-to-peer electronic cash system*. https://bitcoin.org/bitcoin.pdf.

Partz, H. (December, 2019). *R3's marco polo runs largest trade finance trial with over 70 members*. Cointelegraph. Retrieved November 20th, 2020, from https://cointelegraph.com/news/r3s-marco-polo-runs-largest-trade-finance-trial-with-over-70-members.

PitchBook Data, Inc. (June, 2020). *Hyperledger overview*. https://pitchbook.com/profiles/investor/180468-10.

Pure play asset management | Robeco.com. (2020). *Spending One Bitcoin = 330,000 Credit Card Transactions*. Retrieved September 7th, 2020, from https://www.robeco.com/en/insights/2019/04/spending-one-bitcoin-330000-credit-card-transactions.html. Accessed 7 September 2020.

Quinn, C. (2020). *Business consortia: A lesser known but important layer in blockchain governance* [online]. Retrieved September 7th, 2020, from https://medium.com/inside-r3/business-consortia-a-lesser-known-but-important-layer-in-blockchain-governance-9f3d1bfd5dd4.

R3. (October, 2018). *Trade finance solution Contour launches open platform on Corda blockchain* [Press release]. Retrieved November 20th, 2020, from https://www.r3.com/press-media/trade-finance-solution-contour-launches-open-platform-on-corda-blockchain/.

Schwabe, G. (2019). *The role of public agencies in blockchain consortia: Learning from the Cardossier*. Information Polity. 1-15. 10.3233/IP-190147.

Skidelsky, R. (September, 2018). Ten years on from the financial crash, we need to get ready for another one. *The Guardian*. Retrieved November

19th, 2020, from https://www.theguardian.com/commentisfree/2018/sep/12/crash-2008-financial-crisis-austerity-inequality.

The Block. (2020). *Ethereum transaction fees reached an all-time high of $6.87 million yesterday* [online]. Retrieved September 7th, 2020, from https://www.theblockcrypto.com/linked/74804/ethereum-transaction-gas-fees-all-time-high.

The Unbounded Network. (July, 2020). *Consortiums*. https://unbounded.network/consortiums.

Venegas P. (2018). *Asymmetric trust and causal reasoning in blockchain-based AIs. Editor: Alfredo Morales, New England Complex Systems Institute Cambridge, USA*. STEM Academic Press.

Venegas, P. (2017). *Economy monitor guide to smart contracts: Blockchain examples*. Macmillan Holtzbrinck Publishers.

VISA. (2020). *VISA fact sheet* [online]. Retrieved September 7th, 2020, from https://www.visa.co.uk/dam/VCOM/download/corporate/media/visanet-technology/aboutvisafactsheet.pdf.

Welfare, A. (2019). *Commercializing blockchain: Strategic applications in the real world*. Wiley.

Wolfram Research, Inc. (2020). *Interacting with blockchains* [online]. Retrieved September 11th, 2020, from https://www.wolfram.com/wolfram-u/catalog/wl042/.

Wolfram Research. (2020). *Wolfram language & system—Working with blockchains*. Retrieved September 11th, 2020, from https://reference.wolfram.com/language/guide/Blockchain.html.

World Economic Forum. (August, 2016). *The future of financial infrastructure: An ambitious look at how blockchain can reshape financial services*. Retrieved July 20th, 2020, from http://www3.weforum.org/docs/WEF_The_future_of_financial_infrastructure.pdf.

Zavolokina, L., Ziolkowski, R., & Bauer, I., & Schwabe, G. (2020). *Management, governance and value creation in a blockchain consortium*. MIS Quarterly Executive. https://doi.org/10.17705/2msqe.00022.

Informational Efficiency and Cybersecurity: Systemic Threats to Blockchain Applications

Constantin Gurdgiev and Adam Fleming

1 Introduction: Informational Efficiency of Cryptocurrencies Markets and Technology Threats to Social Impact Finance Intermediaries

The origins of crypto-assets can be traced to early 1980s (Chaum, 1983) and the digital money regulatory innovations (Dykes, 1995). These roots have been strengthened by the continuously evolving and expanding concept of privacy in the age of electronic communications. In this, the very beginnings of the crypto-assets can be viewed as anchored in social impact-targeting innovations that, according to their proponents, are promising to develop more secure systems for managing public and

C. Gurdgiev (✉)
College of Professional Studies, Monfort College of Business, University of Northern Colorado, Greeley, CO, USA
e-mail: gurdgic@tcd.ie

Trinity Business School, Trinity College Dublin, University of Dublin, Dublin, Ireland

A. Fleming
Trinity College Dublin, University of Dublin, Dublin, Ireland

T. Walker et al. (eds.), *Innovations in Social Finance*,
https://doi.org/10.1007/978-3-030-72535-8_16

private data, enhancing public trust in data collection, and enhancing the transmission and analytics systems (Peck, 2012).

Then, in 2008, a developer known only by the name of Satoshi Nakamoto released a white paper entitled "Bitcoin: A peer-peer electronic payment system" Nakamoto (2008) that resulted in the development of the first decentralized cryptocurrency, Bitcoin. This led to the emergence of a large new asset class and cryptocurrency markets. It also ushered in the new era of technological innovation which resulted in a wide range of blockchain-based applications (also known as Distributed Ledger Technologies, or DLTs) in financial services, back-office management, and private contracting and public identity provision services. The new technology also captured the minds of social impact-related innovators and service providers (Galen et al., 2019). The latter include the use of blockchain technologies to increase financial inclusion and access to basic financial services for those currently left unbanked, provide basic digital identity to the refugees and migrants, create new avenues for raising capital for smaller and indigenous entrepreneurs operating in remote and economically less developed communities, and increase the efficiency in instrument supply chains in delivery of food and disaster relief, among many others.

As of January 2020, there were 2,957 cryptocurrencies trading on 500 different cryptocurrency exchanges worldwide. Many of these instruments are directly linked to specific service provision platforms. Others support general data processing and storage infrastructure in public blockchains. Multiples of the cryptocurrencies exist as non-publicly traded tokens supporting private blockchains (also known as permissionless blockchains).[1]

This growth momentum has been underpinned by two major fundamentals.

Firstly, cryptocurrencies in general have offered new and exciting platforms for using DLTs in supporting transactions management as well as data recording and storage services across a broad range of sectors.

[1] Permissionless blockchains are based on a pool of cryptocurrency used as a transactions currency to pay service providers, or miners who update the general ledger with transactions records. Since anyone with access to requisite technology can be a miner, there are no standard financial services intermediaries checks (e.g., know-your-customer or KYC checks, or background checks) to safeguard against black-hat intermediaries being involved in verification of transactions (Santhana & Biswas, 2017).

Although much of these promises have gone unfulfilled, as is consistent with the first stages of introduction of the pioneering technologies (the so-called hype phase of the Kondratieff innovation curve), supply of potential new applications development presented by the blockchain technology continues to drive longer-term investors' interest in the technology and the underlying cryptocurrencies.

Secondly, the new asset class of cryptocurrencies that emerged from the introduction of Bitcoin has led to a large-scale expansion of investor and speculative interest in the currency.

One of the areas in which the promise of the widespread applicability of blockchain solutions continues to evolve is social impact finance and, as a result, increases hype in the expected adoption of cryptocurrencies. Niche applications in the sub-fields of refugee's and migrant's assistance provision, financial inclusion, social payment supports, public transfers administration, and data management are some of the more commonly argued areas for the deployment of public blockchains and cryptocurrencies as well as tokens. Since the beginning of the Bitcoin maturation curve in 2014, a number of these promises have been at least partially implemented. Galen et al. (2019) identify the primary areas of deployment of blockchain technologies in social impact-linked activities to date. They show that as of early 2019, the primary uses of blockchain in social impact services relate to records and verification of data, as well as in facilitating payments (combined share of these two services pillars amounting to 51% of overall DLT activities). At the same time, primary benefits promised by the blockchain deployment in the areas of social impact include either the reduction of risk and fraud, or an increase in integrity/transparency (38% of all applications) and increased efficiency of transactions (24%).

Despite the promise of greater security and improved integrity of data and records storage, the rise in the inherent value of Bitcoin and the explosive growth in crypto-assets have resulted in an increased number of attacks on major cryptocurrency exchanges and, since May 2017, attacks on cryptocurrencies themselves. Centralized exchanges are attractive targets for hackers due to the irreversible nature of cryptocurrency transactions and transfers, as well as the fact that the majority of deposits that are left on exchanges by novice investors are rarely insured (Devi Bhaskar & Kuo Chuen, 2015). The increasing value of cryptocurrencies, such as Bitcoin, and rising concentration in crypto-assets holdings per each active account on major exchanges add to the 'black-hat' actors' incentives (Kharif, 2020).[2] Currently, an estimated 2 percent of all active Bitcoin accounts hold 95 percent of the entire cryptocurrency by value, making cyberattacks, when successful, extremely effective.

Per Selfkey (2020, p. 1), “2019 saw a record number of twelve crypto-exchanges being hacked. That being said, across the board the amounts of crypto-stolen were worthless. In total, $292,665,886 worth of cryptocurrency and 510,000 user logins were stolen from crypto-exchanges in 2019. One would hope that as time goes on cryptocurrency exchanges would become more secure. The unfortunate reality is that more exchanges are hacked every year. As cryptocurrency and exchanges remain largely unregulated, it is unclear as to who has jurisdiction over cryptocurrency markets.”

The lack of security and accompanying regulation in DLT-based public systems, alongside the related issue of the lack of regulatory oversight over data acquisition, storage, and transfers within and between the blockchain ledgers and accounts, as well as to the third parties, presents an ever-escalating risk to the aforementioned applications. In this chapter, we explore this dimension of risk and uncertain environment presented by the new technology and discuss its saliency to the area of social impact finance and social impact FinTech applications.

More specifically, we look at the history of major cybersecurity breaches involving a range of cryptocurrencies and exchanges from 2014 through 2019. We identify 25 major cybersecurity events, based on the volume of crypto-assets impacted, as well as an additional two events based on the volume of clients’ or investors’ records stolen. The frequency of such events rose from two annual events in 2014 to nine in 2019. Galen et al. (2019) provide some tangible examples of social impact finance use of some of the crypto-assets covered in this research. These include: fundraising activities based on cryptocurrencies (such as Bitcoin, Ethereum, and Ripple), using these cryptocurrencies in blockchain solutions deployed in empowering emerging markets’ farmers, and in underwriting supply chain management for social impact in food production and delivery in the United States. Other cases surveyed by Galen et al. (2019) reference the use of smart contracts built on the Ethereum platform, in providing access to banking services to those currently excluded

[2] For a definition of the black hat cyber security actors, see Montaine (2020).

from traditional lenders' coverage. In addition, a range of cryptocurrencies issuers including Zcash, Bitcoin, Ethereum, Dash, Litecoin, and Ripple have launched their own impact-focused foundations.

Using fractal analysis, in line with Peters (1994), Kristoufek (2012), and Celeste et al. (2018), we show that these events have had a material impact on underlying cryptocurrency markets, namely via the largest cryptocurrency, Bitcoin. We also show that the markets have, to date, failed to acquire the higher informational efficiencies necessary to sustain these technologies' deployment in impact finance during the wake of these cybersecurity breaches. In other words, despite increasing cyber threats, public or permissionless blockchain systems appear to be more vulnerable to informational inefficiencies today, than they were in the past.

This lack of learning from the security threats is worrying. Cyber breaches in the cryptocurrency markets create major risk like contagion pathways, which are dramatically increasing volatility of both directly attacked currencies and other major cryptocurrencies, as well as present an increased risk of system-wide attacks that threaten not only the accounting and transactional accuracy and efficiency of the crypto-based FinTech solutions, but also the data stored using public blockchain protocols.

These findings lead us to conclude that, due to the absence of dramatic improvements in the regulation of cryptocurrencies and exchanges, public blockchains based on traded crypto-assets (currencies and tokens) are not suitable for large-scale deployment in social impact finance applications.

With this in mind, our paper is organized as follows. Section 2 presents a brief literature review in relation to the blockchain and cryptocurrency markets' informational efficiencies and applicability to impact finance. Section 3 outlines our data and methodological approach to testing the effects of the cybersecurity attacks on cryptocurrencies' informational efficiencies. This section draws key empirical conclusions, while Sect. 4 provides a discussion of our empirical findings in the context of the evolutionary dynamics of the cryptocurrencies, and Sect. 5 offers a discussion of their usability in social impact finance applications.

2 Literature Review: Crypto-Markets and Informational Inefficiencies

Before advancing to the empirical evidence, we should examine prior work that led to the development of the Fractal Market Hypothesis (FMH), the theoretical framework within which more contemporary research positions the technical analysis of cryptocurrencies. The FMH offers important intuitive and behaviorally-anchored insights into this new asset class—in the context of crypto-assets strengths and vulnerabilities in their potential applications in broader finance, including social impact finance. The FMH also presents the basis for policy-linked analysis of the crypto-assets.

2.1 *Bitcoin, Blockchain, and the Rise of Crypto-Hacking*

The Global Financial Crisis of 2008 was the beginning of the cryptocurrency era (Nakamoto, 2008). In the years to follow, Bitcoin became the first, and the most widely accepted, decentralized digital currency based on a peer-to-peer ledgering that allows the users to eliminate the need for third-party transaction interference from institutes such as banks.

Despite waves of subsequent innovations in blockchain technology, to date, Bitcoin is still being recognized as the gold standard crypto-asset. Bitcoin-backed transactions are similar to the online payment systems, such as PayPal, but are carried out in a currency other than a traditional, government-backed fiat currency. Digital records of the transactions on public blockchain, such as Bitcoin, are stored and verified in a public-ledger. As a main security feature, before a transaction is added as a record into the blockchain, the transaction itself must be verified. This verification takes place through an open-source mining. The open-source nature of this process means that, in theory, anyone using the Bitcoin network can verify a transaction before it is added to the blockchain by executing algorithmic 'work' of solving a cryptographic or algorithmic problem presented to all miners. This is known as a Proof-of-Work protocol, or POW protocol. Successful miners who solve the cryptographic problem associated with verification receive payment for their effort in the form of Bitcoin (Nakamoto, 2008).

Open-source blockchain, or public blockchain, such as the one underlying Bitcoin has, therefore, two key perceived or alleged advantages from the security point of view. Firstly, the anonymous nature of Bitcoin means that individual privacy is maintained in recording the transaction. Secondly, the publicly decentralized procedure for verification of the transaction reduces opportunities for fraudulent behavior. In traditional transactional systems, records of a transaction between two parties are verified and stored by the third parties. This creates two key disadvantages of the traditional payments and records-keeping systems in comparison with the decentralized blockchains, such as Bitcoin: traditional systems require payments to third-party intermediaries, and security of traditional systems is fully dependent on security of data verification and storage intermediaries. Being centralized at the intermediary point of entry and storage, traditional records-keeping system is vulnerable to a hacking or cybersecurity attack on the singular point of storage. In theory, decentralized systems, such as public blockchain, are only vulnerable to the attacks that require hackers to achieve majority consensus to override the established 'block' of records. These types of attacks are known as a 51 percent attack, because they require hackers to possess 50 percent-plus dominance over the entire blockchain users' community.

Owing to the promise of the above advantages over traditional transaction facilitators, over the last twelve years, the crypto-assets market and the underlying markets for blockchain technology have experienced an exponential growth. At the time of writing, there are 1,586 different cryptocurrencies trading on more than 500 internationally-distributed exchanges, with the total market-cap at US$256 billion. Garcia et al., (2014) notes that deregulation, widespread media attention, the promise of rapid technological development of crypto-assets-based applications, and the algorithmically-fixed supply have been the major factors behind the remarkable appreciation in Bitcoin price. Investment in blockchain-based solutions for records keeping, transaction facilitation, and data processing has expanded dramatically in recent years. Many of these investments are flowing into technologies that use blockchain to deliver social impact-mandated financial and governance services, including applications for non-profit payments, digital identity, and supply chain management systems (Galen et al., 2019).

Growth of the cryptocurrency market and the blockchain technology applications has also been associated with an increase in crypto-based cybercrime. This growth took place across a range of channels, including: (i) cybersecurity crime targeting crypto-assets, such as theft and fraud; (ii) cybersecurity crime relating to the use of cryptocurrencies in terrorism financing, money laundering, and tax evasion; and (iii) cybersecurity crime relating to data theft and disruption. From 2014 through 2019, cybercriminals have stolen at least US$1.283B in crypto-assets (see Table 2), although the full extent of cybercrime in the cryptocurrencies markets remains unknown due to the lack of regulation on the disclosure of criminal activities and losses associated with them in a number of countries where cryptocurrencies trading tends to be concentrated.

Our study aims to measure the impact that cybersecurity breaches have on the price dynamics of Bitcoin and to assess the potential adverse costs that cybersecurity threats can present to the financial intermediaries, including the social impact finance community. Before we do so, we need to summarize core theoretical frameworks used to explain market behavior of the crypto-assets and more specifically the FMH.

2.2 From the Efficient Market Hypothesis to the Fractal Markets Hypothesis

For decades, the idea of the financial markets and assets traded on these markets follows a random walk, originally postulated by Osbourne (1959), which dominated our view of the dynamics in prices of financial assets. This idea was formalized in the Efficient Market Hypothesis (EMH) by Eugene Fama (1965). The theory is built on a number of core assumptions, including that (1) all investors share the same investment time horizon, and (2) all investors process new information efficiently and at zero cost. The Fama (1965) theory states that at any given moment in time, markets are informationally efficient. As market prices are driven by arbitrage, it is impossible for any investor to outperform or beat the market. Hence, financial assets always trade at their fair value. Subsequent formulations of the EMH took various forms: weak, semi-strong, and strong, allowing researchers to incorporate the inclusion of private information and market inefficiencies into market prices (Ball, 1978; Black et al., 1972; Fama et al. 1969; Jensen, 1968).

Overtime, the EMH came under a sustained and more fundamentally-anchored criticism. Kahneman (2011) reveals that emotions and behavioral psychology have a significant influence on investors/traders' decisions. This behavioral view of decision-making highlights herding, prospect theory, and loss aversion as some of the possible explanations for the highly unpredictable and large in-scale shocks or crises, commonly dubbed the "Black Swan" events, that are frequent in the markets but cannot be explained by the EMH (Kahneman, 2011). Building on the view that individual behavior can deviate from the traditional rational expectation models, De Bondt and Thaler (1985) argue that most people overreact to negative news, as opposed to positive news. They demonstrate that such over-reaction was evident in the stock market, leading to market inefficiencies. More recently, Lee et al. (2010) looked at the stock markets in 32 developed and 26 developing countries from January 1999 to May 2007. They concluded that global stock markets are inefficient and do not behave in line with the core predictions of the EMH.

Other researchers challenged the fundamental assumptions of the EMH, such as assumed lack of information costs (Grossman & Stiglitz, 1980), the irrelevance of the transaction costs (Roll, 1984), and the insider trading (Maskin & Laffont, 1990), showing that EMH does not hold in the presence of these violations. Malkiel (2003, 2005) examines challenges to the EMH, concluding that stock markets are irrational and show signs of predictable behavior; however, these features are rare and do not persist forever. Using high frequency data for the New York Stock Exchange, Toth and Kertesz (2006) show that markets are becoming more efficient over time, while Bariviera et al. (2012) confirm similar findings for bond markets during the period of markets' uncertainty and shocks. Overall, therefore, most of the empirical evidence suggests that the EMH is insufficient in describing all of the asset price dynamics observed in the capital markets.

As a result, other theories and hypotheses have been put forward to provide better basis for modeling price and return dynamics in financial markets. The most notable of these, and the more recent one, is the FMH. Technically, the FMH is anchored in fractal geometry, using it to capture asset price dynamics.

Fractal geometry allows us to model complex dynamic systems by identifying specific properties of these systems, including self-similarity and dimensionality. These characteristics allow the fractal system to capture cyclical processes as they evolve over time (Mandelbrot et al., 1997). As outlined by Gurdgiev and Harte (2016), financial time series' fractal dimension (D) properties are captured by the Hurst exponent (H). The fractal dimension ranges from 1 to 2 and measures how 'jagged' the time series is. If $1 < D < 1.5$, the time series is less jagged than a random walk, implying the existence of a detectable trend in the series—a pattern that violates the EMH assertion that all market-generated data is a random noise. For $1.5 < D < 2$, the time series is more similar to a random walk, showing no signs of an identifiable trend and consistent with the EMH. The fractal dimension, therefore, is a useful benchmark for testing whether time series, such as cryptocurrencies prices, behave randomly (EMH satisfied) or according to a predictable trend in response to an exogenous shock. Such a shock can be a cryptocurrency exchange hack or a cybersecurity breach, and if asset price responds to this shock in a predictable or systemic way, the EMH is violated.

FMH is a theory of financial market behavior outlined by Peters (1994), based on the assumption that (1) capital markets are dynamic, complex, nonlinear, and cyclical chaotic systems. Under FMH, the markets are not purely random in their responses to shocks or news. Peters (1994) speculated that market agents (investors and traders) have different investment time horizons. This means they differ in interpretation of public and private information, inducing differences in the way they react to news and shocks. These differences, in turn, lead to the violation of the EMH. The FMH also aims to describe the high degree of volatility and frequent panics associated with market crashes and price corrections, such as the one experienced in the equity markets in October 1987 (Peters, 1994), as well as during the Global Financial Crisis and the peak of the COVID-19 pandemic.

According to FMH, in periods of market stability, new information material to price formation has no correlation with investors' time horizons. This is because markets are liquid, in so far as there are always long-term investors willing to immediately transact with short-term investors and vice versa. However, during market crashes and corrections, investor become sensitive and react abruptly to new information. This results in shortening of the investors' time horizons; thus, there is a decline in the number of investors willing to trade with one another and there is a subsequent disappearance of liquidity in the markets.

This problem is especially prevalent in the cryptocurrencies markets and the issue is salient to the impact-targeting service providers who rely on public blockchains built on these cryptocurrencies. If sell-offs and panics in the cryptocurrencies markets can be induced by cyber-security breaches and events, then impact investors and service providers can face severe risks of excessive volatility of the exchange rates and transaction costs when dealing in crypto-assets. They may also suffer from falling liquidity and thus lower efficiency of blockchain transactions. In addition, cybersecurity risks associated with DLTs can carry potential direct losses to the social impact-targeting services providers, their clients, and investors. With DLTs being increasingly deployed in provision of vital social impact services, such as securing identities of clients, their medical and financial records, and providing backbone for aid and emergency payments provision, these risks can quickly escalate from being a matter of business sustainability to matters of life and death. We discuss some of these risks in Sect. 5 below.

Over time, informational efficiency is restored, trades are transacted, and the fractal patterns of volatility in prices give way to stability in the markets.

FMH, therefore, suggests that financial markets are chaotic systems, thus offering an alternative approach to capturing asset price dynamics using fractal geometry tools. Specifically, as per Peters (1994), the Hurst exponent calculated using the Rescaled Range Analysis (R/S) method can be combined with the V-statistic to identify price behavior patterns, such as long memory (or persistency) and cyclical patterns in the financial time series. Peters (1994) showed that currency pairs exhibited evidence of long memory, finding that USD/GBP and USD/JPY exchange rates had a Hurst exponent $H = 0.6$ and continuous V-statistics consistent with infinite memory. The two exchange rates displayed little correlation with economic fundamentals, indicating that technical information and investors' crowding behavior were the dominant factors explaining their price development. Mulligan (2000) expanded the R/S to 22 exchange rates also observing the presence of long memory in 22 countries. Kristoufek (2012) used FMH to explain the dynamics of the financial markets during the global financial crisis in 2007/2008. He confirmed that the FMH provides a better analytical framework to understanding market's behavior during the crises, rather than the EMH.

Since crypto-assets are traded similarly to foreign currencies, use of R/S and fractal analysis tools in general in the cryptocurrencies markets has been a rapidly developing area for research. Bariviera (2017) used a R/S to examine the behavior of Bitcoin returns and volatility over 2011–2017, showing that from 2011 to 2014 Bitcoin returns exhibited signs of inefficiency supported by the FMH. From 2014, Bariviera (2017) finds that Bitcoin behavior has become more informationally efficient and thus more consistent with the EMH. Celeste et al. (2018) examined the fractal dynamics of various cryptocurrencies for the period 2011 through 2017, concluding that Ethereum and Ripple prices followed a random walk (EMH), while Bitcoin showed signs of persistence and long memory (FMH).

Building on these findings, we examine the impact of major cryptocurrency exchange hacks on the fractal dynamics in Bitcoin in order to detect the extent of markets' inefficiency in crypto-assets. The importance of this research, in terms of its application to the evolving social impact finance area, is manifold. Social finance services providers include a range of payments facilitation companies, providers of information custody services, back-office clearance services, and supply chain management organizations. Whether for-profit or non-profit, these companies deliver direct and second-order social impacts. Many work in supplying support services to NGOs and International Organizations (IOs), including in the fields of social and financial inclusion, disaster assistance, poverty alleviation, minorities empowerment, and more (Galen et al., 2019).

Since the development of the blockchain technology that underpins crypto-assets, the social impact finance services sector has been at the forefront of using blockchain and cryptocurrencies to facilitate its payments, transaction clearing, information processing, and supply chain management operations. A recent Stanford University study (Galen et al., 2019, p. 2) states that "Blockchain initiatives dedicated toward social impact are still in the early days — 34% were started in 2017 or later, and 74% are still in the pilot or idea stage. But, 55% of social-good blockchain initiatives are estimated to impact their beneficiaries by early 2019." According to the study, the most common applications for blockchain initiatives today are found in the areas of payments and money transfer services (25%) and record keeping and verification (26%). Blockchain's primary benefits are being able to reduce risk and fraud (38%) and increase efficiency (24%) (Galen et al., 2019, p. 4).

As such, increasing volumes of transactions in the social impact finance services sector are tied to the price dynamics (valuations, volatility, and liquidity risks) of crypto-assets. This makes these services potentially susceptible to risk and uncertainty associated with technological security threats that impact major crypto-assets and blockchain systems. In other words, if hacks of major blockchain systems, such as Bitcoin and other key crypto-assets exchanges have fractal properties, the shocks from these hacks can have more significant impact on the systems providing key supports to the social impact finance providers.

In order to examine the impact of cryptocurrency hacks on the fractal dynamics in Bitcoin, we first outline data and core methodology used in detecting fractal properties of the Bitcoin. We then proceed to empirically analyze the data for all major hacks on cryptocurrency exchanges between 2014 and 2019 and draw our conclusions based on this data as to whether there is a systemic risk contagion channel from technology breaches to crypto-assets valuations.

3 Detecting Informational Inefficiencies in Crypto-Markets

3.1 Methodology

We use daily frequency price of Bitcoin from 1 January 2014 to 31 September 2019, identifying all key sub-periods covering major cryptocurrency exchange hacks. We consider 'before,' 'during,' and 'after' sub-periods of Bitcoin price reactions to each hacking event. Each 'during' sub-period is analyzed using tick data from the day of the attack. In order to analyze the impact of these hacks on the price dynamics of Bitcoin, we will use various tools, consistent with Bariviera (2017) and Celeste et al. (2018).

First, we use R/S analysis to examine logarithmic returns to Bitcoin for the presence of time-persistence and long memory. The R/S is a commonly-used method for detecting persistence, randomness, or mean reversion in the financial asset prices. As per Celeste et al. (2018), the R/S analysis allows us to distinguish between random and systematic (time-persistent) behavior of asset prices while establishing the duration of cycles in the data. Celeste et al. (2018) derive the details of how the Hurst exponent (H) is calculated using time series of asset prices, linking it to the R/S value (rescaled range of prices normalized by their volatility) through the derived identity linking log of R/S range to the Hurst exponent (H). We use Bariviera (2017) and Celeste et al. (2018) method to identify intraday Bitcoin price volatility.

From the discussion earlier, the Hurst exponent ranges from 0 to 1. For $H = 0.5$, the time series in question is said to follow a random walk. When $0.5 < H < 1$, the time series shows persistency and long-term memory (weak EMH applies). A shock to the price of an asset with H within this range will persist for a long period of time, and any adjustments back to market equilibrium will be slower than for the random walk (EMH). Finally, for $0 < H < 0.5$, the time series shows signs of anti-persistence, exhibiting negative correlation and reversing back to its equilibrium state at a rate greater than that of a random noise series (strong EMH applies).

Finally, we also use Celeste et al. (2018) methodology for correcting our R/S statistic estimates for small sample sizes. This adjustment allows us to consider intraday variation in Bitcoin prices in sub-periods 'during' the hacking attack shocks.

Our second set of measures relates to analyzing the existence and duration of cycles in the Bitcoin price responses to hacking events. Celeste et al. (2018) used the V-statistic for this purpose and their paper outlines how R/S statistic can be converted into a V-statistic. If long-term memory ($H > 0.5$) is found in the data, the resulting V-statistic will be up-trending. Any flattening of the V-statistic over time indicates a break in the memory process as the cycle of disturbances from the equilibrium caused by the original hack draws toward conclusion.

3.2 Key Findings

As previously mentioned, we examine six years of major cryptocurrency exchange hacks that took place between 1 January 2014 and 31 December 2019.

3.2.1 R/S Analysis and V-Statistic

To test our time series data for the presence of long memory, we consider complete time series of daily log-returns to Bitcoin over the entire period 2014–2019. We repeated the same for Bitcoin intraday volatility. Since maturity period of Bitcoin trading starts only around 2014 (Celeste et al., 2018), our time dimension is short, encompassing only 6 years' worth of data. This means that we focus on R/S analysis using corrected Hurst exponent. The results of these initial tests are presented in Table 1.

The corrected Hurst exponent for the complete series was $H = 0.609$, indicating the presence of long memory in the Bitcoin price process, as consistent with Bariviera (2017) and Celeste et al. (2018).

In other words, crowd behavior and technical information dominate the crypto-assets price development for more mature assets such as Bitcoin. In theory, the autocorrelation seen within the data indicates that Bitcoin's returns today are correlated with future returns, implying that any shock to today's Bitcoin valuations persists over a long period of time. Intra-year analysis shows that the Hurst exponent is, generally, increasing over time. From 2017 on, Bitcoin price volatility has a corrected Hurst exponent at 0.8337 over the period under consideration and it is persistently in excess of 0.633 in every annual sub-period. This indicates strong levels of autocorrelation in the daily volatility of Bitcoin returns. Overall, our evidence indicates that Bitcoin price (returns) deviations from pre-shock equilibrium and the volatility in Bitcoin price deviation tend to last for a relatively long period of time following the shocks.

Table 1 Hurst exponents by year

	2014	*2015*	*2016*	*2017*	*2018*	*2019*	*2014–2019*	*2014–2019 change, %*	*2017–2019 change, %*
Hurst Exponents (Log returns)									
Classical	0.6577	0.6496	0.6335	0.6782	0.6973	0.7103	0.6337	8.0	4.7
Corrected	0.5012	0.5014	0.5703	0.534	0.5783	0.5892	0.609	17.6	10.3
Hurst Exponents (Intraday Volatility)									
Classical	0.833	0.9047	0.8535	0.8107	0.8012	0.8322	0.8023	−0.1	2.7
Corrected	0.664	0.873	0.6783	0.6332	0.6398	0.6478	0.8337	−2.4	2.3

Intuitively, this means that any financial values, including the values relating to payments transacted by social impact finance intermediaries via Bitcoin-type blockchains, are, therefore, susceptible to these volatilities.

To check robustness, we use the *V*-statistics to identify the presence of persistence. The *V*-statistic describes the ratio between R/S statistic and the square root of time. If a time series is indicating persistence, the ratio will be up-trending. Our *V*-statistics are calculated using Bitcoin logarithmic returns and intraday volatility. We observe a steady up-trend in both *V*-statistics, confirming the presence of persistence in daily returns and intraday volatility. The results are similar to those obtained by Celeste et al. (2018) for Bitcoin returns over 2011–2017.

In summary, therefore, our analysis of the data shows that Bitcoin price exhibits strong and, over time, growing signs of susceptibility to herd behavior and information shocks—especially during the periods associated with cybersecurity breaches involving major exchanges. As noted above, these findings suggest that social impact financial services solutions based on major publicly traded cryptocurrencies are potentially subject to transmission of volatility and risk from cybersecurity threats to crypto-asset valuations and, ultimately, to the DLTs-based payments and accounting systems used by the financial intermediaries. It is, therefore, warranted for us to look at the specific risk events associated with cybersecurity breaches.

3.2.2 Hacking Events

We identify 25 major cryptocurrency exchanges cybersecurity breaches that had occurred in 2014–2019 and involved multiple permissionless cryptocurrencies and DLT platforms. These are listed in Table 2. Table 2 also identifies sub-periods of interest to our analysis, namely "Before," "During," and "After" sub-periods associated with each hacking event.

Based on Bariviera (2012, 2017) and Celeste et al. (2018), we use the rescaled R/S analysis to calculate all relevant Hurst exponents for these subperiods. The results are displayed in Table 2. We test these results for robustness using *V*-statistic.

We find across 2014–2018, and majority of hacking events, that following a major cryptocurrency cybersecurity breach the Bitcoin price dynamics can be best described as a random walk. However, the picture changes in 2019, showing that from, roughly, mid-2018 on, majority of hacking events resulted in Bitcoin price following a long-term memory path of adjustment. This suggests that in later hacking events, Bitcoin prices are starting to exhibit predictable, non-random response behavior

Table 2 Major cyber security events and their impacts on informational efficiency of Bitcoin

Major Cyber Events				Hurst Exponents (HE)						Hack Effects		
Exchange	Event	USD Value, million	Event Year	Before the Hack		During the Hack		After the Hack		Impact	Post-Impact	Event Window
				HE	Market Environment	HE	Market Environment	HE	Market Environment			
Bitstamp	Hack	5.1	Jan-15	0.501	FMH(w)	0.446	EMH(w)	0.548	FMH(s)	−0.110*	0.228*	0.093*
BTER	Hack	1.5	Feb-15	0.559	FMH(w)	0.503	FMH(w)	0.544	FMH(s)	−0.100*	0.080*	−0.028*
2014–2015		**6.6**										
Gatecoin	Hack	2	May-16	0.548	FMH(w)	0.287	EMH(s)	0.511	FMH(s)	−0.476*	0.776*	−0.069*
Bitfinex	Hack	73	Aug-16	0.518	FMH(w)	0.506	FMH(w)	0.64	FMH(s)	−0.023	0.264*	0.235*
2016		**75**										
Coinbin/Yapzon /Youbit	Hack	5	Apr-17	0.614	FMH(s)	0.505	FMH(w)	0.603	FMH(s)	−0.177*	0.194*	−0.017
Bithumb	Hack	7	Jul-17	0.594	FMH(s)	0.483	EMH(w)	0.574	FMH(s)	−0.186*	0.187*	−0.034*
Tether	Hack	31	Nov-17	0.64	FMH(s)	0.437	EMH(w)	0.582	FMH(s)	−0.318*	0.333*	−0.090*
Coinbin/Yapzon /Youbit	Hack	17	Dec-17	0.592	FMH(s)	0.447	EMH(w)	0.557	FMH(w)	−0.245*	0.245*	−0.059*
NiceHash	Hack	80	Dec-17	0.589	FMH(s)	0.394	EMH(w)	0.527	FMH(w)	−0.332*	0.338*	−0.107*
2017		**140**										
Coincheck	Hack	533	Jan-18	0.527	FMH(w)	0.34	EMH(s)	0.544	FMH(w)	−0.356*	0.603*	0.033*
Bitgrail	Theft/Hack	170	Feb-18	0.524	FMH(w)	0.415	EMH(w)	0.538	FMH(w)	−0.208*	0.296*	0.026
Bitcoin Gold	51% attack	18	May-18	0.512	FMH(w)	0.481	EMH(w)	0.511	FMH(w)	−0.061*	0.063	−0.002
Bithumb	Hack	31	Jun-18	0.509	FMH(w)	0.504	FMH(w)	0.494	EMH(w)	−0.010	−0.020	−0.029*
Coinrail	Hack	40	Jun-18	0.491	EMH(w)	0.5	FMH(w)	0.497	EMH(w)	0.019	−0.008	0.011
Zaif	Hack	60	Sep-18	0.508	FMH(w)	0.499	EMH(w)	0.501	FMH(w)	−0.017	0.004	−0.013
QuadrigaCX	Theft	250	Dec-18	0.574	FMH(s)	0.51	FMH(w)	0.509	FMH(w)	−0.110*	−0.002	−0.112*
2018		**1,102**										
Cryptopia	Hack(1)	4.8	Jan-19	0.533	FMH(w)	0.501	FMH(w)	0.493	EMH(w)	−0.060*	−0.015	−0.074*
Coinmama	Hack(2)	0.9	Feb-19	0.528	FMH(w)	0.511	FMH(w)	0.511	FMH(w)	−0.033	−0.001	−0.033*
Coinbin/Yapzon /Youbit	Theft	30	Feb-19	0.523	FMH(w)	0.521	FMH(w)	0.522	FMH(w)	−0.004	0.002	−0.003
CoinBene	Theft/Hack	100	Mar-19	0.528	FMH(w)	0.498	EMH(w)	0.529	FMH(w)	−0.058*	0.063	0.002

(continued)

Table 2 (continued)

Coinrail	Hack	40	Jun-18	0.491	EMH(w)	0.5	FMH(w)	0.497	EMH(w)	0.019	-0.008	0.011
Zaif	Hack	60	Sep-18	0.508	FMH(w)	0.499	EMH(w)	0.501	FMH(w)	-0.017	0.004	-0.013
QuadrigaCX	Theft	250	Dec-18	0.574	FMH(s)	0.51	FMH(w)	0.509	FMH(w)	-0.110*	-0.002	-0.112*
2018		**1,102**										
Cryptopia	Hack(1)	4.8	Jan-19	0.533	FMH(w)	0.501	FMH(w)	0.493	EMH(w)	-0.060*	-0.015	-0.074*
Coinmama	Hack(2)	0.9	Feb-19	0.528	FMH(w)	0.511	FMH(w)	0.511	FMH(w)	-0.033	-0.001	-0.033*
Coinbin/Yapzon /Youbit	Theft	30	Feb-19	0.523	FMH(w)	0.521	FMH(w)	0.522	FMH(w)	-0.004	0.002	-0.003
CoinBene	Theft/Hack	100	Mar-19	0.528	FMH(w)	0.498	EMH(w)	0.529	FMH(w)	-0.058*	0.063	0.002
Bithumb	Theft	13	Mar-19	0.54	FMH(w)	0.474	EMH(w)	0.523	FMH(w)	-0.122*	0.103*	-0.032*
Binance	Hack	40	May-19	0.537	FMH(w)	0.507	FMH(w)	0.564	FMH(w)	-0.056*	0.112*	0.049*
GateHub	Hack	10	Jun-19	0.53	FMH(w)	0.523	FMH(w)	0.554	FMH(w)	-0.014	0.06	0.045*
Bitpoint	Hack	30	Jul-19	0.567	FMH(w)	0.557	FMH(w)	0.511	FMH(w)	-0.017	-0.083*	-0.099*
Upbit	Hack	51	Nov-19	0.551	FMH(w)	0.548	FMH(w)	0.531	FMH(w)	-0.005	-0.031	-0.036*
2019		**280**										
	Average			0.545		0.476		0.537		-0.123	0.152	-0.014
	STDEV			0.037		0.062		0.036		0.132	0.205	0.073
	Frequencies	FMH(s)			6		0		7			
		FMH(w)			18		13		15			
		EMH(w)			1		10		3			
		EMH(s)			0		2		0			

*5%

to attacks. In other words, informational efficiency of blockchain-based assets may be deteriorating over time in response to increasing magnitude and frequency of cyber-attacks. Put differently, more recent vintages of cybersecurity threats appear to have a systematic risk impact on Bitcoin.

From social impact finance sector perspective, Bitcoin—a more mature, publicly traded cryptocurrency-based blockchain solutions platform it represents—potentially carries an inherent risk of cybersecurity attacks that trigger shocks to transactions and asset valuations involved in provision of impact finance (Lee, 2019; Orcutt, 2019). This risk spillover channel is even more pronounced for crypto-platforms not as widely distributed as Bitcoin, implying that less popular crypto-assets are highly likely to experience sustained losses as the result of cybersecurity breaches (Dion-Schwarz et al., 2019; Galen et al., 2019, Pompon & Vinberg, 2019). These losses will, in turn, transmit more volatility and uncertainty to financial intermediaries, including social impact finance companies, who opt to use these blockchain systems.

Cybersecurity breaches involving public cryptocurrencies exchanges are rising in numbers and volumes of assets involved, in line with growing popularity of these assets among investors and users. As summarized in Table 2, these breaches are associated with frequent switching of the dynamics of Bitcoin price formation from FMH to EMH and back to FMH before, during, and after the hacks, making it difficult for cryptocurrencies users to manage volatility and uncertainty associated with potential technological threats to the exchanges.[3]

[3] Additional channels for risk transmission from blockchain solutions to social impact services providers involve the following: (1) many blockchain solutions that exist today rely on traditional system's infrastructure that is vulnerable to cyber security breaches, and (2) with the advent of the blockchain innovation age, we are seeing increasing use of cryptocurrencies as source of funding and donations in the social impact sphere. Galen et al. (2019) note that "blockchain is also providing new sources of fundraising and revenue for non-profits through mechanisms such as crowdfunding and tokenized giving." The authors reference Fidelity Charitable, a large U.S.-based grants underwriter which witnessed a tenfold increase in cryptocurrencies donations in 2017, compared to 2016. Platforms "such as BitGive enable donors to make Bitcoin donations to specific charities and projects through crowd-fundraising campaigns. Other organizations have created their own charity cryptocurrencies that serve as a donation mechanism while providing a potential return for the donor" (Galen et al., 2019, p. 62).

4 From the Evidence of Markets Inefficiency to Risk Transmission in Social Impact Finance

As our analysis shows, from January 2014 until the end of 2019, Bitcoin returns time series indicate the presence of long memory and market inefficiencies. Based on discussions in Gurdgiev and Harte (2016), this pattern of behavior suggests that the time series for Bitcoin valuations has an easily identifiable trend before and after major security breaches involving exchanges on which the cryptocurrencies are traded. On average, during 2014-2019 period, Bitcoin price formation process follows the Fractal Market Hypothesis theory, exhibiting behavior consistent with predominance of herd behavior biases, reacting strongly to technical information as opposed to the underlying macro- and microeconomic fundamentals. Bitcoin, of course, is the most developed, highly liquid, and mature cryptocurrency of all other assets traded within the asset class of cryptocurrencies. As such, it should be showing signs of market maturation and stabilization, as well as offer the best-in-class levels of protection from both technological breaches and spillover of risks from such breaches. In reality, our data suggests that the opposite is happening over time.

Our data also supports the conclusion that cryptocurrency exchange hacks tended to increase the informational efficiency of Bitcoin in the short run by significantly reducing the Hurst exponent 'during' the breach event, prior to 2019. This relationship, however, appears to have broken down during late 2018 and through 2019. We can, therefore, distinguish two periods of Bitcoin evolution with respect to the dynamics of its price formation. On average, prior to mid-2018, a major cyber-exchange breach tended to shift Bitcoin prices from being informationally inefficient prior to the breach, to informational efficiency during the breach, and back to informational inefficiency after the breach. Since mid-2018, however, majority of the hacks resulted in only relative weakening of informational inefficiencies from the pre-breach phase to throughout the breach, with subsequent re-amplification of inefficiencies in the periods after the breach. These findings suggest that potential vulnerabilities to impact finance intermediaries that may arise from the use of major cryptocurrencies-backed blockchain solutions in managing payments, accounting, and supply chain management transactions are not easily eroded over time following the cybersecurity shock.

Overall, our empirical evidence suggests that after years of markets' development and continued growth in adoption by investors and blockchain users, Bitcoin price formation processes are still being dominated not by fundamentals of supply and demand, but by crowd behavior and exogenous shocks. Absent robust and sustained efforts to regulate crypto-assets and associated exchanges, our findings imply that Bitcoin and, to a greater extent, less liquid publicly traded cryptocurrencies present a risk contagion channel from cybersecurity attacks to the social impact finance intermediaries that intend to use these blockchain platforms for transacting payments or managing supply chains. More egregiously, this risk contagion involves cybersecurity attacks that are increasing in their numbers and severity over time.

5 A Path for More Secure Applications of Crypto-Assets in Social Finance

Adoption of blockchain technologies and associated crypto-assets (both private and public) presents substantial opportunities for the social impact finance sector. However, with rapid deployment of new technology and the accelerating development of its applications in impact finance space, the risks associated with blockchain solutions and their ecosystem of cryptocurrencies are growing as well. Our research shows that cryptocurrencies markets relating to public or permissionless crypto-assets are witnessing growing pressures from hackers and other 'black-hat' actors intent on theft and use of technology for money laundering and terrorism financing. This concern is also reflected in the shift in law enforcement activities to target these concerns, cyber-attacks, and other criminal activities that use crypto-assets trading and investing platforms, more aggressively.[4]

Focusing on core technological and 'black-hat' actors threats, public blockchain technology (also known as 'permissionless blockchain') deployment in impact finance space has the following major vulnerabilities:

[4] The proposed U.S. Federal Budget 2021 explicitly links the term "cryptocurrency"—the main asset underwriting public blockchain solutions—to terrorism financing, money laundering, and other criminal activities.

1. **Exposure to exchanges-related risks**. Hacking of contract records and theft of funds represent the remote (in terms of likelihood), but nonetheless material risk that is hard to mitigate for companies using public blockchain technologies. While cybersecurity breaches of public crypto-asset exchanges still represent a tail risk (low probability, but high impact events); the volumes of clients' records involved in these solutions and the sensitive nature of data[5] require use of precautionary principle in engaging public platforms-based new technologies in key sectors.
2. **Exposure to counterparties and vendors risks**. Cybersecurity risks can transmit to back-office support services providers (e.g., payments, data recording and analytics, logistics and identity verification services platforms) through the use of these platforms by the counterparties to the transactions. As services relating to social impact finance scale and reach less regulated and poorly governed jurisdictions, the counterparties risks rise (Galen et al., 2019, Holbrook, 2020; Santhana & Biswass, 2017).[6]

[5] Numerous sources reference the potential rates of blockchain technology utilization on identity services provision, retail payments services support, and health care—the sectors characterized by large-scale data utilization and highly private nature of data used (see Galen et al., 2019; Kawar, 2018; Millard, 2017).

[6] On the one hand, blockchain solutions pose promise of lowering some counterparties risk by reducing the number of counterparties involved in financial transactions. This allows blockchain technologies to lower cost and accelerate the speed of financial and physical transactions involved in shipping goods and services across borders. On the other hand, social impact finance solutions that utilize blockchain technologies are predominantly focused on providing services in the emerging and frontier markets, where regulatory and supervisory framework governing contractual agreements, goods and services flows, international trade, and clients data protection are less robust than their counterparts in the advanced economies (Holbrook, 2020). Specifically, permissionless blockchain platforms promise to reduce costs of transactions rests on eliminating the need for traditional payments intermediaries. In the emerging and frontier markets, these intermediaries, however, are more heavily regulated and supervised, often acting as the barriers to cyber and other 'black hat' agents. Blockchain technology cannot eliminate other counterparties from the transactions, including counterparties more frequently associated with high technological, regulatory and governance risks, such as product and services suppliers, supply chain management servicing firms, legal, planning and permissioning authorities and intermediaries, local government authorities, and so on. In traditional social impact finance transactions, existent and regulated infrastructure of banking and payments services providers acts as a break line for fraud and illicit financial flows, while other compliance and supply chain management intermediaries act as a barrier to illegal

3. **Exposure to markets / investors risks**. One of the key risks involving public or permissionless blockchains is that the crypto-assets used to back these technologies are highly risky in terms of their valuations (high volatility of exchange rates), can involve extremely variable and often prohibitive costs, and can be subject to liquidity risks (Santhana & Biswass, 2017). They are also exposed to potential abuse by the 'black-hat' crypto-assets users.[7]
4. **Risks associated with smart contracts.**[8] As discussed by Santhana and Biswiss (2017), smart contracts represent the main point of vulnerability for cybersecurity breaches and technological failures in any blockchain, whether public or private.

It is imperative that social impact finance services providers are aware of the key risks involving public (and also private) blockchains and, more broadly, the entire space of technological innovation involving the DLTs. Santhana and Biswass (2017) and Galen et al. (2019) provide good entry points for considering risk strategies, analysis, and mitigation measures as relating to the blockchain deployment in impact finance. From our research perspective, given the scaling up in the number of cybersecurity attacks and breaches involving even the most popular public blockchain-backing assets, such as Bitcoin, and considering the widening breadths of the typologies of these attacks and their systematic (as opposed to localized) impacts, social impact finance intermediaries and services suppliers

flows of goods and services (e.g., counterfeit and illegal goods flows, international sanctions regime enforcement, etc.). By reducing reliance on traditional intermediaries in social impact finance transactions, blockchain systems can increase cybersecurity, data, and legal risks, while lowering the cost of transactions.

[7] Investors and traders acquiring cryptocurrency on the public blockchain can transact with any entity on the blockchain, raising the risk of terrorism financing, money laundering, and illicit activities contaminating the transactions space that can be used by the social impact finance services providers. Additionally, as noted in Santhana and Biswass (2017, p. 4), public blockchains "have scalability and privacy issues that pose a significant risk to the use of this framework by financial institutions."

[8] Independent of the blockchain format (public or permissioned/private), smart contracts form the basis for the business applications using blockchain technology. Per Santhana and Biswass (2017, p. 4), mart contracts represent "a self-executing code on the blockchain framework that enable straight-through processing, which means that manual intervention is not required to execute transactions. Smart contracts rely on data from outside entities referred to as "oracles," and can act on data associated with any public address or with another smart contract on the blockchain."

should completely avoid public (permissionless) ledger technologies. This precautionary principle should apply until such time when regulatory and supervisory frameworks, guarding their users and investors, evolve sufficiently enough to allow for effective and efficient mitigation of these key risks.

References

Ball, R. (1978). Anomalies in relationships between securities' yields and yield-surrogates. *Journal of Financial Economics, 6*(2–3), 103–126.

Bariviera, A. F. (2017). The inefficiency of Bitcoin revisited: A dynamic approach. *Economics Letters, 161,* 1–4.

Bariviera, A. F., Guercio, M. B., & Martinez, L. B. (2012). A comparative analysis of the informational efficiency of the fixed income market in seven European countries. *Economics Letters, 116*(3), 426–428.

Black, F., Jensen, M. C., & Scholes, M. (1972).The capital asset pricing model: Some empirical tests. In M. C. Jensen (Ed.), *Studies in the theory of capital markets*. Praeger.

Celeste, V., Corbet, S., & Gurdgiev, C. (2018). Fractal dynamics and wavelet analysis: Deep volatility properties of Bitcoin, Ethereum and Ripple. *The Quarterly Review of Economics and Finance, 76,* 310–324.

Chaum, D. (1983). Blind signatures for untraceable payments. *Advances in Cryptology, Proceedings of Crypto, 82,* 199–203.

De Bondt, W. F., & Thaler, R. (1985). Does the stock market overreact? *The Journal of Finance, 40*(3), 793–805.

Devi Bhaskar, N., & Kuo Chuen, D. L. (2015). Bitcoin exchanges: Chapter 28 In D. L. Kuo Chuen (Ed.), The *handbook of digital currency* (pp. 529–552). Elsevier.

Dion-Schwartz, C., Manheim, D., & Johnston, P. B. (2019). *Terrorist use of cryptocurrencies: Technical and organizational barriers and future threats*. RAND Corporation.

Dykes, J. M. M. (1995). *Digital cash and the development of the apolitical currency: Ethics and law on the electronic frontier* (Discussion Paper). MIT, MA.

Fama, E. (1965). The behavior of stock market prices. *The Journal of Business, 38*(1), 34–105.

Fama, E., Fisher, L., Jensen, M. C., & Roll, R. J. (1969). The adjustment of stock price to new information. *International Economic Review, 10*(1), 1–21.

Galen, D., Brand, N., Boucherle, L., Davis, R., Do, N., Eel-Baz, B., Kimura, I., Wharton, K., & Lee, J. (2019). *Blockchain for social impact: Moving beyond the hype*. Stanford Graduate School of Business, Center for Social Innovation.

Garcia, D., Tessone, C. J., Mavrodiev, P., & Perony, N. (2014, October). The digital traces of bubbles: Feedback cycles between socio-economic signals in the Bitcoin economy, *Interface, 11*(99). https://doi.org/10.1098/rsif.2014.0623.

Grossman, S. J., & Stiglitz, J. E. (1980). On the impossibility of informationally efficient markets. *The American Economic Review, 70*(3), 393–408.

Gurdgiev, C., & Harte, G. (2016). Tsallis entropy: Do the market size and liquidity matter? *Finance Research Letters, 17,* 151–157.

Holbrook, J. (2020). Blockchain governance, risk, and compliance (GRC), privacy, and legal concerns. In J. Holbrook, John Wiley & Sons, Inc. (Eds.), *Architecting enterprise blockchain solutions* (pp. 257–277). https://doi.org/10.1002/9781119557722.

Jensen, M. C. (1968). The performance of mutual funds in the period 1945–1964. *Journal of Finance, 23*(2), 389–416.

Kahneman, D. (2011). *Thinking slow and fast*. Farrar, Straus and Giroux. ISBN-10: 0374533555.

Kawar, G. (2018). *Blockchain for social impact*. MaRS Centre for Impact Investing. Retrieved from https://www.socialfinanceforum.ca/2018/10/23/blockchain-for-social-impact/ on October 23, 2018.

Kharif, O. (2020). *Bitcoin Whales' ownership concentration is rising during rally*. Bloomberg. Retrieved from https://www.bloomberg.com/news/articles/2020-11-18/bitcoin-whales-ownership-concentration-is-rising-during-rally on 18 November, 2020.

Kristoufek, L. (2012). Fractal market hypothesis and the global financial crisis: Scaling, investment horizons and liquidity. *Advances in Complex Systems, 15*(6).

Lee, C.-C. (2010). Stock prices and the efficient market hypothesis: Evidence from a panel stationary test with structural breaks. *Japan and the World Economy, 22*(1), 49–58.

Lee, J. H. (2019). *Systematic approach to analyzing security and vulnerabilities of blockchain systems* (Working Paper). MIT Sloan Management School, MA. Retrieved from https://web.mit.edu/smadnick/www/wp/2019-05.pdf.

Malkiel, B. G. (2003). The efficient market hypothesis and its critics. *Journal of Economic Perspectives, 17*(1), 59–82.

Malkiel, B. G. (2005). Reflections on the efficient market hypothesis: 30 years later. *The Financial Review, 40,* 1–9.

Mandelbrot, B., Fisher, A., & Calvet, L. (1997). *A multifractal model of asset return* (Discussion Papers 1164). Cowles Foundation. Cowles Foundation for Research in Economics, Yale University.

Maskin, E., & Laffont, J. (1990). The efficient market hypothesis and insider trading on the stock market. *Journal of Political Economy, 1,* 70–93.

Millard, M. (2017). How does blockchain actually work for healthcare? *Healthcare IT News*. Retrieved from https://www.healthcareitnews.com/news/how-does-blockchain-actually-work-healthcare on April 13, 2017.

Montaine. (2020). *Information and cyber security threat actors*. Montaine PS. Retrieved from https://www.montaneps.com.au/post/information-and-cyber-security-threat-actors on January 16, 2020.

Mulligan, R. F. (2000). A fractal analysis of foreign exchange markets. *International Advances in Economic Research, 6*, 33–49.

Nakamoto, S. (2008). Bitcoin: A peer-to-peer electronic cash system. *Bitcoin.org*. https://bitcoin.org/bitcoin.pdf.

Orcutt, M. (2019). Once hailed as unhackable, blockchains are now getting hacked. *MIT Technology Review*. Retrieved from https://www.technologyreview.com/2019/02/19/239592/once-hailed-as-unhackable-blockchains-are-now-getting-hacked/ on February 19, 2019.

Osbourne, M. (1959). Brownian motion in the stock market. *Operations Research, 7*(2), 145–173.

Peters, E. E. (1994). *Fractal market analysis: Applying Chaos theory to investments and economics*. John Wiley & Son Inc.

Peck, M. (2012). Bitcoin: The cryptoanarchists' answer to cash. *IEEE Spectrum*. Retrieved from https://spectrum.ieee.org/computing/software/bitcoin-the-cryptoanarchists-answer-to-cash on 30 May 2012.

Pompon, R., & Vinberg, S. (2019). *Cryptocurrency hacks 2019. f5 Labs*. Retrieved from https://www.f5.com/labs/articles/threat-intelligence/cryptocurrency-hacks-2019 on September 11, 2019.

Roll, R. (1984). A simple implicit measure of the effective bid-ask spread in an efficient market. *Journal of Finance, 39*(4), 1127–39.

Santhana, P., & Biswas, A. (2017). *Blockchain risk management: Risk functions need to play an active role in shaping blockchain strategy, Deloitte*. https://www2.deloitte.com/content/dam/Deloitte/us/Documents/financial-services/us-fsi-blockchain-risk-management.pdf.

Selfkey (2020). *A comprehensive list of cryptocurrency exchange hacks*. Retrieved from https://selfkey.org/list-of-cryptocurrency-exchange-hacks/ on February 13, 2020.

Toth, B., & Kertesz, J. (2006). Increasing market efficiency: Evolution of cross-correlations of stock returns. *Physica a: Statistical Mechanics and Its Applications, 360*(2), 505–515.

Governance and the Role of Institutions

Who Should Fund Social Innovation?

Molly Sinderbrand

1 Introduction

Innovation within the three economic sectors—for-profit, social, and government—is both sector-specific and related to the creative strides of other sectors, either through explicit partnership or spontaneous interaction. This chapter focuses on both the discrete innovative processes and the interconnected inventive developments, in two of these three economic sectors: the social economy and government. In doing so, I argue that social economy enterprises are better suited to fund innovation than are governments within the sphere of social services, for both ethical and practical reasons. Indeed, my normative conclusion is that social enterprises should fund social innovation and that government should not. This conclusion is consistent with, and complementary to, the idea that governments are in the best position to provide, rather than innovating, social services.

The argument revolves around how innovation is funded, and how funding decisions are made. The main funding mechanism for the social

M. Sinderbrand (✉)
Online Nonprofit Leadership Program Coordinator, School of Social Policy and Practice, University of Pennsylvania, Philadelphia, PA, USA
e-mail: molsi@upenn.edu

T. Walker et al. (eds.), *Innovations in Social Finance*,
https://doi.org/10.1007/978-3-030-72535-8_17

economy is philanthropic donation, while the main funding mechanism for government is tax revenue. The distribution of philanthropic funds to particular organizations is generally controlled by the donors, while the distribution of tax revenue to particular agencies is usually determined by a legislative body and then approved by an executive. In addition, even within organizations, donors may have some control over allocation, such as giving to particular causes, whereas legislatures may not. The "who" and "how" of funding in these sectors lead to three reasons that innovation should be in the purview of the social economy (nonprofit) sector and not in that of the government sector. The first reason relates to responsiveness: philanthropic funds are more flexible. The second reason concerns mission: individuals within social enterprises share a common goal, set forth in the vision and mission of the enterprise. The third reason is associated with risk: given duties to taxpayers and citizens, innovation is too risky for government to ethically undertake.

The article is structured as follows. I begin with a discussion of social service innovation and how its funding differs in the nonprofit and government sectors. Using the three arguments listed above—responsiveness, mission, and risk—I demonstrate that the social economy is the ideal sector for social service innovation. I close by discussing implications and further questions including, what should government's role be in the innovation process? Should there be social service innovation at all?

2 The "Who" and "What" of Social Innovation

2.1 What Is Social Innovation?

Innovation, at its core, is the implementation of a new idea in an established area. Newness implies a type of disruption, which is what distinguishes innovation from a process of gradual improvement. In other words, innovation alters a method or process in goods or service provision and upsets the current process, rather than incrementally altering it (Mulgan et al., 2007). Social innovation is a subset of this disruptive type of alteration that focuses on solving social problems. One oft-cited definition is that of Phills et al. (2008, p. 36):

> We contend that social innovation is the best construct for understanding–and producing–lasting change. In order to gain more precision and insight, we define social innovation to mean: *A novel solution to a social problem*

> *that is more effective, efficient, sustainable, or just than existing solutions and for which the value created accrues primarily to society as a whole rather than private individuals.*

The problem with this definition is that it does not account for failed innovation, that is, a new and disruptive alteration to a method or process that does not end up solving the social problem, or is not as effective, efficient, sustainable, or just than the existing solution. Phills and colleagues argue that innovation is the best way to achieve social change, but they have built this conclusion into their definition. Innovation is clearly best if it is defined as more effective, efficient, sustainable, or just than alternatives. The negative aspects of innovation, including risk of failure, are not addressed by this definition. The ways that different funding mechanisms respond to failure affect both the efficiency and the ethics of funding new practices that may fail. The notion of failed innovation is crucial to both the argument of responsiveness and the argument of risk discussed later in this chapter.

In order to talk about risk and failed innovation, we need a definition of social innovation that accounts for such concepts. We may achieve this by defining social innovation in terms of intention: innovators intend for their solution to be better than the norm, even if it is not. However, this excludes social innovation in the private sector, in which innovators primarily envision the increased generation of private capital as a marker of successful innovation. Hence, the definition should allow for either intent or effect. I offer the following amendments to the above definition:

> Social innovation is a novel method to address a social problem that is *or is intended to be* more effective, efficient, sustainable, or just than current ways of addressing the problem, and for which the value it creates *or is intended to create,* and accrues *or is intended to accrue,* to society generally.

I use this amended definition throughout this chapter.

2.2 Who Innovates in Social Services? Who Funds Innovation?

Social innovation, according to the definition, can happen in all three economic sectors. Often, however, innovation transcends sector, either through explicit partnerships (e.g., in 2010, when Mayor Cory Booker partnered with Mark Zuckerberg's private foundation to transform public education in Newark, NJ (Russakoff, 2015)), or spontaneously through interaction (as seen in 1991, when the state of Minnesota started allowing private management organizations to operate public schools, thereby creating charter schools (Zinsmeister, 2014, p. 9)).

Cross-sector innovation looks different depending on which sectors are involved. A large part of the reason that innovation differs across sectors is that the funding mechanisms for innovation tend to vary across sectors. In general, in the for-profit sector, private capital funds innovation, either by reinvesting profit into innovative ventures, or in the case of entrepreneurship, by raising capital from private investors by promising returns if the innovation is successful. An entrepreneur raises capital by promising returns on the investment to the investor. In government, tax revenue primarily funds innovation. Such tax-funding, allocated by Congress through a budget process, supports government bureaus and laboratories (Center on Budget and Policy Priorities, 2017).[1] However, it should also be noted that private investment finances many capital-intensive government projects as well, through means such as bonds.

Innovation in the nonprofit sector is more complicated, especially since the introduction of new financing mechanisms like social innovation funds, which aim to mimic the private sector entrepreneur-investor relationship. Traditionally, private or government grants fund nonprofit social innovation. For our purposes, we focus on public charities, which make up the majority of the nonprofit sector and are the most likely candidates for pursuing social innovation. As innovation requires capital before services are provided, funding for innovation is unlikely to come primarily from fees for service. When we take out fees for service, which account for 72% of nonprofit revenue, private donations make up about half of the remainder in revenue (McKeever, 2015). As a result, I posit that funding for social innovation is most likely to come from the nonprofit's investment income or from private donations.

[1] In fiscal year 2016, tax revenue financed about 85% of the $3.9 trillion US federal budget, leaving 15% financed through borrowing. The vast majority of tax revenue (81, or 69% of the budget) came from individual income and payroll taxes.

2.3 Who Should Fund Social Innovation?

So far, we know that there are multiple funding mechanisms for social innovation, even for achieving the same goal. For the remainder of the chapter, I argue that we should prioritize certain funding sources over others, both on practical grounds and on ethical grounds. Namely, I compare philanthropic funding sources to government funding and argue that private philanthropic capital is better suited to social innovation than government funding.

The argument against government funding of social innovation stems from Rob Reich's work on philanthropy and democracy. Reich, in multiple articles and volumes, argues against using philanthropic capital for services that are rightly provided by a democratic government, including public education, basic science research, and core safety nets (e.g., Bernholz et al., 2016; 2011, 2016). At the center of the argument is the ethical use of power: when philanthropy funds basic services, they are provided at the discretion of the philanthropist, not the citizens or their elected representatives, in accordance with the preferences of the philanthropist (Bernholz et al., 2016). By comparison, government-funded services, in a democracy, are provided at the discretion of citizens, who voice their preference through voting, either through referenda or electing representatives. Others argue that private provision may actually erode confidence in government provision, which in turn undermines democratic legitimacy (Horvath & Powell, 2016).

However, Reich does allow for philanthropy to fund social innovation, which he terms "discovery," arguing that foundations in particular are "a potent discovery mechanism for innovation and experimentation in social policy" (Reich, 2016). In this chapter, I expand on that argument, using a similar negative argument. Just as philanthropy is unsuitable for public service provision in a democracy, democracies are not suited to funding social innovation, leaving philanthropy as the best candidate. I offer three arguments against democratic funding of social innovation. I term them the arguments of responsiveness, mission, and risk, and I address each in turn.

2.4 The Argument from Responsiveness

The argument of responsiveness is a practical one. The democratic process is not appropriately responsive to the success and failure of innovations, and responsiveness is necessary for innovations to be effective. The basic claim is that the pace at which government works is too slow to keep pace with innovation. This slow pace is problematic because it means government is unable to quickly end investment in unsuccessful innovations without stifling successful ones.

The argument of responsiveness rests on the idea that law lags behind innovation and technology. This "law lag" causes "regulatory gaps," or a misalignment between the regulatory frameworks required to enact legislation and a rapidly changing environment (Wadhwa, 2014). There are numerous examples of law failing to keep pace with innovation. For example, social media has created numerous regulatory gaps. An employer may not be allowed to require an applicant to disclose their ethnicity, which helps to avoid discrimination in hiring, but the same employer might discriminate on the basis of a LinkedIn profile picture (Wadhwa, 2014).

Even within government, regulatory gaps exist. For example, an innovative tax on sugar-sweetened beverages in the city of Philadelphia cannot keep Philadelphians from buying sodas in suburbs or neighboring states (McCrystal, 2017). Regulatory gaps represent a failure of policy to adapt to changing environments. They empirically exemplify policy's inability to quickly respond to failing innovation in a particular setting.

Regulatory gaps do not themselves prove that democratic governments cannot quickly respond to failing innovations, but rather that, in some instances, they do not. However, I argue that there is something inherent within democratic governance that ideally prevents timely adaptation to failure (or success) to mitigate harm (or expand benefit). There are two reasons for the lack of responsiveness: legislature's incentive and responsibility to diffuse, and the structure of constitutional checks and balances.

In a democracy, citizens express their preferences through voting, and elected representatives ideally carry out those preferences. These processes of voting and policymaking in general preserve a status quo—before a change is made, representatives must be confident that the electorate supports it. This process creates an incentive for inaction, especially when many legislators share the opportunity to regulate. Responsibility becomes diffuse and difficult to assign, making it challenging for voters and advocates to demand action. The preference for inaction on the part of legislatures makes policy sticky—bad policy is unlikely to change, and even good policy is unlikely to adapt to new circumstances (Buzbee, 2003).

Furthermore, in the US, the process of checks and balances exists to prevent bad legislation. However, this process makes it more difficult to enact any legislation. Constitutional democracies like the US, or the UK, were set up to protect against bad leaders doing harm by creating checks at every step (Wilson, 1744/2007). Large bureaucracy has much the same effect, though it is generally less transparent and accountable to citizens (Glennon, 2016). Unfortunately, these checks also prevent good leaders from taking positive action.

What does responsiveness, then, have to do with financing social innovations? It slows response, and when paired with the uncertainty associated with innovation, can lead to waste and harm when innovations fail. For example, No Child Left Behind, passed in 2001, was an innovative way to incentivize public schools to help their lowest-performing students succeed. It sanctioned schools in which students did not adequately perform on standardized tests by taking away funding or local control. For some schools, the threat of sanctions worked, particularly schools that generally performed well but had a subset of students that did not. For most low-performing schools, however, the law did much more harm than good. Yet, despite widespread evidence and popular opinion against the law, it did not change until 2015, fourteen years after it was enacted and eight years after it had technically expired (Turner, 2015).

There are reasons beyond the speed of government operation that can further lead to lagging. This includes the relative "safety" of government positions, which do not turn over as quickly, limiting responsiveness in the workforce. Practices such as log rolling and lobbying, both arguably important to the democratic process, often favor lagging reactions. Even political optics may mean the support for failing practices simply to avoid admitting mistakes were made, or to avoid appearing uncaring for the social issues being pursued. A good example of a problem of political optics is the drug prevention program D.A.R.E., an in-school drug education initiative. D.A.R.E. began in 1983, and as early as 1991, there were multiple studies that showed little to no effectiveness in preventing substance use (West & O'Neal, 2004). However, into the early 2000s, D.A.R.E. was still incredibly popular among schools and among parents, so legislators kept funding it. Schools wanted parents to believe that they were taking a stand against drug use, which endorsing D.A.R.E achieved, regardless of the program's inefficiency in practice (Mead, 2004).

Law and policy are blunt instruments and the democratic process is slow, leading to potential waste and even harm from continuing to invest in interventions that have been proven to be unsuccessful. Since they are not determined by the legislative process, philanthropic funds do not have this problem. When an innovation fails, they can mitigate damage by redirecting funds.

2.5 *The Argument from Mission*

The previous argument concerns efficiency; the argument of mission is concerned with effectiveness. The argument of mission states that social enterprises are more effective at innovation than government because they are mission-driven in a way that governments are not. Given that they operate with narrow missions, social enterprises may have more agreement on what to do. In government, the choice of policy is rarely between limited set options, whereas in social enterprises, the choice set is limited by the priorities of the organization. Such enterprises do not have to choose what to prioritize. Similarly, once the wishes of a philanthropic organization are established by members or by trustees, there is generally (more) agreement on priorities. Agreement provides focus and stability to funding. Stability, along with reactivity, means that philanthropy can experiment in innovation investment.

Members of a social enterprise all work toward the same concrete goal, whatever the goal may be. The mission defines the enterprise. An education nonprofit, for example, has the broad goal of improving education for a certain subset of students. Yet, the mission is usually narrower, in terms of methodology or geographic location. For example, the KIPP Foundation, which runs a network of successful charter schools for low-income students, focuses on a college-preparatory mission:

> To create a respected, influential, and national network of public schools that are successful in helping students from educationally underserved communities develop the knowledge, skills, character, and habits needed to succeed in college and the competitive world beyond. (KIPP Foundation, 2018)

Philanthropic organizations, whether a private foundation or a mass-philanthropy public charity, often have similarly specific missions, though these may focus on more areas. The William Penn Foundation, a private family foundation in Philadelphia, outlines three main funding priorities:

> Our mission is to help improve education for low-income children, ensure a sustainable environment, [and] foster creative communities that enhance civic life and advance philanthropy in the Greater Philadelphia region. (William Penn Foundation, 2018)

Mass philanthropy, or community foundations, may have more priorities and are more similar in this respect to local governments. Such foundations are nevertheless focused on helping their donors be more successful in their own sets of goals for community improvement (Council on Foundations, 2018). Community foundations are unlike government in that they enable individual donors to be mission-driven in the same way as private philanthropy does. For example, the mission of the Greater Milwaukee Foundation is to "inspire philanthropy, serve donors, strengthen communities now and for future generations" (Greater Milwaukee Foundation, 2018). Social enterprises, whether they are grant makers or grantees, have set and agreed-upon missions that govern their activities and their funding.

Democratic government, on the other hand, does not have a set mission or goal. Rather, it is a process for citizens to set priorities and act on them. Citizens share only a "meta-goal," the goal that each should be able to pursue his or her own goals, consistent with the maintenance of social order, so that citizens can coordinate with each other. This view of government can be found throughout Western philosophical tradition, as summarized by John Rawls in *A Theory of Justice* (1971) and *Lectures on the history of political philosophy* (2007). The "mission" of government is to allow each citizen to create a mission and act upon it (Rawls, 1971). Citizens decide on the scope of government, and its activities, through electing representatives or voting directly on referenda. Given that citizens have different goals and preferences, democracies must balance many competing interests. Mission-driven enterprises focus on a limited number of goals, on which everyone involved agrees; democracies focus on weighing a vast number of goals without agreement.

How do missions impact innovation? First, mission-driven enterprises may be more likely to engage in innovation because they can agree that innovation is a priority—they are tasked with solving a difficult social issue and agree that it needs to be solved. However, the reason to favor mission-driven enterprises for innovation has to do with the stability of funding for a specific goal amid shifting activities aimed at fulfilling that goal.

Ideally, given agreement on a mission, social enterprises are flexible in the best way to achieve that mission. When one method does not work, social enterprises are incentivized to choose another simply by their shared goal. Funding for the particular problem (though not necessarily the solution) is stable. Education philanthropists continue to fund education, even if a particular experiment does not work. Foundations thus have a longer time horizon, which is beneficial to experimentation, because they do not need to weigh other priorities when they account for the failure that necessarily comes with experimentation (Reich, 2016).

Hence, social enterprises can innovate toward a specific goal upon which all members agree, whereas government innovation will require compromise and weighing competing goals, especially in light of failed experimentation. An example of efficient problem-solving using social enterprises as opposed to government comes from Elinor Ostrom's (1990) work on preventing overfishing and common-pool resource dilemmas. A common-pool resource dilemma is when individuals cannot exclude others from resources, but are nonetheless competing for those resources. In other words, resources are finite, but access to them is unrestricted. Individuals have an incentive to use as much as they can before others do. The group then quickly depletes the resource. Ostrom's example is overfishing: individuals have an incentive to overfish, to harvest as many fish as possible before competitors do, thus depleting the population of fish before it can replenish itself.

To solve common-pool resource dilemmas, Ostrom shows that communities come up with their own informal (or semi-formal) agreement and enforcement mechanisms. That is, they create an institution, outside of government, to regulate their behavior on a specific issue. People who work in fishing create agreements to stop overfishing, along with informal and formal sanctions. Instead of using top-down enforcement, they each have an incentive to sanction one another and in turn expect to be sanctioned by one another. These mission-driven institutions, Ostrom argues, are more effective at curtailing problematic behavior because they are limited to a specific group and focused on solving a particular problem that exists within that group.

In these common-pool resource dilemmas, mission-specific institutions simply work better (Ostrom, 1990). They are bottom-up; they are more stable than top-down government approaches partly because they are not subject to the shifts in priorities that come from individuals with other interests. Everyone has the same goals. The same reasoning can be used with social enterprises. They are not subject to outside shifts in priorities because everyone has the same mission at the onset.

2.6 *The Argument from Risk*

The final argument against democratic government innovation—and in favor of philanthropically funded innovation—is an ethical, as opposed practical or efficiency-based, argument. I argue that non-voluntary democratic institutions are not in an ethical position to innovate in the social sector because innovation necessarily implies too much risk. This relates to the idea of harm mitigation in the argument of responsiveness and to the idea of the necessity of failure in experimentation in the argument of mission. I expand on both of these ideas in the argument from risk.

The argument of responsiveness shows us that there is no effective feedback mechanism when an intervention is not successful, so there is no way to minimize continued investment in unsuccessful programs. Since innovation is by definition new, we cannot assign a probability of success (in this way, it stands in contrast to the concept of continued improvement). The stickiness of policy magnifies any harm, making it less likely that the good outweighs the harm that comes from experimentation.

Harm is further magnified by the scale of government. If we take the equal consideration of citizens seriously, government cannot provide interventions arbitrarily to some citizens and not to others. Government-funded programs must be, in principle, open to all citizens within a particular category or demographic. Hence, the scale of government innovation may be large relative to nonprofit interventions, including those innovating with government funding. The scale of the intervention means that harmful policies risk harming a large number of people. Again, the scale of potential harm makes it more likely to outweigh the good that eventually comes from experimentation.

On the other hand, in a democracy we assume that, when innovation is funded, it is because we support funding innovation. This counter-argument is based on the idea of consent to government. Even if it is risky, we, as voters, have chosen to assume that risk, or at least most of us have, by authorizing our representatives. If we believe in a social contract, then we can say we have consented to the system, and thus consent to the outcome of the system. If that outcome is funding something risky, then we have consented to that risk.

Barring arguments against social contract theory, or against the idea that a majority of citizens can authorize risky investments on behalf of all citizens, there is still reason to be wary of the claim that if we consent to government investment in risky innovations, then they receive ethical permissions as well. The reason is that unsuccessful programs take capital away from services that governments are morally obligated to provide. Innovation, though it may grow the tax base in the long run, cannot generate revenue immediately. Resources are finite, at least in the short term, and funding innovation claims a part of those resources. Governments are required, as per the argument of mission, to weigh many competing interests. Thus, funding one option necessarily diminishes the resources available to fund others.

Why, then, favor funding the status quo over funding innovation, especially if the status quo is ineffective, unjust, or otherwise problematic? An innovation is by definition an attempt to improve the status quo because the status quo does not solve the social problem. It cannot be that we should prefer a policy that we know is problematic over an innovation that only might be problematic.

A way to navigate this dilemma is to challenge the dichotomy. The choice is not between the status quo and innovation. The choice is between the status quo, which is by definition problematic; innovation, which is risky; gradual improvement, which is less risky; or scaling previously tested innovation, which is also less risky. When philanthropy funds innovation, it provides another option for government, namely adopting and scaling innovations that have higher probabilities of success because they have already been tested. The argument is that government has an obligation to minimize risk so that it can instead use funding to provide services that we have evidence-based reasons to believe are superior.

3 Conclusion and Further Thoughts

My arguments in this chapter, building on the work of Reich and others, lead us to assign distinct roles to social enterprises and government. Social enterprises are charged with innovation—they are the incubators—whereas government is charged with the provision of services and the adoption of new practices when they have sufficient evidence to establish that they are superior to the status quo. This conclusion, of course, leaves many questions unanswered, including whether such a sharp dichotomy can ever exist in practice, and if not, how social enterprises should relate to government, and in particular philanthropy. These are practical questions, which much of the literature on effective philanthropy already addresses (Frumkin, 2008).

There is, however, another related question that I have not addressed so far: should we, as a society, invest in social innovation at all at this point in time? There are reasons to believe that we need to shrink the scope of philanthropy and exclude it from social services altogether; namely, we do not need innovative solutions to problems. We already have a plethora of known, tested, evidence-based solutions. The trick is to enact them (Ross, 2014).

Given the large number of evidence-based solutions to social problems that exist in databases like the What Works Clearinghouse for education, or SAMHSA's National Registry of Evidence-based Programs and Practices for mental health, I am inclined to think that, for some social issues, this objection to innovation might be at least partially valid. Perhaps the focus should be on enacting what we know rather than innovating. However, the fact that known solutions are not enacted is itself a social problem, one that could possibly be addressed through innovation. The role of social innovation, and thus philanthropy, might be different in each field, requiring more or less partnership among sectors. Certainly, there is room for nuance and for collaboration. Regardless, just as we should be careful about philanthropy overstepping its bounds in terms of public service provision, we should not let government overstep its bounds in terms of innovation. To do so is to take unnecessary risk and great scale, inconsistent with the goal of government to provide for citizens.

References

Bernholz, L., Cordelli, C., & Reich, R. (2016). Introduction. In R. Reich, C. Cordelli, & L Bernholz (Eds.), *Philanthropy in democratic societies: History, institutions, values* (pp. 1–18). University of Chicago Press. https://doi.org/10.7208/9780226335780-002.

Buzbee, W. W. (2003). Recognizing the regulatory commons: A theory of regulatory gaps. *Iowa L. Rev., 89*(1), 1–64. https://doi.org/10.2139/ssrn.447700.

Center on Budget and Policy Priorities. (2017, August 6). *Policy basics: Where do federal tax revenues come from?* Center of Budget and Policy Priorities. https://www.cbpp.org/research/federal-tax/policy-basics-where-do-federal-tax-revenues-come-from.

Council on Foundations. (2018). *Community foundations.* Council on Foundations. https://www.cof.org/foundation-type/community-foundations-taxonomy.

Frumkin, P. (2008). *Strategic giving: The art and science of philanthropy.* University of Chicago Press.

Glennon, M. J. (2016). *National security and double government.* Oxford University Press.

Greater Milwaukee Foundation (2018). *About us: Our mission, vision and values.* Greater Milwaukee Foundation. https://www.greatermilwaukeefoundation.org/about-us/our-mission/.

Horvath, A., & Powell, W. W. (2016). Contributory or disruptive: do new forms of philanthropy erode democracy? In R. Reich, C. Cordelli, & L Bernholz (Eds.), *Philanthropy in democratic societies: History, institutions, values*. (pp. 87–122). University of Chicago Press https://doi.org/10.7208/chicago/9780226335780.003.0004.

KIPP Foundation (2018). *KIPP Foundation: About*. KIPP Foundation. https://www.kipp.org/kipp-foundation/.

McCrystal, L. (2017, December 23). Philly's soda tax has spawned multiple studies. Here's what we've learned. *The Philadelphia Inquirer*. http://www.philly.com/philly/news/pennsylvania/philadelphia-soda-tax-impact-studies-what-weve-learned-20171222.html?arc404=true.

McKeever, B. (2015). *The nonprofit sector in brief 2015: Public charities, giving, and volunteering.* Urban Institute, National Center for Charitable Statistics. https://www.urban.org/research/publication/nonprofit-sector-brief-2015-public-charities-giving-and-volunteering.

Mead, J. (2004, February 1). DARE program: Sacred cow or fatted calf? *The New York Times*. https://www.nytimes.com/2004/02/01/nyregion/dare-program-sacred-cow-or-fatted-calf.html?_r=0.

Mulgan, G., Tucker, S., Ali, R., & Sanders, B. (2007) *Social innovation: What it is, why it matters and how it can be accelerated.* Skoll Centre for Social Entrepreneurship.

Ostrom, E. (1990). *Governing the commons: the evolution of institutions for collective action.* Cambridge University Press. https://doi.org/10.1017/cbo9781316423936.

Phills, J. A., Deiglmeier, K., & Miller, D. T. (2008). Rediscovering social innovation. *Stanford Social Innovation Review, 6*(4), 34–43.

Rawls, J. (1971). A theory of justice. *Harvard University Press*. https://doi.org/10.1017/cbo9780511814099.

Rawls, J. (2007). Lectures on the history of political philosophy. *Harvard University Press*. https://doi.org/10.2307/j.ctvjnrtqz.
Reich, R. (2011). Toward a political theory of philanthropy. In P.M. Illingworth, T. Pogge, & L. Wenar (Eds.), *Giving well: The ethics of philanthropy* (pp. 177–195). Oxford University Press. https://doi.org/10.1093/acprof:oso/9780199739073.003.0010.
Reich, R. (2016). Repugnant to the whole idea of democracy? On the role of foundations in democratic societies. *PS: Political Science and Politics*, *49*. https://doi.org/10.1017/s1049096516000718.
Ross, R. K. (2014). We need more scale, not more innovation. *Stanford Social Innovation Review*, *12*(2), 18–19. https://ssir.org/articles/entry/we_need_more_scale_not_more_innovation.
Russakoff, D. (2015). *The prize: Who's in charge of America's schools?* Houghton Mifflin Harcourt.
Turner, C. (2015, October 27). No child left behind: What worked, what didn't. *National Public Radio*. https://www.npr.org/sections/ed/2015/10/27/443110755/no-child-left-behind-what-worked-what-didnt.
Wadhwa, V. (2014, April 15). *Laws and ethics can't keep pace with technology*. MIT Technology Review. https://www.technologyreview.com/s/526401/laws-and-ethics-cant-keep-pace-with-technology/.
West, S. L., & O'Neal, K. K. (2004). Project DARE outcome effectiveness revisited. *American Journal of Public Health*, *94*(6), 1027–1029. https://doi.org/10.2105/ajph.94.6.1027.
William Penn Foundation. (2018). *About us*. William Penn Foundation. https://www.williampennfoundation.org/about-us.
Wilson, J. (2007). Considerations on the nature and extent of the legislative authority of the British parliament. In K.L. Hall & M.D. Hall (Eds.), *Collected works of James Wilson, Volume 1* (pp. 3–31). Liberty Fund. (Original work published in 1744).
Zinsmeister, K. (2014). *From promising to proven: A wise giver's guide to expanding the success of charter schools*. The Philanthropy Round Table.

The Financial Intermediary Role of Peer-To-Peer Lenders

Barbara Dömötör and Tímea Ölvedi

In the last few decades, the financial market has changed significantly. Not only has the market embraced new innovative forms of financial services, but it also benefits from new types of institutional design. In the past, the conventional banking sector served as the financial intermediary that links depositors and borrowers. More recently, financial services have witnessed a disintermediation trend, accelerated by the technological development of FinTech. Other than traditional financial service providers, such as the banking system and capital markets, alternative finance models emerge that affect not just the payment and settlement services, but also the very core of financial intermediation: capital-raising activities, including lending and investment. The social impact of the emergence of new services is twofold. Smaller clients who are unable to access financial markets directly, and fall out of the scope of traditional banks, can gain access to better financial services by leveraging the more flexible features of the platforms. This process then instigates banks to improve their services.

B. Dömötör · T. Ölvedi (✉)
Department of Finance, Corvinus University of Budapest, Budapest, Hungary

B. Dömötör
e-mail: barbara.domotor@uni-corvinus.hu

T. Walker et al. (eds.), *Innovations in Social Finance*,
https://doi.org/10.1007/978-3-030-72535-8_18

The chapter is organized as follows: the first section introduces the various forms of alternative financing, and the second section describes the size, dynamics, and geographical coverage of the actual market. We then focus on the potential explanations as to why P2P lending can create value for both the lender and the borrower and summarize the empirical results of the literature. We present regulatory issues in a separate section.

1 Disruption of Financial Intermediation

Crowdfunding refers to the phenomenon of entrepreneurs seeking funding not from a small group of wealthy investors, but rather from a broader audience that offers smaller amounts. According to Belleflamme's (2014, p. 588.) definition, "Crowdfunding involves an open call, mostly through the Internet, for the provision of financial resources either in the form of donation or in exchange for the future product or some form of reward to support initiatives for specific purposes." Although crowdfunding-type financing is not entirely novel (indeed, the Statue of Liberty in New York was financed using small donations obtained through several money-raising events), online platforms accelerate the spread of disintermediated financing (Hemer, 2011).

1.1 Business Models of Alternative Finance

Related literature describes many types of crowdfunding that can be ordered into four main groups (Walter, 2019). The first is donation-based crowdfunding, a charity program without any financial interest and profit. The second is reward-based crowdfunding, in which investors receive material or immaterial benefit from their investment. The third is equity-based crowdfunding, which is part of the corporate's equity offered for the funding. The fourth type is peer-to-peer (P2P) lending, which is the focus of this chapter.

In the following sections, we employ the terminology of the Cambridge Centre for Alternative Finance (2020) and use the term "alternative finance" to refer to all types of financing that are outside of both the traditional banking sector and the capital market. Alternative finance can be debt-based or equity-based. The former is a lending relationship between partners and extends the above-mentioned crowdfunding groups through balance sheet lending and securitized financing. The latter refers to providing funds without any reward, or for a share in a project or venture. Table 1 presents the different business models and their market shares as of 2018 (CCAF, 2020).

Financing source providers are individuals or institutional investors in all forms, except in the case of balance sheet lending models, in which the platform itself offers the loan. The borrowers can be private or business partners. Consumer and business lending cover unsecured loans. In the case of property lending, the loan is secured against property.

P2P consumer lending represents the highest market share, accounting for almost two-thirds of the whole outstanding volume globally. As Table 1 shows, excluding China changes the picture: P2P consumer lending is still in first place, but the shares of other types of P2P lending and balance sheet lending are more balanced.

Table 1 Forms of alternative finance

Category	*Business model*	*Market share excl. China (%)*	*Market share incl. China (%)*
P2P/Marketplace lending	Consumer lending	36	64
	Business lending	9	17
	Property lending	4	2
Balance sheet lending	Consumer lending	11	3
	Business lending	17	7
	Property lending	12	4
Invoice trading	Invoice trading	3	1
Securities	Debt-based securities	1	0
	Mini bonds	0	0
Investment-based	Equity-based crowdfunding	2	0
	Real Estate crowdfunding	3	1
	Profit sharing	0	0
Non-investment-based	Reward-based crowdfunding	1	0
	Donation-based crowdfunding	1	0
Other		0	0

Source CCAF, 2020, Table 1.1 page 40

1.2 Comparison of Banks and P2P Lending Platforms

Both traditional financial intermediaries (banks) and P2P lending platforms serve to implement the reallocation of financial sources. However, their approaches to regulation, operation, and risk management differ in many aspects. Financial intermediation includes two different roles. The first is brokerage, including transaction services, financial advice, screening and certification of quality (i.e., rating), origination, issuance, and funding. The second is risk and maturity transformation, which happens when banks collect (almost) riskless short-term deposits and offer risky, long-term credit to their clients (Havrylchyk & Verdier, 2018). P2P platforms perform the brokerage function not just by matching lenders and the borrowers, but also by offering services to reduce information asymmetries and to monitor costs. Table 2 compares the main features of banks and P2P platforms.

Although some platforms provide capital protection to their investors in the form of buyback guarantees, P2P platforms, unlike banks, primarily serve as brokers. Such platforms achieve this by matching lenders and borrowers without taking positions on their own balance sheets. As platforms do not collect or create money, their risk profile is not as complex, and consequently, they are less of a target for financial regulation.

2 Market Overview

P2P lending has rapidly expanded in recent years and several platforms have appeared on the market. In general, cross-border lending, which involves borrowers and investors from neighboring countries, is possible. However, a few platforms operate solely at the national level. The purposes of the platforms are quite diverse: the majority of the platforms facilitate consumer credit for private individuals or business lending for SMEs, while others provide real estate loans or student loans. It is also possible that a single platform offers a wide range of these services. As a result of this variance, it is not possible to fully differentiate the platforms that focus merely on consumer lending. Nonetheless, approximate statistics regarding the segment are available. Figure 1 presents the distribution of platforms by geographic location as of July 2020 (P2 PMarketData, 2020).

As per the Fig. 1, a significant number of platforms are located in Europe. The European market is highly developed in the United

Table 2 Characteristics of banks and P2P Platforms

	Bank	*P2P platform*
Regulation	Since banks finance loans from collected deposits, they are exposed to several risk factors. In order to manage risks appropriately, international standards were introduced for banking regulation (the Basel Accords)	There is no comprehensive regulatory framework in the P2P segment. However, some initial regulations have appeared in Europe, specifically in the United Kingdom, Lithuania, and Switzerland. The main issues that these laws cover are transparency and risk management
Investors	Depositors are protected. Different authorities are responsible for deposit insurance in each country	In general, investors assume the risk as the decision to fund is theirs'. Some platforms have introduced investor protection measures, such as buyback guarantees and payment guarantees
Capital allocation and economic role	Banks play a crucial role in the efficient allocation of capital in the economy. A few decades ago, financial institutions were the only entities to offer these services in the market. Banks also provide a buffer in the economy in case of an external macroeconomic shock	These platforms apply innovative technologies, such as machine learning and artificial intelligence, in the credit assessment process in order to improve efficiency. The funding process is based on an online auction, in which supply and demand determine the final interest rate. Such platforms also serve the underbanked-customer segment with lower credit ratings
Liquidity and payment services	Banks offer money-changing services and manage the savings of depositors. Further, through their clearing activity, they facilitate the money transfer process	Platforms do not provide money-changing and payment services Some platforms operate in a secondary market to ensure liquidity for the lenders
Asset transformation	Banks perform several asset transformations. They can transform the size of the product, e.g., by providing loans in small amounts from a large deposit investment. Quality transformation refers to the fact that the risk-return characteristics of the deposits and loans can differ Maturity transformation is also essential, as it turns short-term deposits into long-term loans	Platforms do not perform asset transformation in the classic interpretation of the term. However, they enable investors to compile diversified portfolios. In addition, large loan requests can be funded with small investments. There is no possibility for maturity transformation, as the platforms do not own capital and funding is given directly, without intermediary transformation

(continued)

Table 2 (continued)

	Bank	*P2P platform*
Risk management	Banks have a comprehensive risk management framework that covers credit risk, liquidity risk, market risk as interest rate risk, and operational risk. Regulators carefully monitor risk management practices	Platforms apply different risk management measures, e.g., credit assessment, secondary market, buyback guarantee, and rejection for those under a certain score, etc. Currently, market risk is not relevant to them, while credit and liquidity risks are passed to the investors. However, operational risk, including risks regarding cybersecurity, is high for these platforms
Information processing and monitoring	Due to information asymmetry between investors and borrowers, banks play a key role in monitoring potential applicants and their performances	Platforms as well as investors perform monitoring. Platforms perform credit risk assessment based on the information provided by the borrower and on data from credit bureaus. The decision to fund is made by the investor; thus, some platforms set their portfolio data to be publicly available to investors, so that they might investigate historical performance. Further, more data used for information processing, such as the picture of the applicant, is available on these platforms

Source Based on Freixas and Rochet (2008)

Kingdom where the whole segment was implemented. Twenty platforms are currently operating in Europe, all offering a wide range of products. Through robust expansion and boasting 29 players, the Baltic countries further strengthen the northern continent. Western Europe is also progressing, with dominance in Germany, Switzerland, and France, which have 36 participants together. In southern Europe, Spain is leading with 11 platforms, followed by seven in Italy. Eastern Europe is lagging behind with ten platforms, mostly located in the Czech Republic. Europe is followed by Asia, where Indonesia and South Korea dominate the segment with 15 and nine platforms, respectively. According to the number of platforms, the North American market seems smaller in comparison. However, it is worth noting that the total lending volume

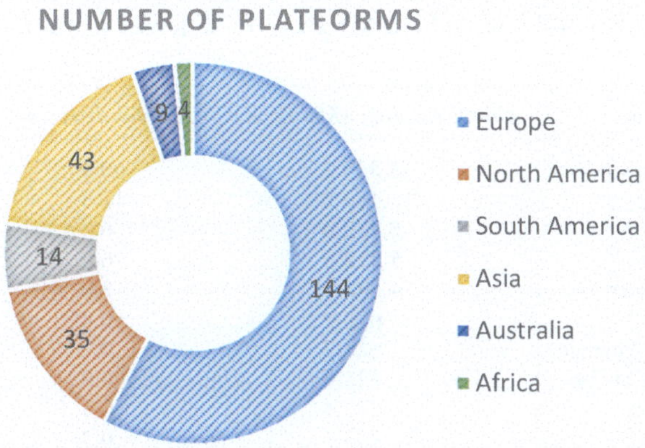

Fig. 1 Extension of the market as of July 2020 (*Source* p2pmarketdata.com)

is much higher in North America, due to the significant number of institutional investors. Most North American platforms are located in the United States, home to 20 platforms. The market is modest in the rest of the world: 14 lending platforms operate in South America, nine in Australia, and only four in Africa (P2PMarketData, 2020).

In terms of loan volume, LendingClub is the market leader with a total issuance of EUR 53.3bn, which accounts for more than half of the market. The platform is centered in San Francisco and emerged as one of the first American sites in 2007 (LendingClub, 2020a). Its introduction to the New York Stock Exchange in 2014 and the appearance of a significant number of institutional investors supported its vigorous expansion (NYSE, 2014). Prosper, the main competitor in the United States, boasts a 17.5% market share. The rest of the significant players are mostly concentrated in the United Kingdom and the Baltic region. Zopa was the first P2P platform. Since its creation in 2005, Zopa has enhanced transparent operations and supported the introduction of government regulations in the segment (Zopa, 2020), currently accounting for 6.7% of the market. Mintos is a relatively new platform, founded in 2015 (Mintos, 2020a). In five short years, it has rapidly become the largest site in the Baltic region, with a 6% market share (Table 3).

Overall, the total contribution of the P2P segment is still modest compared to the lending volume of commercial banks. In the case of the US market, the total consumer credit provided by financial

Table 3 Lending volume and market share of different platforms, as of July 2020

No	*Platform*	*Total funding (Mn EUR)*	*Market share (%)*	*Country*
1	LendingClub	53,329.2	60.4	USA
2	Prosper	15,448.2	17.5	USA
3	Zopa	5,885.0	6.7	UK
4	Mintos	5,252.5	6.0	Latvia
5	RateSetter	4,388.4	5.0	UK
6	TWINO	673.9	0.8	Latvia
7	Fellow Finance	621.2	0.7	Finland
8	CreditGate24	441.0	0.5	Switzerland
9	Bondora	372.4	0.4	Estonia
10	Peerberry	265.5	0.3	Latvia

Source p2pmarketdata.com; the top 39 consumer credit platforms are considered as the whole market and market share is estimated as portion of the total lending volume of these platforms

institutions is approximately EUR 3,666.2bn (FED, 2020). The loan origination of the top P2P platforms operating in the United States approached EUR 68.8bn as of July 2020 (P2PMarketData, 2020), which represents roughly 2% of the total bank lending.[1] The proportion is similar to that in the European market. Total consumer lending is approximately EUR 840.4bn, while platform lending is EUR 19.3bn, representing slightly more than 2% (European Credit Research Institute, 2019; P2PMarketDate, 2020). In spite of the relatively low portion of P2P lending, the growth rate of the segment is quite precipitous. Figure 2 showcases this dynamic growth, which accounts for the cumulated lending volume from inception for the main platforms that publish loan statistics regularly. The right axis shows the figures for LendingClub, the highest in volume.

A frequently made argument in favor of these platforms is that they provide lower prices for the borrowers and also serve those clients who are not accepted by banks. So, on the one hand, P2P platform lending might be advantageous for underbanked borrowers. On the other hand, debtors who have stable credit profiles would like to obtain cheaper funding. Table 4 summarizes the weighted average interest rates and lending volumes by rating the two main consumer lending marketplaces.

[1] The top 39 platforms based on lending volume are considered as the whole market.

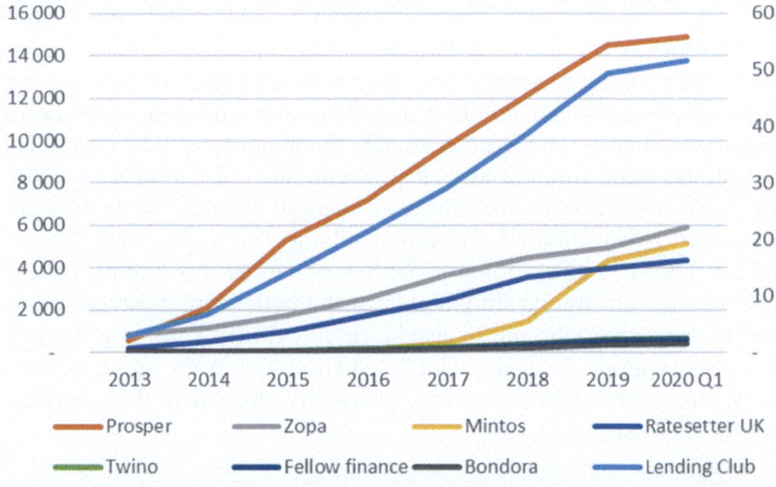

Fig. 2 Total lending volume from inception to July 2020 (*Source* Lending Club 2020b, Mintos 2020b, Bondora 2020, Ratesetter 2020, Twino 2020, Fellow Finance 2020 and p2pmarketdata.com)

Table 4 Average interest rates as of Q1, 2020b

LendingClub			*Prosper*		
Rating	*Interest rate (%)*	*Volume (thousand USD)*	*Rating*	*Interest rate (%)*	*Volume (thousand USD)*
A	7.28	9,666,049	AA	6.98	1,738,925
B	10.94	12,553,303	A	9.57	3,480,886
C	14.48	12,094,583	B	12.48	4,212,929
D	18.90	6,529,057	C	16.78	4,423,160
E	21.87	2,415,368	D	22.81	2,010,421
F–G	26.09	1,046,612	E	28.09	766,950
			HR	31.38	207,125

Source Lending Club statistics 2020b,Prosper Funding LLC, 2020

The average interest rate in commercial banks in the United States is 9.63% for personal loans and 15.09% for credit cards (FED, 2020). Consequently, P2P conditions, compared to commercial bank rates, are cheaper for borrowers only when classified in the upper-rating categories. Debtors in bad standing have to pay significantly higher interest. However, they might be rejected by the banks regardless of their paying of higher interest, which would leave them with no other choice in funding. According to empirical evidence, the majority of P2P borrowers are eligible for bank funding as well. Roughly 85% of consumer lending debtors have full access to conventional financial services, while 13% are underbanked, having limited access to banking services and only 2% are unbanked (CCAF, 2020). Table 4 further evidences this finding, where lending volumes are significantly higher in the better-rating categories, in the case of borrowers who might also be eligible for bank funding. Empirical findings support the fact that P2P clients, within the same income category, are more debt-laden and financially distressed than average borrowers (Morse, 2015).

3 Relevance of P2P Lending

P2P platforms facilitate the interaction of the two sides of the lending market by offering them a simple algorithm. Borrowers can apply for a loan online, and based on the platform's credit rating and pricing offer, lenders can choose the amount, as well as the borrowers they are willing to finance.

Through advertisement, these platforms claim that the transaction is beneficial for both parties. The suggestion is that by removing the intermediation, investors receive higher returns for their investments, while borrowers pay lower interest rates as compared to a banking loan. On the other hand, in the case of platform funding, the risk is higher, transparency is lower, and the level of risk management is not significantly developed (Milne & Parboteeah, 2016).

Some obvious questions arise, such as: Is P2P lending actually more advantageous for the lending partners, or is the higher return of the investment just a reflection of the fair price for the credit and liquidity risks? Are the funding costs actually cheaper? As given in Table 4, this is not necessarily the case. Simply formulated, what added value or advantage do the platforms boast that provides the rationale of their existence? What do they know that banks do not? Are the two forms competing with or complementing each other?

Banks play a central role in the economy, which is difficult to explain in a frictionless market, where the supply and the demand for financial sources locate each other directly in an optimal setting. The existence of and the rationale for banks are consequences of market imperfections that make perfect diversification impossible. In the following sections, we analyze the main explanations that justify financial intermediation and investigate P2P lending from those perspectives.

3.1 Transaction Costs

The original reason for the emergence of intermediaries in financial services was the essential physical and technological costs connecting to those services. Due to the transaction costs, a separate unit (the bank) could be profitable by offering financial services because of the economies of scope and scale. Transaction costs are partly exogenous, but the costs of searching and monitoring are also relevant here (Freixas & Rochet, 2008). The economies of scope and scale motivate borrowers and lenders to form coalitions to reduce fixed costs and to achieve a perfect diversification.

Philippon (2016) investigates cost of intermediation in the US market and Bazot (2018) examines the same in the European market. They both find that intermediation costs are around 2% of the intermediated assets and that this level has remained stable since the end of the nineteenth century, despite technological changes. Based on these findings, one can argue that traditional banks generate extra profit that the appearance of P2P platforms can reduce. These platforms are free of the considerable fixed costs of branch networks or employers and are often described as having a competitive advantage in access to technology. Cost efficiency is not clear if we look at the charges used by the platforms. The origination fee costs 1–5%, depending on the credit rating that is subtracted from the loan amount, and platforms usually also charge a collection fee of 1% (Morse, 2015). Based on the data, the average cost of 3–4% to the platforms seems to exceed the 2% calculated for banks.

One argument in favor of P2P platforms is that they are faster and more flexible in adopting new data and technological solutions than banks with hierarchical structures and strict rules. Another important factor of the platforms' cost efficiency is the fact that in the absence of their own exposures, they are not subject to financial regulation's prescribing of costly capital requirements and other risk management rules. We explore this aspect in Sect. 5.

3.2 *Information Asymmetry*

Information asymmetry refers to the problem that the lender has constrained knowledge of the borrower's creditworthiness. Information asymmetry takes three forms:

- Ex ante: an adverse selection, meaning that the average price of the loan will be attractive only for the less-creditworthy portion of the given credit segment;
- Interim: a moral hazard refers to the fact that the borrower does not have enough incentive to make an effort to enhance the probability of success, as he/she shares both the return and the risk of the project with the lender;
- Ex post: the verification of the outcome is costly.

We consider the consequences of information asymmetry as specific forms of transactional costs that monitoring may help to reduce, and thus serve to improve the efficiency of lending. Financial intermediaries create value by economizing monitoring costs and by having better access to the borrowers' credit and account history, or to other public sources like bad debtor registries or records of legal processes (Diamond, 1984). Banks, using their own capital to finance the borrowers, also give signals about the quality of the debtor.

P2P platforms have no or less access to the previous financial history of the borrower. The verification of this information, if available, is also costly, sometimes even impossible. Offering no credit from their own sources, the signaling effect is also less significant than in the case of banks.

On the other hand, platforms have the aforementioned advantage of applying big data analysis techniques and what is more important they can collect "soft information," which banks are not allowed to gather. In the case of earlier crowdfunding campaigns, the borrowers and lenders knew each other; the social relationship thus facilitates the screening of borrowers. Today, this kind of proximity is not typical among the borrowers and lenders. Yet, the narratives that borrowers submit can contain sensitive information and as shown in the next section, have a high impact on investors' decisions. The fact that platform lending is the most intense in consumer lending when informational asymmetry is at its highest (see Table 1) also confirms the importance of the information that banks are prohibited from collecting.

3.3 *Liquidity Shocks*

As depositors face uncertain future consumption needs, a depository institution can create value by providing insurance against idiosyncratic liquidity shocks, unless utility-maximizing depositors choose short-term investments and the long-term higher return investments fail to get enough financing. Platforms exist primarily to match investors and borrowers, so investors must be prepared to meet liquidity needs by holding cash in separate reserves. Recently, many platforms operate a secondary market that encourages lenders to enter into longer-term contracts and sell their investment in the case of a liquidity shortage. It is also important to note that in contrast to banks, platforms are not exposed to bank runs, which can happen if more depositors withdraw their funds not because of liquidity needs but for fear of the other depositors' actions.

3.4 *Benefits of P2P Lending*

P2P lending is a rapidly expanding phenomenon, even if its whole market is only a fraction of the entire credit market. Such growth suggests that it should be advantageous in some aspects compared to the banks. However, none of the listed market imperfections emerge as the obvious rationale for the existence of these platforms. The most important argument in favor of P2P marketplaces may be that they are not subject to regulations as strict as those imposed on banks, so they operate more cost-efficiently.

P2P platforms can also offer funding solutions to those who are not targets of bank lending, as they can better reduce information asymmetry by using soft information and the technological development of data processing. Some borrowers turn to P2P platforms after exhausting their banking financing possibilities, or after being rejected by banks due to the procyclical nature of the banking system's risk management practices. The latter shrinks the banks' risk appetite when it is mostly needed by the small-sized borrowers. Less-regulated platforms are not exposed to the changes of the regulation, and they are not forced to reduce their credit supply if regulatory requirements become stricter, so they can offer less volatile access to financing than banks.

Investors, on the other hand, are attracted by the achievable return. In recent years, the near-zero interest rate environment pushed investors toward riskier alternative investments that have the potential to offer superior returns. As the platforms allow for diversification by financing small fractions of many individual loans, both active and passive investment strategies can be followed. Besides the already listed rational explanations, behavioral effects can also play a role on the lenders' side; for example, investors may suppose that they can better judge the borrowers' creditworthiness. This self-confidence is an irrational explanation for the popularity of direct financing that is not enhancing utility.

4 Empirical Results on P2P Lending

P2P lending is in its early stages. However, interested parties have already conducted a number of studies, focusing on the different dimensions of the segment. In general, studies investigate the following three issues: the nature and role of the platforms in the financial market (e.g., De Roure et al., 2016; Milne & Parboteeah, 2016), the main factors driving the decisions of investors (e.g., Gavurova et al., 2018; Larrimore et al., 2011), and portfolio performance (e.g., Emekter et al., 2015; Klafft, 2008).

4.1 The Role of P2P Lending

Although there are some aspects in which P2P platforms have an advantage when compared to banks, as shown in the previous section, it is not obvious whether platforms serve the credit demand that is unmet by banks, or whether they compete for the same clients.

De Roure et al. (2016) examine a banking and a P2P portfolio dataset and conclude that platforms serve the underbanked segment of customers with low credit ratings, which is out of the scope for conventional banks. Thus, such platforms play a complementary role to this customer group. While funding customers with low credit ratings and a high probability of default is not worth it for banks, it can still be profitable for lending platforms.

Milne and Parboteeah (2016) support this concept of collaboration, predicting that platforms have a complementary function in lending activity. Specifically, they supplement traditional banks because banks possess few comparative advantages, which exclude platforms to compete with them. The two parties may cooperate in the future; however, the research emphasizes that P2P marketplaces should develop their risk management practices and keep in mind prevailing regulatory requirements.

In contrast to the above results, Tang (2019) found that when investigating the unsecured consumer loan market in the United States, a negative shock in the bank's credit supply lowered the quality of P2P platforms' credits. The author concluded that platforms are substitutes for bank lending in terms of serving infra-marginal bank borrowers, yet they also complement bank lending when it comes to small loans. These results also suggest that the credit expansion of P2P lending was based on the borrowers who already have access to bank credit.

Morse (2015) shows that the majority of the loans were used for credit card debt retirement (25%) and debt consolidation (61%). By comparing the size and the terms of the loans, P2P borrowers prove to be highly indebted individuals who are not likely to be extended further loans by their banks. Finally, Hemer (2011) argues that crowdfunding can be the right solution for early-stage start-up financing, and that it is at the very least complementary to classical forms of financing.

4.2 *Factors Influencing Investment Decisions*

Based on the number of researches, the most commonly researched topic deals with the success of lending, due to the fact that several platforms publish a wide range of data regarding their portfolio table and loan requests. The literature investigates various features of potential borrowers' candidacies that might support funding success. Some of them are quite intuitive; for example, Herzenstein et al. (2008) draw the conclusion from Prosper data that the financial strength of the applicant and the loan characteristics significantly impact the outcome. Specifically, higher borrower credit rating impacts the decision positively, resulting in a lower interest rate, while a high debt-to-income ratio had an adverse impact on funding. Gavurova et al. (2018) echo this conclusion. However, their analysis, conducted on the dataset of the European platform Bondora, implies that there are similarities in investment decisions regardless of the region.

The social lending application process provides the opportunity for several unlinked data sources to be considered in the decision. One of these data sources is the narrative, which is a brief note added to the application in order to personalize the request and to persuade lenders. Larrimore et al. (2011) prove the importance of word usage in posturing financial stability and ability to repay the loan as a positive indicator, and argue that including irrelevant information covering personal details comprises a negative indicator. Herzenstein et al. (2011) also investigate a number of narratives and support arguments for the relevance of narrative content.

Another influencing factor is the appearance of the potential debtor. Ravina (2008) found that "good-looking" applicants are more likely to receive funding compared to those determined to be "average-looking" by prospective lenders. Interestingly, the probability of default is higher among "attractive" debtors compared to "average-looking" applicants with similar financial backgrounds. This fact confirms that appearances have a strong influencing power and result in irrational investor decisions. Duarte et al. (2012) prove the importance of a "credible" appearance. Based on their analysis, debtors that look "trustworthy" are more likely to obtain a loan and to pay a lower interest rate. The authors test the performance of trustworthy borrowers with historical portfolio data, leading to the result that debtors with credible appearances have better credit ratings and are less likely to default. Moreover, Pope and Sydnor (2011) highlight the influence of race: Black applicants are funded with a lower probability and a higher final interest rate compared to white debtors with the same credit characteristics. However, they find that the default rate is also higher among Black borrowers. Barasinska and Schäfer (2014) investigate gender in a German site's dataset and conclude that there is no significant difference between male and female applicants in terms of funding.

An often-mentioned benefit of social lending is the knowledge of the crowd. Lin et al. (2013) find that social connectors serve as a good indicator of the credit quality of the borrower. Specifically, debtors with a broad friendship network, including friends with better credit rating grades, are more successful at receiving loans; their default rate is also lower. Freedman and Jin (2008) strengthen the claim that social relations and group membership within the platform lead to a higher chance of funding coupled with lower interest rates. Groups can conduct monitoring activities and incite borrowers for good performance.

4.3 Performance of P2P Portfolios

Another direction that a subsection of P2P literature explores is credit risk, which covers portfolio performance and the probability of default. Emekter et al. (2015) deduce that financial stability measures are good predictors of future performance. Concretely, debt-to-income ratio, revolving credit utilization, and FICO score prove to be significant in terms of the paying capacity of the debtor.

In terms of investment return, Klafft (2008) shows that by following a few basic investment rules, lenders can expect higher returns. Currently, good returns are observable only in high rating category loan cases; the decisions of investors should be made with due care.

Interestingly, by examining the narratives, Herzenstein et al. (2011) find that although identity claims like "trustworthy" or "successful" improve the funding availability and the condition of the credit for the borrower, they are not correlated with the loan performance. This result also confirms our hypothesis that unsubstantiated assumptions can impact funding decisions.

5 Regulatory Framework

One of the main challenges in terms of the expansion and long-term maintenance of marketplace lending is compliance with regulatory requirements. This segment has barely been regulated. However, in recent years, more and more supervisory authorities have started to monitor social lending and some of these have attempted to implement a comprehensive regulatory framework for the market. Most regulatory materials mainly discuss associated challenges and suggest recommendations rather than concrete regulations. Yet, a few laws have already been passed, which provide a framework for the operations of marketplace lending.

In the case of the US market, the most commonly referenced regulation act is the Securities Act of 1933. To understand the regulation's relevance, we must clarify the business model of US platforms. According to the practice of the largest platforms, loans are provided through a bank and the platform acts as an intermediary between the parties. As a first step, the bank issues the loan. Following this step, the platform purchases the obligation and sells it to the investor. In this model, the issued notes are considered securities, meaning that they fall under the Securities Act. This solution circumnavigates the need for a lending license in each state, as the bank deals with different regulatory requirements (LendingClub Corporation, 2014). The Securities Act states that each security traded in the United States has to be registered and a prospectus has to be issued regularly, the latter covering the primary information regarding the company and the investments in order to properly inform investors (SEC, 2013). As of 2008, the Securities and Exchange Commission (SEC) determined that Prosper violated these regulations and issued a cease-and-desist order, which highlights that the notes provided by Prosper are considered as investments and that these require registration (SEC, 2008). This order is considered a milestone in the P2P segment of the United States; it also caused a temporary shutdown of the marketplaces in 2008 (Schonfeld, 2008). From that point on, all platforms had to register their notes and publish the required reports, which increased transparency around their operations and somewhat decreased risk for investors. However, it is worth noting that compliance with the SEC requirements is quite expensive for the platforms (from administrative point of view) and also constrains new players from entering the market (Magee, 2011). Later, platforms sought regulatory facilitation from the Dodd-Frank Wall Street Reform and Consumer Protection Act of 2010. Prosper lobbied to appoint the Consumer Financial Protection Bureau (CFPB) as the main supervisory authority of the segment, in order to be exempt from the Securities Act. In the end, however, the proposal was refused (Tsai, 2018).

The United Kingdom's regulatory perspective requires a separate discussion. The market is quite developed in this region. As previously mentioned, the very first platform was implemented in the United Kingdom in 2005 (Zopa, 2020). The entity responsible for regulating marketplace lending is the Financial Conduct Authority (FCA). According to the FCA, social P2P lending is considered a financial intermediary; comprehensive regulation is thus applied to the segment. In line with market evolution, the rules expended and tightened and social lending officially became a regulated activity. The most recent related law was published in 2019 by FCA. The ultimate goal of the regulations is to protect investors and to ensure the sustainable operation of marketplaces. Measures include the introduction of an investment limit for new-to-market customers in order to control risk, where a maximum of 10% of the lender's net investible asset may be invested through P2P lending. Further restrictions relate to the risk management process and cover the requirements for credit risk assessment as well as a fair valuation method. Another crucial part of the regulations is the proper informing of investors; platforms have to assess the potential lenders' knowledge of the segment and specify the minimum information, which they should share with investors in order to support their decision (FCA, 2019).

In the case of Europe, when regulations exist, they are mostly on a national level. At the EU level, the European Commission published a proposal for crowdfunding in 2018. However, the paper principally focused on lending platforms for SMEs (European Commission, 2018). In the case of consumer lending, regulation depends on the internationality of the marketplace. Inasmuch as the platform provides cross-border services, it can be regulated by the European Securities and Markets Authority (ESMA) as a single supervisor, which provides integrated regulation for operations. Otherwise, the platform can choose to operate on a domestic basis, where national regulations apply instead of a unified set of rules. Since platforms hold the customers' funds when they link the two parties, this activity falls under the Second Directive on Payment Services. According to the regulations, marketplaces should provide sufficient information to the customers about how they ensure the protection of the funding (Jorgensen, 2018). Overall, while there is a broad EU-wide framework for marketplace lending operations, there is still space for further clarification in the case of existing legislation.

6 Summary

P2P lending is a form of alternative finance which refers to direct finance between lenders and borrowers through an online platform without an intermediary institution. Online P2P marketplaces are intended to operate more inexpensively by saving the cost of intermediation. Removing a layer of the lending process reduces cost, but as banks still generate the majority of credit relationships (98%), the cost efficiency of disintermediation only partly exceeds the benefits of an intermediary institution. The most significant advantages of these platforms are their flexibility in implementing the newest technological solutions, such as artificial intelligence and big data processing, as well as their ability to collect sensitive data, which reduces information asymmetry in the segment with less transparent borrowers. They are also free from the costly capital requirements of banks, as they have no credit exposure in their balance sheet. In addition to the above arguments, behavioral factors also contribute to the popularity of these platforms, which often results in problematic investment decisions. There is no comprehensive regulatory framework in the P2P segment; yet, initial regulations have been implemented in some countries. The future of P2P lending depends both on how regulation develops in the coming years, as well as on banks' participation in meeting challenges associated with this still-developing lending framework.

Acknowledgements This research was supported by the Higher Education Institutional Excellence Program 2020 of the Ministry for Innovation and Technology in the framework of the "Financial and Public Services" research project (reference number: TKP2020-IKA-02) at Corvinus University of Budapest.

References

Barasinska, N., & Schäfer, D. (2014). Is crowdfunding different? Evidence on the relation between gender and funding success from a German peer-to-peer lending platform. *German Economic Review, 15*(4), 436–452. https://doi.org/10.1111/geer.12052.

Bazot, G. (2018). Financial consumption and the cost of finance: Measuring financial efficiency in Europe (1950–2007). *Journal of the European Economic Association, 16*(1), 123–160. https://doi.org/10.1093/jeea/jvx008.

Belleflamme, P., Lambert, T., & Schwienbacher, A. (2014). Crowdfunding: Tapping the right crowd. *Journal of Business Venturing, 29*(5), 585–609. https://doi.org/10.1016/j.jbusvent.2013.07.003.

Bondora. (2020). *Statistics*. Bondora. https://www.bondora.com/en/public-statistics.

Cambridge Centre for Alternative Finance. (2020). *The global alternative finance market benchmarking report: Trends, opportunities and challenges for lending, equity, and non-investment alternative finance models*. https://www.jbs.cam.ac.uk/wp-content/uploads/2020/08/2020-04-22-ccaf-global-alternative-finance-market-benchmarking-report.pdf.

Diamond, D. W. (1984). Financial intermediation and delegated monitoring. *The Review of Economic Studies, 51*(3), 393–414. https://doi.org/10.2307/2297430.

De Roure, C., Pelizzon, L., & Tasca, P. (2016). *How does P2P lending fit into the consumer credit market?* https://www.bundesbank.de/resource/blob/704046/b53dc281b4666672e6d526a35e50fd50/mL/2016-08-12-dkp-30-data.pdf.

Duarte, J., Siegel, S., & Young, L. (2012). Trust and credit: The role of appearance in peer-to-peer lending. *The Review of Financial Studies, 25*(8), 2455–2484. https://doi.org/10.1093/rfs/hhs071.

Emekter, R., Tu, Y., Jirasakuldech, B., & Lu, M. (2015). Evaluating credit risk and loan performance in online Peer-to-Peer (P2P) lending. *Applied Economics, 47*(1), 54–70. https://doi.org/10.1080/00036846.2014.962222.

European Commission. (2018). *Proposal for a regulation of the European Parliament and of the Council on European Crowdfunding Service Providers (ECSP) for business*. https://eur-lex.europa.eu/legal-content/EN/TXT/?uri=CELEX%3A52018PC0113.

European Credit Research Institute. (2019). *Lending to European households and non-financial corporations: Growth and trends*. http://www.ecri.eu/sites/default/files/key_findings_ecri_2019_final.pdf.

FCA. (2019). *Loan-based ('peer-to-peer') and investment-based crowdfunding platforms: Feedback to CP18/20 and final rules*. https://www.fca.org.uk/publication/policy/ps19-14.pdf.

FED. (2020, November 6). *Consumer credit - G.19*. Board of governors of the federal reserve system. https://www.federalreserve.gov/releases/g19/current/.

Fellow Finance. (2020). *Statistics*. Fellow Finance. https://www.fellowfinance.com/for-investor/statistics..

Freedman, S., & Jin, G. Z. (2008). *Do social networks solve information problems for peer-to-peer lending? Evidence from Prosper.com* (NET Institute Working Paper No. 08–43). Indiana University, Bloomington: School of Public & Environmental Affairs Research Paper No. 2008–11–06. https://papers.ssrn.com/sol3/papers.cfm?abstract_id=1936057.

Freixas, X., & Rochet, J. C. (2008). *Microeconomics of banking*. MIT Press.

Gavurova, B., Dujcak, M., Kovac, V., & Kotásková, A. (2018). Determinants of successful loan application at peer-to-peer lending market. *Economics & Sociology, 11*(1), 85–99. https://doi.org/10.14254/2071-789X.2018/11-1/6.

Hemer, J. (2011). *A snapshot on crowdfunding* (No. R2/2011). Arbeitspapiere Unternehmen und Region. https://www.econstor.eu/bitstream/10419/52302/1/671522264.pdf.

Havrylchyk, O., & Verdier, M. (2018). The financial intermediation role of the P2P lending platforms. *Comparative Economic Studies, 60*(1), 115–130. https://doi.org/10.1057/s41294-017-0045-1.

Herzenstein, M., Andrews, R. L., Dholakia, U. M., & Lyandres, E. (2008). The democratization of personal consumer loans? Determinants of success in online peer-to-peer lending communities. *Boston University School of Management Research Paper, 14*(6), 1–36.

Herzenstein, M., Sonenshein, S., & Dholakia, U. M. (2011). Tell me a good story and I may lend you money: The role of narratives in peer-to-peer lending decisions. *Journal of Marketing Research, 48*(SPL), S138–S149. https://papers.ssrn.com/sol3/papers.cfm?abstract_id=1840668.

Jorgensen, T. (2018). Peer-to-Peer lending-a new digital intermediary, new legal challenges. *Nordic Journal of Commercial Law, 1*, 231–260. https://doi.org/10.5278/ojs.njcl.v0i1.2491.

Klafft, M. (2008). Online peer-to-peer lending: A lenders' perspective. *In Proceedings of the international conference on E-learning, E-business, enterprise information systems, and E-government, EEE*. Proceedings of the International Conference on E-Learning, E-Business, Enterprise Information Systems, and E-Government. https://papers.ssrn.com/sol3/papers.cfm?abstract_id=1352352.

Larrimore, L., Jiang, L., Larrimore, J., Markowitz, D., & Gorski, S. (2011). Peer to peer lending: The relationship between language features, trustworthiness, and persuasion success. *Journal of Applied Communication Research, 39*(1), 19–37. https://doi.org/10.1080/00909882.2010.536844.

LendingClub. (2020a). *About LendingClub*. LendingClub. https://www.lendingclub.com/company/about-us.

LendingClub. (2020b). *LendingClub statistics*. Lending Club. https://www.lendingclub.com/info/statistics.action.

LendingClub Corporation. (2014). *Registration statement*. https://www.sec.gov/Archives/edgar/data/1409970/000119312514323136/d766811ds1.htm.

Lin, M., Prabhala, N. R., & Viswanathan, S. (2013). Judging borrowers by the company they keep: Friendship networks and information asymmetry in online peer-to-peer lending. *Management Science, 59*(1), 17–35. https://doi.org/10.2139/ssrn.1355679.

Magee, J. R. (2011). Peer-to-peer lending in the United States: Surviving after Dodd-Frank. *NC Banking Inst., 15*, 139.

Milne, A., & Parboteeah, P. (2016). The business models and economics of peer-to-peer lending. *European Credit Research Institute*. https://doi.org/10.2139/ssrn.2763682.

Mintos. (2020a). *About us*. Mintos. https://www.mintos.com/en/about-us/about-us/.

Mintos. (2020b). *Statistics*. Mintos. https://www.mintos.com/en/statistics/.

Morse, A. (2015). Peer-to-peer crowdfunding: Information and the potential for disruption in consumer lending. *Annual Review of Financial Economics, 7*, 463–482. https://doi.org/10.3386/w20899.

NYSE. (2014). *Trust & transparency: How LendingClub serves an evolving marketplace*. NYSE. https://www.nyse.com/network/article/nyse-lendingclub.

P2PMarketData. (2020). *Top 90 alternative financing platforms by funding volumes: Crowdfunding investments, peer-to-peer lending & online lending*. P2PMarketData. https://p2pmarketdata.com/.

Philippon, T. (2016). *The fintech opportunity*. National Bureau of Economic Research. http://pages.stern.nyu.edu/~tphilipp/papers/FinTech.pdf.

Pope, D. G., & Sydnor, J. R. (2011). What's in a picture? Evidence of discrimination from Prosper.com. *Journal of Human Resources, 46*(1), 53–92.

Prosper Funding LLC. (2020). *$1,000,000,000 borrower payment dependent notes*. https://www.prosper.com/Downloads/Legal/Prosper_Prospectus_2020-07-21.pdf.

Ratesetter. (2020). *Ratesetter statistics*. Ratesetter. https://www.ratesetter.com/invest/statistics.

Ravina, E. (2008). Love & loans: The effect of beauty and personal characteristics in credit markets. *Journal of Finance*. https://papers.ssrn.com/sol3/papers.cfm?abstract_id=1107307.

Schonfeld E. (2008). *SEC outlines its reasoning for shutting down P2P lender prosper*. TechCrunch. https://techcrunch.com/2008/11/26/sec-outlines-its-reasoning-for-shutting-down-p2p-lender-prosper/.

SEC. (2008). *Order instituting cease-and-desist proceedings pursuant to Section 8a of the Securities Act of 1933, making findings, and imposing a cease-and-desist order*. https://www.sec.gov/litigation/admin/2008/33-8984.pdf.

SEC. (2013). *The laws that govern the securities industry*. https://www.sec.gov/answers/about-lawsshtml.html#secact1933.

Tang, H. (2019). Peer-to-peer lenders versus banks: Substitutes or complements? *The Review of Financial Studies, 32*(5), 1900–1938. https://doi.org/10.1093/rfs/hhy137

Tsai, C. H. (2018). To regulate or not to regulate: A comparison of government responses to peer-to-peer lending among the United States, China, and Taiwan. *University of Cincinnati Law Review, 87*(4), 1077.

Twino. (2020). *Statistics*. Twino. https://www.twino.eu/en/statistics.

Walter, G. (2019). Vállalatfinanszírozás a gyakorlatban-Lehetőségek és döntések a magyar piacon.Alinea Kiadó.

Zopa. (2020). *About us*. Zopa. https://www.zopa.com/about.

The Role of Social Financing in Sustainable Development: The Case of Nigerian Co-operatives

Ajibola Anthony Akanji

1 Introduction

There have been several attempts at bridging class disparity and addressing disempowerment in Nigeria. A frontline model in this regard is cooperativism, as it encompasses cooperatives and solidarity economics. The model has shown resilience in elevating individuals and groups from the lower rungs of the socio-economic pyramid because of its capacity to bridge socio-economic divides (particularly between the working class and the owners of the means of production) and to sustain development. Cooperativism achieved a high degree of success in Nigeria's defunct Western region, particularly from 1954 to 1966. The cooperatives' structures, especially at the grassroots level, have been known to pull scattered, and sometimes even diverse, micro-resources into fewer units of macro-resources. With this approach, marginalized classes of society, when acting in solidarity, can undertake socio-economic adventures that were previously unthinkable because of their lack of individual power. Due to the complexities of the conventional financial market in obtaining loans, such

A. A. Akanji (✉)
Lead City University, Ibadan, Nigeria

T. Walker et al. (eds.), *Innovations in Social Finance*,
https://doi.org/10.1007/978-3-030-72535-8_19

as the requirements for registration, the magnitude of collateral security, and high interest rates, alternatives like cooperatives have evolved. This practice provides basic financing at minimal cost and the model supports the socio-economic mobility of the working class as well as the sustainable development of society. Although an impressive phenomenon, economic, social, and political dynamics introduce aggravating factors that must be addressed periodically. Hence, the Nigerian cooperative movement's intersections with social financing and sustainable development are significant in charting paths to further frontiers.

2 Conceptual Clarifications

2.1 Cooperatives and the Social Economy

The International Co-operative Alliance (ICA, 1995) and the International Labour Organization (ILO, 2015) both define cooperatives as autonomous organizations of persons that unite voluntarily to meet their common economic, social, and cultural needs and aspirations through jointly owned and democratically controlled enterprise. Cooperatives are managed by seven principles and six values jointly known as cooperative ethics.[1]

Cooperatives play socio-economic and political roles in communities; through these communities, cooperatives reach subnational, national, and international levels. They have been known to offer complementary resources and, in some cases, alternatives to the governmental institutions in the provision of social overheads. The term social economy qualifies the cooperatives' activities in various sectors and subsectors, such as agriculture, banking, insurance and mutuals, credit unions, education, industries, and trade unions. By applying their principles and values, they reconcile any divisions that may arise due to different life experiences (social factors such as ethnicity, religion, race, educational background) using profits; they are distinct in their combination of business enterprises and social institutions. The integration of social considerations into profitability is at the center of the social solidarity economy and is the cooperative movement's main target.

[1] The principles are: voluntary and open membership; democratic member control; member economic participation; autonomy and independence; education, training, and information; cooperation among co-operatives; and concern for community. The values are self-help, self-responsibility, democracy, equality, equity, and solidarity.

2.2 *Financial Services and Social Financing*

Financing services refer to the commercial involvement of banks, insurance companies, stockbrokers, and fund managers in the economy. They are, in the strict sense, profit-oriented businesses mainly dominated by private sector investments. The imperative of maximizing returns on investments to guarantee survival, growth, and expansion, while integrating social considerations into their operations, often sees the latter kept to barest minimum (UNCTAD, 2015). The consequence is that a part of the population, particularly those in lower socio-economic classes, cannot afford their services and are thus excluded. Unfortunately, it is this excluded population that requires the very financial assistance for economic survival and upward socio-economic mobility that they are denied. Hence, there is need for services that align with their specific needs. Social financing runs on one of the core characteristics of cooperatives: the reconciliation of social consideration and profitability. It comes in variants, such as through community banks, microfinance banks, and cooperative banks. They seek to offer solutions to the challenges faced by those excluded by conventional institutions. A good example is the provision by LAPO Microfinance Bank of soft loans with low interest rates and without collateral securities to traders in their group capacities or with moveable collateral in the case of individual traders.

2.3 *Sustainable Development*

A 1987 UN report by the Brundtland Commission defines sustainable development as "the development that meets the needs of the present without compromising future generations' ability to meet their own needs" (WCED, 1987). It centers on the goals of reconciling diverse needs, for example, the needs of the environment and the needs of the economy, as well as the needs of different classes. This negotiation is similar to the practice of reconciling profitability with social peculiarities. In conjunction with other development partners, the United Nations Development Programme (UNDP, 2015) advances the current Sustainable Development Goals (SDGs) as an international public policy instrument. The SDGs have since been integrated into public and private policy frameworks at various tiers across the world. Cooperatives and social financing initiatives have been identified as major mechanisms in actualizing of the SDGs.

3 Social Financing and the Nigerian Cooperative Movement

The terms microfinance, sustainable finance, micro-enterprise finance, and micro-credit can be used interchangeably (Oluyombo, 2007). All these terms capture the essence of social financing in Nigeria, because the institutions involved provide small-scale alternatives to conventional financial services. In recent times, these terms are all captured under the umbrella of "microfinance banks." Otero and Rhyne (1994) describe these banks as the result of the revolutionary involvement of the large-scale provision of small loans and deposit services to low-income people through secured, conveniently located, and competing commercial, financial institutions; these generate the process needed to democratize capital. The outcome that this comprehensive definition implies is desirable but, unfortunately, does not always come to pass.

In 2001, the Central Bank of Nigeria (CBN) began the complete deregulation of Nigerian banks through the release of circular reference BSD/DO/CIR/Vol. 1/10/2000, which, among other goals, mandated banks to recapitalize to the minimum base of N25 billion. This reform pushed out many players from the market; the number of banks reduced from 89 to 21 as many was unable to meet the capital base minimum. However, this also led to the introduction of a new model of banking in Nigeria: the microfinance bank.

In 2005 the CBN, following the CBN Act's provisions and those of the Banks and Other Financial Institutions Acts (BOFIA), released a microfinance policy. Before this policy, microfinance banks were not statutorily recognized. According to the policy, the financing instruments or products of microfinance banks include the following:

1. Deposit: The availability to deposit generates an aggressive savings mobilization from the grassroots level. Microfinancing may be operated on a daily, weekly, or monthly saving (deposit) basis.
2. Credit: Low-income groups or individuals and micro-, small-, and medium-scale enterprises can use their credit (deposit) as capital. This improves access to loan facilities.
3. Collateral substitution: The traditional immovable collateral required by conventional banks for loan acquisition, which is often beyond the reach of the micro-, small-, and medium-scale enterprises, is substituted. The substitutions are moveable collaterals,

group guarantees, community collateralization, and compulsory savings.

According to Oluyombo (2007), the CBN identified the following in 2006 as the features of social financing in Nigeria:

1. Small loans for customers;
2. Small contributions from customers;
3. The absence of asset-based collateral;
4. Simple operations;
5. The extension of banking services beyond the economic toward the social;
6. The promotion of an interpersonal relationship between the bank and its customers as means to build trust; and
7. The programming of a bank's products and services around micro- and small-scale, local enterprises.

Prior to the arrival of microfinance banks in Nigeria, cooperative societies operated according to the offshoots of traditional/informal models of social financing in forms of Esusu/Itutu/Adashin or daily/periodic contributions. These, according to Nwanyawu (2011), were contribution-based savings schemes that functioned on the basis of loans, rotating savings, and regular saving deposits to a thrift collector. The introduction of modern cooperatives in Nigeria has gradually reduced these to the bare minimum.

Cooperatives have played a significant role in Nigeria's socio-economic development in the colonial and post-colonial eras; they were particularly impactful on the agricultural sector's development and viability, which was then a cornerstone of the Nigerian economy. They were integral to the socio-economic development achieved by the defunct Western (not to be confused for Westernized) region of Nigeria.

The flow of these developments was altered by the discovery of crude oil in 1966 and its gradual integration into the mainstream Nigerian economy. Consequently, the agricultural sector was relegated from its erstwhile position as the mainstream of the Nigerian economy. On the one hand, crude oil offers enormous earnings in the short run; it is capital-intensive and not labor-intensive. On the other hand, agriculture, which is less capital-intensive, requires more laborers and offers more employment opportunities. Furthermore, the 1980s brought an economic recession, and one of the solutions was the adoption of the International Monetary Fund's (IMF) Structural Adjustment Program. This allowed for a reduction of public sector spending on social intervention programs, and therefore a decrease in government subsidies, on which cooperatives were reliant (Schwettmann, 2014).

During the 1980s, agitations for the return to civil rule from military rule and allegations of corrupt practices in government beamed accusatory light onto the management of public finances. This appraisal of government finances exposed the realities that cooperatives were not only a development partner to government, but also conduit pipes for the corrupt practices of government officials. This fueled fierce criticism of cooperatives from civil rights organizations and reduced government patronage (Schwettmann, 2012).

Nonetheless, this scandal did not decrease Nigeria's need for cooperatives and other allied mechanisms in the fight to democratize the economy. Due to economic downturn, it became imperative to strengthen the economy with more social financing. Some of these initiatives, which eventually served as social financing mechanisms, started before the economic downturn of the 1980s and lasted through the 1990s. A first example of such a mechanism is the Nigerian Agricultural and Cooperative Bank (NACB). It was established in 1973 for the purpose of providing financial services through the utilization of structures from the cooperative movement to identify qualified agricultural cooperatives that were then granted loans for agricultural and allied purposes, on terms in accordance with social financing. The NACB disbursed agricultural loans to 6,286 farmers between 1990 and 1994. A second example is the Agricultural Credit Guarantee Scheme Fund (ACGSF), a CBN response to the inability of micro and small farms to secure loans from conventional banks. The initiative was programmed to fill the vacuum between farmers and conventional financial institutions with packages from the collateral of CBN for credit acquisition. This proved successful between rural farmers and urban-based financial institutions.

More recent initiatives include community banks, the Family Economic Advancement Programme, the National Economic Reconstruction Fund, the National Directorate of Employment, the Small and Medium Enterprises Equity Investment Scheme, the Small and Medium Enterprises Development Agency of Nigeria, and the National Poverty Eradication

Programme (NAPEP). Of these, the following have been particularly effective:

1. Community banks: They were established and managed by communities, cooperative societies, social clubs, and town associations, among others. They are self-sustaining and work toward the provision of financial services to host communities or identified groups so as to foster individual and group survival, growth, and enhanced socio-economic development at the grassroots level.
2. The National Directorate of Employment (NDE): The emphasis of the NDE was on the development of vocational skills for the unemployed and the promotion of quality artisanship. Beneficiaries were given soft loans at the completion of their training and were encouraged to work in unions (cooperatives).
3. The National Poverty Eradication Programme (NAPEP): It was designed to replace the Poverty Alleviation Programme of the federal government of Nigeria, which was launched earlier in 2000. NAPEP was established in 2001 with 3 goals: (a) skill acquisition, (b) agricultural development and extension, and (c) the provision of micro-credits to beneficiaries. A striking feature of NAPEP is that it supported the first mass tricycle transportation program in Nigeria. This began in the commercial capital of Lagos. The tricycles, nicknamed "Keke NAPEP" (which translate to NAPEP tricycles, as *keke* is the local vocabulary word for bicycle or tricycle), were given as loans to the beneficiaries. It provided jobs for many as well as a cheap and fast means of transportation for many more. Gradually, however, these became dangerous on the roads of Lagos and several other cities due to their overwhelming number and the reckless driving of some of their operators.

Since 2000, Nigerian cooperatives have become more resilient through the adoption of innovative social financing, particularly with the adoption of the multipurpose model of cooperative societies. The emergence of manufacturing cooperatives as well as the advancement in marketing, thrift, and savings cooperatives has been instrumental to the agricultural industry and rural development (Nnadozie, 2015). Sustainable development in Nigeria's rural areas is an integral part of addressing the parasitic rural–urban drift, and by consequence retaining the gains accruable from urban development. Moreover, Akanle and Busari (2014) identify that cooperatives function as important mechanisms to the discourse of development in South-western Nigerian. They premise this assertion with the fact that cooperatives have proved important to socio-economic functionalism and social capital development both in years past and in contemporary times. The authors' assertions gain more traction with the growing reception accorded to cooperatives since the return of civil rule to Nigeria in 1999. The growing relevance of cooperatives to national development saw the admission of two new Nigerian apex cooperative societies: Odua Cooperative Conglomerate (OCC) and Nigerian Cooperatives Multipurpose Society Limited (NNPC CMS). Both of these were admitted into the International Cooperative Alliance in 2013, bringing the number of Nigerian members to three.

In recent times, one of the domains in which cooperatives are most active is within the field of housing and property development, a field in which Nigeria is currently disadvantaged under the weight of massive deficit. It is now commonplace to see cooperatives acquire large expanses of land for housing purposes and thereafter apportion such land to their members. Another emerging trend is the building of shopping malls and residential estates for commercial purposes by cooperative societies. Examples of such developments are:

1. The acquisition of land for housing purposes by the following cooperatives societies:
   a. Lead City Cooperative Society;
   b. Nigerian Institute of Social and Economic Research Cooperative Society;
   c. Federal College of Agriculture, Ibadan Cooperative Society, etc.
2. The building of shopping malls and residential estates:
   a. University College Hospital, Ibadan Cooperative Society;
   b. Nigerian National Petroleum Corporation Cooperative Society;
   c. Sumal Foods Nigeria Limited Cooperative Society, etc.

These initiatives exist alongside the increasing number of giant cooperative societies, such as the Nigeria Police Cooperative Society and the Nigerian Security and Civil Defense Corps Cooperatives Society. These large cooperatives (primary cooperative societies with very high number of members, e.g., over a thousand) possess the capability to own and run their social finance institution or to channel their resources into a single social finance institution. Examples of the latter are the Nigerian Police Microfinance Bank and the Nigerian Police Insurance Company.

The growing relevance of the cooperative model and social financing is, however, impeded by the current state of Nigerian laws. Various solutions are currently proffered to address the challenges of inadequate legal framework on cooperatives and allied matters in Nigeria. At the forefront of the campaign is the Coop4Dev, an initiative of the partnership of the International Cooperative Alliance and the European Union-sponsored Nigerian Legal Framework Analysis Report.

4 Challenges of Social Financing/Cooperatives in Nigeria

Cooperatives have become more integral to social financing in Nigeria, with more people willing to adopt the model. Nevertheless, social financing in Nigeria has not been able to optimize its potential due to a broad spectrum of challenges caused by the following problems:

1. Poor synergy between the private and the public sectors: The public sector in Nigeria is tremendously bureaucratic and it is not run with profit in mind. Rather, it is often run as an expenditure and at a loss. For example, socio-economic overheads such as education, health, and roads are built with government funding and maintained with heavy government subsidies. These sectors rent from the petroleum industry, which offers a relatively stable source of government revenue to sustain this nonprofit, non-commercial, and heavily subsidized public sector. The contrast to the case of the private sector is clear, where business capitals are sourced competitively, such as through loans from commercial banks. Moreover, there is less bureaucracy, which allows for fast decision-making processes. The disparity in these modes of operation stands as a hindrance to possible synergy between the two sectors, but is preferable to an unbalance relationship in favor of the private sector. In such instances, subsidies meant for the public are channeled through the private sector and the private sector is part of the beneficiaries.

2. Poor synergy between the informal and the formal sectors: The formal sector consists of registered businesses and registered companies. These actors are enabled by relevant laws and other rules of engagement. A significant portion of their business must be documented in accordance with laws such as the Companies and Allied Matters Act, which puts a constraint on their capacity to engage in business with the informal sector. Unlike the informal sector, members of the formal sector are often without any form of documented identity and are at best a registered business name. Its informality encumbers the informal sector in many of its attempts to engage in business with the formal sector. For example, commercial banks give loans only to formal organizations or individuals associated with formal organizations. Consequently, the large number of members of the Nigerian informal sector cannot access loans from commercial, although they operate accounts with such banks by virtue of registering their business names.
3. Diversion of funds: Public funds that are meant to subsidize either government officials or departments often divert the cost of doing business, particularly in the agricultural sector and the micro-, small-, and medium-scale enterprises, private businesses employed as intermediaries, and on some occasions by the beneficiaries to endeavors which are not within the scope of specific programs. Such misappropriation of funds defeats well-conceived initiatives.
4. Political interference: This refers to both the public administration carried out through the activities of the various government ministries, departments, and agencies as well as the roles of politicians and political parties. While governance might put in place well-thought out policies, the execution might be constrained by politicians' involvement. For example, the ruling political party often attempts to sustain party members' patronage by giving them unwarranted advantages in the review of applications for government subsidies. Moreover, changes in government could imply changes in government policies, because the governance structure is built more around individuals (politicians) and less around institutions.
5. Low level of technical expertise: Although expertise in conventional finance is at a reasonably high level in Nigeria, due to long years of practice and the reconciliation of their needs into the educational system, the opposite is the case with modern cooperatives and social

financing. Cooperatives and social financing occupy a smaller space in comparison with conventional finance in Nigeria. Virtually, all the postsecondary educational institutions have at least an undergraduate level course with the aim of serving the need of conventional finance. However, there are only three federal cooperative colleges in Nigeria.

5 The Intersection Between Cooperatives, Social Financing, and Sustainable Development in Nigeria

A feature common to many countries of the global south is that they face a plethora of regional, national, and international policy frameworks in which to operate during their pursuit of sustainable development. In many of these countries, there are waves of increased economic development, which are often harnessed by the upper socio-economic and political classes and, to some extent, by the middle class. In such instances, lower classes are left behind. Consequently, gains from economic development are concentrated in the hands of a few. As a result, such economies grow but develop at a slower pace, which in turn breeds inequalities. The multiple effects of these inequalities lead to repeated processes aimed at economic survival and growth without economic development. The cooperatives, through social financing, have provided solutions to readdress inequalities as emphasized by SDG 5 (Gender Equality) and SDG 10 (Reduced Inequality), through the following:

1. The application of cooperative principles, which seek to abolish restrictions to membership of cooperatives on the grounds of race, religion, gender, etc. The inequalities which result from a patriarchal tradition are addressed by the first of the cooperative principles: open membership. This has increased the involvement of women, particularly within the informal sector of the economy. To a large extent, it has contributed to the promotion of women's right to participate in economic activities within Nigerian society. Social financing complements this increased participation with the provision of soft loans to women in their bid to enter their various trades. Thus, cooperatives improve women's entry into business entrepreneurship, and social financing promotes their actual participation. Moreover, the cooperative principle of democratic member

control democratizes the administration and management of cooperative societies. Education, training, and access to information have been applied toward informing members of recent and emerging trends that pertain to their businesses, exemplified by the organizing of formal and informal training, where required.

2. The application of cooperative values, particularly self-help and self-responsibility, fosters hope among members of cooperative societies, both in their individual and joint capacities, so as not to resort to discouragement because of their disadvantaged economic position. Instead, these values encourage solidarity in working toward upward socio-economic mobility. Importantly, this also translates to the adoption of equity into the allocation of rights and responsibilities, assets, and liabilities.

Furthermore, private sector initiatives such as establishing community banks, microfinance banks, thrift and credit societies, credit practices by cooperative societies, and community/group loan schemes have been instrumental to the consolidation of these gains. The provision of social loans by the cooperatives and other allied enterprises has elevated the lower and middle classes in Nigeria, preventing both the collapse of these classes into abject poverty and the entire system's descent into chaos from aggravated inequalities. For example, the Nigerian Union of Teachers (NUT) Co-operative Society to the welfare of teachers, in particular the teachers' housing schemes, is a viable initiative supported by various cooperative societies that exist on Nigerian university campuses for both staff and faculty in support of their acquisition of properties. A more practical example is the relationship between organizations like the Lead City Cooperative Society and the Lead City Microfinance Bank, and the positive impact they have on the welfare of the staff and faculty of the Lead City University, Ibadan, Nigeria.

6 Social Financing in Other Developing Countries

Cooperatives and social financing contribute to sustainable development in many countries of the global south. Although social financing in these countries is still fraught with challenges, it has made its mark as an indispensable player in these countries' affairs. Two case studies serve to illustrate this point:

6.1 India

India and Nigeria are both former British colonies with similar social fabrics. Both have heterogeneous ethno-religious components and British-influenced civic institutions (Wani, 2016). Modern cooperatives were introduced into India by British colonialists. Thereafter, British colonialists introduced modern cooperatives into Nigeria based on their experience in India. The variant of modern cooperatives introduced by the British could be classified as a British-Indian hybrid (Lawal & Kamaldeen, 2013). India has some socio-economic challenges that are similar to those in Nigeria, such as mass poverty and suboptimal utilization of resources, particularly labor (Lawal & Kamaldeen, 2017). The country has, however, adopted more innovative approaches with its cooperatives and other social financing institutions. These institutions operate through regional-rural banks, cooperative banks, and small finance banks. These banks share a similar framework with the above-mentioned social banks. According to Sridevi (2014), other forms of social financing in India are:

1. Tamilnadu Adi Dravidar Housing Development Corporation (TAHDCO): This is a scheme for the improvement of the standard of living for those disadvantaged by the practice of the caste and tribal systems. It seeks to improve their artisanal, professional, and behavioral skills as a pathway toward upward socio-economic mobility.
2. Self-Employment Scheme for Ex-Servicemen (SEMPEX): This is a program designed for military members and affiliates (servicemen, ex-servicemen, widows of servicemen, and widows of ex-servicemen) with disabilities. It aims to create opportunities for them to access micro-credits for agricultural purposes or other businesses that are domiciled in rural areas.

A striking feature of both TAHDCO and SEMPEX is the reconciliation of the operations of regional-rural banks, cooperative banks, and small finance banks, specifically with respect to the operations of two out of the three conventional banks, i.e., public sector banks (national banks) and the private sector banks. This reconciliation integrates the substance of cooperatives into the banks and uses sustainable development. This contrasts the situation in Nigeria, where the operation of social banks is not coordinated along both horizontal and vertical structures.

6.2 Kenya

Although Kenya is located in East Africa, it is often considered part of the global south. The country shares a lot of similarities with Nigeria, such as legacies of British colonialization as well as both religious and ethnic heterogeneity. Unlike Nigeria, which has the fortune of rent revenue from the petroleum industry, Kenya has had to rely more on agriculture and allied industries to sustain its economy. Cooperatives and the social economy are an integral part of the Kenyan economy. The Kenyan cooperative movement is the largest in Africa, with its activities transcending virtually every area of national life, except for policing, external defense, and a few other areas. Cooperative activities in Kenya have been built with social financing. The Cooperative Bank of Kenya holds the second-largest customer base in Kenya and is the largest cooperative bank in Africa (CFI, 2020).

A striking feature of the Cooperative Bank of Kenya is how it shares the Indian model's integration of social banking into conventional banking, which is done by adopting a framework in which formal social financing is linked to conventional banking. The Cooperative Bank of Kenya is at once a conventional financial institution and a social financial institution. The Bank's vision is to become the dominant bank in Kenya and the East African region, riding on its unique cooperative model. The bank was established in Nairobi in 1968 as a cooperative bank and was listed in the Nairobi Stock Exchange in 2008. The bank integrated conventional banking into its operations in 1994. It currently operates in two countries, Kenya and South Sudan, with about 100 branches and 5 million customers. The bank's cooperative banking section provides financial solutions to the following: large Savings and Credit Co-operative Societies (SACCOs), housing SACCOs, agricultural and other cooperatives, transport SACCOs, and investment SACCOs. It also provides consultancy and capacity building services to cooperative societies.

The Cooperative Bank of Kenya has a stake in the insurance industry, as it holds 35.71% shareholding of the Co-operative Insurance Society Limited of Kenya. There is also a retail banking division that provides financial solutions to individual customers, as well as micro, small, and medium enterprises. The CoopHoldings Co-operative Society Limited is the largest shareholder of the Bank, with a holding of 64.50% (CBK, 2018).

The CoopHoldings Co-operative Society Limited is the group's strategic investor. Its shareholding is the amalgamation of shares previously held by 3,805 cooperative societies and unions, which were ring-fenced under the investor as a mechanism to retain the bank's critical cooperative identity. Although there is a functional over-the-counter (OTC) trading of shares held by cooperative societies, an iconic feature of this arrangement is that, although the bank's shareholding is allowed to be sold, it must be retained within the cooperative movement. Both the Indian and the Kenyan examples are precedents, supporting the assertion that social financing is practicable in the global south, while the Kenyan example goes further to support its practicability in sub-Saharan Africa. Both offer models that could be imported into Nigeria and integrated into the fabric of its local peculiarities.

7 Prospects of the Cooperatives and Social Financing in Nigeria

Social financing, particularly through the cooperative movement platform, has been effective in the sustainable development of many countries. It is highly relevant in the global south, which is an argument in support of its further integration and utilization in Nigeria. There have been some identified challenges with cooperatives and social financing in Nigeria, which occupy spaces within at the intersection of the conventional financial sector and sustainable development. Despite these problems, the prospects appear bright and can be situated as follows:

1. Upward socio-economic mobility: Social financing anchored in the cooperatives presents a horizontal ring through which micro, small, and scattered resources are mobilized into fewer but more effective units. This reduces waste and maximizes resources with results such as the economic empowerment of low-income earners, the increase in employment, and poverty reduction. The next stage is the vertical progression of the movement, which guarantees the upward socio-economic mobility of virtually all, the resources captured earlier by

the horizontal ring. A unique feature of these progressions is that while they often lack the capability to attain the highest level of the socio-economic ladder, they are non-pyramidal and maintain their hedges in its upward movement until they attain their full potential.

2. Support for the actualization of the Sustainable Development Goals (SDGs): In the global south, the prevalence and vicious cycle of poverty as well as the inability to maximize the use of resources are at the forefront of unsustainable development. These factors also constitute a major drawback for poverty alleviation in Nigeria, as many resources are under-employed, including labor, which is the main resource of the working class. The low return on labor and its numerous and multifaceted multipliers (such as the alienation of laborers from the services they render as well as the owners of other factors of production) are some of the core impediments to the actualization of the SDGs. The solution lies in advancements made in the practices of cooperatives and social financing, because both hold the capacity to provide solutions. Such solutions are found in the mobilization of suboptimally utilized micro, small, and medium resources into fewer but more significant productive units.
3. Globalization: Nigeria is an import-dependent country with a massive trade deficit, which negates gains from the rent accruable from the exploration of crude oil. The country stands at a disadvantaged position in global trade. Discontentment with globalization is synonymous with suboptimal utilization of resources and, in many cases, poverty. These create the very problems that necessitate the existence of cooperatives and social financing. Successes with the utilization of social financing in Nigeria demonstrate the capability to redress the rural urban drift by promoting rural development, skill acquisition, skill development, innovation, effective utilization of local resources, and output expansion. One of the envisaged cumulative effects of social financing, in this regard, is the promotion of local production of certain goods, thus the reduction in imports of such goods, and a consequent reduction in loss to foreign exchange. Homegrown initiatives that build from the bottom to the top, as represented by cooperatives and social financing, hold the key to reversing the current trend of trade deficit. This will also align with the repositioning of Nigeria for more inclusion and impactful contributions to globalization.

8 Conclusion and Recommendations[2]

This paper explores social financing in Nigeria as a concept within the larger scope of cooperatives. It reinforces the idea that cooperatives, social economy, financial services, and the actualization of the SDGs are imperative to the upward socio-economic mobility of Nigerians living below and within the poverty line. It further establishes the need for more innovative social financing to be built on the following recommendations:

8.1 Upward Review of Cooperative and Allied Legislation in Nigeria

Some of the legislation that requires review includes the Nigerian Co-operative Societies Act, the Co-operative Development Act, the Central Bank of Nigeria Act, the Banks and Other Financial Institutions Act, and the Companies and Allied Matters Act. These acts, among others, are the laws that enable cooperatives and financial institutions in Nigeria. Currently, their provisions are not in tandem with contemporary demands. A precedent needs to be set by the ongoing review of relevant legislation in both the countries of the global south and the global north. It is time that Nigeria starts this process in order to optimally benefit from the ongoing harmonization of cooperative laws, which are currently anchored by the Co-operative Law Committee (CLC) of the ICA.

8.2 Improved Supervision

At the national level in Nigeria, the Federal Ministry of Agriculture and Natural Resources and the Federal Ministry of Labour and Productivity both supervise cooperatives through the Federal Department of Co-operatives. Interestingly, banks and other financial institutions are supervised by the Federal Ministry of Finance through the CBN. At the subnational level, state governments supervise only the cooperatives that are registered with the state. They do this through the relevant state ministries. The ministries of finance at the subnational level lack the power to supervise financial institutions because the financial institutions

[2] The recommendations proposed are products of fieldwork. The fieldwork was part of my duties to support the drafting of the proposed "Nigerian Microfinance Act," a bill which is pending before the Nigerian national assembly.

are registered and regulated through the federal government's relevant agencies. Hence, most activities occur at the subnational level, but the bulk of the supervision rests with the federal government, which is not visible at the subnational level. The disconnect in supervision creates a gap for partisan politicians interested in ruling political parties' harnessing of cooperatives' structures and social financing for political interest. Loans and other palliatives are channeled through cooperatives and social financial institutions into the hands of political party loyalists who, in many cases, have no link to the primary intentions of the scheme. For example, individuals or groups with no interest in farming could be beneficiaries of agricultural loans at farmers' expense. In addition, groups of political party loyalists could form cooperatives for the sole purpose of collecting loans or other deliberate misappropriations of such loans. Only a regime of strict supervision by regulatory authorities could reduce this identified threat to the bare minimum.

8.3 Integration of the Structures of Conventional and Social Finance

As observed with the Indian example and the Cooperative Bank of Kenya, the integration of conventional and social banking promotes the efficiency and effectiveness of social financing. Social banking is deemed low profit and would not ordinarily fit into the frameworks of conventional banks. However, the increased poverty that results from the collapse or inefficiency of social banking invariably reduces the size of the economy, which negatively impacts the size of conventional banks. Therefore, it seems logical to have an integrated traditional and social financial modeled banking system to assure a win–win synergy.

8.4 Integration of Programs

There is a threefold need to integrate the efforts of the cooperatives and social financing: within private initiatives, across public initiatives, and between private and public initiatives. Private initiatives, which include cooperative societies and microfinance banks, are solitary in their operations. Their solitariness is contrary to the sixth principle of cooperatives (cooperation among cooperatives) and creates circumstances that, in part, defeat the very essence of cooperatives and the social solidarity economy. Similarly, except for the federal (national) government that often utilizes the structures of the states (subnational) and local governments (third-tier government in Nigeria) when harnessing cooperatives and social financing for socio-economic development, the other tiers of government tend to run their affairs independently, often resulting in suboptimal utilization of resources. Furthermore, a significant number of initiatives at the local and subnational government levels are private initiatives independent of the government. This lack of synergy among levels does not support the truest purposes of cooperatives and social financing. Except for the CBN, which is the federal government's banker and the statutory banker to all other banks in Nigeria, virtually all other banks are private/non-government entities. Whereas the government's role should ordinarily not exceed regulatory functions, the Nigerian states' peculiarities and the requirements for more impactful social financing demand symbiotic relationships between the governments, particularly the federal government and the private sector.

8.5 Personnel Planning and Development

Nigeria has a large pool of professionals in various fields, such as lawyers, insurers, accountants, stockbrokers, and bankers (to serve the conventional financial institutions), but few possess the required training to support social financing. There are three Federal Cooperative Colleges in Nigeria (located in Ibadan, Enugu, and Kaduna) that train personnel up to the graduate level on cooperatives and allied matters. This small number is inadequate to support the sector. Graduates from the Federal Cooperative Colleges are rarely employed by the relevant government departments and private initiatives. Instead, graduates of other academic programs are preferred. Unfortunately, this widens the knowledge gap in the field of cooperatives and social financing in Nigeria. Lastly, there is the need to develop the current level of expertise on cooperatives and social financing in Nigeria to build on the current low level of appreciation.

References

Akanle, O., & Busari, D. (2014). Cooperative societies in the development discourse of Ibadan, South-western Nigeria. *The Nigerian Journal of Sociology and Anthropology, 12*, 48–65.

Banks and Other Financial Institutions Act (BOFIA), 1991, as amended in 1997, 1998, 1999, 2002, 2007. https://www.cbn.gov.ng/out/2014/lsd/bofia.pdf.

Central Bank of Nigeria. (2005). *Microfinance policy, regulatory and supervisory framework for Nigeria*. https://www.cbn.gov.ng/out/publications/guidelines/dfd/2006/microfinance%20policy.pdf.

Central Bank of Nigeria. (2006). *Important notice on the deadline for conversion of existing community banks (CBs) to microfinance finance (MFBs)*. https://www.cbn.gov.ng/OUT/CIRCULARS/OFID/2007/OFID-08-2007.PDF.

Central Bank of Nigeria Act, 2007, no. 7. https://www.cbn.gov.ng/OUT/CIRCULARS/CSD/2007/CBN%20ACT%202007.PDF.

Co-operative Bank of Kenya Limited. (2018). *Integrated report*. https://www.co-opbank.co.ke/sites/default/files/document-downloads/CO-OP%20BANK%202018%20ANNUAL%20REPORT-compressed.pdf.

Corporate Finance Institute [CFI]. (2020). https://corporatefinanceinstitute.com/.

International Co-operative Alliance. (1995). *Cooperative identity, values and principles*. https://www.ica.coop/en.

International Labour Organization. (2015). *The story of the ILO's Promotion of Cooperatives Recommendation, 2002 (No. 193)—A review of the process of making ILO Recommendation No. 193, its implementation and its impact*. ILO.

Lawal, & Kamaldeen, A. A. (2013). Cooperative development in Europe, America and Africa. In O. O. Oluyombo (Ed.), *Cooperative and microfinance revolution*. Soma Publishers.

Lawal, & Kamaldeen, A. A. (2017). *Comparative cooperative course guide*, National Open University of Nigeria.

Nnadozie, A. K. O. (2015). Nigerian agricultural co-operatives and rural development. In L. G. A. Ivo (Ed.), *Global Journal of Management and Business Research*. Nigeria.

Nwanyawu, O. J. (2011). Microfinance in Nigeria: Problems and prospects. *African Research Review*, *5*(2), 106–111.

Oluyombo, O. O. (2007). Developing microfinance banking in Nigeria. *Babcock Journal of Management and Social Sciences*, *6*(1), 126–134.

Otero. M., & Rhyne. E. (1994). *The new world of microenterprise finance: Building healthy financial institutions for the poor*. West Hartford Conn Kumarian Press.

Schwettmann, J. (2012). Capacity building for Africa's cooperatives and social economy organization. *Proceedings of the expert group meeting cooperatives in social development and beyond*. Ulaanbaatar, Mongolia.

Schwettmann, J. (2014). *Cooperatives in Africa: Success and challenges. A contribution to the international symposium on cooperatives and sustainable development goals: The case of Africa*. ILO.

Sridevi, K. (2014). *Social banking in public sector commercial banks: A case of state bank of Hyderabad* (Doctoral dissertation). Osmania University, India.

United Nations Conference on Trade and Development [UNCTAD]. (2015). *Investment policy framework for sustainable development*. https://unctad.org/system/files/official-document/diaepcb2015d5_en.pdf.

United Nations Development Programme. (2015). *Sustainable development goals*. https://www.undp.org/content/undp/en/home/.

Wani, H. (2016). Transforming ethnic divide: Comparative analysis of India and Nigeria. *American International Journal of Contemporary Research, 6*(5), 47–58.

World Commission on Environment and Development [WCED]. (1987). *Our common future*. https://sustainabledevelopment.un.org/content/documents/5987our-common-future.pdf.

Evaluating Impact Investments: Frameworks and Applications for Social Ventures

Alessandro Rizzello, Elisabetta Scognamiglio, Ludovica Testa, and Lorenzo Liotta

1 Introduction

In the aftermath of the 2008/2009 financial crisis, an expansive debate led to questions of how, where, and why financial actors invest. As a result, the inclusion of practices that promote issues such as environmental stewardship, consumer protection, human rights, quality of labor and jobs, as well as the consideration of the sustainable use of natural resources into investment choices has been increasingly recognized by the investment industry (Geels, 2013). An increasing number of socially oriented

A. Rizzello (✉)
Department of Law, Economics and Sociology, University Magna Græcia of Catanzaro, Catanzaro, Italy
e-mail: rizzello@unicz.it

E. Scognamiglio · L. Testa · L. Liotta
Italiacamp, Rome, Italy
e-mail: e.scognamiglio@italiacamp.com

L. Testa
e-mail: l.testa@italiacamp.com

L. Liotta
e-mail: lorenzo.liotta@hotmail.it

T. Walker et al. (eds.), *Innovations in Social Finance*,
https://doi.org/10.1007/978-3-030-72535-8_20

investors consequently sought to influence the companies in which they invest to create more social value as a result of their investment (Talan & Sharma, 2019). Unlike an investment approach that seeks value alignment (by owning stocks only in companies whose business and practices accord with the investors' moral or social values), investors who wish to create social value deploy their capital to increase an investee company's socially valuable externalities. Such a form of socially oriented investing is known as Social Impact Investing (SII), also referred to by the simplified expression Impact Investing. SII is a fast-developing investment strategy in which capital is used to maximize the combined value of social and environmental impact alongside financial return (Balkin, 2016; Clarkin & Cangioni, 2016).

A broad range of investors is engaged in impact investments: impact funds, social banks, foundations, family offices, and individuals. These investors create social value by increasing the amount of an investee company's social impact rather than simply aligning their portfolio decisions with the company's social values (Walker et al., 2017); there is, therefore, a necessary causal link between the investor's social outcome expectations and the increase in social impact deriving from the investment (Chiappini, 2017). This emphasis on social and environmental outcomes distinguishes SII from other forms of responsible investment (Lieberman, 2020).

In existing academic literature, SII research receives attention from three main theoretical perspectives: sustainable finance, sustainable entrepreneurship, and public policy in the social sector (Rizzello et al., 2016). Earlier research in this field focuses on clarifying definitions and concepts (Höchstädter & Scheck, 2015; Vecchi et al., 2017). However, this field of research is still in a pre-paradigmatic state and many research questions concerning, for example, standardization and inconsistency in the area of impact evaluation and reporting remain underexplored (Agrawal & Hockerts, 2019; Lehner, 2016; Rizzi et al., 2018). SII centers on achieving positive social and/or environmental outcomes, but must nonetheless balance these goals with that of financial return.

Policy-making studies extensively address the concept of Social Impact Assessment (SIA); however, there are as many studies as there are meanings of SIA in the SII field. SIA approaches can be qualitative, quantitative, or both (mixed methods), and there is no common standard application in the SII field (Dufour, 2019). As a result, a wide spectrum of approaches and levels of rigor toward the measurement of impacts and non-financial returns exists (Choda & Teladia, 2018). Impact investors can adopt SIA schemes at various points in the investment process, such as in the ex-ante phase as well as in the ex-post investment phase. In other cases, they can adopt SIA as a framework to communicate the social mission's achievement with their stakeholders (O'Flynn et al., 2019). At the same time, the integration of impact measurement into financial strategies and tools also requires robust research efforts to clarify its definition, as well as practices related to its management, evaluation, and reporting. The issue of social impact (and its evaluation) has inspired growing interest from both academics and practitioners (Choda & Teladia, 2018; Epstein & Yuthas, 2017; Lazzarini, 2018; Reeder et al., 2015; Reisman et al., 2018). Furthermore, there is an increasing demand to both have formal and standardized measures of performance, as well as to identify the expected social and/or environmental outcomes for an impact investor (Choda & Teladia, 2018; Verrinder et al., 2018). Indeed, few academic contributions discuss specific best practices and methodologies that impact investors can use to evaluate the social impact in their investments, particularly in the ex-ante phase of their investments (Migliavacca, 2018; Viviani & Maurel, 2019).

By addressing these gaps in the literature, this research provides an answer to the following research questions:

1. How is an ex-ante qualitative impact assessment built in the case of impact investment in social ventures?
2. Is it possible to identify a "one-size-fits-all" model applied within SII in impact-oriented start-ups?
3. How is this qualitative step integrated with quantitative metrics that inform investment decisions?

With these objectives in mind, this research aims to:

1. Provide an overview of different approaches of impact assessment categorized in the SII literature.
2. Identify assessment methods usefully adaptable to the ex-ante stage of impact investment.
3. Present an experimental approach adopted for an Italian social venture.

The study performs qualitative and exploratory analyses by presenting a case study application of ex-ante impact evaluation for Mygrants, an Italian social venture focused on migrants' and refugees' integration. The study's results contribute to understanding how theoretical perspectives concerning the creation of social value in the financial system can converge with the definition of impact evaluation schemes in the field of SII.

This paper is divided as follows. Section 2 reviews the different approaches of impact evaluation categorized in the SII literature. Section 3 considers the method adopted. Section 4 presents findings. Section 5 provides discussion and suggests a series of propositions to advance our knowledge in the field. Finally, Section 6 concludes the paper.

2 Social Impact Assessment in Impact Investing: Concepts, Methods, and Barriers

SIA is an object of growing interest and academic debate as a result of the increasing pressure for accountability from governments, donors, and citizens, all of whom ask non-profit and for-profit organizations to demonstrate their effectiveness in addressing social problems (Mook et al., 2015). The SIA academic landscape is multidisciplinary as it combines social policy, management of social change, and social research topics. Essentially, this discipline emerged with the primary objective of identifying and predicting the impacts of projects, especially within policy interventions (Vanclay, 2003). Largely, SIA application studies include different bodies of literature, such as those dedicated to the public sector, environmental impact, performance and accountability, developing economies, social enterprise and, more recently, impact finance studies (Grieco et al., 2015). A popular avenue of SIA exploration is that of social enterprise performance and accountability (e.g., Arvidson & Lyon, 2014). The main challenge in SIA processes concerns the conversion of qualitative social impact achievement data into quantitative metrics (Grieco et al., 2015). However, no common understanding or consensus underpins the concept "social impact" (Hlady-Rispal & Servantie, 2018; Quélin et al., 2017). In fact, social impact has been described variously as "the total outcome attributed to the organisations' interventions" (Clark et al., 2004: 7); "the inclusion of the positive and negative effects of interventions" (Victora et al., 2011: 3); and as "the combination of resources, inputs, processes or policies for achieving desired outcomes" (Grieco et al., 2015: 7). Scholars interested in this field identify different approaches as well as metrics and indicators (Bengo et al., 2016; Rawhouser et al., 2019; Sammarco et al., 2018).

More recently, reverberations from the focus on the "creation of social value" inspired the niche social enterprise field to uncover connections between economic value creation and an organization's social dimension (Kramer & Porter, 2011: 16). Also in the financial context, investment performance measurement is starting to include, beyond risk and return, impact evaluation and measures, as in the case of SII. In particular, impact investors intend to create positive impact beyond financial return; it is vital for the investment to include an intentional, and therefore predetermined, social impact. For these reasons, SII necessarily calls for measuring social and environmental returns alongside financial returns, per Fig. 1.

In recent years, several academic publications have highlighted the challenges associated with the impact measurement methods of SII, while simultaneously introducing possible solutions and emphasizing the progress made so far. With this in mind, in SII, impact investors need to quantify the social/environmental impact generated by impact investees into non-financial measures. Furthermore, some studies register a conceptual opacity with regard to the nature of impact that the SII field considers, essentially due to the fact that the impact generated from investments can be attributable, directly or not, to such capital (Hehenberger et al., 2013; Leborgne-Bonassié et al., 2019). In particular, the impact referred to by the term "Impact Investing" is related to a "net-effect," implying those "outcomes over any timescale compared to

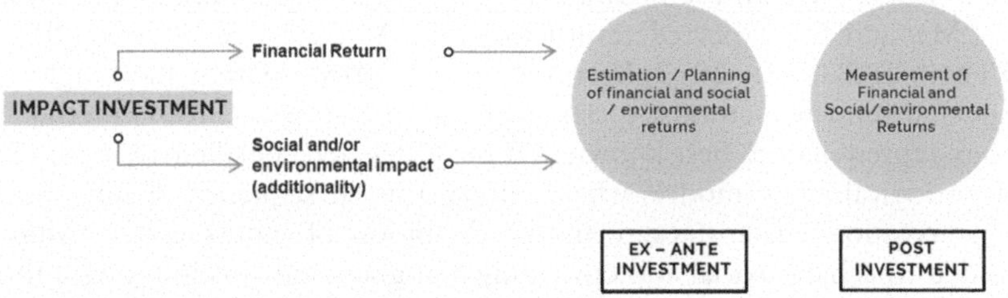

Fig. 1 Social and financial returns in impact investing (*Source* Adapted from Reeder et al. [2015])

what would have occurred without any action taking place" (Reeder & Colantonio, 2013: 13).

Conducting quantitative analysis (which adopts statistical reasoning) or qualitative analysis (derived from anecdotes) can attribute data to casual connections with impact investments and can be based overall on the theory of change (based on logical chains of arguments). Within the impact investing field, impact assessment activities span a continuum which includes different objectives suitable for different phases of the impact investment cycle (Vo & Christie, 2018).

In SII, impact assessment may be conducted ex-ante to predict the social and/or environmental outcomes in the short- and medium-term by identifying the main affected stakeholders, as well as strategies to enhance positive consequences and mitigate negative ones. Nevertheless, in SII, the evaluation of impact often also has an ex-post dimension. For these reasons, it is possible to identify four main blocks along an ideal spectrum of SIA activities in impact investing: estimation, planning, monitoring, and evaluation (Brest & Born, 2013; So & Staskevicius, 2015). Estimation assesses potential social return before committing to an investment; impact planning defines the metrics and data collection methods that the investor uses to monitor a program's effects; impact monitoring runs once the program is underway; and finally, impact evaluation measures an investment's social consequences after the programe concludes and assesses portfolio performance.

Scholars have determined a multitude of tools for and approaches to, measuring impact across the sector, categorized into four main types: mission alignment, experimental and quasi-experimental, qualitative methods (e.g., the theory of change or ToC, also identified interchangeably with the broader category of the logic model framework or LM), and the expected return method (Abrahams & Walaza, 2018; O'Flynn & Barnett, 2017; Verrinder et al., 2018). Within the range of expected returns methods, social return on investment (SROI) methodology represents the best known and most debated. Qualitative methods adopt logical chain models where, along a linear sequence of steps, the value creation chain starts with the definition of inputs and activities needed to achieve social and environmental goals and concludes with the identification of outcomes and positive net impact. Clark et al. (2004) introduce such a framework, identify the expression "impact value chain," and refine this concept within SII by the European Venture Philanthropy Association (EVPA) in 2013 (Hehenberger et al., 2013; see Fig. 2).

Fig. 2 Visualization of an impact value chain (*Source* Adapted from Hehenberger et al. [2013]))

Per Fig. 2, we define an impact value chain as a translatable evaluative tool for the measurement of impact in SII based on the theory of change and include both positive and negative net-effects produced by the organization, directly or indirectly, intended or unintended.

However, practical applications of such theoretical frameworks in the SII field are fragmented and present scarce evidence about the transformation of qualitative measures into quantitative metrics useful to inform investment decisions (Lee et al., 2020). Other scholars highlight limitations and barriers in the conceptual development of this field by encouraging further explorations regarding the time-horizon of the impact that should be evaluated, the need for a specific and standardized process for ex-ante impact evaluations that are theory-of-change-based, and the inclusion, in impact investment decisions, of consideration concerning risks associated with the underachievement of the expected impact (Cole et al., 2020; McCallum & Viviers, 2020; Scognamiglio et al., 2019).

3 Research Design

Our study aims to fill the gap in the empirical literature about social impact assessment and metric systems that the SII field adopts, with particular attention to ex-ante approaches, wherein significant opacity exists. We design this empirical study as an exploratory action research project by presenting a case study application of a social venture. Moreover, the study performs qualitative and exploratory analysis through the case study application of an ex-ante impact assessment for Mygrants, an Italian social venture focused on refugees' integration. Single case studies are more effective when the research aims to provide a deeper understanding of the subject explored and when it intends to create a high-quality theory by richly describing the existence of the phenomenon (Donmoyer, 2000).

The approaches that we use here are typical of action research that, according to Dickens and Watkins (1999), sees the researcher directly involved in fostering a change on organizational or societal levels while observing and reflecting upon the unfolding processes. Action research has been traditionally defined as research that is based on a "collaborative problem-solving relationship between researcher and client which aims at both solving a problem and generating new knowledge" (Coghlan, 2019: 9). In this study, the collaboration aims to inspire and support the ongoing development of SIA within the SII field, especially in the ex-ante investment phase, through concrete experimentation. The unit of analysis is the ex-ante SIA process in impact investment. This research design allows the researchers to examine the selected unit extensively as it unfolds and to collect rich data about the observed activities (Orum, 2001; Yin, 2017). With this objective in mind, our research intends to provide empirical insight from the concrete building of an ex-ante impact assessment of a social venture suitable for impact investment.

3.1 Case Selection and Description

Founded in 2017, Mygrants is an Italian start-up with several objectives: to train and provide migrants and refugees with new skills and abilities, as well as enhance their existing ones; to help them be productive members of society; to be included in their hosting communities; and, broadly speaking, to ensure they have the best possible living conditions. Mygrants' web platform offers educational content through interactive quizzes that help its users with language learning and train them in issues such as rights, asylum, social challenges, and entrepreneurship. In addition to "Education" offerings, Mygrants provides three other services that constitute its core business: "Career Placement" (thanks to an accurate mapping of migrants' skills, both enhanced and acquired), "Pocket Money" (meant to empower migrants with economic independence through the chance to open up bank accounts), and "50 K/Talent" (includes scholarships and incubation paths to promote entrepreneurial capacities). Beyond the financial sustainability of its activity, the start-up can thus generate a positive impact for many different stakeholders including the migrants themselves, welcome centers, host and home countries, and the community as a whole.

We select Mygrants as a case study for two main reasons. Firstly, Mygrants' business model is oriented to both social objectives and financial returns and therefore represents an ideal example of an investment

Table 1 Differences between the theory of change and logic model approaches

Theory of change (ToC)	*Logic model (LM)*
General vision at the strategic level	Specific vision at the program implementation level
Captures complex processes	Neat and structured
Explanatory	Descriptive
Backwards induction approach	Bottom-up approach
Pathway of change	Lists components
Requires critical thinking	Is a logic and linear representation

Source Adapted from Brown (2016) and Clark and Anderson (2004)

target for impact investors. Secondly, at the time[1] of the impact evaluation, Mygrants is an early-stage impact-oriented start-up. This status sees impact investments with a need to receive an ex-ante impact evaluation, suitable to define its expected outcome, in both qualitative and quantitative ways, and is useful for the impact investors' due diligence.

3.2 Data Gathering and Analysis Process

According to the academic literature, for the selected case, the adoption of the theory of change (ToC) as well as the logic model (LM) is appropriate (So & Staskevicius, 2015). However, for the evaluation of this case, we ultimately face a choice between applying the ToC approach versus the LM (or logical framework, as presented by Brown, 2016) approach. Although the two terms are used interchangeably and the two approaches do present some similar characteristics, they also differ in several relevant ways, as Table 1 summarizes.

The first major difference between the two models is that the ToC approach results in a more general, strategic vision of the change one wants to make, showing all of the different paths that may lead to change, even if not strictly related to a specific program. The LM, conversely, focuses on one specific process within that mapping and discloses the single steps for its implementation as well as the causal link between them (Kellogg, 2006). For this case, we deem ToC to be the most appropriate

[1] January 2019.

approach to evaluate the company's potential impact. We made this choice as the objective of the estimation of social impact is to make projections on Mygrants' ability to generate positive changes and the areas in which the company could have the most significant effect, given its infancy stage of development. Furthermore, given Mygrants' still-developing core business aspects (at the time of the evaluation), we integrate the ToC approach with two further dimensions. First, distinguishing the outcomes into short-term (one to three years), long-term (four to seven years), and impact per se (seven to ten years) enhances the ToC, following the Logic Model Development Guide (Kellogg, 2006). Furthermore, this type of specification seems necessary due to Mygrants' maturity and core business traits. These traits lead us to believe that the change they could generate in their market and community in the next year would differ significantly from the change they could generate in five years. In this way, the model provides a "step-by-step" breakdown within the outcomes, underlining the causal nature of the ToC (Clark & Anderson, 2004). Second, as in the case of financial returns, we include risks concerning the social return associable to Mygrants. Indeed, our ex-ante impact evaluation enables us to define the expected social outcome by adding this useful information for investors to identify social risk associated with the financial risk of their investment into Mygrants (Scognamiglio et al., 2019). With these considerations in mind, we map Mygrants' impact on the base of our integrated ToC approach.

3.3 Data and Results

The map of Mygrants' most relevant outcomes, which the ToC represents, is the result of an analytical study phase. This phase consists of two steps: internal and external analysis. The internal analysis starts with a thorough understanding and data gathering concerning the company's core business and daily activities by adopting a two-fold approach. Firstly, we ask Mygrants' team, including its co-founder and CEO, to provide us with relevant documents and materials (such as pitch presentation, an investors' deck, Mygrants' business plan, web-platform structure, as well as relevant partnerships and competitors) that enable us to understand Mygrants' principal tasks and, consequently, identify its core business activities and outputs. After carefully reviewing the documents, we then interview Mr. Richmond N'zi, CEO. The interview aims to ensure that our understanding of the business is correct and accurate. Ultimately, thanks to both our analysis and Mr. Richmond N'zi's perspective, we clearly define Mygrants' vision, mission, strategic objectives, and core business activities. Table 2 summarizes these results.

As we draft Mygrants' most relevant outcomes, we want to have points of comparison to make sure that we focus on aspects and areas generally

Table 2 Mygrants' business structure

Vision	"Opportunity in Adversity"/from Mygrants capitalizing on resources to Mygrants generating resources
Mission	Transforming migration for economic causes into a profitable opportunity, for both migrants and hosting communities, as well as for the home countries
Strategic objectives	• Improve access to permanent education in informal contexts • Update knowledge, skills and previous competences • Transform unexpressed talent into a profitable resource for the community • Reduce the host country's expenses, e.g., reducing time spent in welcoming centers, promoting investments in economic, social, civic and cultural growth
Core business activities	• Education: quizzes on the web platform focused on rights and asylum, social challenges, and entrepreneurship • Career placement: internships in partner companies • Pocket money: the opening of bank accounts after appropriate financial education • 50 K/Talent: scholarships and incubation paths
Outputs	• N°. migrants trained • N°. migrants whose previous skills are updated for the Italian market • N°. migrants with new language skills • N°. internships activated • Tot. grants supplied • N°. investments realized • N°. requests satisfied via geo-localization • Time spent on the web platform • N°. bank accounts opened • N°. quizzes passed by users on financial education • N°. scholarships awarded • N°. incubation paths activated

Source Authors' elaboration derived from the analysis

considered important in the sector of immigrants' and refugees' integration, so as to grant our work as much validity as possible. Therefore, we proceed to the second step by performing a benchmark analysis in terms of Mygrants' competitors, mostly useful to in identifying outputs, rather than impact areas or outcomes. The competitors Mygrants identify are InfoStranieri, Asylum Access, and Start Refugees. The publicly available documents concerning the competitors allow us to have an effective benchmark in terms of relevant impact areas to identify for Mygrants.

Furthermore, we validate our research by integrating this information with a specialized report focused on migrants' integration to shed light on the main areas where it is paramount to create a positive impact (Ernst & Young, 2016). It follows that filling the gaps in the identified areas means producing intended outcomes through outputs and creating a positive impact. In conclusion, we notice that by analyzing Mygrants' direct competitors, we identify mostly outputs, rather than impact areas or, better yet, outcomes. As a result of this enhanced analysis, we identify further impact areas to include in the impact evaluation of Mygrants, namely: legal education and training, the number of jobs created, as well as social and economic integration. At the end of the analytical matrix phase and based on the evidence that emerges, it is possible to implement the second phase of research. Its objective is to map the social risks associated with the identified outcomes; in essence, to determine the contextual risks that could limit or hinder the achievement of the desired impact.

4 Findings

By performing both internal and external analyses of Mygrants' business and the context in which it operates, we design and map its ToC. As mentioned above, we first distinguish "outcomes," or effects produced in the long-term (four to seven years) and short-term (one to three years) from "impact," or the change achieved in the long run (seven to ten years). The latter includes significant changes in social, cultural, and economic environments, both in the host country and the migrants' original communities (e.g., a general improvement in living and economic conditions) as well as a consequent reduction of costs for the hosting country (e.g., for security reasons).

Mygrants' impact vision is encapsulated by the phrase "Opportunity in Adversity," as Fig. 3 showcases: Such an expression aptly expresses the change the company wishes to make to in community and society.

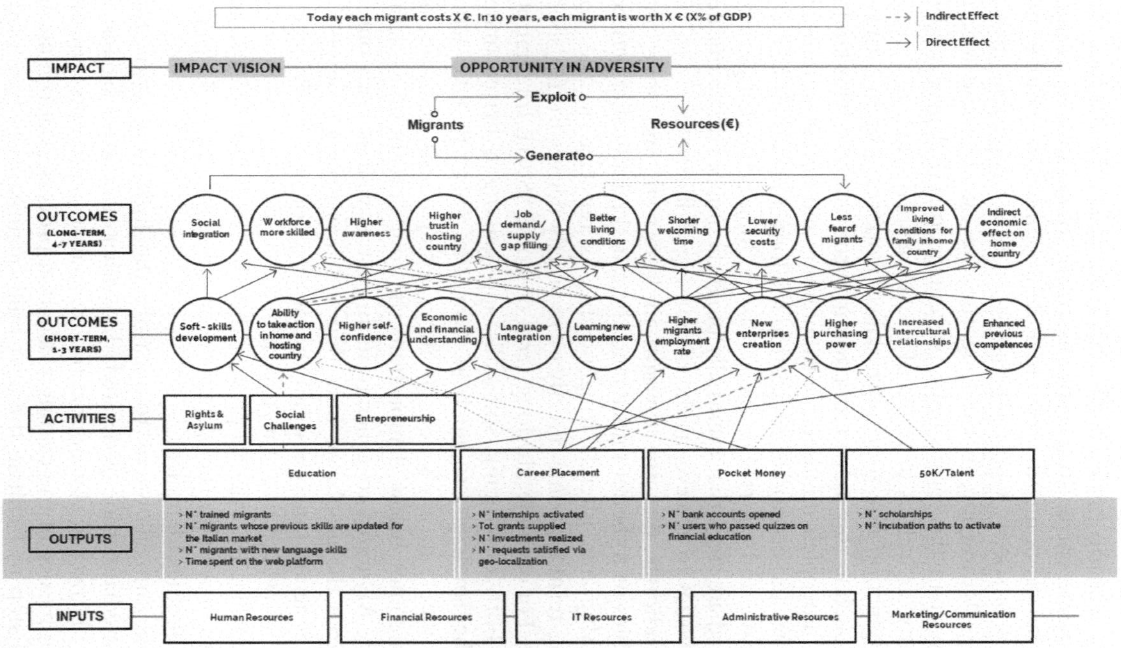

Fig. 3 Mygrants' theory of change map (*Source* Authors' elaboration derived from the analysis)

Some groups are perceived as an inconvenience in a best-case scenario and more often as a threat that could potentially become a resource for Italy as a worst-case scenario (and any other hosting state). In the long run, migrants that some currently consider as costly to the hosting country could become an economically generative demographic, developing into active members of society who contribute to national economic growth and well-being. Meanwhile, in the long run, we calculate and identify Mygrants' impact in the form of the percentage of GDP produced by trained migrants, as well as in terms of money gained (such as from an increase in production due to a more skilled workforce) or in terms of money saved (such as through a reduction in security costs). This kind of major change in people's mindsets (both migrants and host communities) in terms of social and economic integration is a long and complex process that requires time and effort. For these reasons, long-term changes need several intermediate steps that eventually build the impact that a business organization wishes to achieve, as the map in Fig. 3 illustrates.

Figure 3 indicates that the division in long-term and short-term outcomes enables us to better understand the causal relationship between the changes Mygrants intends to generate. As reported in the ToC map, each long-term outcome directly or indirectly derives from a short-term outcome. For example, the long-term outcome "Social Integration" derives from both developing soft-skills and gaining a better understanding of the language, as much as from the ability to take action (or be independent) in one's new country. For synthesis purposes, the short-term outcomes below demonstrate the four core business activities that enable Mygrants to generate its impact as well as both output and inputs. From the graph, we infer that activities generate outputs as much as they generate outcomes, but the two do not necessarily depend on each other. However, each short-term outcome generates at least one long-term outcome. In order to present the ToC map more clearly and logically, and to provide further details of the outcomes, Table 3 contains a list of the outcomes identified.

This identification allows us to measure the final long-term effect and the intermediate value generated that otherwise could be lost in the evaluation. However, this double-timing analysis represents a further element of complexity in the ex-ante evaluation process; it also indicates a fundamental step to facilitate the next (and quantitative) phase of the evaluation, allowing for a more accurate measurement process.

Table 3 Mygrants' outcomes definitions

Outcome	*Definition*
(ST) Soft-skills development	Increase in social and personal skills
(ST) Ability to take action in home and hosting country	Economic and social empowerment and independence
(ST) Higher self-confidence	Belief in oneself through professional and personal accomplishments
(ST) Economic and financial understanding	Stronger financial competences through completed quizzes
(ST) Language integration	Higher linguistic skills through completed quizzes
(ST) Learning new competencies	Entrepreneurial and business education
(ST) Higher migrants' employment rate	Increase in employment rates due to better-trained workforce
(ST) New enterprises creation	Migrants as start-up entrepreneurs due to specific training
(ST) Higher purchasing power	Migrants able to be financially independent due to job placement
(ST) Increased intercultural relationships	Relationships might come easier due to linguistic and economic integration
(ST) Enhanced previous competences	A better understanding of previous skills that may otherwise be unknown
(LT) Social integration	Migrants are better included in hosting communities due to linguistic and economic integration
(LT) Workforce more skilled	Resulting from the web platform training that provides new competences
(LT) Higher awareness	The "Rights & Asylum" training might create more respect and awareness of rights and duties as citizens
(LT) Higher trust in hosting country	Migrants might have more faith in a country in which they are welcomed and can work
(LT) Job demand/supply gap filling	Mygrants allows for better matching between skills obtained and job positions
(LT) Better living conditions	A generally higher standard of living due to social and economic integration
(LT) Shorter welcoming time	Trained migrants have easier access to the job market and gain independence from welcome centers
(LT) Lower security costs	Decrease in crime rates due to greater financial security
(LT) Less fear of migrants	Resulting from economic and social integration and consequent understanding

(continued)

Table 3 (continued)

Outcome	*Definition*
(LT) Improved living conditions for the family in the home country	Resulting from money received from migrants
(LT) An indirect economic effect on home country	Ability to send money back to the home country due to receiving a salary

Source Authors' elaboration derived from the analysis

We complete the ToC analysis by sequencing outputs and outcomes along the impact value chain (see Fig. 4) where, in a much clearer way, it is possible to observe how the pieces of the ToC map connect to each other.

In its last step, our evaluation considers the mapping of risks associated with the achievement of the identified expected impact. As specified in the methods section, we believe it appropriate to analyze the social risks mostly related to our short-term outcomes, keeping in mind that

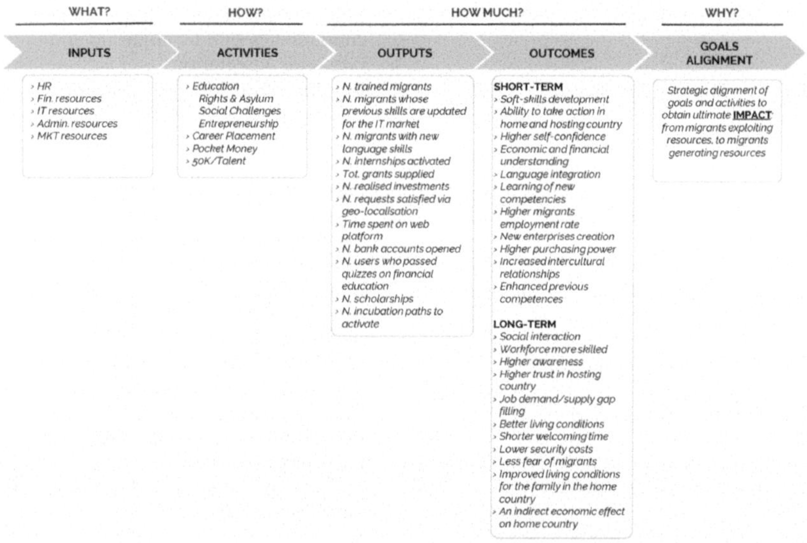

Fig. 4 Mygrants' impact value chain (*Source* Authors' elaboration derived from the analysis)

outcomes are to be intended as sequential steps that lead to one's ultimate impact. Therefore, not achieving short-term outcomes necessarily implies reaching neither long-term outcomes nor significant impact itself.

The correct and precise identification of ex-ante risks allows the organization to manage and mitigate them so that the organization can reach its impact aim. At the same time, such activity is useful to inform the investor about the social value that could derive from investment (from reading the ToC) and the risks associated with a possible underachievement of the expected social performance.

We identified social risks in two macro-categories: internal and external risks. By internal risks, we refer to factors that could damage the achievement of short-term outcomes, strictly related to Mygrants' organization and structure. External risks relate to those economic, social, and political factors that do not directly depend on the company but might nonetheless hamper its desired change. Table 4 summarizes the risks identified.

Within the two macro-categories, we divide social risks into three subgroups: The "Organization's Risks" group are those that strictly relate to the execution of Mygrants' core business activities. "Scenario Risks" refer to unexpected changes in policies, economic decisions, and legal environment. "Community Risks" are those that depend on the people's mental attitude and their behavior, both the hosting communities and the migrants themselves.

Table 4 Mygrants' map of social risks associated with its impact value chain

Social risks	
Internal	*External*
Organization's risks • Attempt to "cheat" the platform • Quizzes only taken in the native language • A mismatch between education offer and market/migrants' needs • Partial exclusion of those not identified as 'talents'	*Scenario risks* • Policies harmful toward inclusion • Lack of incentives to employ migrants/create new businesses • Increased difficulty in bureaucracy • Stagnant job market *Community risks* • Lack of an inclusive mindset • Incapacity to integrate oneself • Absence of structures to promote inclusion

5 Discussion

This study applies an ex-ante impact evaluation suitable for impact investment to a social venture by employing the methodology that, according to the literature, represents the most adaptable and useful approach in this case.

The analysis that this paper conducts sheds light on the relevance of the qualitative impact analysis for the assessment in ex-ante impact investment. Specifically, in order to put the findings of the study in context, we focus our attention on: (a) the importance of a qualitative impact assessment to build a credible set of quantitative metrics (the following step of an impact evaluation process); (b) the standardization of the framework, suitable for different national and business contexts; and (c) the integration of qualitative measures with quantitative metrics that inform investment decisions. Investigating these three aspects allows us to provide a preliminary analysis, which is useful in answering all three of this study's research questions.

5.1 *Qualitative-Based Process*

The study's framework provides an initial picture of how the analysis is organized and represents a fundamental step to integrate, with a successive assessment of quantitative character, an assessment that follows some characteristics of the traditional financial/economic assessment. The ex-ante evaluation is qualitative for two reasons: First, not all the value generated by the organization is quantitative in nature and, therefore, not all the effects produced are measurable. Second, mapping the qualitative effects is a fundamental step to arrive at a later quantitative evaluation, as the graphic representation of the ToC shows. In the long-term, in fact, changes generated can be measured quantitatively; this is the case of the indirect gain of the socio-economic system, thanks to the trained workforce described in the case study. Highlighting the causal links that exist in an activity model thus makes it possible to focus on (and correctly identify) the qualitative effects and, consequently, the quantitative effects.

5.2 *Validation and Standardization of the Framework*

The explored framework presents a standardizable operative set of steps and a method, by offering to potential impact investors a qualitative and strategic reading of one or more organizations subject to evaluation. Moreover, the approach, although experimental, is valid for two reasons. First, it adopts the ToC, an instrument already recognized by academics and practitioners alike for its ability to highlight causal links and, therefore, improve the reliability of the results. Furthermore, we obtain the definition of the outcomes through backward mapping, which determines all the changes of a qualitative nature that must happen before a change is generated. This tool can be used to correctly identify the impact that an organization generates. Second, we carry out a structured benchmark analysis with respect to similar organizations, individual effects (to correctly identify the social risks associated with each), and the main international assessment frameworks that allow each element of the analysis to be validated in the progress. This approach can be replicated by all organizations because its potential for standardization is based not solely on the results obtained, but rather on the stages leading to the results.

5.3 *Integration of Qualitative Assessment in the Impact Investment Process*

The analysis that emerges from the qualitative evaluation presents the first results that can be considered as indications of "risk-social return" related to an organization. In this sense, therefore, the joint reading of the results that the ToC obtains and the analysis of social risks replicates, with due differences, is the traditional investment valuation model. This analogy may be useful to ensure an easier analysis for an investor. The social risk-return assessment also indirectly affects economic performance, especially in the case of impact investing, where the two sides (social plus financial) of the total value are indissolubly matched. In some cases, as for "Social Impact Bond," the missed achievement of a pre-determined impact threshold generates financial losses for investors of all or part of their investment. Thus, identifying the expected effects and risk factors that could prevent their implementation makes it possible to foresee, manage, and modify actions to achieve the expected objectives as well as to encourage the remuneration of investors. In this sense, this associated qualitative risk-performance assessment lays the foundation for the development of a ranking system that gives each organization a value or a score related to level of risk and performance (Scognamiglio et al., 2019).

6 Conclusion

Our analysis represents a preliminary step in enlarging and empowering the definition of a standard framework that maps the expected outcome for a social venture in an ex-ante impact investment evaluation. The study models a framework useful not only to investors, but also to other social ventures seeking impact investments. The model represents a valid assessment tool useful in monitoring self-improvement as well as the impact investment readiness of these organizations.

By considering the application of an integrated framework that looks beyond financial risks to social risks, our results offer valuable suggestions for the impact investing industry, useful for the understanding of what should be evaluated through qualitative impact assessment, especially in the case of social ventures. Our findings suggest that the application of the ToC approach represents a solution that could, on the one hand, capture the complexity of potential social outcomes and, on the other hand, integrate this evaluation with further considerations that provide a holistic perspective. Furthermore, the qualitative assessment represents a fundamental base for further quantitative analysis before an impact investment. We base the building of a quantitative set of indicators or metrics on this qualitative step. It is useful in identifying and mapping all relevant achievable outcomes.

A second implication of this analysis, particularly useful for the impact investing industry, is a deeper understanding of how an integrated impact assessment framework orients impact investment decisions by adding a qualitative analysis of social risks related to the achievement of the expected impact. Our findings provide insights on how such analyses can be conducted into quantitative indicators, by adopting key performance indicators (KPIs) or key risk indicators (KRIs). In this way, it is possible to monitor risks over time and develop risk management policies that allow for a safer achievement of social outcomes.

Finally, the framework approach represents the first attempt to identify common elements for impact evaluations in the case of a social for-profit organization. Future replications and implementations of this model could explore SII investments in other business sectors and national contexts, with the aim to build a database clustered by sector and associated risk. Such a database would present an important benchmark: It would allow for not only the improvement of the validation for future ex-ante evaluations, but also the existence of a ranking system (including quantitative measures of impact and associated risks), useful in informing the community of impact investors with international standardized quantitative indicators based on a qualitative metrics-identification process.

Future academic research could address this theme to verify and validate the model for the impact investing industry by testing and implementing this mixed approach in myriad business sectors as well as different, and similar, organizations. Future research efforts in this field could add further data, which would assist in understanding how theoretical perspectives, with respect to the creation of social value in the financial system, can find a convergence in the definition of impact evaluation schemes in the field of Social Impact Investing.

References

Abrahams, M., & Walaza, S. (2018). Measuring social impact investment. *African Evaluation Journal, 6*(2), 3.

Agrawal, A., & Hockerts, K. (2019). Impact investing: Review and research agenda. *Journal of Small Business & Entrepreneurship, 33*(2), 153–181.

Arvidson, M., & Lyon, F. (2014). Social impact measurement and non-profit organisations: Compliance, resistance, and promotion. *VOLUNTAS: International Journal of Voluntary and Nonprofit Organizations, 25*(4), 869–886.

Balkin, J. (2016). *Investing with impact: Why finance is a force for good*. Routledge.

Bengo, I., Arena, M., Azzone, G., & Calderini, M. (2016). Indicators and metrics for social business: A review of current approaches. *Journal of Social Entrepreneurship, 7*(1), 1–24.

Brest, P., & Born, K. (2013). When can impact investing create real impact? *Stanford Social Innovation Review, 11*(4), 22–31.

Brown, A. M. (2016). *Differences between the theory of change and the logic model*. Ann-Murray Brown Consultancy. https://www.annmurraybrown.com/single-post/2016/03/20/Theory-of-Change-vsThe-Logic-Model-Never-Be-Confused-Again.

Chiappini, H. (2017). *Social impact funds—Definition, assessment and performance*. Palgrave Macmillan.

Choda, A., & Teladia, M. (2018). Conversations about measurement and evaluation in impact investing. *African Evaluation Journal, 6*(2), 1–11.

Clark, C., Rosenzweig, W., Long, D., & Olsen, S. (2004). *Double bottom line project report: Assessing social impact in double bottom line ventures*. Rockefeller Foundation. https://community-wealth.org/sites/clone.community-wealth.org/files/downloads/paper-rosenzweig.pdf.

Clark, H., & Anderson, A. A. (2004, November). *Theories of change and logic models: Telling them apart*. In American Evaluation Association Conference.

Clarkin, J. E., & Cangioni, C. L. (2016). Impact investing: A primer and review of the literature. *Entrepreneurship Research Journal, 6*(2), 135–173.

Coghlan, D. (2019). *Doing action research in your own organization*. Sage.

Cole, S., Melecky, M., Molders, F., & Reed, T. (2020). *Long-run returns to impact investing in emerging market and developing economies* [No. 9366]. The World Bank. https://openknowledge.worldbank.org/handle/10986/34383.

Dickens, L., & Watkins, K. (1999). Action research: Rethinking Lewin. *Management Learning, 30*(2), 127–140.

Donmoyer, R. (2000). Generalizability and the single-case study. In R. Gomm, M. Hammerslay, & P. Foster (Eds.), *Case study method: Key issues, key texts* (pp. 45–68). Sage.

Dufour, B. (2019). Social impact measurement: What can impact investment practices and the policy evaluation paradigm learn from each other? *Research in International Business and Finance, 47*, 18–30.

Epstein, M. J., & Yuthas, K. (2017). *Measuring and improving social impacts: A guide for nonprofits, companies and impact investors*. Routledge.

Ernst & Young. (2016). *Managing the EU migration crisis. From panic to planning*. EY. https://www.ey.com/Publication/vwLUAssets/ey-managing-the-eu-migration-crisis/%24FILE/ey-managing-the-eu-migration-crisis.pdf.

Geels, F. W. (2013). The impact of the financial–economic crisis on sustainability transitions: Financial investment, governance and public discourse. *Environmental Innovation and Societal Transitions, 6*, 67–95.

Grieco, C., Michelini, L., & Iasevoli, G. (2015). Measuring value creation in social enterprises: A cluster analysis of social impact assessment models. *Nonprofit and Voluntary Sector Quarterly, 44*(6), 1173–1193.

Hehenberger, L., Harling, A. M., & Scholten, P. (2013). *A practical guide to measuring and managing impact*. European Venture Philanthropy Association.

Hlady-Rispal, M., & Servantie, V. (2018). Deconstructing the way in which value is created in the context of social entrepreneurship. *International Journal of Management Reviews, 20*(1), 62–80.

Höchstädter, A. K., & Scheck, B. (2015). What's in a name: An analysis of impact investing understandings by academics and practitioners. *Journal of Business Ethics, 132*(2), 449–475.

Kellogg, W. K. (2006). *Logic model development guide*. WK Kellogg Foundation Web site.

Kramer, M. R., & Porter, M. (2011). *Creating shared value* (Vol. 17). FSG.

Lazzarini, S. G. (2018). The measurement of social impact and opportunities for research in business administration. *RAUSP Management Journal, 53*(1), 134–137.

Leborgne-Bonassié, M., Coletti, M., & Sansone, G. (2019). What do venture philanthropy organisations seek in social enterprises? *Business Strategy & Development, 2*(4), 349–357.

Lee, M., Adbi, A., & Singh, J. (2020). Categorical cognition and outcome efficiency in impact investing decisions. *Strategic Management Journal, 41*(1), 86–107.

Lehner, O. M. (2016). *Routledge handbook of social and sustainable finance*. Routledge.

Lieberman, D. (2020). Impact investing 2.0—Not just for do-gooders anymore. *The Journal of Investing, 29*(2), 58–69.

McCallum, S., & Viviers, S. (2020). Exploring key barriers and opportunities in impact investing in an emerging market setting. *South African Journal of Business Management, 51*(1), 11.

Migliavacca, A. M. (2018). Social impact measurement practices; A meta-analysis. *International Journal Series in Multidisciplinary Research (IJSMR), 2*(3), 1–17.

Mook, L., Maiorano, J., Ryan, S., Armstrong, A., & Quarter, J. (2015). Turning social return on investment on its head: The stakeholder impact statement. *Nonprofit Management and Leadership, 26*(2), 229–246.

O'Flynn, P., & Barnett, C. (2017). *Evaluation and impact investing: A review of methodologies to assess social impact* (No. IDS Evidence Report; 222). IDS. https://www.researchgate.net/publication/325049649_Evaluation_and_Impact_Investing_A_Review_of_Methodologies_to_Assess_Social_Impact.

O'Flynn, P., Higdon, G. L., Besamusca, D., & Shetty, A. (2019). *Deepening impact through a participatory due diligence process*. IDS. https://www.ids.ac.uk/publications/deepening-impact-through-a-participatory-due-diligence-process/.

Orum, A. M. (2001). Case study: Logic. In N. J. Smelser & P. B. Baltes (Eds.), *International encyclopedia of the social and behavioral sciences* (Vol. 3, pp. 1509–1511). Elsevier.

Quélin, B. V., Kivleniece, I., & Lazzarini, S. (2017). Public-private collaboration, hybridity and social value: Towards new theoretical perspectives. *Journal of Management Studies, 54*(6), 763–792.

Rawhouser, H., Cummings, M., & Newbert, S. L. (2019). Social impact measurement: Current approaches and future directions for social entrepreneurship research. *Entrepreneurship Theory and Practice, 43*(1), 82–115.

Reeder, N., & Colantonio, A. (2013). *Measuring impact and non-financial returns in impact investing: A critical overview of concepts and practice*. The London School of Economics and the European Investment Bank Institute. https://lsecities.net/wp-content/uploads/2013/10/Measuring_Impact-full-length-Oct-20131.pdf.

Reeder, N., Colantonio, A., Loder, J., & Rocyn Jones, G. (2015). Measuring impact in impact investing: An analysis of the predominant strength that is also its greatest weakness. *Journal of Sustainable Finance & Investment, 5*(3), 136–154.

Reisman, J., Olazabal, V., & Hoffman, S. (2018). Putting the "impact" in impact investing: The rising demand for data and evidence of social outcomes. *American Journal of Evaluation, 39*(3), 389–395.

Rizzello, A., Migliazza, M. C., Carè, R., & Trotta, A. (2016). Social impact investing: A model and research agenda. In O. M. Lehner (Ed.), *Routledge handbook of social and sustainable finance* (pp. 102–124). Routledge.

Rizzi, F., Pellegrini, C., & Battaglia, M. (2018). The structuring of social finance: Emerging approaches for supporting environmentally and socially impactful projects. *Journal of Cleaner Production, 170*, 805–817.

Sammarco, F., Liotta, L., Scognamiglio, E., Testa, L., & Vitale, S. (2018). *Valutazione d'impatto ed imprese sociali: caratteristiche a confronto*, IRIS Network XII Colloquio Scientifico (Trento). https://irisnetwork.it/wp-content/uploads/2018/06/sammarco-liotta-scognamiglio-testa-vitale.pdf.

Scognamiglio, E., Di Lorenzo, E., Sibillo, M., & Trotta, A. (2019). Social uncertainty evaluation in social impact bonds: Review and framework. *Research in International Business and Finance, 47*, 40–56.

So, I., & Staskevicius, A. (2015). *Measuring the "impact" in impact investing*. Harvard Business School, Social Enterprise. http://www.hbs.edu/socialenterprise/Documents/MeasuringImpact.pdf.

Talan, G., & Sharma, G. D. (2019). Doing well by doing good: A systematic review and research agenda for sustainable investment. *Sustainability, 11*(2), 353.

Vanclay, F. (2003). International principles for social impact assessment. *Impact Assessment and Project Appraisal, 21*(1), 5–11.

Vecchi, V., Balbo, L., Brusoni, M., & Caselli, S. (Eds.). (2017). *Principles and practice of impact investing: A catalytic revolution*. Routledge.

Verrinder, N. B., Zwane, K., Nixon, D., & Vaca, S. (2018). Evaluative tools in impact investing: Three case studies on the use of theories of change. *African Evaluation Journal, 6*(2), 9.

Victora, C. G., Black, R. E., Boerma, J. T., & Bryce, J. (2011). Measuring impact in the Millennium development goal era and beyond: A new approach to large-scale effectiveness evaluations. *The Lancet, 377*(9759), 85–95.

Viviani, J. L., & Maurel, C. (2019). Performance of impact investing: A value creation approach. *Research in International Business and Finance, 47*, 31–39.

Vo, A. T., & Christie, C. A. (2018). Where impact measurement meets evaluation: Tensions, challenges, and opportunities. *American Journal of Evaluation, 39*(3), 383–388.

Walker, T., Kibsey, S. D., & Lee, S. (2017). Impact investing. In C. Krosinsky & S. Purdom (Eds.), *Sustainable investing: Revolutions in theory and practice* (pp. 17–24). Routledge.

Yin, R. K. (2017). *Case study research and applications: Design and methods*. Sage.

Social Investment in the UK: The Emergence of a Hollow Field

Belinda Bell

1 Introduction

The notion of using financial mechanisms to achieve pro-social goals fits well with the neo-liberal zeitgeist, in that it is a powerful idea representing innovation at the intersection of social and financial paradigms and potentially even shining a light on a new economic era. These are the ideas that have underpinned the emergence of social investment in the UK over the last two decades.

Over the last 20 years, the concept of social investment has emerged and been the focus of much public goodwill and increasingly of academic research (Daggers & Nicholls, 2016). Significant government funding and legislative support (H.M. Government, 2016) have been directed toward social investment, and it has been argued that, taken together, the series of interventions and institutional development have contributed to social investment emerging as a distinct and recognizable field of practice, particularly in the UK (Bell & Haugh, 2016).

However, all is not as would be expected in such an institutionalized field. There is significant dissonance between the experience of field

B. Bell (✉)
Cambridge Judge Business School, Cambridge, UK
e-mail: bb326@cam.ac.uk

T. Walker et al. (eds.), *Innovations in Social Finance*,
https://doi.org/10.1007/978-3-030-72535-8_21

actors, such as finance providers, government and policy representatives and the supposed beneficiaries or investees in the field. The gray literature on the subject, practitioners, and sector blogs have long argued that social investment is not having an impact on the ground. Key actors acknowledge that social investment is not succeeding in delivering on its promise (O'Donohoe, 2016). Despite the appearance of a coherent and established field, meaningful activity in UK social investment—in terms of the value of social investment deals completed—is unexpectedly low.

This chapter illustrates the low activity level and draws on institutional theory to apply a critical perspective to analyze the field of social investment. This illustrates the existence of a novel phenomenon that I term "Hollow Fields."

A hollow field is one which, despite initial appearances, is not substantiated. In the case of social investment, the field has been characterized by a significant amount of institutional work leading to a high degree of institutionalization and the outward trappings of an established field, and yet a low degree of meaningful or productive activity.

By definition hollow fields are hard to identify from the outside, as they appear to contain all the institutions and actors expected; it is only through detailed examinations that their hollowness in terms of activity becomes apparent. I set out to establish why this situation exists and what types of institutional work have contributed to creating it.

In this chapter, I examine some key actors and explore the institutional work they undertook that contributed to social investment emerging as a hollow field. I will posit some suggestions of likely pre-conditions leading to the emergence of similar hollow fields. Alongside the academic literature, I utilize secondary data including reports from the Social Investment Task Force and its successor bodies, gray literature from within the sector and governmental departments, and the websites of key actors.

Subsequent to this introduction, the paper is structured as follows: The second section introduces field theory and the core concepts of institutional work; in the third section, the empirical context of social investment in the UK is explored; the fourth section illustrates the lack of actual social investment activity; in the fifth section, I identify three key actors and outline the institutional work they undertook to contribute to the development of the field; in the sixth section, I draw all this together to argue that social finance is a hollow field and identify factors relating to institutional work that may have led to this happening; and finally, I conclude in section seven by giving my impressions of likely pre-conditions for the emergence of hollow fields, outlining why this is important and relevant more broadly to field studies, and making some suggestions for the next steps in research.

2 Field Theory and Institutional Work

An institutional field is a "recognized area of institutional life" (DiMaggio & Powell, 1983, p. 148) in which there is "a community of organizations that partakes of a common meaning system and whose participants interact more frequently and fatefully with one another than with actors outside the field" (Scott, 2001, p. 84). The practices of an institutional field develop through interactions between actors within the community of organizations making up the field (DiMaggio & Powell, 1991; Lawrence et al., 2002; Scott, 2001). The concept of an institutional field is considered a "cornerstone of institutional theory" (Zietsma et al., 2014, p. 2).

Fields are formed of institutions. The processes by which institutions are themselves created, maintained, and disrupted are known as "institutional work" (Lawrence & Suddaby, 2006). Institutional work acknowledges that individual actors purposefully set out to create institutions by engaging in a wide range of practices over time. The concept of institutional work is an influential approach to focus on the many practical and real actions individual actors take in the process of institution and subsequently, field-building (Tracey et al., 2011; Zietsma & Lawrence, 2010).

Despite its relative youth, the field of social investment presents itself as an established institutionalized field with elaborate institutional infrastructure. Over the last two decades, a considerable amount of institutional work has been undertaken in service of building the field of social investment. The rapid field development can perhaps be seen as a purposeful attempt to become sufficiently legitimized and institutionalized to whether any potential changes ahead, including a drop in government support.

Lawrence and Suddaby (2006) propose several different forms of institutional work that create institutions and these can be separated into three groups. The first group includes advocacy, defining, and vesting. These focus on engaging political support, constructing rules and identity, and allowing, for instance, the government to confer property rights. Ultimately, these three forms of work are mutually reinforcing of each other and often involve “the dramatic, wholesale reconstruction of institutions or institutional structures and practices” (2006, p. 223).

The second group is more focused on rules, values, and norms within the peer group and their practices in the field. This group includes activity such as constructing identities, changing normative associations, and constructing normative networks.

The final group includes mimicry, theorizing, and education that seek to provide meaningful patterns which result in a reduction in the costs and risks of institutional creation (Lawrence & Suddaby, 2006, p. 228).

Taken together, these three groups of institutional work are undertaken by actors as fields develop. Lawrence and Suddaby’s proposed categories are used in section five to explore the specific institutional work undertaken by three key actors in the social investment field.

3 The Development of the Field of Social Investment in the UK 1997–2020

While people have always found ways to use money for social good, social investment, as it is currently conceived, emerged in association with the rise of interest in social enterprise and social innovation in the late 1990s (Bell & Haugh, 2016; Nicholls & Emerson, 2015). Social enterprise’s overarching philosophy was about being “market-driven, client-driven and self-sufficient” (Tracey et al., 2005, p. 355), and proponents of social enterprise were considered to be “enabling alternative capitalist possibilities” (Dey & Teasdale, 2015, p. 11). Social investment arose within this specific context where there was a perceived increase in demand for social investment by social entrepreneurs and also an increasing interest in social investment from government and investors (Nicholls, 2014).

Over the last 20 years, there have been significant increases in practice, policy, and research around social investment (Bishop & Green, 2010; Bell & Haugh, 2016; SIIT, 2014). As Casanovas and Ventresca (2016, p. 694) observe, “The fact of these activities is well documented and well known, and the UK is regularly referred to as a global leader in this space.”

Lawrence and Phillips (2004) have shown how macro-cultural discourse can pave the way for the emergence of new fields. In the case of social investment, the external political and social context enabled and encouraged its emergence as a result of the prevailing zeitgeist. The election of the New Labour government in 1997 was a precursor to the public exploration of many new ideas and practices. The possibility of resolving social problems by using the power of markets appeals to a wide spectrum of actors and, in particular, the political climate was favorable for exploring ways to link disadvantaged communities with the mainstream economy (Bell & Haugh, 2016; Dayson, 2004), including through social enterprise.

One of the defining moments in the establishment of social investment in the UK was the convening of the Social Investment Task Force (SITF) in 2000. The SITF was an initiative created by the UK Social Investment Forum, in partnership with three non-profit organizations focused on social impact, community development, and poverty alleviation. However, the SITF was close to the government too, as its formation was announced by the Chancellor of the Exchequer and the Treasury held observer status. The members of the SITF included senior figures from the charitable and private sectors.

While it has been argued that institutional entrepreneurship is contingent and emergent, i.e., reactive and by chance (Lawrence & Phillips, 2004), the institutionalization of social investment has been somewhat more purposeful than that. Specifically, governmental support, which is frequently prominent in financial markets, has been very significant. From initially launching the SITF to introducing new legal structures and tax reliefs, as well as legislating to create a wholesale social investment institution and directly funding multiple programs, government support has stretched over nearly two decades in different phases (Spear et al., 2015). This has included specific program interventions on the demand side, the supply side, and in the intermediation of the market as well as playing the role of promotion, which is common for governments who act as convenors and create legitimacy by acting as market champions (Casanovas & Ventresca, 2016; Vermeulen et al., 2007). Ultimately, this governmental support builds both a market and policy setting. The government, or actors within the government, are actively members of the field itself.

A range of cross-sector actors have been involved in developing social investment, but it has been largely catalyzed or enabled by the consistent support of the government, informed by connections to private sector financiers among others. Throughout, the legitimacy of senior finance figures and finance logics *per se* have not been seriously questioned. Since 1997, successive governments led by different political parties have supported social enterprise (Dey & Teasdale, 2015, p. 3).

They purposefully sought to develop the field of social investment and played a dominant role in it by investing very considerable resources into it (Casanovas & Ventresca, 2016). Since 2001, the UK government committed well over £10 billion of public funds to subsidize the social investment market (Flip Finance & The Access Foundation, 2017).

4 Activity Levels in the Field of Social Investment

Given the development of the institutions, practices, and products in social investment over a two-decade period, with the government funding to support it, observers may reasonably expect there to be a concomitant rapid development of meaningful activity within the field, i.e., actual investments being made. However, this has not occurred. The field has consistently underperformed in expectations, and there are many examples of unmet projections and underutilized apparatus.

Underutilized apparatus include two tax reliefs: Community Investment Tax Relief (CITR) and Social Investment Tax Relief (SITR). CITR was intended to incentivize investment into Community Development Finance Institutions. The relief was brought in 2002, and the initial proposal for CITR claimed it would lead to an additional £1bn in investment over a five-year period. However, in practice it has substantially undershot that £1bn, and the reported investment is more likely to be around £145m to date.[1] Similarly, SITR has also been massively underutilized: introduced in 2014 against a prediction of £83m of resultant investment, only £5m was raised in the following three years (Floyd, 2019; Rotheroe & Lomax, 2016).

Activity without expected impact can be illustrated by Social Impact Bonds (SIBs). SIBs are outcome mechanisms that were first launched in 2010 and they "captured the collective imagination of a range of actors" (Addis, 2015, p. 448), leading to the rapid commissioning of around 200 SIBs around the world (Fraser et al., 2016). Early SIBs are now recognized as expensive and overengineered (Maier et al., 2018). The House of Lords Select Committee on Charities took evidence in October 2016 from several sector leaders including Geoff Burnand, the Chief Executive of Investing for Good, a social investment intermediary.

[1] Estimate from Responsible Finance, July 2020. https://responsiblefinance.org.uk/.

He stated that SIBs were "incomprehensible to mainstream investors and broadly irrelevant to many front-line, smaller organisations" (Parliament, 2016). SIBs operate over multi-year timeframes and so the evidence base is still emerging; however, it seems that a cautionary approach to their effectiveness is imperative (Edmiston & Nicholls, 2018; Fraser et al., 2016).

Big Society Capital (BSC) is the largest player in the social investment market in the UK, as well as being a market champion and significant influencer. It had a long gestation period, in that it was first mooted in 2005 through The Commission on Unclaimed Assets until it eventually launched in 2012. BSC has two core streams of work: Firstly, it invests its funds through wholesaling into social finance intermediaries, and secondly, it acts as a champion for the sector by promoting social investment, sharing best practice, providing education, and networking initiatives. BSC is explored in more detail in the next section. In terms of it underdelivering on expectations, it was launched in 2012 with available funds of £625m and had more committed from dormant bank accounts. By 2020, BSC's investment portfolio stood at £373m. BSC's lack of success in deploying capital triggers a note of concern for the whole social investment sector.

Within the overall social investment market, a lack of definitions and a lag in data being collected somewhat hinder analysis; however, it is demonstrably much smaller than anticipated. In 2012, Brown and Swersky projected that the market would amount to £1bn in 2016. BSC reported in 2015 a market that is roughly comparable to Brown and Swersky's projection, amounting to £427m. They equate this to a "not spectacular" 20% annual growth rate (Big Society Capital, 2016, p. 11).

By 2019, BSC reported the UK social investment market had grown to £3.5bn; however, this was after changing the definition being used that resulted in the inclusion of more investments. Additionally, over recent years, government subsidies have continued amounting to a total of at least £10bn (Flip Finance & The Access Foundation, 2017). According to the BSC website (2020), there has been no systematic analysis of the "value for money" of the government subsidies.

Some will contend that building a new field will inevitably be a long journey, and subsequently, the low transaction volume is not of concern. Mulgan et al. (2007) suggest that social investment will face challenges including the struggle against "vested interests" (p. 4). This heroic dialog, i.e., preparing for a long process with the need for persistence, is a call to be patient with the lack of progress. It has been argued that there remains a need for more intervention including intermediaries to enable the market to operate, functional stock exchanges to create liquidity, more time to develop demand pipelines, additional and bespoke products, and most of all, more investment capital (Schwartz et al., 2016).

A contrasting view is that as social investment has consistently failed to gain the anticipated traction, it is only sensible to reexamine the underlying assumptions. For instance, much of the early reasoning on the need for social investment was because there was a need to correct market failure. Subsequent market interventions have been in supply, demand, and intermediation. These are not elements of market failure being corrected, but rather the (attempted) wholesale construction of a market. Such widespread interventions, without notable success, lead us to question the original verdict of market failure. Indeed, the conclusion that there was or is a shortage of finance for social enterprise is inaccurate and many social enterprises secure bank lending in the traditional way (Floyd & Gregory, 2016; Lyon, 2016). If there is not a genuine shortage of finance for social enterprise, then the social investment sector has been built upon an essential misunderstanding.

I have demonstrated the low levels of meaningful social investment activity in the UK as well as the repeated disconnect between projections and actual delivery. Among practitioners, this is not news. Nick O'Donohoe, on standing down as Chief Executive of BSC, writes that "the volume of political rhetoric, consulting work, academic research, and global convening that [social investment] has created is disproportionate to the amount of money that has actually moved" (O'Donohoe, 2016, p. 49). In writing this, it appears that O'Donohoe foreshadows my own description of social investment activity as a hollow field.

5 Key Actors and Their Institutional Work

To explore the process of creating the field of social investment and the institutional work involved, I have chosen three actors that each possess key strategic resources, power, and thus a significant influence on the development of the field. Each of these actors used creative ways to achieve their desired ends over a period of many years. As such, they undertook what has been conceptualized as "intelligent, situated" institutional work (Lawrence & Suddaby, 2006, p. 219).

5.1 *Social Investment Task Force (and Successor Bodies)*

The SITF was highly influential; its establishment in 2000 represents the starting point of the current wave of interest in social investment in the UK. The SITF and successor bodies released a series of reports providing a substantial body of data.

The initial SITF report (2000) laid out a series of policy proposals that catalyzed the development of the social investment sector. The SITF continued to meet and produce additional reports (2003, 2005, and 2010) for over 10 years, setting the agenda for the development of the sector. It merged into the successor body of the Social Impact Investment Taskforce in 2013, which released an influential report (2014) and itself merged into a further successor body, the Global Steering Group for Impact Investing (GSG) in 2015, which continued to release reports (2018).

Initially, the SITF's institutional work was focused on *advocacy*. Through its reports, it made recommendations to the government about specific legislative interventions. The impact of its initial recommendations is a result of mobilizing both political and regulatory support. The power of the SITF is manifest, in that four of the five policy proposals in the initial report were enacted within three years (Bell & Haugh, 2016, p. 55).

This fundamental advocacy work was a key method by which marginal actors acquired legitimacy. For instance, Community Development Finance Institutions (CDFIs) were marginal, young, and fragile organizations. The recommendations in the first SITF report legitimized them by calling for both general governmental support, particularly a trade body, and also a tax relief that would benefit CDFIs. These recommendations made CDFIs more visible and their enactment helped to validate their work with marginalized communities.

The SITF also undertook *definitional* institutional work. Institutional work is often "language centred" (Lawrence & Suddaby, 2006, p. 239) and developed through physical reports and documentation. The first in the series of SITF reports specifies types of organizations that will form part of the field (Bell & Haugh, 2016, p. 57) including a fairly extensive glossary and the introduction of new terms, many borrowed or adapted from the US. By using new language, the SITF contributed to creating an identifiable space, separate from that which previously existed. Additionally, the introduction of a tax relief came with the associated necessity for accreditation to be able to utilize it. In time, holding this accreditation became equated with being part of the field (2003, p. 4).

The SITF and its successors also helped to *change normative associations*, in two particular ways: firstly, by reframing finance as a possible source of social good, and secondly, by suggesting it was important and right for the traditional third sector to become more entrepreneurial/professional.

The institutional work of reframing finance as a "social good" runs throughout the publications of the SITF. The introduction to the first report states: "Social investment, intended to achieve both social objectives and financial returns, can work alongside conventional commercial finance and business, to the advantage of the whole community" (2000, p. 4). Similar statements continue throughout the reports, and by 2014, rather inflated analogies are being drawn: "It harnesses the forces of entrepreneurship, innovation and capital and the power of markets to do good. One might with justification say that it brings the invisible heart of markets to guide their invisible hand" (SIIT, 2014, p. 1).

Similarly, over the span of these reports, the institutional work of encouraging change in the traditional third sector is reported to have developed. "The long-term aim of the Social Investment Task Force is to achieve a move away from this culture of philanthropy, paternalism and dependence towards one of empowerment, entrepreneurship and initiative." (2000, p. 4). The SITF considered that "Entrepreneurial behaviour in the voluntary sector tends to be fettered by its traditions, laws and established practices" (2000, p. 14) and made some specific recommendations to change these. Ten years later, the SITF reported "…a shift in mindset and culture amongst voluntary sector organisations, which have become more entrepreneurial and more focused on the sustainable achievement of their targeted social result" (2010, p. 2). In this, the SITF is effectively reporting the success of its institutional work of changing the traditional normative associations of the third sector.

Another piece of institutional work undertaken by the SITF is that of *mimicry*. Many of the proposals to develop social investment explicitly draw on the example of the US and also of the venture capital industry. In the Appendix of one of its reports (2000, p. 27), the SITF includes a table directly comparing elements of the UK and US community development finance systems. This strategy seeks to reassure the reader by both demonstrating that it is possible to develop a sector as proposed by the SITF and making explicit the opportunities for growth.

In terms of mimicking the venture capital industry, the SITF states "successful principles of the venture capital industry… should be applied to community investment," then adds, "In the last 20 years, venture capital has made a major contribution to the growth of wealth and employment in the UK" (2000, p. 5) and therefore encourages the mimicry of these techniques in developing the social investment sector. I will return to this issue later when discussing Sir Ronald Cohen.

The 2014 report continued much of the advocacy and defining work (particularly in an international context) but also additionally undertook the institutional work of *theorizing*. This report includes attempts to build the "cognitive map" (Lawrence & Suddaby, 2006, p. 226) of the field by adopting a new term ("social impact investment") and providing charts and diagrams of, for instance, the ecosystem (SIIT, 2014, p. 3) and individual social impact investment products (SIIT, 2014, p. 4).

I have shown then how the SITF used a variety of techniques of institutional work to promote advocacy, new definitions, the change of normative associations, mimicry, and theorizing over an extended time period. The advantage of the SITF repeatedly releasing reports and revisiting progress is that these processes are well documented, and the reports themselves contain timelines of actions undertaken in the process of building the field of social investment.

5.2 *Big Society Capital*

Big Society Capital (BSC) is an independent financial institution with a social mission. It was set up in 2012 to help grow the social investment market in the UK. BSC was capitalized with funds from dormant bank accounts, plus debt finance from mainstream banks making a total of over £600m (Schwartz et al., 2016). It is a wholesaler of finance, investing in intermediaries that onward invest into social sector organizations.

BSC benefitted from the ongoing institutional work of advocacy undertaken by the SITF. The SITF helped to create a climate in which further work that is crucial to BSC's existence could be undertaken, referred to as "vesting." The Commission on Unclaimed Assets, which emerged from the SITF, made the case that funds in dormant bank accounts could be put to use for social investment. To do this, it was necessary for the government to appropriate these assets and pass them to BSC. This clear example of vesting led to an unprecedented inflow of capital into the social investment sector.

One of BSC's founding principles is that it seeks to be self-sustainable from its activities and thus demonstrates that the model of social investment is sustainable. Given this principle, it is perhaps not surprising that BSC has produced a considerable number of publications focusing on itself. These include publicly available annual reviews, financial reviews, and stakeholder feedback about BSC. These are further examples of language-based institutional work. The publications and activities undertaken across BSC's many projects can be understood as undertaking the institutional work of *advocacy, theorizing* and *education*.

BSC also makes and publicizes investments, developing case studies of social investments aimed at both potential investees and investors. It has produced a number of documents focused on public policy and on promoting social investment. BSC holds events and conferences, sponsors sector initiatives, holds webinars, and has a social media presence. These elements of BSC's activities can be viewed through an institutional work lens as being focused on *constructing identities*, *changing normative associations*, and *constructing normative networks*.

In its role as a champion, BSC has undertaken considerable work promoting Social Investment Tax Relief (SITR). BSC has produced multiple case studies, reports, and videos, as well as held events focused on SITR. Through these materials, the institutional work of *mimicry, theorizing*, and *education* emerges.

5.3 Sir Ronald Cohen

Sir Ronald Cohen has been heavily involved in the development of the social investment sector. Initially working in venture capital and known as the "father of British venture capital," he has also often been referred to as the "father of social investment" (Casasnovas & Ventresca, 2015). Cohen holds a pivotal role in the social investment sector because he was the founding Chair of both the SITF and BSC. Lawrence and Phillips (2004) have previously shown how the decisions of one influential individual can have a crucial impact on an emerging field.

Cohen has had a direct influence in almost all of the significant developments in the sector and has been in a governance role on all the most significant (non-governmental) organizations. Following the initial SITF report, he went on to be the founding Chair of two organizations that were a direct result of SITF recommendations: the Community Development Finance Association and Bridges Ventures. He also acted as

Chair of the Commission on Unclaimed Assets from 2005, which recommended the establishment of BSC, before becoming BSC's founding Chair. He is currently Chair of Global Steering Group for Impact Investment (GSG). He has played many other relevant roles perhaps most noteworthy being co-founder of Social Finance UK, a financial advisory organization that designed and promoted Social Impact Bonds among other social investment products.

Cohen's presence has been identified as having a strong legitimizing impact on both politicians and financiers (Spear et al., 2015, p. 462). He has been involved in politics as a parliamentary candidate for the Liberal Party, subsequently becoming a supporter and donor to the Labour Party. Nevertheless, his influence continued with the subsequent Conservative/Liberal Democrat coalition government, and he has thus demonstrated an ability to span the political landscape.

In terms of the institutional work he has undertaken, much of Cohen's work has been through the organizations he Chairs. His actions are a fine example of how to "creatively navigate" within organizational fields (Lawrence & Suddaby, 2006, p. 219). In particular, he liaised between successive governments and the sector, developed his views and practices iteratively, and mediated between the different logics of the government, the social sector, and the finance sector.

Cohen's background is in venture capital, and he has promoted that model within social investment. Venture capital as a field has built myths around itself, meaning that it exists and is respected despite poor performance (Mulcahy, 2013). In the development of social investment, there has been hierarchical diffidence to a pre-existing logic (that of venture capital) (Purdy & Gray, 2009, p. 357), which is not founded on evidence of success. Cohen's career is inseparable from venture capital and, similarly, the ideas, models, and language of venture capital have become inseparable from social investment.

6 Hollow Fields Emerging from Institutional Work

Social finance presents as an institutionalized field in the sense that there are multiple organizations, consultants, regulations and regulatory agencies, conferences and academic papers; therefore, the field is recognizable to onlookers (DiMaggio & Powell, 1983, p. 148). It has also been demonstrated that the amount of meaningful activity in terms of transactions and volume of capital deployed is far lower than projected. Theoretically, it seems that a high degree of institutionalization has occurred, which would usually indicate field emergence, and yet without the expected associated activity. I have been unable to identify previous examples in the literature of field emergence and structuration in the absence of the expected relevant, meaningful activity. I label this new phenomenon a hollow field.

Field study scholars recognize that nuanced understandings are difficult to elicit without deep embeddedness in a field. The extant literature has an *a priori* assumption that the interactions between field actors are meaningful and contribute to the ongoing legitimization of the field. Having explored some of the institutional work that was undertaken as social investment developed, I seek here to elaborate on why such hollow fields exist.

Firstly, the environmental conditions were receptive to the emergence of social investment. The New Labour government in 1997 ushered in an era of innovation that was focused on social change in keeping with Labour policy. People genuinely wanted to solve issues of social inequality. Social investment was a natural extension of the social enterprise logic which was embraced at that time. Interestingly, this enthusiasm continued through the financial crash of 2008 when public questioning of the financial markets led to the concept of social investment being looked upon favorably as an ethical alternative to the financial activities which were perceived to have led to the crash.

The fact that there were genuine problems to solve and that the prevailing zeitgeist considered social enterprise as a key part of a potential solution laid the groundwork for the emergence of social investment. Social investment both built on the mainstream neo-liberal logics of finance and markets as well as introduced a socially beneficial element. This was appealing and comprehensible across government, private, and community sectors.

Secondly, the individuals and the coalition of actors that supported social investment held strong legitimacy. While initially including actors from the community sector, in time the voices of the private sector, particularly in finance, came to dominate and were respected by the government, which was a key actor itself and more importantly, a very major funder.

The SITF, BSC, and Ronald Cohen undertook well-crafted, extensive institutional work, over extended time periods. They used various approaches to practically and technically prepare the ground, to change the values and social norms, then to demonstrate how the sector could be embedded for scale and longevity through the use of appealing rhetorical arguments and ambitious and inspiring claims.

The ongoing existence of the field over a certain time period does not demonstrate it is solid, and suboptimal institutions and practices can be maintained for considerable periods of time (DiMaggio & Powell, 1991). In the case of social investment, the institutional work has become somewhat self-sustaining since more actors want to engage with this appealing idea. Indeed, it can be argued that the more vested interests are involved in the field, the more disincentives there are to openly dispute its success, especially when the public sector subsidy continues to support social investment.

7 Conclusion

The existence of hollow fields is theoretically novel and adds to the current debate within field theory. Prior work has not proposed the existence of hollow fields. My contention is that among some of the contestation and ambiguity of field studies, there may be other hollow fields. They are, by definition, hard to identify. Perhaps an embedded actor, who is close enough to tap the wall and unencumbered enough to label it as hollow, is required.

The identification of social investment, in particular, as a hollow field is important due to the amount of public subsidy that has and is flowing into it. With multiple calls on limited available public funds, it is imperative that they are spent in an effective manner. The context within which social investment has developed is specific, and the external socio-cultural factors (for instance the fit with contemporary ideologies) may be pertinent to the development of hollow fields. Additionally, I have demonstrated how the specific institutional work of certain actors resulted in impressive and effective field-building. It seems that in the case of social investment, the successful and purposeful institutional work undertaken by multiple actors combined with the specific macro-cultural context, i.e., there was a real desire to create the field and social outcomes, resulted in the creation of a hollow field.

To extend the utility and usefulness of this work and add theoretical prescience (Corley & Gioia, 2011), I attempt to predict characteristics that may imply or encourage the development or existence of a hollow field:

- Building on Lawrence and Phillips (2004), a scenario in which the new field is in keeping with broader macro-cultural developments. In the case of social investment, it was appealing from a social and cultural perspective, in terms of an innovative approach, to solve intractable social problems.
- In particular, a scenario in which powerful actors, such as those from government or policy, are particularly focused on new and innovative solutions either through opportunity (e.g., the beginning of the New Labour government) or desperation (e.g., post financial crash of 2008).
- Following that, a situation in which there are highly legitimate actors who hold power and can undertake significant institutional work, including that which exerts influence over less knowledgeable power holders (e.g., civil servants). This may be exacerbated if individual actors are highly influential, (i.e., information asymmetry between government and other fields has been identified [Vermeulen et al., 2007]).
- Where there is an element of portmanteau on the cusps of sectors where previously antagonistic areas of practice are being brought together, allowing for a lack of clear definition. It is possible that the coalition of actors will either forge a genuinely new sector or simply rebrand old logics.

This chapter has been an initial attempt to use knowledge and access to data in the field to highlight the status of social investment as a hollow field. There are a number of avenues for further research building on this thesis, such as a data-rich study of actors in the field, which could reveal how it has developed in this manner, or a discourse analysis approach of extant documents, which could shed more light on the possible process of legitimization that I consider a precursor to the development of this hollow field. Therefore, I call on other researchers with deep familiarity with other fields to propose other hollow fields and to both test and add to my propositions about the likely factors leading to the emergence of hollow fields.

References

Addis, R. (2015). The roles of government and policy in social finance. In A. Nicholls, R. Paton, & J. Emerson (Eds.), *Social finance* (pp. 383–459). Oxford University Press.

Bell, B., & Haugh, H. (2016). The emergence and institutionalization of the field of social investment in the United Kingdom. In O. M. Lehner (Ed.), *Routledge handbook of social and sustainable finance* (pp. 50–67). Routledge.

Big Society Capital. (2016). *The size and composition of social investment in the UK. Social investment insights series*. Big Society Capital. https://golab.bsg.ox.ac.uk/knowledge-bank/resources/size-and-composition-social-investment-uk/.

Big Society Capital. (July, 2020). *For third year in a row UK social investment market grows by 30, now worth over 35 billion*. BSC. https://bigsocietycapital.com/latest/for-third-year-in-a-row-uk-social-investment-market-grows-by-30-now-worth-over-35-billion.

Bishop, M., & Green, M. (2010). *Philanthro-capitalism: How giving can save the world*. Bloomsbury.

Brown, A., & Swersky, A. (2012). *The first billion: A forecast of social investment demand*. Boston Consulting Group. https://mkt-bcg-com-public-images.s3.amazonaws.com/public-pdfs/legacy-documents/file115598.pdf.

Casanovas, G., & Ventresca, M. J. (2015, February 11). *Building a robust social investment market*. Stanford Social Innovation review. https://ssir.org/articles/entry/building_a_robust_social_investment_market.

Casanovas, G., & Ventresca, M. J. (2016). Formative dynamics in the UK social investment market, 2000–2015. In O. M. Lehner (Ed.), *Routledge handbook of social and sustainable finance* (pp. 693–709). Routledge.

Corley, K. G., & Gioia, D. A. (2011). Building theory about theory building: What constitutes a theoretical contribution? *Academy of Management Review, 36*(1), 12–32.

Daggers, J., & Nicholls, A. (2016). Academic research into social investing and impact investing. In O. M. Lehner (Ed.), *Routledge handbook of social and sustainable finance* (pp. 68–82). Routledge.

Dayson, K. (2004). *Community finance initiatives: A policy success story*. University of Salford, Salford.

Dey, P., & Teasdale, S. (2015). The tactical mimicry of social enterprise strategies: Acting 'as if' in the everyday life of third sector organizations. *Organization, 23*(4), 485–504.

DiMaggio, P. J., & Powell, W. W. (1983). The iron cage revisited: Institutional isomorphism and collective rationality in organizational fields. *American Sociological Review, 48*(2), 147–160.

DiMaggio, P. J., & Powell, W. W. (1991). Introduction. In W. W. Powell & P. J. DiMaggio (Eds.), *The new institutionalism and organizational analysis* (pp. 1–38). University of Chicago Press.

Edmiston, D., & Nicholls, A. (2018). Social impact bonds: The role of private capital in outcome-based commissioning. *Journal of Social Policy, 47*(1), 57–76.

Flip Finance & The Access Foundation. (2017). *Grant designs: Mapping the use of subsidy in the UK social investment market*. https://access-socialinvestment.org.uk/wp-content/uploads/2017/09/SubsidyReport.pdf.

Floyd, D. (2019). *What a relief! A review of social investment tax relief for charities and social enterprises*. Social Investment Business. https://www.sibgroup.org.uk/resources/what-relief-review-social-investment-tax-relief-sitr-charities-and-social-enterprises.

Floyd, D., & Gregory, D. (2016). *The forest for the trees: UK banks' investment in a social purpose*. RBS/Social Spider. http://flipfinance.org.uk/2016/07/23/forest-for-the-trees/.

Fraser, A., Tan, S., Lagarde, M., & Mays, N. (2016). Narratives of promise, narratives of caution: A review of the literature on social impact bonds. *Social Policy & Administration, 52*(1), 4–28. https://doi.org/10.1111/spol.12260.

Global Steering Group for Impact Investing. (2018). *Ideas for impact: 2018* working group papers. https://gsgii.org/news/.

H.M. Government. (2016). *Social investment: A force for social change, 2016 Strategy*. H. M. Government. https://assets.publishing.service.gov.uk/government/uploads/system/uploads/attachment_data/file/507215/6.1804_SIFT_Strategy_260216_FINAL_web.pdf.

Lawrence, T. B., Hardy, C., & Phillips, N. (2002). Institutional effects of interorganizational collaboration: The emergence of proto-institutions. *Academy of Management Journal, 45*(1), 281–290.

Lawrence, T. B., & Phillips, N. (2004). From *Moby Dick* to *Free Willy*: Macro-cultural discourse and institutional entrepreneurship in emerging institutional fields. *Organization, 11*(5), 689–711.

Lawrence, T. B., & Suddaby, R. (2006). Institutions and institutional work. In S. R. Clegg, C. Hardy, W. R. Nord, & T. B. Lawrence (Eds.), *The SAGE Handbook of Organizational Studies*. (2nd ed., pp. 215–254). Sage.

Lyon, F. (2016). Lending to social ventures: Existing demand for finance and the potential roles of social investment. In O. M. Lehner (Ed.), *Routledge handbook of social and sustainable finance* (pp. 177–188). Routledge.

Maier, F., Barbetta, G. P., & Godina, F. (2018). Paradoxes of social impact bonds. *Social Policy & Administration, 52*(7), 1332–1353.

Mulcahy, D. (2013, May). Six myths about venture capital. *Harvard Business Review*.

Mulgan, G., Tucker, S., Rushanara, A., & Sanders, B. (2007). *Social innovation: What it is, why it matters, how it can be accelerated.* Young Foundation. https://www.youngfoundation.org/publications/social-innovation-what-it-is-why-it-matters-how-it-can-be-accelerated/.

Nicholls, A. (2014). Filling the capital gap: Institutionalizing social finance. In S. Denny & F. Seddon (Eds.), *Social enterprise: Accountability and evaluation around the world.* (pp. 161–195). Routledge.

Nicholls, A., & Emerson, J. (2015). Social finance: Capitalizing social impact. In A. Nicholls, R. Paton, & J. Emerson (Eds.), *Social finance.* Oxford University Press.

O'Donohoe, N. (2016). A big new market? *Stanford Social Innovation Review.* https://ssir.org/articles/entry/a_big_new_market

Parliament, House of Lords. (2016, October 25). *Oral evidence to the select committee on Charities.*

Purdy, J. M., & Gray, B. (2009). Conflicting logics, mechanisms of diffusion, and multilevel dynamics in emerging institutional fields. *Academy of Management Journal, 52*(2), 335–380.

Rotheroe, A., & Lomax, P. (2016). *Social Investment Tax Relief (SITR): Two years on.* New Philanthropy Capital. https://www.bl.uk/collection-items/social-investment-tax-relief-sitr-two-years-on.

Schwartz, R., Jones, C., & Nicholls, A. (2016). Building the social finance infrastructure. In A. Nicholls, R. Paton, & J. Emerson (Eds.), *Social finance.* (pp. 488–517). Oxford University Press.

Scott, W. R. (2001). *Institutions and organizations.* Sage.

Social Impact Investment Taskforce (SIIT). (2014). *Impact investment: The invisible heart of markets, harnessing the power of entrepreneurship, innovation and capital for public good.* G8, Social Impact Investment Taskforce. Cabinet Office. https://gsgii.org/reports/impact-investment-the-invisible-heart-of-markets/.

Social Investment Task Force (SITF). (2000). *Enterprising communities: Wealth beyond welfare.* Social Investment Task Force. Cabinet Office. https://www.scrt.scot/wp-content/uploads/2019/03/SITaskForce_Enterprising-CommunitiesOct_2000.pdf.

Social Investment Task Force (SITF). (2003). *Enterprising communities: Wealth beyond welfare, A 2003 update on the Social Investment Task Force.* Social Investment Task Force. Cabinet Office. https://static1.squarespace.com/static/5a6f0b584c0dbf370367c95a/t/5b27cd1ef950b7fedf445e0f/1529335086558/SITF_July_2003.pdf.

Social Investment Task Force (SITF). (2005). *Enterprising communities: Wealth beyond welfare, A 2005 update on the Social Investment Task Force.* Social Investment Task Force. Cabinet Office. https://static1.squarespace.com/sta

tic/5a6f0b584c0dbf370367c95a/t/5b27ce070e2e7236482eb363/152933 5305895/SITF_July_2005.pdf.

Social Investment Task Force (SITF). (2010). *Social investment: Ten years on*. Social Investment Task Force. Cabinet Office. https://static1.squarespace.com/static/5a6f0b584c0dbf370367c95a/t/5b27ce32562fa7107cd1469e/1529335349485/SITF_10_year_review.pdf.

Spear, R., Paton, R., & Nicholls, A. (2015). Public policy for social finance in context. In A. Nicholls, R. Paton, & J. Emerson (Eds.), *Social finance*. (pp. 460–487). Oxford University Press. https://doi.org/10.1093/acprof:oso/9780198703761.003.0015.

Tracey, P., Phillips, N., & Haugh, H. (2005). 'Beyond philanthropy: Community enterprise as a basis for corporate citizenship. *Journal of Business Ethics, 58*, 327–344.

Tracey, P., Phillips, N., & Jarvis, O. (2011). Bridging institutional entrepreneurship and the creation of new organizational forms: A multilevel model. *Organization Science*, *22*(1), 60–80. https://doi.org/10.1287/orsc.1090.0522.

Vermeulen, P., Buch, R., & Greenwood, R. (2007). The impact of governmental policies in institutional fields: The case of innovation in the Dutch concrete industry. *Organization Studies, 28*(4), 515–540.

Zietsma, C., Groenewegen, P., Logue, D., & Hinings, A. R. (2014). Field or fields? Building the scaffolding for cumulation of research on institutional fields. *Academy of Management Annals*. ANNALS-2014–0052.R4.

Zietsma, C., Lawrence, T. B. (2010). Institutional work in the transformation of an organizational field: The interplay of boundary work and practice work. Administrative Science Quarterly, 55(2), 189–221. https://doi.org/10.2189/asqu.2010.55.2.189.

The New Venture Philanthropy

Sureyya Burcu Avci

1 Introduction

Venture philanthropy (VP) combines traditional philanthropy (grant-making activities) with the tools and methods of venture capitalism. Similar to traditional philanthropy, VP funds new innovations creating social impact. Similar to venture capitalism, VP remains engaged with its target social enterprises (SE) over extended periods at high levels in order to achieve predetermined levels of success. Venture philanthropists provide tailored financing support, non-financial support, and impact measurement tools to SEs (EVPA Knowledge Centre, 2018; John, 2006). The term, VP, was first introduced to the public in 1960s (Letts et al., 1997); however, it became popular in the 1990s in North America, in the 2000s in Europe (EVPA Knowledge Centre, 2018), and in the 2010s in Asia (AVPN Annual Review, 2019). Even though the approach to funding is similar to post-World War II generation of donations (Larson, 2002), it is a new and emerging method in the entrepreneurs' portfolio to support social innovation (EVPA Knowledge Centre, 2018). The execution and several distinguishing characteristics, such as recipients' nature, tailored

S. B. Avci (✉)
Sabanci University School of Management, Istanbul, Turkey
e-mail: burcu.avci@sabanciuniv.edu

T. Walker et al. (eds.), *Innovations in Social Finance*,
https://doi.org/10.1007/978-3-030-72535-8_22

financing, non-financial support, and impact measurement, are similar to venture capital activities (Gordon, 2014; Grossman et al., 2013).

Social entrepreneurs form organizations to improve the social and economic conditions of the poor and oppressed groups and scale up with innovations to realize social transformation (Alvord et al., 2004). VP organizations (VPOs) invest in SEs to realize their plans by employing market-based activities that create social value (Daly, 2008, 2012; Lehner & Nichols, 2014; Wirgau et al., 2010). SEs can be categorized as impact-only or impact-first entrepreneurial organizations. Impact-only organizations are charities, whose most or entire income comes from grants. Impact-first organizations are revenue-generating social enterprises and socially driven business. Commercially-oriented social sector organizations, such as nonprofits, voluntary organizations for public services, profit-making organizations addressing social problems and economic goals or operating in public welfare sectors, and community enterprises, fall into this category (EVPA OECD netFWD, 2014; Survey, 2013). The common terms among these enterprises are trading income and social benefit (Peattie & Morley, 2008). Impact investors seek social return along with financial return by investing in new innovations (Brest, 2012).

VPOs do not invest in traditional businesses, which are categorized as finance-first organizations, even though the traditional businesses provide social benefits. VP is not suitable for all SEs, just like venture capital is not suitable for all businesses. VP is most useful when SEs require an injection of capital along with "change management" in their operations, markets, distribution, or marketing channels. VPOs prefer young and dynamic SEs that require a turnaround in strategy, an increase in scale, or synergies through mergers and acquisitions (EVPA Knowledge Centre, 2018).

VPOs provide tailored financing to recipients with equity and debt, just like venture capital companies do for commercial ventures. In addition to debt and equity, VPOs often use grants and seldom use hybrid financial instruments to fund recipients. Grants are cash allocations to recipients without an expectation of repayment or financial return (EVPA Knowledge Centre, 2018). VPOs prefer funding of newly established SEs, which do not have enough funding and capacity to receive debt or equity. Debt and equity investments are preferred in financing more established and lucrative companies. Hybrid financial instruments are contracts used to align risks on SEs developing innovative products and services (Spiess-Knafl & Struewer, 2015). Mezzanine financing, convertible loans, and recoverable grants are some examples of hybrid financial instruments (EVPA Knowledge Centre, 2018).

The tailored financing term combines a thorough assessment of financing needs of SEs and available financing tools of VPOs. VPOs satisfy the needs of SEs with available and appropriate types of funds at hand. Moreover, it is also possible to co-invest in SEs to vary financing tools. Co-investment of VPOs with other philanthropic organizations, financial institutions, development agencies, and/or corporations spread risks makes it possible to invest in several SEs at the same time, increase VPO popularity, and enable diverse skills to many SEs on the positive side. On the negative side, it increases management costs, makes decision-making harder, compels dependency, causes free-riding issues, and consumes time (EVPA Knowledge Centre, 2018).

To achieve their predefined goals, VPOs provide non-financial support to SEs. Non-financial support can be in various forms, such as strategic, operational, governmental, and human capital support. VPO staff or third-party advisers (intermediaries) can be employed in these services (Moore et al., 2012). SEs may need strategic support to achieve change management, increase abilities to boost funds, use available funds better to increase revenues, strengthen staff and directors, and have better legal and operational support (EVPA Knowledge Centre, 2018).

After providing support and co-managing the SE, the VPO measures the impact created based on their predefined criteria. If the investment has achieved the target social/blended impact and the SE has learned how to keep financial sustainability and operational resiliency, the VPO successfully exits from the SE with the pleasure of reaching its targets (EVPA Knowledge Centre, 2018).

2 Where Does Venture Philanthropy Stand Within the Philanthropy Industry?

Traditional philanthropy can be defined as donating time, talent, or treasury to improve other people's lives (Fidelity Charitable, 2020). Narrowing this broad definition, traditional philanthropy usually focuses on "giving grants" for specific projects or social ventures to fill a need gap or alleviate a suffering in society (Grossman et al., 2013). Donors can be individuals, corporations, and philanthropic foundations. The donor selects the projects or social venture to invest. The primary motive of philanthropy is to generate societal value for the recipients, who are usually nonprofit service organizers. The philanthropist neither targets a change in the organizational structure, nor provides supervision or advice to the recipient. The philanthropist does not target any financial benefits as well; however, states/jurisdictions may provide tax benefits to philanthropists (Rosenman, 2019).

Individual philanthropists are usually high-net-worth individuals who invest nationally or internationally for traditional philanthropic purposes, such as disaster relief, sustainability, or development (Adelman, 2009). Contemporary individual philanthropists, such as business angels, microfinance providers, or crowd-funders, look for blended value (social and financial return together), whereas the purpose of traditional philanthropists is to achieve societal value only (Rosenman, 2019).

Recent decades have witnessed a growing number of corporate philanthropists. It is important to distinguish between nonprofit organizations and corporations. Corporations are traditional businesses (for-profit organizations), and they invest only a fraction of their revenues on philanthropic purposes. Philanthropic expenditures of corporations are categorized under environmental, social, or governance (ESG)-focused social responsibility activities intended to increase company performance. Improving social impact can be a secondary objective of traditional business or ESG companies (OECD netFWD, 2014). Corporations participate in philanthropic activities because there is evidence that philanthropic expenditures may increase stakeholder value (Logsdon et al., 1990; Wang & Qian, 2011) through firm reputation (Adams & Hardwick, 1998; Berman et al., 1999; Brammer & Millington, 2005; Fombrun & Shanley, 1990; Williams & Barrett, 2000; Wood & Jones, 1995); environmental issues and product safety (Chen et al., 2008); managerial incentives (Choi & Wang, 2007); firm financial performance (Abzug & Webb, 1997; Choi & Wang, 2007; Shaw & Post, 1993; Stendardi, 1992; Wang & Qian, 2011); shareholder value (Liang & Renneboog, 2017); tax advantages (Avci et al., 2016; Lowndes, 1960); and provide competitive advantages (Porter & Kramer, 2002). Engaging in corporate gifts has become widespread among corporations, in contrast to earlier bottom-line focused practices (Davis, 1973; Friedman, 1970; Gautier & Pache, 2015; Helme & Laurilla, 2009).

Philanthropic foundations and charitable institutions are the fundamental traditional donors. Their income is provided by individual/corporate donors and their assets are spent for socially useful purposes (Britannica, 2020). They were the largest donors in North

America throughout the twentieth century. However, as new models of philanthropy, such as VP, challenge traditional giving patterns, their share in the total global gifts has reduced dramatically after the 2000s (Powell et al., 2019). Institutional philanthropy gained importance after the 1980s when the social cutbacks and financial limitations of the welfare state caused need gaps for security, education, health, and poverty in Western societies (Rath & Schuyt, 2014; Shaw et al., 2010).

In the 1980s, more entrepreneurs emerged to fill the social-need gaps created by welfare state policies' abandonment. Neoliberalist ideologies are supported by the mega success of the Internet business to create new wealth and new capitalists in the 1990s and 2000s (Grossman et al., 2013; Johnson, 2010; Krugman, 2009; Rath & Schuyt, 2014; Shaw et al., 2013). The new socio-economic policies and the new tax code enlarged the income gap between the rich and the poor (Krugman, 2009; Shaw et al., 2013). As markets liberalized, entrepreneurs accumulated more wealth than ever. Part of the accumulated wealth was directed to philanthropy due to tax benefits and personal choices (Havens & Shervish, 1999; Rath & Schuyt, 2014). The newly minted billionaires were also eager to make a difference in the world during their own lifetimes. Coming from a business background, they further wanted to combine business techniques with philanthropy in order to ensure that their donations were used most efficiently and strategically (Frumpkin, 2003; Grossman et al., 2013; Johnson, 2010). Socially innovative products/services served by SEs built a new bridge between the rich and the poor (Gordon, 2014). In brief, VPs took over some of the responsibilities of the welfare state after the 1990s.

The demand for philanthropy can be described as a product of the increase in global wealth, the opening of the political space, the shifting roles of the market, the state and civil society, and the increased visibility of philanthropy and its influential leaders (Johnson, 2010). The entrepreneurs' philanthropy is both strategic and good natured. Strategic philanthropy brings philanthropist and recipient closer, and it is a new form of giving, with more responsibility on the philanthropist (Gautier & Pache, 2015). This kind of giving is complemented by contributions from philanthropists and recipients (Sulek, 2010). Compared to traditional philanthropy applications, entrepreneurs are more flexible in their approach: they apply tailored giving. The blurred boundaries of individual, corporate, and institutional giving allow them to find the most effective way for their donations (Larson, 2002).

3 Innovations of Venture Philanthropy

Traditional philanthropist organizations are generally small, disconnected, and they lack the assessment methods to measure impact. They compete to earn more funds from donors, and as a result, they do not learn each other's best practices. Due to their small size, they cannot influence the government and cannot achieve a national impact. Irrespective of the amount of generous funds or how hard-working the staff is, they do not fulfill the desired expectations from the society (Kramer, 2009). While grant provision is a primary activity in the philanthropy sector, the organization of giving was looked down upon as a secondary level effort in traditional philanthropy. As a result, traditional philanthropy ignores VP's non-financial activities with a conclusion of inefficient donations (Letts et al., 1997).

The new "venture" type of philanthropy is different in its approach to giving: first, the philanthropists are usually the new wealthy, who made billions through innovative ways and are ready to make a difference in the world. These people know well how venture capital works, and they apply venture capital or business angel methods to their donations. They put themselves in the positions of venture capitalists, treat giving as an investment, and manage recipients with a consultative engagement like in a venture capital deal. People from different backgrounds, such as business, philanthropy, and development sectors, who have large networks of other people and organizations, come together. They adopt a proactive approach to find the best opportunities to fit their institutional targets, based on their predefined strategy (Gordon, 2014). Giving is referred to as an investment because philanthropists seek a social return, which benefits society somehow (Dacin et al., 2010). Philanthropists intervene in the business of the recipient, make it more efficient by changing organizational structure, and exit after achieving the desired outcomes (Frumpkin, 2003; Gautier & Pache, 2015; Grossman et al., 2013). The philanthropist donates time and talent along with money to achieve a goal.

According to an OECD netFWD report (2014), the differences between VP and traditional philanthropy can be summarized as follows:

1. Charity or non-for-profit giving in traditional philanthropy shifts to for-profit or private sector giving in VP. VPOs usually invest in entrepreneurs in contrast to traditional philanthropy, which usually

provides grants to nonprofit organizations. This context distinguishes VP as complementary to the traditional philanthropy rather than a rival. VPOs do not directly serve the least developed countries/people; it serves markets and sectors where there is potential to evolve into a more efficient one. Funding financially fertile investments can have different impact on development than funding people in need. The new approach may increase inequality, and VPOs may bias certain sectors and regions where they see potential for monetarized outcomes.

2. Project-based transfers become systems- or sectors-based investments. Investment strategies lead VPOs to determine which sectors or businesses to invest in. Instead of funding diverse recipients, VPs adopt a systems approach to manage investments: VPOs organize co-investors, partners, and allies to intervene in the business whenever necessary, keep them focused, and keep in touch with stakeholders to run the business smoothly.

3. Cash donations are replaced with targeted investing in VP. Allocating grants to people who cannot effectively use them causes inefficiencies and unsatisfying outcomes, such as loss of funds, low level of innovations, and continual operational problems. VPOs not only allocate money, but also do strategic investments and use funds more effectively.

4. The tailored financing of VPOs replaces grants: a blend of grants, debt, equity, and hybrid financial instruments are employed to satisfy various needs of SEs in various investment stages. Grants are widely used in early stage investments, while other financing tools are used for later stages. The use of various financial tools effectively funds the recipients and hedges businesses against several potential risks.

5. The engagement style has changed. While traditional philanthropy has a light engagement with the management of the recipient, VPO and its partners have a maximum engagement almost in all managerial avenues from strategic, governmental, legal, and financial advice to marketing, production, and human resources management. VPOs keep in touch with the recipient to detect deficiencies that would block success. If a deficiency is detected, the required advice and resources are provided to run the business flawlessly.

6. Short (1–2 years) engagement periods are replaced with longer (5–10 years) engagement periods with VP. Engagement continues until SEs can sustain the businesses on their own. The duration

exceeds 10 years for some businesses posing several problems for VP, such as attached funds, and staff. Additionally, the timing of exit and unclear exit strategies are other potential problems that do not exist for traditional philanthropy (Grossman et al., 2013).

7. The altruistic, administrative, and financial giving type becomes innovative, multi-disciplinary, and commercial. People from business background in VPOs select more innovative projects with market-based solutions. Certain practices require some time to catch up to the cultural changes.

8. Success criteria shift to outcomes and impact from inputs and outputs. Success criteria of traditional philanthropy are inputs (or grant size) and sometimes outputs (or immediate results such as the number of trained volunteers). Grant size is used to measure the success, and sometimes grant size is compared to outputs to measure success. The input of a VPO is leverage, which denotes financial or non-financial support to take the initiative to a next stage of maturity. Outcomes and impact are measured by scale. Outcomes can be defined as benefits to users, such as volunteers' services to end-users, and impact is the greater awareness of a created social effect. Leverage is compared to scale to measure success in VP.

A summary of differences between traditional philanthropy and VP is presented in Table 1. In a nutshell, VP distinguishes from traditional philanthropy in terms of sentiment of the philanthropist, strategy, investment and financing method, engagement style, duration and closeness of the relationship, success measurement, and exit process. The new VP is more strategic than traditional philanthropy: philanthropist and recipient make strategic decisions together to transform the entrepreneurial idea into a robust business.

4 Organizational Structure of VP

The investment process of VP has several steps which can be summarized as below (EVPA, 2014). These steps are similar to venture capital and business angel investment stages in dealing with social enterprises (EVPA Survey, 2018; Gordon, 2014).

Table 1 Differences between traditional philanthropy and venture philanthropy

Traditional philanthropy	*Venture philanthropy*
Recipient is a nonprofit organization; target group is least developed people/countries	Recipient is a social enterprise; target group is people/projects with potential to evolve into a profitable business
Projects are supported. Target development is achieved	Systems/sectors are supported. As a result, aggregate development is achieved
No interference with business management	Interferes with business management and strategic decision-making process
Means of donation are grants	Means of donation are tailored financing and non-financial support
Light engagement with the recipient	Intensive engagement with the recipient including controlling and advising
Short-term (1–2 years) engagement	Long-term (5–10 years) engagement
Altruistic, administrative, and financial giving	Innovative, multi-disciplinary, and commercial giving
Success measure is outputs (immediate results)	Success measure is outcomes (benefits to users) and impact

Source OECD netFWD (2014)

1. *Investment strategy*: At this initial stage, the VPO describes the type of social/blended impact that it wants to achieve and assesses risk/return tradeoff associated with not achieving impact. To establish achievable goals, it assesses conditions about legal and tax structure, funders, recipients, and duration of investments; sets objectives about impact measurement; determines investment focus; analyzes stakeholders; and sets up operational processes, such as employees, directors, monitoring and reporting systems, and portfolio-level indicators (EVPA, 2014).
2. *Deal screening*: In this step, VPO screens alternative investment opportunities and assesses the characteristics and needs of SEs. Prospective projects are determined and projects that do not match the VPO's objectives are eliminated. SEs should set objectives about their target social/blended impact clearly and provide a detailed list of required resources to run the project in this stage to find the best matching VPO.
3. *Due diligence*: After a light assessment of potentially suitable projects, a limited number of projects are reserved for due diligence

process. In this process, VPOs and SEs collect information about each other and exchange information (Gordon, 2014). The business plan is analyzed by the VPO in detail, an official investment proposal is presented by SE, and the final decision is made with the compromise of the two parties. VPOs sometimes select none, one, or multiple projects to support.

4. *Deal structuring*: The VPO reaches a formal decision to make an investment. A formal contract is prepared after the decision is announced. The contract outlines stages and timelines of the investment, conditions for financing, non-financial support, reporting, and measurement. The contract includes details about impact measurement indicators, along with outputs and outcomes.
5. *Investment management*: VP manages the investment at both the SE and portfolio levels. VPOs keep strong communication with the SE to achieve the investment. The promised financial and non-financial support is provided; new risks are monitored, and flexibility to deliver the product/service is evaluated during the lifetime of the project. This is a continued co-creation and co-evaluation process (Hill & Levenhagen, 1995). As the process advances, value impact for key stakeholders is measured, and VPO assesses to exit as the goals of the project are achieved.
6. *Exit and post-exit follow-up*: VPOs exit if the predefined social/blended impact is achieved or cannot be achieved, even with additional investment. If the project is not successful, the VPO should minimize losses as much as possible. If the project was successful, the VPO should exit the company in a strong position. Some of the possible methods of positive disengagement is to ensure that the SE generates funds enough to survive or to provide new funding from third parties through initial public offerings, private sales, or takeovers by government or social development programs. VPOs may follow up the SE if both parties agree on conditions (EVPA, 2014; Gordon, 2014).

5 Impact Measurement

Impact measurement is important for the VP industry in determining which ideas and applications are viable (Rath & Schuyt, 2014). Impact measurement is challenging yet comparing the impact of an investment to another is more challenging. Because VPOs use a system-wide approach rather than a project-based approach, it is hard to determine the inputs and outputs. Non-financial investments are hard to quantify (OECD netFWD, 2014). Impact measurement is the first step, yet the most challenging part of impact investing is to assess the impact. Impact can appear in different forms; it is usually called "social/blended impact" because it is more than just financial benefits. However, financial benefits are important tools to identify and evaluate investment opportunities, and they should not be ignored. Foundation's program officers, investment staff, and legal expertise should collaborate to plan and assess the social and financial outcomes of the projects (Brest, 2012). Because traditional charities did not target social impact measurement before, it is a new and somewhat vague step in VP investments.

The first step of impact measurement is to set objectives for the SE. After the problem is defined, its roots and possible solution methods are classified. Methods to change the current situation are determined and selected to create change management. The second step is to identify the stakeholders. Stakeholders are parties who will benefit from the project, for example, SE, partners, the VPO, and the enlarged ecosystem for entrepreneurship. In the third step, stakeholders' benefits are measured at quantities if possible. It is not easy to monetize social benefits, but VPOs try to achieve it. Quantified outcomes are compared to inputs. The fourth step is to verify and value impact. This step is a more subjective step, in which stakeholders value the benefits of the program in interviews or questionnaires. They assess the change in their lives to value impact. The last step is to monitor and report the results (EVPA, 2018).

The degree of betterment in an organization can be units of impact depending on the project (Brest, 2012; Grossman et al., 2013; Maas & Liket, 2011; Moore et al., 2012; Rath & Schuyt, 2014). Quantifying social benefits makes it easier to measure. However, how to monetarize social impact matters. Specific examples can be the number of people whose lives are improved (Brest, 2012; Grossman et al., 2013), the number of jobs increased in a specific community (Gordon, 2014), the amount of medicine to a specific group of sick people (Gordon, 2014), the amount of assistance to school children (Gordon, 2014), the number of climate change resilience strategies created (OECD netFWD, 2014), and the amount of energy consumption due to a new technology (Brest, 2012). Once monetarization of social impact is achieved, social returns on investments (SROI) can be computed for comparison (Lehner & Nichols, 2014; Rath & Schuyt, 2014).

It is not easy to compare the impact of VP and other philanthropic activities yet because there is not sufficient longitudinal data available (OECD netFWD, 2014). There is evidence that impact measurement improves in time, yet it cannot be measured fully (Maas & Liket, 2011).

6 Risks and Critics

The worst possible outcome of a VP investment is the failure of the investment project. Three types of risks can cause failure: organizational, strategic, or execution risks. Organizational risk refers to challenges in internal environment of the VP, such as problems with funding, governance model, staff, or other stakeholders. Strategic risk refers to problems with the investment strategy, such as investment focus, type of the SE, financing instruments, co-investment policy, and intervention policy. Execution risk relates to failures in the implementation of the investment process. Failure in any one of the execution steps, which are listed in Sect. 5 of this chapter, falls into this category (EVPA, 2014). A thorough risk management approach requires determining and assessing risks of all steps in an investment project and hedging if possible.

There are a wide range of other risks associated with VP. A typical risk factor is financing of terrorism, which is a common risk for all donations. Terrorist organizations can divert and skim funds from legitimate resources such as philanthropist organizations (Crimm, 2004). Globalization, large transitory workforce of charitable organizations, and a high level of public trust make charitable organizations attractive to terrorist organizations (FATF, 2014). Due to its close relationship with the SE, it is tough for a terrorist organization to abuse a VP; however, there is some probability. For example, a volunteer without a strict background check can wire funds to an illegal account.

Another VPO risk is moral hazard as a consequence of low investment returns. If the investment strategy is based on donations only, the SE will not repay the VPO. In this case, the investment may be subject to moral hazard problems of perks and stealing by the management, and loss in social impact focus (Scarlata & Alemany, 2010). One way to reduce moral hazard problems is to have strong bonds with the SE. However, the closeness of the relationship between the VP and SE may cause frustration and creates board division and divergence from its core values (Larson, 2002).

A critique of VP is that operational methods and performance measures copied from business do not translate into the public benefit sector. Public sector and civil society have intangible goals and a more complex structure, in which needs and success criteria are different (Edwards, 2010; Herro & Obeng-Odoom, 2019; Larson, 2002). Monetizing social benefits is deficient in the way it is executed.

Modern philanthropy is sometimes named "philanthrocapitalism" by critics. The name evokes philanthropy as a tool to support capitalism, rather than trying to solve the social problems. By its unique method, philanthrocapitalism disguises the causes of social problems (Herro & Obeng-Odoom, 2019) and tries to find market-based solutions to the problems of the poor and the marginalized (World Bank, 2011). It might be a better move to find structural market improvements for the oppressed groups rather than supporting the marketwise solutions. Philanthropists believe that their methods will transform society; however, they only achieve increased access to some goods and services (Edwards, 2010; Herro & Obeng-Odoom, 2019).

Another critique of VP comes from tax issues. Corporations and individuals use charity organizations to minimize their tax payments as tax laws provide tax benefits for philanthropists in many countries/jurisdictions. However, there is evidence that corporate managers play games to minimize their tax bases by means of donations (Avci et al., 2016). Compliance of donations with requirements of anti-fraud provisions is important to maximize social benefits.

7 VP in Europe

VP is a popular form of philanthropic institutions in North America and West Europe. It is emerging in Asia but is less known in other parts of the world. Even though there are examples of VPOs in almost every region, it is not easy to find reliable and systemic data about philanthropic institutions in several regions, such as Latin America, Africa, Middle East, and Asia. These regions have several common factors: philanthropy is based on religious and historical roots and comprised of mostly individual grants for the poor. In the last few decades, corporate philanthropy has flourished, complementary to corporate social responsibility (CSR) in many parts of the world. Institutional philanthropy is not as widespread, mainly because of negative public perception, low confidence and credibility, low transparency, possible government intervention, and a lack of incentives for legal and tax policies (Johnson, 2010). A large portion of academic literature on VP is built upon the information obtained from only North America and Western Europe so far.

The adoption—in part or in full—of the VP approach by existing foundations happened in Europe only in mid-2000s. The practice became widespread toward the end of 2000s. The G8 countries established the Taskforce on Social Impact Investment in 2013, and the European Commission signed a partnership agreement with the European Venture Philanthropy Organization (EVPA) in 2014 to enhance the social impact investment market. Today, the market has blurry boundaries with finance, philanthropy, government, and large sectors of corporations. It is growing in Western Europe and enlarging toward Eastern European countries, in which there was no strong tradition of philanthropy (EVPA Knowledge Centre, 2018).

EVPA collects and disseminates sectoral information in Europe since 2011. This section uses the latest available data from the EVPA 2017 Survey that describes the European VP sector. According to the survey results, VP investments reached €767 million, and 11,951 SEs (corporations and individuals) receive these funds. Each SE received €7.8 million on average in 2017 (EVPA Survey, 2018). The industry has grown two and a half fold since 2011 as Fig. 1 displays.

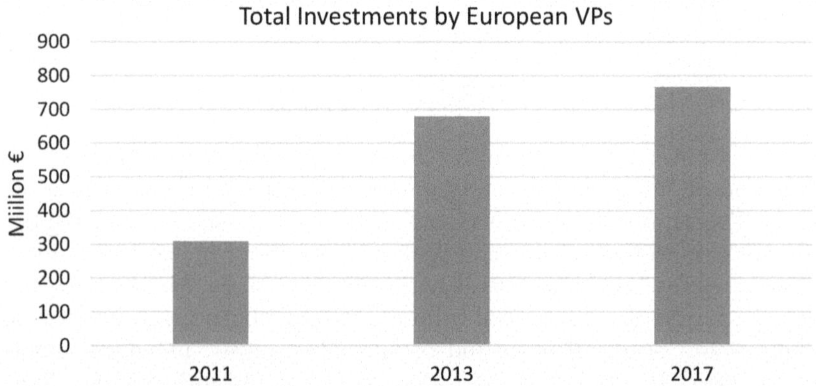

Fig. 1 Total investments by European venture philanthropists in 2011 and 2017 (*Sources* EVPA Survey [2013, 2016, 2018])

Among all funds, 54% is disseminated within Western Europe, 16% is transferred to Africa, 14% is transferred to Asia, 8% is transferred to Latin America, and 7% is transferred to Eastern Europe. VPs have a portfolio of investments in different sectors, such as economic and social development (29%), financial inclusion (27%), and education (12%). About 49% of VPs invest in people experiencing poverty, 45% in children and youth, 35% in people with disabilities, and 26% in migrants, asylum seekers, and refugees.

Around 35% of VPs invest in social impact-only SEs, while the rest invests in blended value SEs. Budget sizes and financial investments of VPs increase through the years. About half of the funds are invested in projects with financial requirements less than €200,000, and a third is invested in mid-level budget required projects (€200,000–550,000). Target investment type changes in time. The percentage of VPs invested in nonprofits decreased to 20% in 2017 from 35% in 2013. More and more VPs prefer to invest in SEs, generating some revenues. Around 56% of VPs invested in SEs, generating some revenues in 2013, compared to 78% in 2017.

The funding methods of organizations vary. Grants are used to fund nonprofits, whereas organizations generating some revenue receive grants, debt, and equity at equivalent amounts to their revenues, on average. Short-term projects up to 4 years receive more grants, while longer-term projects receive debt and equity investments. Investments that last 8 years or longer receive more equity investments. SEs usually receive cash grants in the incubation periods (0–2 years) while the funding portfolio turns to be a mix of grants, debt, equity, and hybrid financial instruments in their later years of existence.

About 49% of VP funding is realized via debt, 29% via grants, 16% via equity, and 5% via hybrid financial instruments. Return expectation of VPOs shows that they are far from being only a charity: only 38% of debt providing VPOs and 20% of equity providing VPOs expect zero return from investments. Only 2% expect negative returns, while the rest expects positive returns from their investments. Results show that debt investments reach expectations: 79% of debt providing VPOs have met or exceeded their expected returns from debt in 2017; 63% and 50% of VPOs did not meet their expectations from equity and hybrid financial instrument investment for the same period, respectively.

The income of VPs comes from a diverse set of providers. Around 23% of total income comes from the VPs' own endowment or trust,

23% comes from individual donors/investors, 14% comes from corporations, and 8% comes from governments. The rest is coming from earned income, financial institutions, external foundations, recycled return on investments, multilateral organizations, private equity/venture capital firms, and others.

Partnering with other philanthropists is widespread in the industry. While 55% of VPOs co-invests with other VPs, 60% co-invests with foundations engaged in other forms of philanthropy. VPs establish partnerships with public financing institutions, venture capitalists, finance-first impact investors, companies, mainstream banks, microfinance institutions, and other institutions.

VPs become more professional year by year. The number of paid employees in VPs increases, while pro-bono contributors and unpaid volunteers decrease in recent years. Additionally, decision-making mechanism improves to be more efficient; compared to the 2013 numbers, VPs screened less companies and funded more companies in 2017.

Some VPs in Europe invest in social impact funds, which have a market size of €16.1 million. More than half of these funds seek financial returns along with the social return. The management fees of these funds (around 3%) are higher than those of venture capital funds (2–2.5%). However, on average, they underperform expectations.

8 Discussion and Conclusion

After listing the many attributes of the new VP, we can now discuss VP's place in the philanthropy sector. The benefits and deficiencies of VP have created a field of debate. Advocates of the model focus on the benefits of it over traditional philanthropy. They claim that VP projects are more sustainable compared to traditional giving, and VPOs encourage the development of new technology. VPOs satisfy local priorities and needs using global resources. As a result, VPOs are a tool to reduce poverty and development gaps between regions (Adelman, 2009; Rosenman, 2019). Even though traditional and venture philanthropy will both survive and exist side by side, adopting a VP approach provides the means to change the world more than traditional philanthropy (Kramer, 2009).

The other approach focuses on the inadequate features of VP. Opponents of the model argue that it is not a well-specified and articulate operating model to improve social benefits. It is rather a term that defines a new worldview that incorporates various principles from management science to increase the impact of resources at hand. The high level of engagement between VP and SE, strategic funding and governance, and the partnering role of VP have potential benefits in the philanthropy world. However, setting up and sustaining such a complex system to serve diverse investment projects appear to be difficult tasks. Indeed, VPOs may lack at least a part of the necessary resources. Moreover, the inclusion of for-profit social enterprises and the pro-market approach cast some doubt on the model's social benefits (OECD netFWD, 2014). It is still unclear if VP can create a large-scale or society-level change, if it is sustainable, and if the SEs supported by VP are more sustainable than the SEs supported by traditional philanthropists. The role of government in VP is still blurry, and agreements regarding the measurement of what works for the SEs are lacking (Grossman et al., 2013).

One realized benefit of VP is its impact on the philanthropy sector overall. To catch up with the new giving models, traditional philanthropists have recently changed their tactics, and they aim to implement more control on their donations. For example, they try to choose time-bound projects with explicit goals, and they maintain surveillance on the project until it ends (Powell et al., 2019). This example shows that VP has changed the direction of philanthropy to a more inclusive and cooperative way.

References

Abzug, R., & Webb, N. J. (1997). Rational and extra-rational motivations for corporate giving: Complementing economic theory with organizations science. *New York Law School Law Review, 41*, 1035–1058.

Adams, M., & Hardwick, P. (1998). An analysis of corporate donations: United Kingdom Evidence. *Journal of Management Studies, 35*(5), 641–654.

Adelman, C. (2009). Global philanthropy and remittances: Reinventing foreign aid. *The Brown Journal of World Affairs, 15*(2), 23–33.

Alvord, S. H., Brown, L. D., & Letts, C. W. (2004). Social entrepreneurship and societal transformation: An exploratory study. *Journal of Applied Behavioral Science, 40*(3), 260–282.

Avci, S. B., Schipani, C. A., & Seyhun, H. N. (2016). Manipulative games of gifts by corporate executives. *University of Pennsylvania Journal of Business Law, 18*(4), 1131–1174.

AVPN. (2019). *Annual review*. https://avpn.asia/insights/annual-review-2019/.

Berman, S. L., Wicks, A. C., Kotha, S., & Jones, T. M. (1999). Does stakeholder orientation matter? The relationship between stakeholder management models and firm financial performance. *Academy of Management Journal, 42*(5), 488–506.

Brammer, S., & Millington, A. (2005). Corporate reputation and philanthropy: An empirical analysis. *Journal of Business Ethics, 61*(1), 29–44.

Brest, P. (2012). A decade of outcome-oriented philanthropy. *Stanford Social Innovation Review, Spring, 10*(2), 42-47.

Britannica. (2020). *Philanthropic Foundation*. https://www.britannica.com/topic/philanthropic-foundation. Accessed on May 16, 2020.

Chen, J. C., Patten, D. M., & Roberts, R. W. (2008). Corporate charitable contributions: A corporate social performance or legitimacy strategy? *Journal of Business Ethics, 82*, 131–144.

Choi, J., & Wang, H. (2007). The promise of a managerial values approach to corporate philanthropy. *Journal of Business Ethics, 75*(4), 345–359.

Crimm, N. J. (2004). High alert: The government's war on the financing of terrorism and its implications for donors, domestic charitable organizations, and global philanthropy. *William and Mary Law Review, 45*, 1341–1451.

Dacin, P. A., Dacin, M. T., & Matear, M. (2010). Social entrepreneurship: Why we don't need a new theory and how we move forward from here. *Academy of Management Perspectives, 24*(3), 37–57.

Daly, S. (2008). Institutional innovation in philanthropy: Community foundations in the UK. *VOLUNTAS: International Journal of Voluntary and Nonprofit Organizations, 19*(3), 219–241.

Daly, S. (2012). Philanthropy as an essentially contested concept. *VOLUNTAS: International Journal of Voluntary and Nonprofit Organizations, 23*(3), 535–557.

Davis, K. (1973). The case for and against business assumption of social responsibilities. *Academy of Management Journal, 16*(2), 312–322.

Edwards, M. (2010). *Small change: Why business won't save the world* (1st ed.). Berrett-Koehler Publishers.

EVPA. (2014). *Learning from failures in venture philanthropy and social investment*. EVPA. https://efc.issuelab.org/resource/learning-from-failures-in-venture-philanthropy-and-social-investment.html.

EVPA. (2018). *VP in a nutshell: Overview*. EVPA. https://evpa.eu.com/download/VP_in_a_Nutshell_1_Overview_2018.pdf.

EVPA Knowledge Centre. (2018). *A practical guide to venture philanthropy and social impact investment* (4th ed.). EVPA. https://www.sdgphilanthropy.org/system/files/2018-12/A_Practical_Guide_to_VP_SII_2018.pdf.

EVPA Survey. (2013). *European venture philanthropy and social investment 2011/2012*. EVPA. https://evpa.eu.com/knowledge-centre/the-evpa-industry-survey.

EVPA Survey. (2016). *The state of venture philanthropy and social investment (VP/SI) in Europe—The EVPA survey 2015/2016*. EVPA.

EVPA Survey. (2018). *EVPA survey 2017/2018: Investing for Impact*. EVPA. https://evpa.eu.com/knowledge-centre/the-evpa-industry-survey.

FATF. (2014). *Risk of terrorist abuse in nonprofit organizations*. https://www.fatf-gafi.org/documents/documents/risk-terrorist-abuse-non-profits.html.

Fidelity Charitable. (2020). *What is a philanthropist?* https://www.fidelitycharitable.org/guidance/philanthropy/what-is-a-philanthropist.html. Accessed on May 14, 2020.

Fombrun, C., & Shanley, M. (1990). What's in a name? Reputation building and corporate strategy. *Academy of Management Journal, 33*(2), 233–258.

Friedman, M. (1970, September 13). The social responsibility of business is to increase its profits. *The New York Times Magazine*. http://umich.edu/~thecore/doc/Friedman.pdf.

Frumpkin, P. (2003). Inside venture philanthropy. *Society, 40*, 7–15.

Gautier, A., & Pache, A.-C. (2015). Research on corporate philanthropy: A review and assessment. *Journal of Business Ethics, 126*(3), 343–369.

Gordon, J. (2014). A stage model of venture philanthropy. *Venture Capital, 16*(2), 85–107.

Grossman, A., Appleby, S., & Reimers, C. (2013). *Venture philanthropy: Its evolution and its future*. HBS Case Collection N9-313-111. Harvard Business School.

Havens, J. J., & Shervish, P. G. (1999). *Millionaires and the millennium: New estimates of the forthcoming wealth transfer and the prospects for a golden age of philanthropy*. Research Report, 19 October, Boston College Social Welfare Research Institute.

Helme, M., & Laurilla, J. (2009). Philanthropy, integration or innovation? Exploring the financial and societal outcomes of different types of corporate responsibility. *Journal of Business Ethics, 84*(3), 325–339.

Herro, A., & Obeng-Odoom, F. (2019). Foundations of radical philanthropy. *VOLUNTAS: International Journal of Voluntary and Nonprofit Organizations, 30*, 881–890.

Hill, R. C., & Levenhagen, M. (1995). Metaphors and mental models: Sense-making and sense giving in innovative and entrepreneurial activities. *Journal of Management, 21*(6), 1057–1074.

John, R. (2006). *Venture philanthropy: The evolution of high engagement philanthropy in Europe*. Skoll Center for Social Entrepreneurship, Said Business School, University of Oxford.

Johnson, P. D. (2010). *Global institutional philanthropy: A preliminary status report*. Worldwide Initiatives for Grandmaker Support (WINGS) and the Philanthropic Initiative (TPI). https://www.issuelab.org/resource/global-institutional-philanthropy-a-preliminary-status-report.html.

Kramer, M. R. (2009). Catalytic philanthropy. *Stanford Social Innovation Review*, Fall, 29–35.

Krugman, P. (2009). *The conscience of a liberal: Reclaiming America from the right*. Penguin Press.

Larson, B. (2002). The new entrepreneurs: New philanthropy or not? *Philanthropic Fundraising, 37*, 79–84.

Lehner, O. M., & Nichols, A. (2014). Social finance and crowdfunding for social enterprises: A public–private case study providing legitimacy and leverage. *Venture Capital, 16*(3), 271–286.

Letts, C. W., Ryan, W. P., & Grossman, A. S. (1997, March–April). Virtuous capital: What foundations can learn from venture capitalists. *Harvard Business Review, 75*, 36–50.

Liang, H., & Renneboog, L. (2017). Corporate donations and shareholder value. *Oxford Review of Economic Policy, 33*(2), 278–316.

Logsdon, J. M., Reiner, M., & L., & Burke, L. . (1990). Corporate philanthropy: Strategic responses to the firm's stakeholders. *Nonprofit and Voluntary Sector Quarterly, 19*(2), 93–109.

Lowndes, C. L. B. (1960). Tax advantages of charitable gifts. *Virginia Law Review, 46*(3), 394–423.

Maas, K., & Liket, K. (2011). Talk the walk: Measuring the impact of strategic philanthropy. *Journal of Business Ethics, 100*(3), 4454–4464.

Moore, M.-L., Westley, F. R., & Brodhead, T. (2012). Social finance intermediaries and social innovation. *Journal of Social Entrepreneurship, 3*(2), 185–205.

OECD netFWD. (2014). *Venture philanthropy in development: Dynamics, challenges, and lessons in the search for greater impact*. OECD Development Center. https://www.oecd.org/dev/Venture%20Philanthropy%20in%20Development-BAT-24022014-indd5%2011%20mars.pdf.

Peattie, K., & Morley, A. (2008). Eight paradoxes of the social enterprise research agenda. *Social Enterprise Journal, 4*(2), 91–107.

Porter, M. E., & Kramer, M. R. (2002, December). The competitive advantage of corporate philanthropy. *Harvard Business Review*.

Powell, A., Seldon, W., & Sahni, N. (2019). Reimagining institutional philanthropy. *Stanford Social Innovation Review*, Spring.

Rath, J., & Schuyt, T. (2014). Entrepreneurial philanthropy: An exploratory review. *The Journal of Wealth Management, 17*(3), 35–46.

Rosenman, E. (2019). The geographies of social finance: Poverty regulation through the 'invisible heart' of markets. *Progress in Human Geography, 43*(1), 141–162.

Scarlata, M., & Alemany, L. (2010). Deal structuring in philanthropic venture capital investments: Financing instrument, valuation and covenants. *Journal of Business Ethics, 95*(2), 121–145.

Shaw, B., & Post, F. R. (1993). A moral basis for corporate philanthropy. *Journal of Business Ethics, 12*(10), 745–751.

Shaw, E., Gordon, J., Harvey, C., & Henderson., K. (2010). Entrepreneurial philanthropy: Theoretical antecedents and empirical analysis of economic, social, cultural, and symbolic capital. *Frontiers of Entrepreneurial Research, 30*(7).

Shaw, E., Gordon, J., Harvey, C., & Maclean, M. (2013). Exploring contemporary entrepreneurial philanthropy. *International Small Business Journal, 31*(5), 580–599.

Spiess-Knafl, W., & Struewer, B. (2015). *Social investing fundamentals of an impact-first investment strategy*. Zeppelin University and Roots of Impact.

Stendardi, E. J. (1992). Corporate philanthropy: The redefinition of enlightened self-interest. *Social Science Journal, 29*(1), 21–30.

Sulek, M. (2010). On the modern meaning of philanthropy. *Nonprofit and Voluntary Sector Quarterly, 39*(2), 193–212.

Wang, H., & Qian, C. (2011). Corporate philanthropy and corporate financial performance: The roles of stakeholder response and political access. *Academy of Management Journal, 54*(6), 1159–1181.

Williams, R. J., & Barrett, J. D. (2000). Corporate philanthropy, criminal activity, and firm reputation: Is there a link? *Journal of Business Ethics, 26*, 341–250.

Wirgau, J. S., Farley, K. W., & Jensen, C. (2010). Is business discourse colonizing philanthropy? A critical discourse analysis of (PRODUCT) RED. *VOLUNTAS: International Journal of Voluntary and Nonprofit Organizations, 21*(4), 611–630.

Wood, D. J., & Jones, R. E. (1995). Stakeholder mismatching: A theoretical problem in empirical research on corporate social performance. *International Journal of Organizational Analysis, 3*(3), 229–267.

World Bank. (2011). *World development report 2000/2001: Attacking poverty.* Oxford University Press.

Index

T. Walker et al. (eds.), *Innovations in Social Finance*,
https://doi.org/10.1007/978-3-030-72535-8

D

The manufacturer's authorised representative in the EU is Springer Nature Customer Service Centre GmbH, Europaplatz 3, 69115 Heidelberg, Germany. If you have any concerns regarding our products, please contact ProductSafety@springernature.com

Printed and bound by CPI Group (UK) Ltd, Croydon, CR0 4YY
30/09/2026
02225456-0016